Praise for ROAD TO PERDITION and Max Allan Collins:

"ROAD TO PERDITION shows, better than anything I've seen, just how powerful and unique a storytelling form the graphic novel can be. This book fulfills the basic requirement of art: it is both surprising and inevitable. And a wonderful read."

Donald Westlake

"Collins has an outwardly artless style that conceals a great deal of art."

The New York Times

"ROAD TO PERDITION represents the final evolution of the form once known as the "comic book," a combination of tough, canny writing and exquisite graphics brought together to tell a story that's 100% American. It's the best movie I've seen in years."

Loren D. Estleman
(author *The Witchfinder* and *Journey of the Dead*)

"Collins is a master."

Publisher's Weekly

"I know mysteries, and I know comics — and ROAD TO PERDITION is one great ride!"

Mickey Spillane

"No one can twist you through a maze with the intensity and suspense of Max Allan Collins."

Clive Cussler

"ROAD TO PERDITION is above all a fine and gripping work of fiction. The artwork is marvelous and the prose masterful. I turned the pages fast enough to get them hot, then went back and savored the illustrations, each like a still from the best of film noir."

John Lutz
(author *Single White Female*)

"One of the new masters of the genre."

Atlanta Constitution

"Collins is the James M. Cain of the '90s!"

Roger L. Simon

Cover illustration by Richard Piers Rayner

SUSTAINABLE FORESTRY INITIATIVE
Certified Sourcing
www.sfiprogram.org
SFI-01042

ROAD TO PERDITION

WRITTEN BY
MAX ALLAN COLLINS

ART BY
RICHARD PIERS RAYNER

LETTERING BY **BOB LAPPAN**

VERTIGO CRIME

To my son, Nathan
—MAX ALLAN COLLINS—

To Richard and Jimmy—
because fathers love their children.
—RICHARD PIERS RAYNER—

POSTCARDS FROM THE ROAD

A shamelessly autobiographical introduction by Max Allan Collins

So, the day before Thanksgiving, 1993, my career decided to implode.

I'd been writing the *Dick Tracy* comic strip since 1977, when — with the blessing of the strip's creator, Chester Gould, who was stepping down after almost fifty years — I joined with his former assistant, Rick Fletcher, to put some life into that dying strip. I'd been told by the head of Tribune Media Services that the strip probably wouldn't survive another five years — the term of my contract.

Not only did the strip survive, we attracted a lot of attention with a return to cops-and-robbers basics, plus an infusion of characters the wildly imaginative Chet Gould had abandoned, and, in particular, by bringing a renewed emphasis to modern themes, like computer crime and video piracy. When the big-time Warren Beatty movie came out in 1990, I was hired as a creative consultant, wrote the novelization (still one of my best-selling books), appeared on all kinds of national TV shows, and generally enjoyed the ride. My five-year contract had turned into a ten-year one, with another five-year stint after that. For a freelance writer, a steady gig like that was a gift.

But in the mail, the day before Thanksgiving, Tribune Media Services curtly informed me my services would no longer be needed. This had a little to do with my involvement in the notorious *True Crime* trading cards, and a lot to do with my having tangled several times with a certain editor at TMS (who had recently replaced the editor who hired me). This probably dated from the time, on the phone, when I told this editor — without expletives deleted — what I

thought of him, his ideas and his abilities, but I had refused to see the handwriting on the wall (my wife Barb, on the other hand, overhearing me reaming my boss on the phone, had long since been looking at the want ads for a part-time job).

Well, I called my agent, on that day before Thanksgiving, to give him the lousy news about losing *Tracy*; he replied with more of the same: a major book contract had just been canceled.

Since the early '80s, much of my career has centered around my Nathan Heller historical detective series. The first Heller novel, *True Detective* (1983), won that year's Best Novel Shamus award from the Private Eye Writers of America. A lengthy first-person account of fictional Chicago private eye Nate Heller mingling with the nonfictional likes of gangster Frank Nitti and Al Capone, *True Detective* explored the so-called attempted assassination of FDR in 1932, which led to the supposedly accidental shooting of corrupt Chicago mayor Anton Cermak.

The most recent Heller novel, *Angel in Black* (2001), finds Heller solving the notorious Black Dahlia murder in 1947; other books have seen my fictional detective cracking such famous real-life mysteries as the Huey Long assassination, the Sir Harry Oakes murder, the Roswell incident, and the disappearance of Amelia Earhart. These books have earned a strong reputation for diligent historical research leading to convincing new solutions for old unsolved mysteries (thanks in no small part to my longtime research associate, George Hagenauer).

But meanwhile, back on the day

before Thanksgiving, 1993, my agent informed me that my current Heller contract had been canceled. A week or so before, the latest Heller, *Stolen Away* — about the Lindbergh kidnapping — had won the series another Best Novel Shamus award, and my Bantam Books editor had spent a three-and-a-half-hour, one-on-one lunch with me, charting the glorious future of Heller at that publishing house. I had just delivered a book that this editor loved; but now that book was being returned, and my contract for two more Heller thrillers... phhhht.

The *why* is not important — one of the periodic changes of regimes so common in publishing was part of it. And how were your holidays in 1993?

Actually, at the Collins household, ours were pretty good. Barb helped me up off the mat, my son Nate kidded me with merciless good humor, my friends Marty Greenberg and Ed Gorman fed me short-story assignments to keep me alive, my agent went out and sold Heller all over again (it took a few months, but he did it), and lots of terrific things have happened since the year Tribune Media Services and Bantam Books decided, independently, to play Scrooge.

It's doubtful I would have written, directed, and co-produced three independent films and two documentaries if I'd still been doing *Dick Tracy*, and I wouldn't have made myself available to the movie tie-in editors if my Heller contract hadn't gone away... meaning I wouldn't have written the New York *Times* bestseller *Saving Private Ryan* for the DreamWorks people, and a number of other novelizations that have sold well and made it to various bestseller charts, expanding my name recognition among readers worldwide.

What the hell does this have to do with *Road to Perdition*, you're wondering?

I'm glad you asked. In 1994, when I attended WonderCon in Oakland, California, I was still in what might charitably be termed a rebuilding phase of my career; I was in particular looking for something to do in the world of comics, now that *Dick Tracy* was no longer my meal ticket.

Over the years I'd done various projects for DC, including some Batman material (not all of it well-received — my version of Robin is the one that, famously, inspired a phone-in campaign that resulted in readers voting to kill the character. How many writers can say that?). With my frequent collaborator, cartoonist Terry Beatty, I had created a super-hero for DC called Wild Dog that caused a stir in the midwest (where the feature was set) and our long-running independent comic book, *Ms. Tree*, shifted to the big-time home of Superman for a series of quarterly graphic novels that ran for several years.

So it made sense that Andrew Helfer — editor of DC's Paradox Press, an ambitious line of sophisticated, non-superhero material — sought me out to create something. As we sat in a hotel lobby in Oakland, Andy explained he was approaching established mystery writers to write new works specifically for comics. These would be serialized in a compact format reminiscent of digest-size Japanese *manga* ("irresponsible drawings," i.e., comics); the three parts would then be collected into a trade paperback. Because I was the only mystery writer (at that time, anyway) who was also doing comics, I was a logical choice.

Perhaps inspired by Andy's *manga* approach, off the top of my head I pitched the editor an idea I'd been mulling over — initially, it was called *Gun and Son*... a title Andy immediately hated, condemning it as "too cute, too comic-booky." Hey, what did he want from the guy who created a female private eye called Ms. Tree and such Dick Tracy characters as Putty Puss, Torcher and Snake Eyes? But Andy liked the concept — liked it a lot — and within weeks we were a going concern.

The new title, incidentally, came to me in something of a flash — I knew the father and son in this story were on the road to hell, and "perdition" popped into my head as the kind of Biblical name that so often turned up in the American heartland, when communities were established in frontier days. It'd be just like the pioneers to head west from religious oppression, and — choosing Godforsaken land to homestead — name it after hell. (I also have to admit that I love the Bob Hope and Bing Crosby "road" pictures, have since childhood, and I doubt this title would have come to me without them. So feel free, during the lighter moments in the narrative ahead, to sing "We're off on the road to Perdition," to the tune of "Road to Morocco.")

While I always knew the story of *Perdition* would not be open-ended, I hadn't planned to bring it to its inevitable, tragic conclusion until I had done several story arcs about the father and son who were simultaneously on the run from mobsters and stealing from them. As in the *manga* epic *Lone Wolf and Cub* (Kozure Okami) — a major influence on *Road to Perdition* — I had envisioned these characters on a long, sprawling journey that would involve them with all sorts of people, with all sorts of problems... like Richard Kimble ducking Inspector Gerard even as he tracks the One-Armed Man, the story was designed to take a while, and include side trips. (Even now, you'll notice that there's a "hole" in the narrative designed for me to eventually go back in and fill with such episodic adventures.)

But editor Andy — who wanted to publish self-contained graphic novels, not ongoing stories — demanded closure; and, God bless him, he was right. He was right artistically — if this narrative has power, much of it comes from the tragic inevitability of the conclusion it marches toward — but also commercially... though the latter wasn't immediately obvious.

Andy's ambitious line of serialized crime novels received its share of critical praise, but generated disappointing sales, so much so that *Road* never did receive serialized publication — the last book to be published as a Paradox Press mystery, it became a single, substantial volume... and we were almost scuttled, anyway, as the last book scheduled in an unsuccessful enterprise, and would have been if Andrew Helfer hadn't made a fuss, pointing out that this long-in-the-works graphic novel was the best he'd developed, with perhaps the greatest potential.

And long-in-the-works it was. Andy had an artist in mind — a Brit named Richard Piers Rayner — whom he described as, "Perfect for this project — he's not fast, just brilliant." I saw samples of Rayner's work and enthusiastically gave my thumbs up. As I write this, I still have not met my fellow *Road* warrior. He remains a cheerful voice on the phone and an intelligent presence in e-mails... and a gifted illustrator. No disrespect meant to any other artist I've worked with in comics, but *Road* is my best work in that field... and it's unimaginable without Richard.

Part of why this collaboration worked so well is the notorious lack of speed this fine artist brought to a project that took until 1998 (!) to complete. I would write 25 or 30 pages of script for the three-hundred-page project, send it to Andy Helfer along with research materials on the real people and places depicted therein, and then months later — sometimes six months later — I'd get a call from Andy. These calls, and there were many of them, went something like this:

"I need pages," Andy would say.

"Pages?"

"You know — for Richard."

"Richard?"

"*Road to Perdition*."

"... Oh! Yeah, yeah, I remember..."

And I would go find my script and re-read everything I'd done to date on the project — to remind myself what the book was about — and sit down and do another 25 or 30 pages. Also, I'd get photocopies of Richard's work — minus any dialogue or captions — and here is where the collaborative, elusive, even magical aspect of this project comes in. The somber, illustrative, very serious tone of the drawings — so suited to what I'd written — kept me on the right track, serving the narrative beautifully. And Richard's amazing contribution is partly why *Road* has a slightly different voice than you'll find anywhere else in my work, with the possible exception of my independent film *Mommy*.

The low-budget *Mommy* features — *Mommy* (1995) and its sequel *Mommy's Day* (1997) — are worth a brief sidebar, because they have thematic similarity to the work at hand... and the original short story predates the conception of *Road*. Designed as a sort of unofficial sequel to novelist William March's classic thriller *The Bad Seed* (1954) — the equally classic movie version starred Patty McCormack, who as a child so memorably played evil Rhoda Penmarck (originating the role on Broadway in Maxwell Anderson's play) — *Mommy* is told from the point of view of Jessica Ann, the little girl who slowly compre-hends that her perfect, country club mommy is a murderer (the box art for this made-for-vid feature describes her as "June Cleaver with a cleaver").

The film is narrated by Jessica Ann (Rachel Lemieux, an eleven-year-old we found at an open audition, an amateur who won raves in *Entertainment Weekly* and other national magazines), and the distance, the poignance, of the child's point of view gives the film much of whatever resonance it may have. The strained relationship between mother and daughter — thanks to the chemistry between Rachel and the incredible Patty McCormack, a criminally underused actress now playing a grown-up sociopath — was similarly powerful.

To some degree, *Road* was always designed as a father/son companion piece to the mother/daughter *Mommy* — and there's irony in the former generating a DreamWorks/Twentieth Century Fox movie starring Tom Hanks, Paul Newman and Jude Law and directed by Sam Mendes, while the lat-ter was a low-budget cult-fave indie held together with chewing gum and shoelaces. Budget issues aside, the parent/child relationship, in a context of danger and violence, has always fascinated me, as does the notion of a child learning of a parent's frailties, dealing with them, and yet continuing to love and even admire that still-larger-than-life — if now, human — figure.

Books written in the first third of my career often had a father-and-son theme. My first published novel, *Bait Money* (1973), charts a surrogate father/son relationship between profes-sional thief Nolan and his young accom-plice, Jon (seven more books about the team followed). The first three Heller novels — often referred to as "The Nitti Trilogy" — explore the detective's awkward, sometimes frightening relationship with surrogate father Frank Nitti, and Heller's guilt over his real father's suicide remains a driving characterization theme in the saga.

These stories all looked at the father-and-son dynamic from the son's point of view. Until my son Nathan was born in 1982 — the same year Nathan Heller was "born" — I had not looked at that dynamic from the father's end of the telescope. And, while the *Mommy* stories (two features, two novels and a short story) and *Road to Perdition* retain the perspective of the child, they are informed by the new emotions, responsibilities and experiences of parenthood I'd encountered.

Of course, in part, *Road* is an unabashed homage to *Lone Wolf and Cub* — both the *manga* and the incredible series of six movies it spawned in the early '70s, written by Kazuo Koike himself, starring quietly charismatic Tomisaburo Wakayama and precocious Akihiro Tomikawa. That epic saga told the story of a samurai betrayed by his shogun, who sets out on a road of bloody vengeance pushing his infant child along in a weapon-accessorized "baby cart." The juxtaposition of tough and tender, of brutality and sensitivity, had seldom been done as well in any storytelling medium, and I hope *Road to Perdition* attracts new readers to what remains my favorite comic-book series and probably the finest movie series ever to be derived from comics.

Another Asian influence was Hong Kong cinema — in particular, the "heroic bloodshed" of director/writer John Woo. In the early '90s, Woo was a cult figure, with Hollywood still in his future, and VHS tapes of his bloody yet poetic movies circulating from film buff to buff; my friend Tom Weisser, editor of *Asian Cult Cinema* magazine (for whom I write a column), was key in spreading the word about this world-class filmmaker. I was taken by Woo's use of over-the-top, beautifully choreographed, carnage-filled action scenes in the context of unabashedly melodramatic epics of family, friendship, loyalty, love, betrayal and redemption, and was struck by his disparate influences — that he was as much influenced by Douglas Sirk and Jean-Pierre Melville as by Sam Peckinpah and Don Siegel. He had even done his own *Lone Wolf and Cub* homage — *Heroes Shed No Tears* (1985) — in which a mercenary and his young son are caught behind enemy lines in a jungle war. I thought a similar fusion of family melodrama and wild bloody action would work well in a graphic novel.

But *Road* — like the Nathan Heller books — is perhaps more rooted in American history than in Japanese comics and movies. I wanted to do something in comics that would be the graphic-novel equivalent of my Nathan Heller novels, and to do a crime novel variation on that approach — as opposed to the classic private eye road Heller was going down.

I had learned of John Looney and his loony son Connor when I was researching the first Heller novel, *True Detective*, a portion of which takes place in the Iowa-Illinois Quad Cities — my own back yard. When I would talk Quad Cities (rather, Tri Cities) gangsters with the likes of Davenport, Iowa newspaper columnist Bill Wundrum and Rock Island, Illinois historian B.J. Elsner, the name Looney would immediately come up.

"Oh, you have to write about Looney," they would say, and off they'd go into wild anecdotes about the tabloid-newspaper publisher who blackmailed the subjects of his stories, controlled local politics, and collaborated with the Capone gang of Chicago in all manner of illegal doings, from bootlegging to prostitution to gambling.

For years I wondered what the right vehicle for the Looney story would be. The father/son dynamic — and knowing that Looney had betrayed a loyal lieutenant — got me thinking about trying an American twist on *Lone Wolf and Cub*; wasn't a Godfather like a shogun, and a mob enforcer like a samurai? I didn't like the idea of an infant child, however, not for this tale — it needed to be a coming-of-age story, including a terrible loss of innocence for both father and son. The son of my protagonist would be an adolescent, capable of comprehending the terrible (and wonderful) things of which his father was capable.

Also, I liked the idea of combining gangsters of the Capone and Nitti ilk with outlaws of the Dillinger and Baby Face Nelson breed. Before George Hagenauer and I got into so much trouble with our *G-Men and Gangsters* trading cards — which a publisher, without our knowledge, packaged with a series about serial killers, and redubbed *True Crime* trading cards — we often commented about the confluence of the gangsters and outlaws of the '30s... but novels and movies (and comics) had treated them as wholly separate entities. I had explored this notion in the second Heller book — ironically also titled *True Crime* (1984) — and saw tremendous visual potential for a graphic novel that charted the twin, occasionally intersecting courses of the '30s gangsters and outlaws.

Another twist would be provided by the Irish background of the Looney gang — long before *The Godfather*, the mobsters of American popular culture had been almost exclusively Italian.

(Another irony: one of the few changes Hollywood would make in my material was changing the name "Looney" to "Rooney" — apparently the former may have sounded too comic-booky. As a guy who spent fifteen years naming *Dick Tracy* villains — and whose DC editor, Andy Helfer, criticized for out-of-control Dickensian punning — I have to say this story would never have been written had I not been irresistibly drawn to the name Looney.)

Of course this all started for me (and many others) with old gangster movies on TV, and in particular the late '50s to early '60s Robert Stack television series *The Untouchables*, the fact-based nature of which had sent me scurrying to libraries and used books stores to find material on the real crimes behind the Hollywood myth. That TV show — after the initial two-part pilot, still probably the most accurate filmed version of Capone's downfall — soon went wildly astray from history, and so exaggerated the real Eliot Ness that revisionist historians have dismissed him as a sham. (Not true — Ness really was as close to Dick Tracy as any real lawman ever came. You may wish to check out the four novels I've written about Ness's real cases.)

With its return to Warner Bros.-style gangster *noir*, *The Untouchables* opened the door for a spate of fact-based crime pictures. A craze of sorts followed, with both gangsters and outlaws filling movie screens for several glorious bullet-spattered years, with Rod Steiger playing Capone, Vic Morrow etching Dutch Schultz, Ray Danton essaying a smooth Legs Diamond, even a re-release of Mickey Rooney's 1957 Don Siegel-directed portrait of a crazed *Baby Face Nelson*. I was surprised when, almost a decade after the fad had faded, Warren Beatty and an unknown actress named

Faye Dunaway showed up in a very late entry in the neo-gangster movie genre.

And no movie ever impacted me more than Arthur Penn's *Bonnie and Clyde* (1967). Arguably, it was the most influential film of the '60s — period. I was just out of high school, and that picture got me excited about movies in a new way. As with *The Untouchables*, it also sent me running to research the real people and crimes behind the moving images. I saw *Bonnie and Clyde* countless times, and one of those times I dragged my father along. Dad (who passed away last year) was a musician — a brilliant one — but he cared more about sports than movies, so getting him to go to *Bonnie and Clyde* took some doing. He was rarely impressed by movies, and frequently voiced his displeasure with what my mother and I talked him into seeing over the years.

But during *Bonnie and Clyde* — specifically, a sequence involving the shooting of Buck Barrow and his blinded wife Blanche in a clearing in a grove, a bloody shoot-out with scattered bandages and bullet holes punched in the metal of a stalled getaway car — my father reacted strangely. Visibly shaken, whitening, he shifted in his seat, his discomfort palpable.

Afterward, he explained: He'd had no memory of it till he saw the movie; but his parents had taken him to that very scene — in rural Iowa — where he, as a very small boy, had seen the bloody morning-aftermath of the shooting, the discarded crimson bandages, the shot-up automobile. The filmmakers had closely patterned their scene on news photos of the time, and had captured it so unerringly that the buried childhood memories — obviously somewhat traumatic ones — came rushing back to Dad.

I believe the Nate Heller novels, and every historical crime story I've written since — including *Road* — began in that moment. My dad's rush of memory was my epiphany: These things had really happened, right where I lived; there was a truth underlying the noir fantasy, more than moldy old books, musty magazines and library microfilm had ever brought to life for me... and that was where my impulse to develop what has been termed the "true-crime fiction" subgenre began.

Already, one of the things characterizing my early crime novels was their heartland settings. In my high school efforts, I had clumsily tried to write about Mickey Spillane's Manhattan and Raymond Chandler's Los Angeles — places where I had obviously never lived (and I didn't yet realize that only Spillane and Chandler ever really "lived" there); and even now the major city I write about is Chicago, the big town I most often visited as a boy. I take a perverse pride in the criminal history of my region — the real events behind *Road to Perdition* happened in the Midwest of the late '20s and early '30s, the paved streets of the Windy City, the dusty rural backroads of Iowa, Illinois, Nebraska, Kansas and the rest.

I took my first driving lesson — on which the driving lesson in this book is based — on a country road in Iowa. My father and his friend Keith Larsen took me out near Keith's farm. Keith was a poet and a fine teacher of English and literature on the college level (he was my first real mentor); but he was also an Iowa farmer — very dry, soft-spoken, understated in that Midwestern way shared by most farmers and some gangsters.

Almost immediately I drove the car into a ditch — a fairly scary moment.

My father was able to take the wheel and back up out of the ditch, and

Keith, in the rear, remained silent throughout. When the car was back on the gravel road, Keith leaned up and said to my dad, "Now, Max, you have to make him stay at it. Get him behind that wheel. He has to get right back up on the horse and ride."

My dad said he agreed with this notion.

Keith said, "Good." Then he got out of the car and walked across the nearest field, back to his farmhouse.

And now *Road to Perdition* is a major motion picture. As I write this, I haven't seen it — but from my visit to the set and my reading of the script, I am confident the filmmakers have stayed true to the letter of our graphic novel — as much as possible — and, what is more important, to its spirit.

Ironically, my father — who, as I've said, did not particularly like movies — always measured me as a writer on whether or not a book of mine would make a good movie. "Would it make a good movie?" he'd invariably ask. He was thrilled whenever something of mine got optioned by Hollywood, though disappointed when nothing would come of it, and he took an active interest in my independent filmmaking. Going to the world premiere of *Dick Tracy* at Disney World was, I believe, a highlight of his life. He knew of the DreamWorks option on *Road to Perdition*, but he did not live to see this particular project actually come to fruition. I regret, terribly, that he did not live to see *Road to Perdition* on the screen. I long to see his look of pride, for this realization of my — and oddly, his — dream.

My son Nathan needs to know that I would not have written this story without him. We watched the *Lone Wolf and Cub* movies together — when he was much younger than any normal parent would have allowed a child to see such bloody, disturbing fare — and our most common bond, as father and son, is our shared love of movies, books, comics and music (with appropriately varying tastes, suitable to our respective generations). I didn't have that with my dad, and it's gratifying to share these enthusiasms with Nate.

My agents Dominick Abel and Daniel Ostrow put this unlikely chain of events into motion, and I am very grateful. Dean Zanuck was the first believer in this material, and his father Richard was the second; that they took this with such confidence to the third believer — DreamWorks — made the dream a reality. That my story had been told visually by the gifted Richard Piers Rayner is no small part of why Hollywood was attracted to this material; this introduction is mine, but the *Road to Perdition* belongs to Richard, too.

And to editor Andrew Helfer.

What I've learned from this — or hope I've learned — is that the illusion of security is blinding. Writing the *Dick Tracy* strip — continuing the work of another creator — gave me a false sense of security; when the security of the strip was stripped away, I tried other things out of that mother, necessity. If things had gone better for me back in the early '90s, I would never have directed independent films or written such books as *In the Line of Fire* and *The Mummy*, much less the graphic novel you hold in your hands and all that it has spawned.

If you're turned away from one road, there's always another — filled with risk but also adventure. Roads less taken are always the most rewarding ones.

— Max Allan Collins
August, 2001

"You must

choose

a road

for yourself."

-Kazuo Koike

CHAPTER ONE:

ARCHANGEL OF DEATH

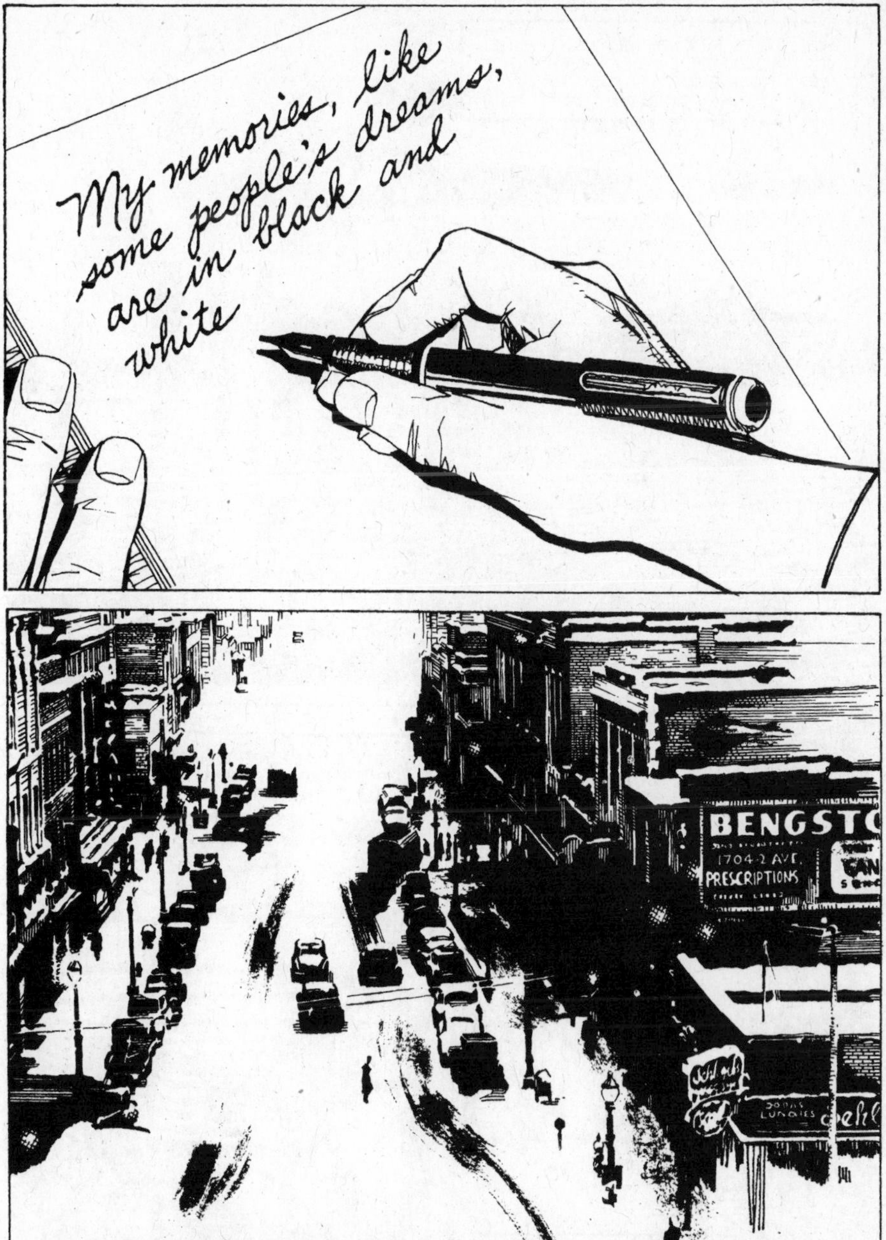
My memories, like some people's dreams, are in black and white
BENGST
1704-2 AVE.
PRESCRIPTIONS
I KNOW WE HAD SUMMER, IN THE TRI-CITIES, BUT WHEN I REMEMBER MY CHILDHOOD, IT'S ALWAYS WINTER... SNOW AND SLUDGE AND SLEET MIXED WITH DIRT AND CINDERS. *THAT* WINTER, OF 1930...

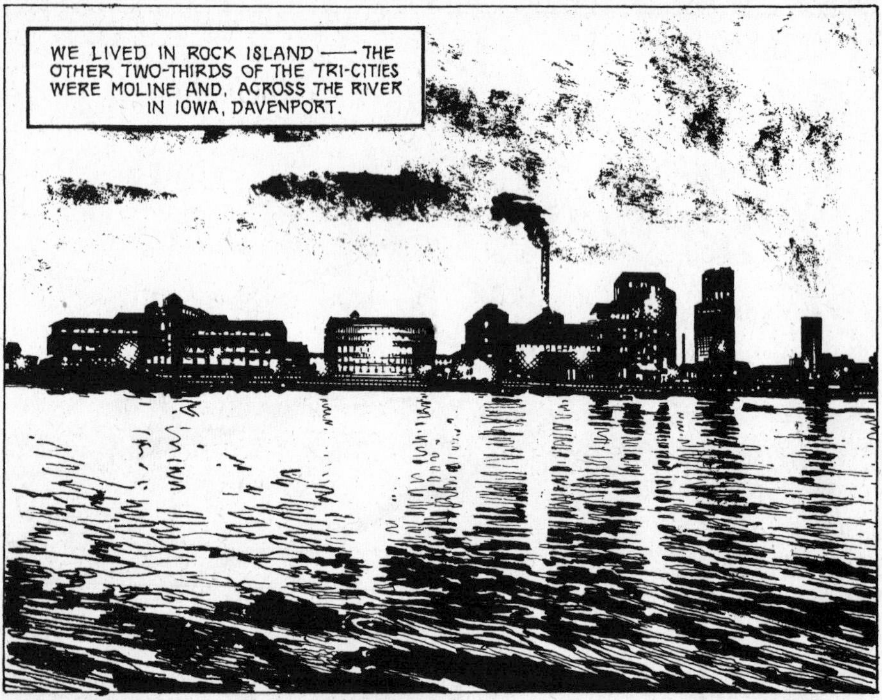
WE LIVED IN ROCK ISLAND — THE OTHER TWO-THIRDS OF THE TRI-CITIES WERE MOLINE AND, ACROSS THE RIVER IN IOWA, DAVENPORT.

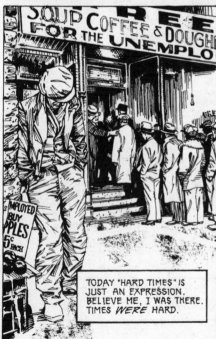

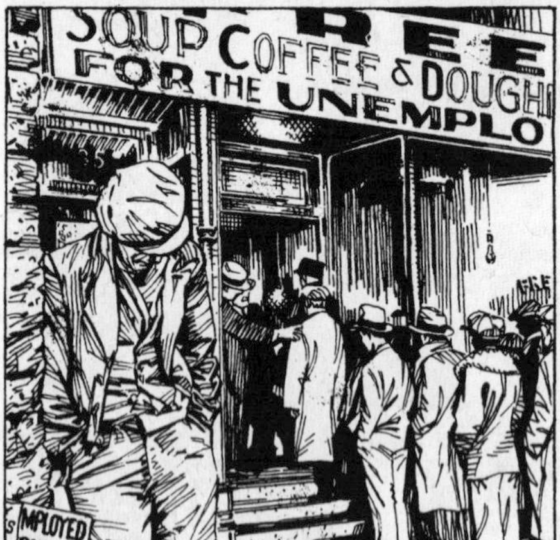
SOUP COFFEE & DOUGH
FOR THE UNEMPLO
TODAY "HARD TIMES" IS JUST AN EXPRESSION. BELIEVE ME, I WAS THERE. TIMES *WERE* HARD.

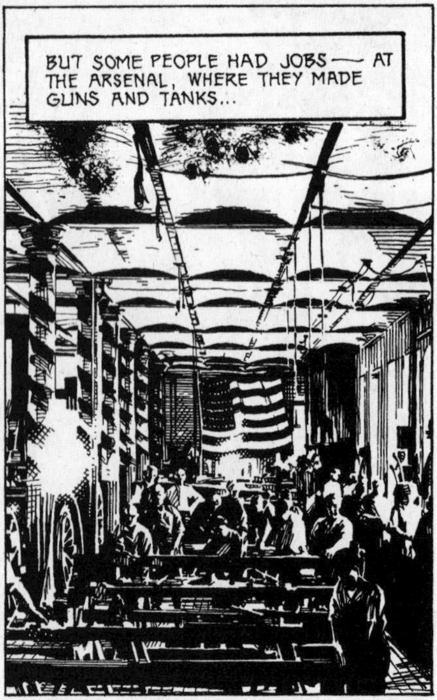
BUT SOME PEOPLE HAD JOBS — AT THE ARSENAL, WHERE THEY MADE GUNS AND TANKS...

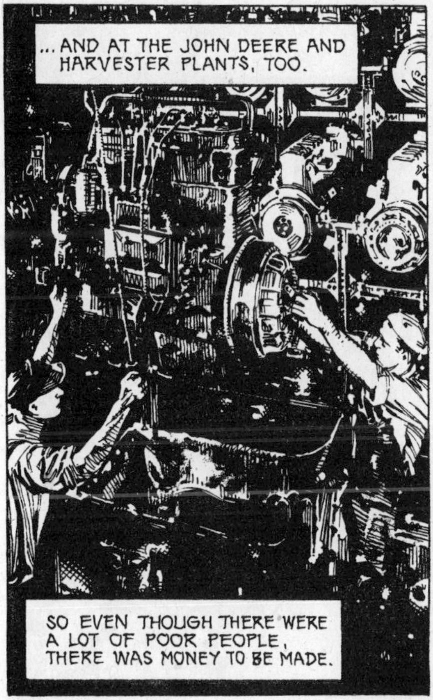
...AND AT THE JOHN DEERE AND HARVESTER PLANTS, TOO.
SO EVEN THOUGH THERE WERE A LOT OF POOR PEOPLE, THERE WAS MONEY TO BE MADE.

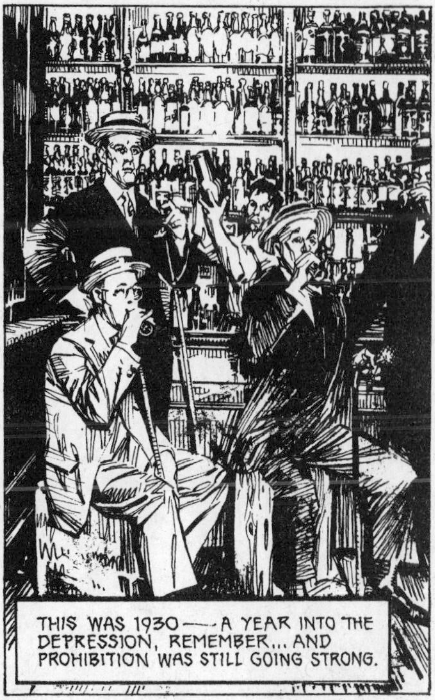
THIS WAS 1930 — A YEAR INTO THE DEPRESSION, REMEMBER... AND PROHIBITION WAS STILL GOING STRONG.

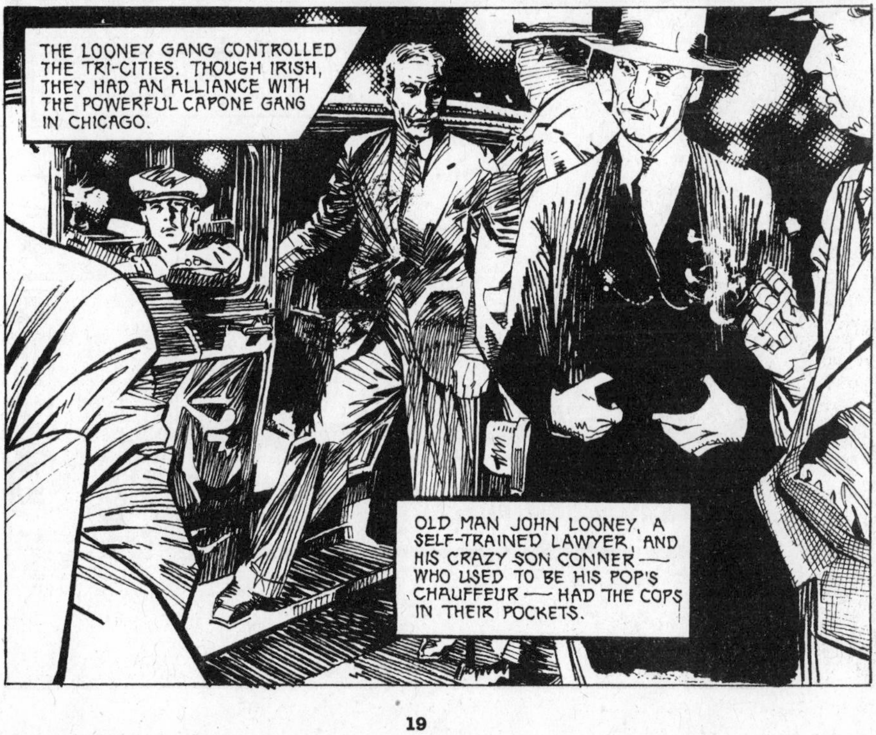
THE LOONEY GANG CONTROLLED THE TRI-CITIES. THOUGH IRISH, THEY HAD AN ALLIANCE WITH THE POWERFUL CAPONE GANG IN CHICAGO.
OLD MAN JOHN LOONEY, A SELF-TRAINED LAWYER, AND HIS CRAZY SON CONNER — WHO USED TO BE HIS POP'S CHAUFFEUR — HAD THE COPS IN THEIR POCKETS.

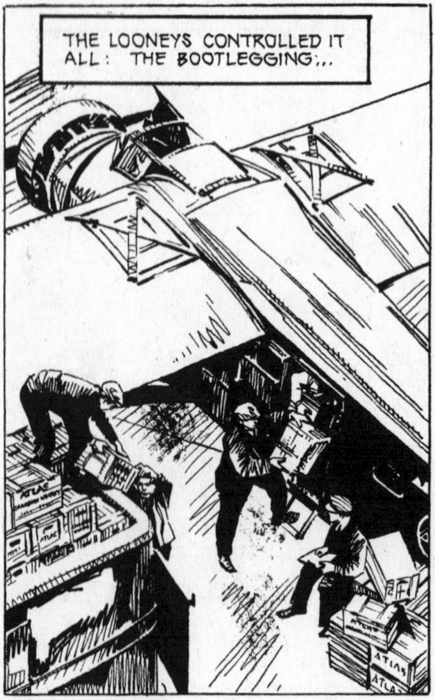
THE LOONEYS CONTROLLED IT ALL: THE BOOTLEGGING...
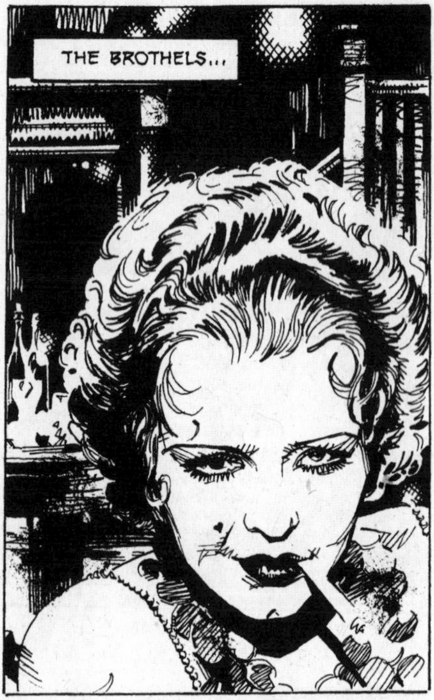
THE BROTHELS...
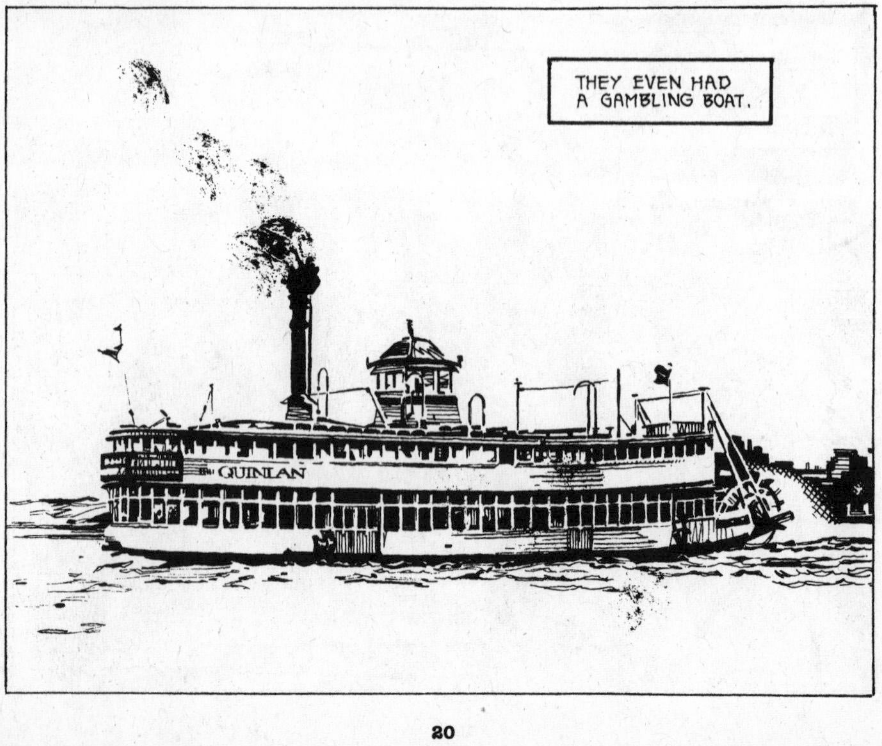
THEY EVEN HAD A GAMBLING BOAT.

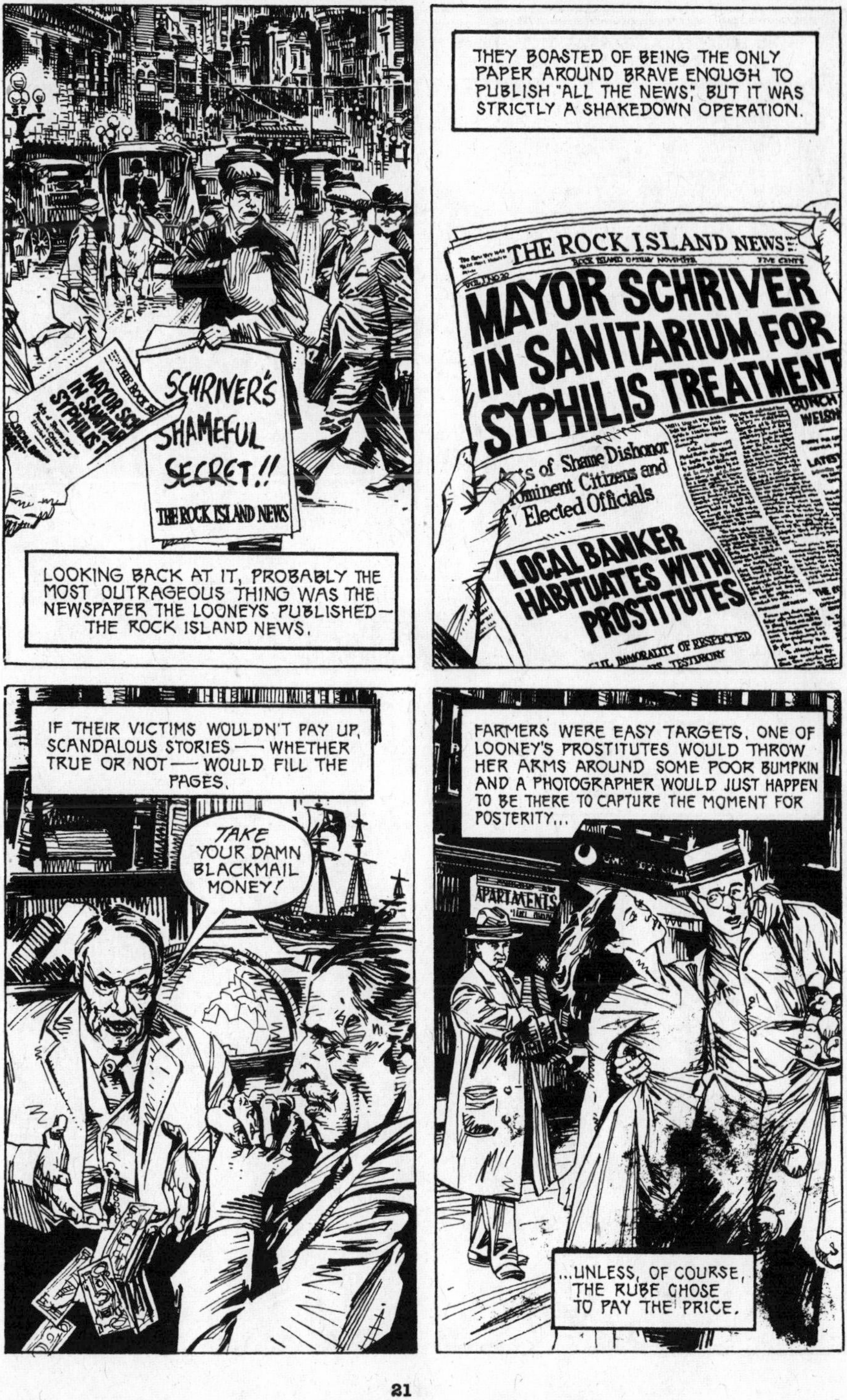

SCHRIVER'S SHAMEFUL SECRET!!
THE ROCK ISLAND NEWS
LOOKING BACK AT IT, PROBABLY THE MOST OUTRAGEOUS THING WAS THE NEWSPAPER THE LOONEYS PUBLISHED— THE ROCK ISLAND NEWS.
THEY BOASTED OF BEING THE ONLY PAPER AROUND BRAVE ENOUGH TO PUBLISH "ALL THE NEWS," BUT IT WAS STRICTLY A SHAKEDOWN OPERATION.
THE ROCK ISLAND NEWS
MAYOR SCHRIVER IN SANITARIUM FOR SYPHILIS TREATMENT
of Shame Dishonor
Citizens and
Elected Officials
LOCAL BANKER HABITUATES WITH PROSTITUTES
IF THEIR VICTIMS WOULDN'T PAY UP, SCANDALOUS STORIES — WHETHER TRUE OR NOT — WOULD FILL THE PAGES.
TAKE YOUR DAMN BLACKMAIL MONEY!
FARMERS WERE EASY TARGETS. ONE OF LOONEY'S PROSTITUTES WOULD THROW HER ARMS AROUND SOME POOR BUMPKIN AND A PHOTOGRAPHER WOULD JUST HAPPEN TO BE THERE TO CAPTURE THE MOMENT FOR POSTERITY...
APARTMENTS
...UNLESS, OF COURSE, THE RUBE CHOSE TO PAY THE PRICE.

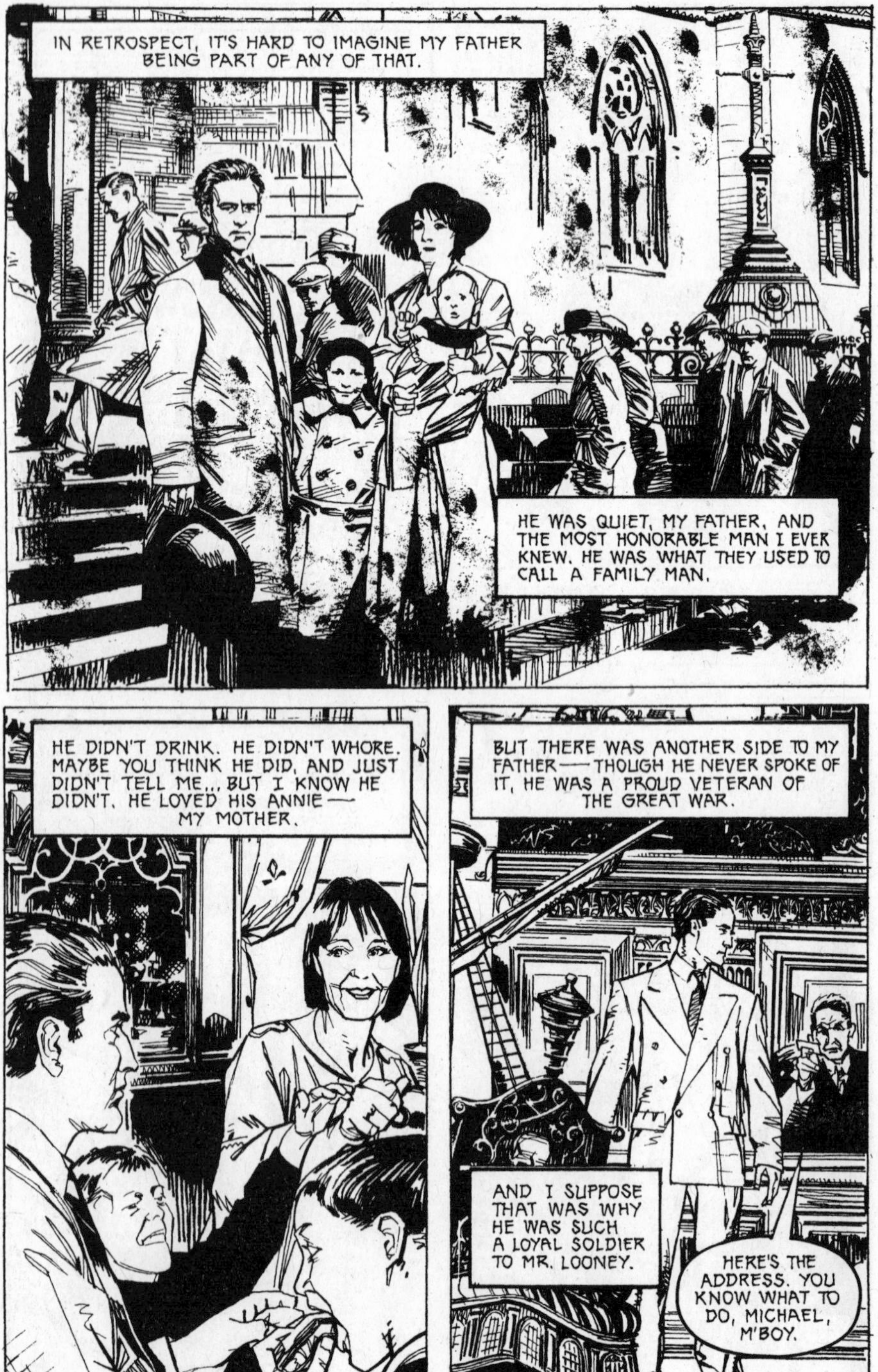
IN RETROSPECT, IT'S HARD TO IMAGINE MY FATHER BEING PART OF ANY OF THAT.
HE WAS QUIET, MY FATHER, AND THE MOST HONORABLE MAN I EVER KNEW. HE WAS WHAT THEY USED TO CALL A FAMILY MAN.
HE DIDN'T DRINK. HE DIDN'T WHORE. MAYBE YOU THINK HE DID, AND JUST DIDN'T TELL ME... BUT I KNOW HE DIDN'T. HE LOVED HIS ANNIE — MY MOTHER.
BUT THERE WAS ANOTHER SIDE TO MY FATHER — THOUGH HE NEVER SPOKE OF IT, HE WAS A PROUD VETERAN OF THE GREAT WAR.
AND I SUPPOSE THAT WAS WHY HE WAS SUCH A LOYAL SOLDIER TO MR. LOONEY.
HERE'S THE ADDRESS. YOU KNOW WHAT TO DO, MICHAEL, M'BOY.

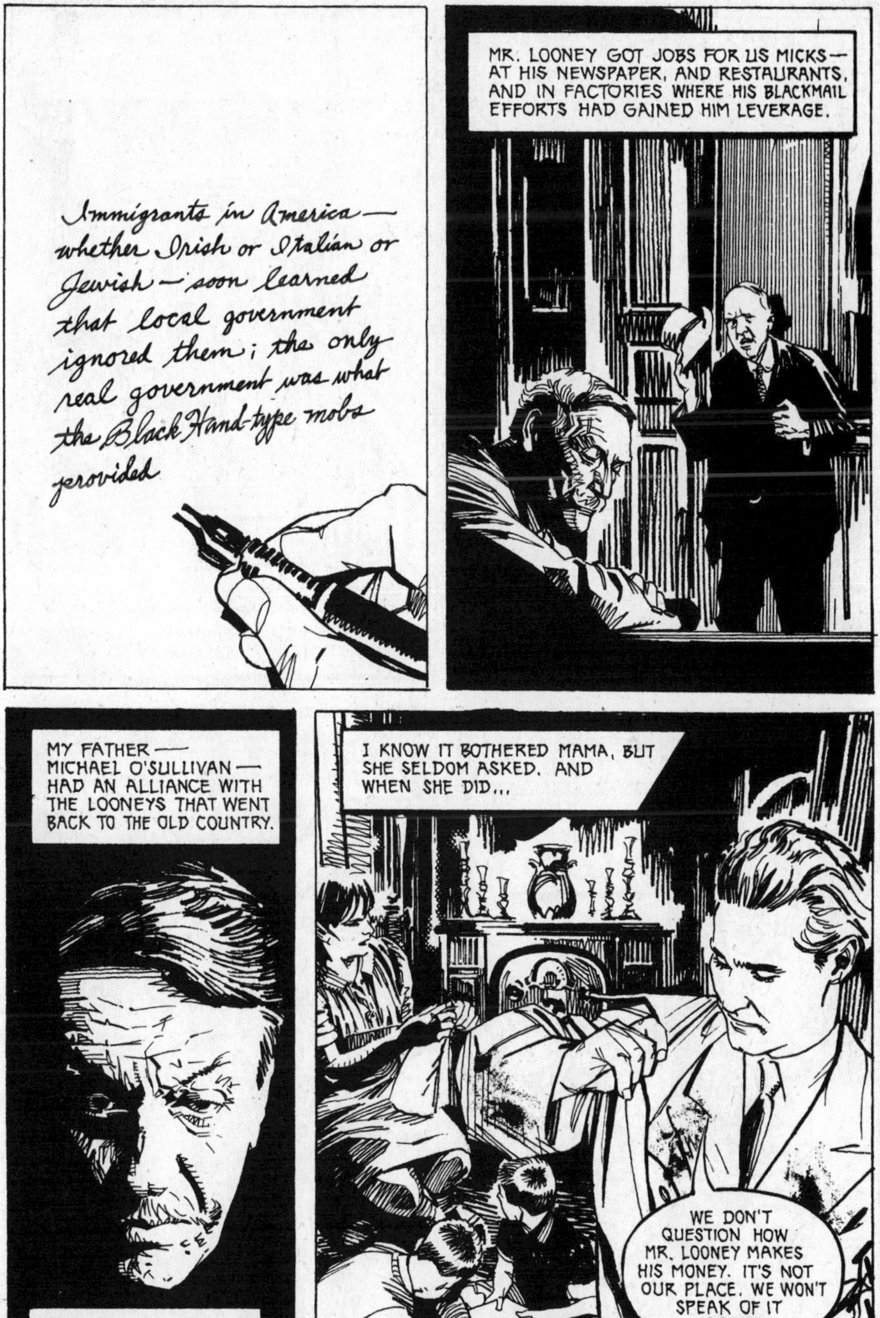
Immigrants in America—whether Irish or Italian or Jewish—soon learned that local government ignored them; the only real government was what the Black Hand-type mobs provided
MR. LOONEY GOT JOBS FOR US MICKS—AT HIS NEWSPAPER, AND RESTAURANTS, AND IN FACTORIES WHERE HIS BLACKMAIL EFFORTS HAD GAINED HIM LEVERAGE.
MY FATHER—MICHAEL O'SULLIVAN—HAD AN ALLIANCE WITH THE LOONEYS THAT WENT BACK TO THE OLD COUNTRY.
TO PAPA, MR. LOONEY *WAS* THE GOVERNMENT.
I KNOW IT BOTHERED MAMA, BUT SHE SELDOM ASKED. AND WHEN SHE DID...
WE DON'T QUESTION HOW MR. LOONEY MAKES HIS MONEY. IT'S NOT OUR PLACE. WE WON'T SPEAK OF IT AGAIN.

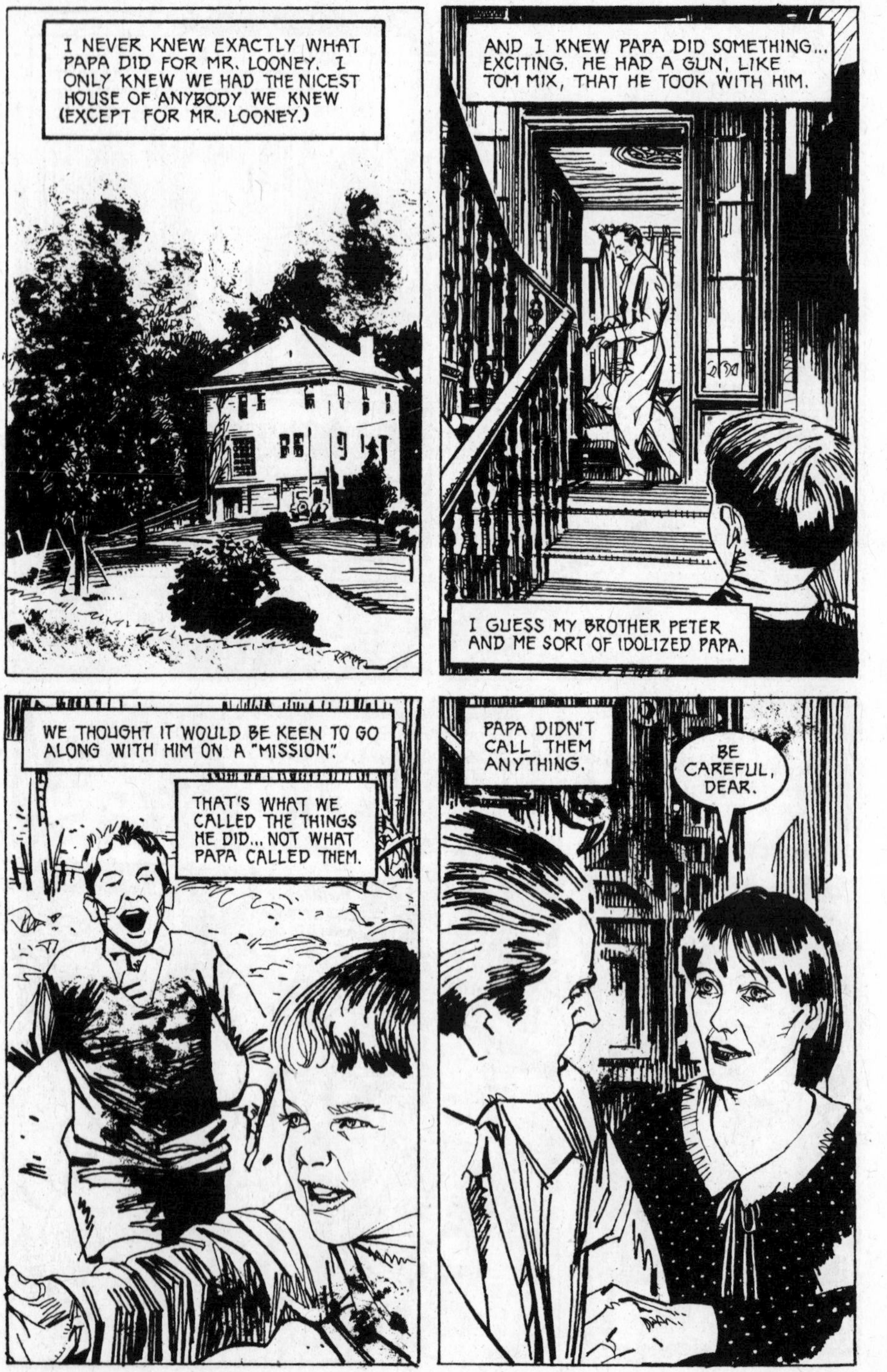
I NEVER KNEW EXACTLY WHAT PAPA DID FOR MR. LOONEY. I ONLY KNEW WE HAD THE NICEST HOUSE OF ANYBODY WE KNEW (EXCEPT FOR MR. LOONEY.)
AND I KNEW PAPA DID SOMETHING... EXCITING. HE HAD A GUN, LIKE TOM MIX, THAT HE TOOK WITH HIM.
I GUESS MY BROTHER PETER AND ME SORT OF IDOLIZED PAPA.
WE THOUGHT IT WOULD BE KEEN TO GO ALONG WITH HIM ON A "MISSION".
THAT'S WHAT WE CALLED THE THINGS HE DID... NOT WHAT PAPA CALLED THEM.
PAPA DIDN'T CALL THEM ANYTHING.
BE CAREFUL, DEAR.

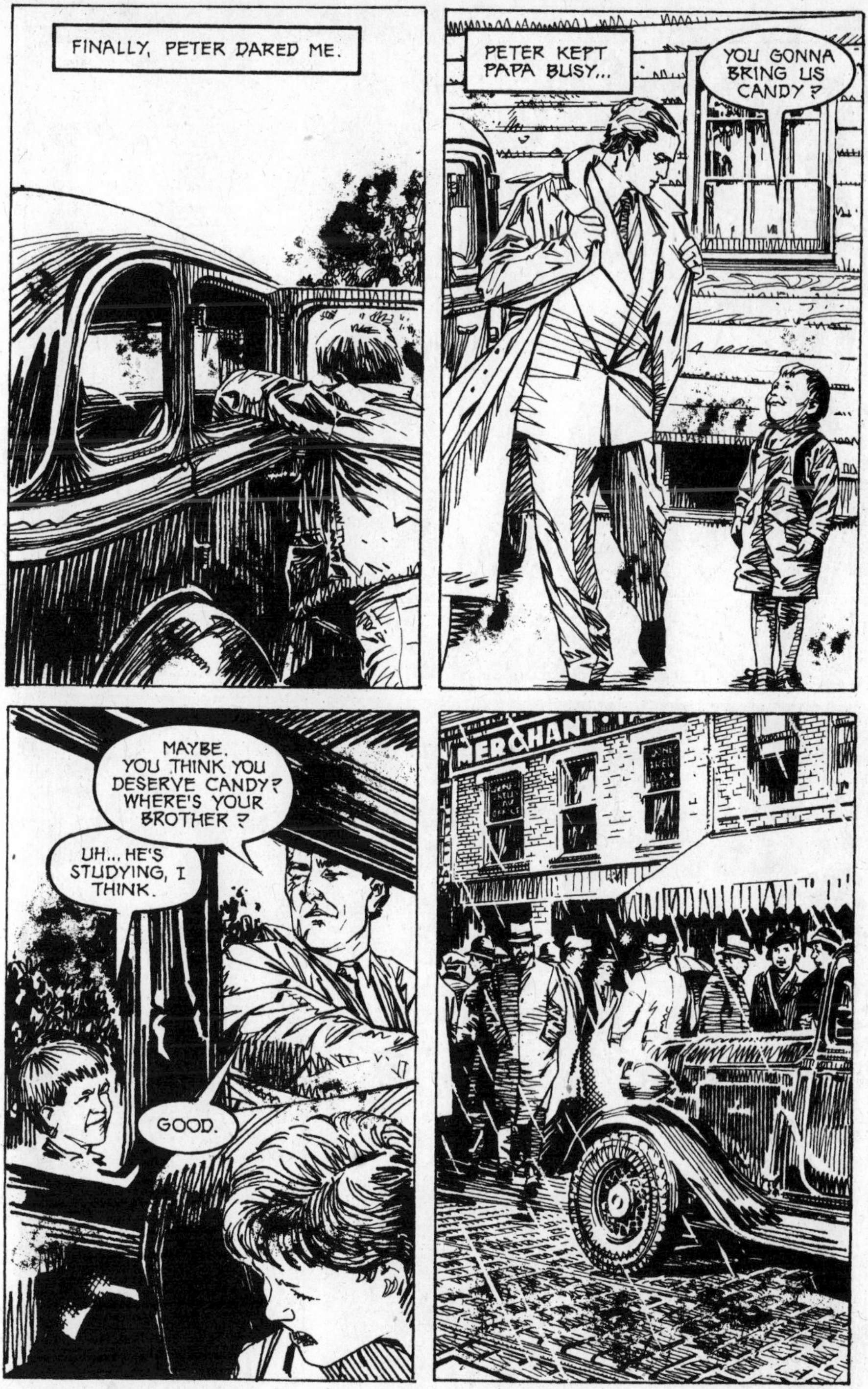
FINALLY, PETER DARED ME.
PETER KEPT PAPA BUSY...
YOU GONNA BRING US CANDY?
MAYBE. YOU THINK YOU DESERVE CANDY? WHERE'S YOUR BROTHER?
UH... HE'S STUDYING, I THINK.
GOOD.
MERCHANT

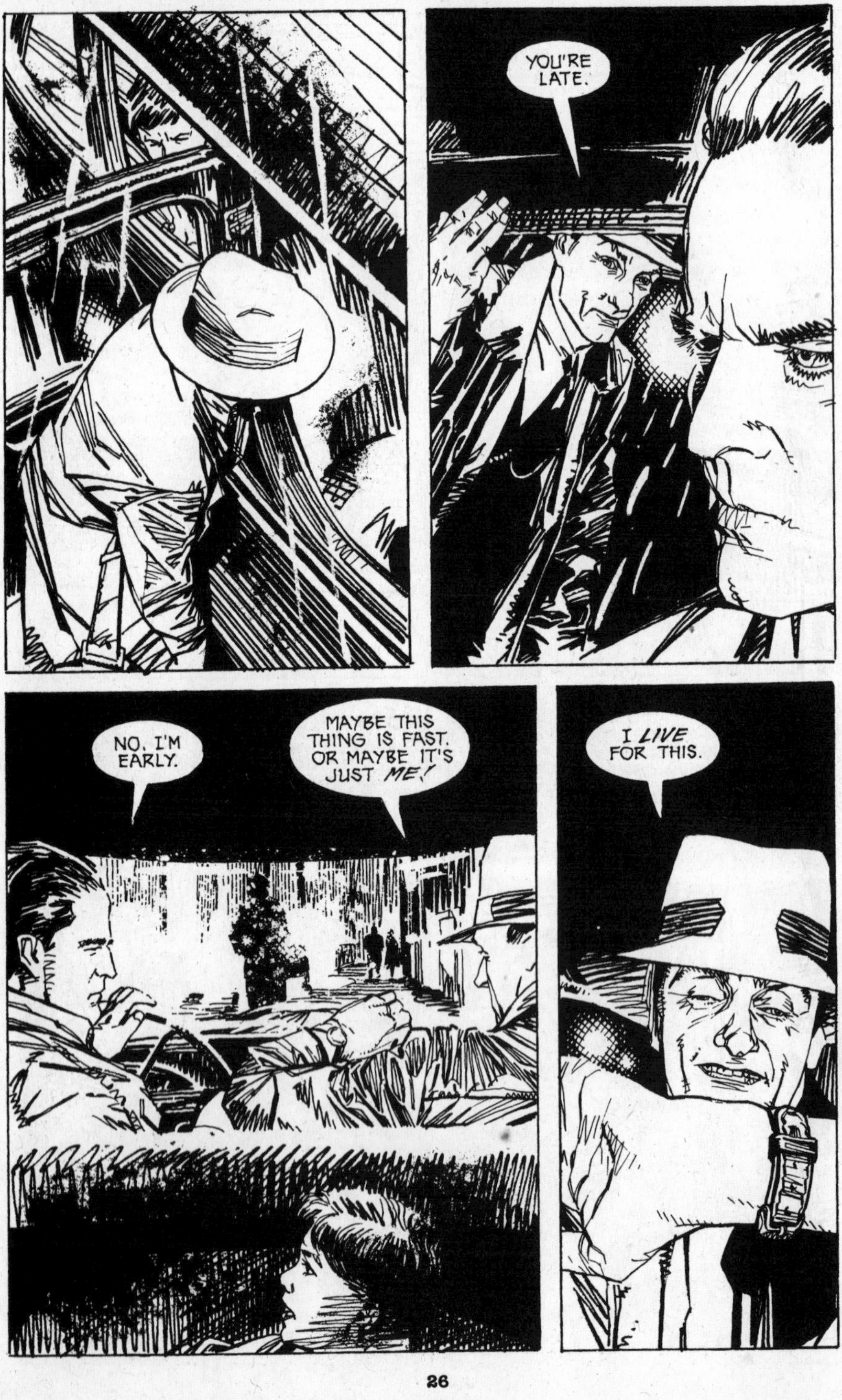
YOU'RE LATE.
NO. I'M EARLY.
MAYBE THIS THING IS FAST. OR MAYBE IT'S JUST *ME!*
I *LIVE* FOR THIS.

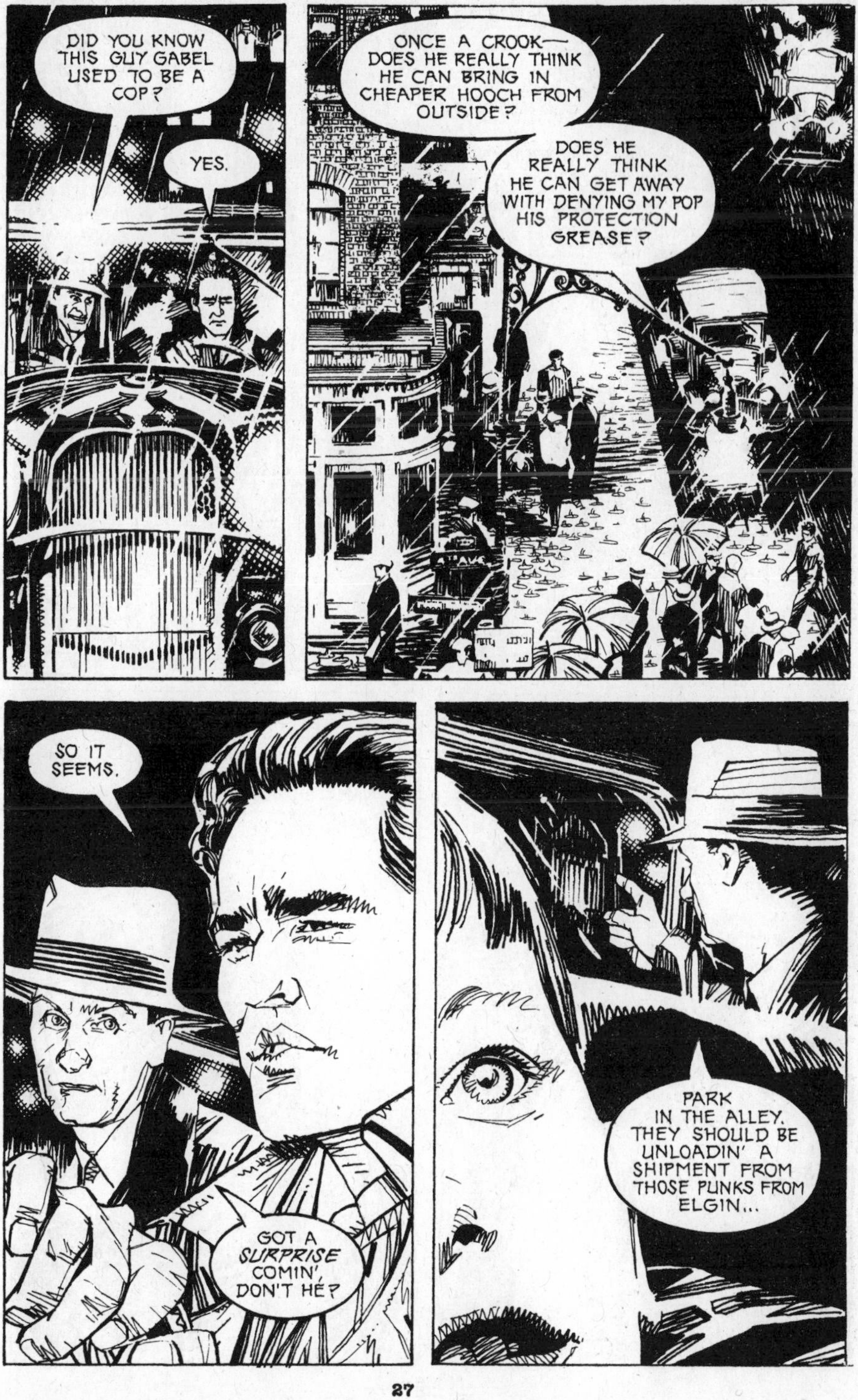
DID YOU KNOW THIS GUY GABEL USED TO BE A COP?
YES.
ONCE A CROOK— DOES HE REALLY THINK HE CAN BRING IN CHEAPER HOOCH FROM OUTSIDE?
DOES HE REALLY THINK HE CAN GET AWAY WITH DENYING MY POP HIS PROTECTION GREASE?
SO IT SEEMS.
GOT A *SURPRISE* COMIN', DON'T HE?
PARK IN THE ALLEY. THEY SHOULD BE UNLOADIN' A SHIPMENT FROM THOSE PUNKS FROM ELGIN...

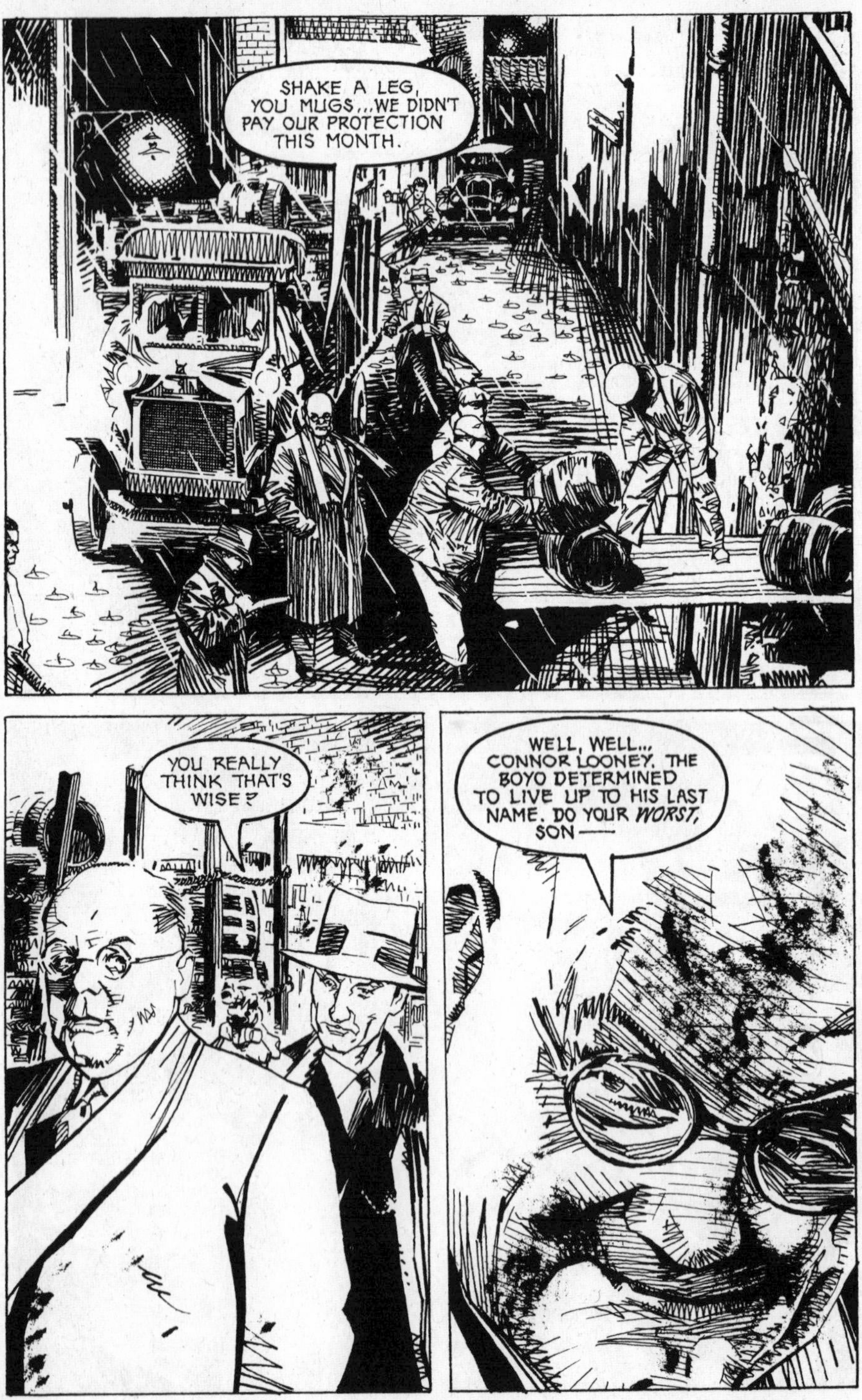
SHAKE A LEG, YOU MUGS,...WE DIDN'T PAY OUR PROTECTION THIS MONTH.
YOU REALLY THINK THAT'S WISE?
WELL, WELL... CONNOR LOONEY. THE BOYO DETERMINED TO LIVE UP TO HIS LAST NAME. DO YOUR *WORST,* SON—

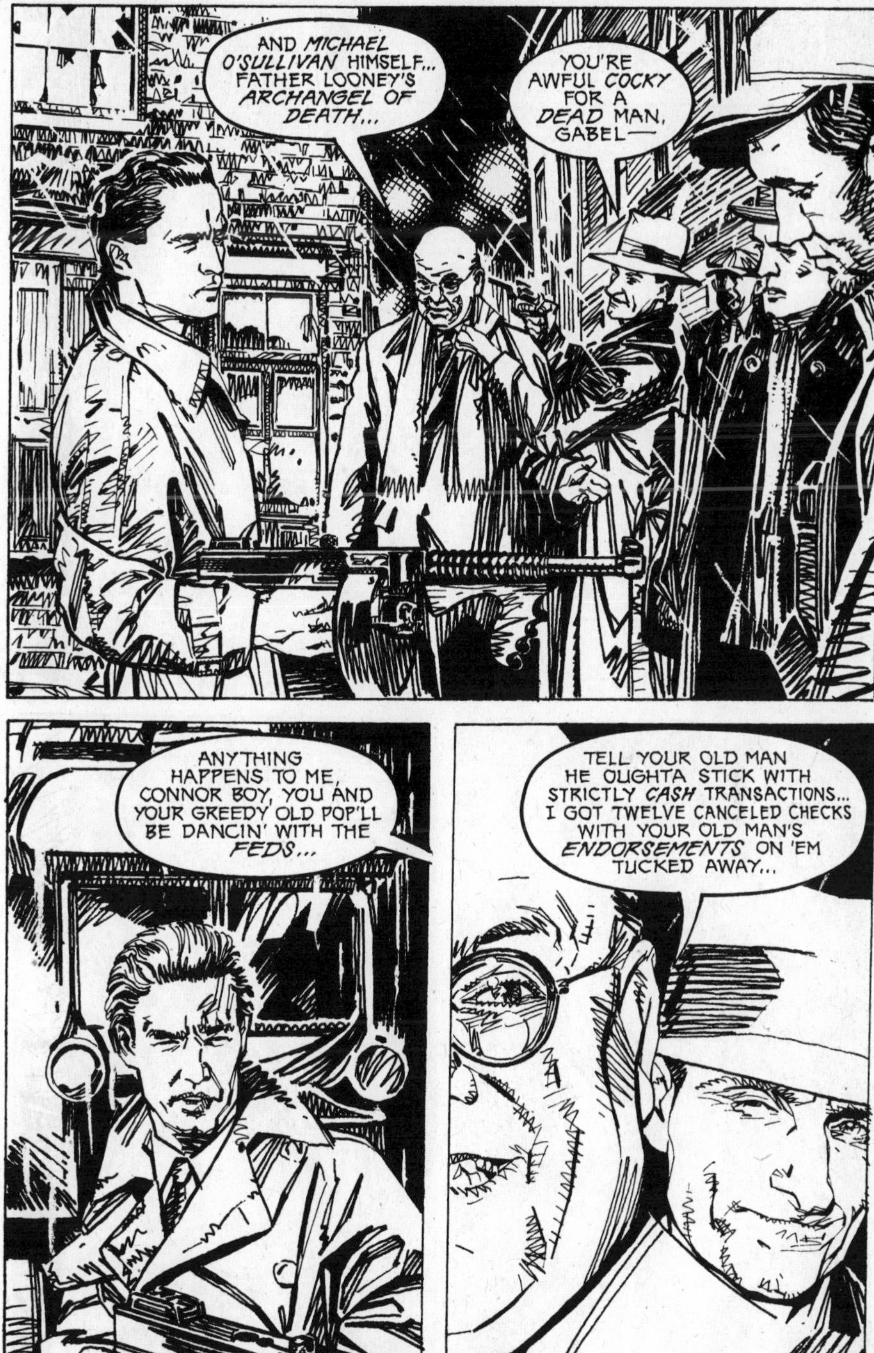
AND MICHAEL O'SULLIVAN HIMSELF... FATHER LOONEY'S ARCHANGEL OF DEATH...
YOU'RE AWFUL COCKY FOR A DEAD MAN, GABEL—
ANYTHING HAPPENS TO ME, CONNOR BOY, YOU AND YOUR GREEDY OLD POP'LL BE DANCIN' WITH THE FEDS...
TELL YOUR OLD MAN HE OUGHTA STICK WITH STRICTLY CASH TRANSACTIONS... I GOT TWELVE CANCELED CHECKS WITH YOUR OLD MAN'S ENDORSEMENTS ON 'EM TUCKED AWAY...

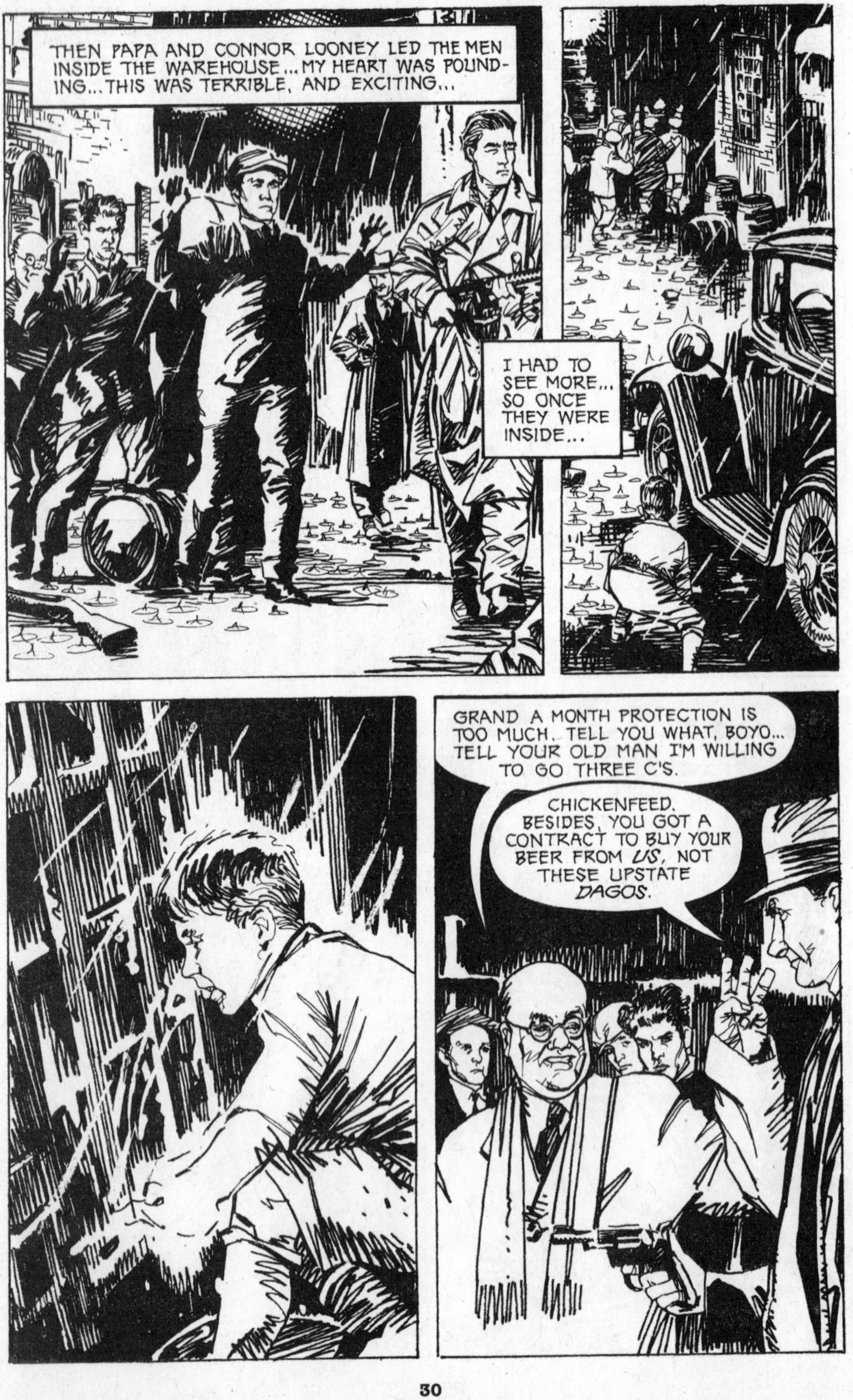
THEN PAPA AND CONNOR LOONEY LED THE MEN INSIDE THE WAREHOUSE... MY HEART WAS POUNDING... THIS WAS TERRIBLE, AND EXCITING...
I HAD TO SEE MORE... SO ONCE THEY WERE INSIDE...
GRAND A MONTH PROTECTION IS TOO MUCH. TELL YOU WHAT, BOYO... TELL YOUR OLD MAN I'M WILLING TO GO THREE C'S.
CHICKENFEED. BESIDES, YOU GOT A CONTRACT TO BUY YOUR BEER FROM *US*, NOT THESE UPSTATE *DAGOS*.

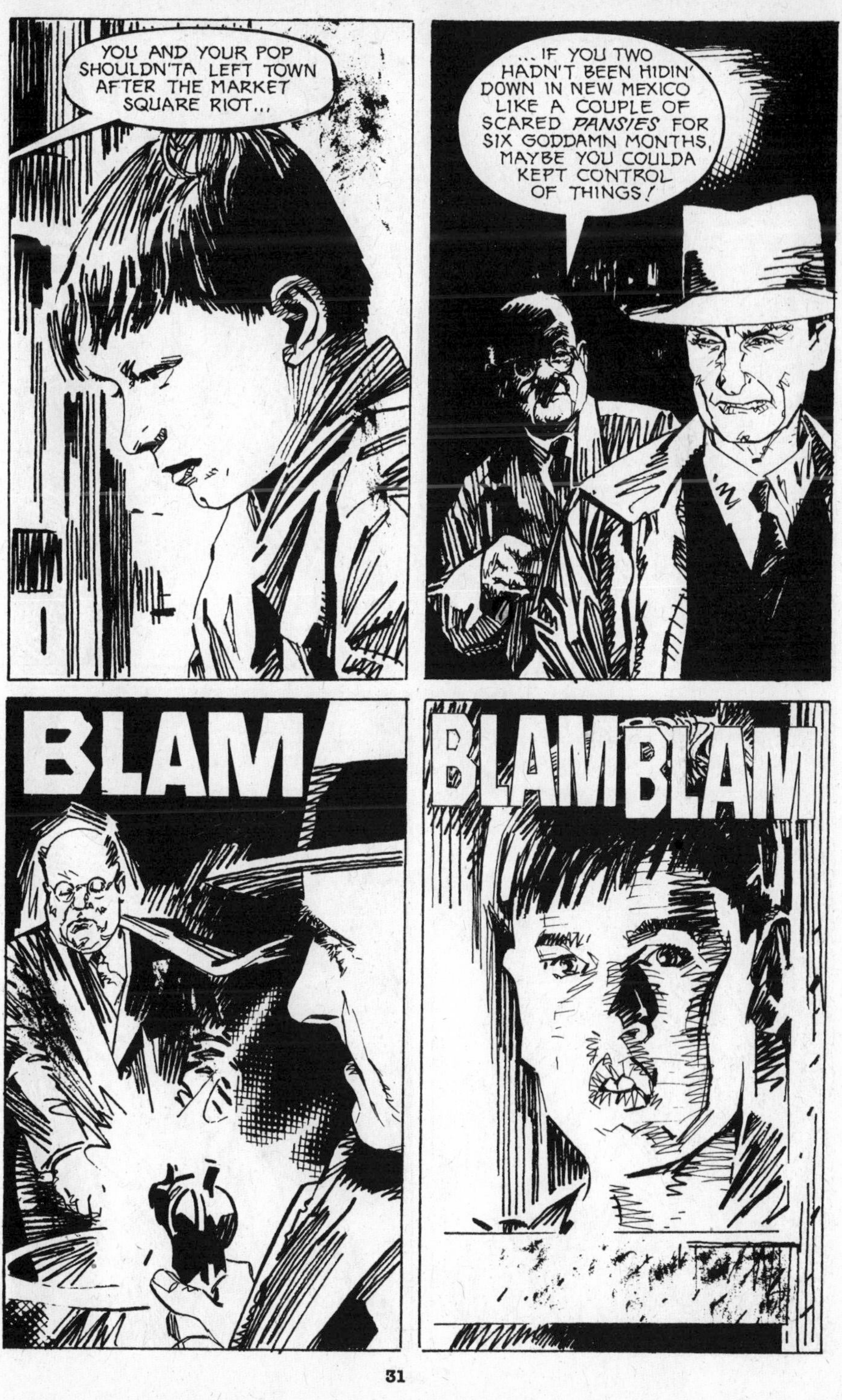
YOU AND YOUR POP SHOULDN'TA LEFT TOWN AFTER THE MARKET SQUARE RIOT...
...IF YOU TWO HADN'T BEEN HIDIN' DOWN IN NEW MEXICO LIKE A COUPLE OF SCARED *PANSIES* FOR SIX GODDAMN MONTHS, MAYBE YOU COULDA KEPT CONTROL OF THINGS!
BLAM
BLAMBLAM

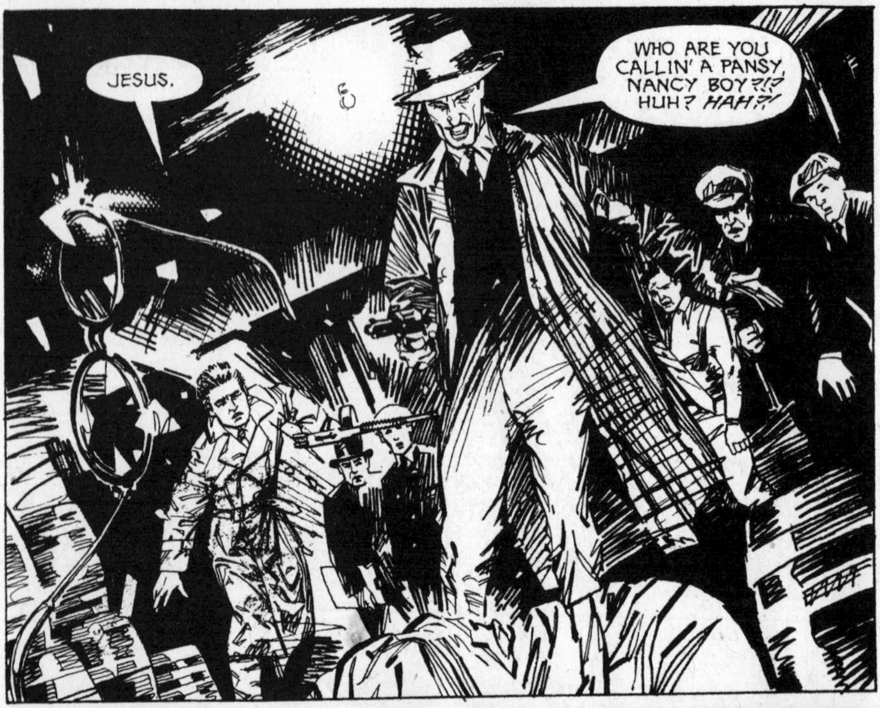
JESUS.
WHO ARE YOU CALLIN' A PANSY, NANCY BOY?!? HUH? HAH?!?

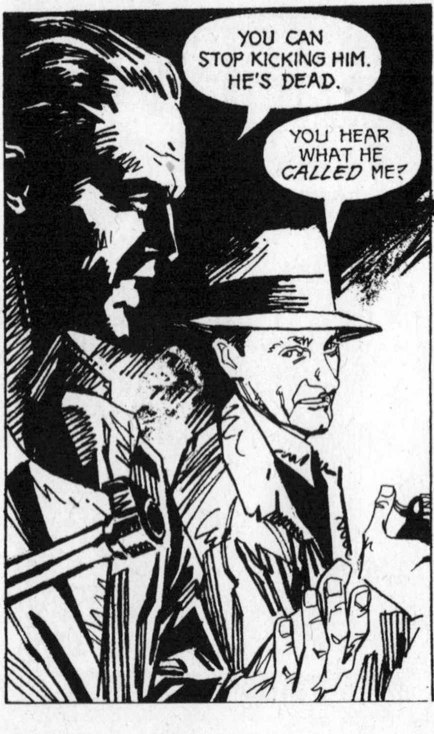
YOU CAN STOP KICKING HIM. HE'S DEAD.
YOU HEAR WHAT HE CALLED ME?

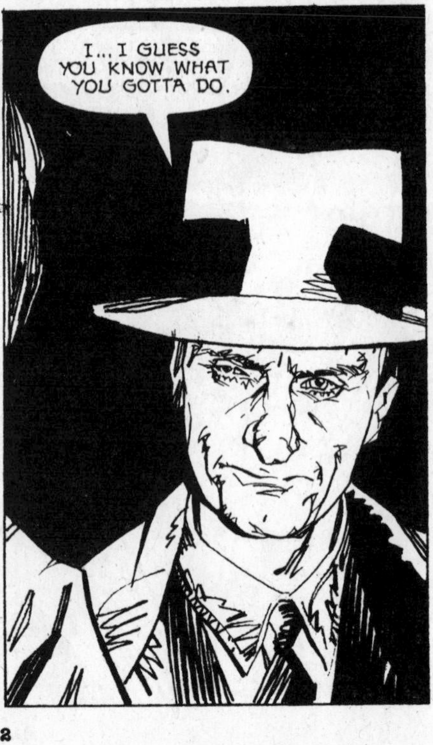
I... I GUESS YOU KNOW WHAT YOU GOTTA DO.

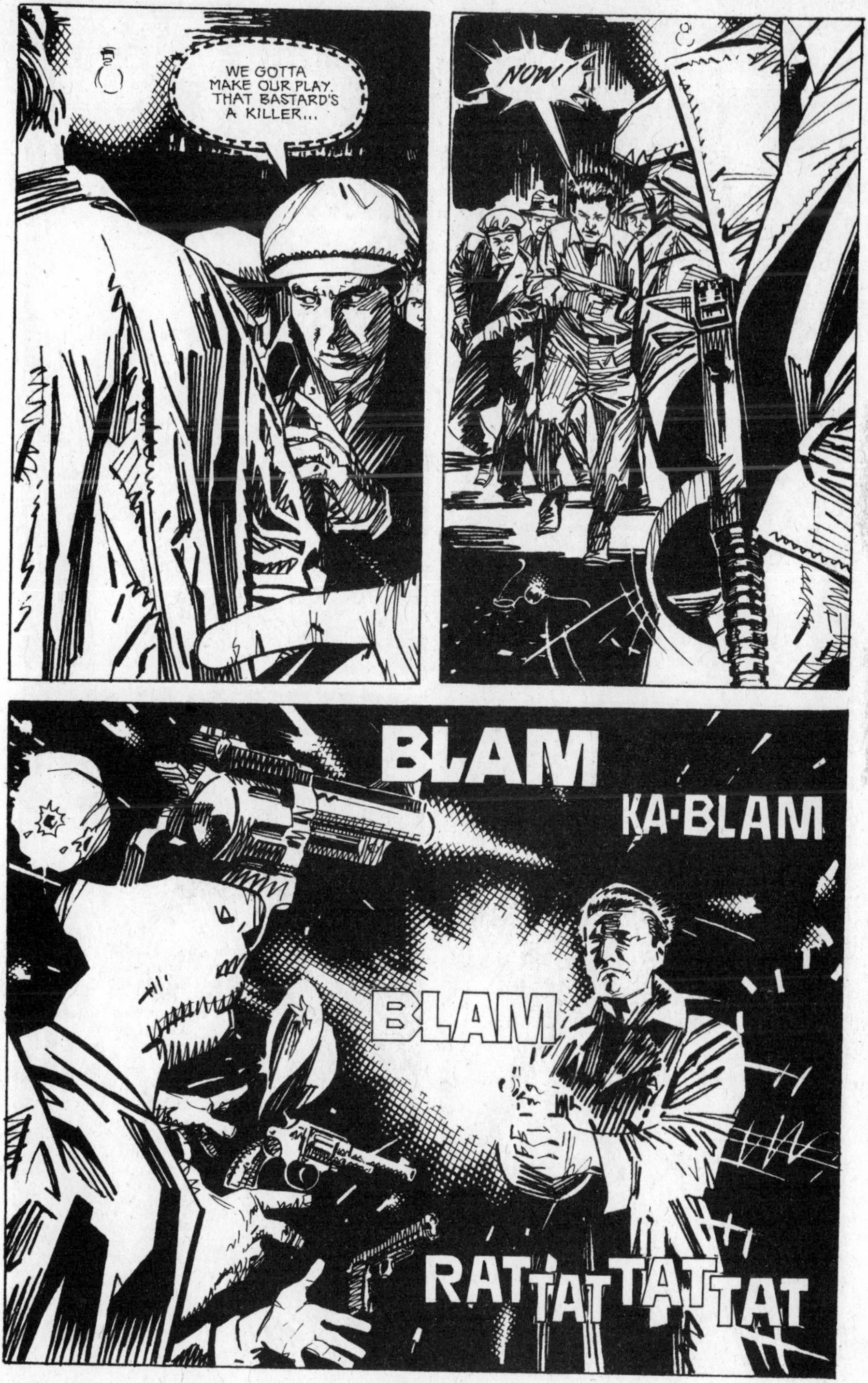
WE GOTTA MAKE OUR PLAY. THAT BASTARD'S A KILLER...
NOW!
BLAM
KA-BLAM
BLAM
RAT TAT TAT TAT

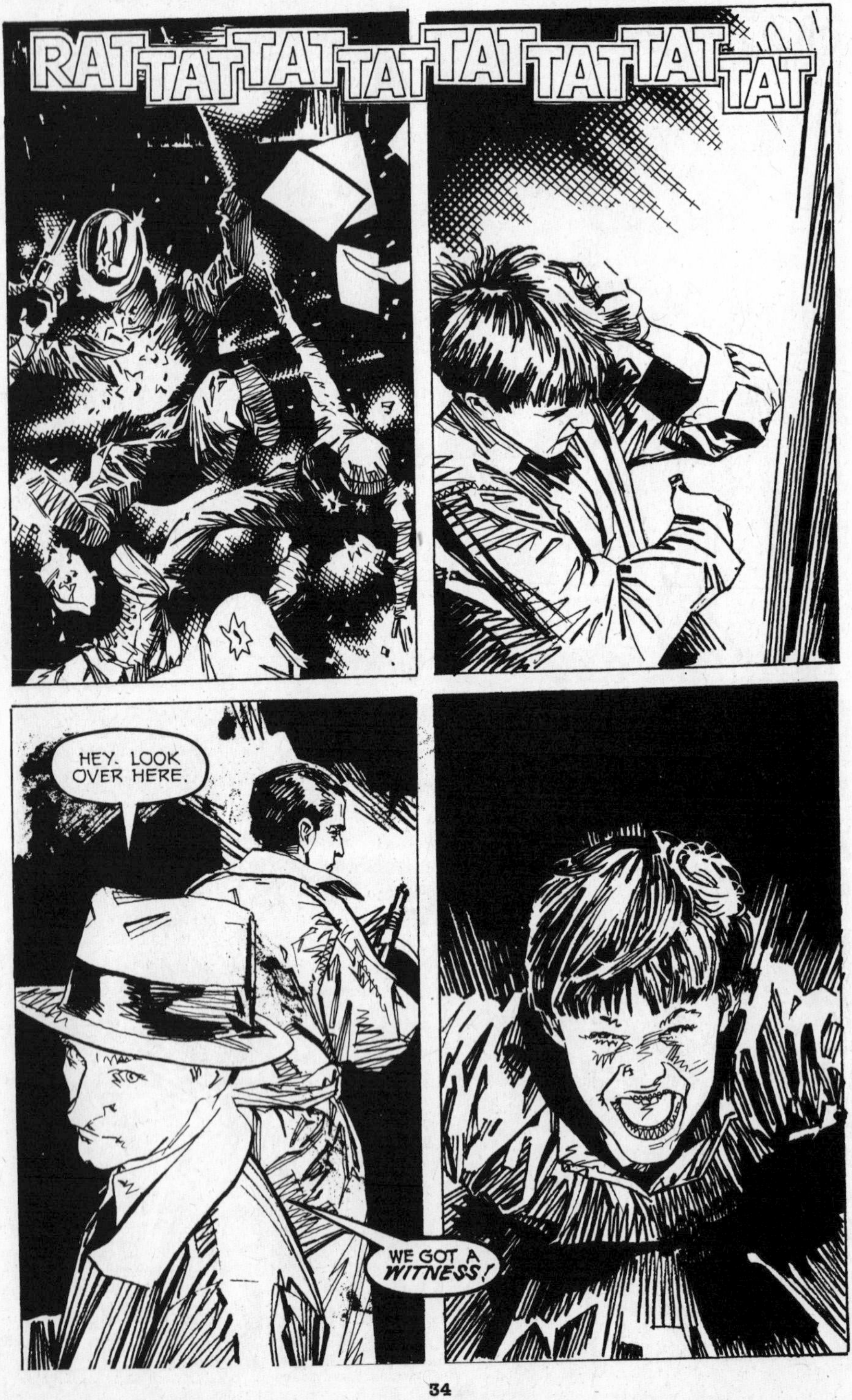
RAT TAT TAT TAT TAT TAT TAT TAT
HEY. LOOK OVER HERE.
WE GOT A *WITNESS!*

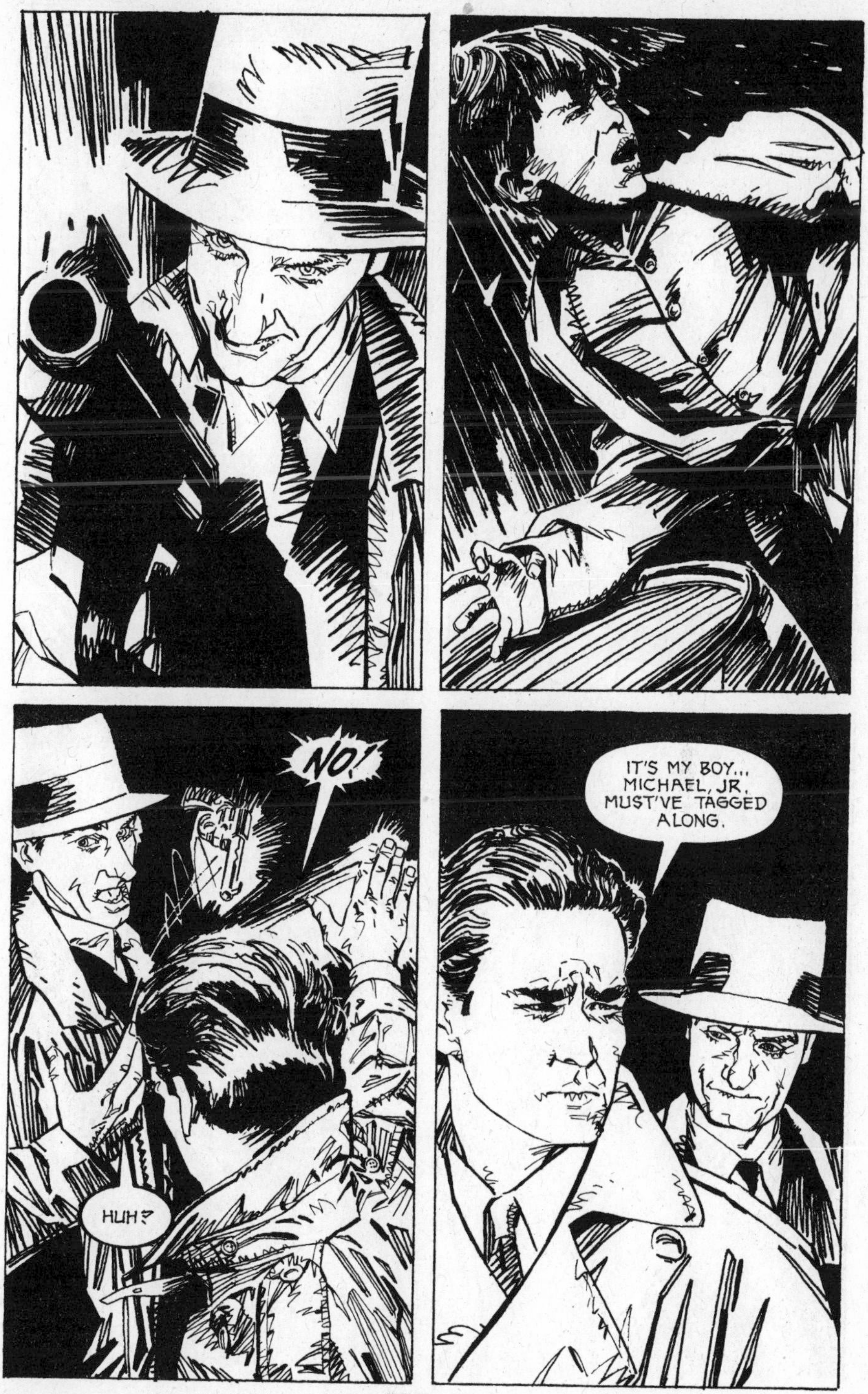
NO!
HUH?
IT'S MY BOY... MICHAEL, JR. MUST'VE TAGGED ALONG.

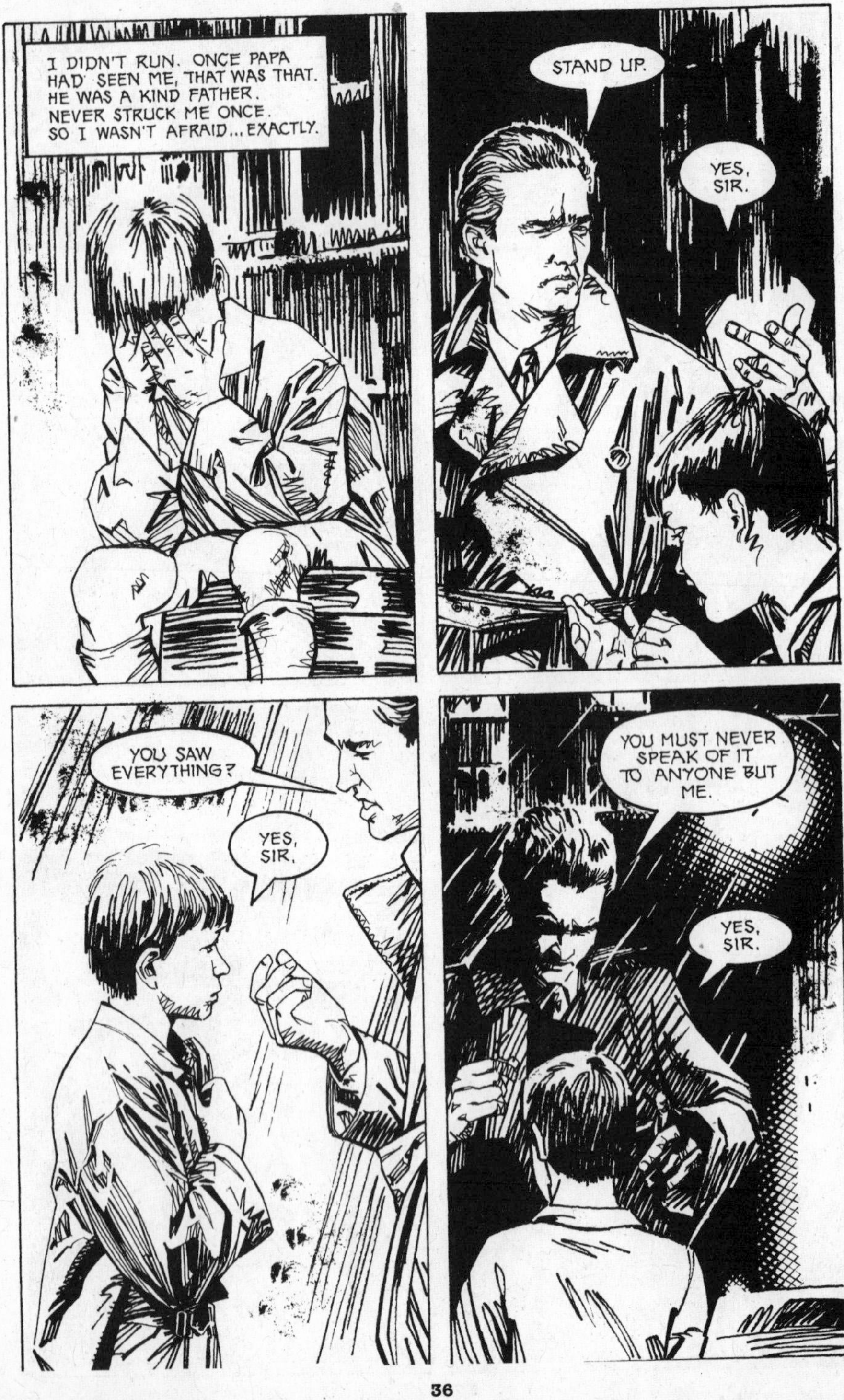
I DIDN'T RUN. ONCE PAPA HAD SEEN ME, THAT WAS THAT. HE WAS A KIND FATHER. NEVER STRUCK ME ONCE. SO I WASN'T AFRAID... EXACTLY.
STAND UP.
YES, SIR.
YOU SAW EVERYTHING?
YES, SIR.
YOU MUST NEVER SPEAK OF IT TO ANYONE BUT ME.
YES, SIR.

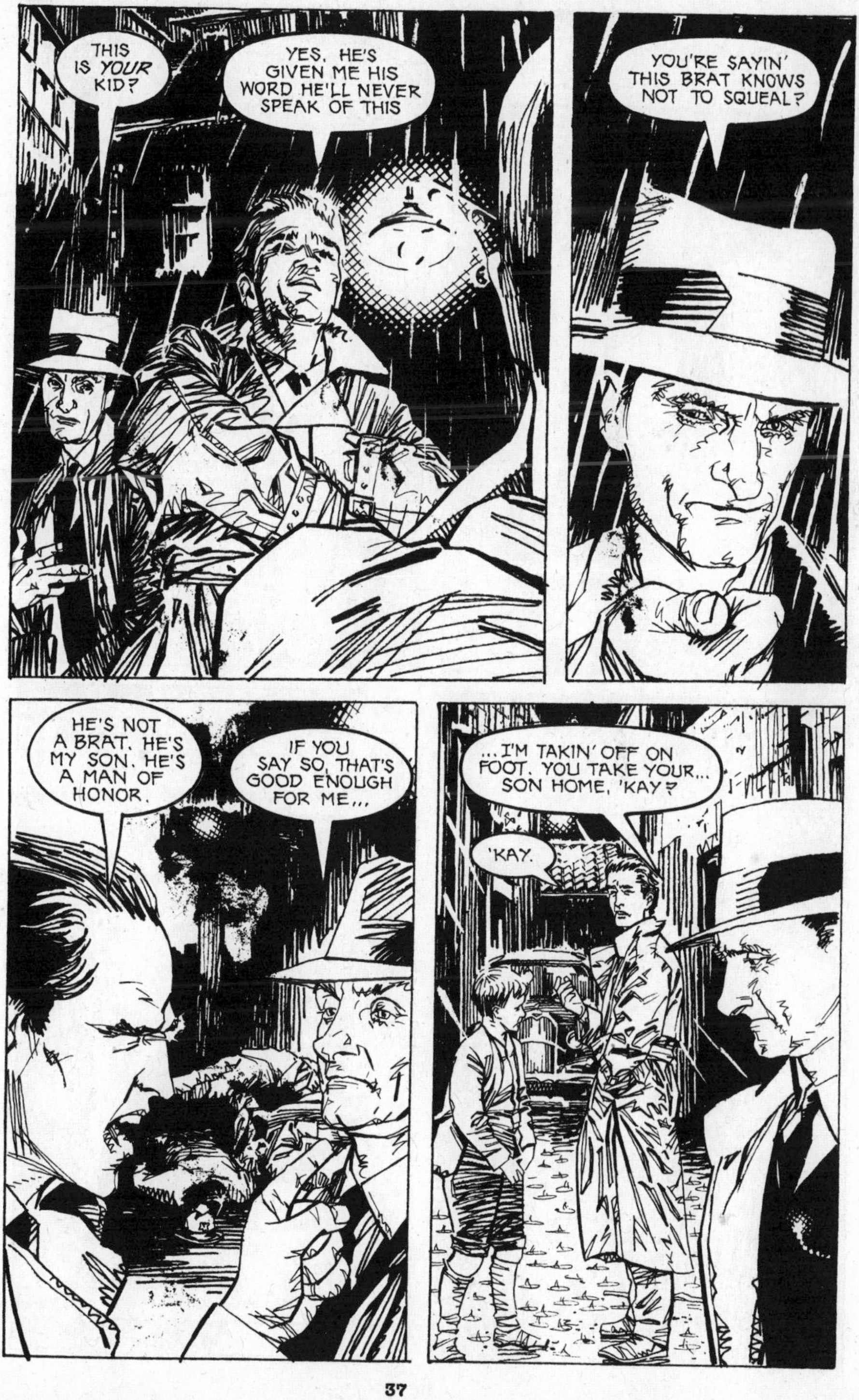
THIS IS *YOUR* KID?
YES, HE'S GIVEN ME HIS WORD HE'LL NEVER SPEAK OF THIS
YOU'RE SAYIN' THIS BRAT KNOWS NOT TO SQUEAL?
HE'S NOT A BRAT. HE'S MY SON. HE'S A MAN OF HONOR.
IF YOU SAY SO, THAT'S GOOD ENOUGH FOR ME...
...I'M TAKIN' OFF ON FOOT. YOU TAKE YOUR... SON HOME, 'KAY?
'KAY.

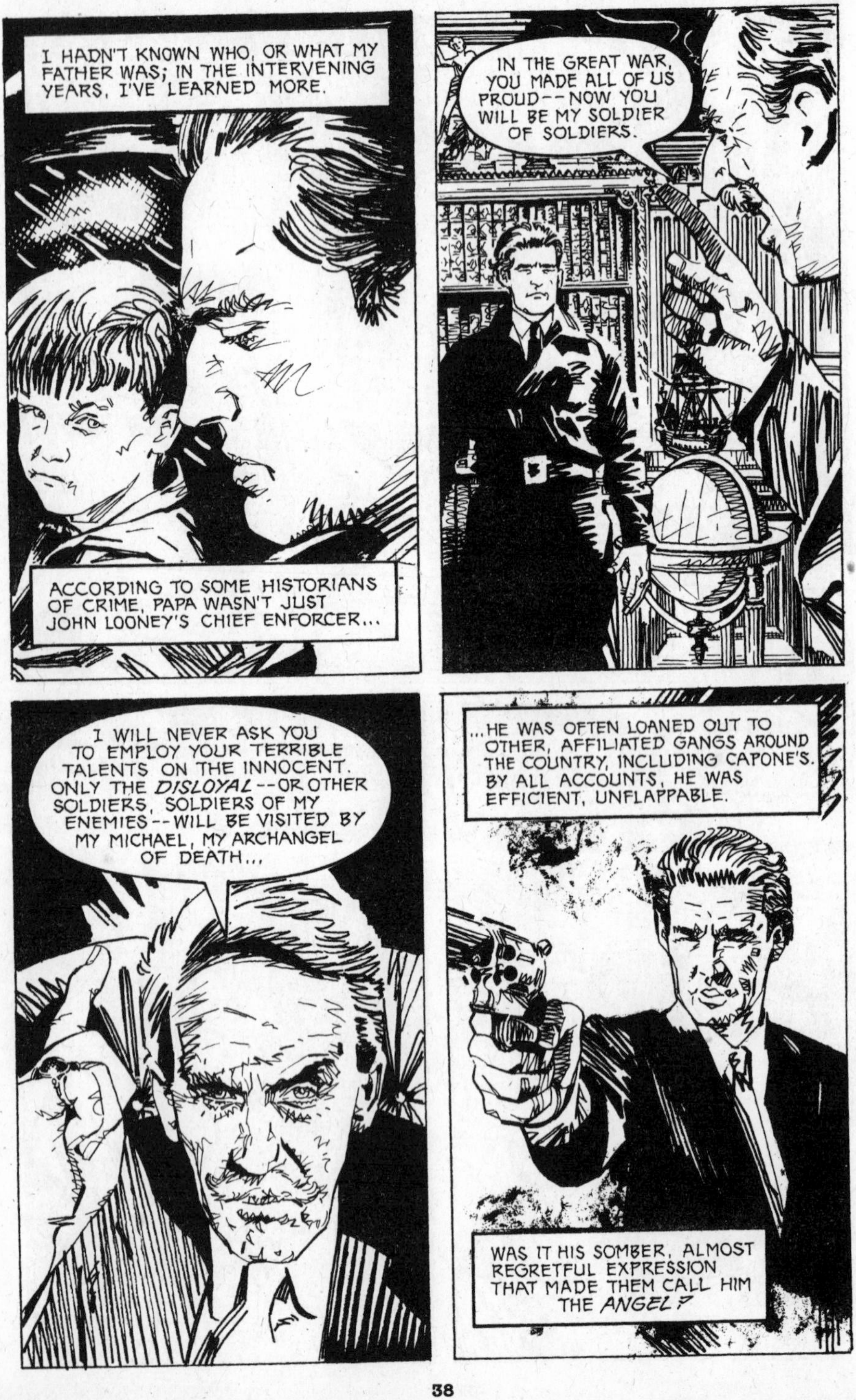
I HADN'T KNOWN WHO, OR WHAT MY FATHER WAS; IN THE INTERVENING YEARS, I'VE LEARNED MORE.
ACCORDING TO SOME HISTORIANS OF CRIME, PAPA WASN'T JUST JOHN LOONEY'S CHIEF ENFORCER...
IN THE GREAT WAR, YOU MADE ALL OF US PROUD--NOW YOU WILL BE MY SOLDIER OF SOLDIERS.
I WILL NEVER ASK YOU TO EMPLOY YOUR TERRIBLE TALENTS ON THE INNOCENT. ONLY THE *DISLOYAL*--OR OTHER SOLDIERS, SOLDIERS OF MY ENEMIES--WILL BE VISITED BY MY MICHAEL, MY ARCHANGEL OF DEATH...
...HE WAS OFTEN LOANED OUT TO OTHER, AFFILIATED GANGS AROUND THE COUNTRY, INCLUDING CAPONE'S. BY ALL ACCOUNTS, HE WAS EFFICIENT, UNFLAPPABLE.
WAS IT HIS SOMBER, ALMOST REGRETFUL EXPRESSION THAT MADE THEM CALL HIM THE *ANGEL*?

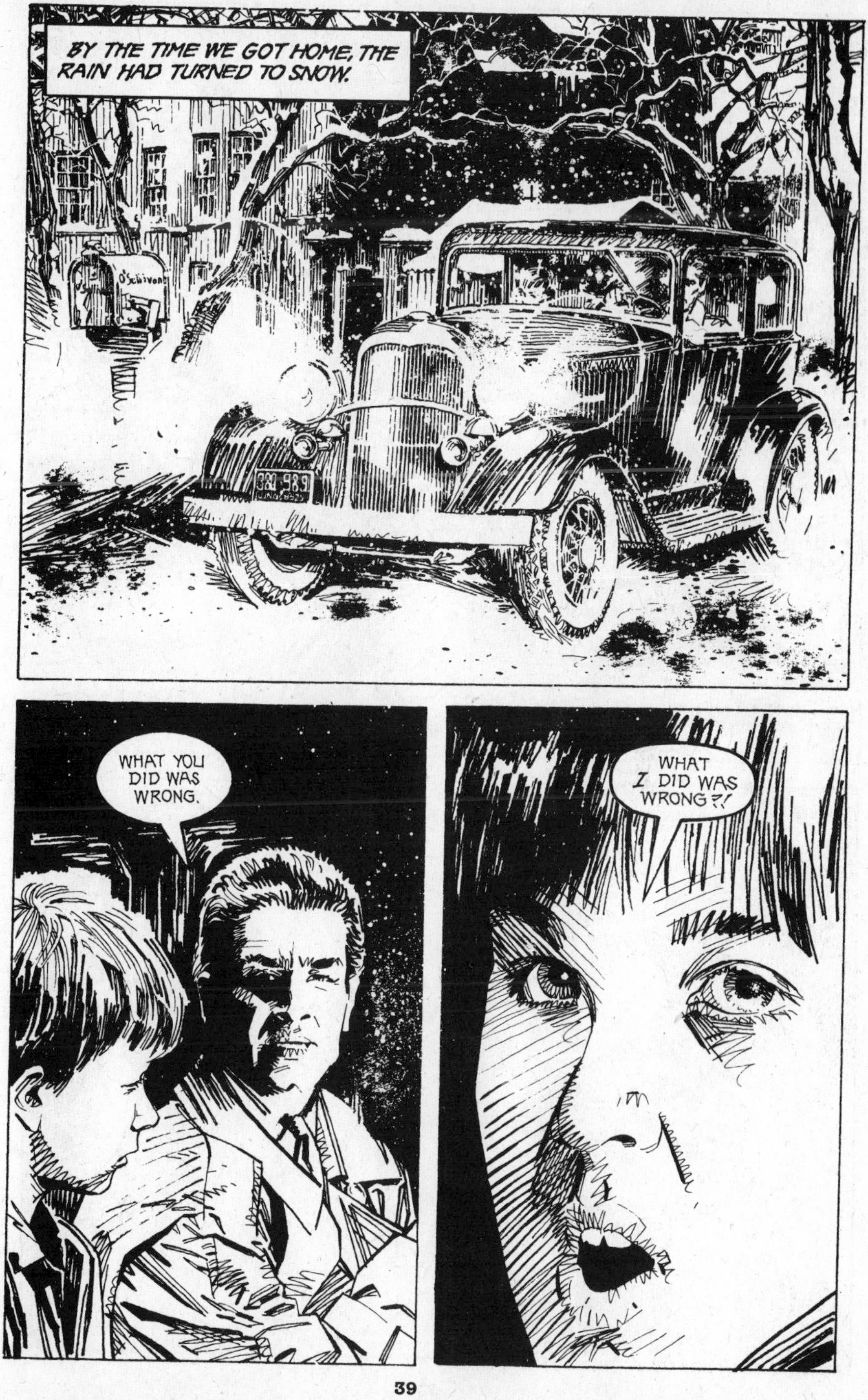
BY THE TIME WE GOT HOME, THE RAIN HAD TURNED TO SNOW.
WHAT YOU DID WAS WRONG.
WHAT I DID WAS WRONG?!

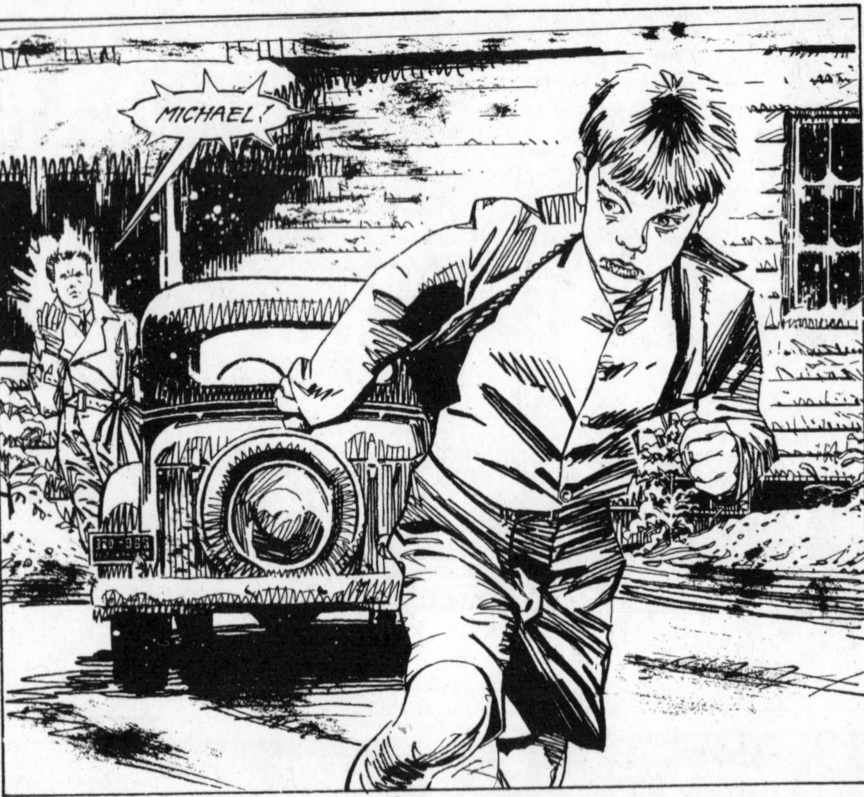
MICHAEL!

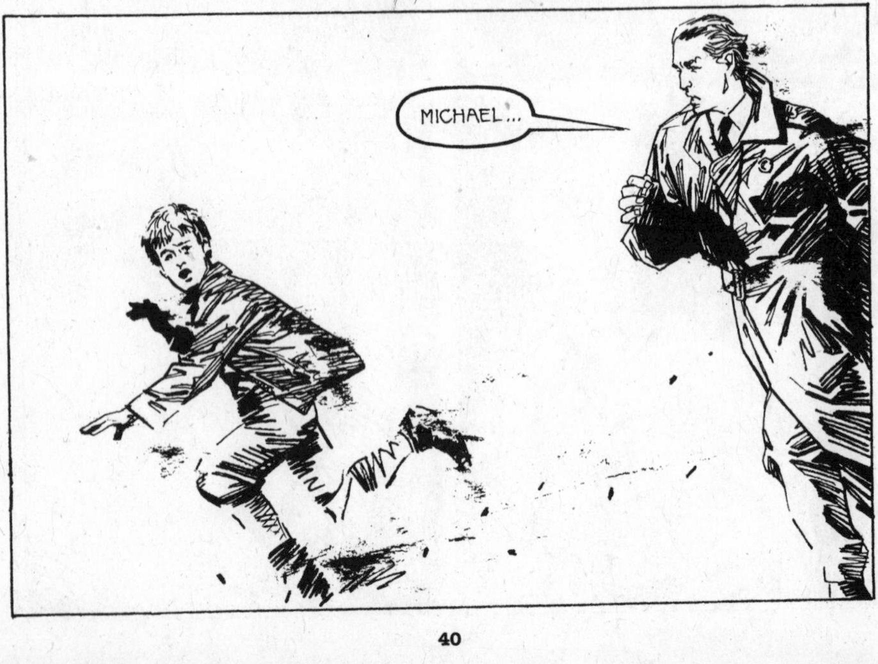
MICHAEL...

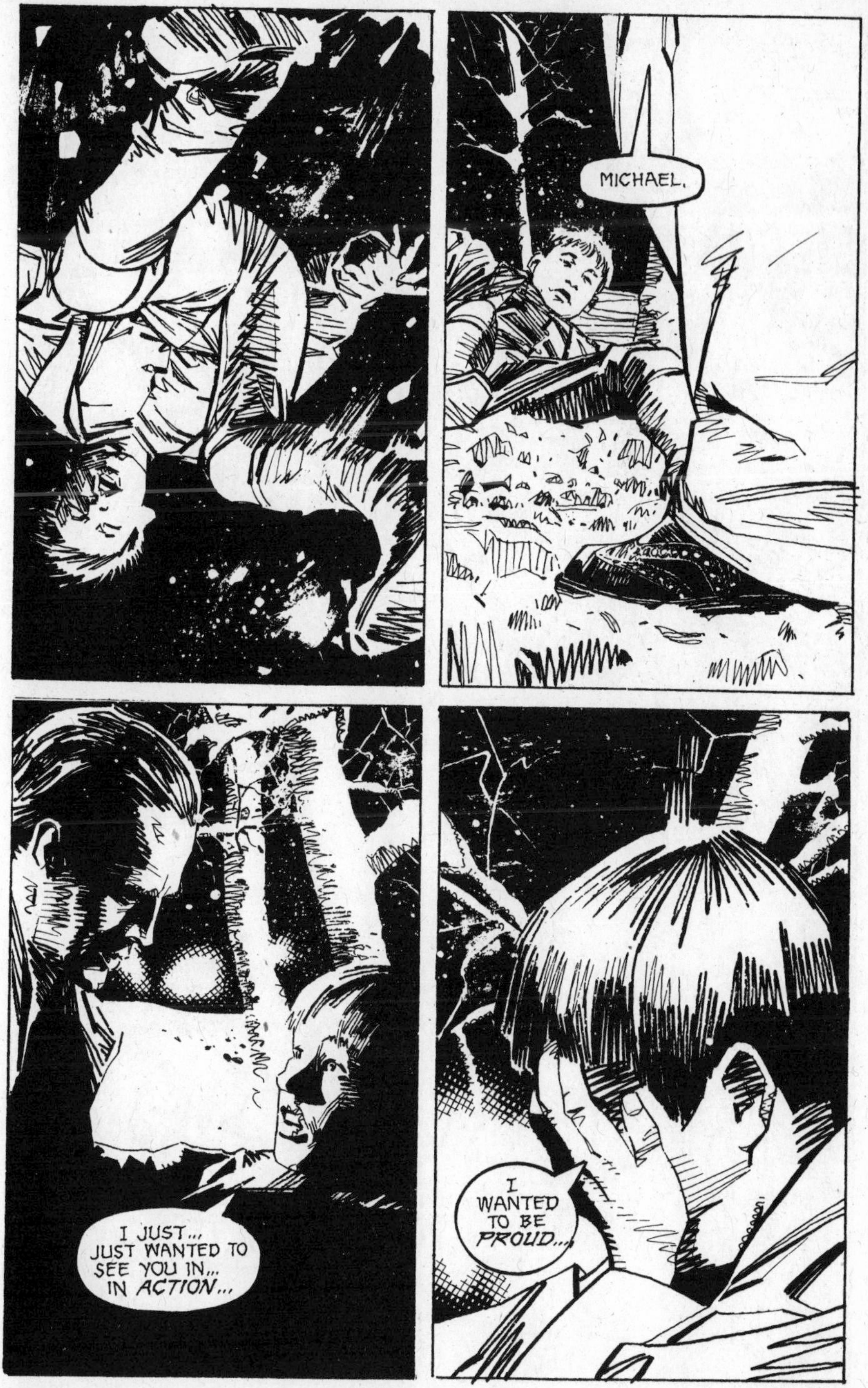
MICHAEL.
I JUST... JUST WANTED TO SEE YOU IN... IN ACTION...
I WANTED TO BE PROUD...

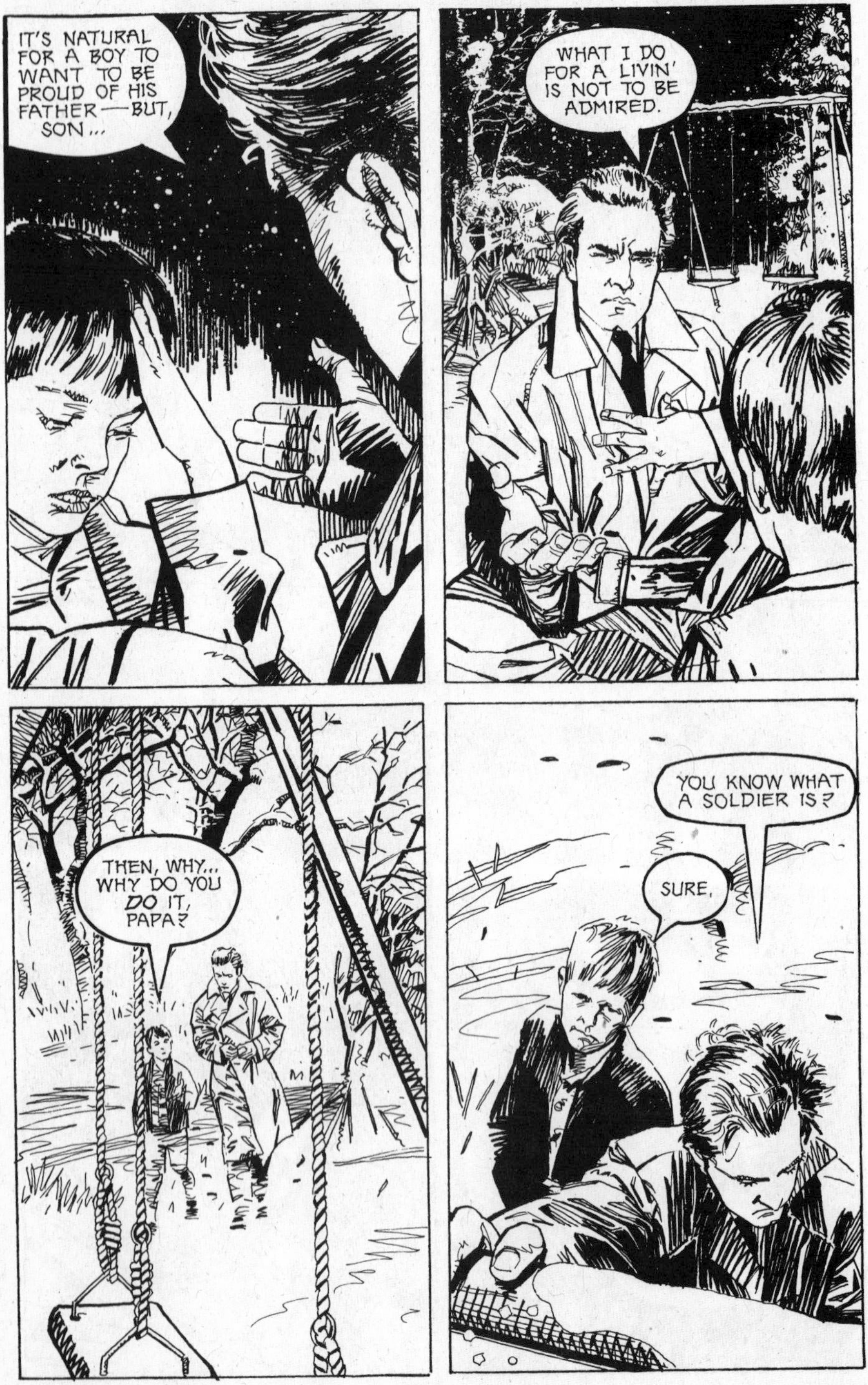
IT'S NATURAL FOR A BOY TO WANT TO BE PROUD OF HIS FATHER—BUT, SON...
WHAT I DO FOR A LIVIN' IS NOT TO BE ADMIRED.
THEN, WHY... WHY DO YOU *DO* IT, PAPA?
YOU KNOW WHAT A SOLDIER IS?
SURE.

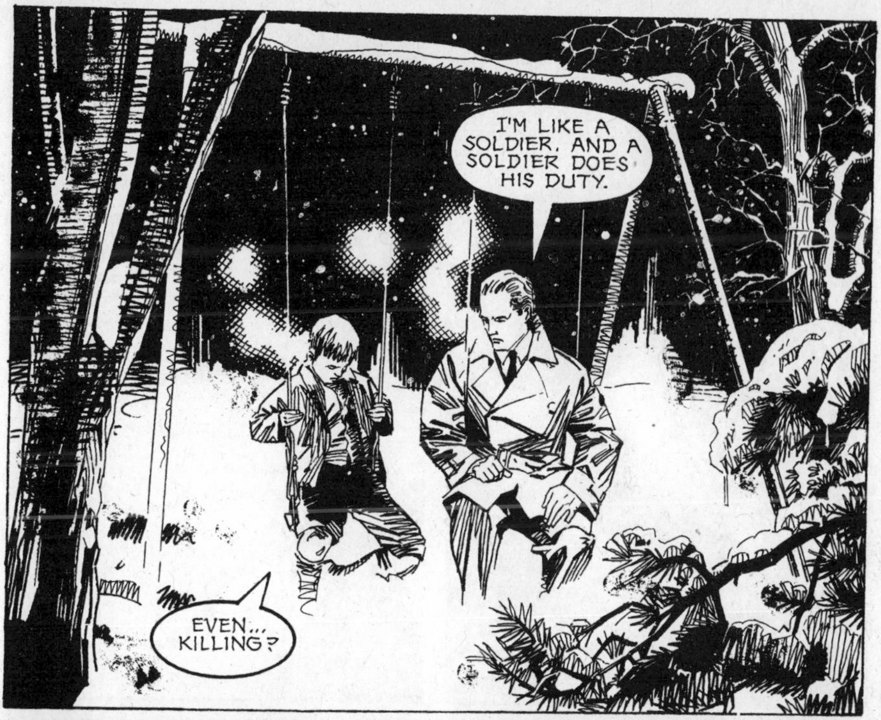
I'M LIKE A SOLDIER. AND A SOLDIER DOES HIS DUTY.
EVEN... KILLING?

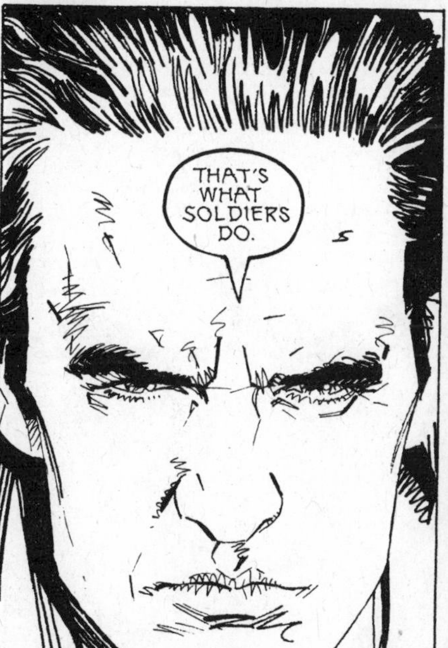
THAT'S WHAT SOLDIERS DO.

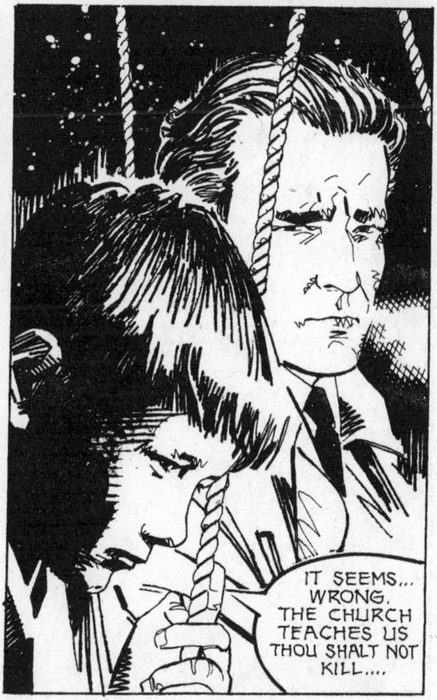
IT SEEMS... WRONG. THE CHURCH TEACHES US THOU SHALT NOT KILL....

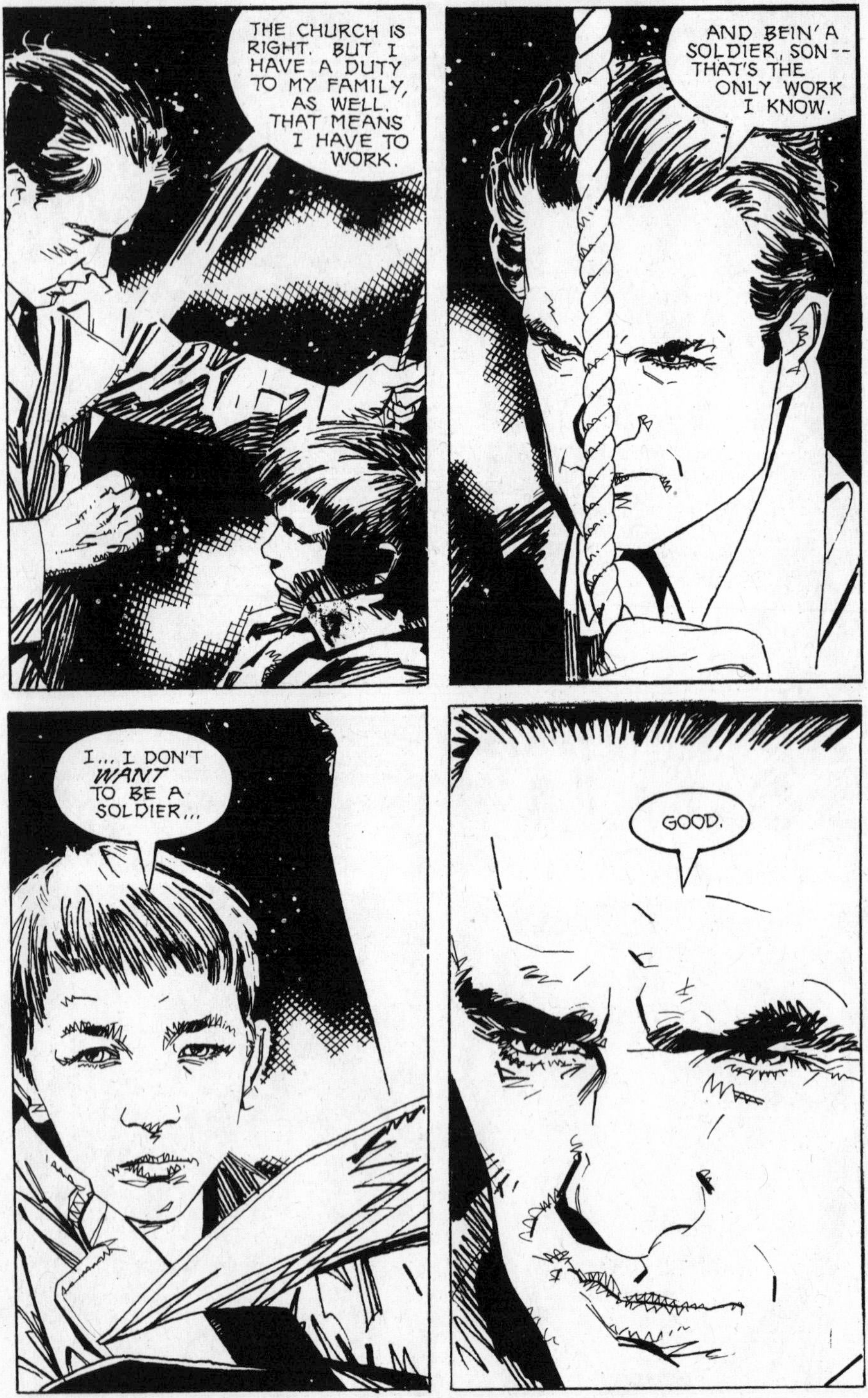
THE CHURCH IS RIGHT. BUT I HAVE A DUTY TO MY FAMILY, AS WELL. THAT MEANS I HAVE TO WORK.
AND BEIN' A SOLDIER, SON-- THAT'S THE ONLY WORK I KNOW.
I... I DON'T *WANT* TO BE A SOLDIER...
GOOD.

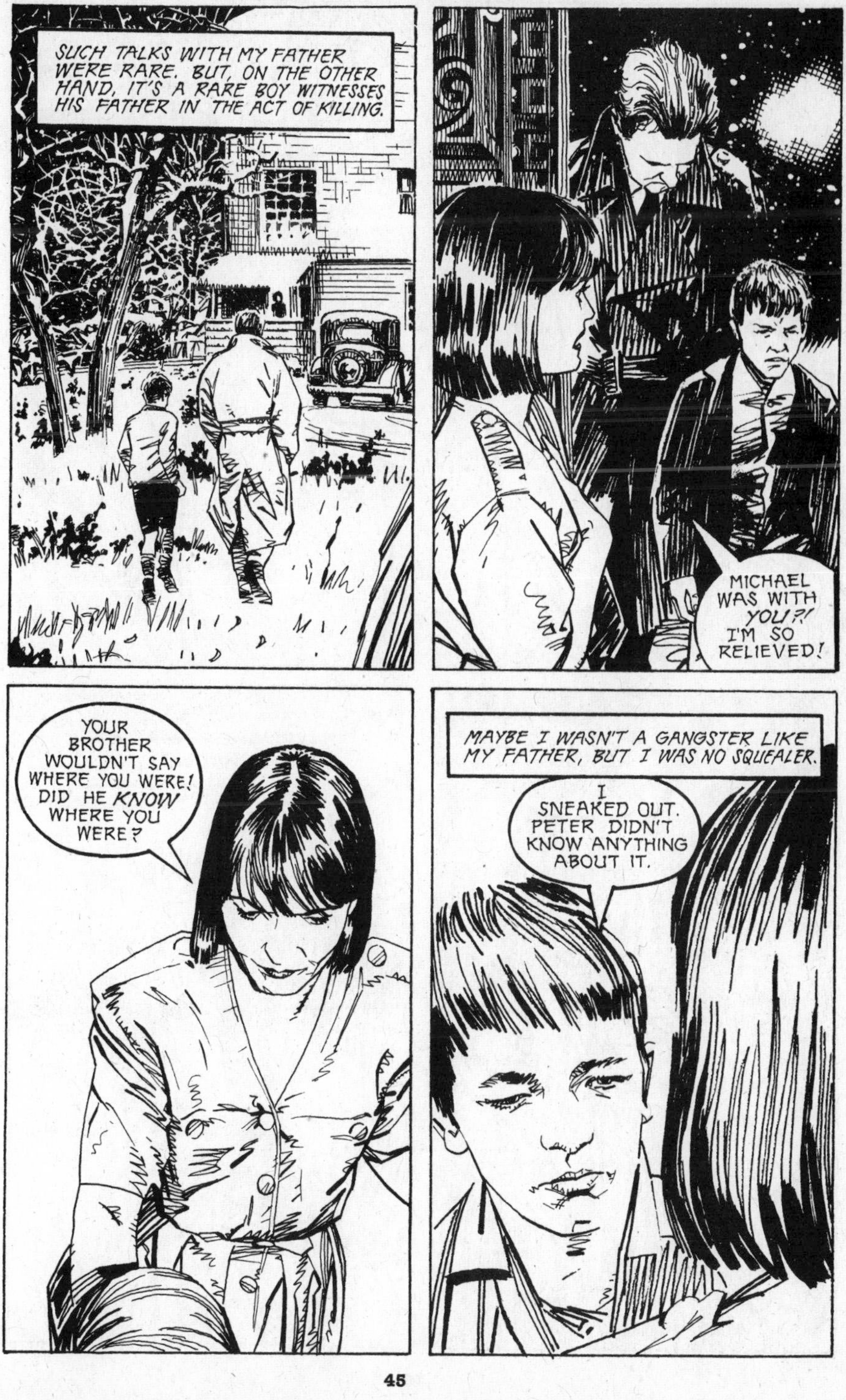
SUCH TALKS WITH MY FATHER WERE RARE. BUT, ON THE OTHER HAND, IT'S A RARE BOY WITNESSES HIS FATHER IN THE ACT OF KILLING.
MICHAEL WAS WITH YOU?! I'M SO RELIEVED!
YOUR BROTHER WOULDN'T SAY WHERE YOU WERE! DID HE KNOW WHERE YOU WERE?
MAYBE I WASN'T A GANGSTER LIKE MY FATHER, BUT I WAS NO SQUEALER.
I SNEAKED OUT. PETER DIDN'T KNOW ANYTHING ABOUT IT.

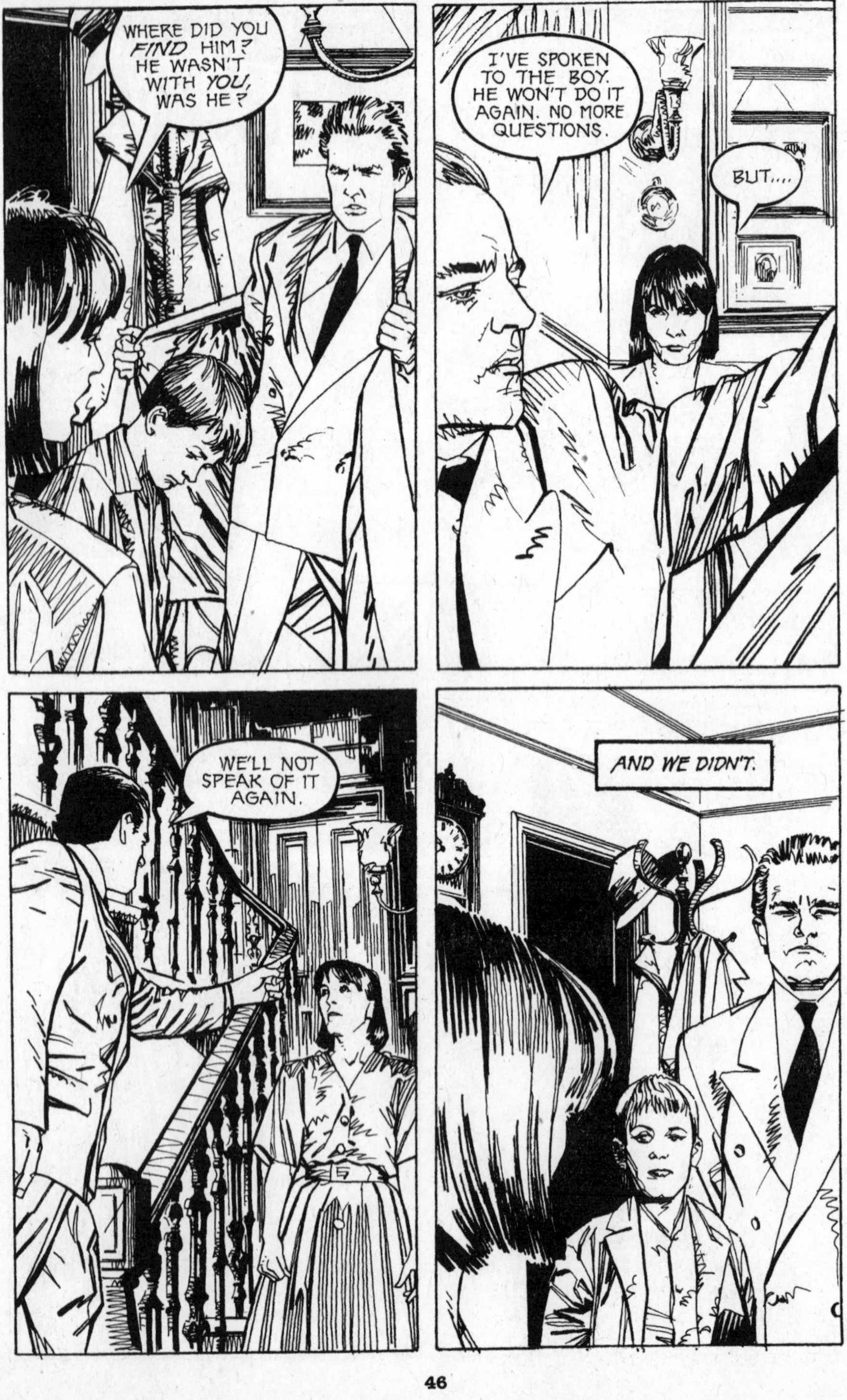
WHERE DID YOU *FIND* HIM? HE WASN'T WITH *YOU*, WAS HE?
I'VE SPOKEN TO THE BOY. HE WON'T DO IT AGAIN. NO MORE QUESTIONS.
BUT....
WE'LL NOT SPEAK OF IT AGAIN.
AND WE DIDN'T.

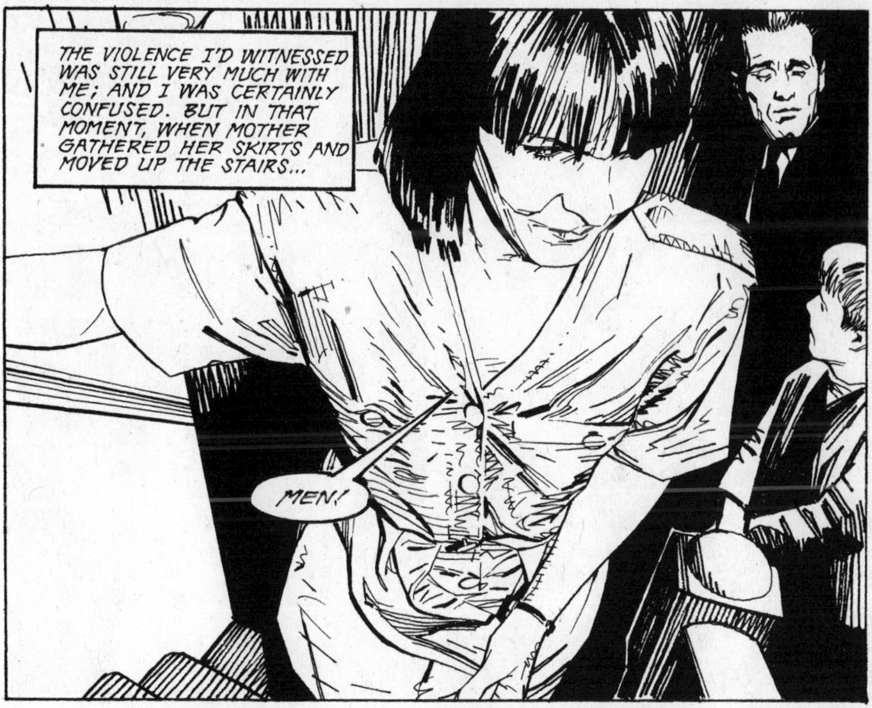
THE VIOLENCE I'D WITNESSED WAS STILL VERY MUCH WITH ME; AND I WAS CERTAINLY CONFUSED. BUT IN THAT MOMENT, WHEN MOTHER GATHERED HER SKIRTS AND MOVED UP THE STAIRS...
MEN!

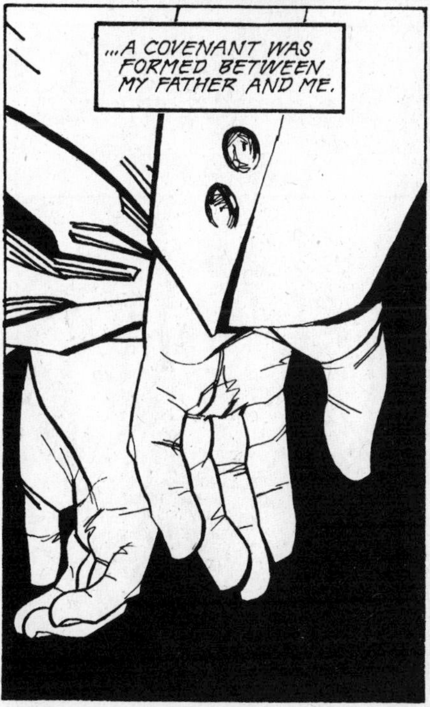
...A COVENANT WAS FORMED BETWEEN MY FATHER AND ME.

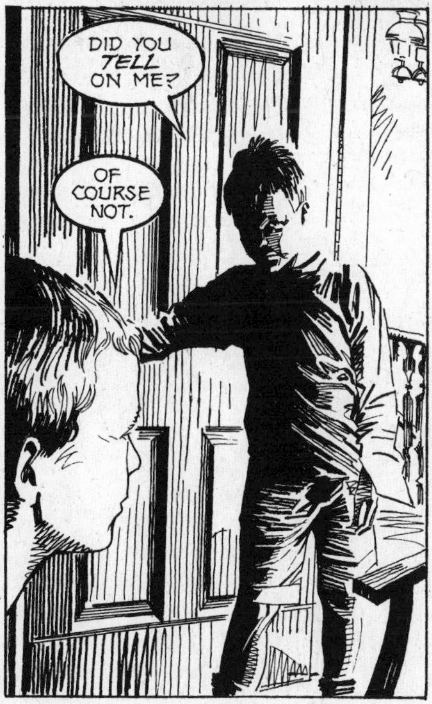
DID YOU TELL ON ME?
OF COURSE NOT.

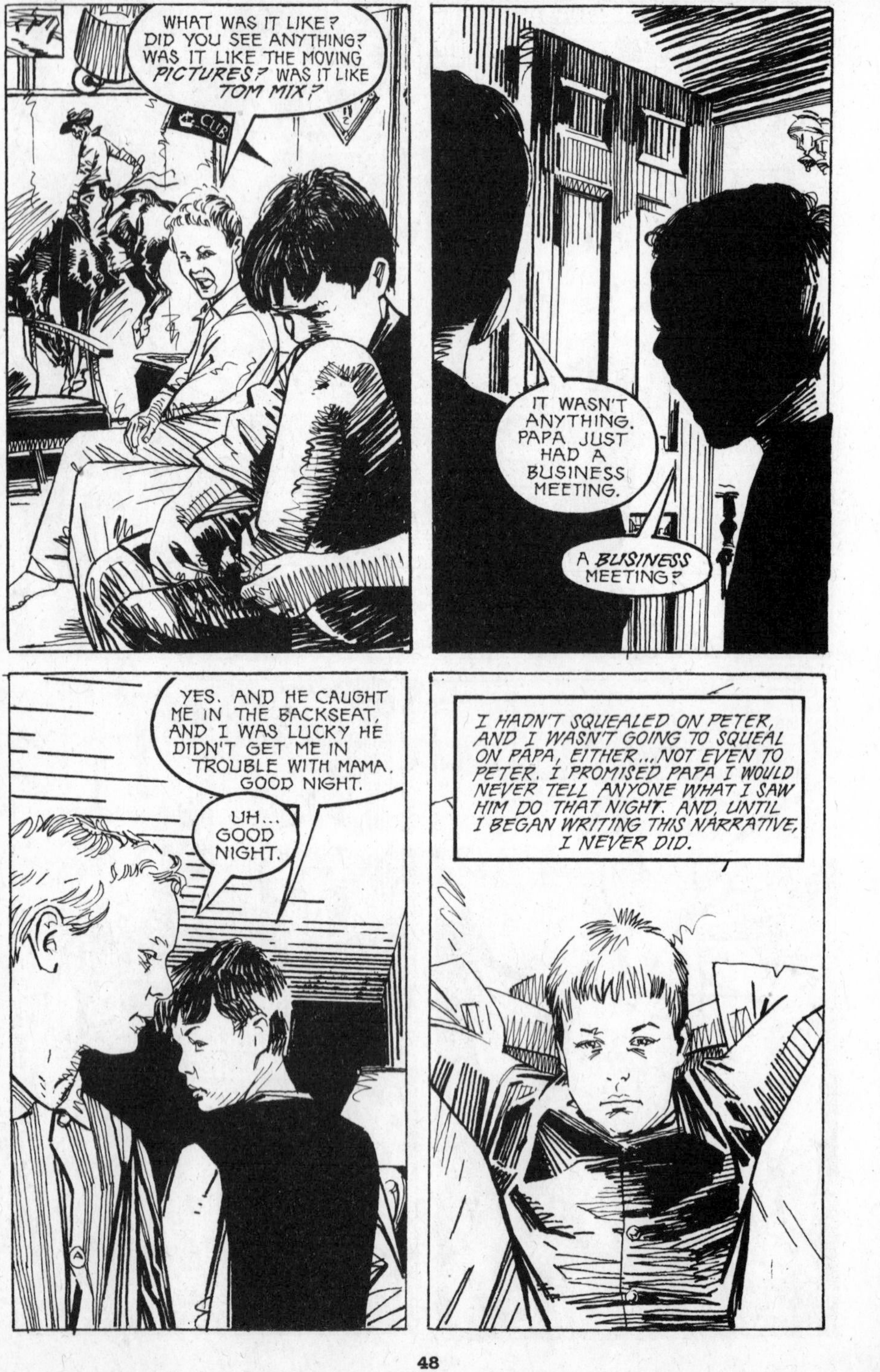
WHAT WAS IT LIKE? DID YOU SEE ANYTHING? WAS IT LIKE THE MOVING *PICTURES?* WAS IT LIKE *TOM MIX?*
CUB
IT WASN'T ANYTHING. PAPA JUST HAD A BUSINESS MEETING.
A *BUSINESS* MEETING?
YES. AND HE CAUGHT ME IN THE BACKSEAT, AND I WAS LUCKY HE DIDN'T GET ME IN TROUBLE WITH MAMA. GOOD NIGHT.
UH... GOOD NIGHT.
I HADN'T SQUEALED ON PETER, AND I WASN'T GOING TO SQUEAL ON PAPA, EITHER... NOT EVEN TO PETER. I PROMISED PAPA I WOULD NEVER TELL ANYONE WHAT I SAW HIM DO THAT NIGHT. AND, UNTIL I BEGAN WRITING THIS NARRATIVE, I NEVER DID.

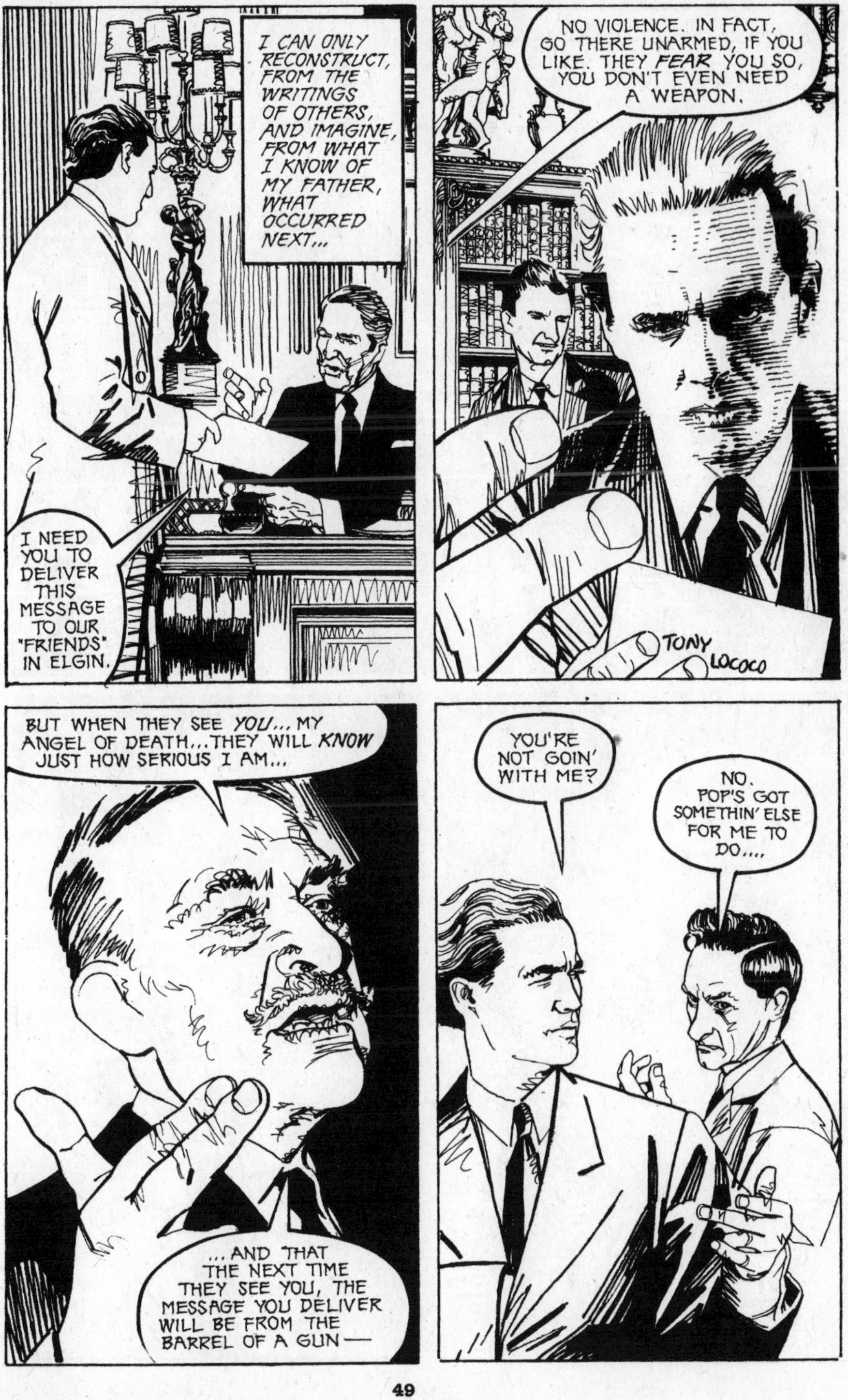
I CAN ONLY RECONSTRUCT, FROM THE WRITINGS OF OTHERS, AND IMAGINE, FROM WHAT I KNOW OF MY FATHER, WHAT OCCURRED NEXT...
I NEED YOU TO DELIVER THIS MESSAGE TO OUR "FRIENDS" IN ELGIN.
NO VIOLENCE. IN FACT, GO THERE UNARMED, IF YOU LIKE. THEY FEAR YOU SO, YOU DON'T EVEN NEED A WEAPON.
TONY LOCOCO
BUT WHEN THEY SEE YOU... MY ANGEL OF DEATH... THEY WILL KNOW JUST HOW SERIOUS I AM...
...AND THAT THE NEXT TIME THEY SEE YOU, THE MESSAGE YOU DELIVER WILL BE FROM THE BARREL OF A GUN—
YOU'RE NOT GOIN' WITH ME?
NO. POP'S GOT SOMETHIN' ELSE FOR ME TO DO....

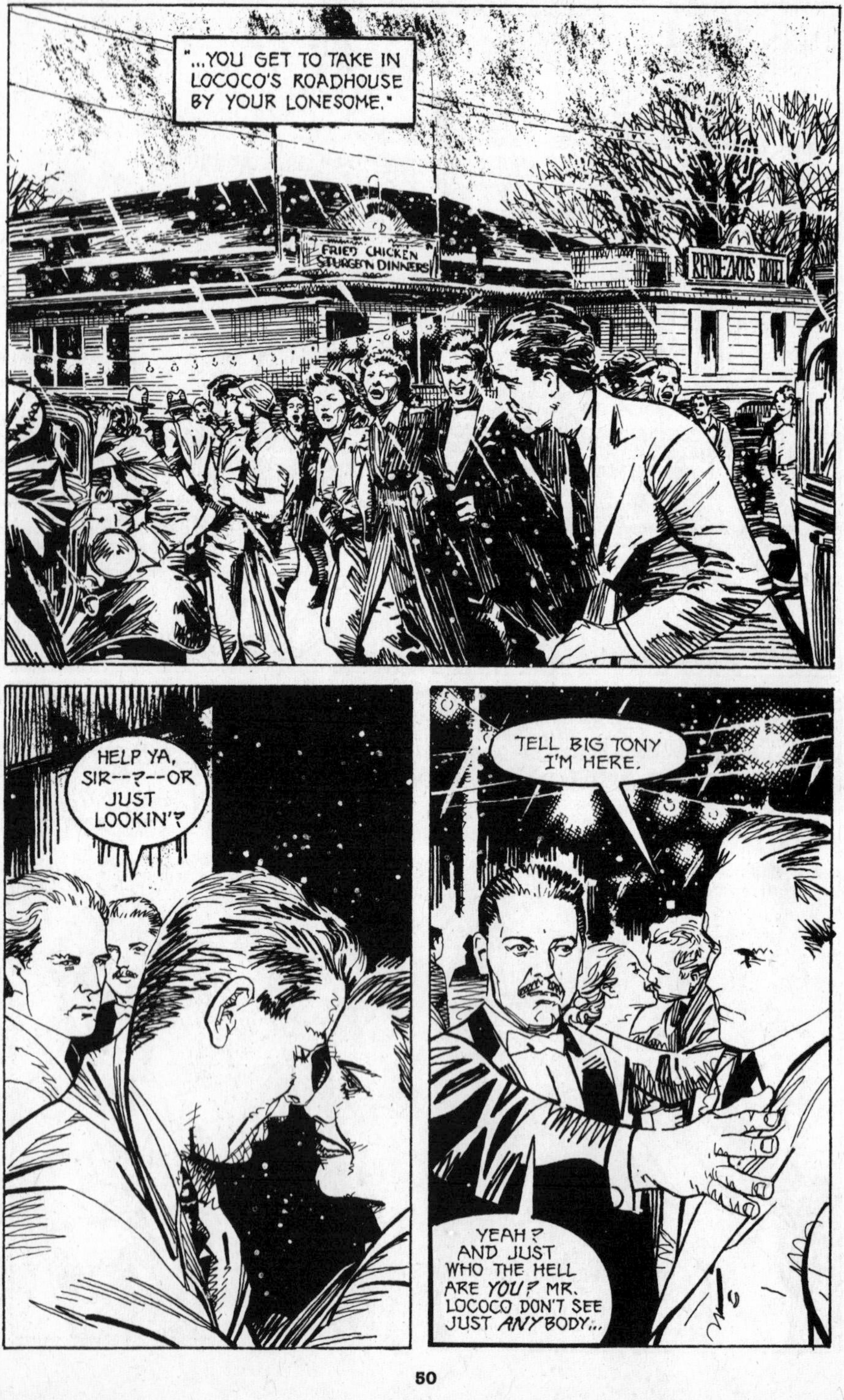
"...YOU GET TO TAKE IN LOCOCO'S ROADHOUSE BY YOUR LONESOME."
FRIED CHICKEN STURGEON DINNERS
RENDEZVOUS HOTEL
HELP YA, SIR--?--OR JUST LOOKIN'?
TELL BIG TONY I'M HERE.
YEAH? AND JUST WHO THE HELL ARE *YOU*? MR. LOCOCO DON'T SEE JUST *ANY*BODY...

MIKE O'SULLIVAN. I WORK FOR MR. LOONEY.

MR. O'SULLIVAN! OF *COURSE!* COME RIGHT THIS WAY... I SHOULDA *RECOGNIZED* YOU...

WHY? HAVE WE MET?

NO, NO, BUT EVERYBODY'S *HEARD* OF THE ANGEL— IF YOU DON'T MIND MY CALLIN' YOU THAT.

JUST TELL BIG TONY I'M HERE.

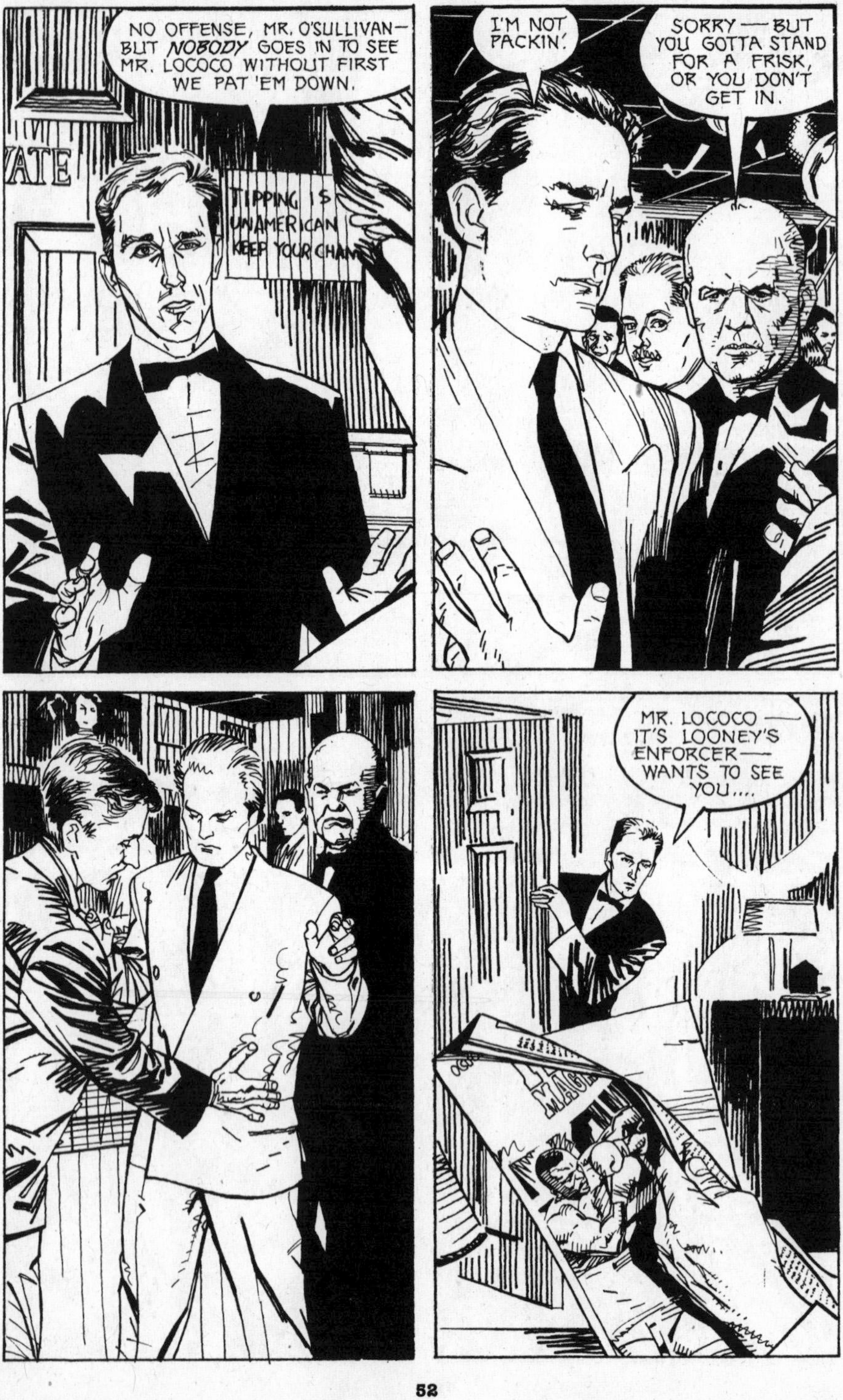
NO OFFENSE, MR. O'SULLIVAN— BUT NOBODY GOES IN TO SEE MR. LOCOCO WITHOUT FIRST WE PAT 'EM DOWN.
TIPPING IS UNAMERICAN KEEP YOUR CHAN
I'M NOT PACKIN'.
SORRY — BUT YOU GOTTA STAND FOR A FRISK, OR YOU DON'T GET IN.
MR. LOCOCO — IT'S LOONEY'S ENFORCER — WANTS TO SEE YOU....

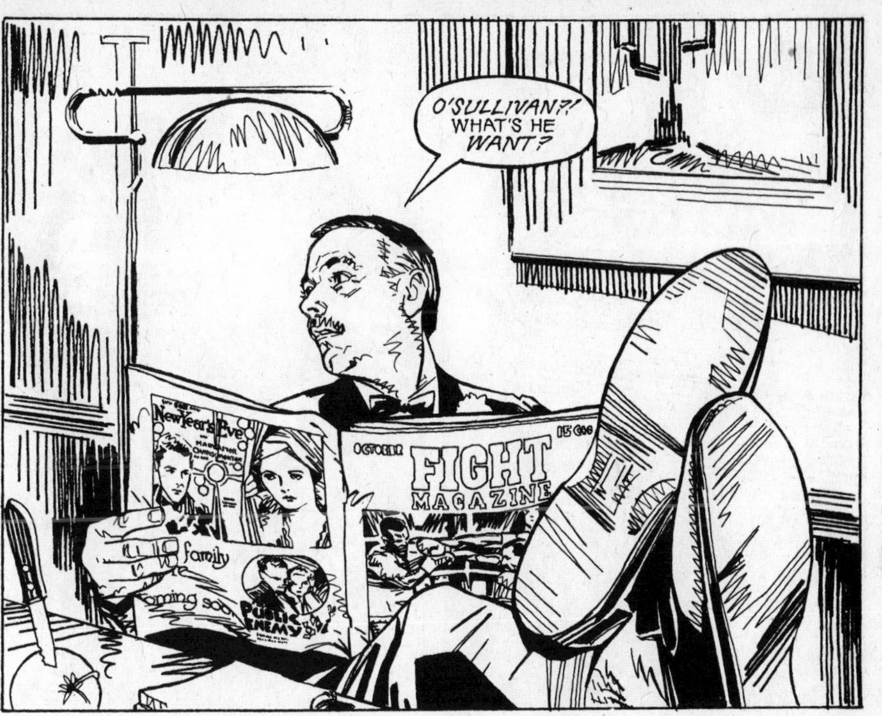
O'SULLIVAN?! WHAT'S HE WANT?
OCTOBER
FIGHT MAGAZINE
15 Cts
New Year's Eve
family
Coming soo
PUBLIC ENEMY
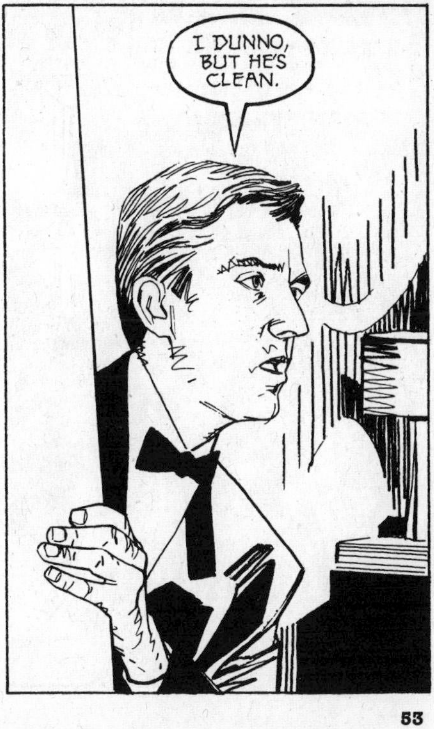
I DUNNO, BUT HE'S CLEAN.
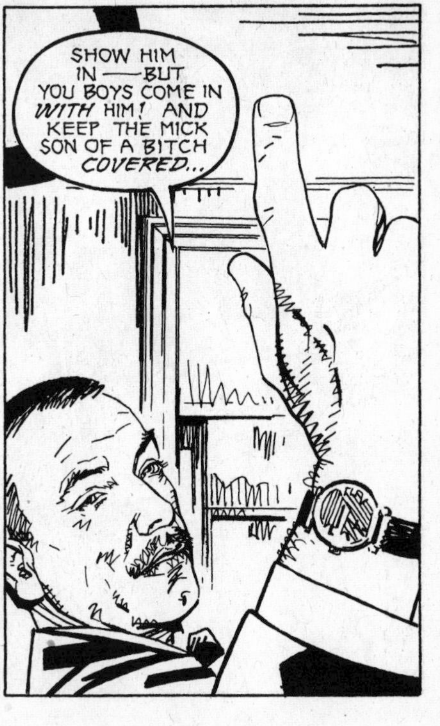
SHOW HIM IN—BUT YOU BOYS COME IN WITH HIM! AND KEEP THE MICK SON OF A BITCH COVERED...

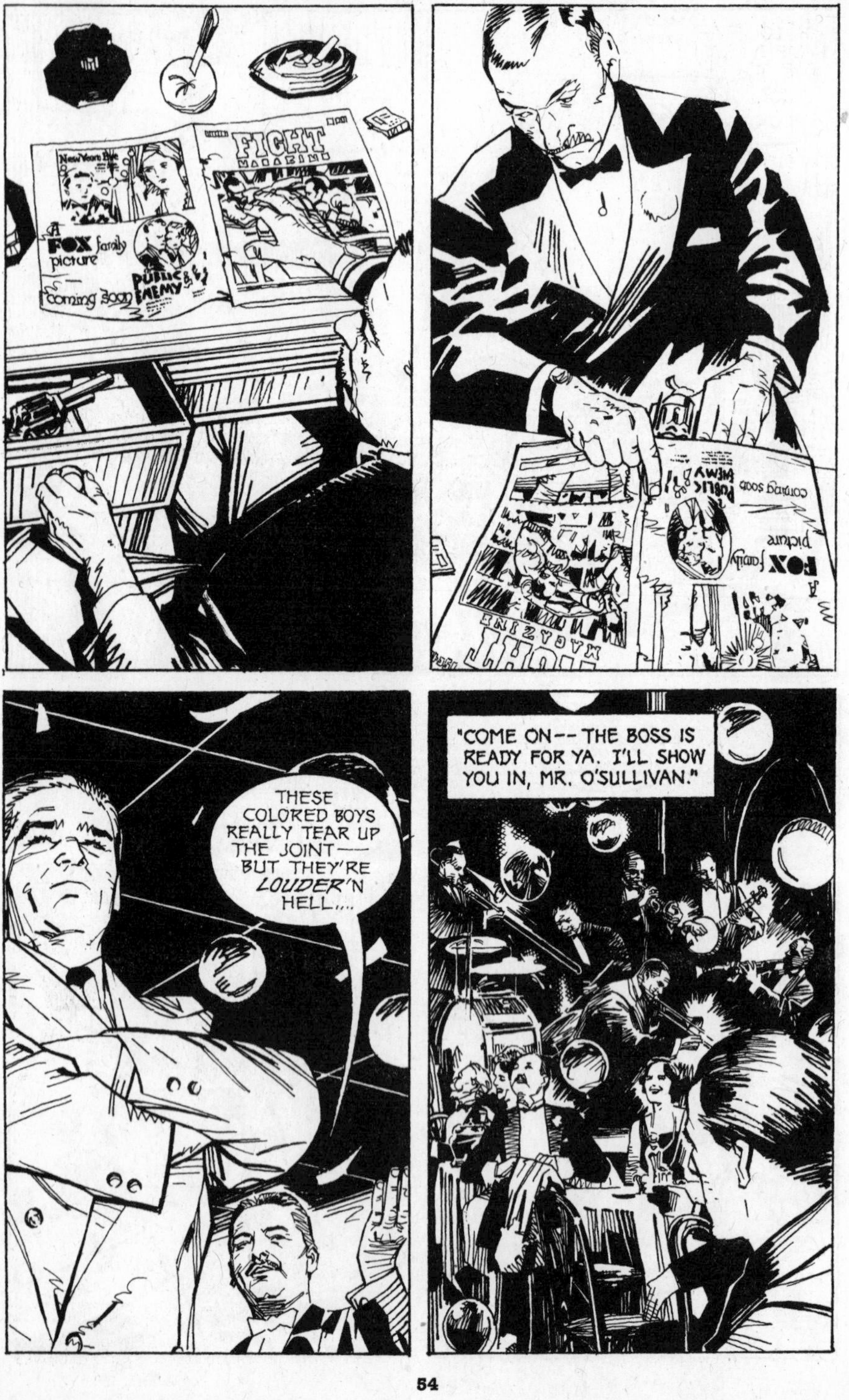
FIGHT
A FOX family picture
PUBLIC ENEMY
coming soon
THESE COLORED BOYS REALLY TEAR UP THE JOINT—— BUT THEY'RE *LOUDER*'N HELL....
"COME ON-- THE BOSS IS READY FOR YA. I'LL SHOW YOU IN, MR. O'SULLIVAN."

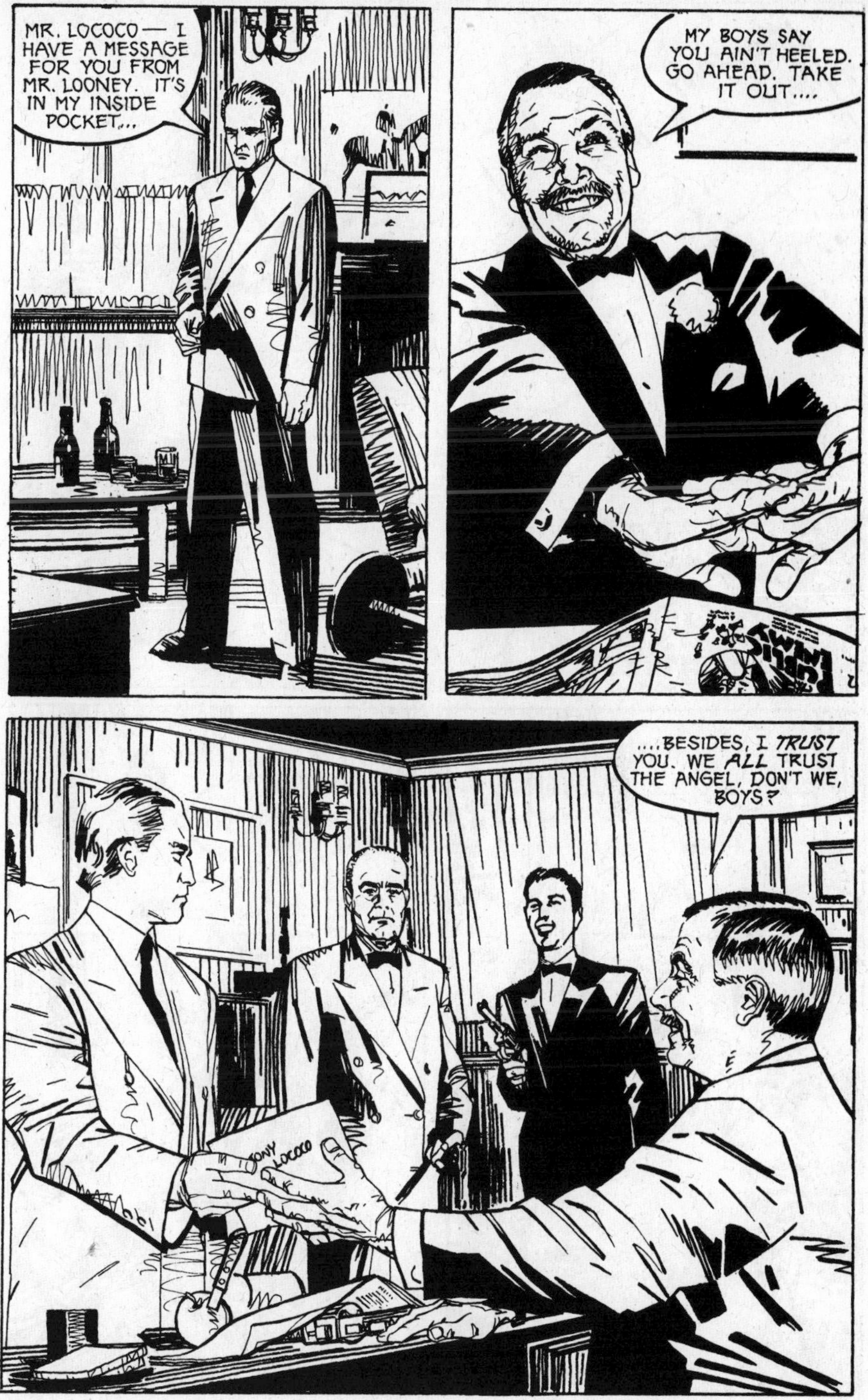
MR. LOCOCO— I HAVE A MESSAGE FOR YOU FROM MR. LOONEY. IT'S IN MY INSIDE POCKET...
MY BOYS SAY YOU AIN'T HEELED. GO AHEAD. TAKE IT OUT....
....BESIDES, I *TRUST* YOU. WE *ALL* TRUST THE ANGEL, DON'T WE, BOYS?

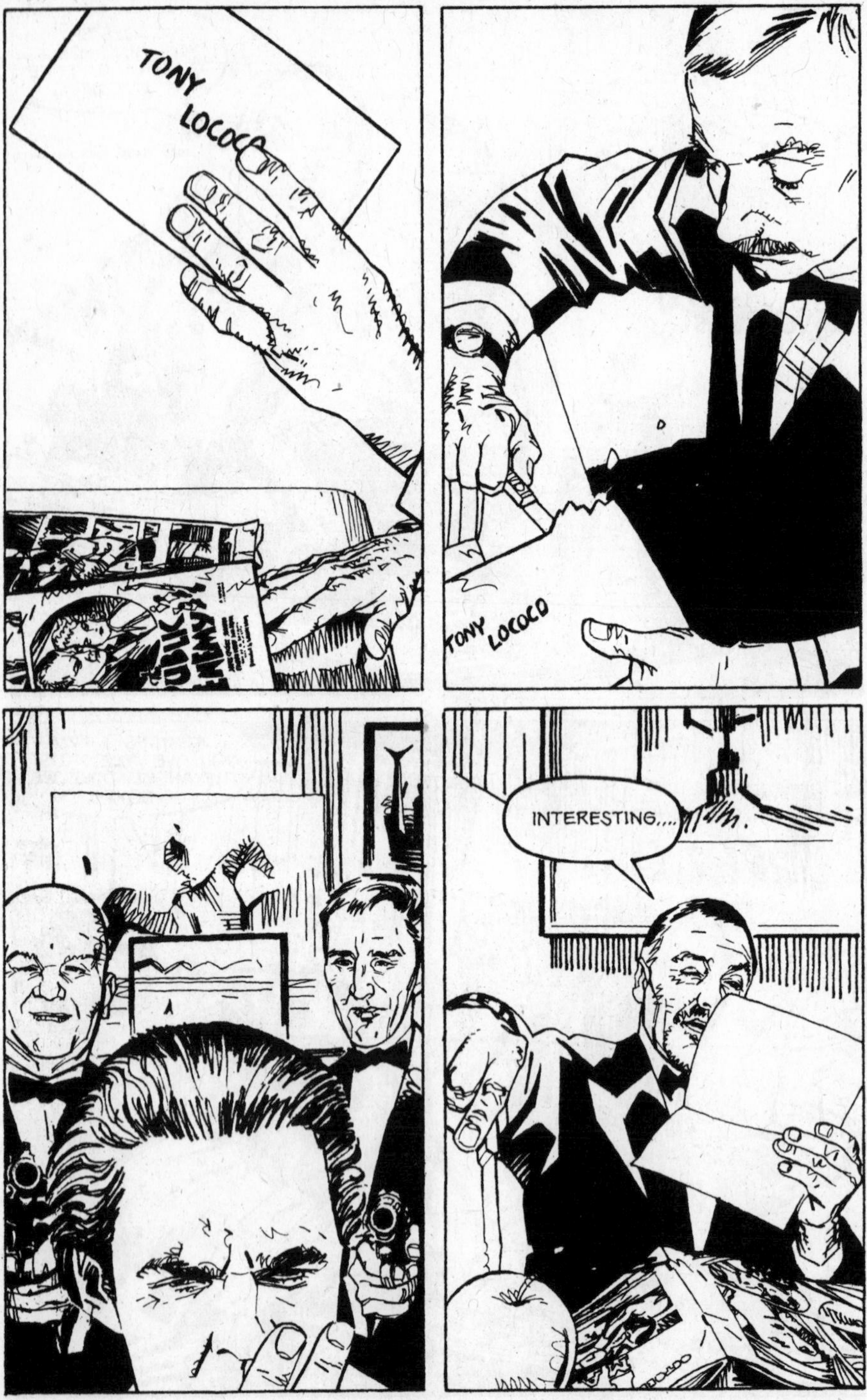
TONY LOCOCO
TONY LOCOCO
INTERESTING....

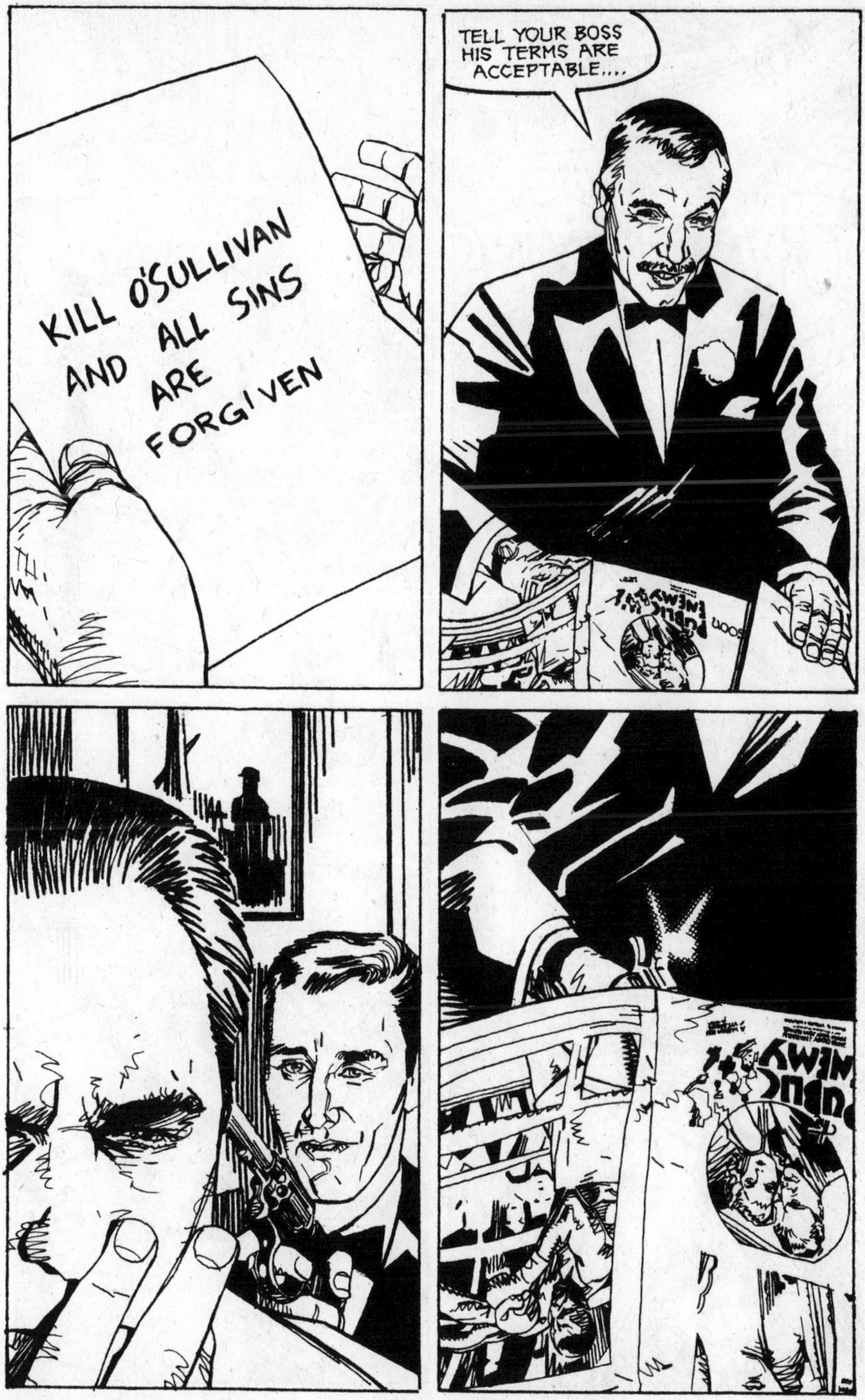
KILL O'SULLIVAN AND ALL SINS ARE FORGIVEN
TELL YOUR BOSS HIS TERMS ARE ACCEPTABLE....

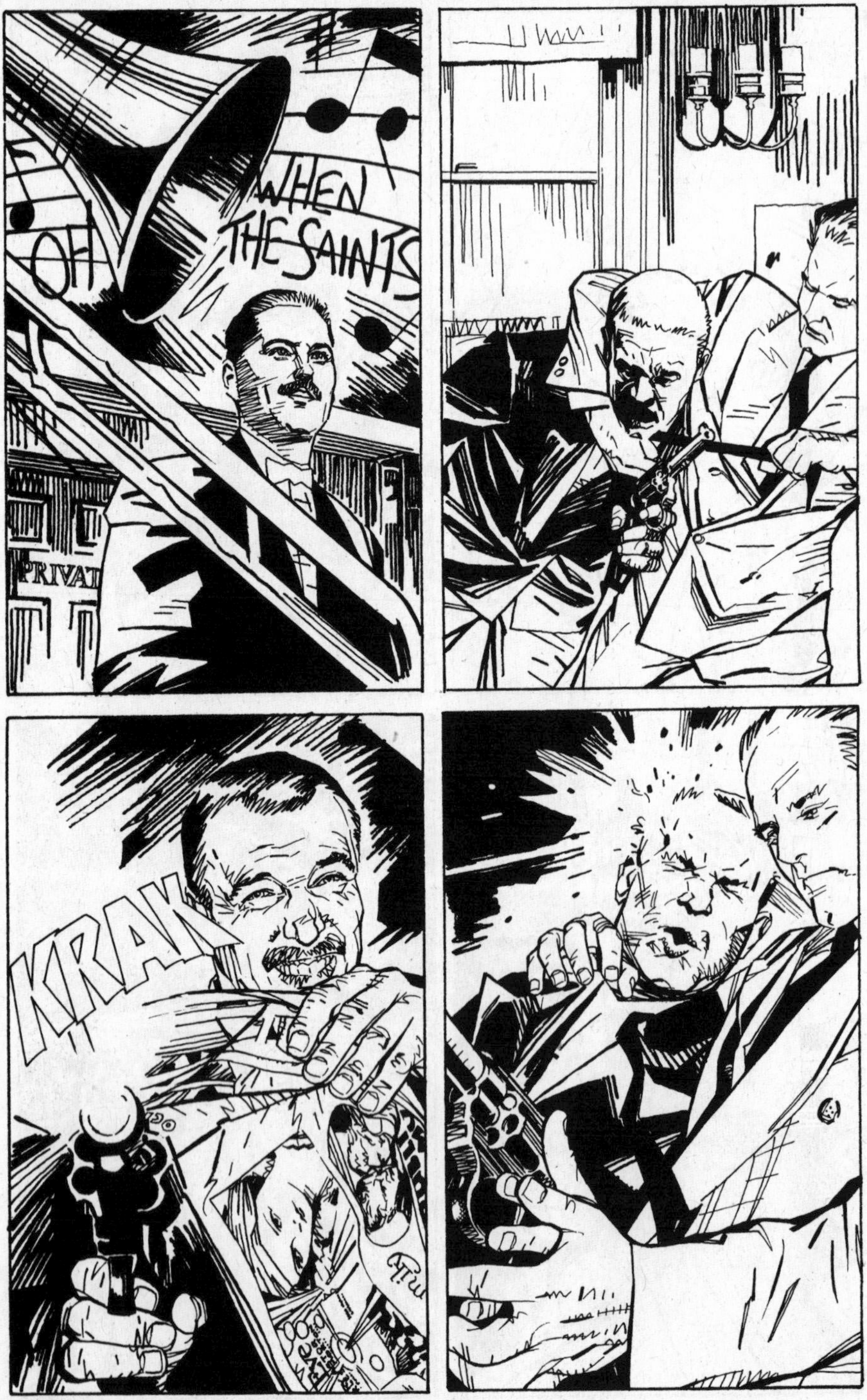
OH WHEN THE SAINTS
PRIVAT
KRAK

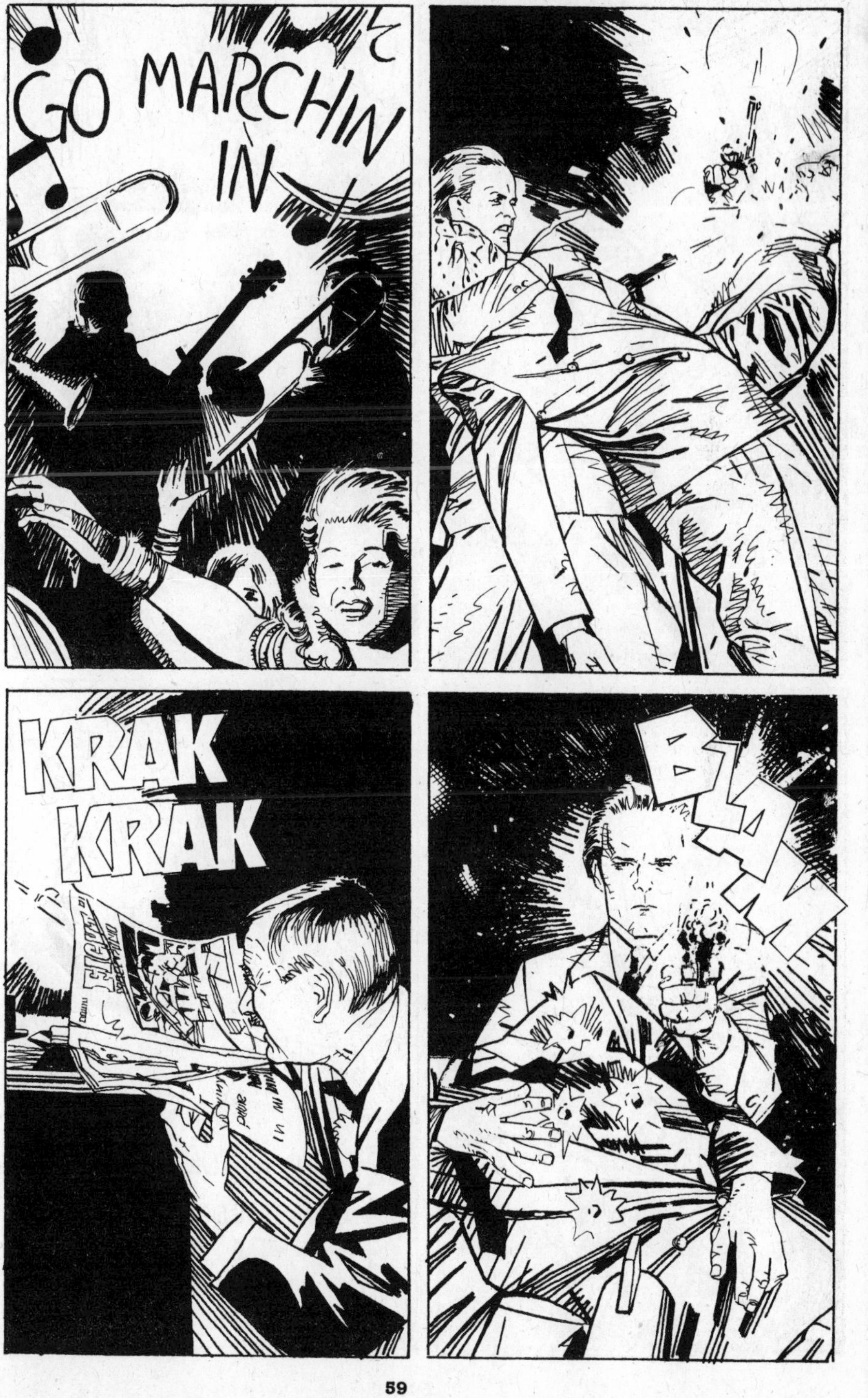
GO MARCHIN IN
KRAK KRAK
BLAM

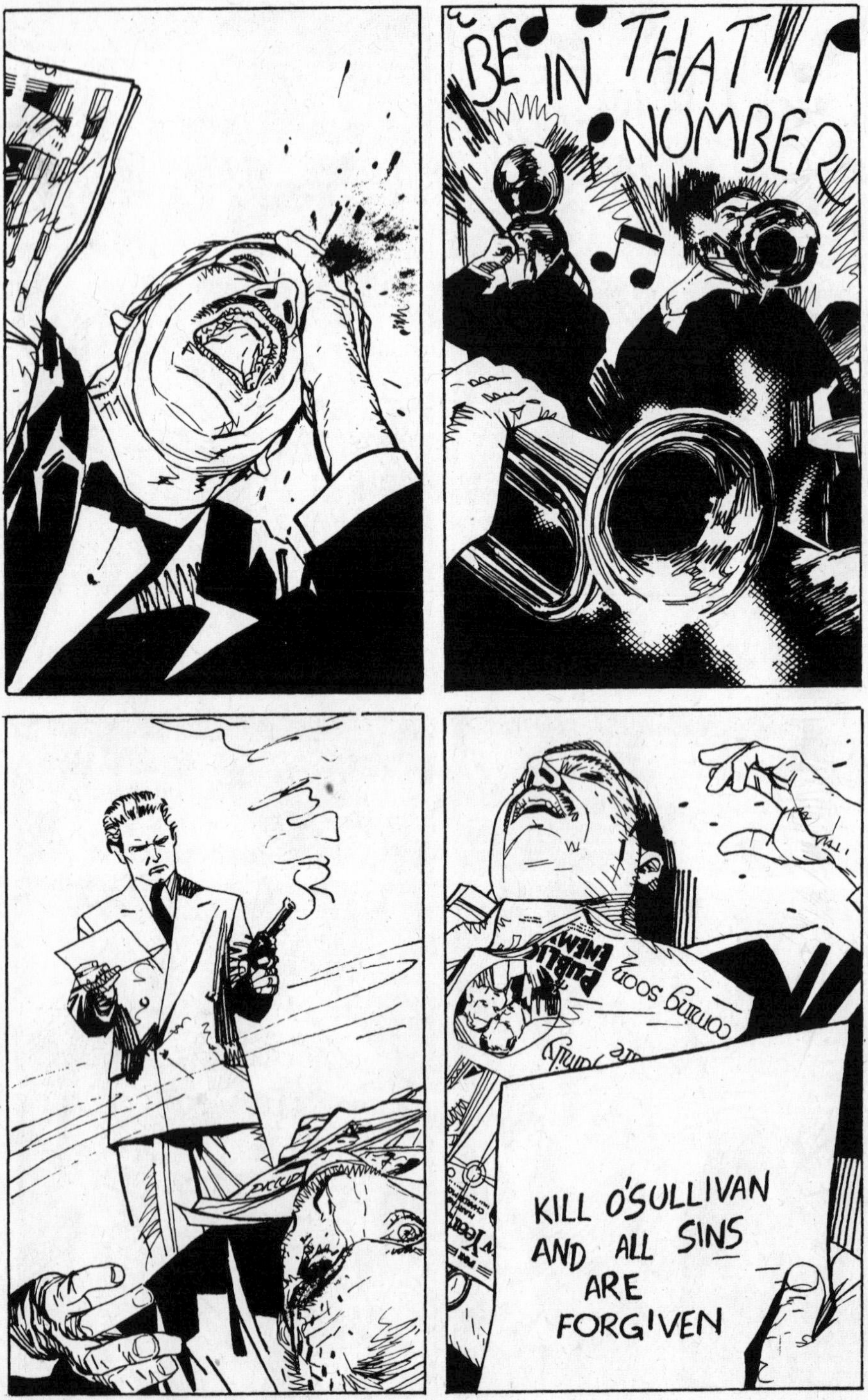
BE IN THAT NUMBER
PUBLIC ENEMY
coming soon
KILL O'SULLIVAN AND ALL SINS ARE FORGIVEN

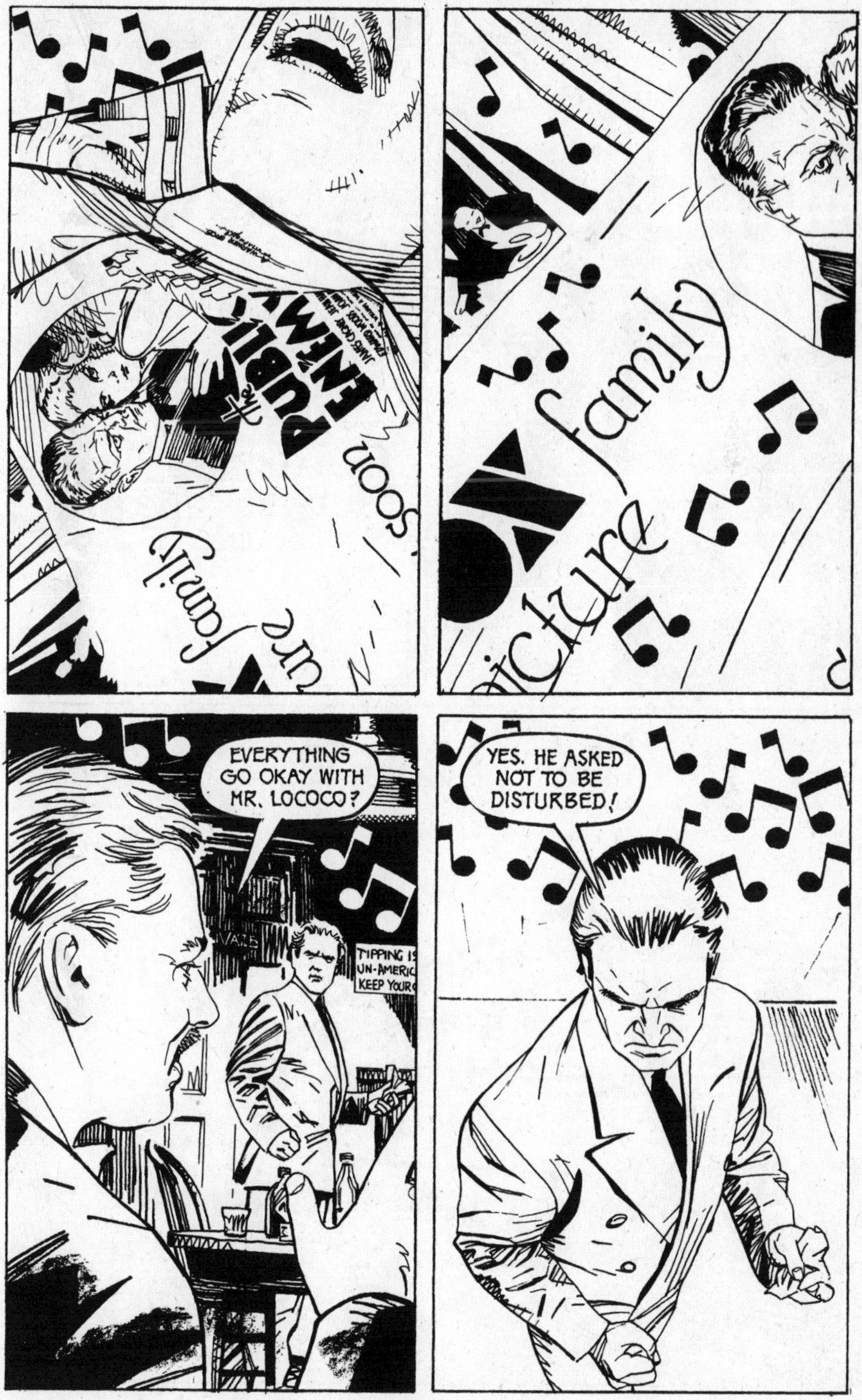
the PUBLIC ENEMY
soon
family
family
picture
EVERYTHING GO OKAY WITH MR. LOCOCO?
TIPPING IS
UN-AMERIC
KEEP YOUR
YES. HE ASKED NOT TO BE DISTURBED!

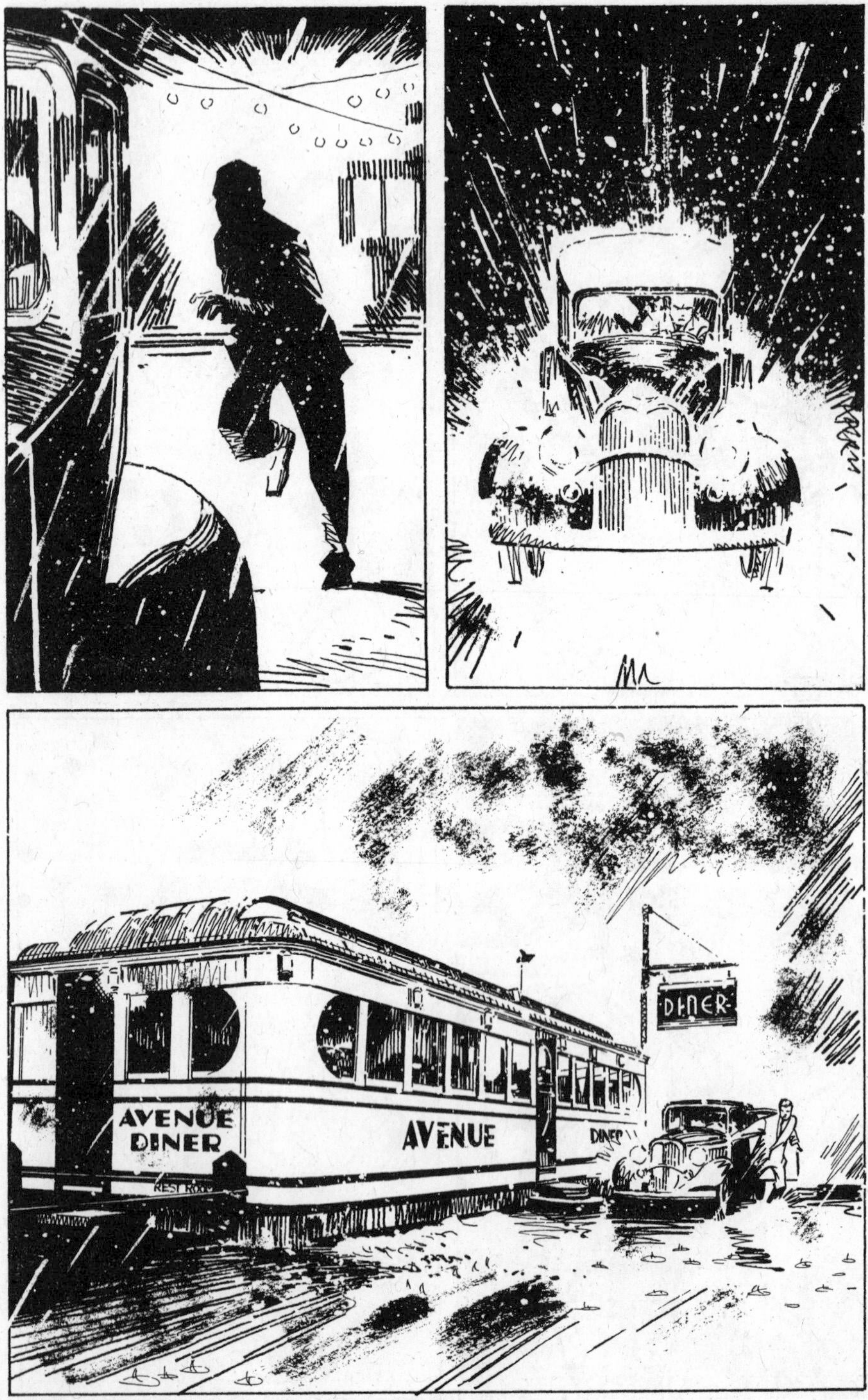
AVENUE
DINER
AVENUE
DINER

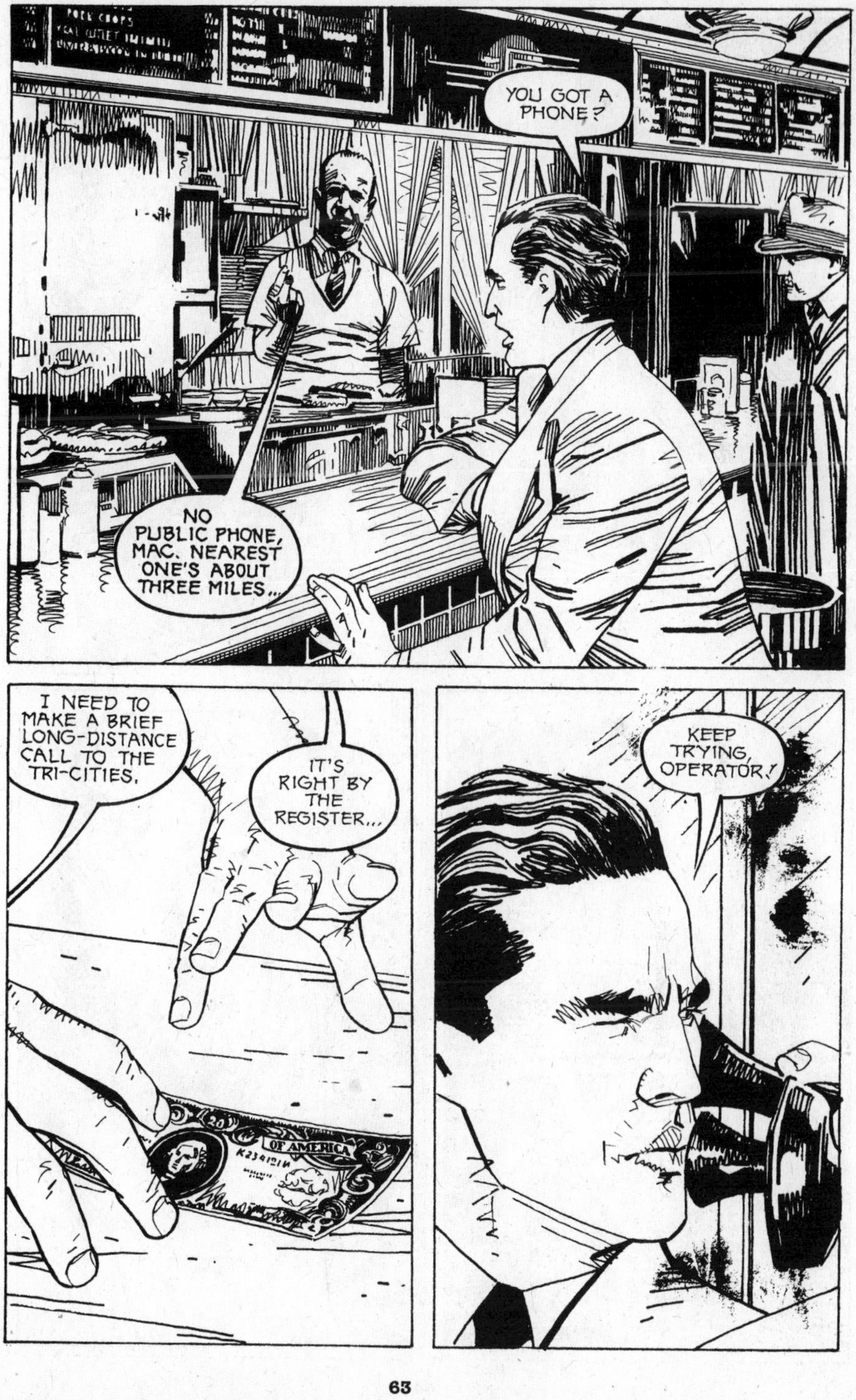
YOU GOT A PHONE?
NO PUBLIC PHONE, MAC. NEAREST ONE'S ABOUT THREE MILES...
I NEED TO MAKE A BRIEF LONG-DISTANCE CALL TO THE TRI-CITIES.
IT'S RIGHT BY THE REGISTER...
KEEP TRYING, OPERATOR!

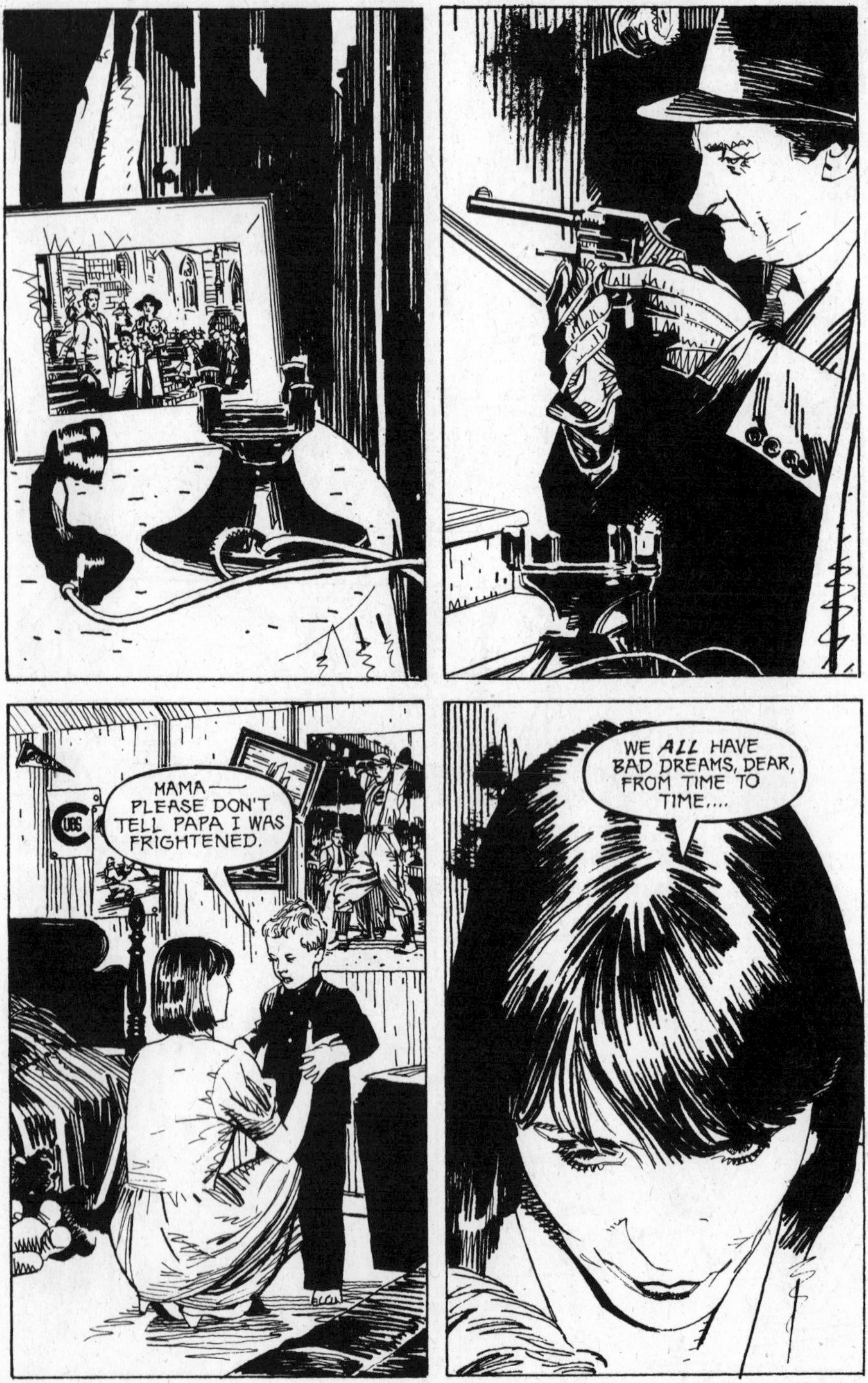
MAMA— PLEASE DON'T TELL PAPA I WAS FRIGHTENED.
WE ALL HAVE BAD DREAMS, DEAR, FROM TIME TO TIME....

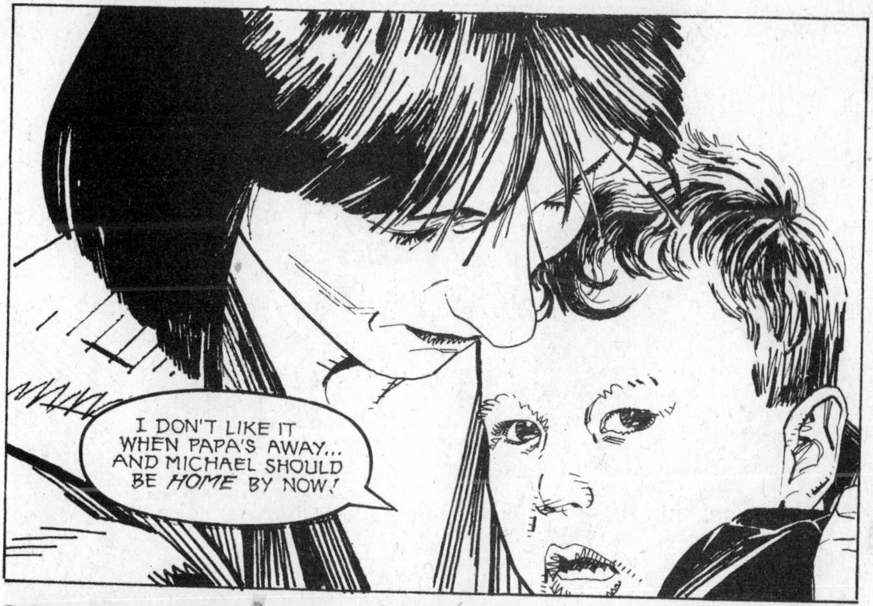
I DON'T LIKE IT WHEN PAPA'S AWAY... AND MICHAEL SHOULD BE HOME BY NOW!

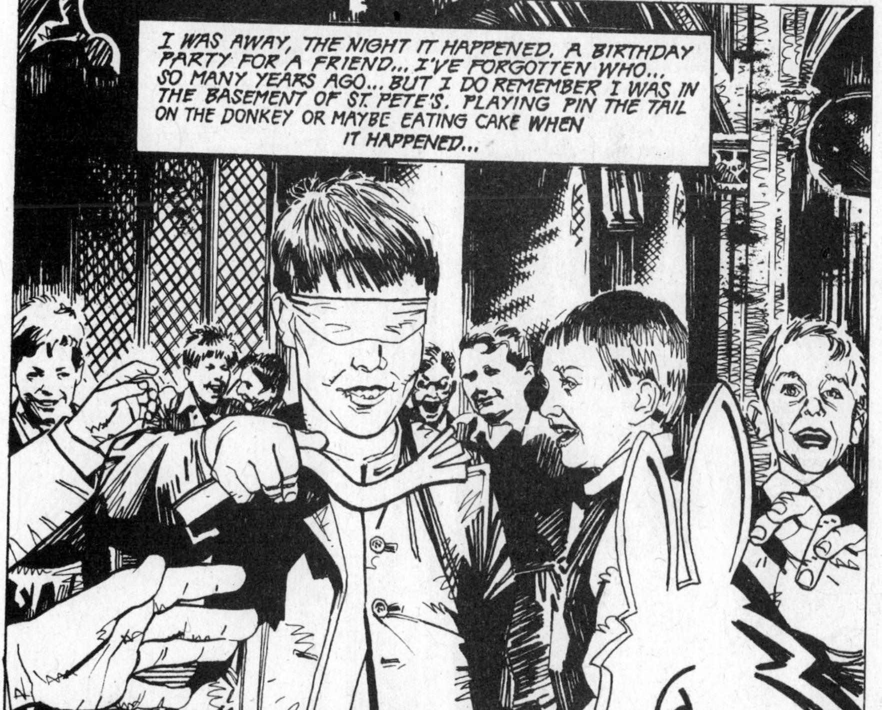
I WAS AWAY, THE NIGHT IT HAPPENED. A BIRTHDAY PARTY FOR A FRIEND... I'VE FORGOTTEN WHO... SO MANY YEARS AGO... BUT I DO REMEMBER I WAS IN THE BASEMENT OF ST. PETE'S. PLAYING PIN THE TAIL ON THE DONKEY OR MAYBE EATING CAKE WHEN IT HAPPENED...

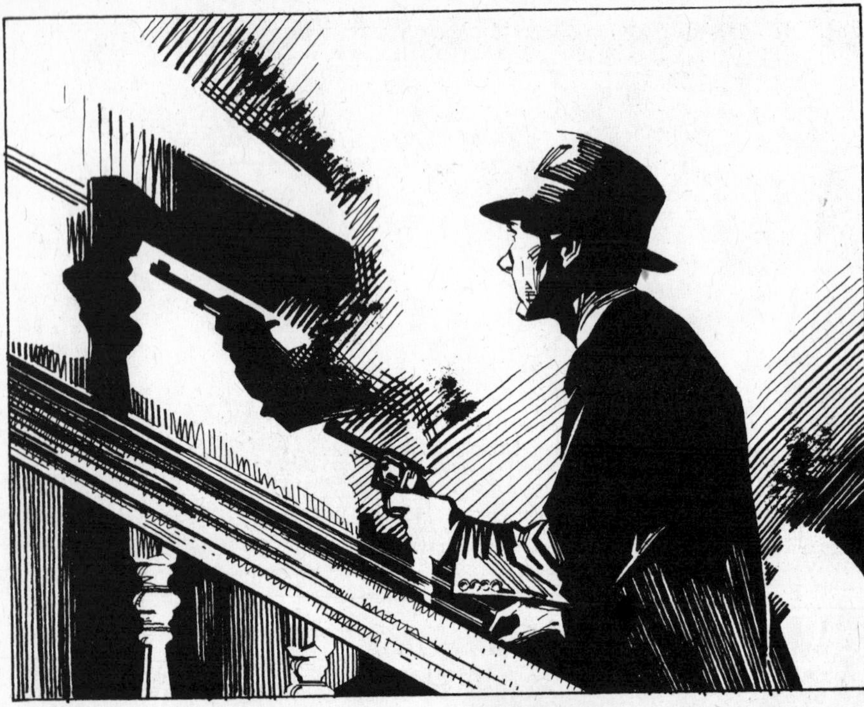

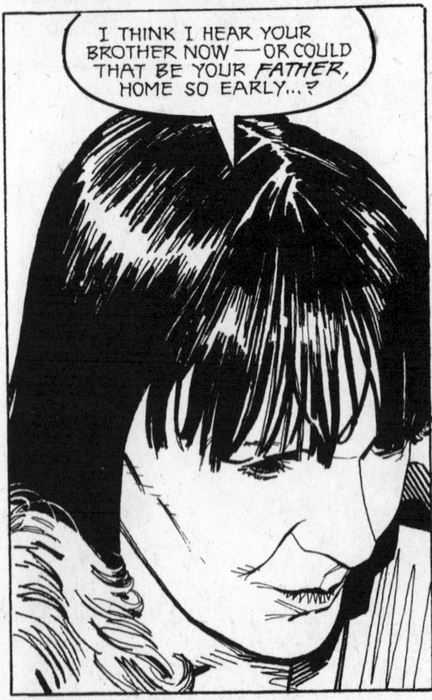
I THINK I HEAR YOUR BROTHER NOW — OR COULD THAT BE YOUR *FATHER*, HOME SO EARLY...?

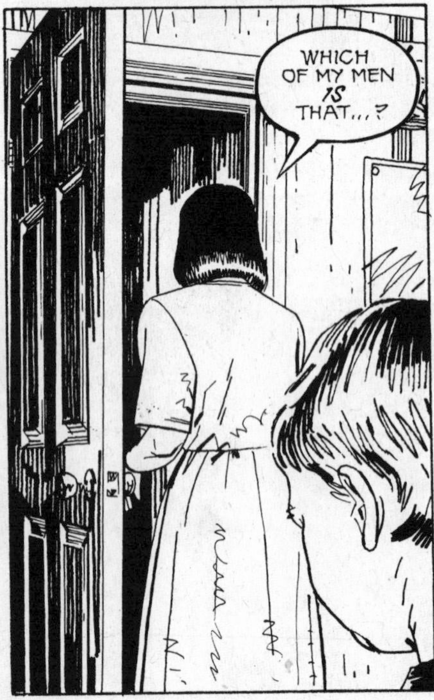
WHICH OF MY MEN *IS* THAT...?

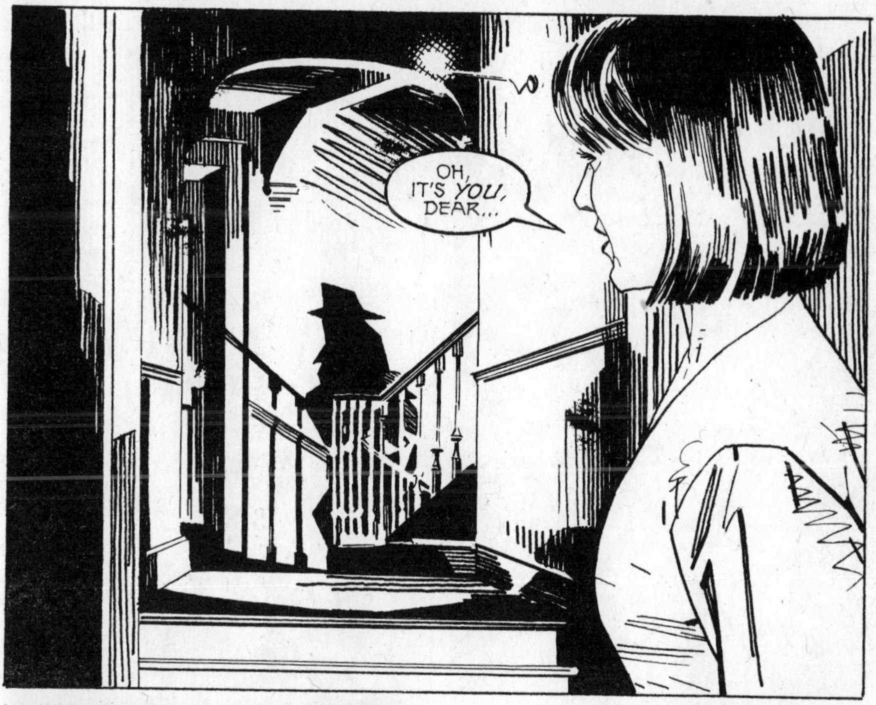
OH, IT'S *YOU,* DEAR...

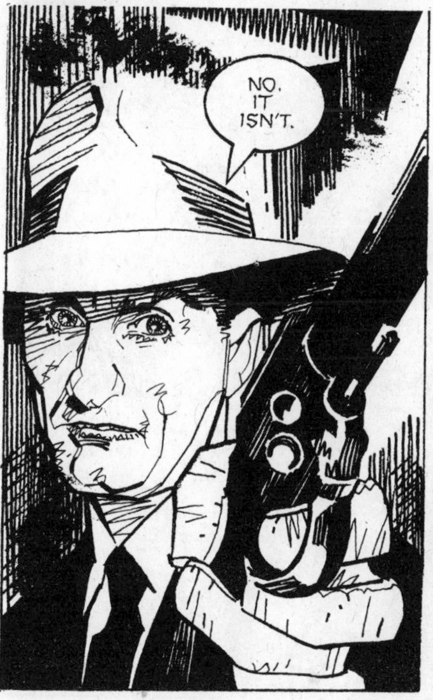
NO. IT ISN'T.

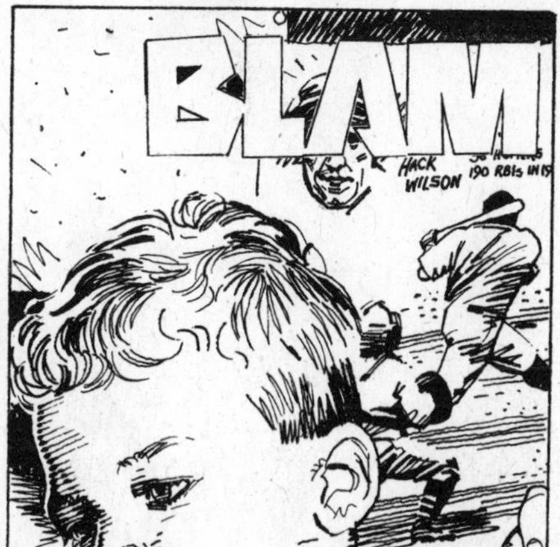
BLAM
HACK WILSON
190 RBIs

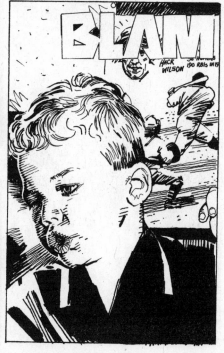

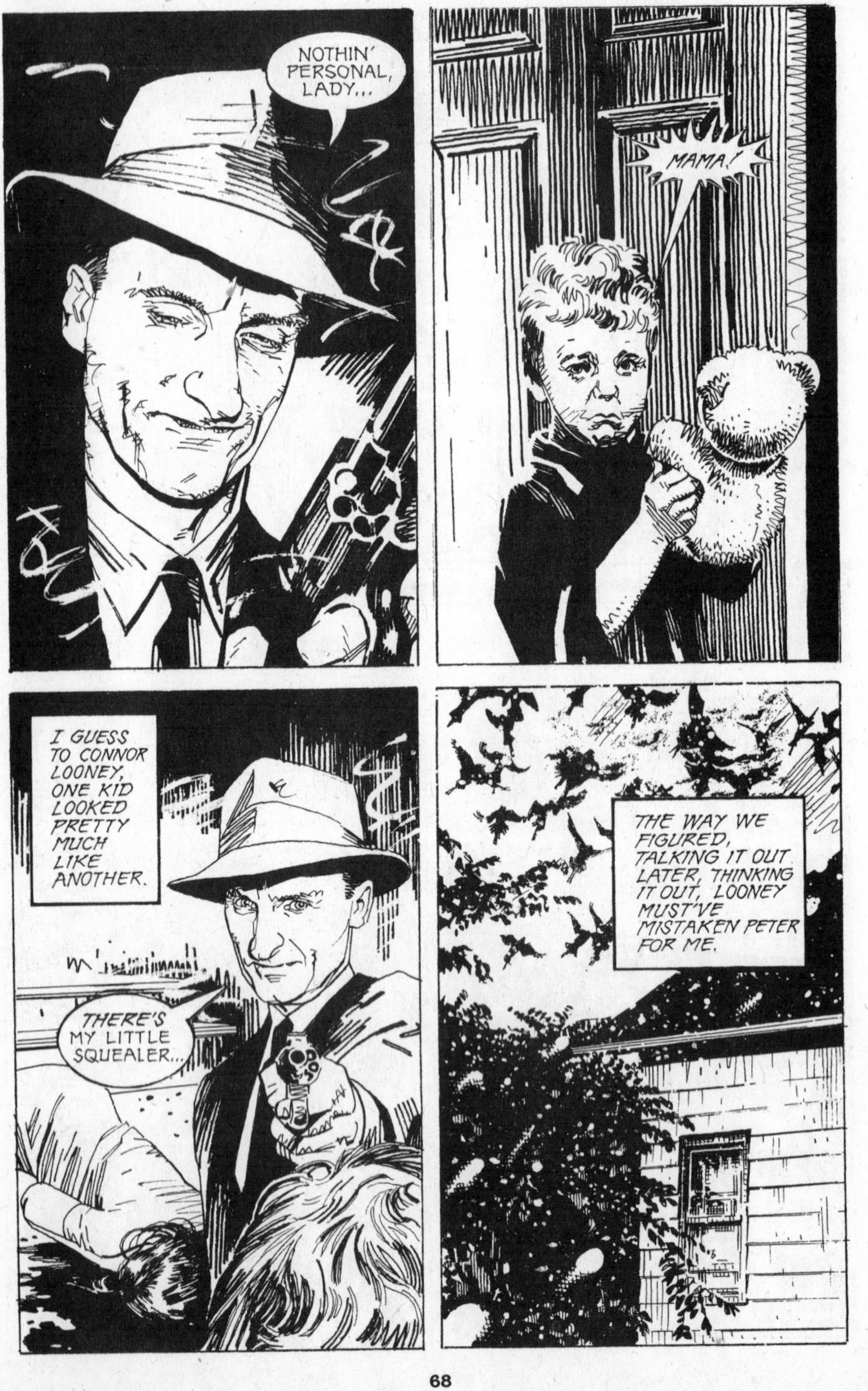
NOTHIN' PERSONAL, LADY...
MAMA!
I GUESS TO CONNOR LOONEY, ONE KID LOOKED PRETTY MUCH LIKE ANOTHER.
THERE'S MY LITTLE SQUEALER...
THE WAY WE FIGURED, TALKING IT OUT LATER, THINKING IT OUT, LOONEY MUST'VE MISTAKEN PETER FOR ME.

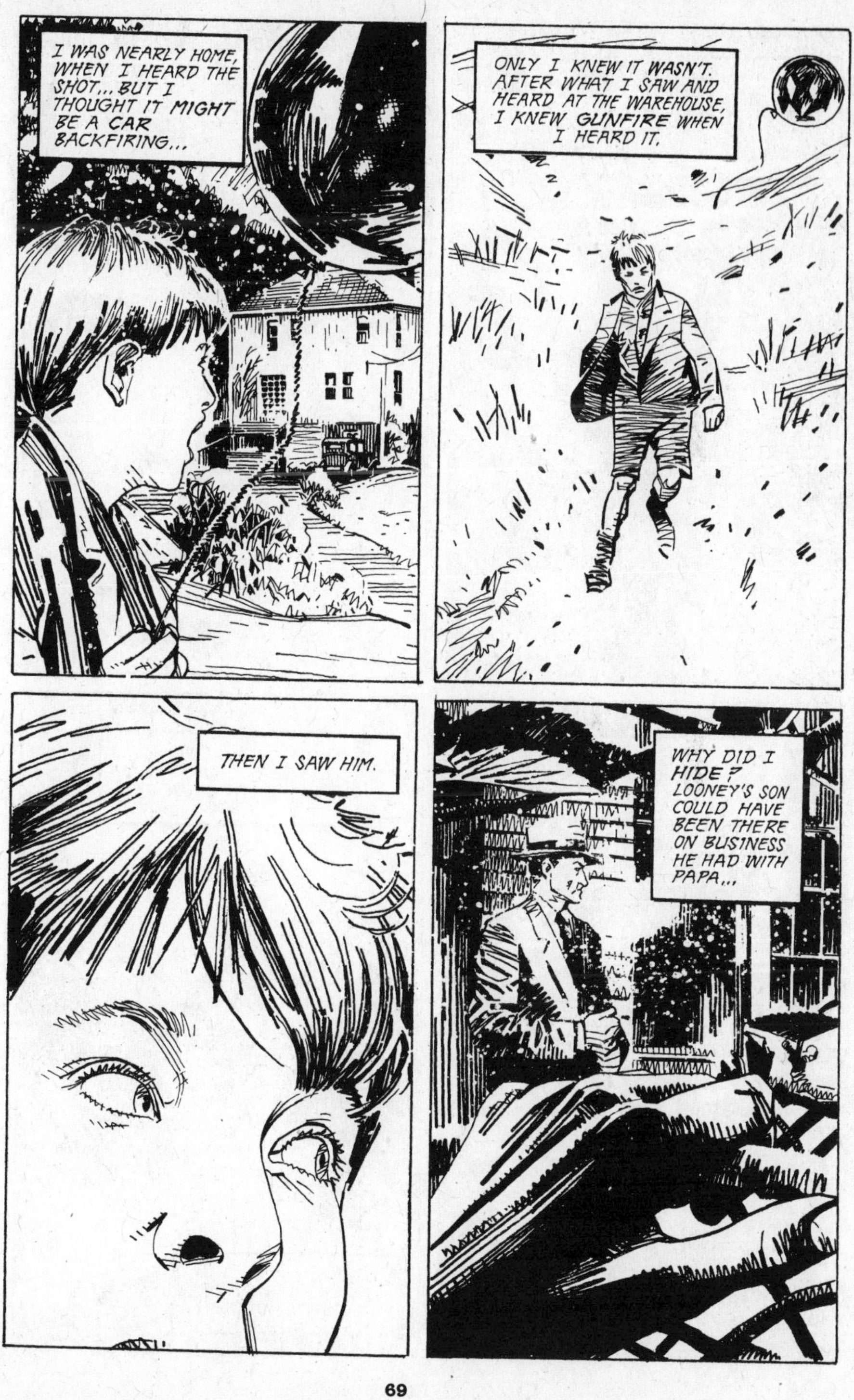
I WAS NEARLY HOME, WHEN I HEARD THE SHOT... BUT I THOUGHT IT MIGHT BE A CAR BACKFIRING...
ONLY I KNEW IT WASN'T. AFTER WHAT I SAW AND HEARD AT THE WAREHOUSE, I KNEW GUNFIRE WHEN I HEARD IT.
THEN I SAW HIM.
WHY DID I HIDE? LOONEY'S SON COULD HAVE BEEN THERE ON BUSINESS HE HAD WITH PAPA...

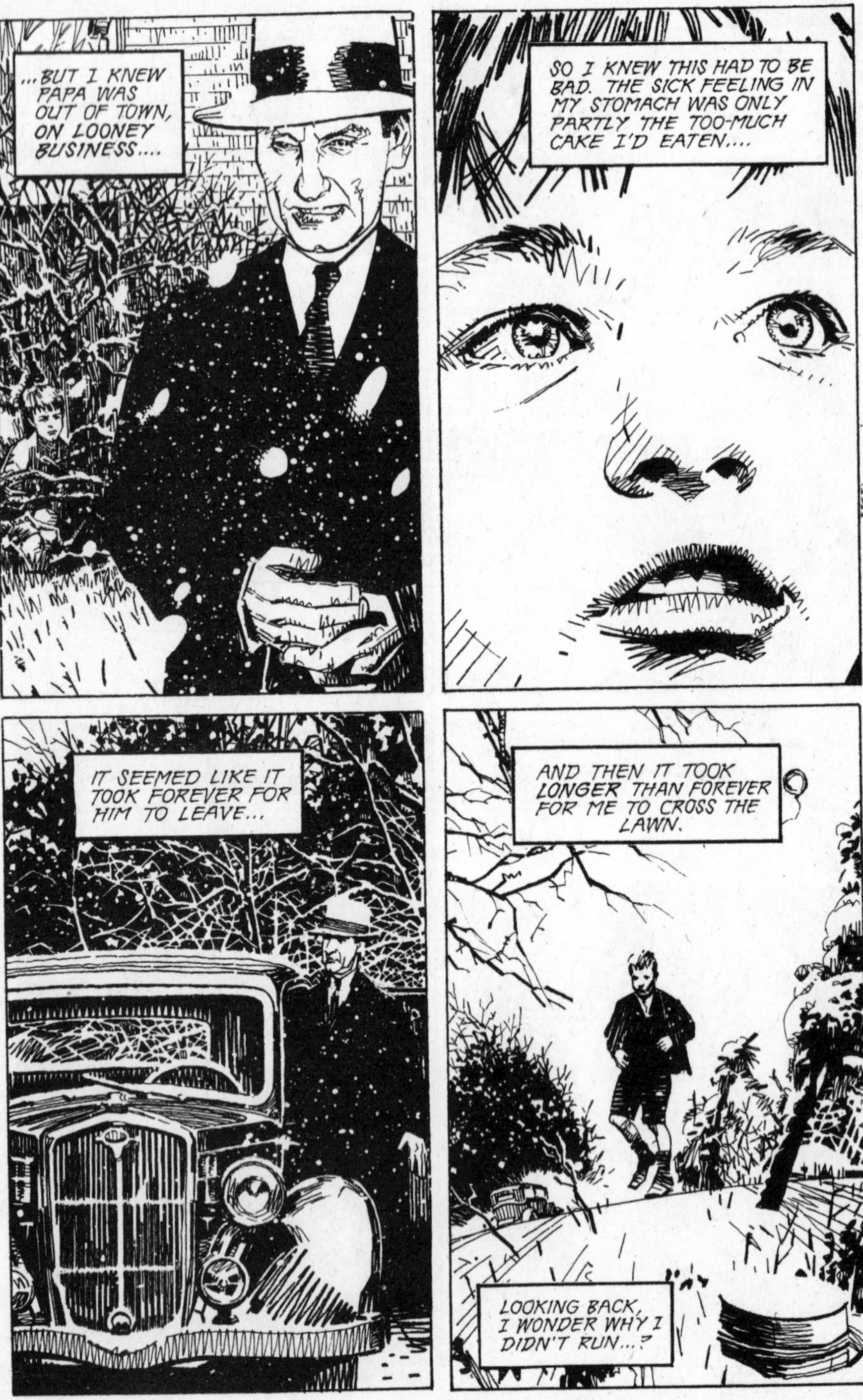
...BUT I KNEW PAPA WAS OUT OF TOWN, ON LOONEY BUSINESS....
SO I KNEW THIS HAD TO BE BAD. THE SICK FEELING IN MY STOMACH WAS ONLY PARTLY THE TOO-MUCH CAKE I'D EATEN....
IT SEEMED LIKE IT TOOK FOREVER FOR HIM TO LEAVE...
AND THEN IT TOOK LONGER THAN FOREVER FOR ME TO CROSS THE LAWN.
LOOKING BACK, I WONDER WHY I DIDN'T RUN...?

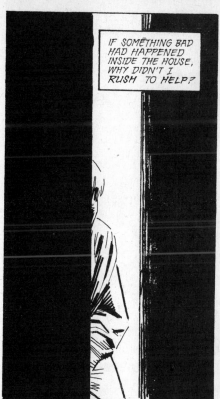

IF SOMETHING BAD HAD HAPPENED INSIDE THE HOUSE, WHY DIDN'T I RUSH TO HELP?

MAYBE IT WAS THAT SOMEHOW I KNEW THAT IF SOMETHING BAD HAD HAPPENED... THERE WAS NO HELP THAT COULD BE GIVEN.

MY INSTINCTS WERE RIGHT, WEREN'T THEY?

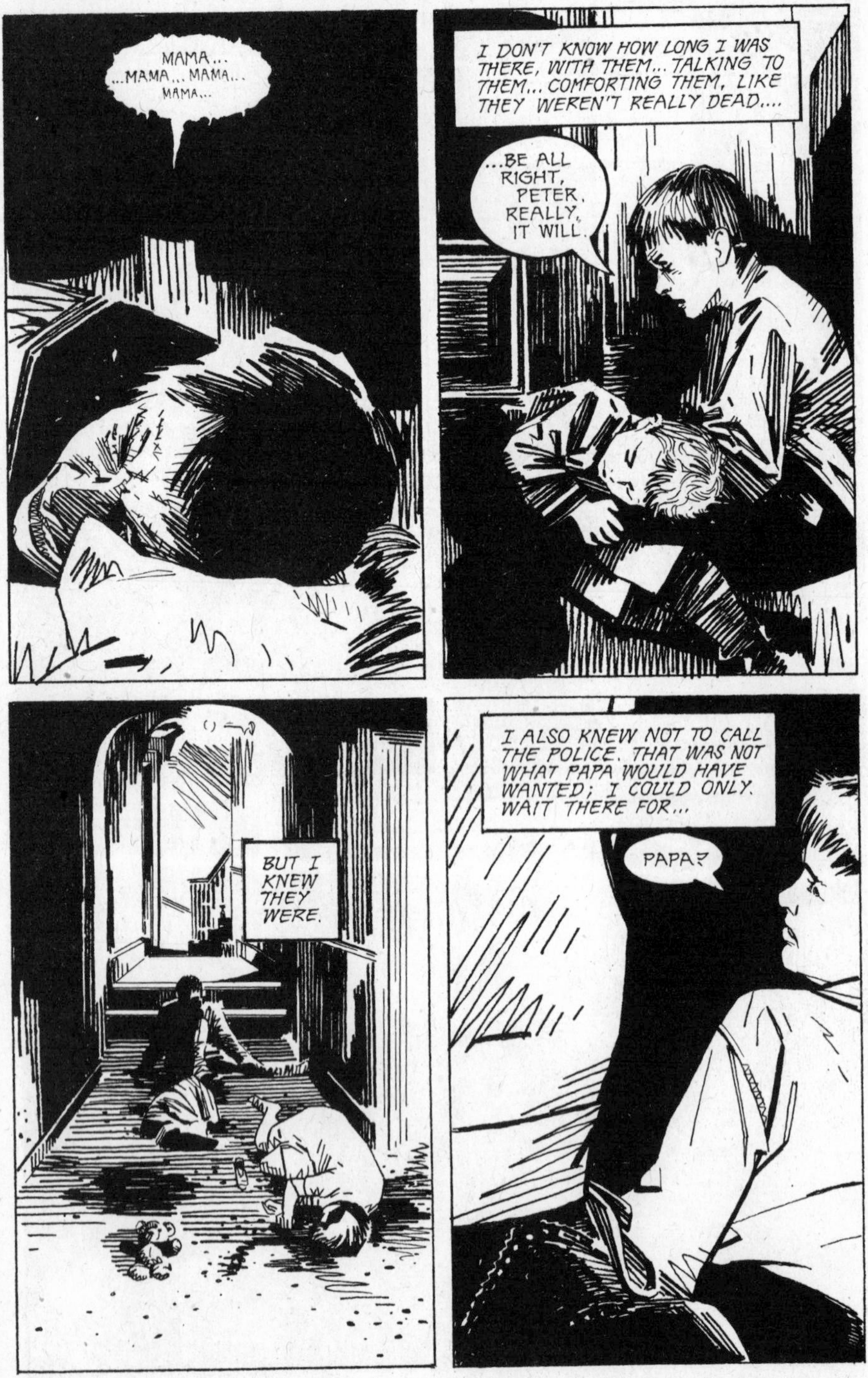
MAMA... ...MAMA... MAMA... MAMA...
I DON'T KNOW HOW LONG I WAS THERE, WITH THEM... TALKING TO THEM... COMFORTING THEM, LIKE THEY WEREN'T REALLY DEAD....
...BE ALL RIGHT, PETER. REALLY, IT WILL.
BUT I KNEW THEY WERE.
I ALSO KNEW NOT TO CALL THE POLICE. THAT WAS NOT WHAT PAPA WOULD HAVE WANTED; I COULD ONLY WAIT THERE FOR...
PAPA?

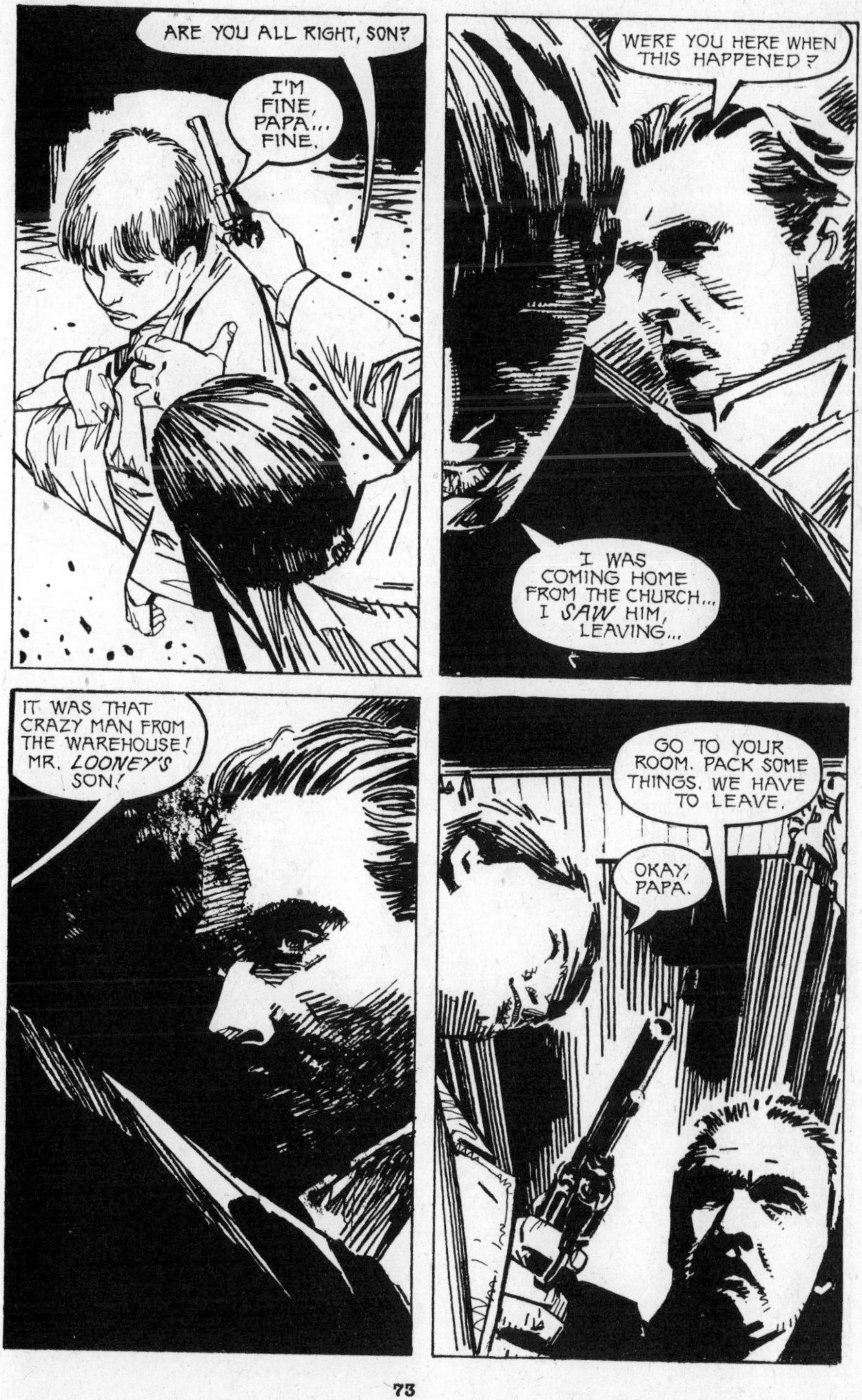
ARE YOU ALL RIGHT, SON?
I'M FINE, PAPA... FINE.
WERE YOU HERE WHEN THIS HAPPENED?
I WAS COMING HOME FROM THE CHURCH... I *SAW* HIM, LEAVING...
IT WAS THAT CRAZY MAN FROM THE WAREHOUSE! MR. *LOONEY'S* SON!
GO TO YOUR ROOM. PACK SOME THINGS. WE HAVE TO LEAVE.
OKAY, PAPA.

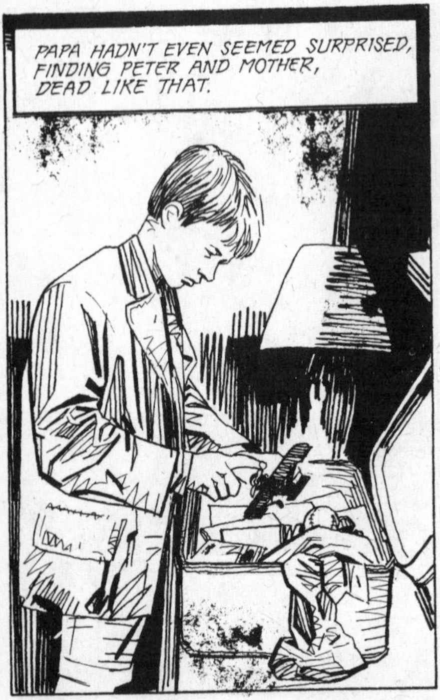
PAPA HADN'T EVEN SEEMED SURPRISED, FINDING PETER AND MOTHER, DEAD LIKE THAT.

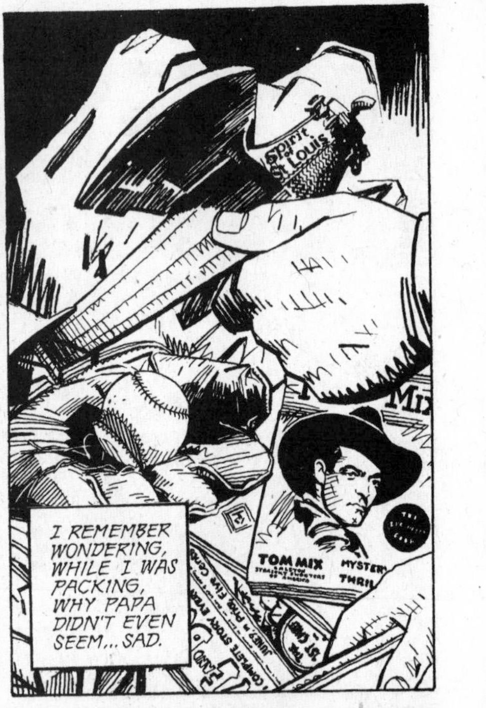
Spirit of St Louis
TOM MIX
I REMEMBER WONDERING, WHILE I WAS PACKING, WHY PAPA DIDN'T EVEN SEEM... SAD.

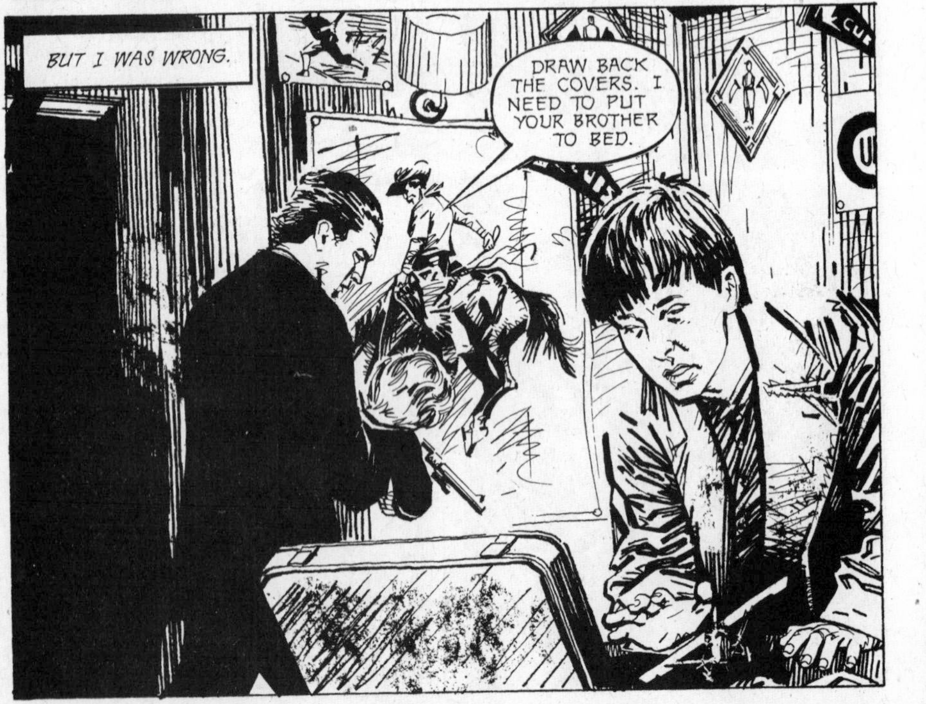
BUT I WAS WRONG.
DRAW BACK THE COVERS. I NEED TO PUT YOUR BROTHER TO BED.

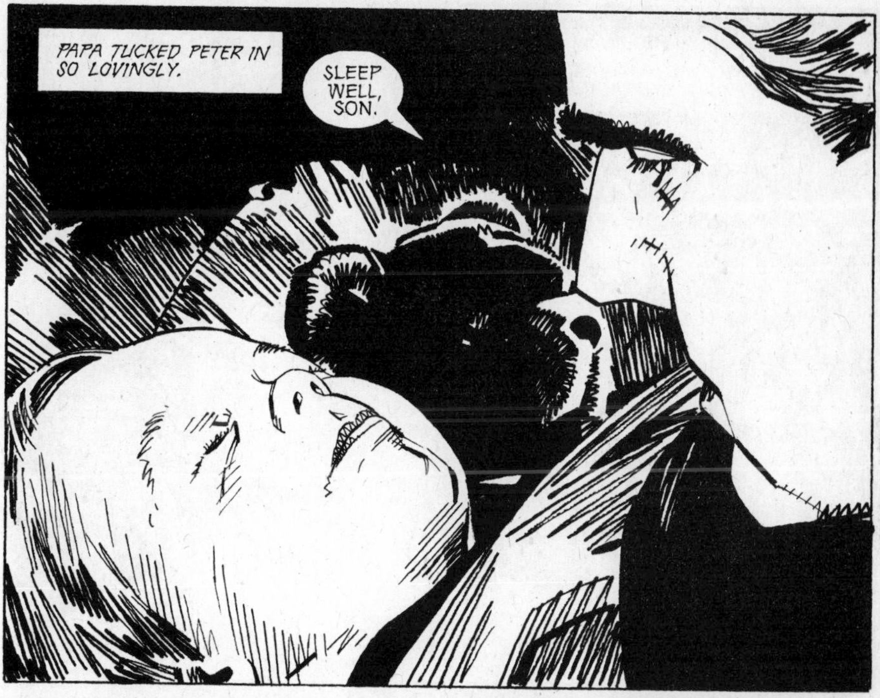
PAPA TUCKED PETER IN SO LOVINGLY.
SLEEP WELL, SON.

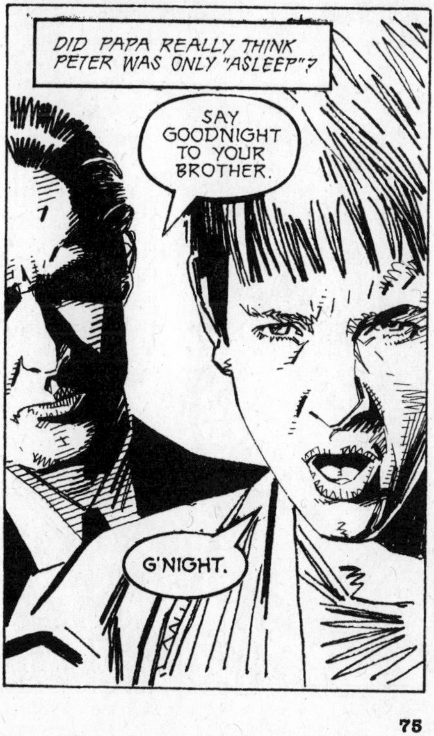
DID PAPA REALLY THINK PETER WAS ONLY "ASLEEP"?
SAY GOODNIGHT TO YOUR BROTHER.
G'NIGHT.

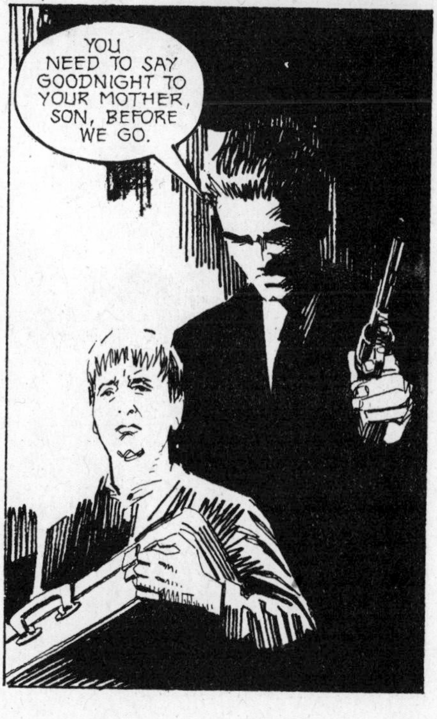
YOU NEED TO SAY GOODNIGHT TO YOUR MOTHER, SON, BEFORE WE GO.

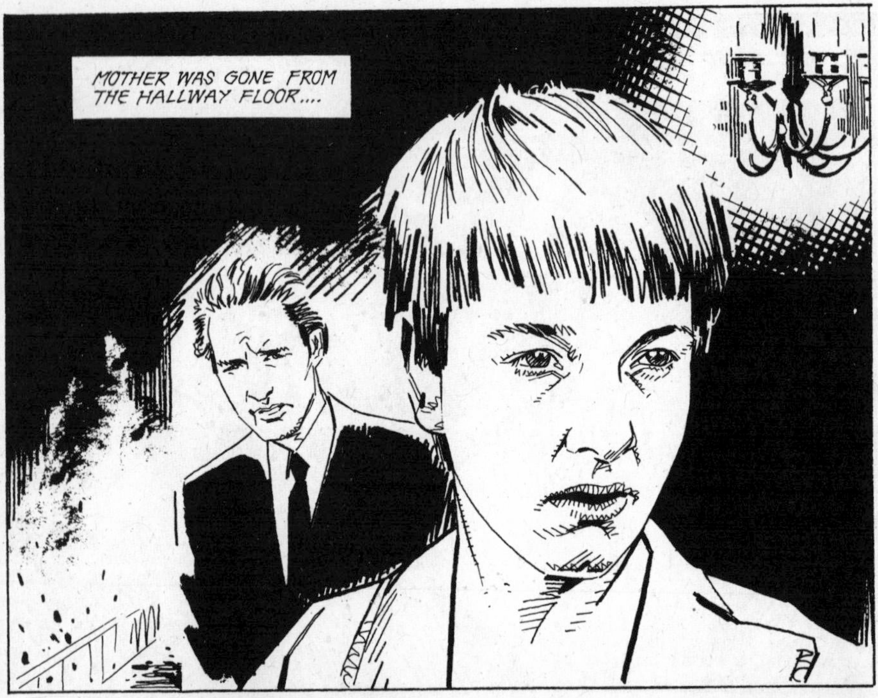
MOTHER WAS GONE FROM THE HALLWAY FLOOR....

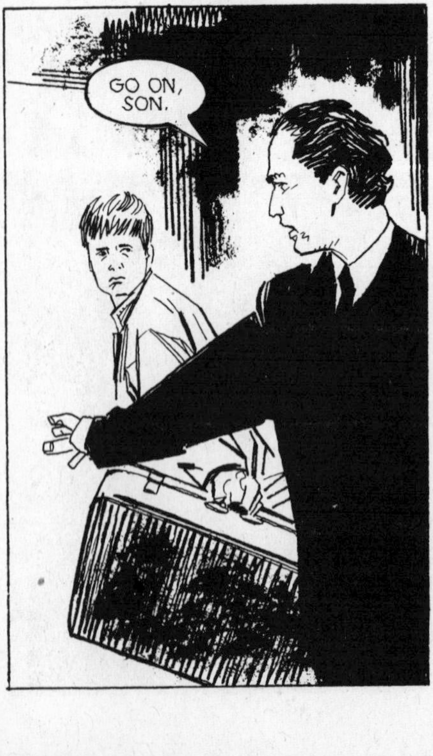
GO ON, SON.

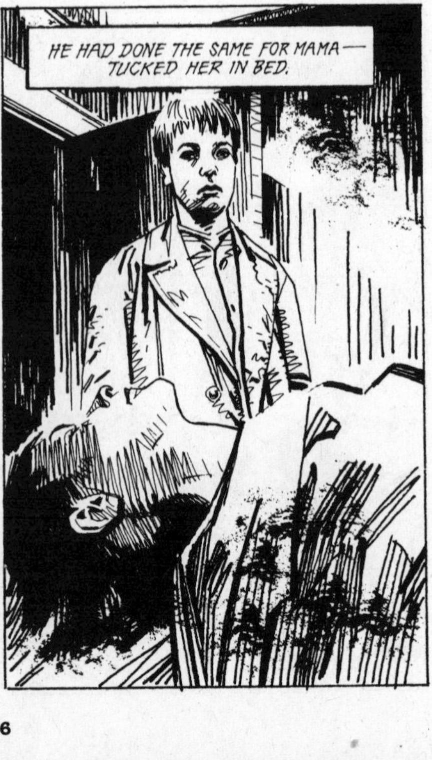
HE HAD DONE THE SAME FOR MAMA— TUCKED HER IN BED.

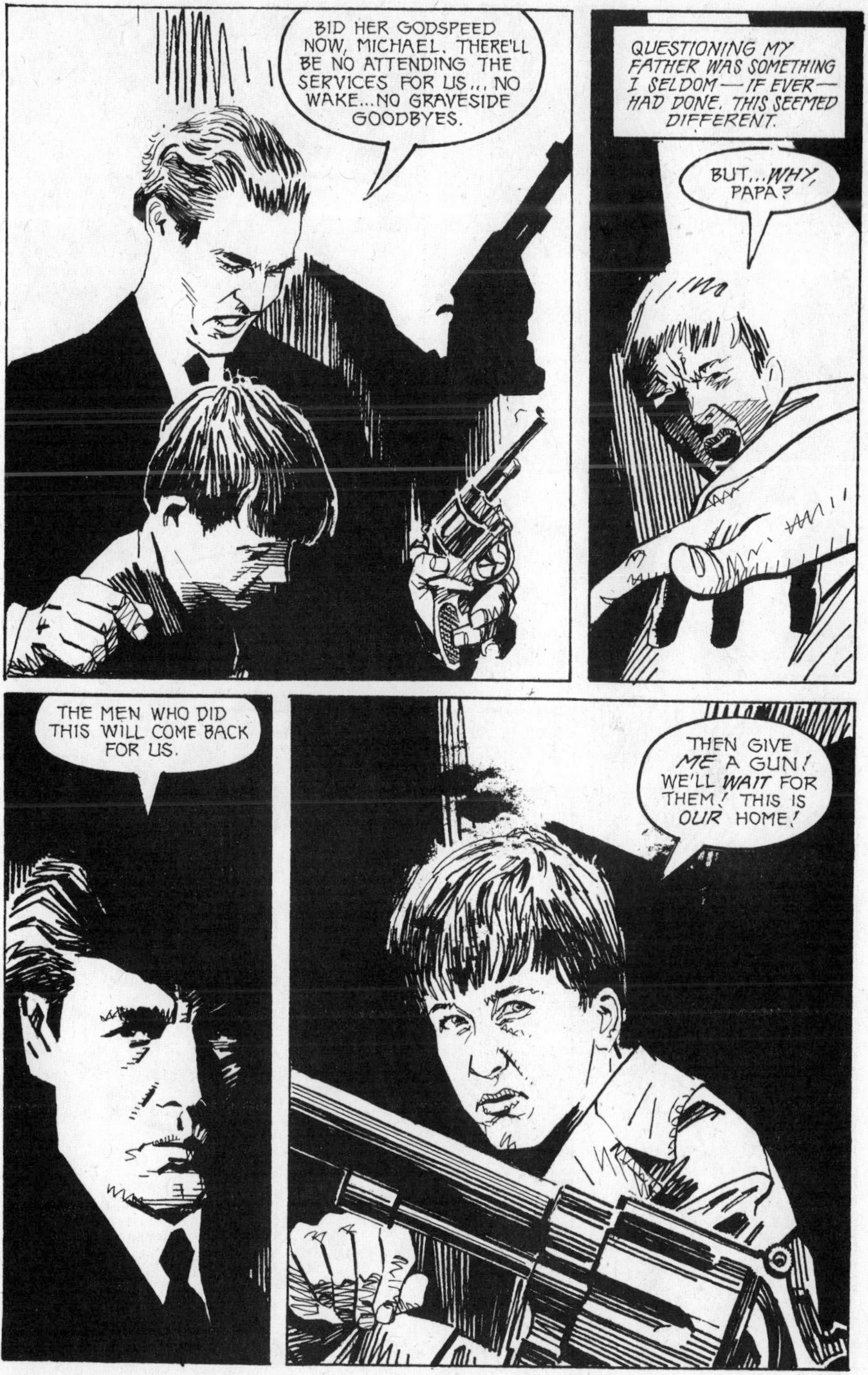
BID HER GODSPEED NOW, MICHAEL. THERE'LL BE NO ATTENDING THE SERVICES FOR US... NO WAKE...NO GRAVESIDE GOODBYES.
QUESTIONING MY FATHER WAS SOMETHING I SELDOM—IF EVER—HAD DONE. THIS SEEMED DIFFERENT.
BUT... *WHY*, PAPA?
THE MEN WHO DID THIS WILL COME BACK FOR US.
THEN GIVE *ME* A GUN! WE'LL *WAIT* FOR THEM! THIS IS *OUR* HOME!

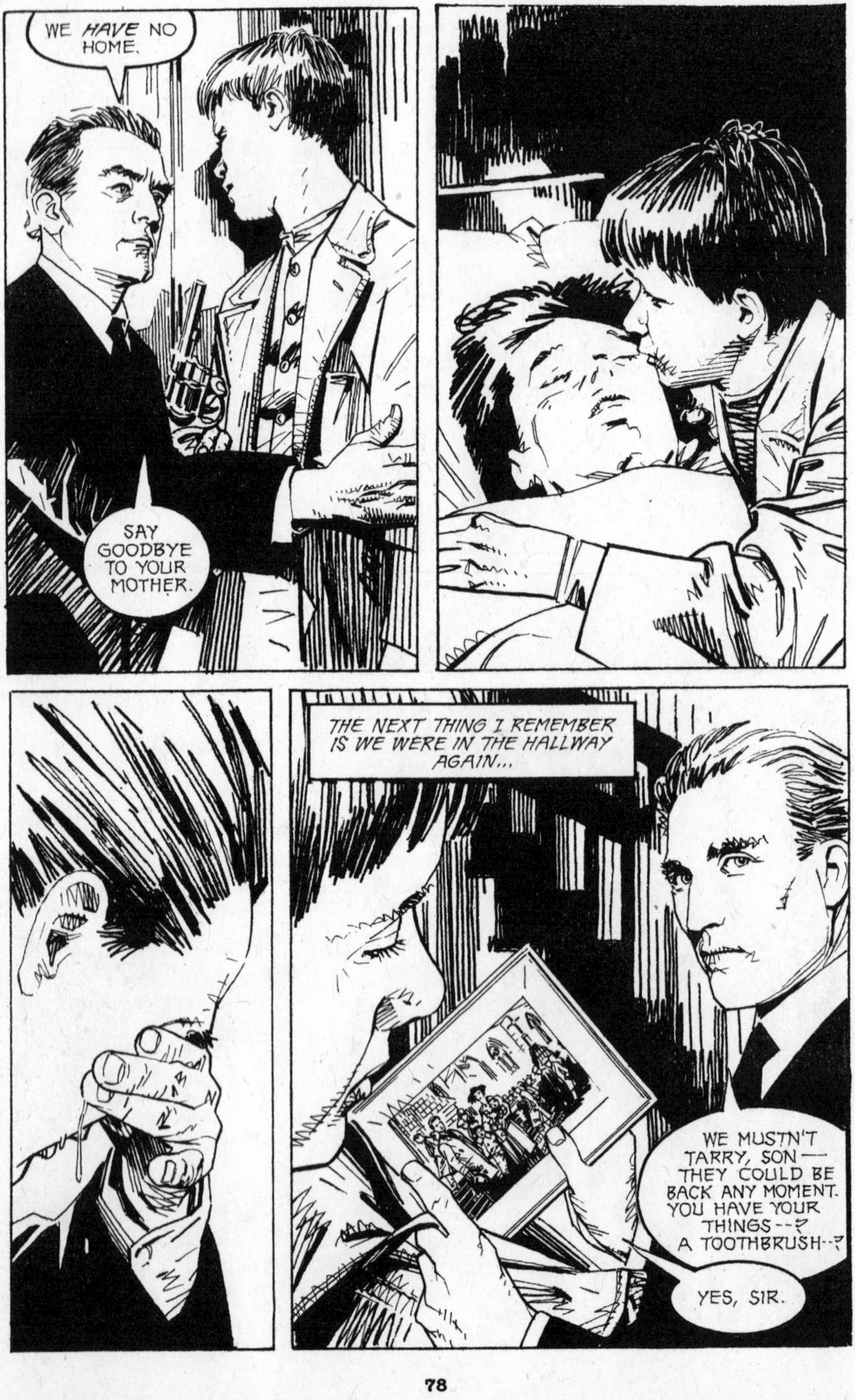
WE *HAVE* NO HOME.
SAY GOODBYE TO YOUR MOTHER.
THE NEXT THING I REMEMBER IS WE WERE IN THE HALLWAY AGAIN...
WE MUSTN'T TARRY, SON— THEY COULD BE BACK ANY MOMENT. YOU HAVE YOUR THINGS--? A TOOTHBRUSH--?
YES, SIR.

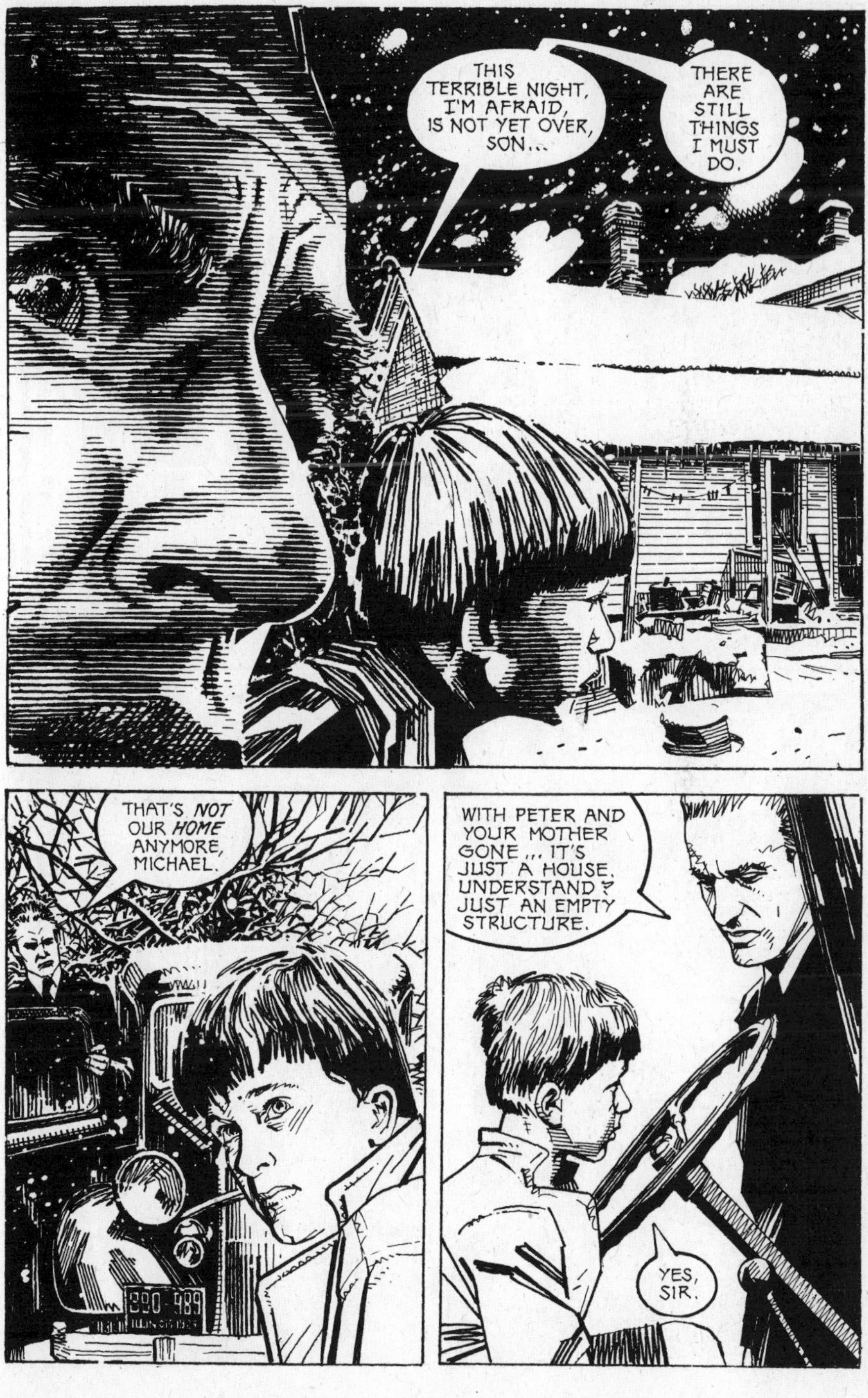
THIS TERRIBLE NIGHT, I'M AFRAID, IS NOT YET OVER, SON...
THERE ARE STILL THINGS I MUST DO.
THAT'S *NOT* OUR *HOME* ANYMORE, MICHAEL.
WITH PETER AND YOUR MOTHER GONE... IT'S JUST A HOUSE. UNDERSTAND? JUST AN EMPTY STRUCTURE.
YES, SIR.

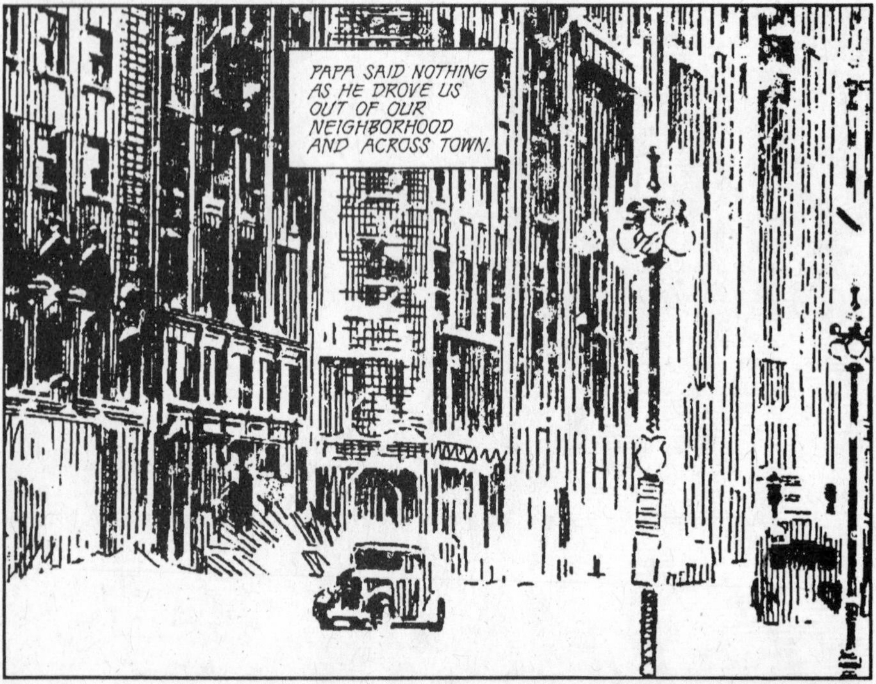
PAPA SAID NOTHING AS HE DROVE US OUT OF OUR NEIGHBORHOOD AND ACROSS TOWN.

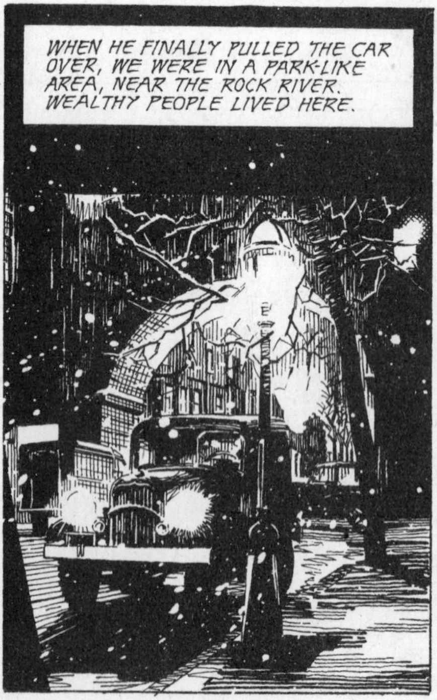
WHEN HE FINALLY PULLED THE CAR OVER, WE WERE IN A PARK-LIKE AREA, NEAR THE ROCK RIVER. WEALTHY PEOPLE LIVED HERE.

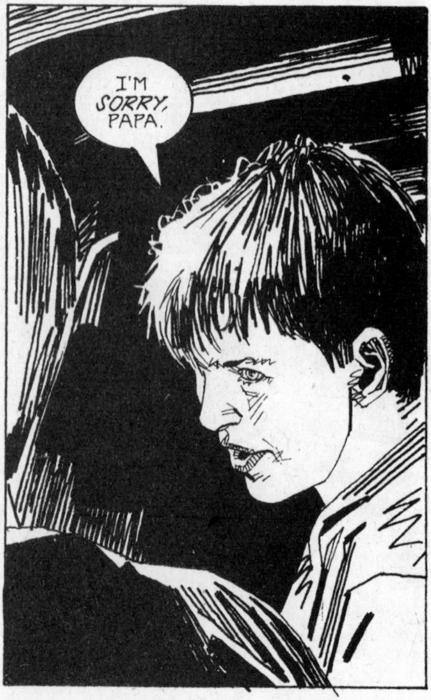
I'M SORRY, PAPA.

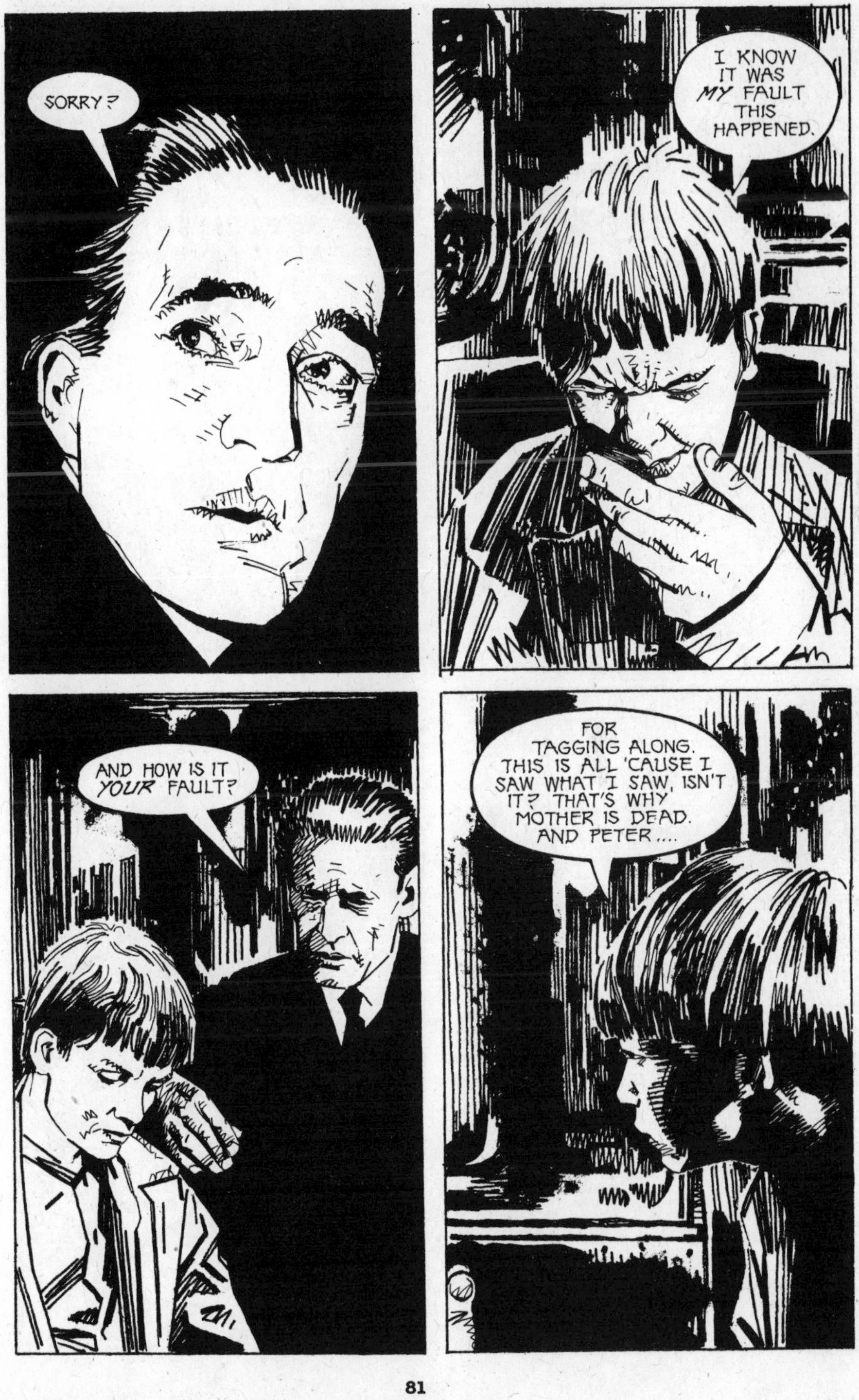
SORRY?
I KNOW IT WAS *MY* FAULT THIS HAPPENED.
AND HOW IS IT *YOUR* FAULT?
FOR TAGGING ALONG. THIS IS ALL 'CAUSE I SAW WHAT I SAW, ISN'T IT? THAT'S WHY MOTHER IS DEAD. AND PETER....

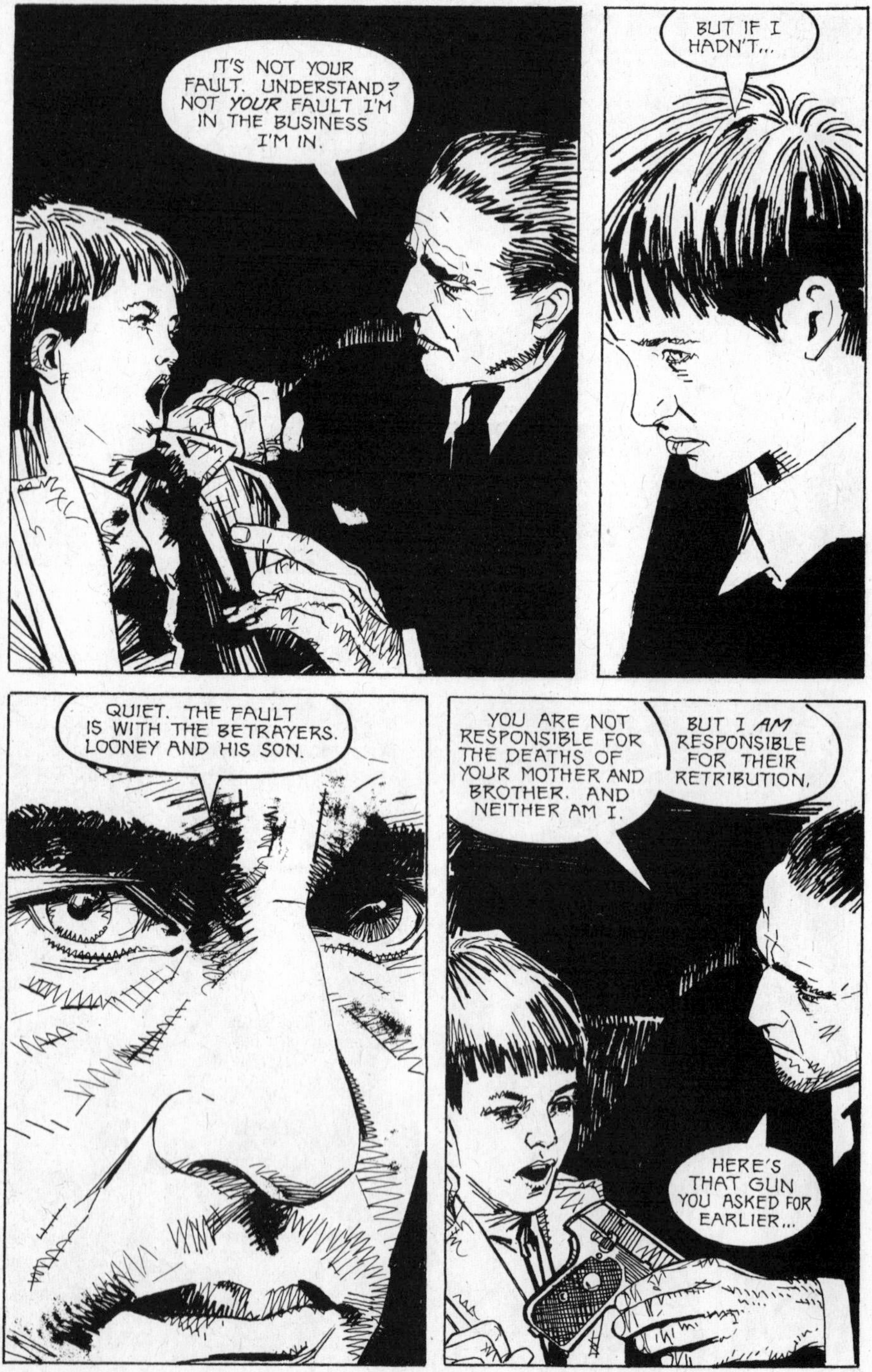
IT'S NOT YOUR FAULT. UNDERSTAND? NOT *YOUR* FAULT I'M IN THE BUSINESS I'M IN.
BUT IF I HADN'T...
QUIET. THE FAULT IS WITH THE BETRAYERS. LOONEY AND HIS SON.
YOU ARE NOT RESPONSIBLE FOR THE DEATHS OF YOUR MOTHER AND BROTHER. AND NEITHER AM I.
BUT I *AM* RESPONSIBLE FOR THEIR RETRIBUTION.
HERE'S THAT GUN YOU ASKED FOR EARLIER...

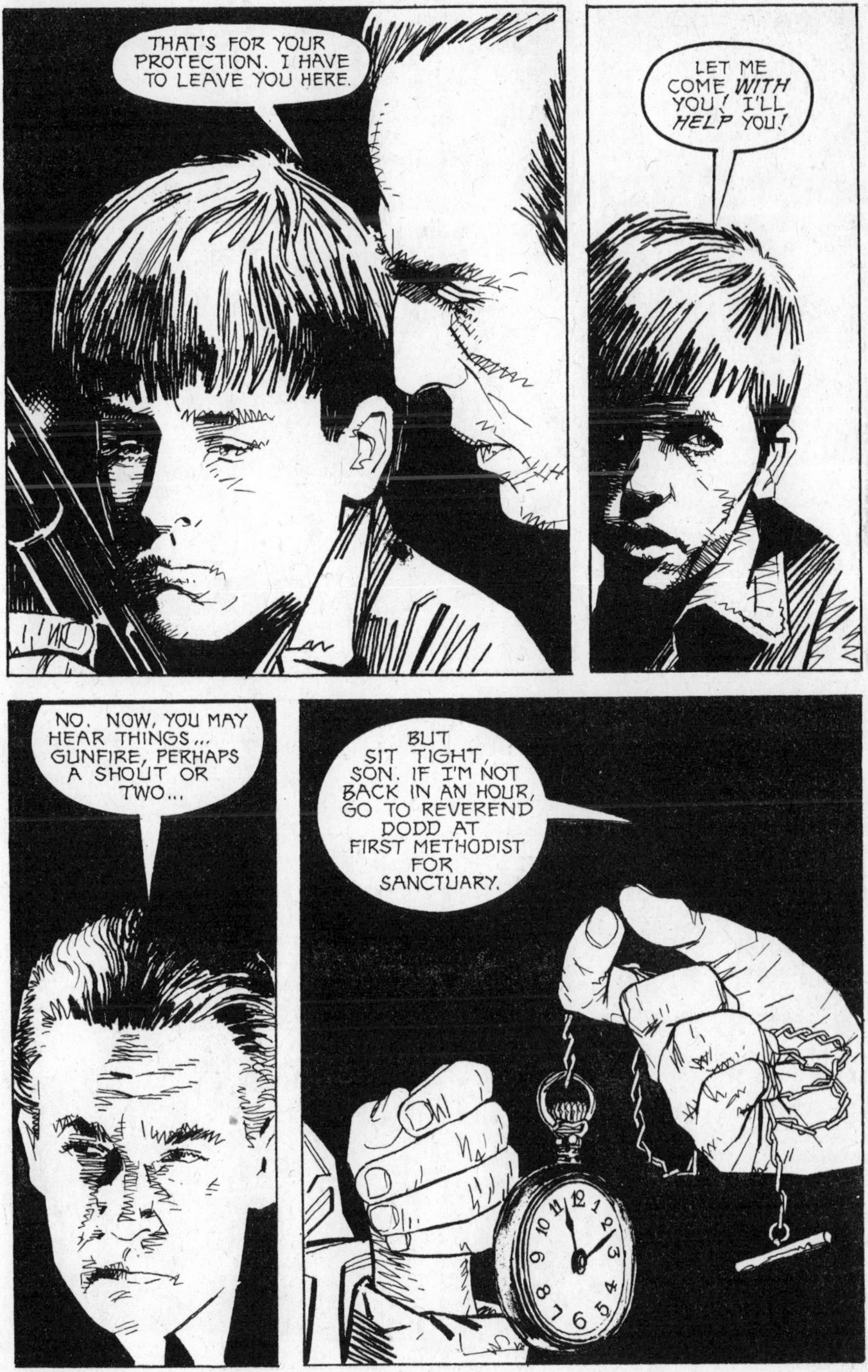
THAT'S FOR YOUR PROTECTION. I HAVE TO LEAVE YOU HERE.
LET ME COME *WITH* YOU! I'LL *HELP* YOU!
NO. NOW, YOU MAY HEAR THINGS... GUNFIRE, PERHAPS A SHOUT OR TWO...
BUT SIT TIGHT, SON. IF I'M NOT BACK IN AN HOUR, GO TO REVEREND DODD AT FIRST METHODIST FOR SANCTUARY.

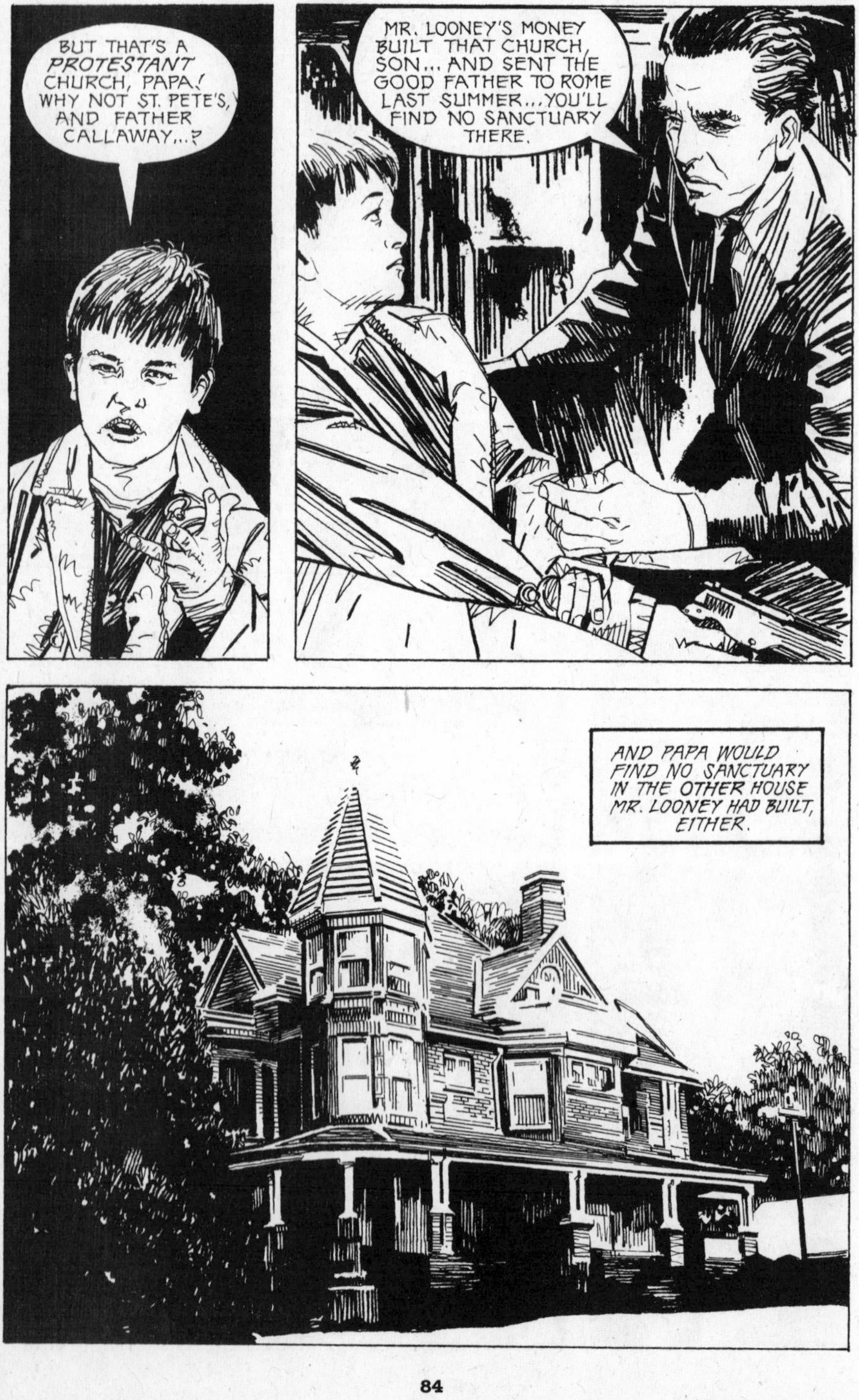
BUT THAT'S A *PROTESTANT* CHURCH, PAPA! WHY NOT ST. PETE'S, AND FATHER CALLAWAY...?
MR. LOONEY'S MONEY BUILT THAT CHURCH, SON... AND SENT THE GOOD FATHER TO ROME LAST SUMMER... YOU'LL FIND NO SANCTUARY THERE.
AND PAPA WOULD FIND NO SANCTUARY IN THE OTHER HOUSE MR. LOONEY HAD BUILT, EITHER.

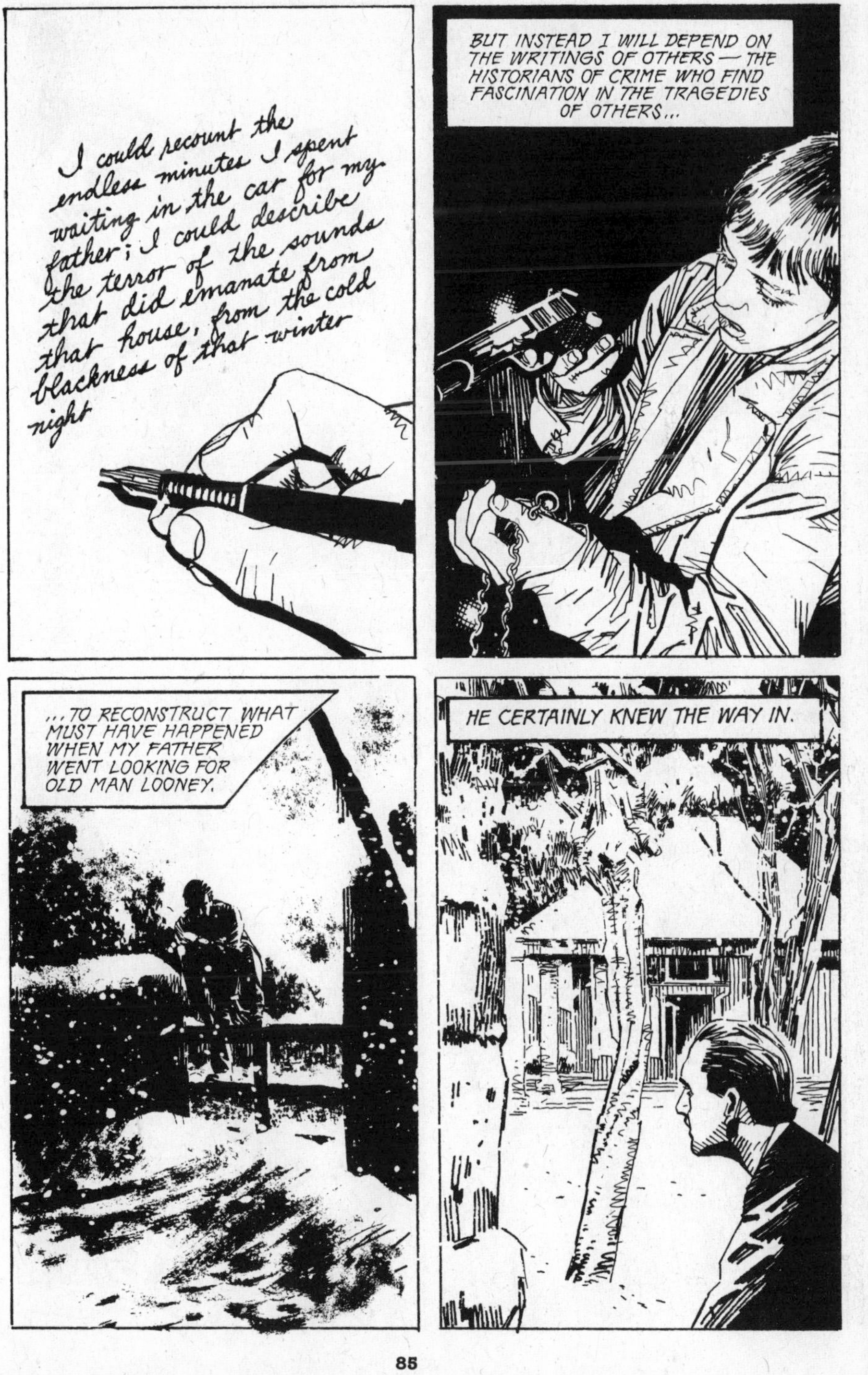
I could recount the endless minutes I spent waiting in the car for my father; I could describe the terror of the sounds that did emanate from that house, from the cold blackness of that winter night
BUT INSTEAD I WILL DEPEND ON THE WRITINGS OF OTHERS — THE HISTORIANS OF CRIME WHO FIND FASCINATION IN THE TRAGEDIES OF OTHERS...
...TO RECONSTRUCT WHAT MUST HAVE HAPPENED WHEN MY FATHER WENT LOOKING FOR OLD MAN LOONEY.
HE CERTAINLY KNEW THE WAY IN.

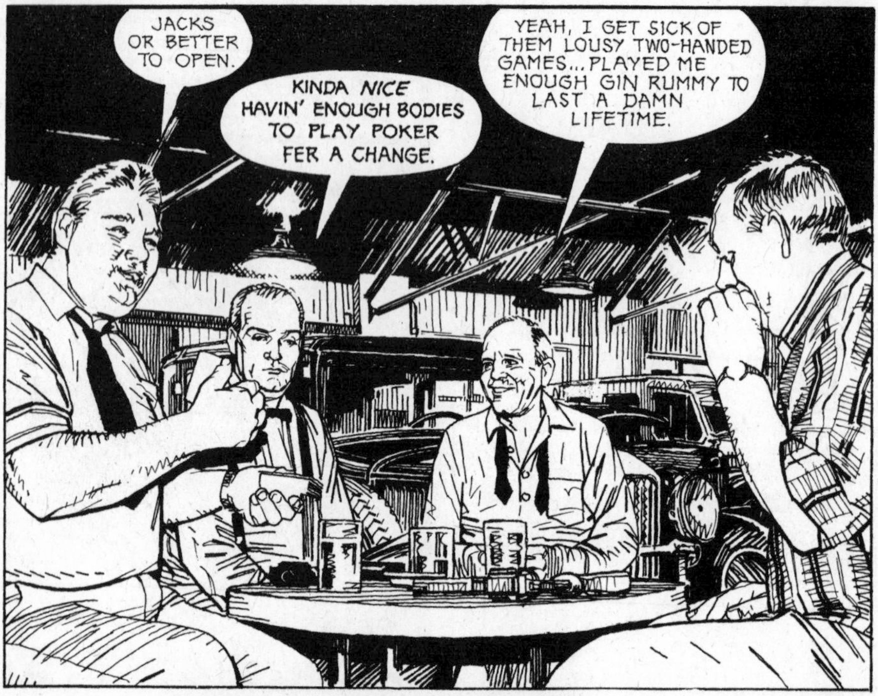
JACKS OR BETTER TO OPEN.
KINDA NICE HAVIN' ENOUGH BODIES TO PLAY POKER FER A CHANGE.
YEAH, I GET SICK OF THEM LOUSY TWO-HANDED GAMES... PLAYED ME ENOUGH GIN RUMMY TO LAST A DAMN LIFETIME.
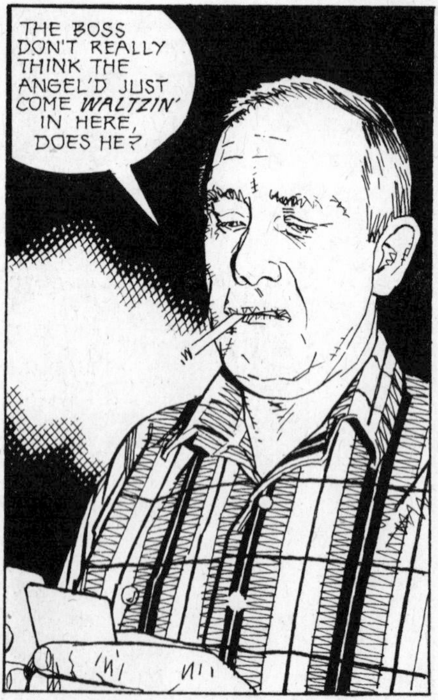
THE BOSS DON'T REALLY THINK THE ANGEL'D JUST COME WALTZIN' IN HERE, DOES HE?
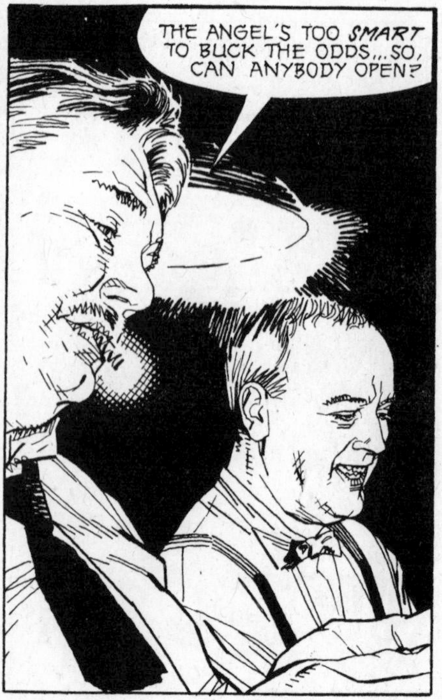
THE ANGEL'S TOO SMART TO BUCK THE ODDS... SO, CAN ANYBODY OPEN?

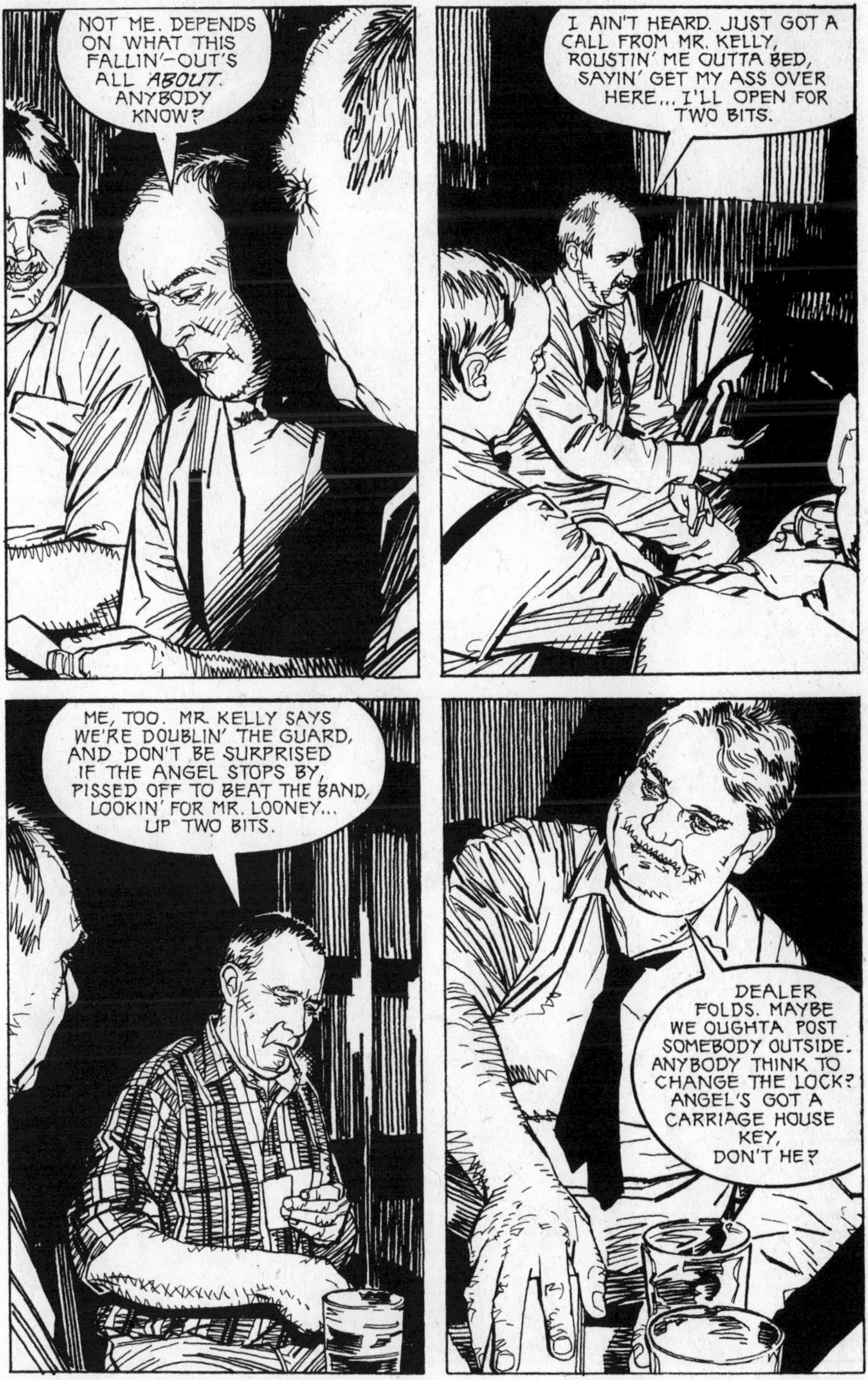
NOT ME. DEPENDS ON WHAT THIS FALLIN'-OUT'S ALL *ABOUT*. ANYBODY KNOW?
I AIN'T HEARD. JUST GOT A CALL FROM MR. KELLY, ROUSTIN' ME OUTTA BED, SAYIN' GET MY ASS OVER HERE... I'LL OPEN FOR TWO BITS.
ME, TOO. MR. KELLY SAYS WE'RE DOUBLIN' THE GUARD, AND DON'T BE SURPRISED IF THE ANGEL STOPS BY, PISSED OFF TO BEAT THE BAND, LOOKIN' FOR MR. LOONEY... UP TWO BITS.
DEALER FOLDS. MAYBE WE OUGHTA POST SOMEBODY OUTSIDE. ANYBODY THINK TO CHANGE THE LOCK? ANGEL'S GOT A CARRIAGE HOUSE KEY, DON'T HE?

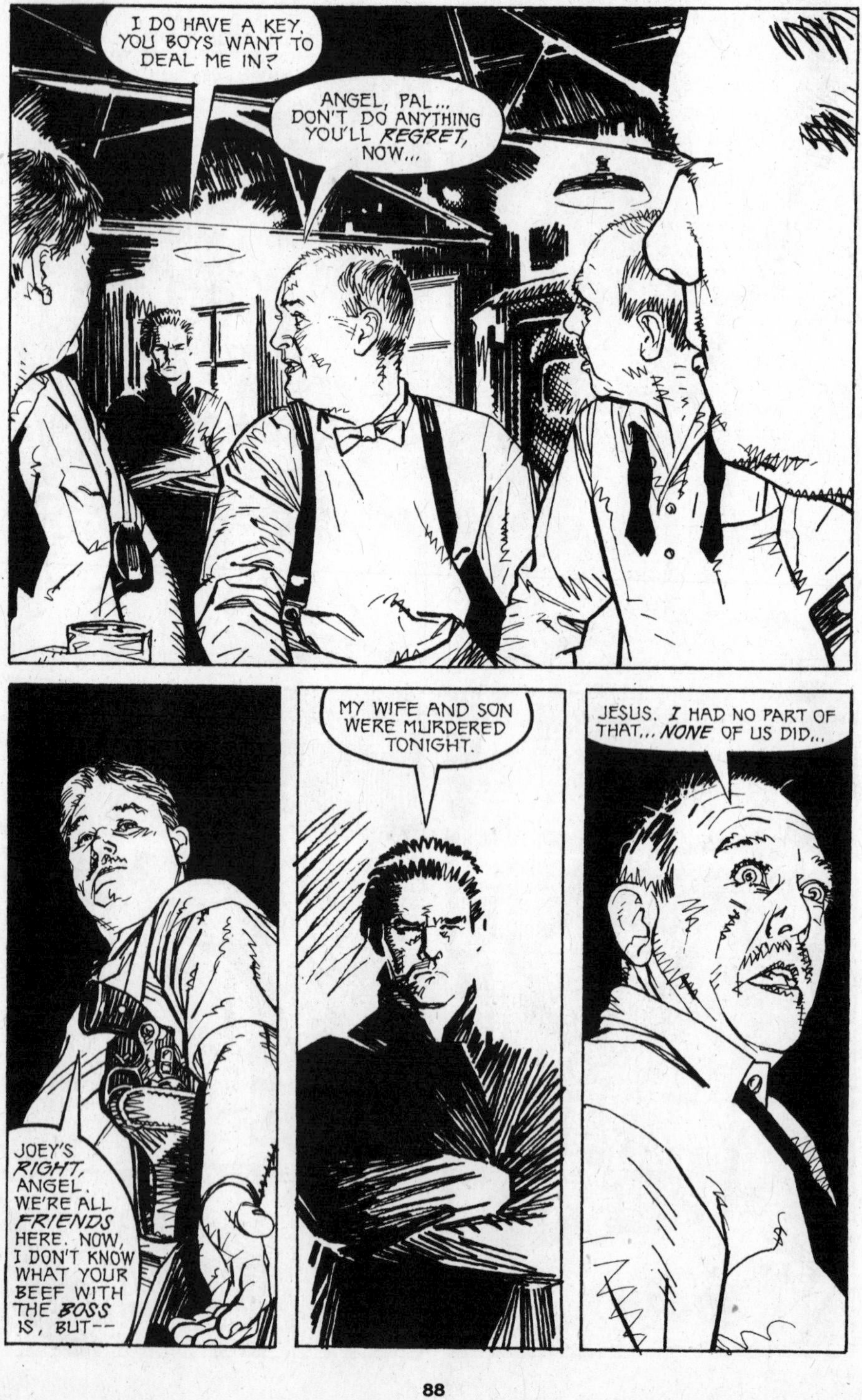
I DO HAVE A KEY. YOU BOYS WANT TO DEAL ME IN?
ANGEL, PAL... DON'T DO ANYTHING YOU'LL *REGRET*, NOW...
JOEY'S *RIGHT*, ANGEL. WE'RE ALL *FRIENDS* HERE. NOW, I DON'T KNOW WHAT YOUR BEEF WITH THE *BOSS* IS, BUT--
MY WIFE AND SON WERE MURDERED TONIGHT.
JESUS. *I* HAD NO PART OF THAT... *NONE* OF US DID...

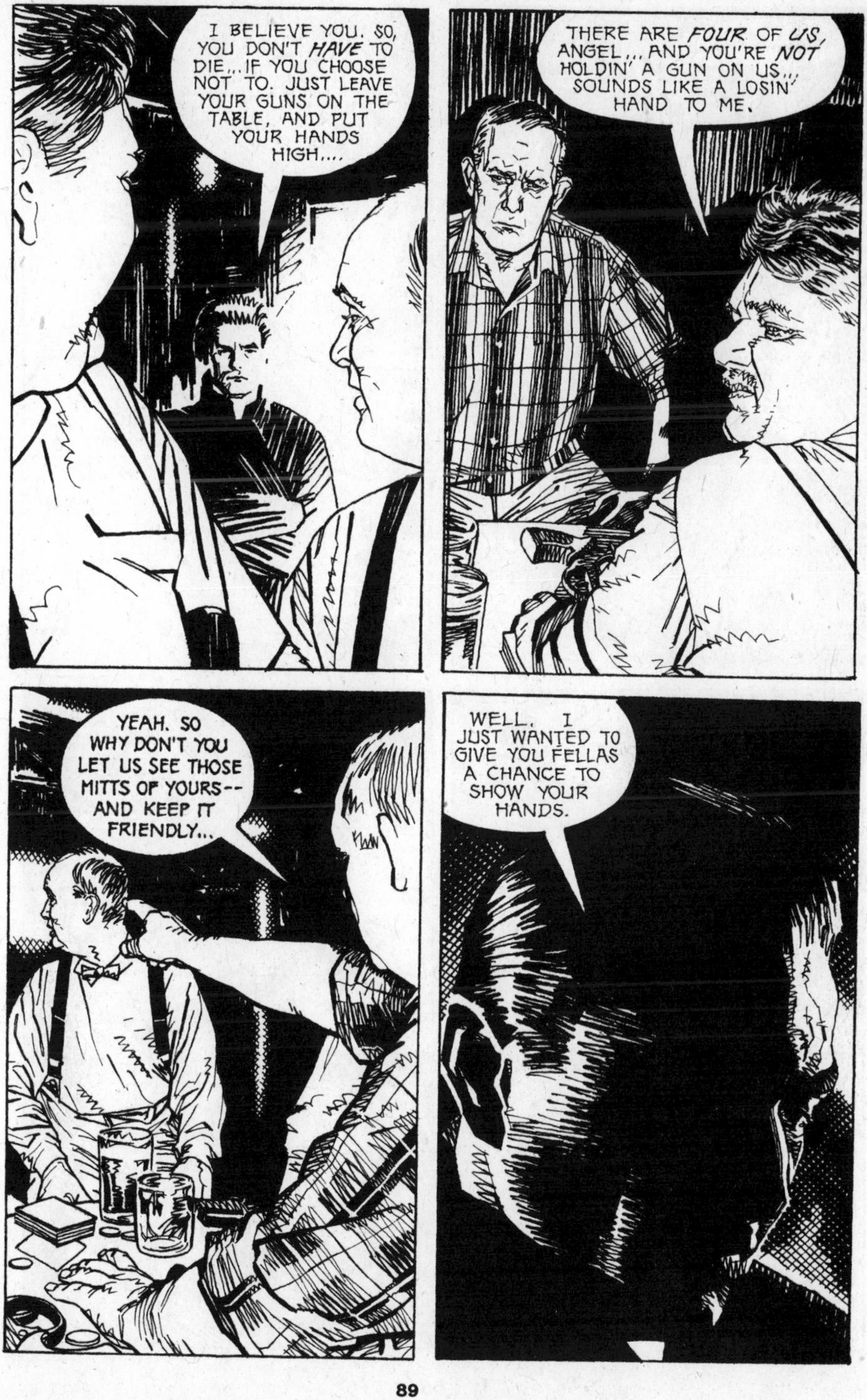
I BELIEVE YOU. SO, YOU DON'T *HAVE* TO DIE... IF YOU CHOOSE NOT TO. JUST LEAVE YOUR GUNS ON THE TABLE, AND PUT YOUR HANDS HIGH....
THERE ARE *FOUR* OF *US*, ANGEL... AND YOU'RE *NOT* HOLDIN' A GUN ON US... SOUNDS LIKE A LOSIN' HAND TO ME.
YEAH. SO WHY DON'T YOU LET US SEE THOSE MITTS OF YOURS-- AND KEEP IT FRIENDLY...
WELL. I JUST WANTED TO GIVE YOU FELLAS A CHANCE TO SHOW YOUR HANDS.

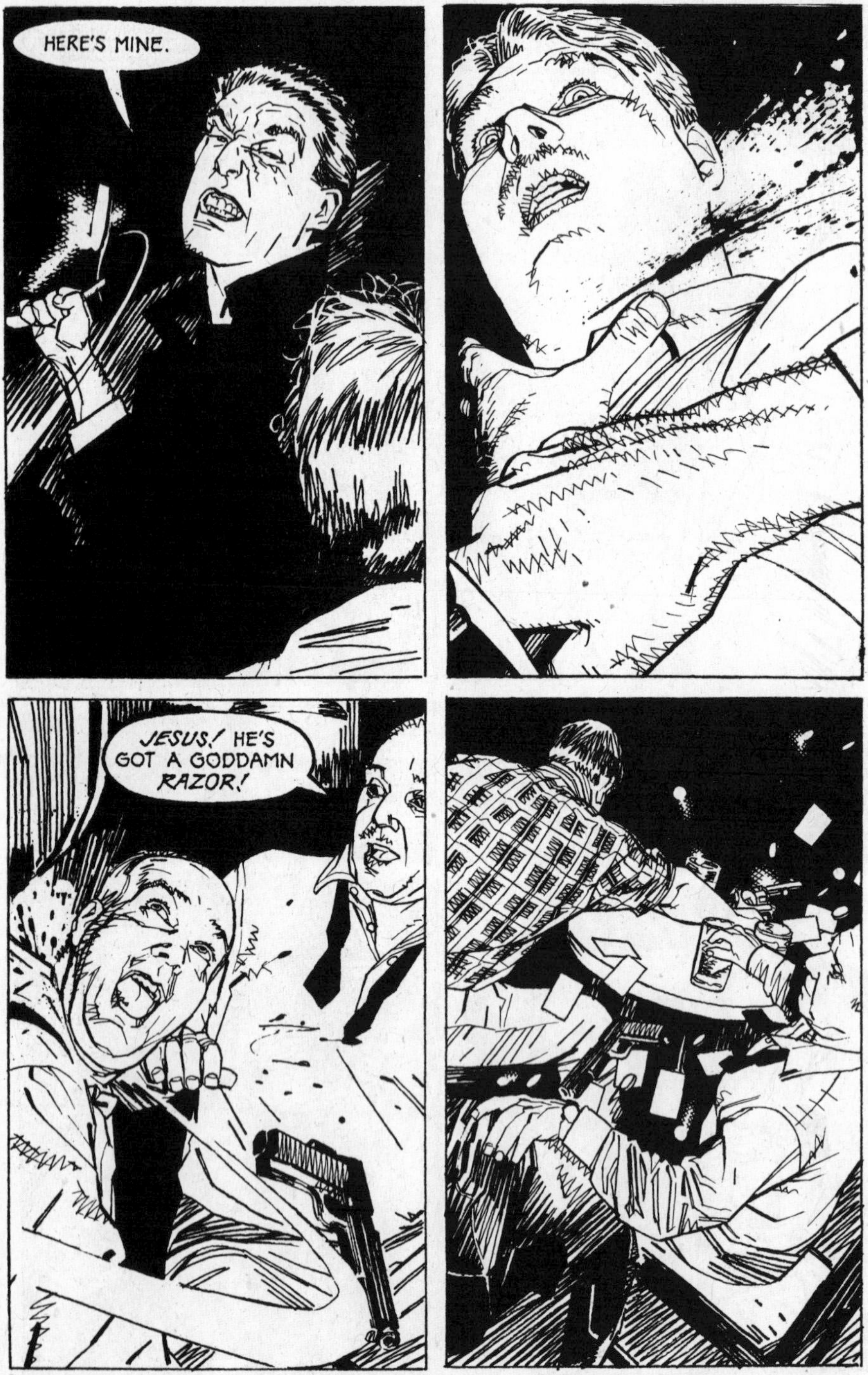
HERE'S MINE.
JESUS! HE'S GOT A GODDAMN RAZOR!

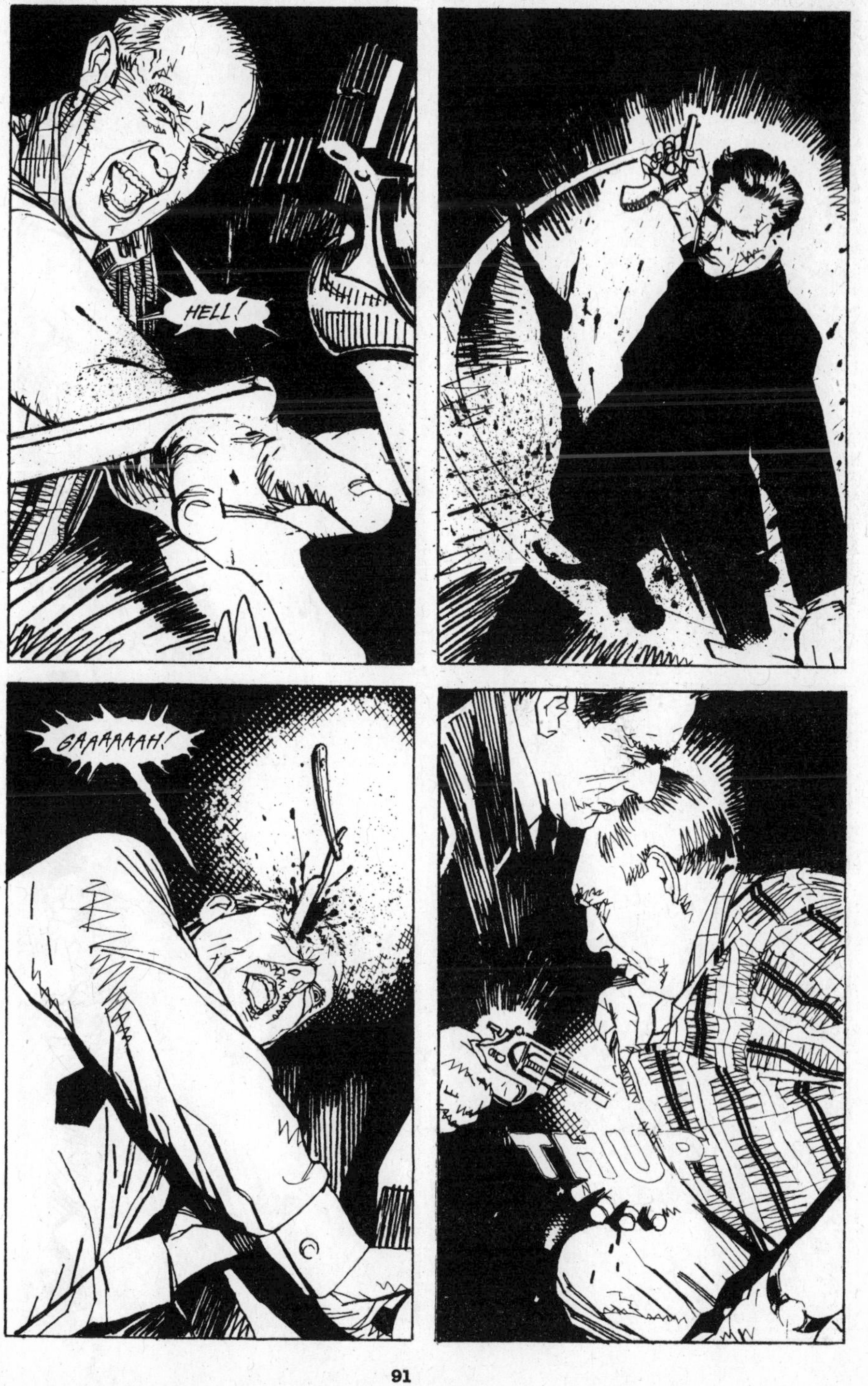
HELL!
GAAAAAAH!
THUP

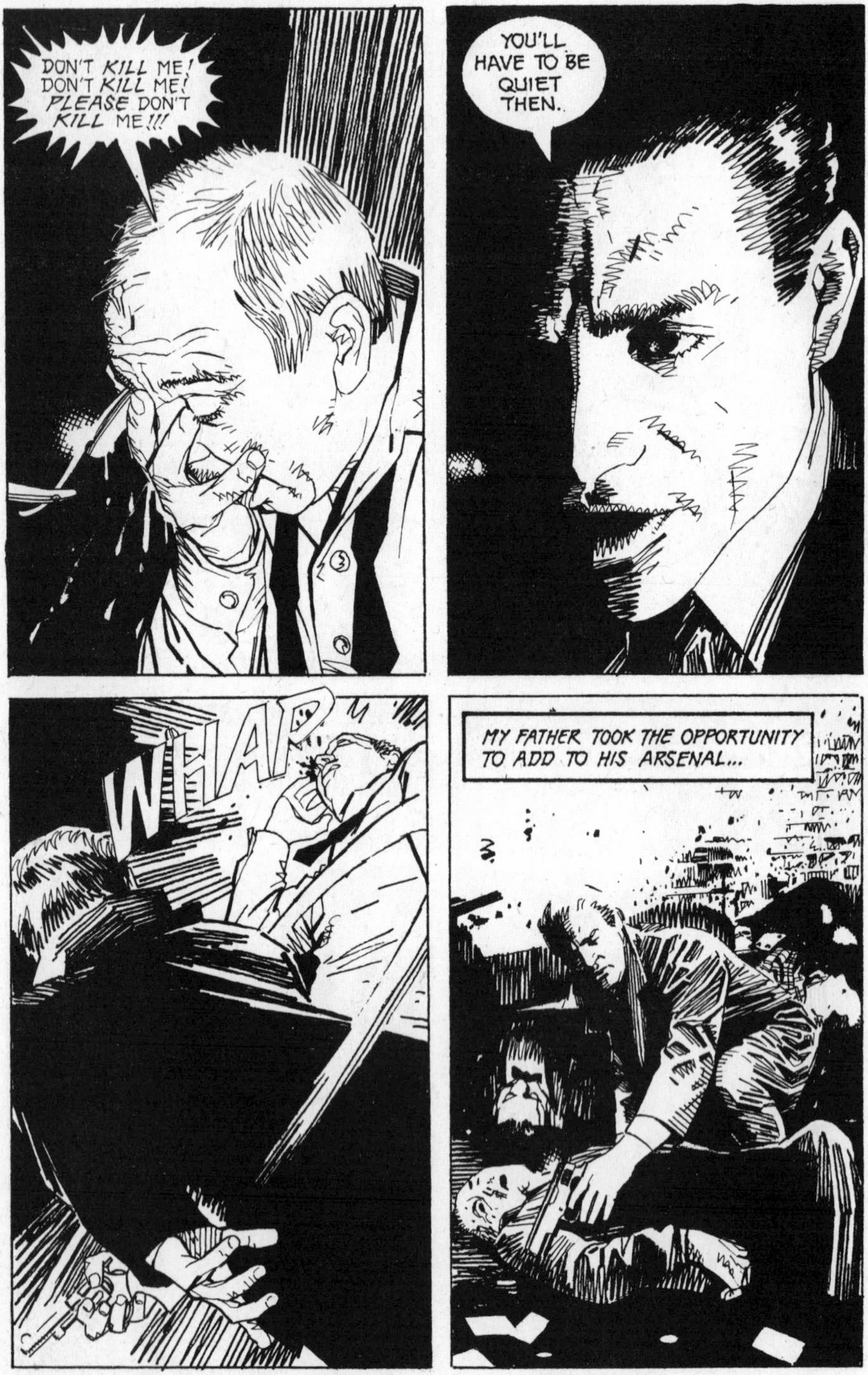
DON'T KILL ME! DON'T KILL ME! PLEASE DON'T KILL ME!!!
YOU'LL HAVE TO BE QUIET THEN.
WHAP
MY FATHER TOOK THE OPPORTUNITY TO ADD TO HIS ARSENAL...

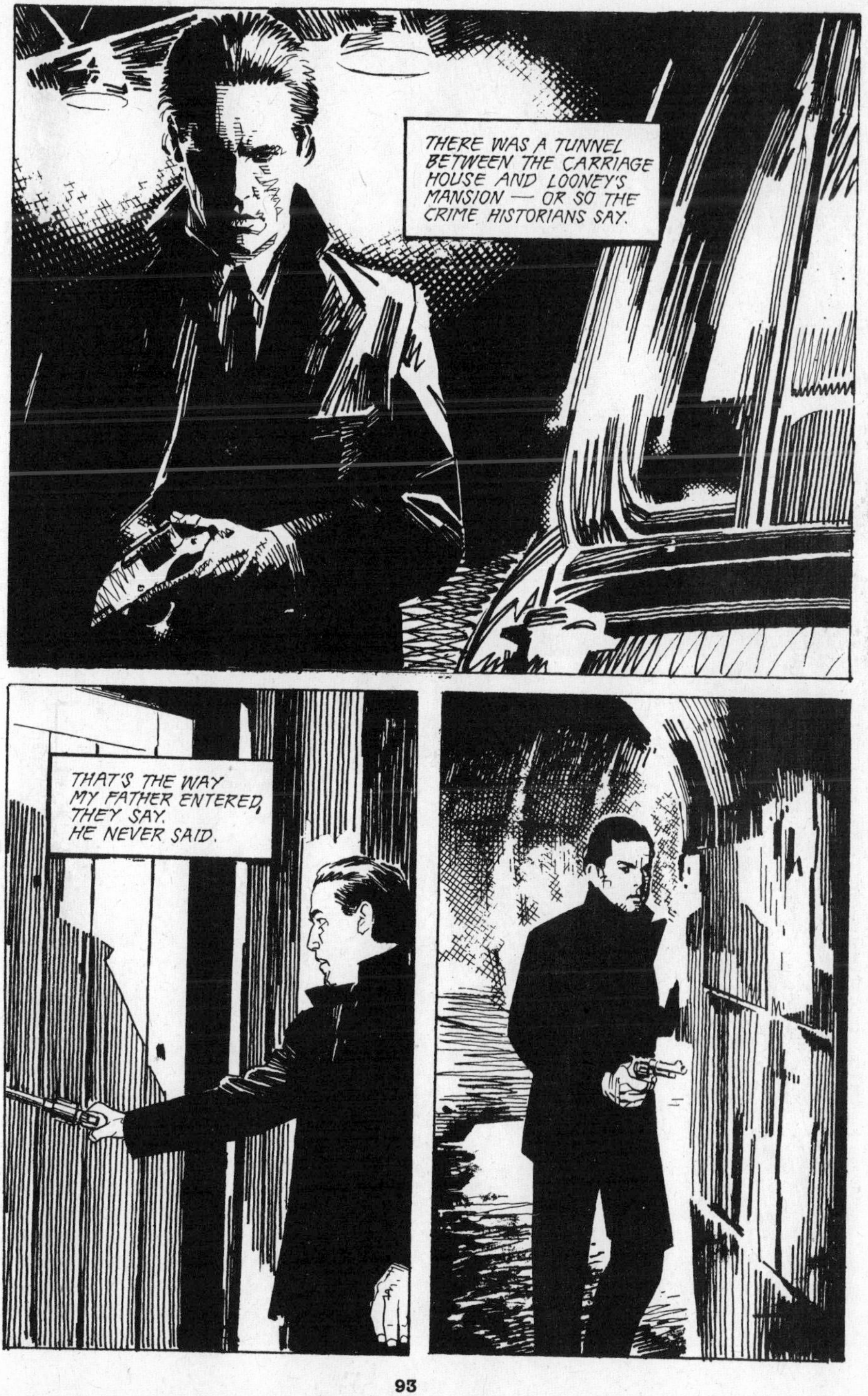
THERE WAS A TUNNEL BETWEEN THE CARRIAGE HOUSE AND LOONEY'S MANSION — OR SO THE CRIME HISTORIANS SAY.
THAT'S THE WAY MY FATHER ENTERED, THEY SAY. HE NEVER SAID.

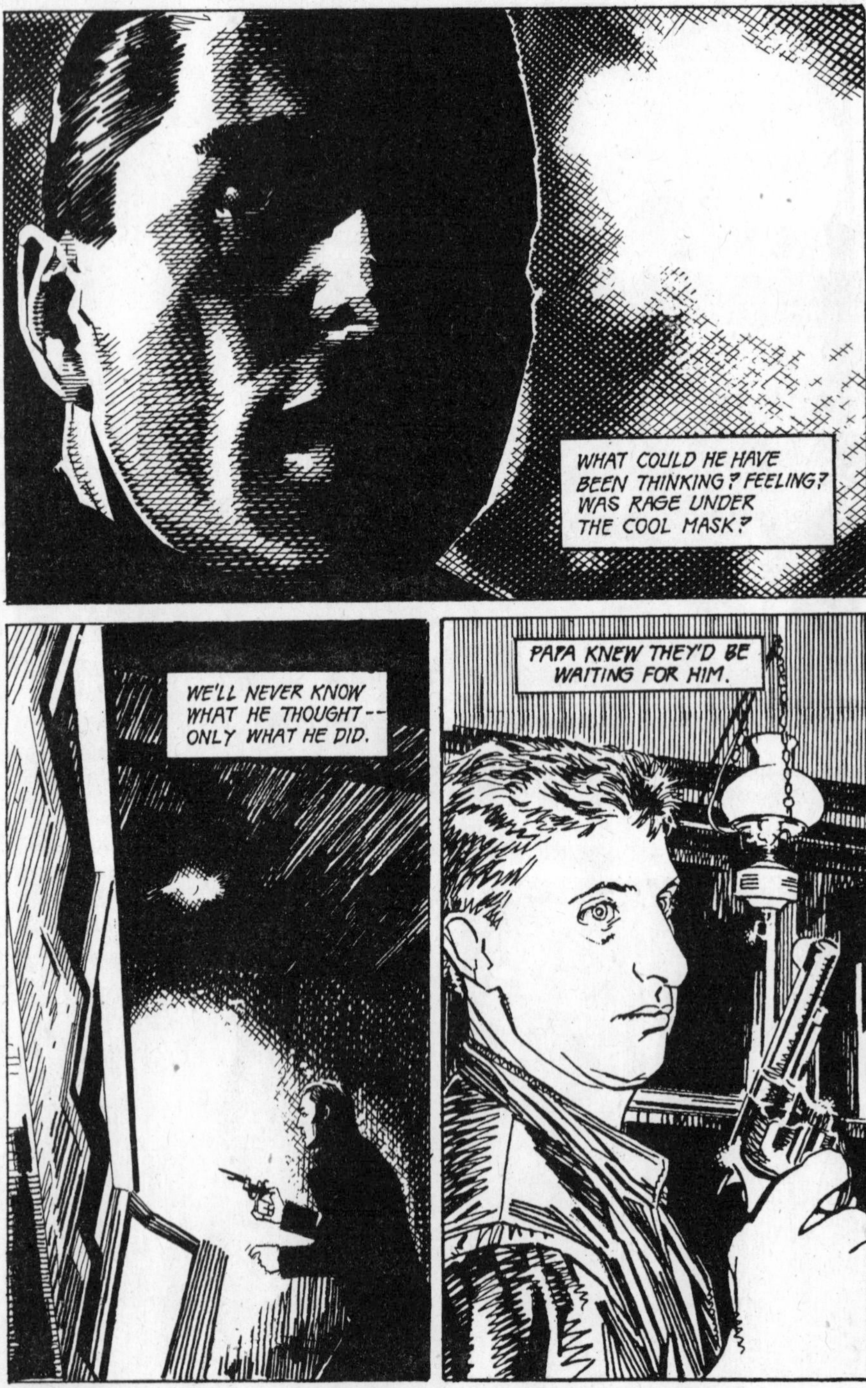
WHAT COULD HE HAVE BEEN THINKING? FEELING? WAS RAGE UNDER THE COOL MASK?
WE'LL NEVER KNOW WHAT HE THOUGHT-- ONLY WHAT HE DID.
PAPA KNEW THEY'D BE WAITING FOR HIM.

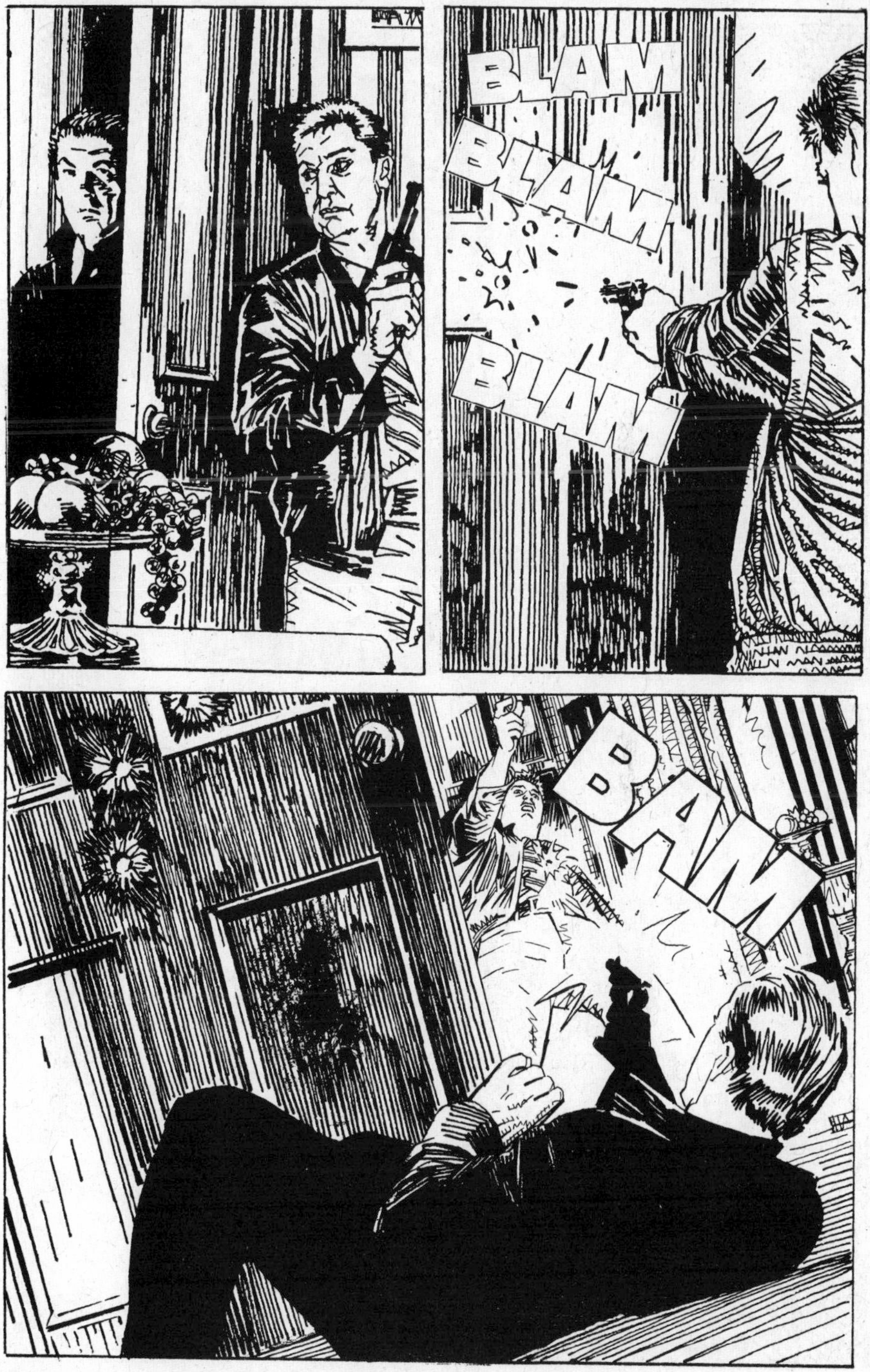
BLAM
BLAM
BLAM
BAM

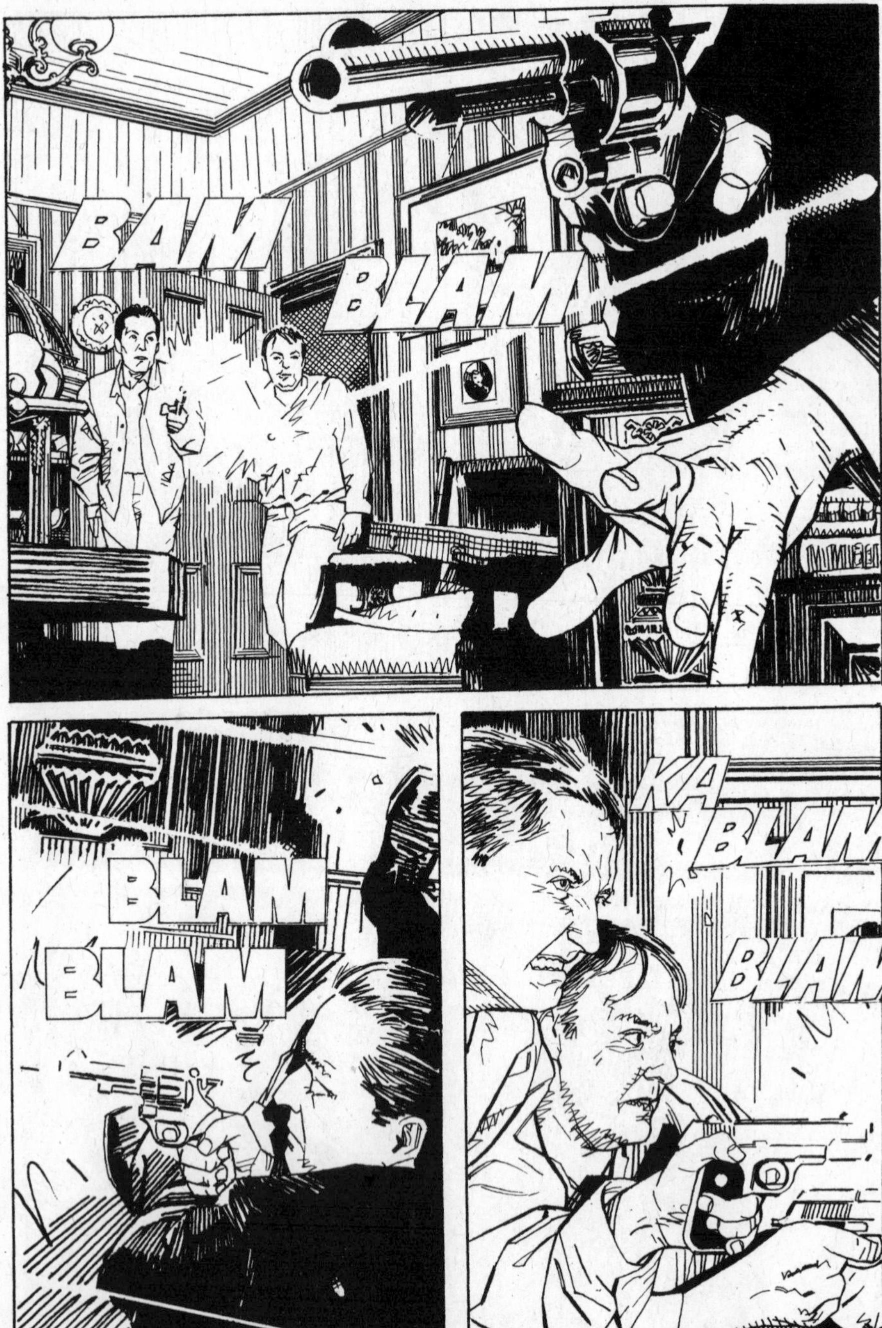
BAM
BLAM
BLAM
BLAM
KA BLAM
BLAM

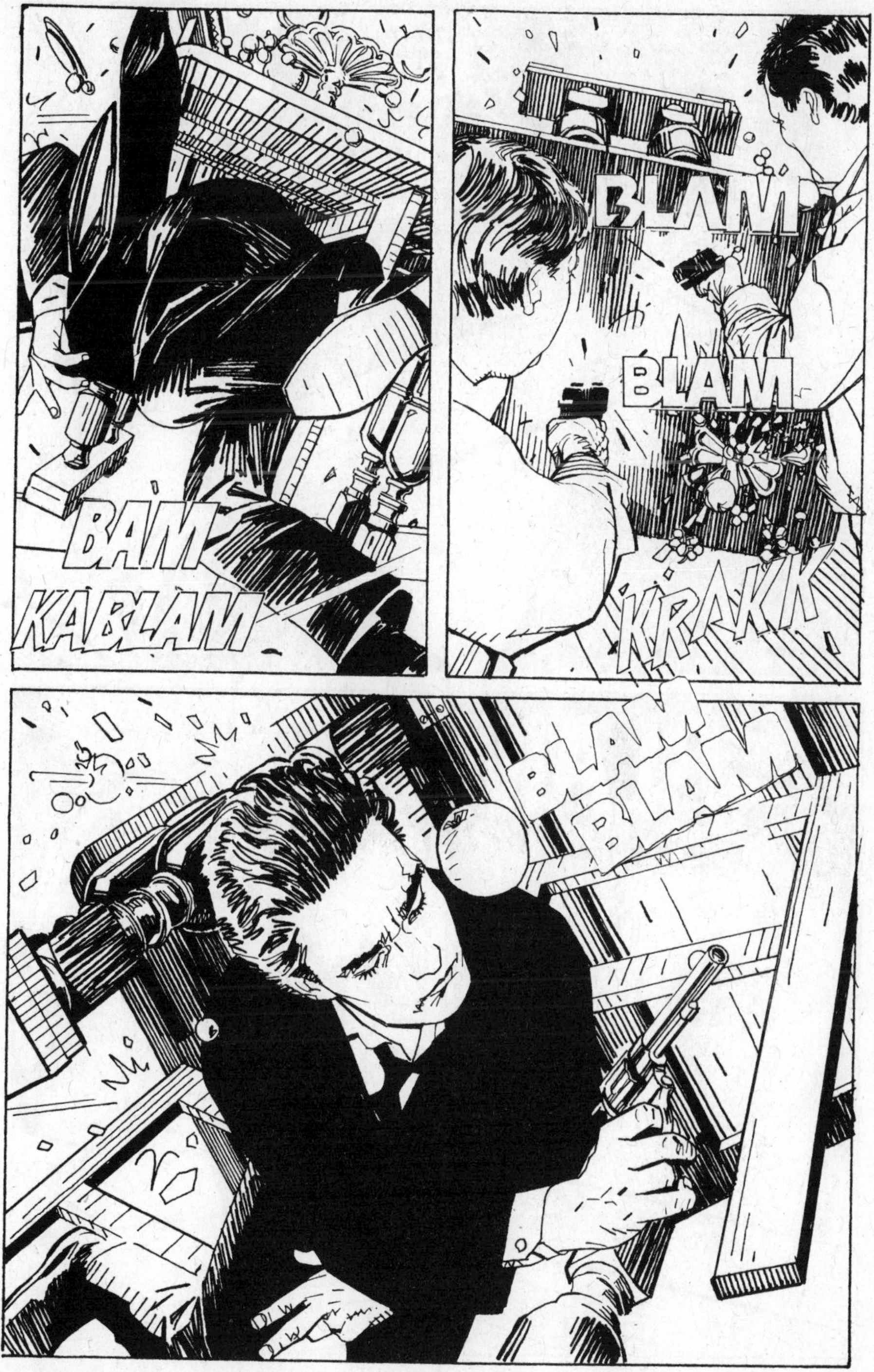
BAM
KABLAM
BLAM
BLAM
KRAKK
BLAM
BLAM

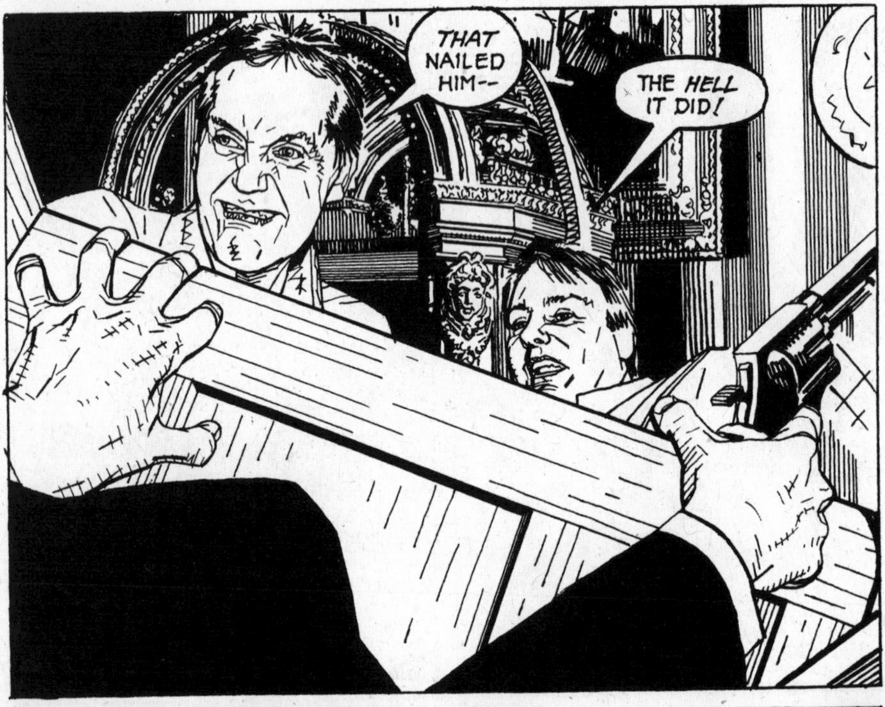
THAT NAILED HIM--
THE HELL IT DID!
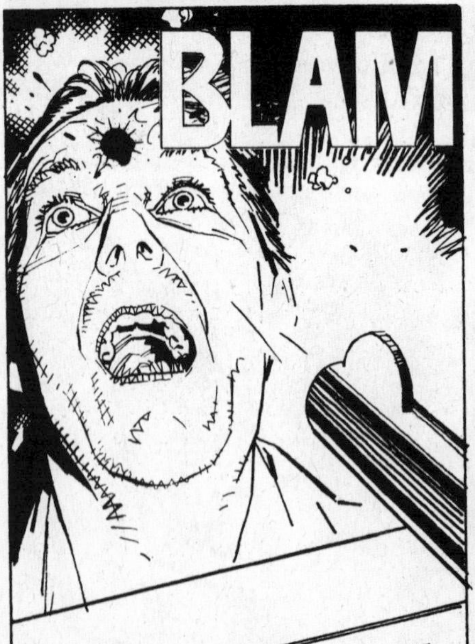
BLAM
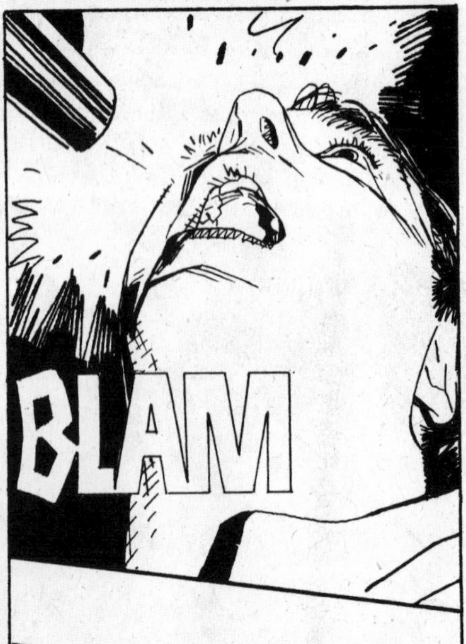
BLAM

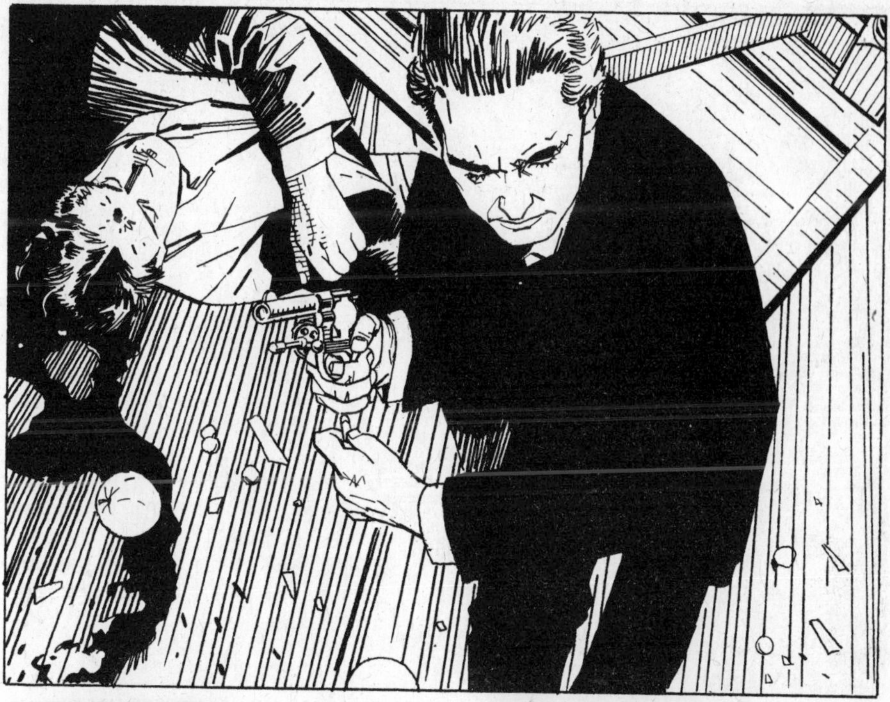

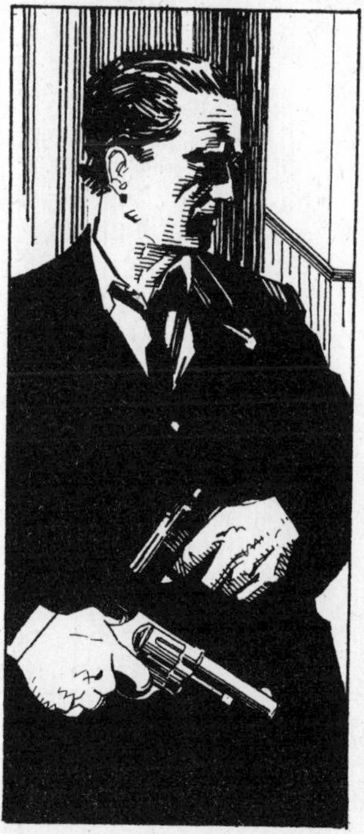

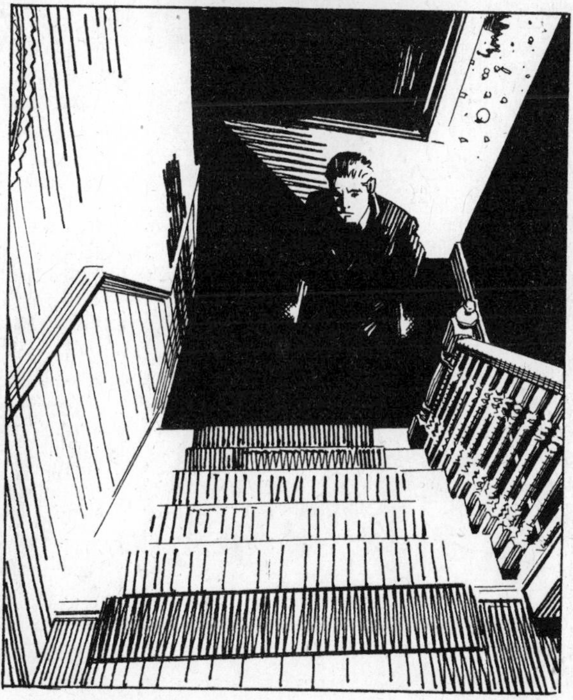

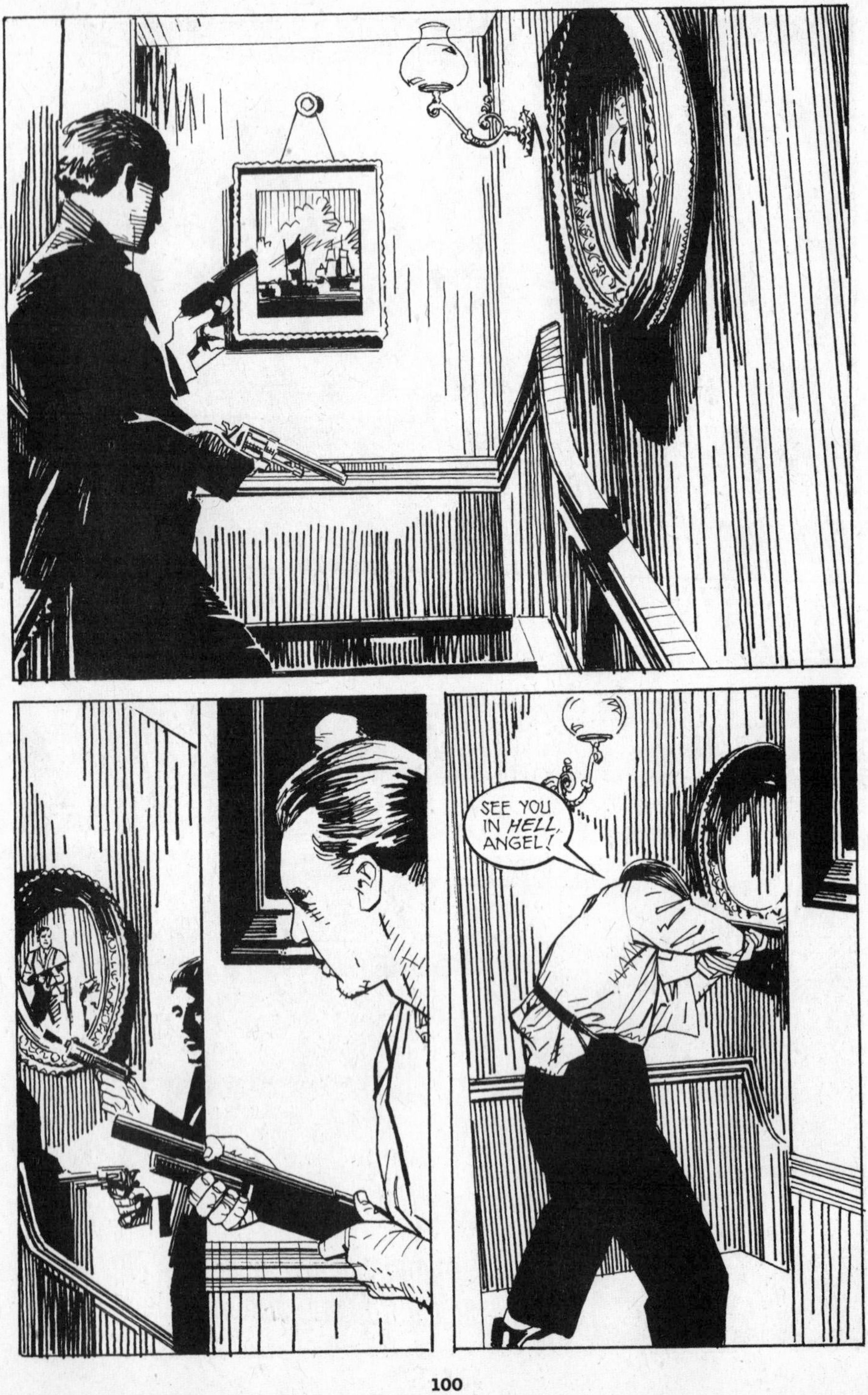
SEE YOU IN *HELL*, ANGEL!

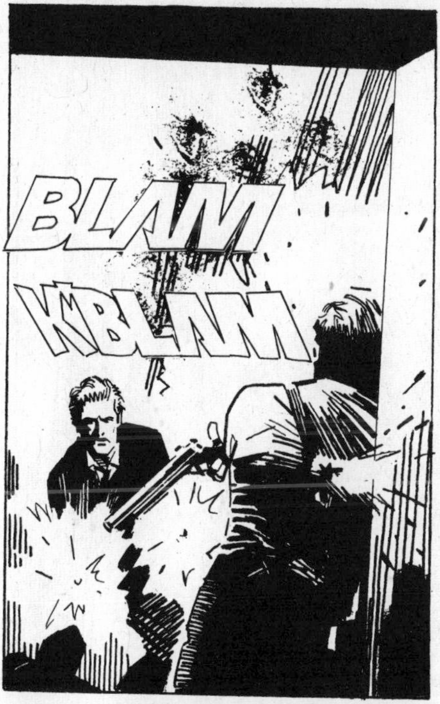
BLAM
KBLAM
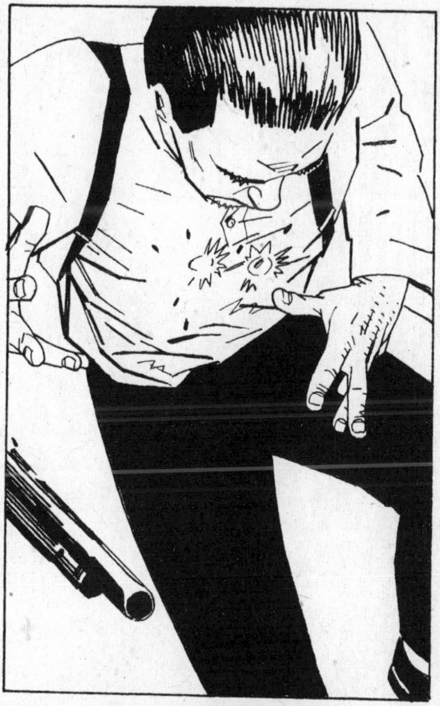
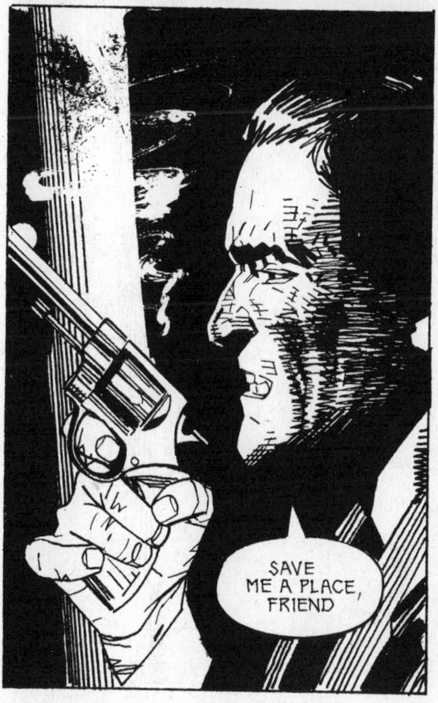
SAVE ME A PLACE, FRIEND
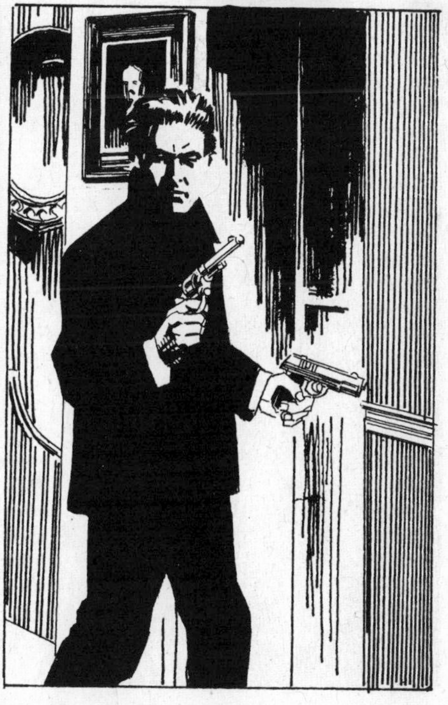

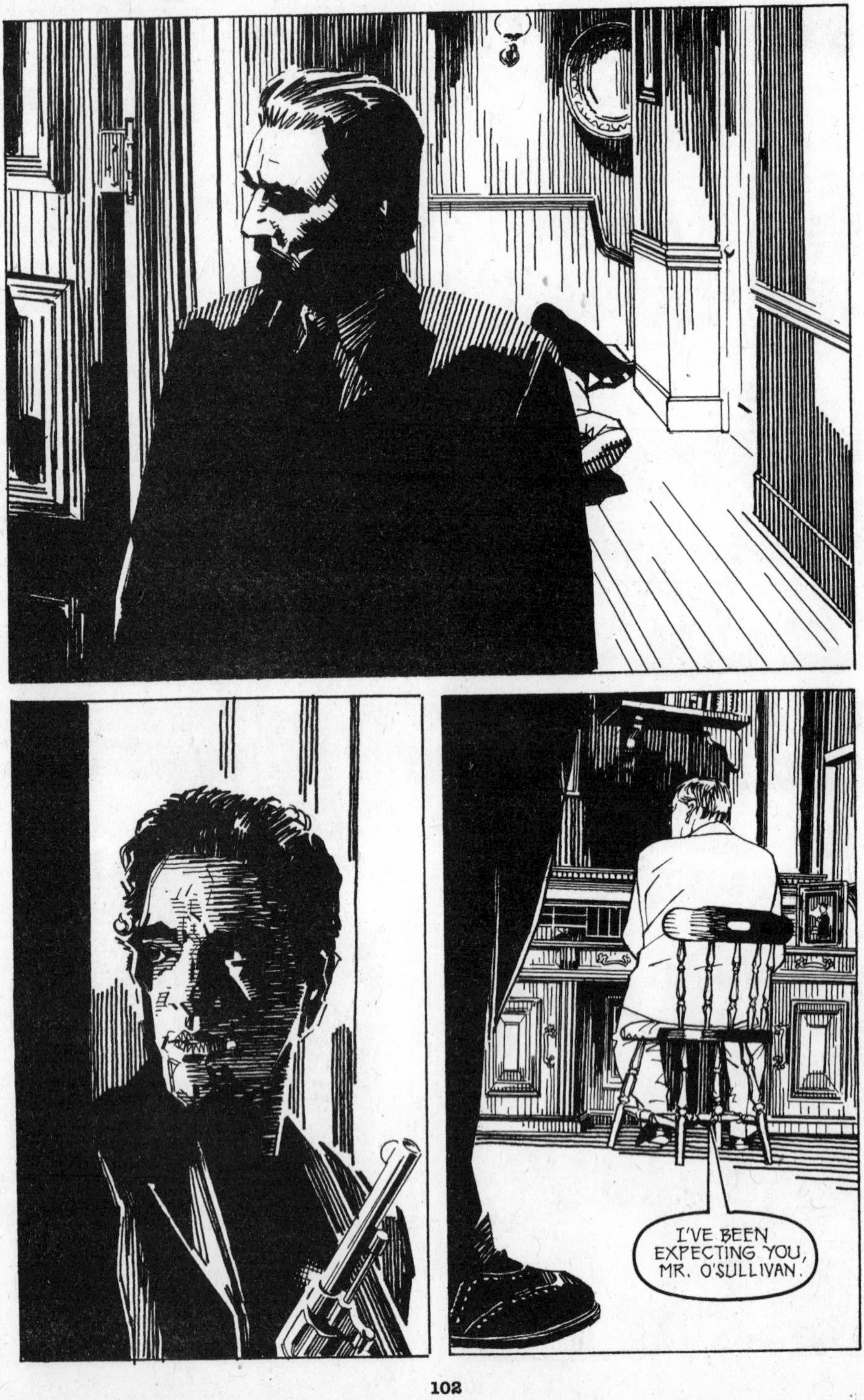
I'VE BEEN EXPECTING YOU, MR. O'SULLIVAN.

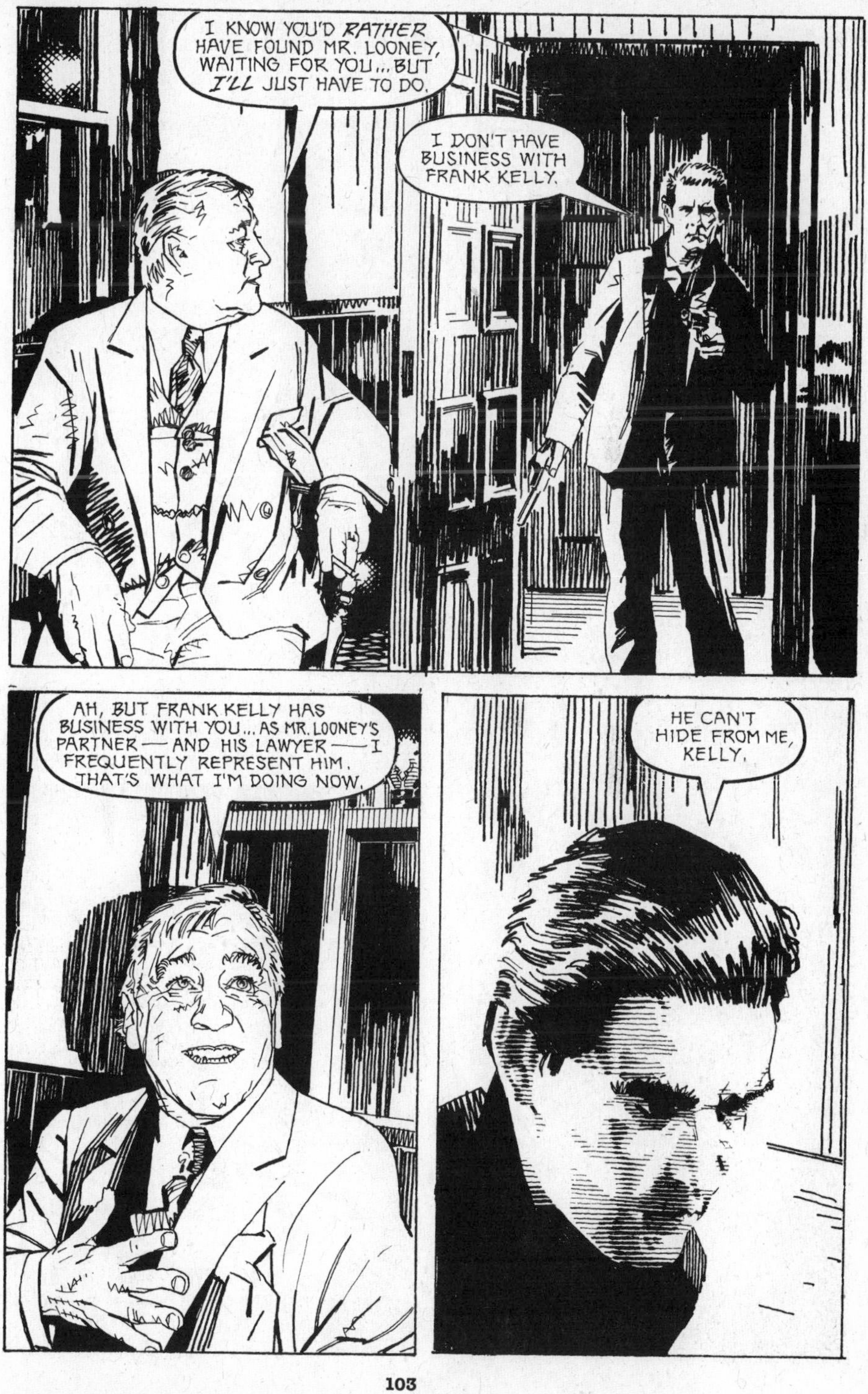
I KNOW YOU'D *RATHER* HAVE FOUND MR. LOONEY, WAITING FOR YOU... BUT *I'LL* JUST HAVE TO DO.
I DON'T HAVE BUSINESS WITH FRANK KELLY.
AH, BUT FRANK KELLY HAS BUSINESS WITH YOU... AS MR. LOONEY'S PARTNER — AND HIS LAWYER — I FREQUENTLY REPRESENT HIM. THAT'S WHAT I'M DOING NOW.
HE CAN'T HIDE FROM ME, KELLY.

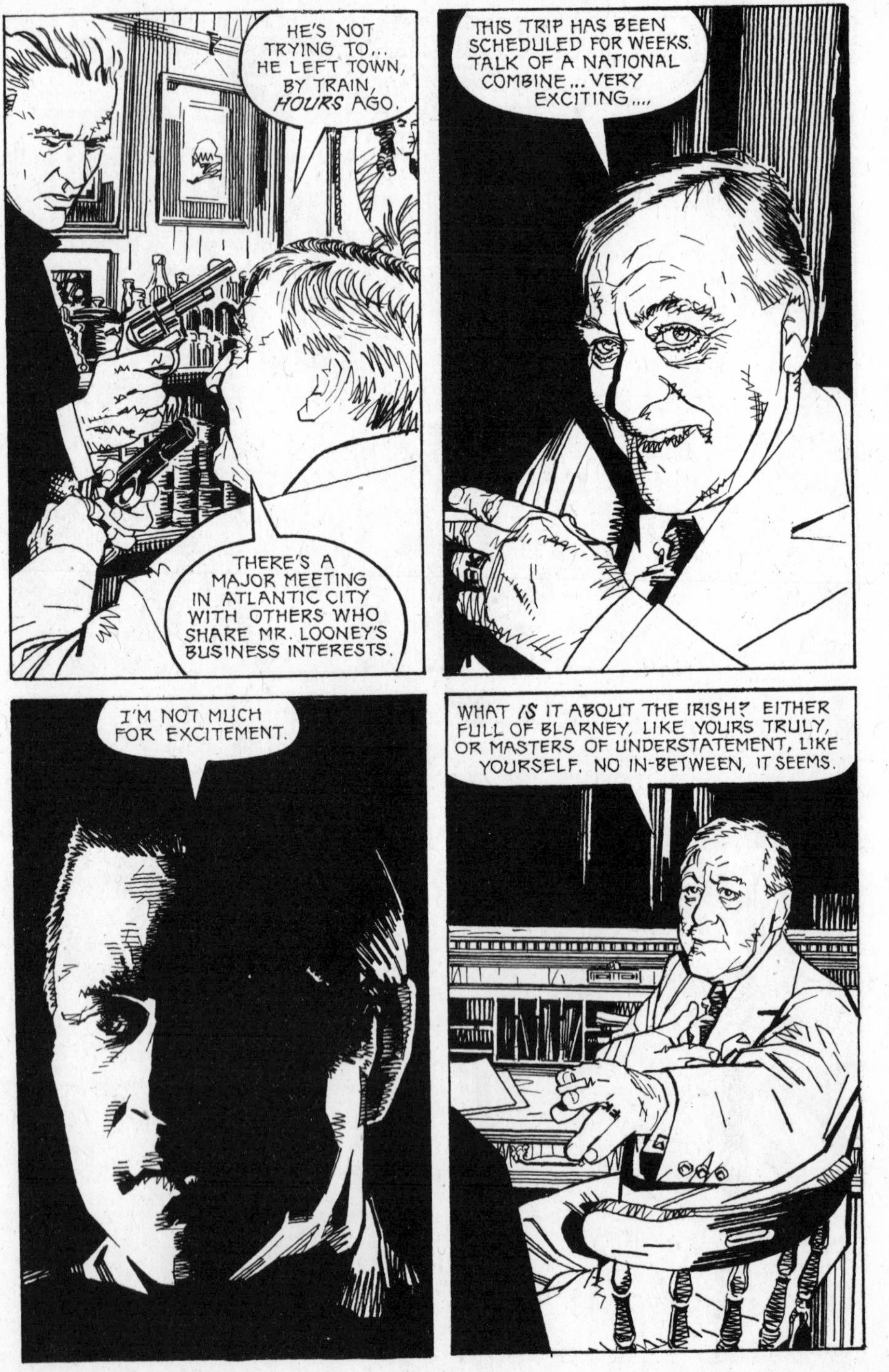
HE'S NOT TRYING TO... HE LEFT TOWN, BY TRAIN, *HOURS* AGO.
THERE'S A MAJOR MEETING IN ATLANTIC CITY WITH OTHERS WHO SHARE MR. LOONEY'S BUSINESS INTERESTS.
THIS TRIP HAS BEEN SCHEDULED FOR WEEKS. TALK OF A NATIONAL COMBINE... VERY EXCITING....
I'M NOT MUCH FOR EXCITEMENT.
WHAT *IS* IT ABOUT THE IRISH? EITHER FULL OF BLARNEY, LIKE YOURS TRULY, OR MASTERS OF UNDERSTATEMENT, LIKE YOURSELF. NO IN-BETWEEN, IT SEEMS.

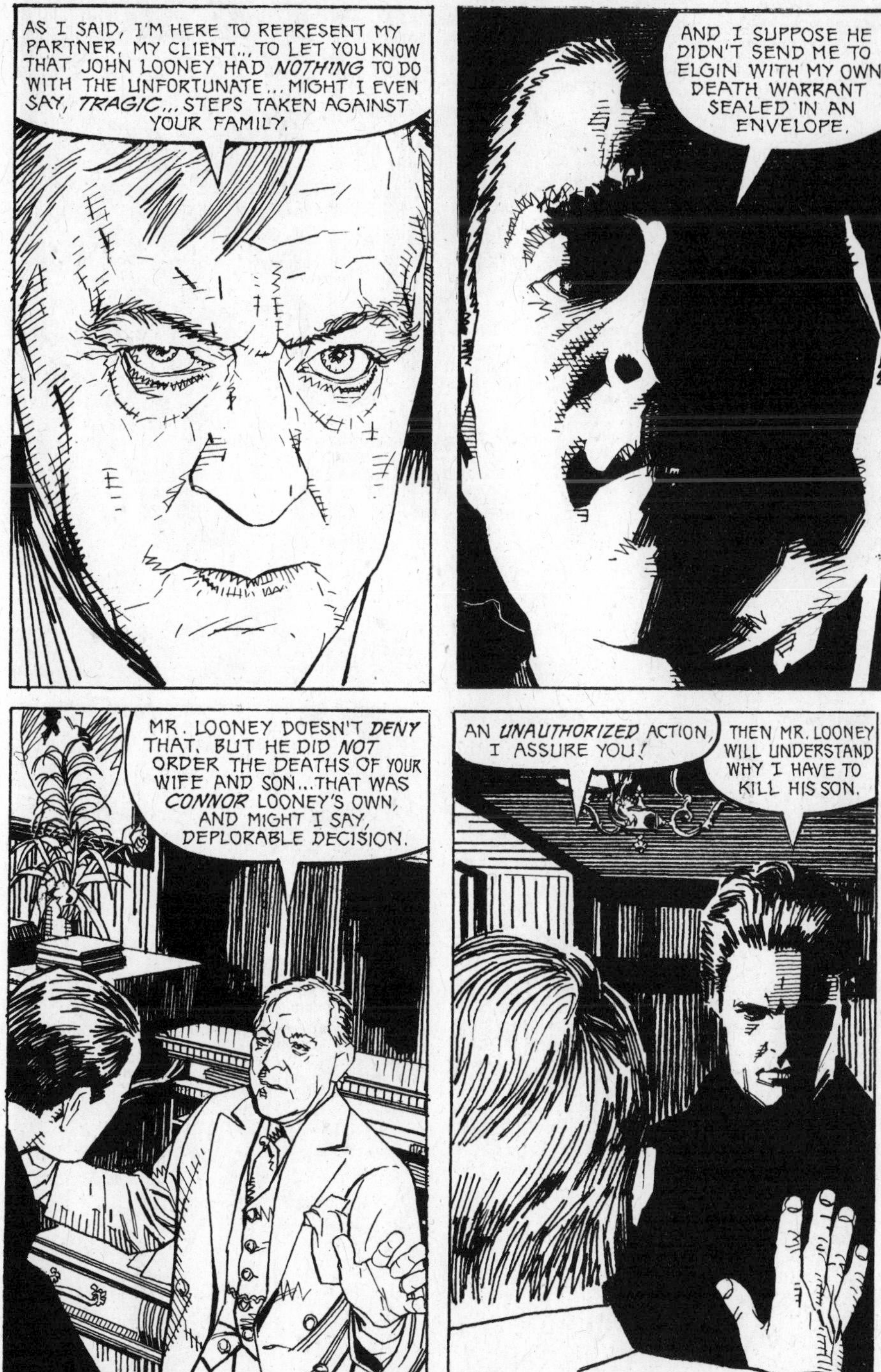
AS I SAID, I'M HERE TO REPRESENT MY PARTNER, MY CLIENT..., TO LET YOU KNOW THAT JOHN LOONEY HAD *NOTHING* TO DO WITH THE UNFORTUNATE... MIGHT I EVEN SAY, *TRAGIC*... STEPS TAKEN AGAINST YOUR FAMILY.
AND I SUPPOSE HE DIDN'T SEND ME TO ELGIN WITH MY OWN DEATH WARRANT SEALED IN AN ENVELOPE.
MR. LOONEY DOESN'T *DENY* THAT. BUT HE DID *NOT* ORDER THE DEATHS OF YOUR WIFE AND SON... THAT WAS *CONNOR* LOONEY'S OWN, AND MIGHT I SAY, DEPLORABLE DECISION.
AN *UNAUTHORIZED* ACTION, I ASSURE YOU!
THEN MR. LOONEY WILL UNDERSTAND WHY I HAVE TO KILL HIS SON.

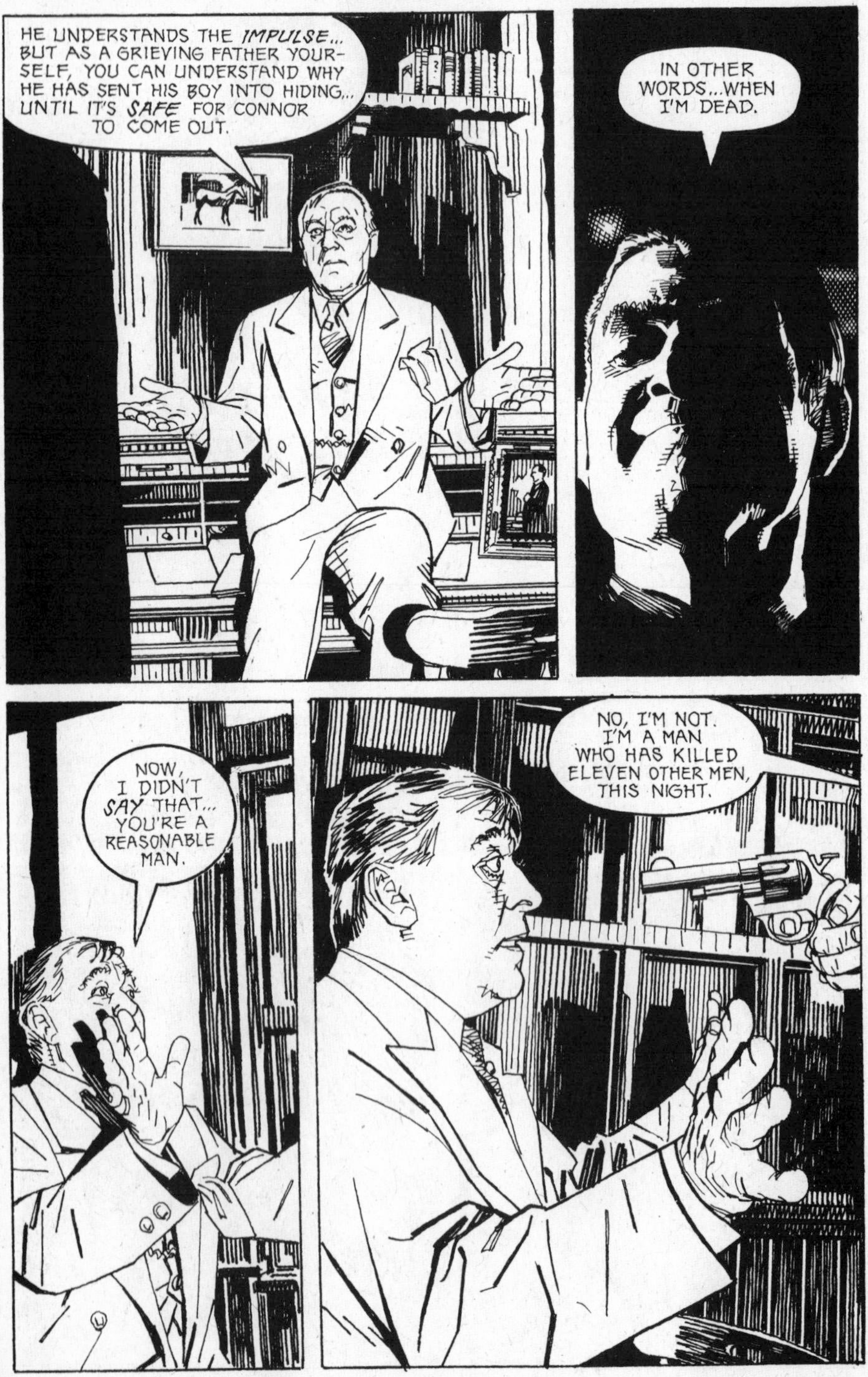
HE UNDERSTANDS THE *IMPULSE*... BUT AS A GRIEVING FATHER YOURSELF, YOU CAN UNDERSTAND WHY HE HAS SENT HIS BOY INTO HIDING... UNTIL IT'S *SAFE* FOR CONNOR TO COME OUT.
IN OTHER WORDS...WHEN I'M DEAD.
NOW, I DIDN'T *SAY* THAT... YOU'RE A REASONABLE MAN.
NO, I'M NOT. I'M A MAN WHO HAS KILLED ELEVEN OTHER MEN, THIS NIGHT.

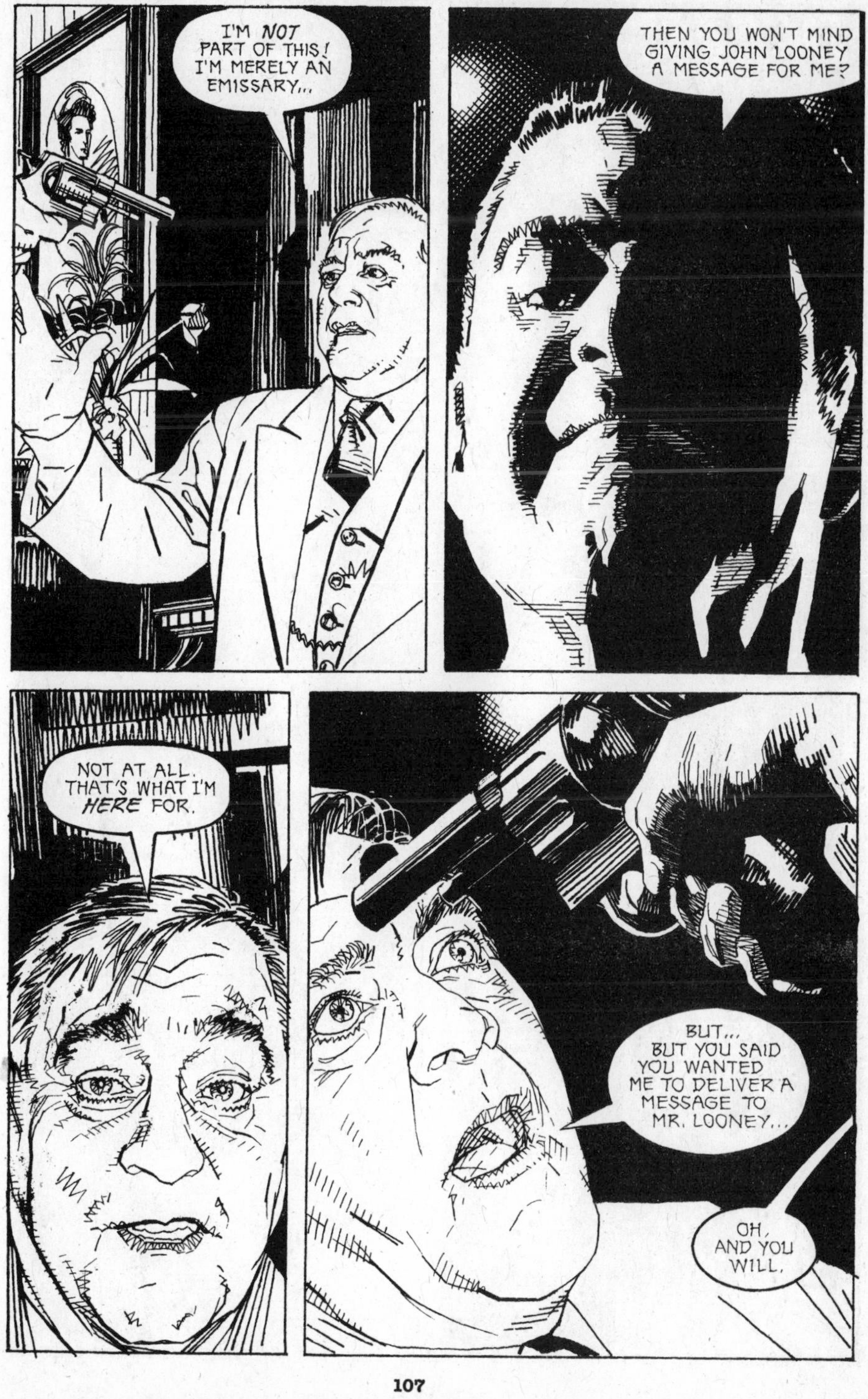
I'M NOT PART OF THIS! I'M MERELY AN EMISSARY...
THEN YOU WON'T MIND GIVING JOHN LOONEY A MESSAGE FOR ME?
NOT AT ALL. THAT'S WHAT I'M HERE FOR.
BUT... BUT YOU SAID YOU WANTED ME TO DELIVER A MESSAGE TO MR. LOONEY...
OH, AND YOU WILL.

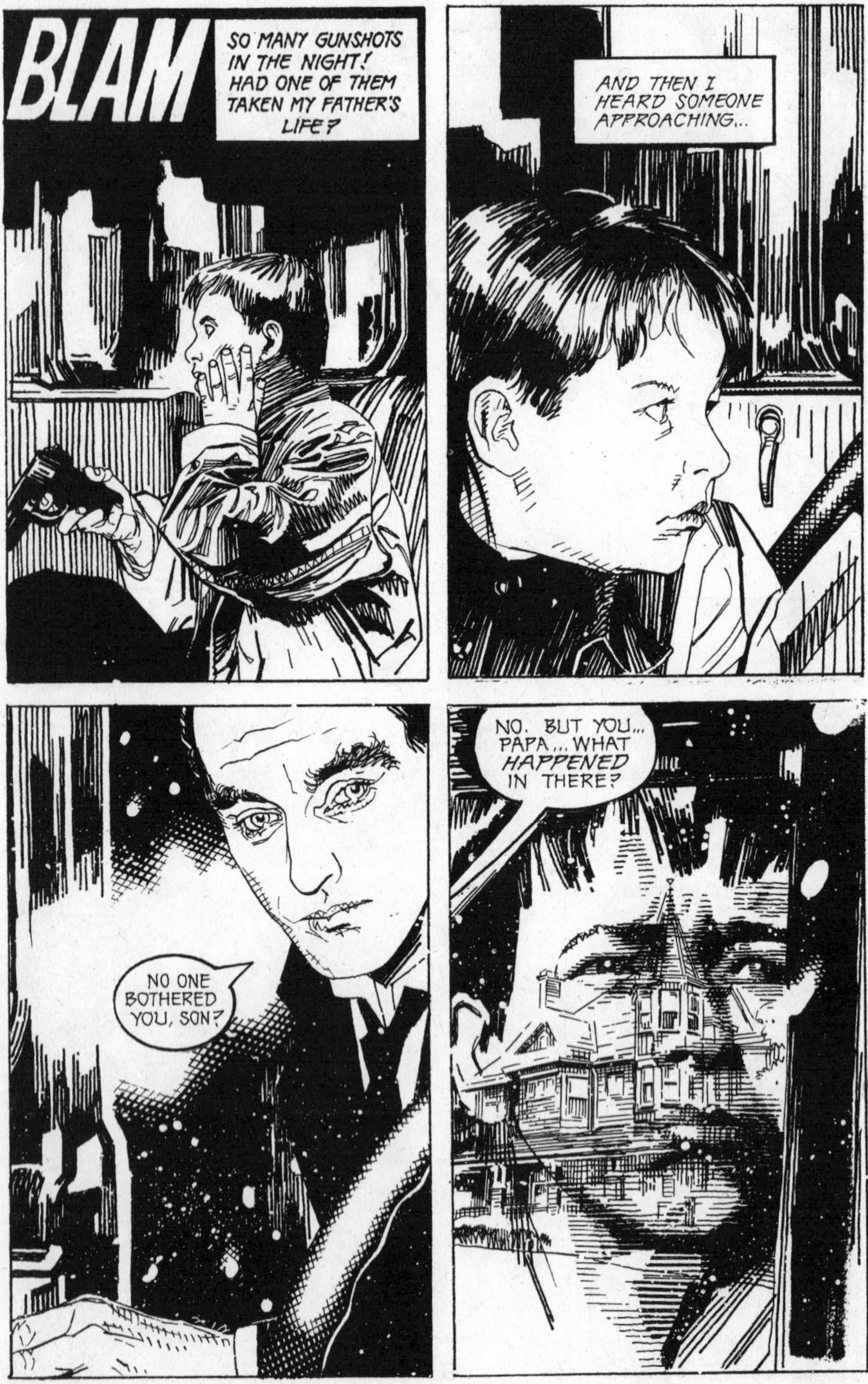
BLAM
SO MANY GUNSHOTS IN THE NIGHT! HAD ONE OF THEM TAKEN MY FATHER'S LIFE?
AND THEN I HEARD SOMEONE APPROACHING...
NO ONE BOTHERED YOU, SON?
NO. BUT YOU... PAPA... WHAT *HAPPENED* IN THERE?

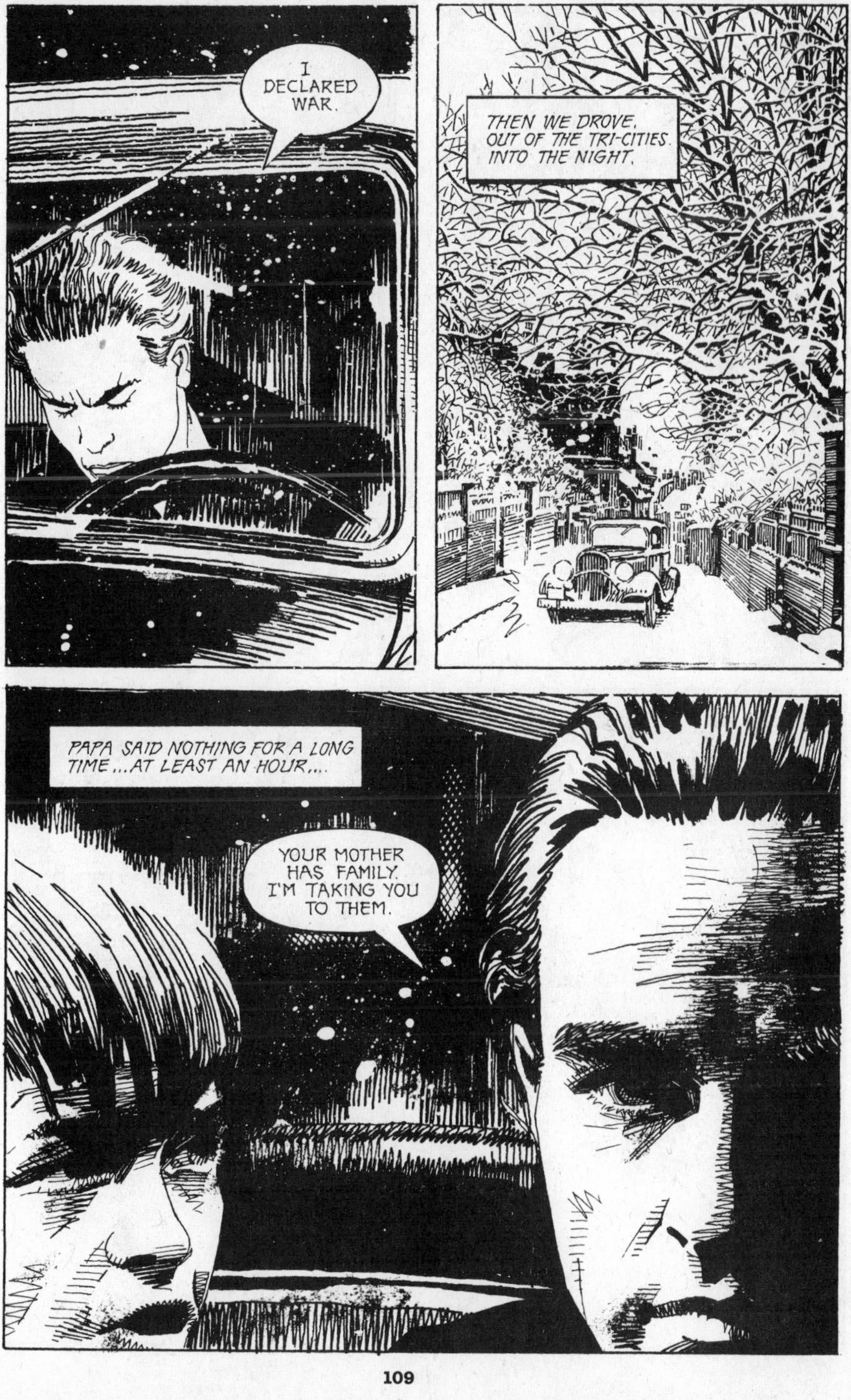
I DECLARED WAR.
THEN WE DROVE, OUT OF THE TRI-CITIES. INTO THE NIGHT.
PAPA SAID NOTHING FOR A LONG TIME... AT LEAST AN HOUR...
YOUR MOTHER HAS FAMILY. I'M TAKING YOU TO THEM.

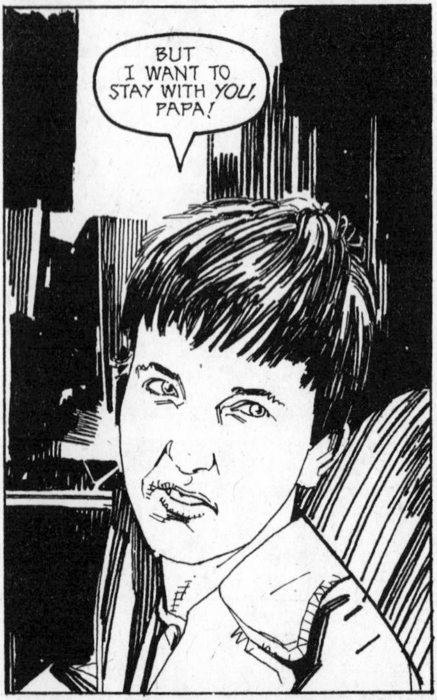
BUT I WANT TO STAY WITH *YOU*, PAPA!

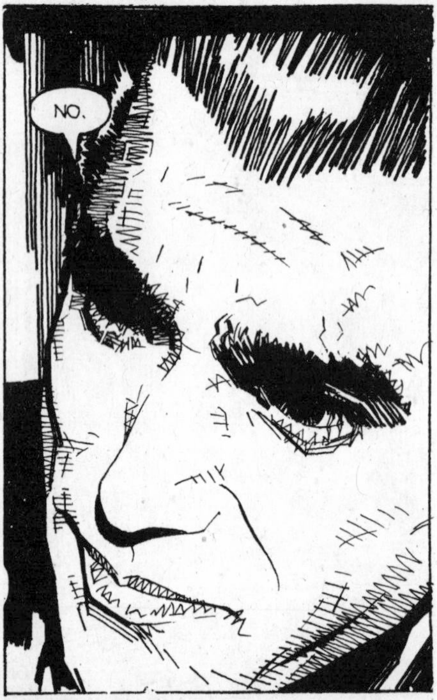
NO.

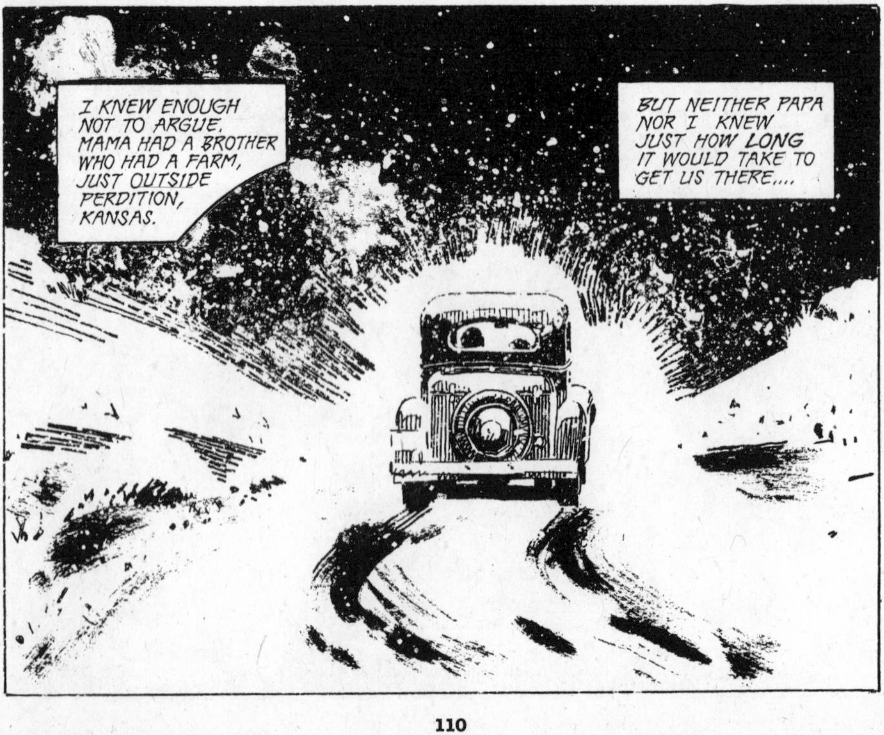
I KNEW ENOUGH NOT TO ARGUE. MAMA HAD A BROTHER WHO HAD A FARM, JUST OUTSIDE PERDITION, KANSAS.
BUT NEITHER PAPA NOR I KNEW JUST HOW **LONG** IT WOULD TAKE TO GET US THERE....

CHAPTER TWO:

VILLAGE OF THE DEAD

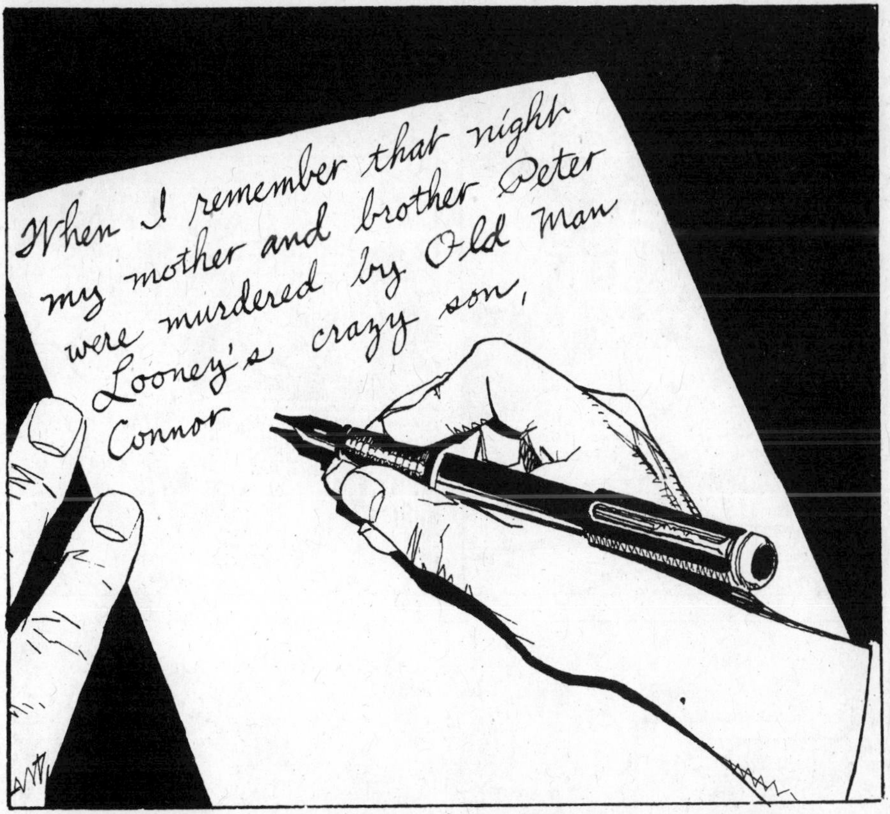
When I remember that night
my mother and brother Peter
were murdered by Old Man
Looney's crazy son,
Connor

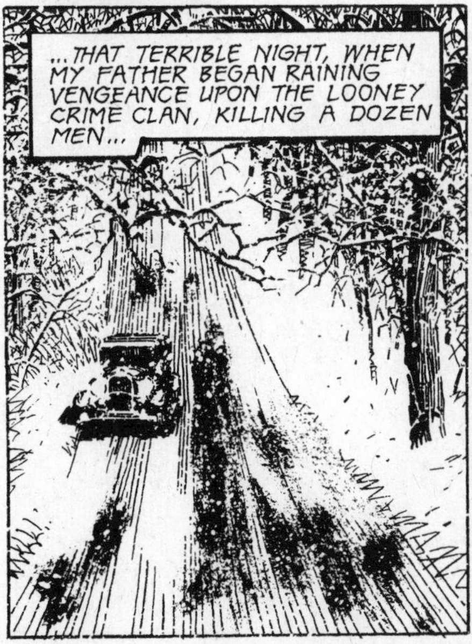
...THAT TERRIBLE NIGHT, WHEN MY FATHER BEGAN RAINING VENGEANCE UPON THE LOONEY CRIME CLAN, KILLING A DOZEN MEN...

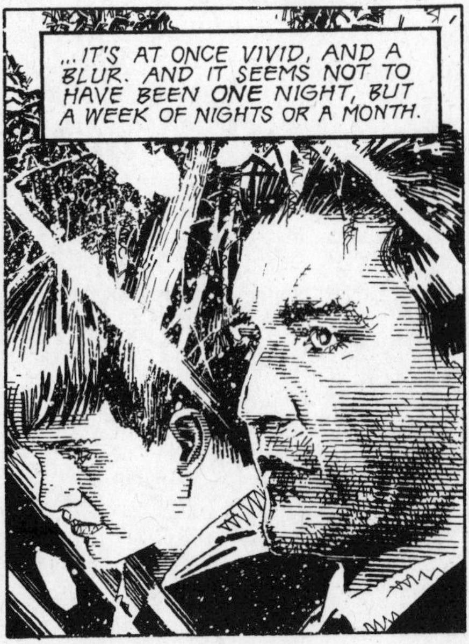
...IT'S AT ONCE VIVID, AND A BLUR. AND IT SEEMS NOT TO HAVE BEEN ONE NIGHT, BUT A WEEK OF NIGHTS OR A MONTH.

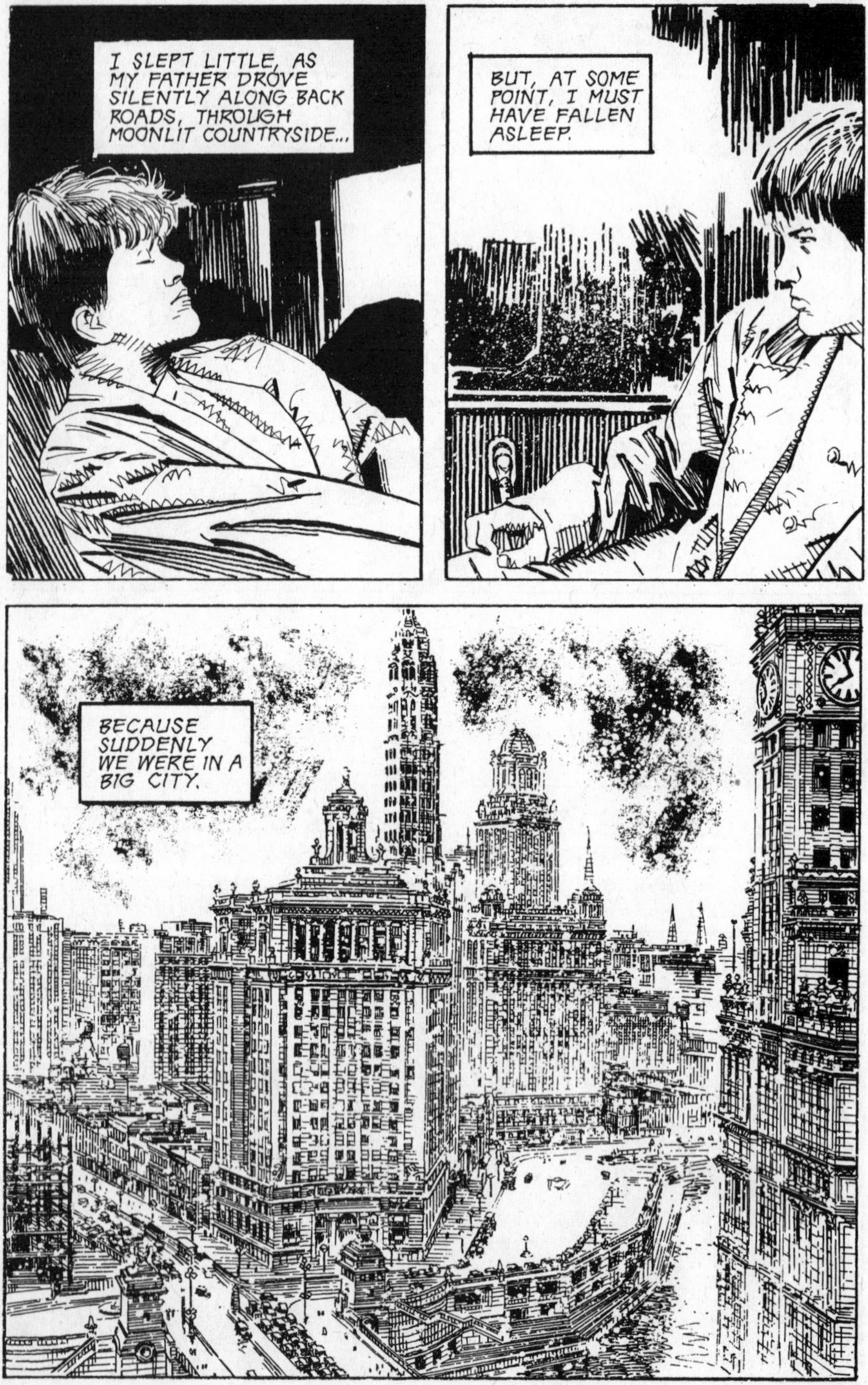
I SLEPT LITTLE, AS MY FATHER DROVE SILENTLY ALONG BACK ROADS, THROUGH MOONLIT COUNTRYSIDE...
BUT, AT SOME POINT, I MUST HAVE FALLEN ASLEEP.
BECAUSE SUDDENLY WE WERE IN A BIG CITY.

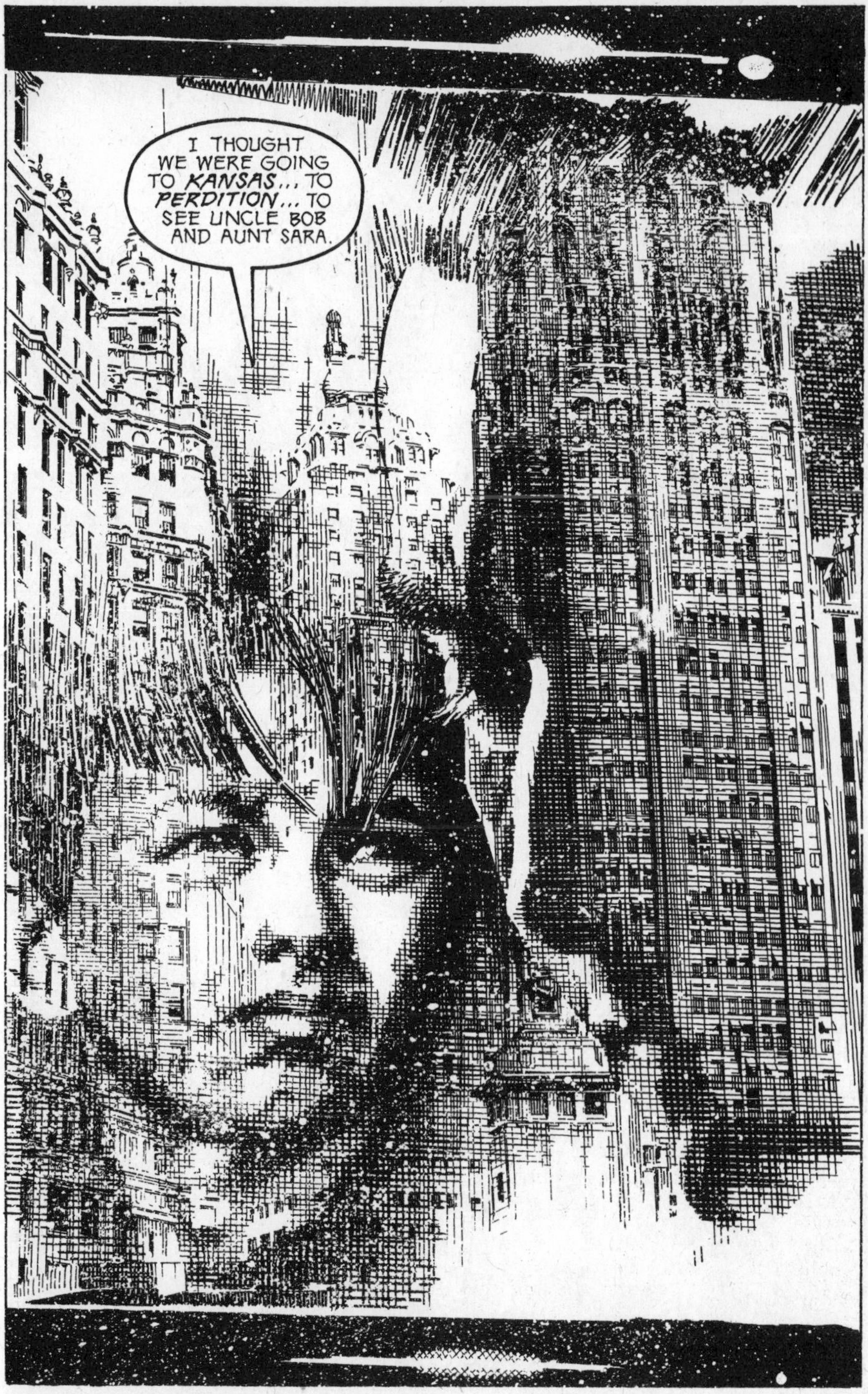
I THOUGHT WE WERE GOING TO *KANSAS*... TO *PERDITION*... TO SEE UNCLE BOB AND AUNT SARA.

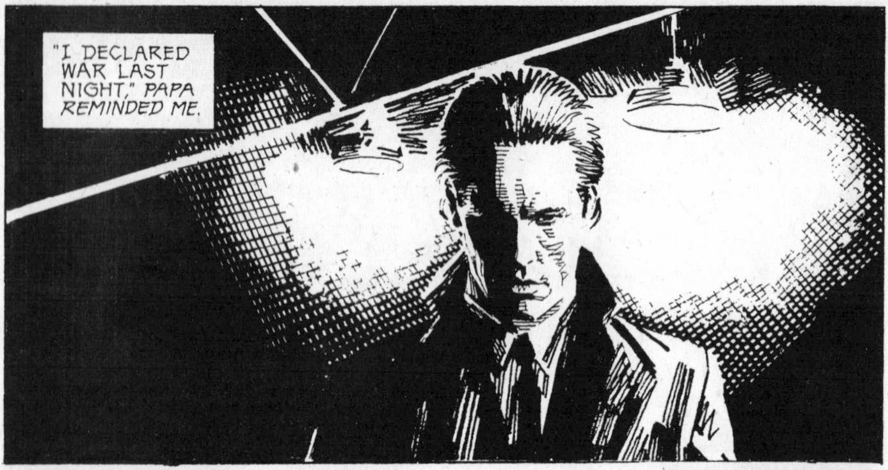
"I DECLARED WAR LAST NIGHT," PAPA REMINDED ME.

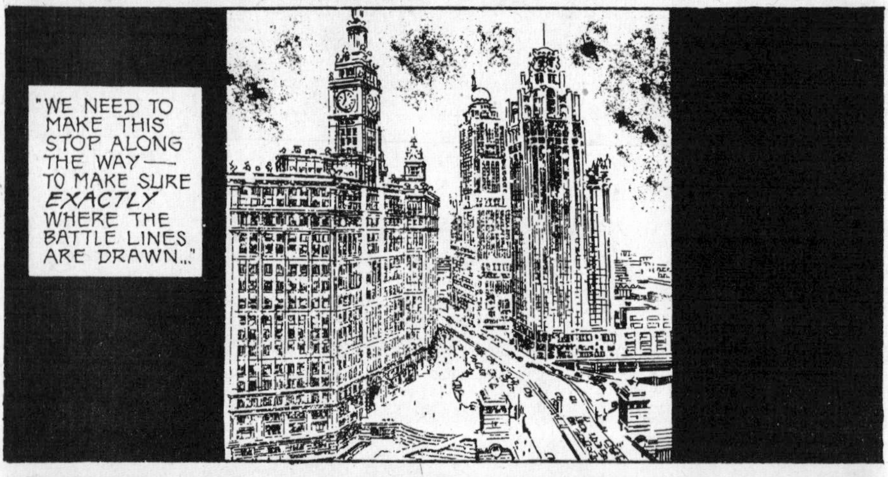
"WE NEED TO MAKE THIS STOP ALONG THE WAY— TO MAKE SURE *EXACTLY* WHERE THE BATTLE LINES ARE DRAWN..."

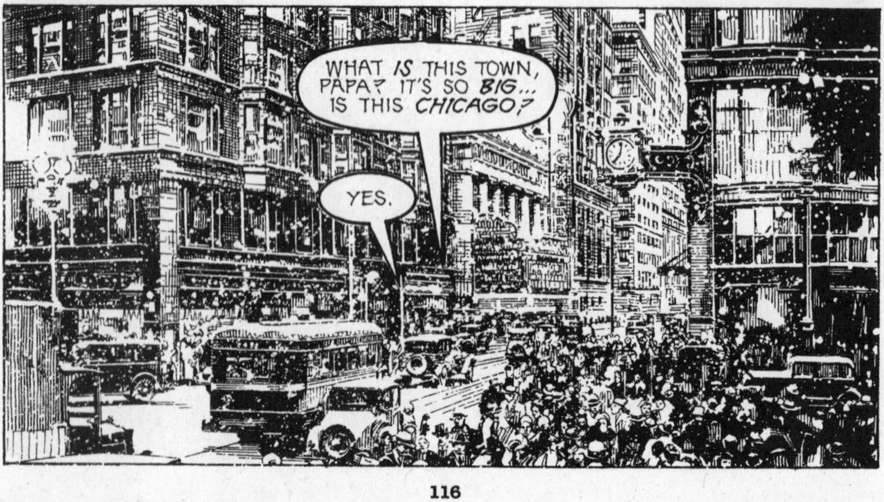
WHAT *IS* THIS TOWN, PAPA? IT'S SO *BIG*... IS THIS *CHICAGO*?
YES.

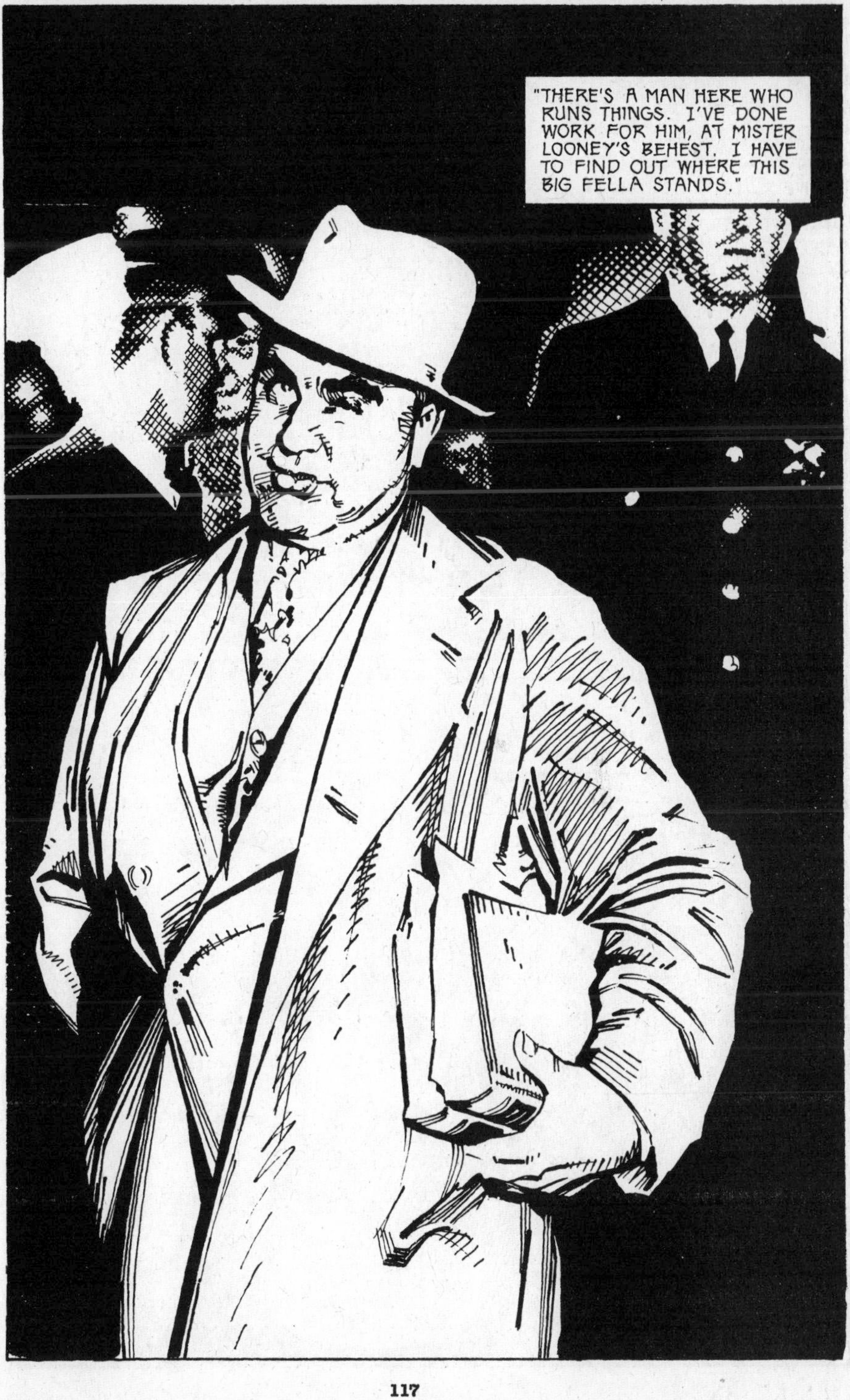
"THERE'S A MAN HERE WHO RUNS THINGS. I'VE DONE WORK FOR HIM, AT MISTER LOONEY'S BEHEST. I HAVE TO FIND OUT WHERE THIS BIG FELLA STANDS."

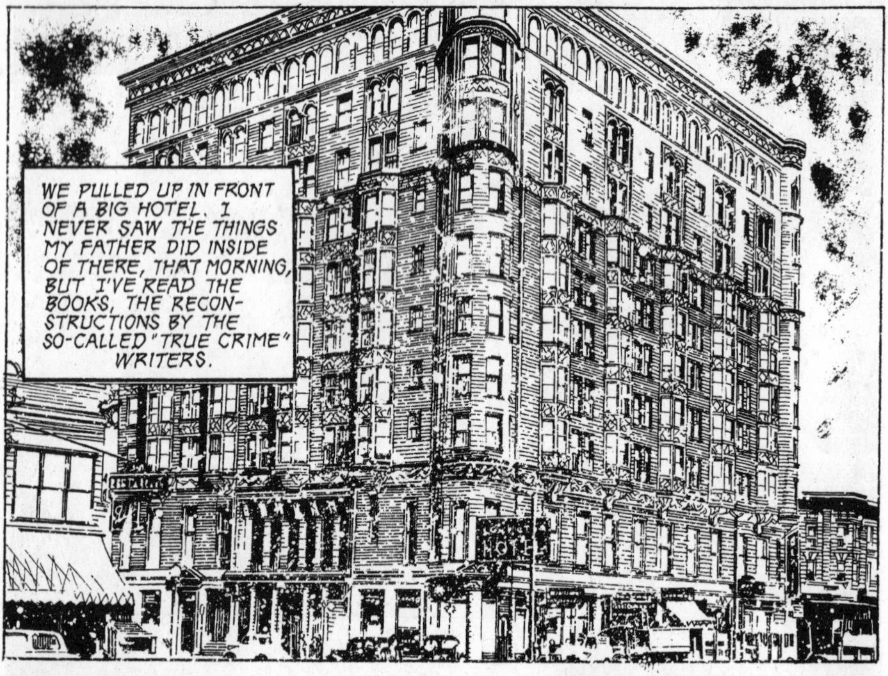
WE PULLED UP IN FRONT OF A BIG HOTEL. I NEVER SAW THE THINGS MY FATHER DID INSIDE OF THERE, THAT MORNING, BUT I'VE READ THE BOOKS, THE RECON-STRUCTIONS BY THE SO-CALLED "TRUE CRIME" WRITERS.

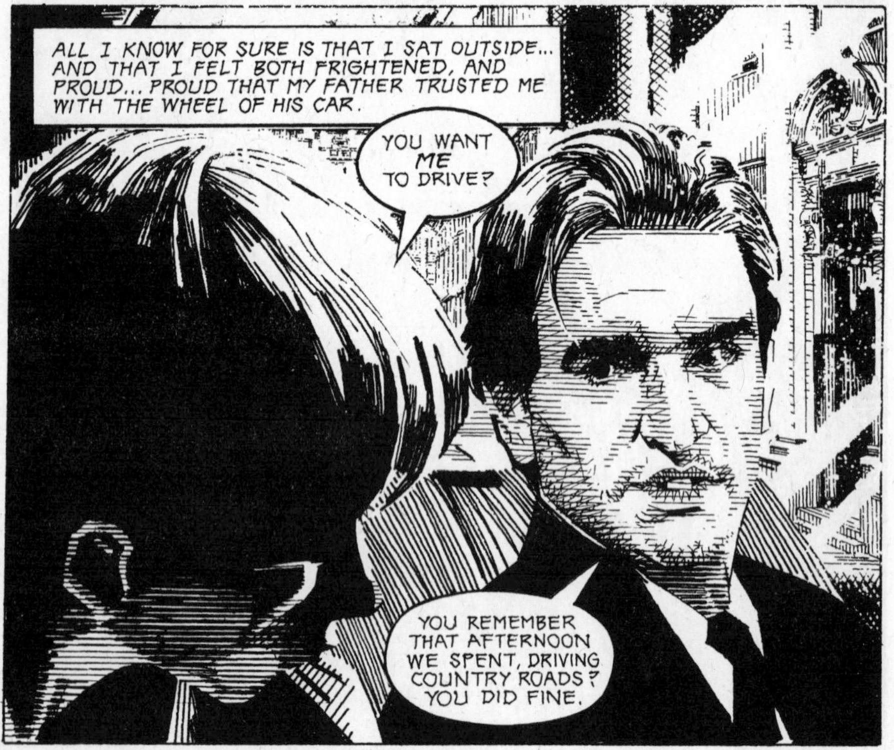
ALL I KNOW FOR SURE IS THAT I SAT OUTSIDE... AND THAT I FELT BOTH FRIGHTENED, AND PROUD... PROUD THAT MY FATHER TRUSTED ME WITH THE WHEEL OF HIS CAR.
YOU WANT *ME* TO DRIVE?
YOU REMEMBER THAT AFTERNOON WE SPENT, DRIVING COUNTRY ROADS? YOU DID FINE.

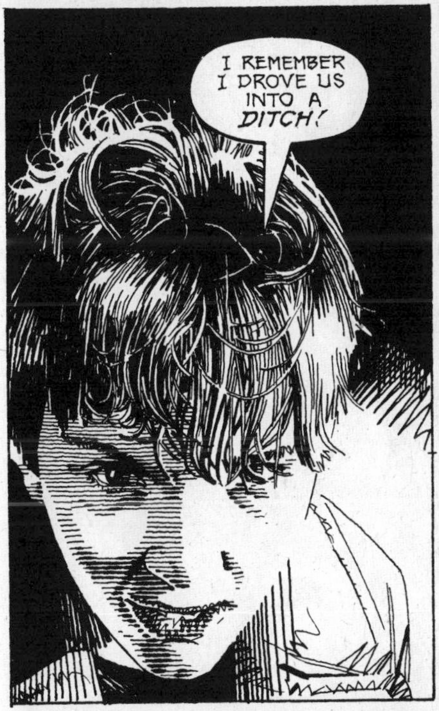
I REMEMBER I DROVE US INTO A *DITCH!*

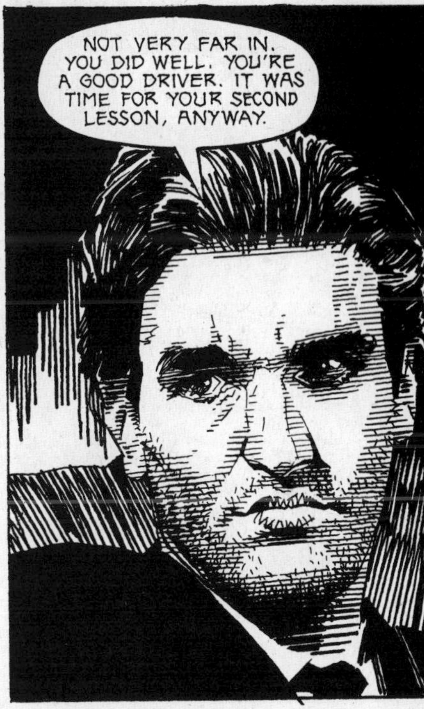
NOT VERY FAR IN. YOU DID WELL. YOU'RE A GOOD DRIVER. IT WAS TIME FOR YOUR SECOND LESSON, ANYWAY.

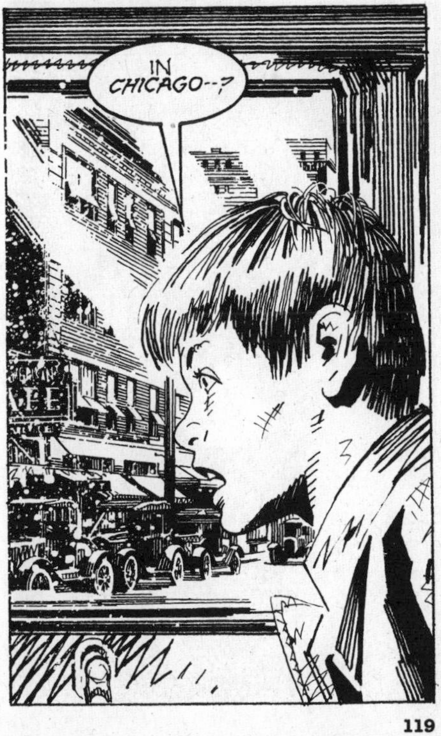
IN *CHICAGO*--?

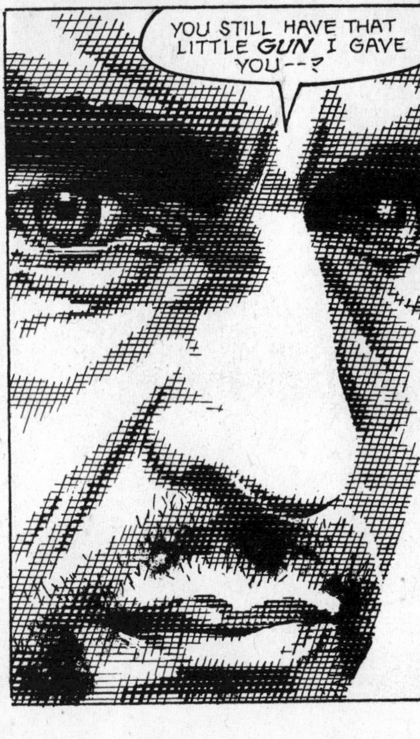
YOU STILL HAVE THAT LITTLE *GUN* I GAVE YOU--?

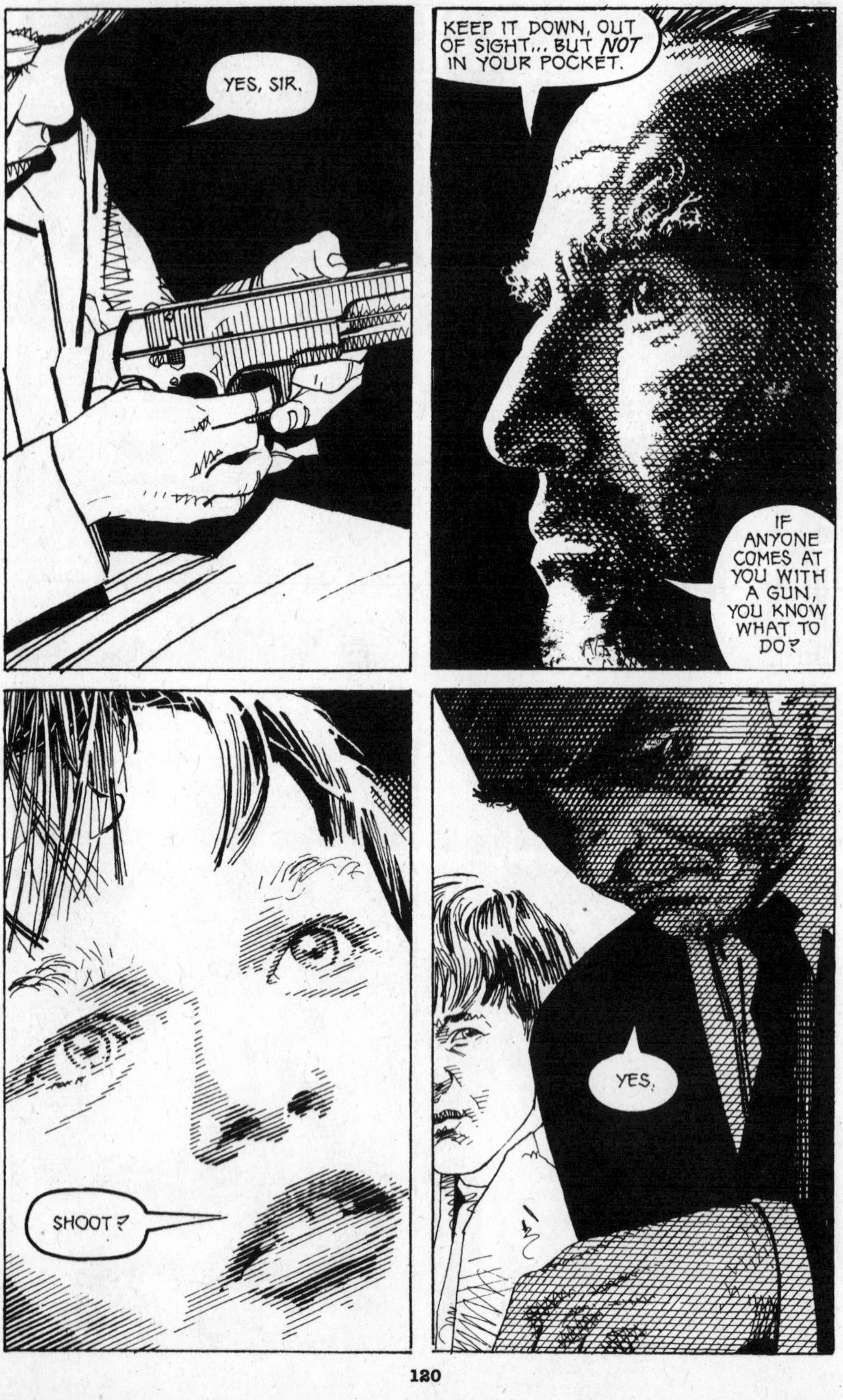
YES, SIR.
KEEP IT DOWN, OUT OF SIGHT... BUT NOT IN YOUR POCKET.
IF ANYONE COMES AT YOU WITH A GUN, YOU KNOW WHAT TO DO?
SHOOT?
YES.

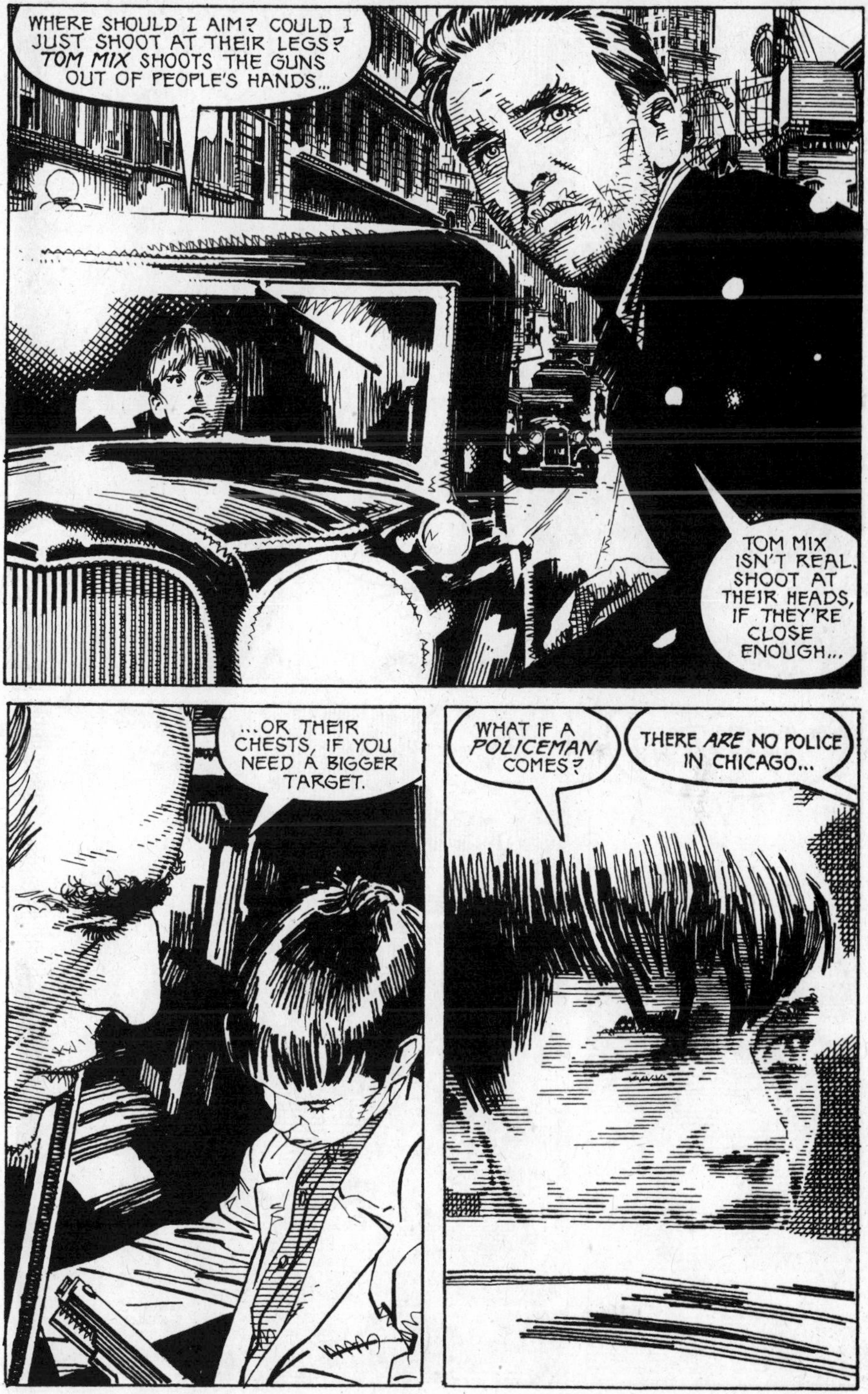
WHERE SHOULD I AIM? COULD I JUST SHOOT AT THEIR LEGS? *TOM MIX* SHOOTS THE GUNS OUT OF PEOPLE'S HANDS...
TOM MIX ISN'T REAL. SHOOT AT THEIR HEADS, IF THEY'RE CLOSE ENOUGH...
...OR THEIR CHESTS, IF YOU NEED A BIGGER TARGET.
WHAT IF A *POLICEMAN* COMES?
THERE *ARE* NO POLICE IN CHICAGO...

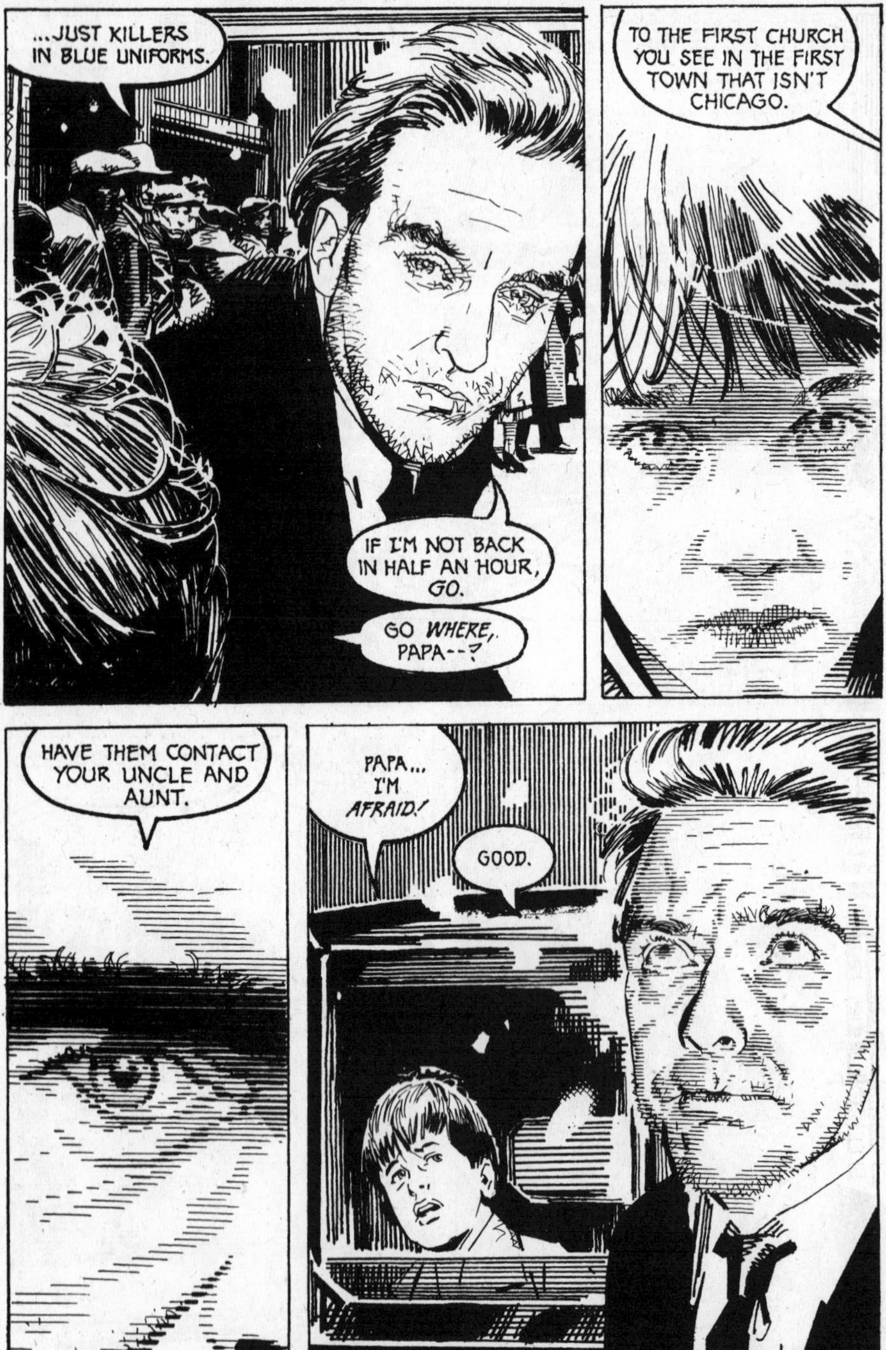
...JUST KILLERS IN BLUE UNIFORMS.
IF I'M NOT BACK IN HALF AN HOUR, *GO.*
GO *WHERE,* PAPA--?
TO THE FIRST CHURCH YOU SEE IN THE FIRST TOWN THAT ISN'T CHICAGO.
HAVE THEM CONTACT YOUR UNCLE AND AUNT.
PAPA... I'M *AFRAID!*
GOOD.

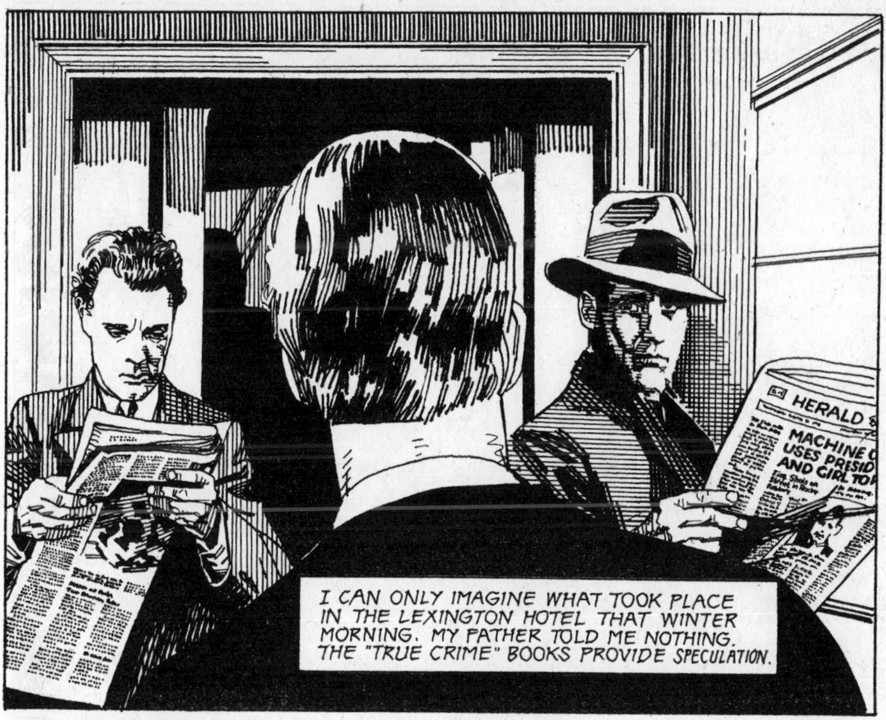
HERALD
I CAN ONLY IMAGINE WHAT TOOK PLACE IN THE LEXINGTON HOTEL THAT WINTER MORNING. MY FATHER TOLD ME NOTHING. THE "TRUE CRIME" BOOKS PROVIDE SPECULATION.

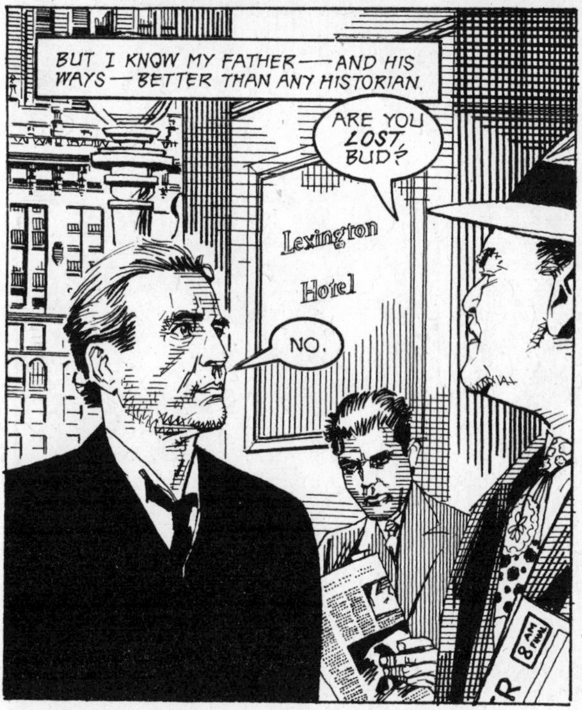
BUT I KNOW MY FATHER — AND HIS WAYS — BETTER THAN ANY HISTORIAN.
ARE YOU *LOST*, BUD?
Lexington
Hotel
NO.
8 AM FINAL

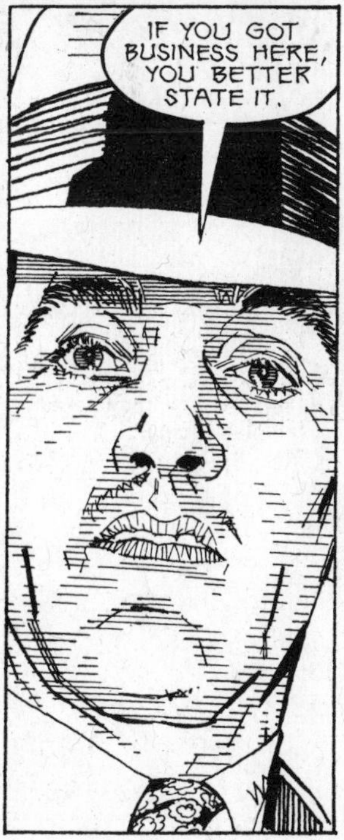
IF YOU GOT BUSINESS HERE, YOU BETTER STATE IT.

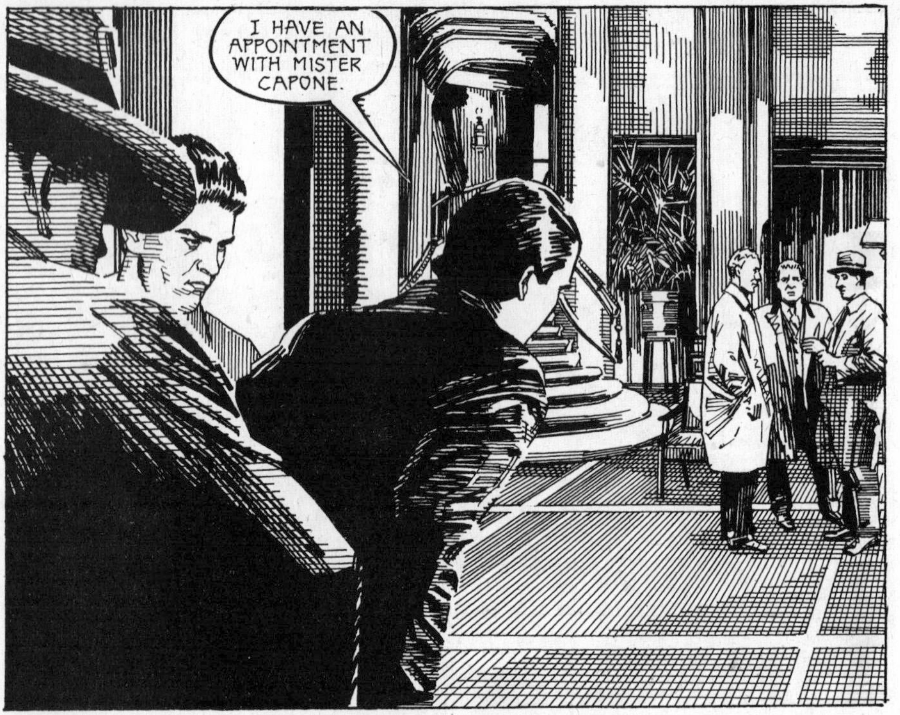
I HAVE AN APPOINTMENT WITH MISTER CAPONE.
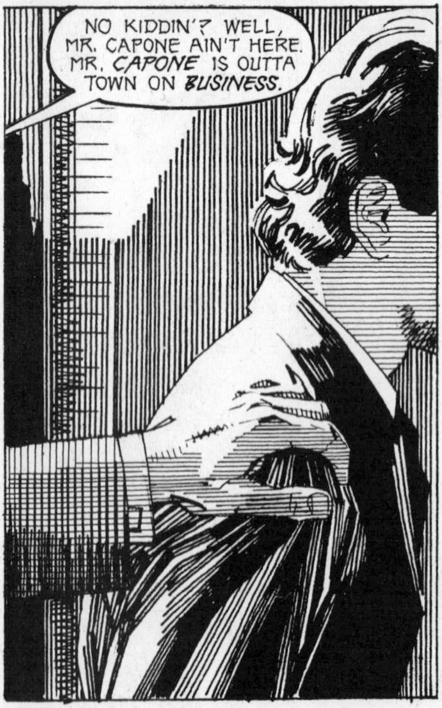
NO KIDDIN'? WELL, MR. CAPONE AIN'T HERE. MR. *CAPONE* IS OUTTA TOWN ON ***BUSINESS***.
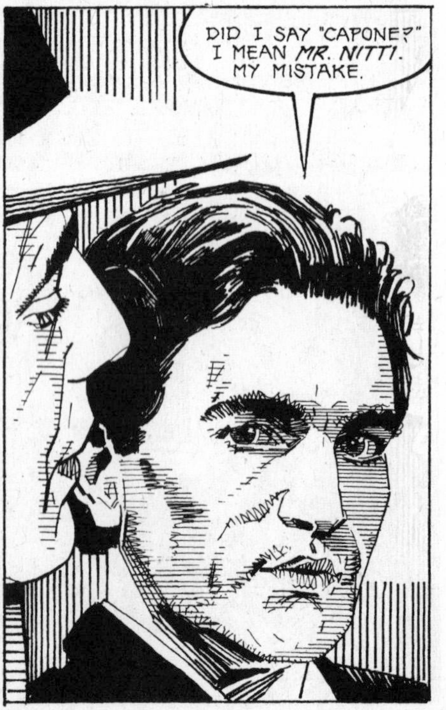
DID I SAY "CAPONE?" I MEAN *MR. NITTI*. MY MISTAKE.

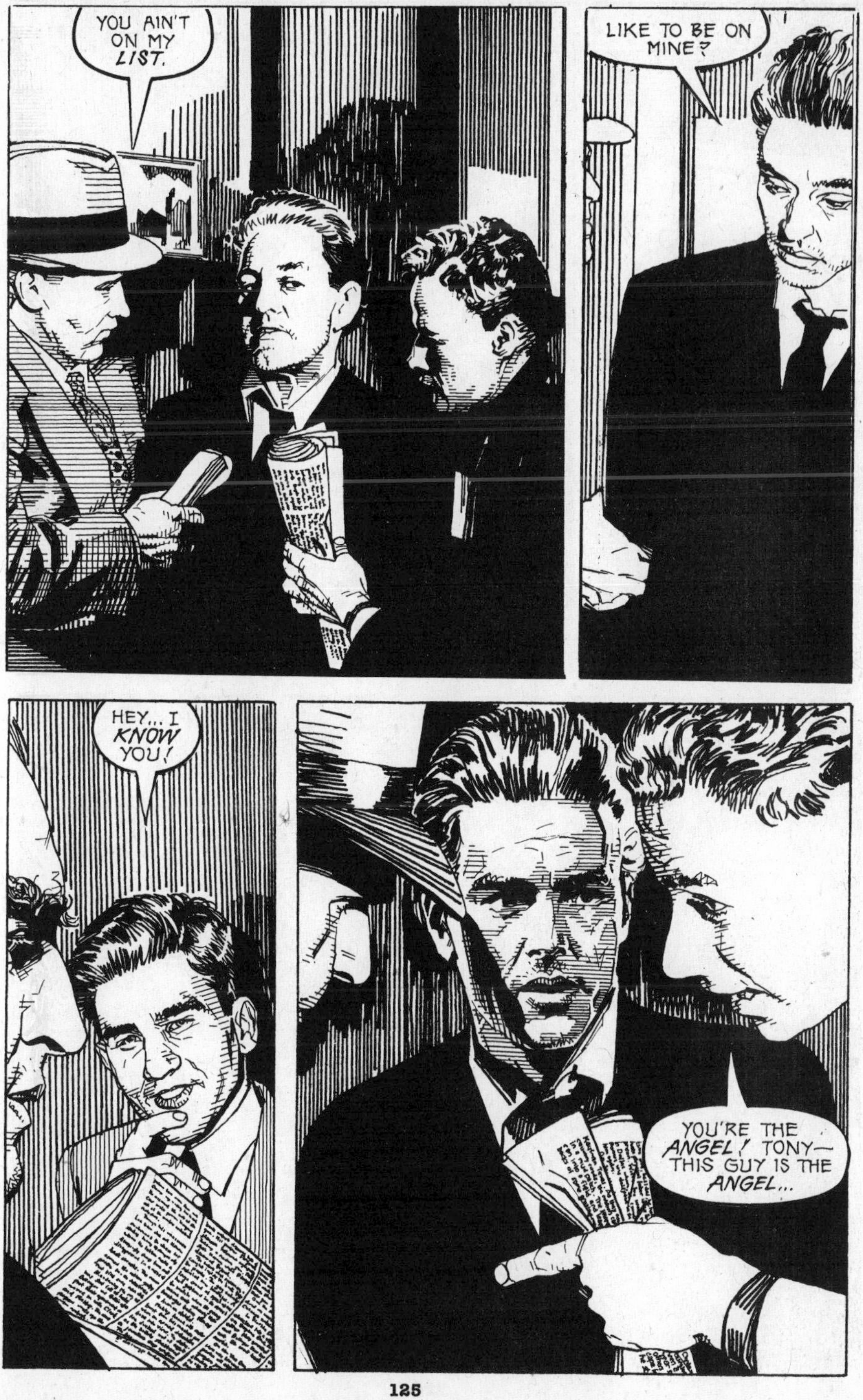
YOU AIN'T ON MY *LIST*.
LIKE TO BE ON MINE?
HEY... I *KNOW* YOU!
YOU'RE THE *ANGEL*! TONY— THIS GUY IS THE *ANGEL*...

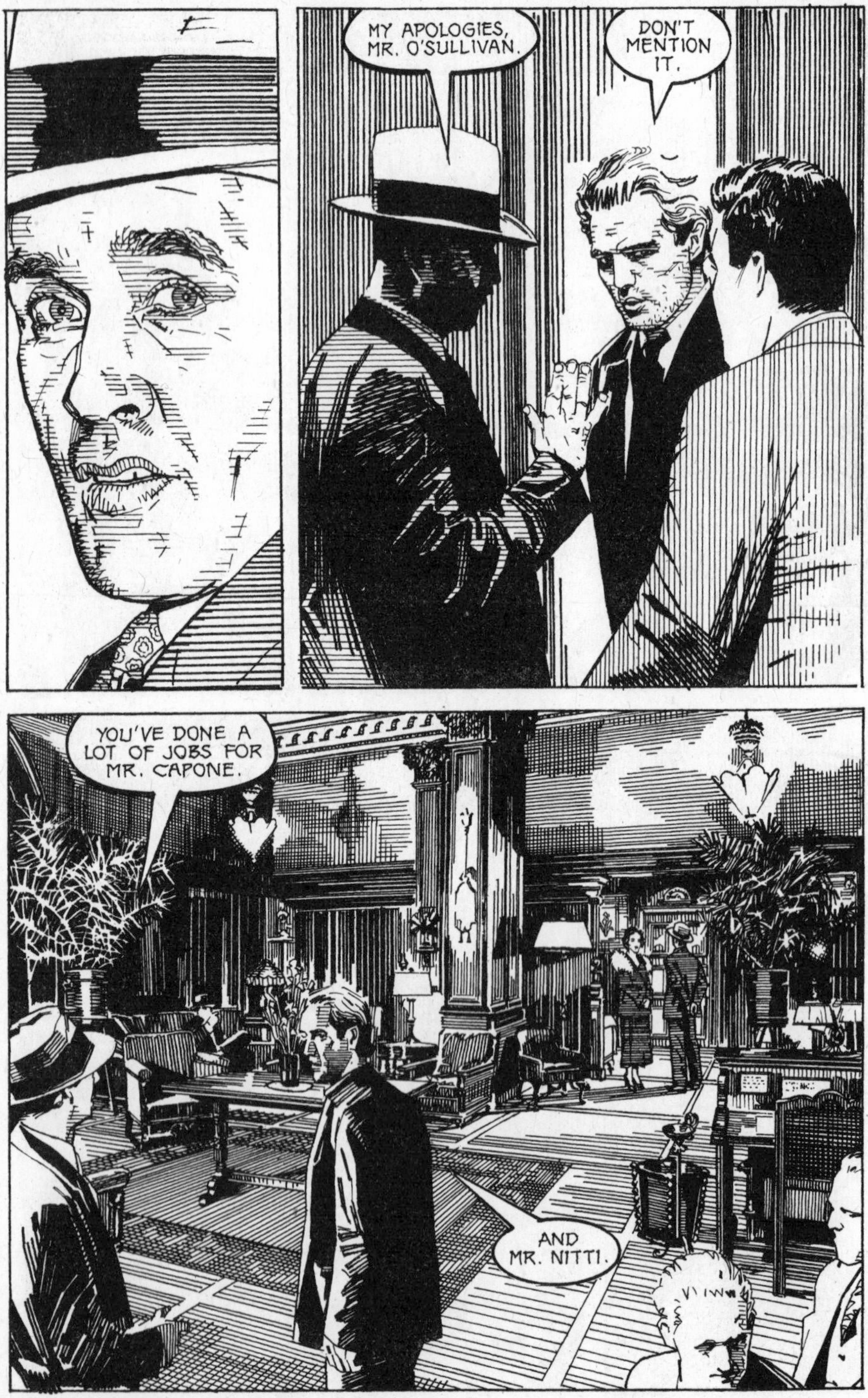
MY APOLOGIES, MR. O'SULLIVAN.
DON'T MENTION IT.
YOU'VE DONE A LOT OF JOBS FOR MR. CAPONE.
AND MR. NITTI.

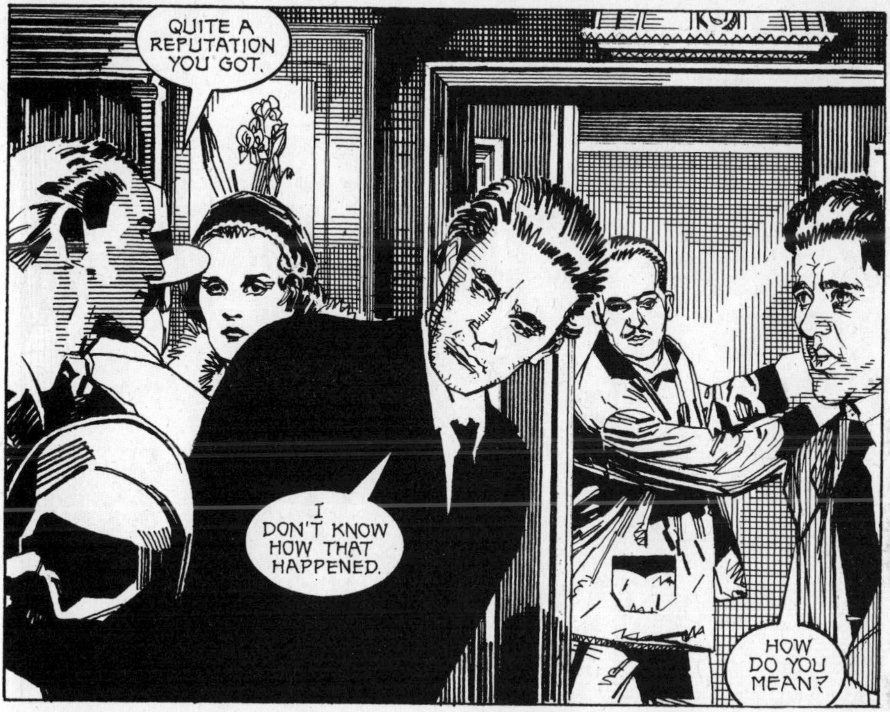
QUITE A REPUTATION YOU GOT.
I DON'T KNOW HOW THAT HAPPENED.
HOW DO YOU MEAN?

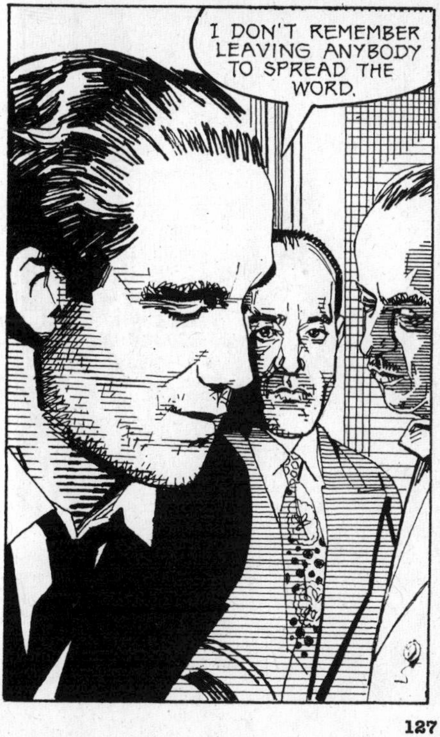
I DON'T REMEMBER LEAVING ANYBODY TO SPREAD THE WORD.

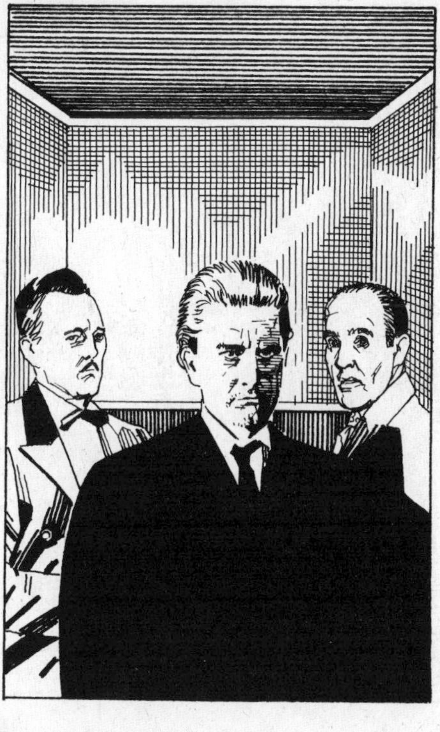

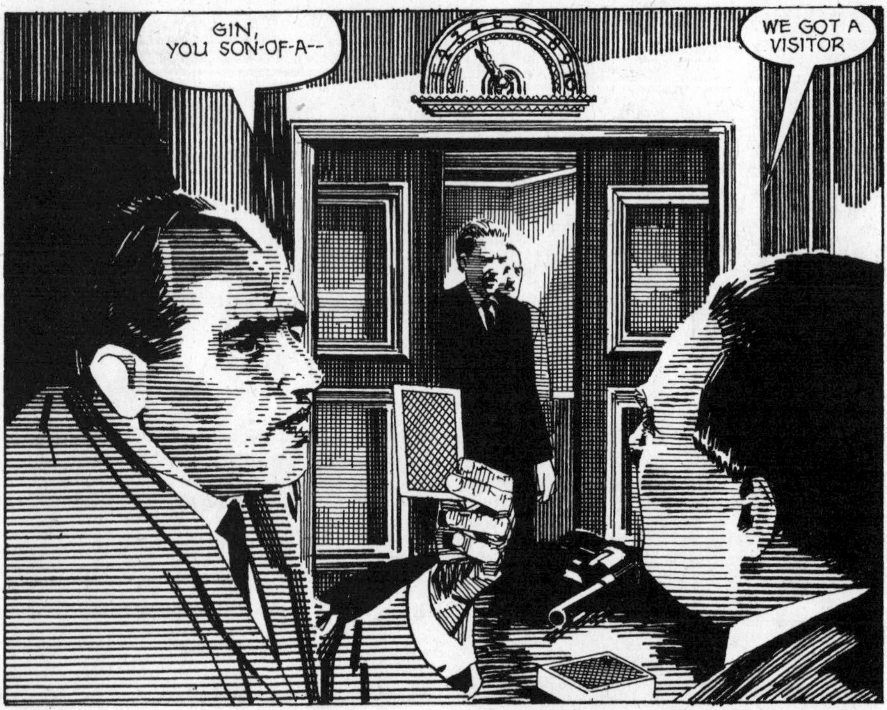
GIN, YOU SON-OF-A--
WE GOT A VISITOR

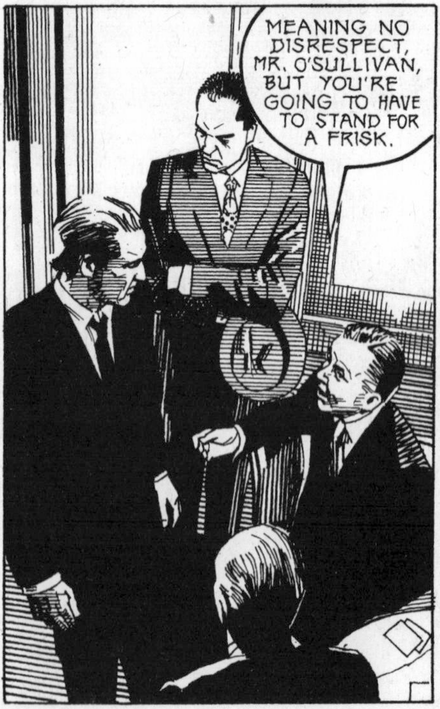
MEANING NO DISRESPECT, MR. O'SULLIVAN, BUT YOU'RE GOING TO HAVE TO STAND FOR A FRISK.

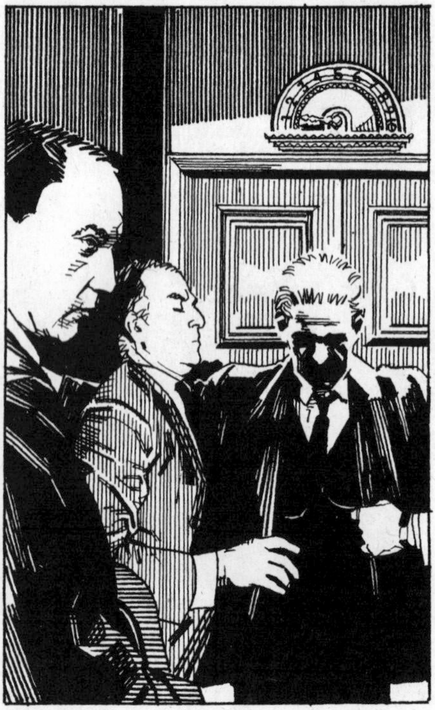

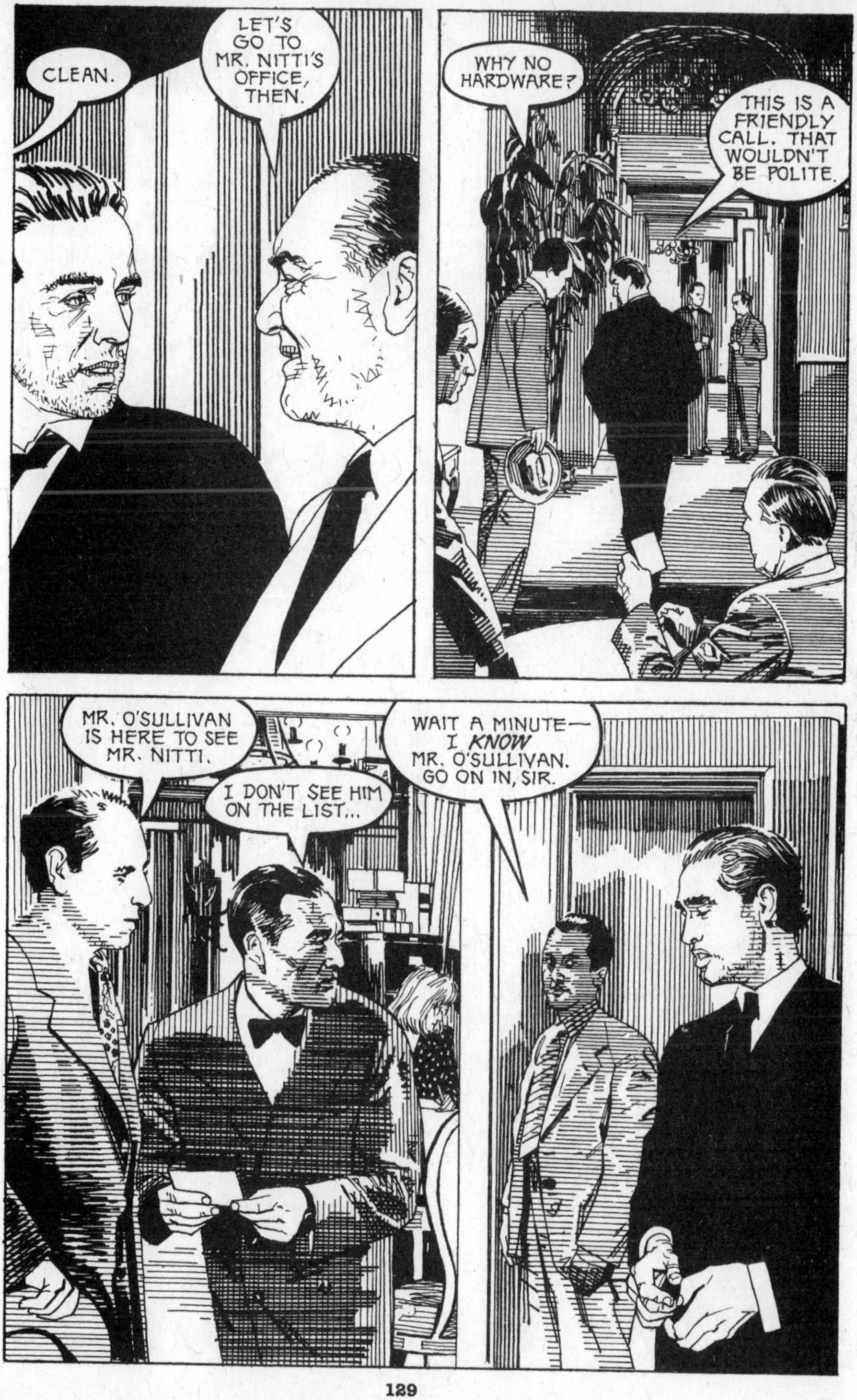
CLEAN.
LET'S GO TO MR. NITTI'S OFFICE, THEN.
WHY NO HARDWARE?
THIS IS A FRIENDLY CALL. THAT WOULDN'T BE POLITE.
MR. O'SULLIVAN IS HERE TO SEE MR. NITTI.
I DON'T SEE HIM ON THE LIST...
WAIT A MINUTE— I *KNOW* MR. O'SULLIVAN. GO ON IN, SIR.

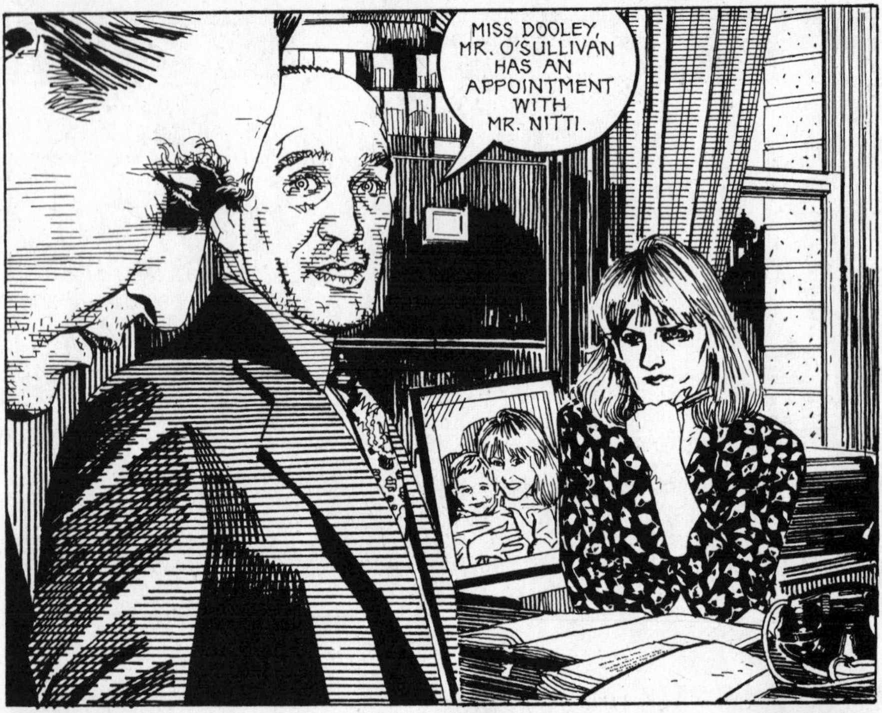
MISS DOOLEY, MR. O'SULLIVAN HAS AN APPOINTMENT WITH MR. NITTI.

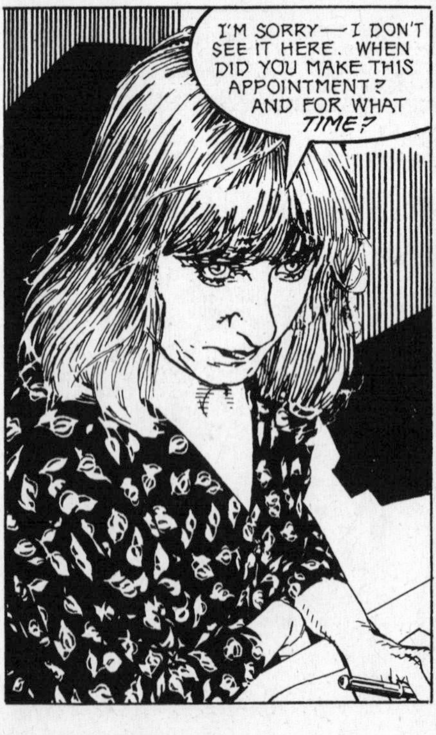
I'M SORRY—I DON'T SEE IT HERE. WHEN DID YOU MAKE THIS APPOINTMENT? AND FOR WHAT *TIME?*

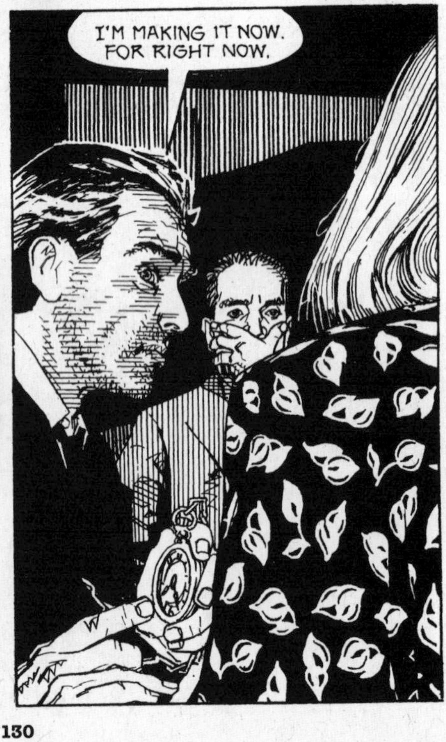
I'M MAKING IT NOW. FOR RIGHT NOW.

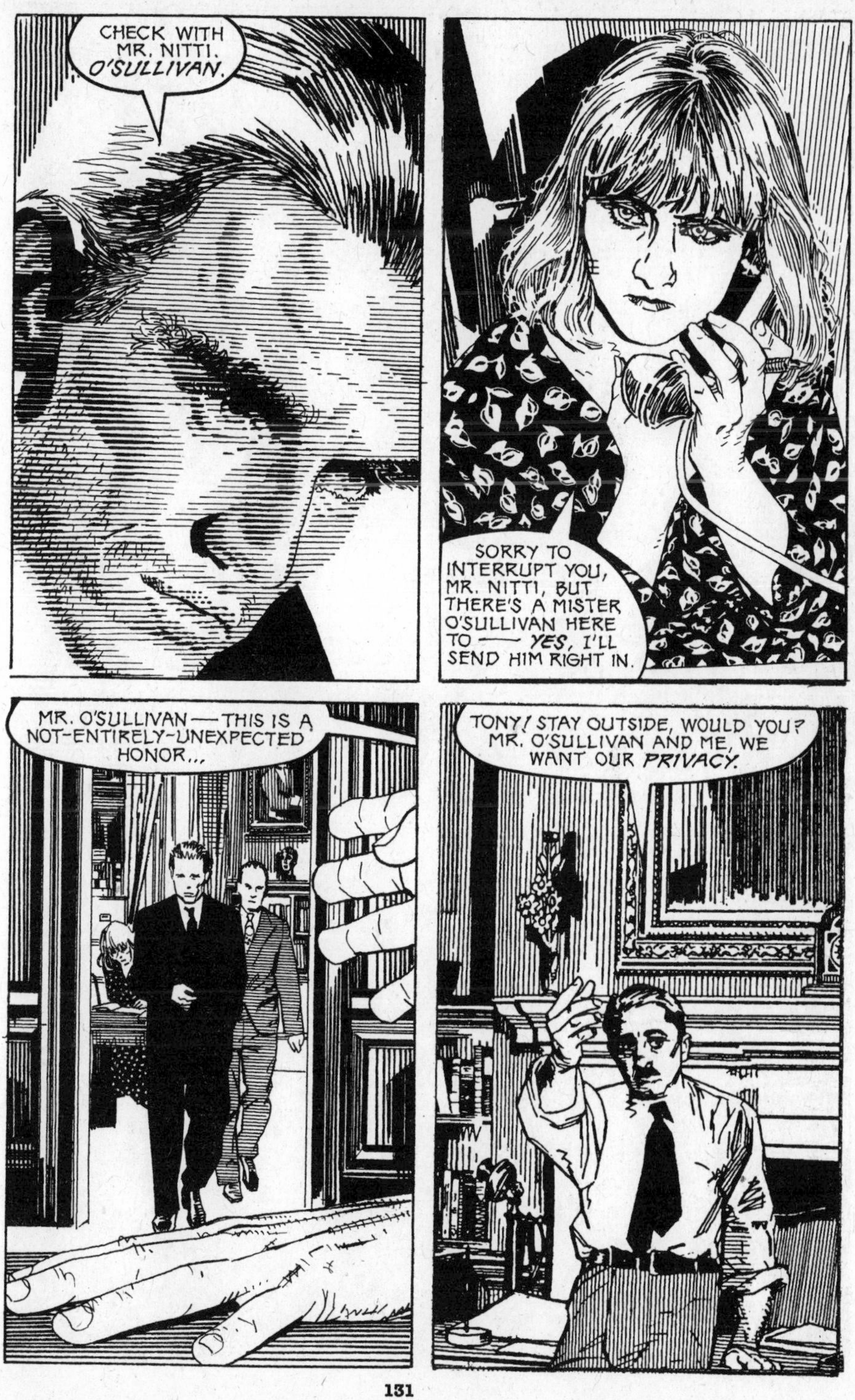
CHECK WITH MR. NITTI. O'SULLIVAN.
SORRY TO INTERRUPT YOU, MR. NITTI, BUT THERE'S A MISTER O'SULLIVAN HERE TO— YES, I'LL SEND HIM RIGHT IN.
MR. O'SULLIVAN— THIS IS A NOT-ENTIRELY-UNEXPECTED HONOR...
TONY! STAY OUTSIDE, WOULD YOU? MR. O'SULLIVAN AND ME, WE WANT OUR PRIVACY.

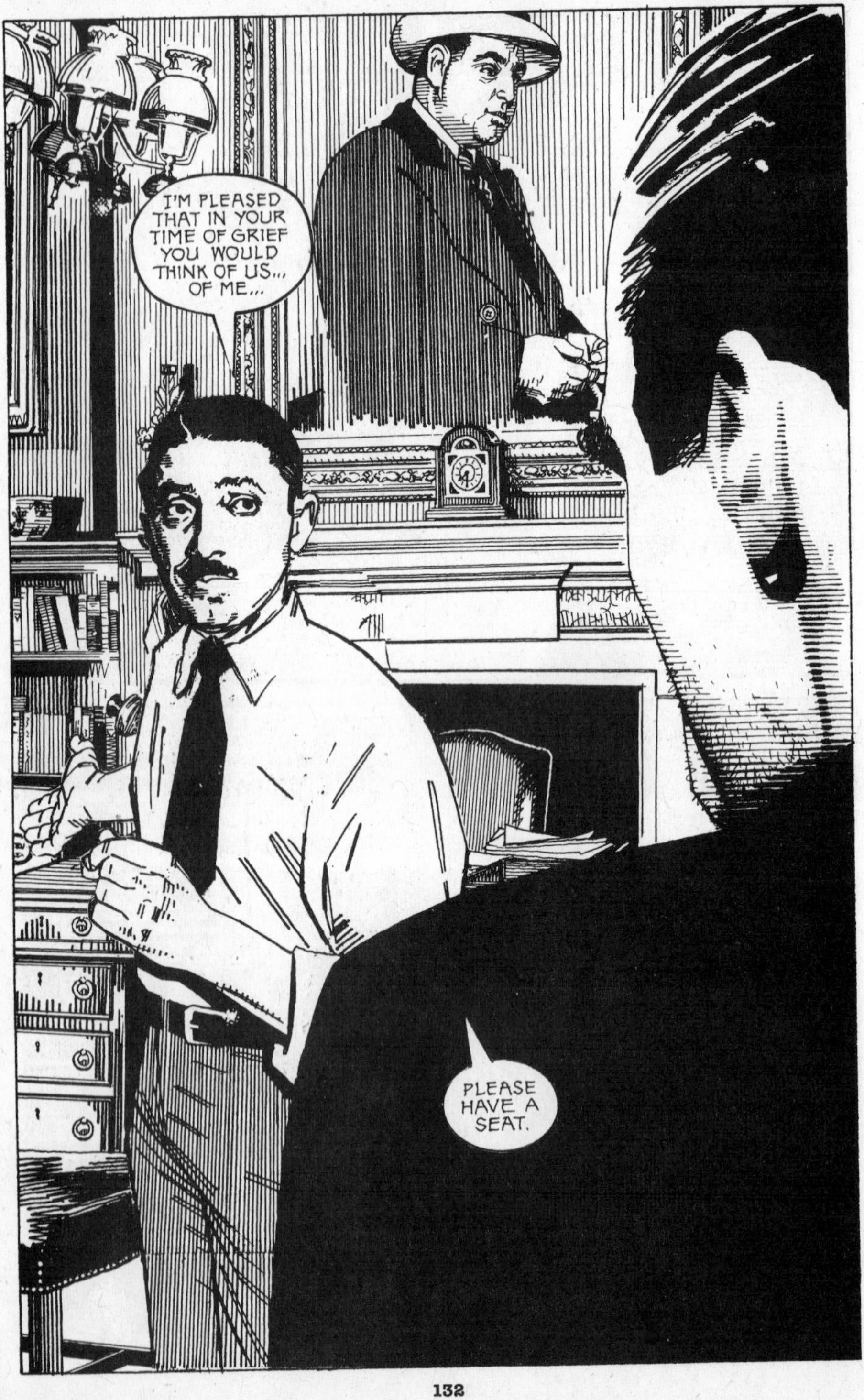
I'M PLEASED THAT IN YOUR TIME OF GRIEF YOU WOULD THINK OF US... OF ME...
PLEASE HAVE A SEAT.

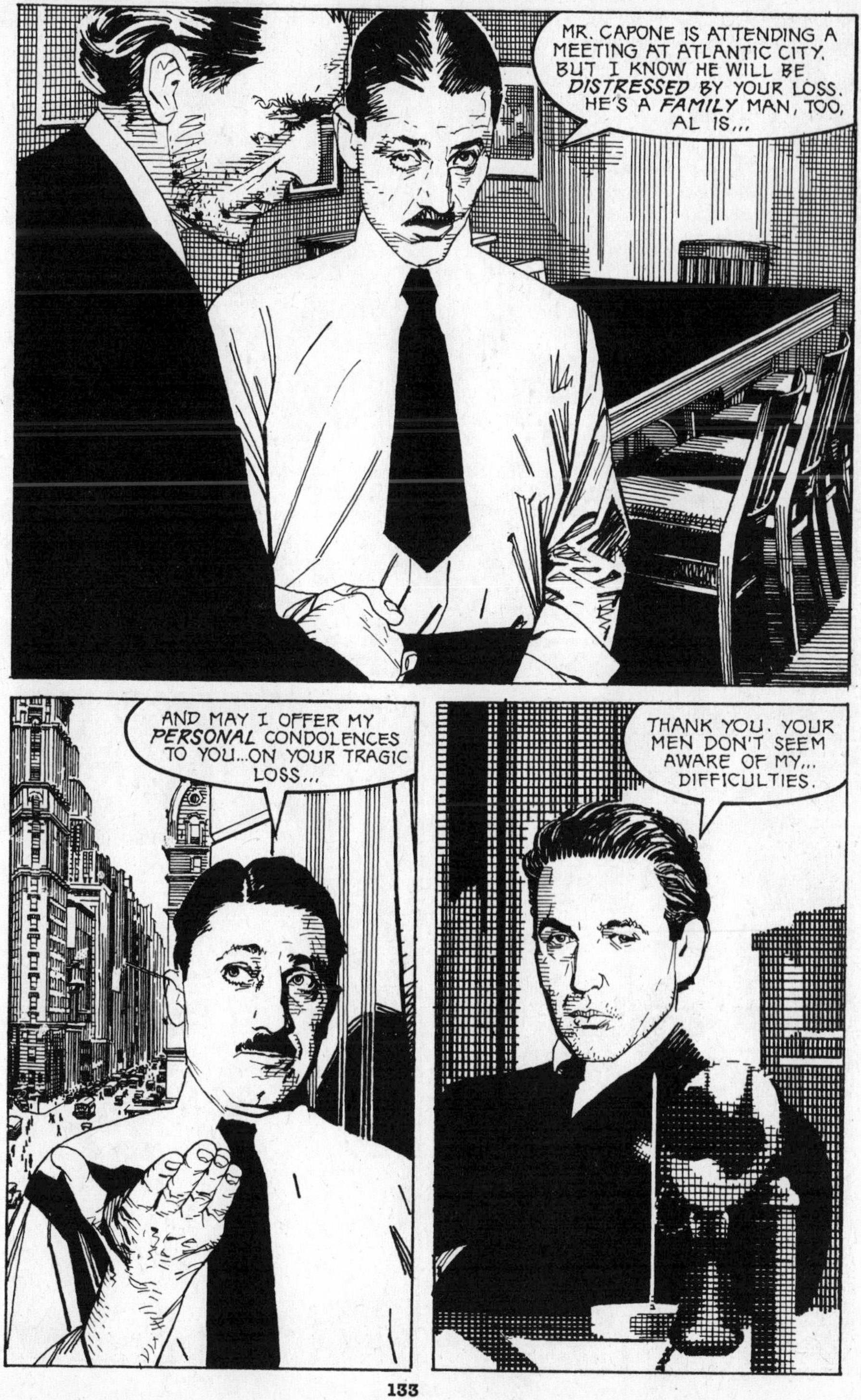
MR. CAPONE IS ATTENDING A MEETING AT ATLANTIC CITY. BUT I KNOW HE WILL BE *DISTRESSED* BY YOUR LOSS. HE'S A *FAMILY* MAN, TOO, AL IS...
AND MAY I OFFER MY *PERSONAL* CONDOLENCES TO YOU...ON YOUR TRAGIC LOSS...
THANK YOU. YOUR MEN DON'T SEEM AWARE OF MY... DIFFICULTIES.

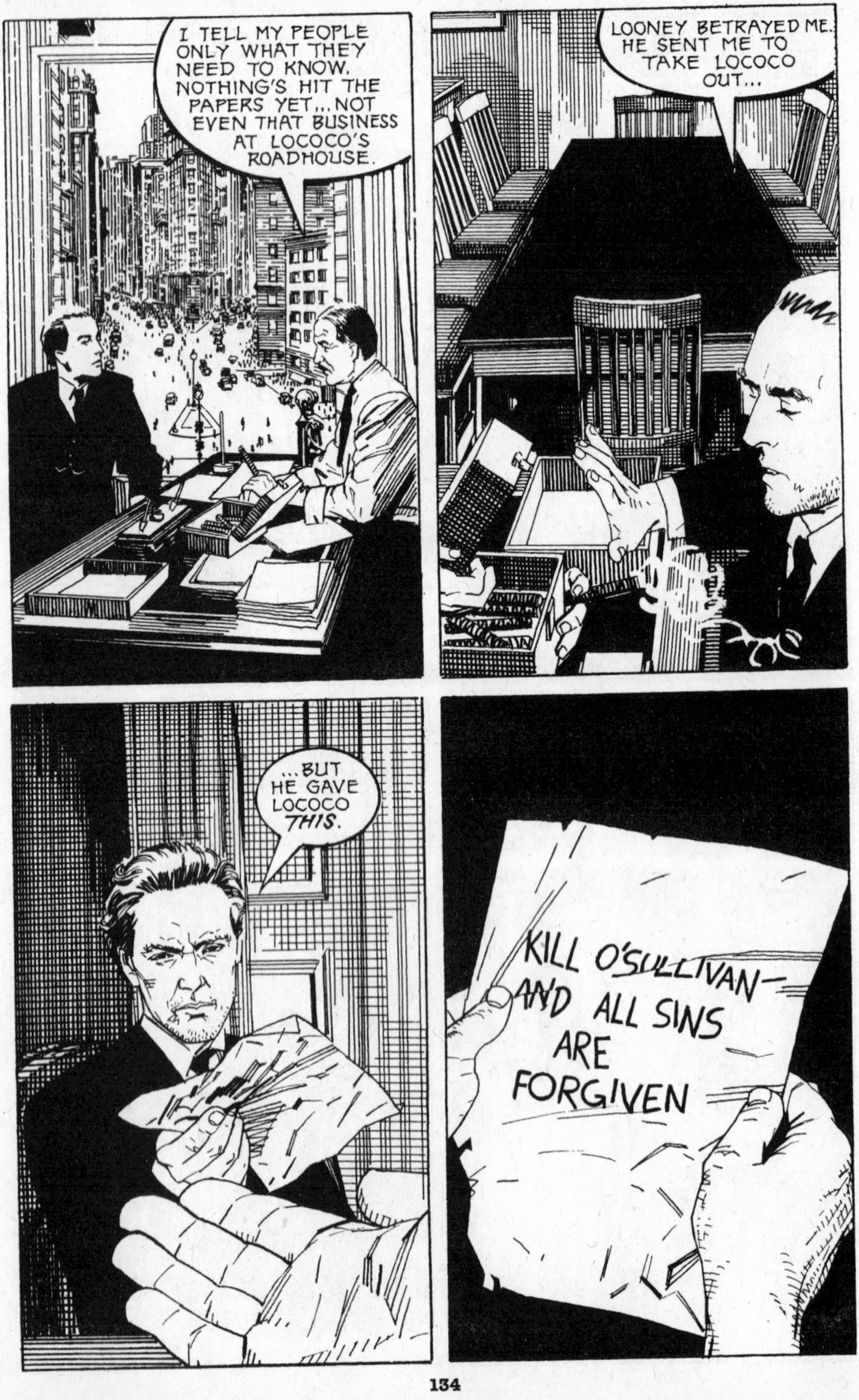
I TELL MY PEOPLE ONLY WHAT THEY NEED TO KNOW. NOTHING'S HIT THE PAPERS YET... NOT EVEN THAT BUSINESS AT LOCOCO'S ROADHOUSE.
LOONEY BETRAYED ME. HE SENT ME TO TAKE LOCOCO OUT...
...BUT HE GAVE LOCOCO *THIS*.
KILL O'SULLIVAN AND ALL SINS ARE FORGIVEN

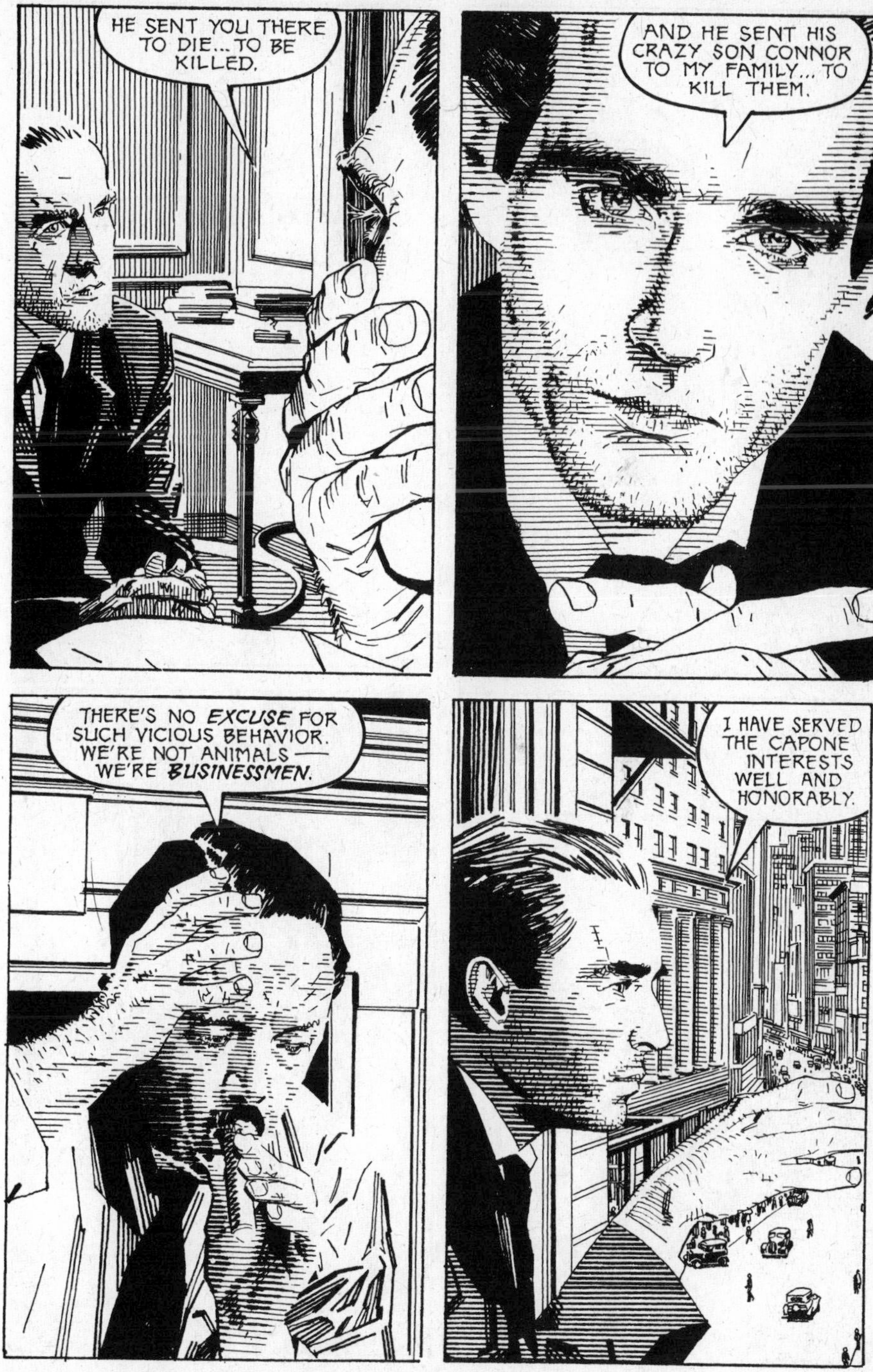
HE SENT YOU THERE TO DIE... TO BE KILLED.
AND HE SENT HIS CRAZY SON CONNOR TO MY FAMILY... TO KILL THEM.
THERE'S NO *EXCUSE* FOR SUCH VICIOUS BEHAVIOR. WE'RE NOT ANIMALS — WE'RE *BUSINESSMEN*.
I HAVE SERVED THE CAPONE INTERESTS WELL AND HONORABLY.

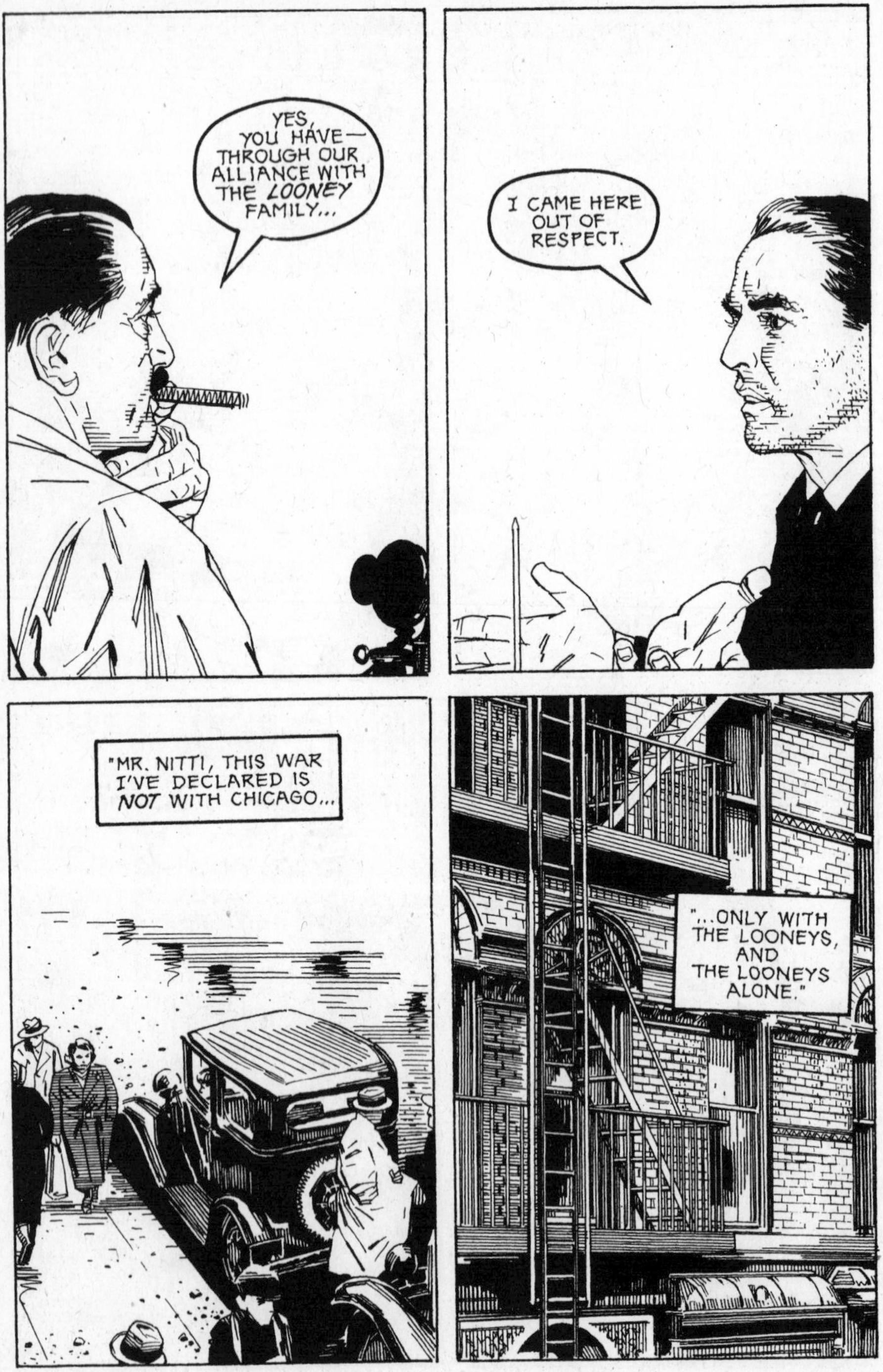
YES, YOU HAVE— THROUGH OUR ALLIANCE WITH THE *LOONEY* FAMILY...
I CAME HERE OUT OF RESPECT.
"MR. NITTI, THIS WAR I'VE DECLARED IS *NOT* WITH CHICAGO...
"...ONLY WITH THE LOONEYS, AND THE LOONEYS ALONE."

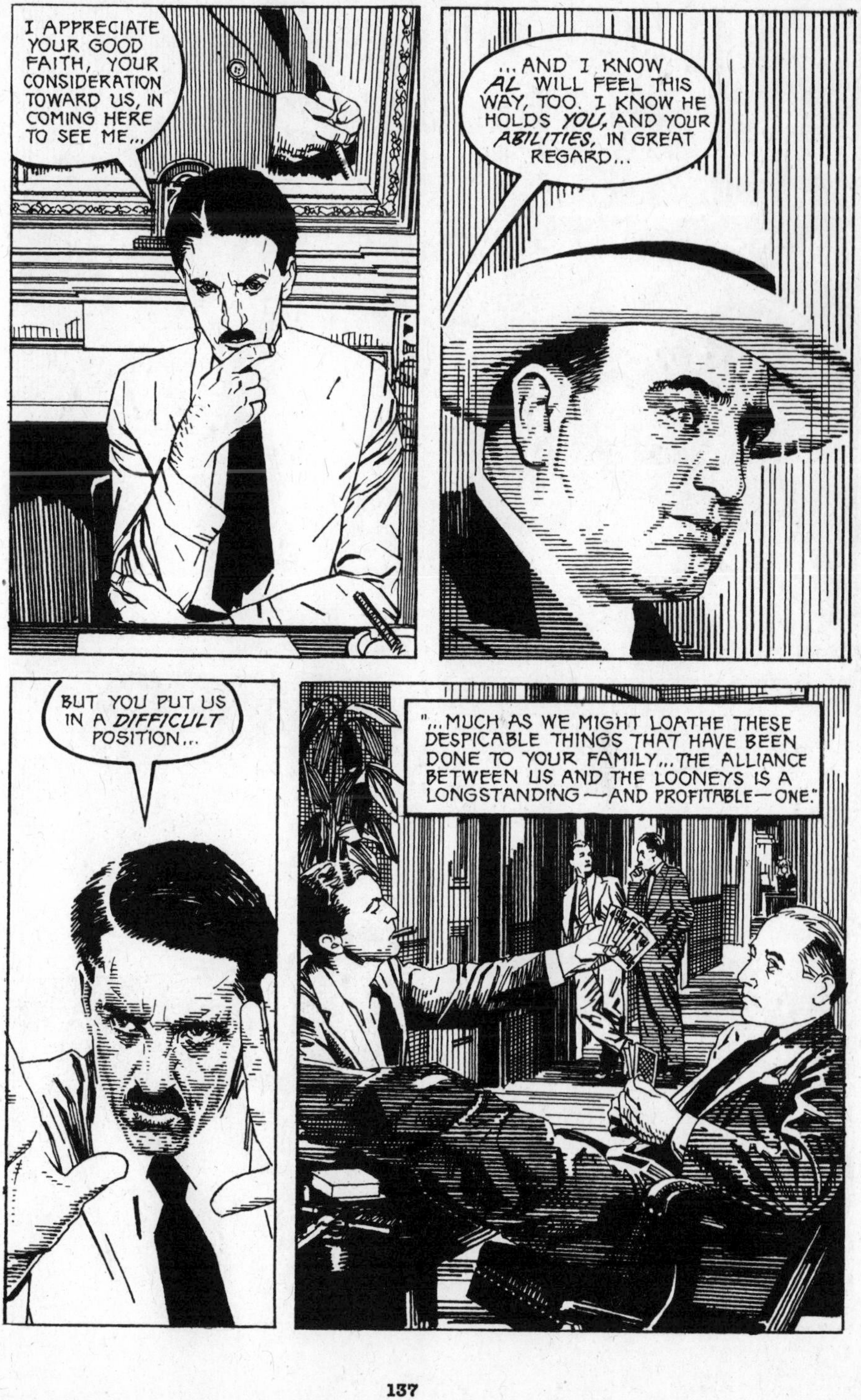
I APPRECIATE YOUR GOOD FAITH, YOUR CONSIDERATION TOWARD US, IN COMING HERE TO SEE ME...
...AND I KNOW AL WILL FEEL THIS WAY, TOO. I KNOW HE HOLDS YOU, AND YOUR ABILITIES, IN GREAT REGARD...
BUT YOU PUT US IN A DIFFICULT POSITION...
"...MUCH AS WE MIGHT LOATHE THESE DESPICABLE THINGS THAT HAVE BEEN DONE TO YOUR FAMILY...THE ALLIANCE BETWEEN US AND THE LOONEYS IS A LONGSTANDING—AND PROFITABLE—ONE."

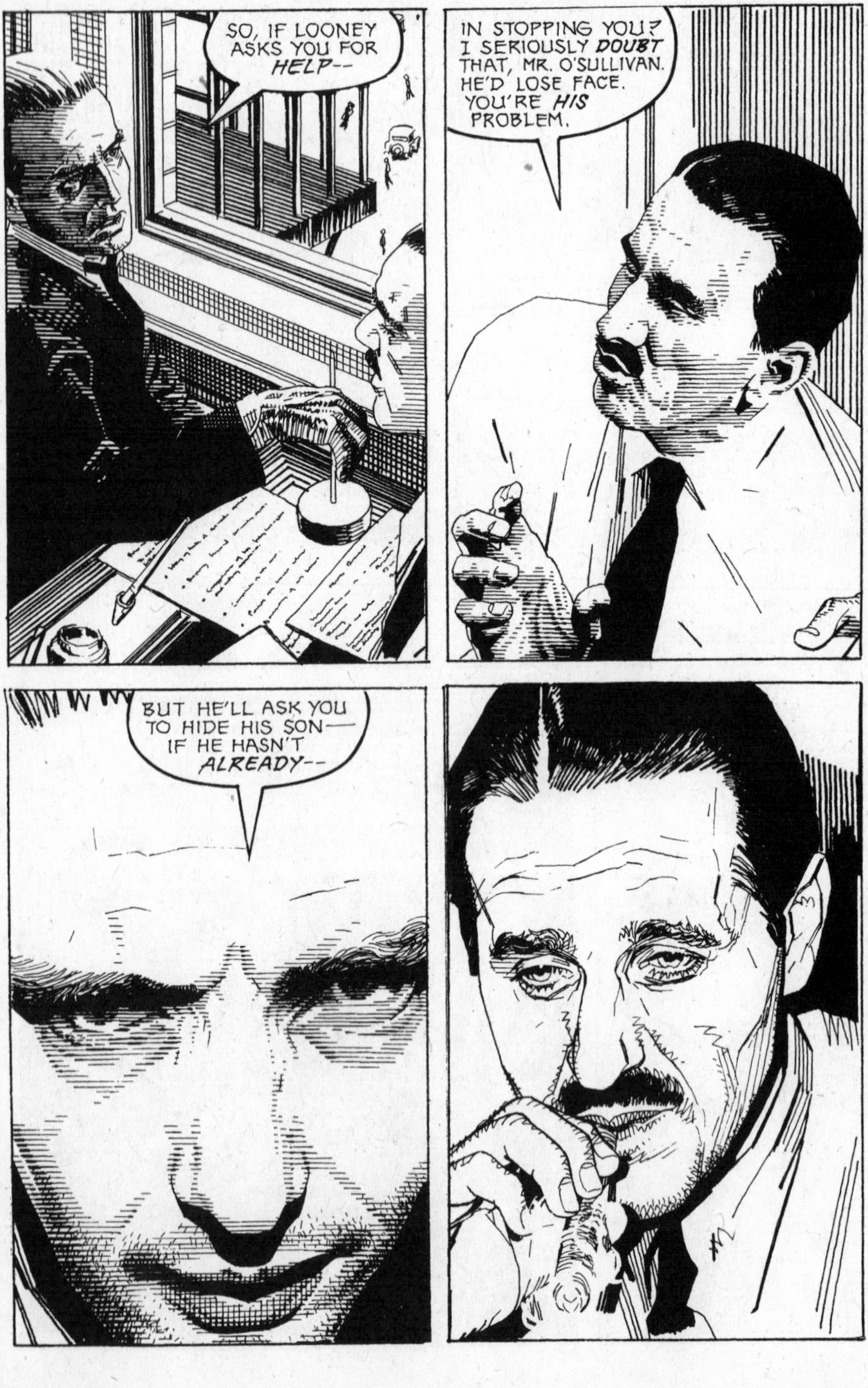
SO, IF LOONEY ASKS YOU FOR HELP--
IN STOPPING YOU? I SERIOUSLY DOUBT THAT, MR. O'SULLIVAN. HE'D LOSE FACE. YOU'RE HIS PROBLEM.
BUT HE'LL ASK YOU TO HIDE HIS SON— IF HE HASN'T ALREADY--

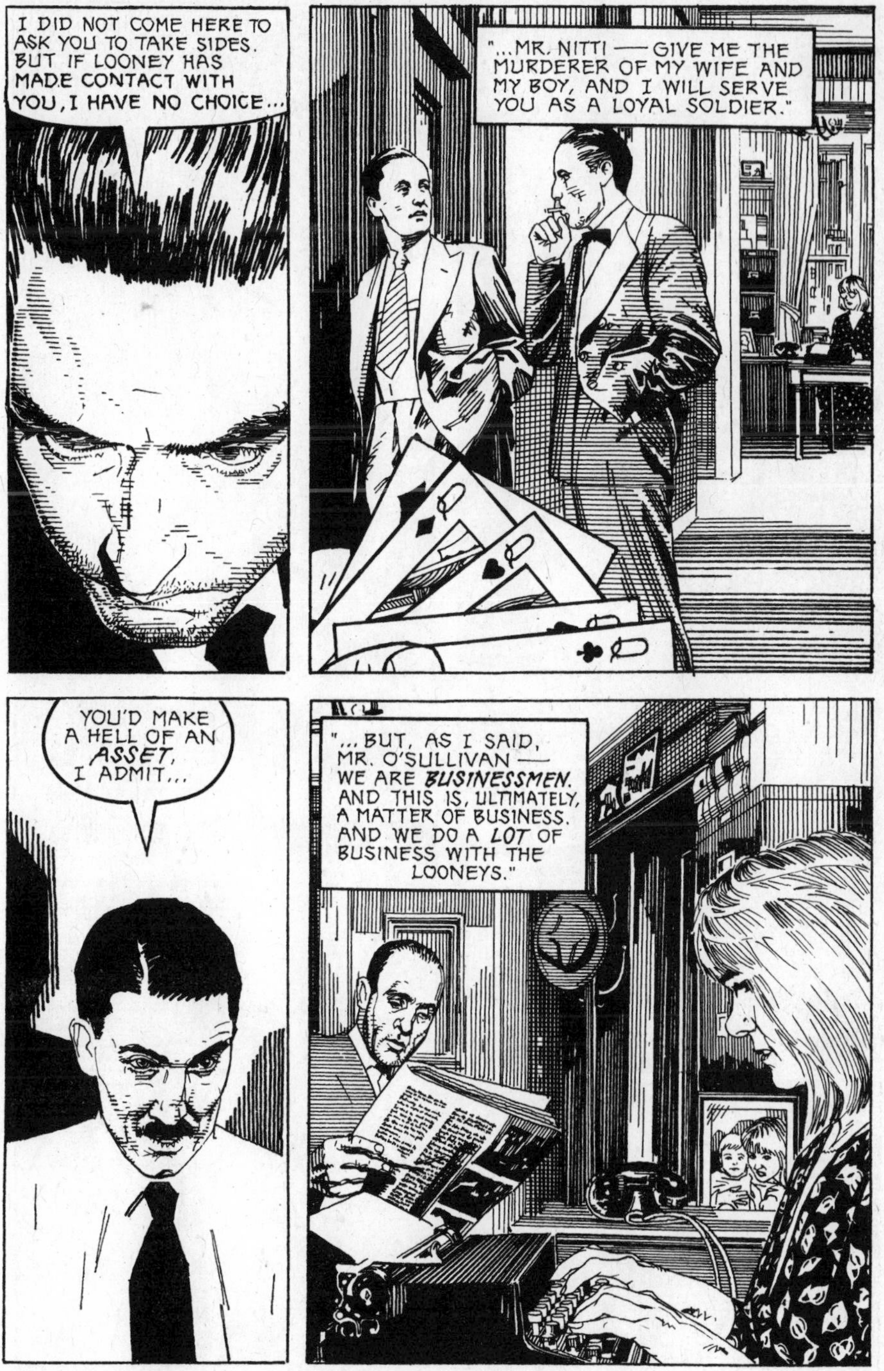
I DID NOT COME HERE TO ASK YOU TO TAKE SIDES. BUT IF LOONEY HAS MADE CONTACT WITH YOU, I HAVE NO CHOICE...
"...MR. NITTI — GIVE ME THE MURDERER OF MY WIFE AND MY BOY, AND I WILL SERVE YOU AS A LOYAL SOLDIER."
YOU'D MAKE A HELL OF AN *ASSET*, I ADMIT...
"...BUT, AS I SAID, MR. O'SULLIVAN — WE ARE *BUSINESSMEN*. AND THIS IS, ULTIMATELY, A MATTER OF BUSINESS. AND WE DO A *LOT* OF BUSINESS WITH THE LOONEYS."

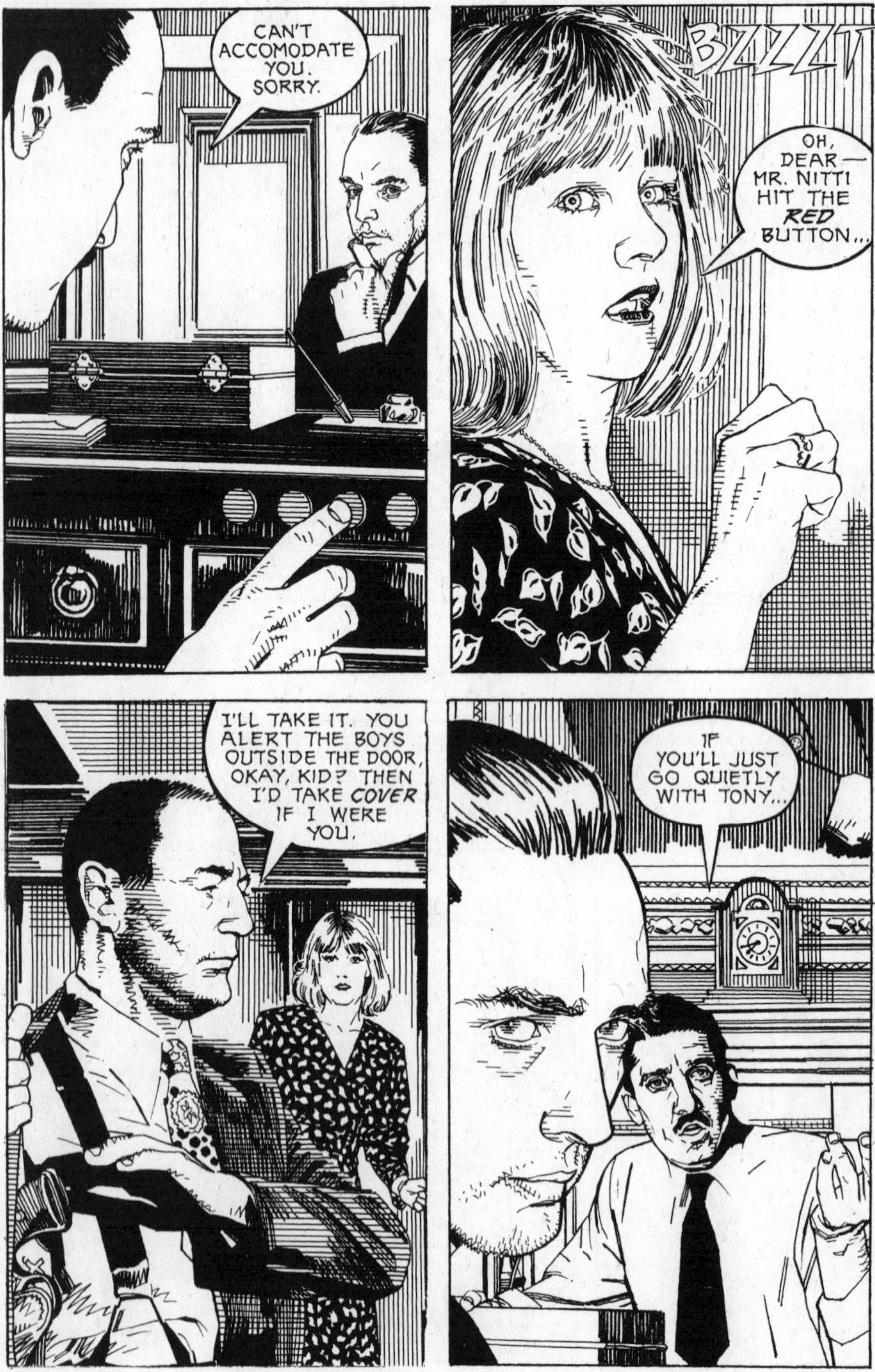
CAN'T ACCOMODATE YOU. SORRY.
BZZZT
OH, DEAR— MR. NITTI HIT THE *RED* BUTTON...
I'LL TAKE IT. YOU ALERT THE BOYS OUTSIDE THE DOOR, OKAY, KID? THEN I'D TAKE *COVER* IF I WERE YOU.
IF YOU'LL JUST GO QUIETLY WITH TONY...

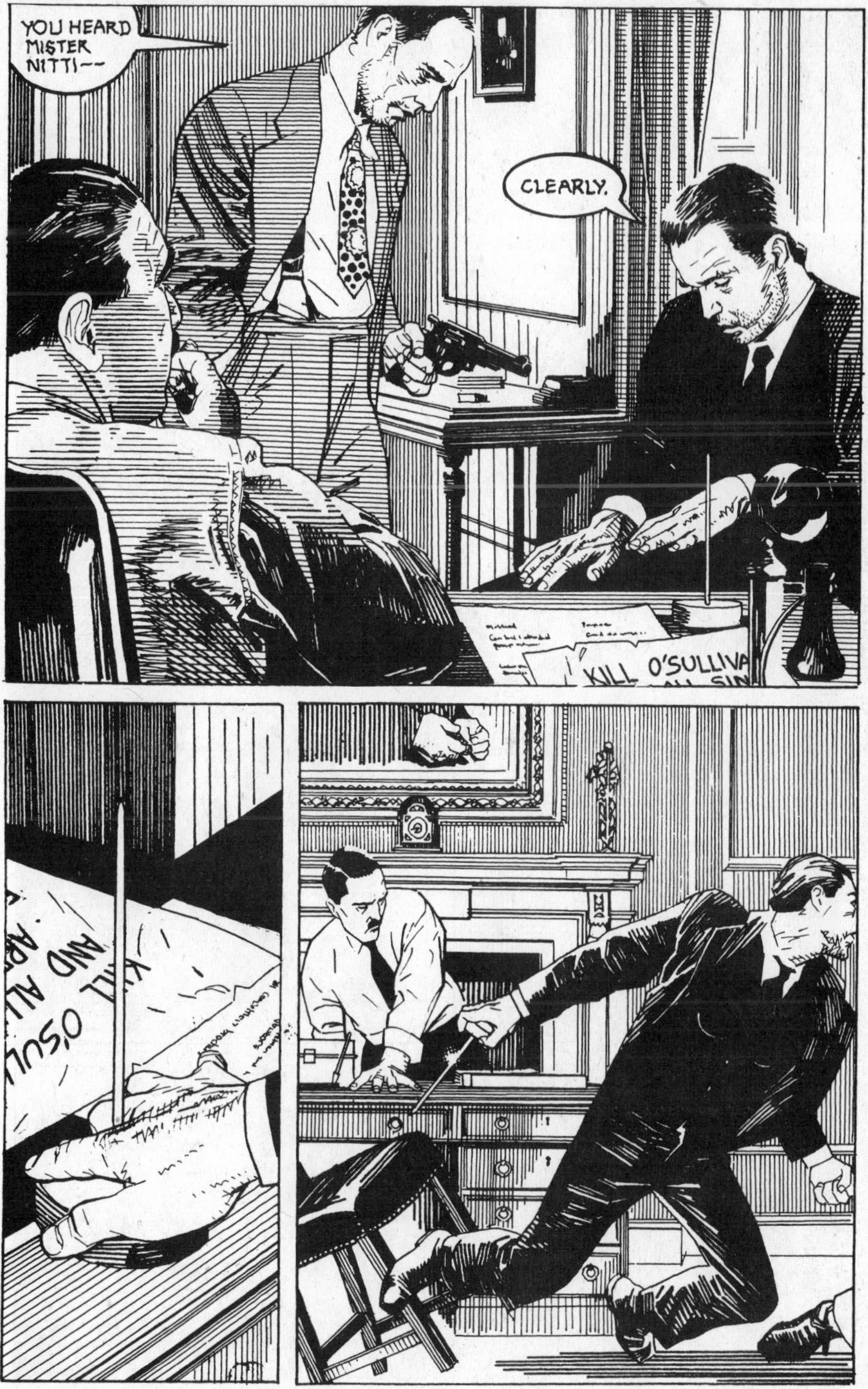
YOU HEARD MISTER NITTI--
CLEARLY.
KILL O'SULLIVA

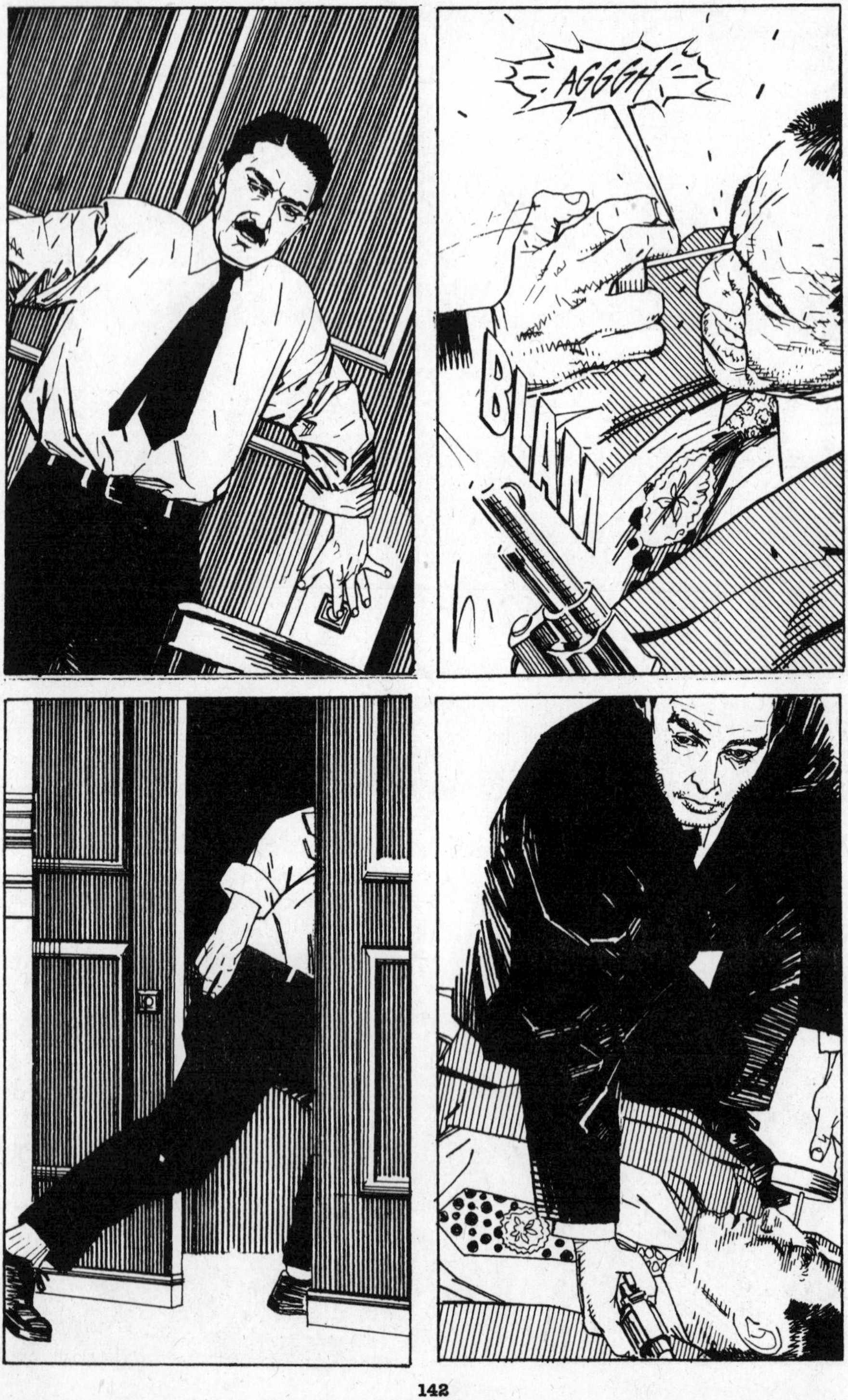
AGGGH
BLAM

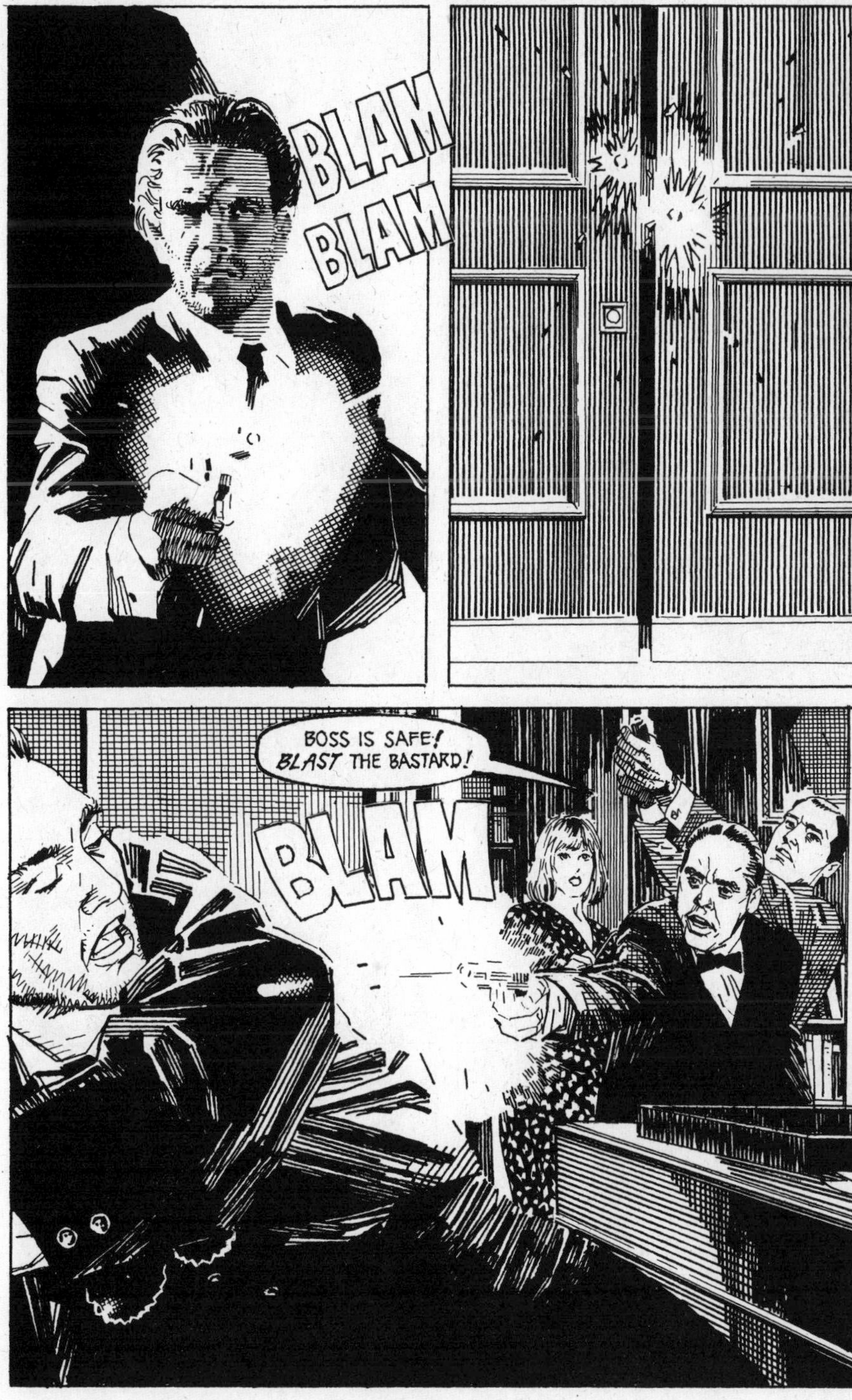
BLAM
BLAM
BOSS IS SAFE! *BLAST* THE BASTARD!
BLAM

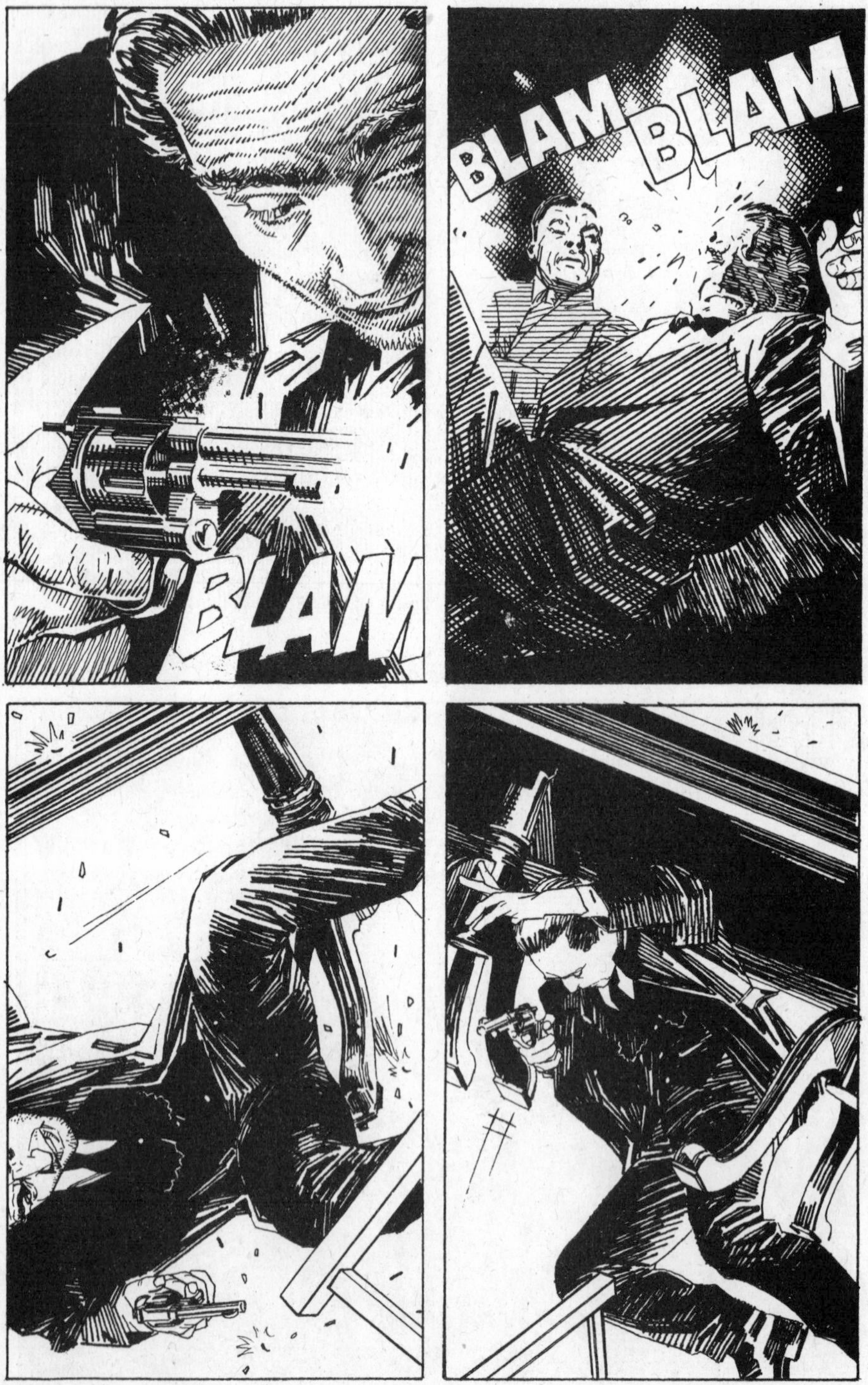
BLAM
BLAM
BLAM

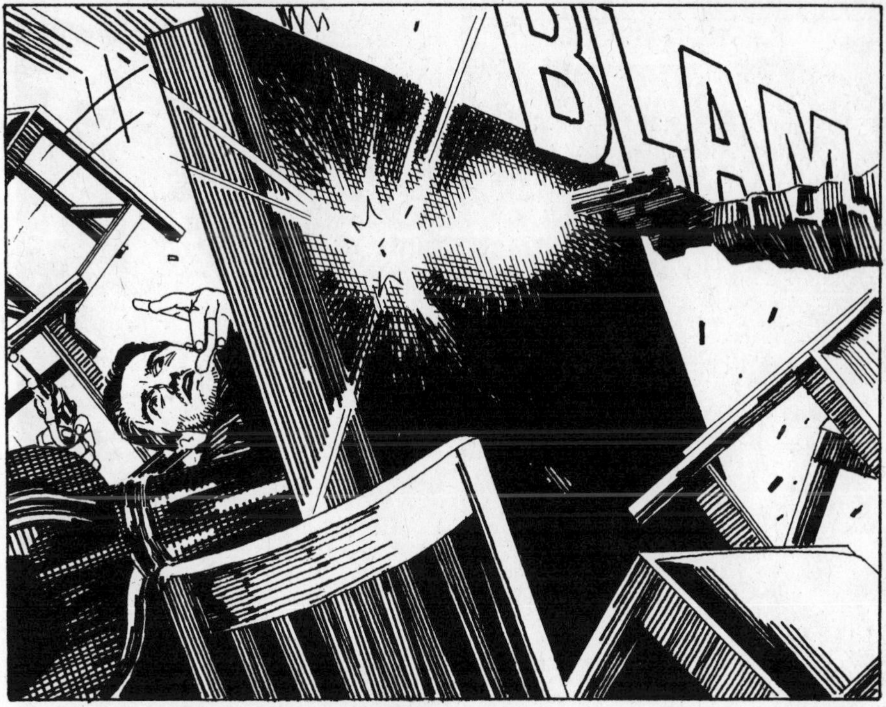
BLAM

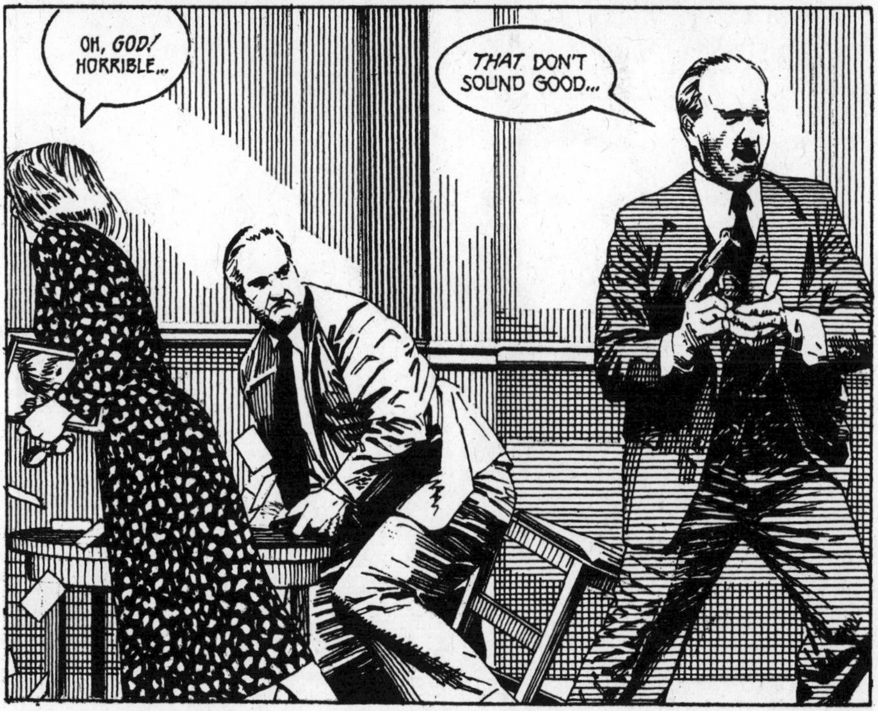
OH, *GOD!*
HORRIBLE...
THAT DON'T SOUND GOOD...

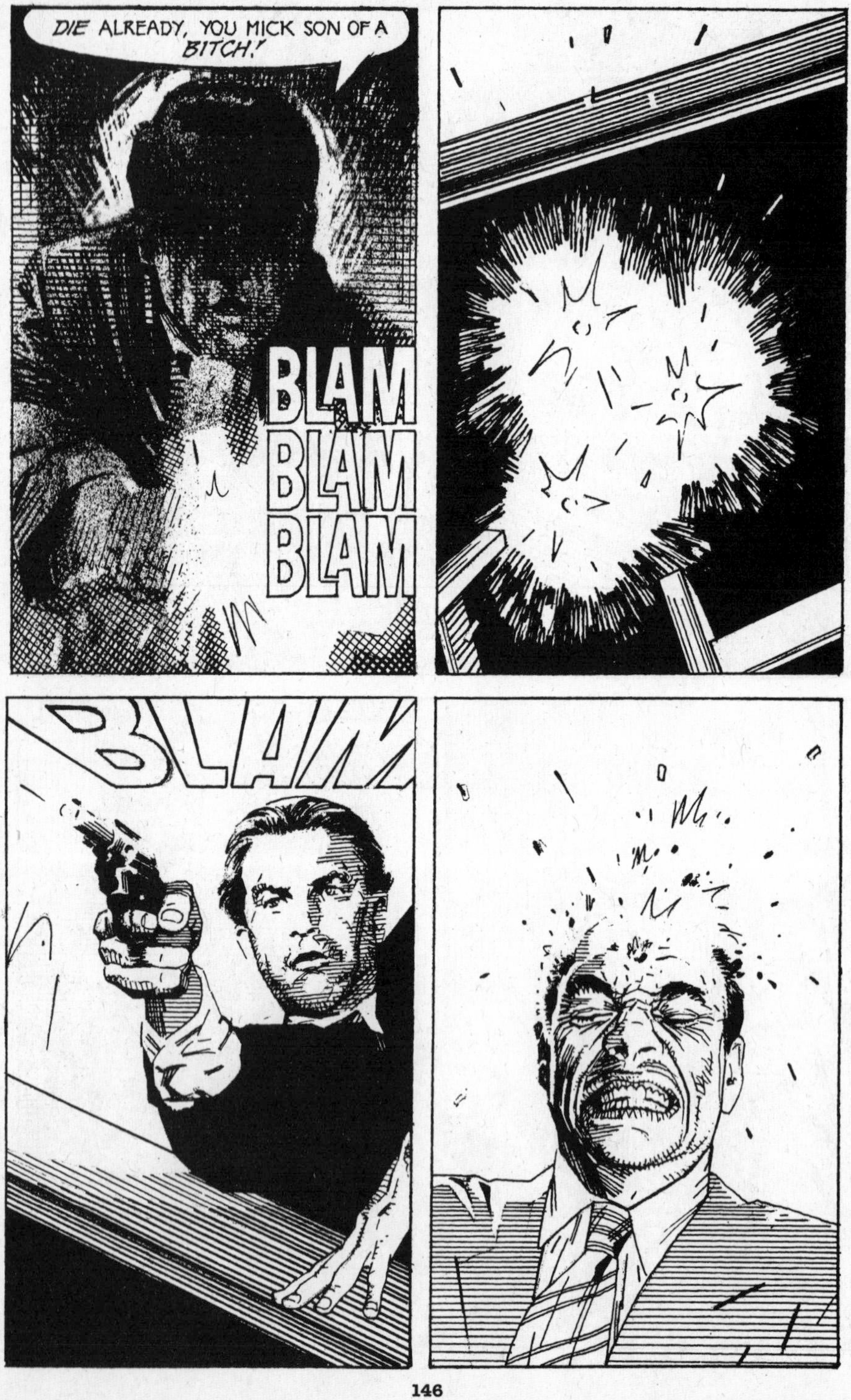
DIE ALREADY, YOU MICK SON OF A BITCH!
BLAM
BLAM
BLAM
BLAM

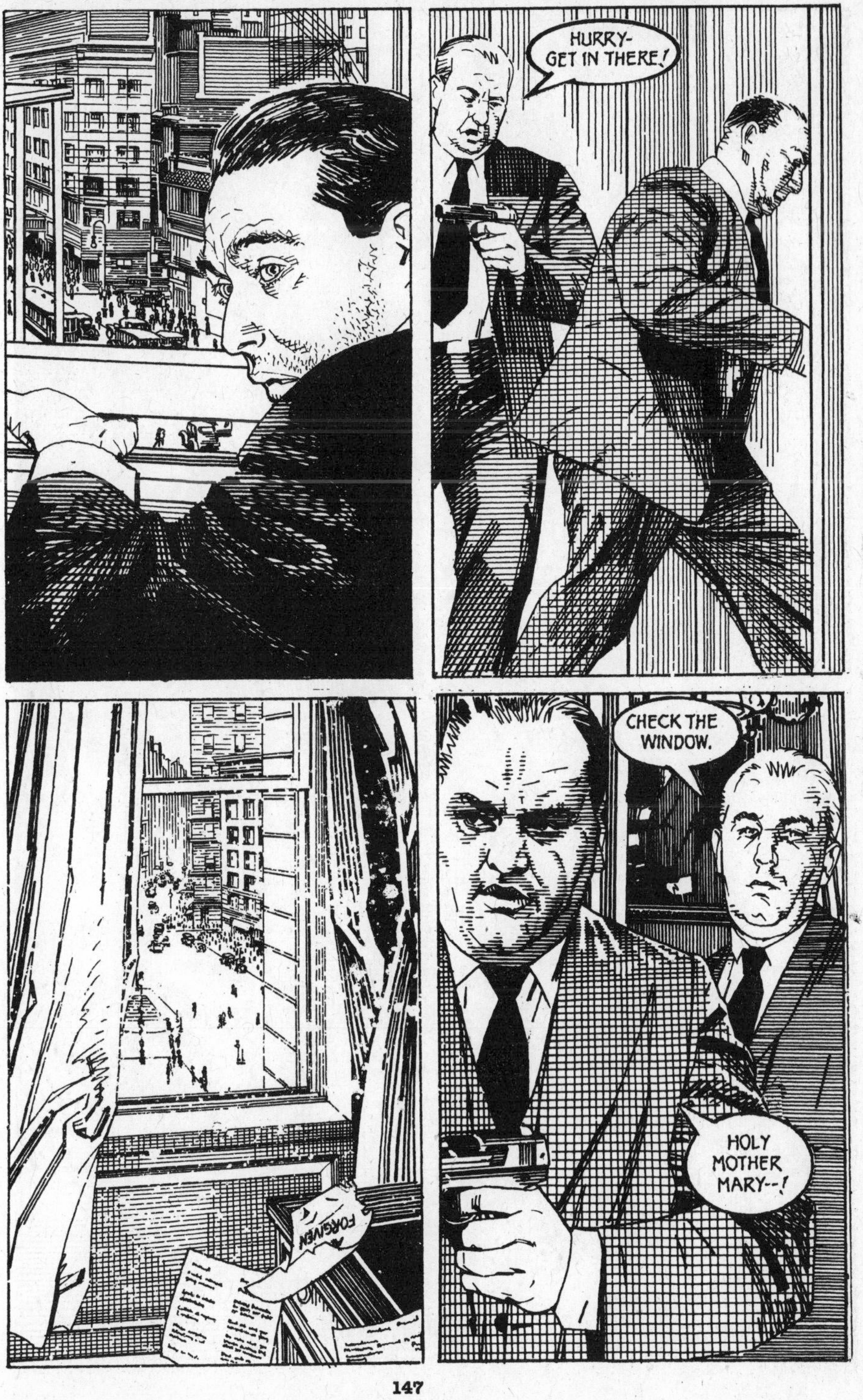
HURRY-
GET IN THERE!
FORGIVEN
CHECK THE WINDOW.
HOLY MOTHER MARY--!

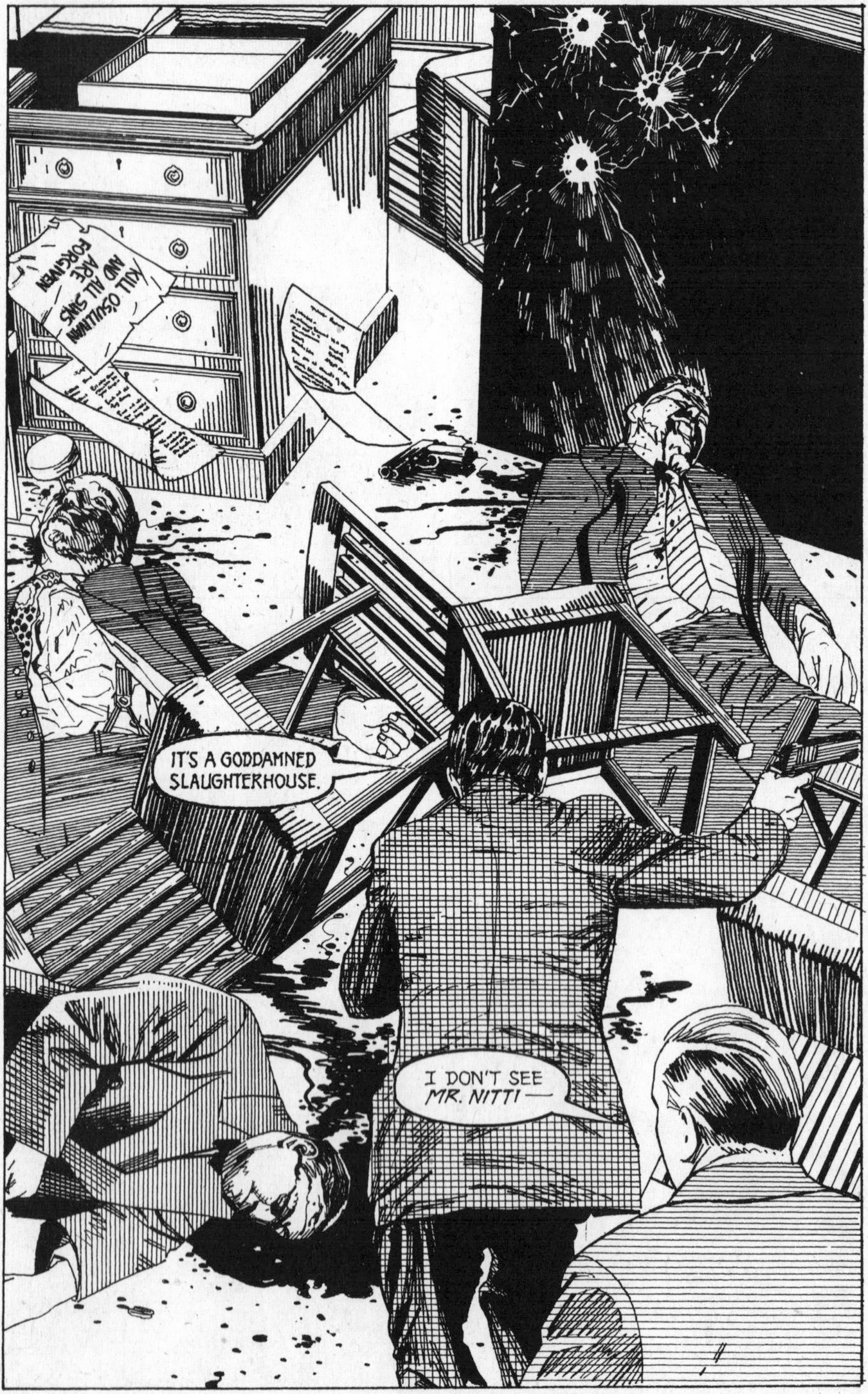
KILL O'SULLIVAN AND ALL SINS ARE FORGIVEN
IT'S A GODDAMNED SLAUGHTERHOUSE.
I DON'T SEE *MR. NITTI* —

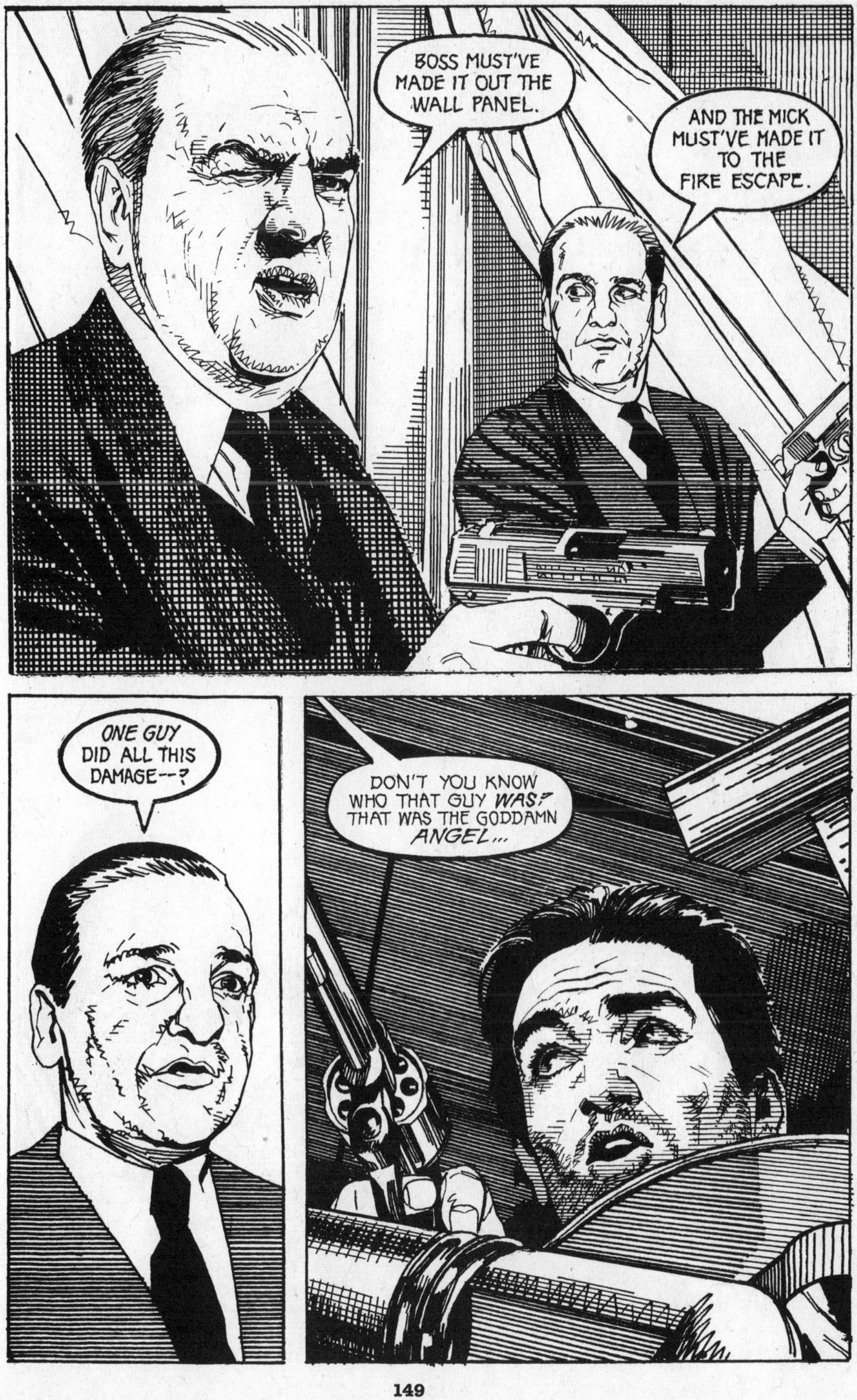
BOSS MUST'VE MADE IT OUT THE WALL PANEL.
AND THE MICK MUST'VE MADE IT TO THE FIRE ESCAPE.
ONE GUY DID ALL THIS DAMAGE--?
DON'T YOU KNOW WHO THAT GUY WAS? THAT WAS THE GODDAMN ANGEL...

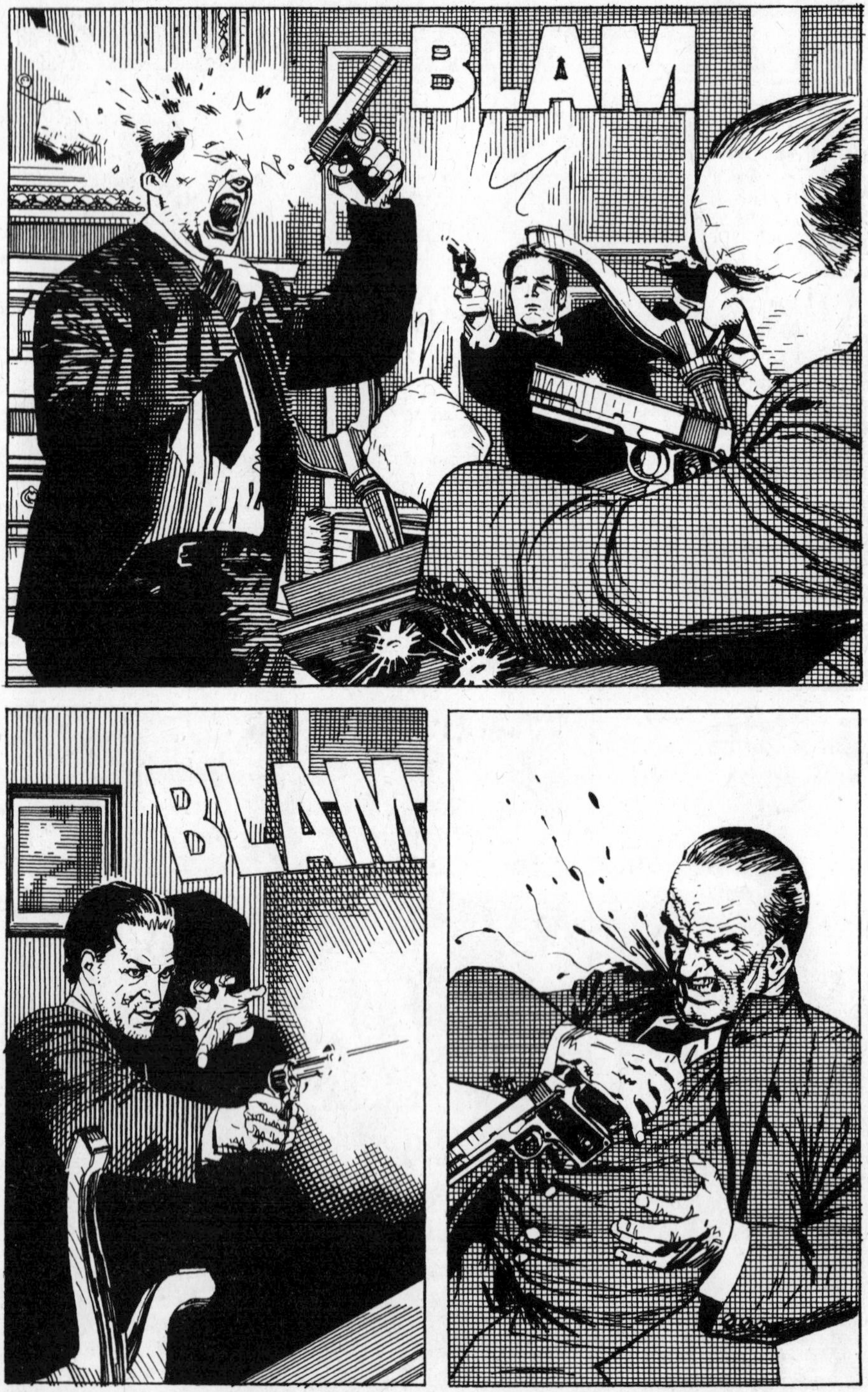
BLAM
BLAM

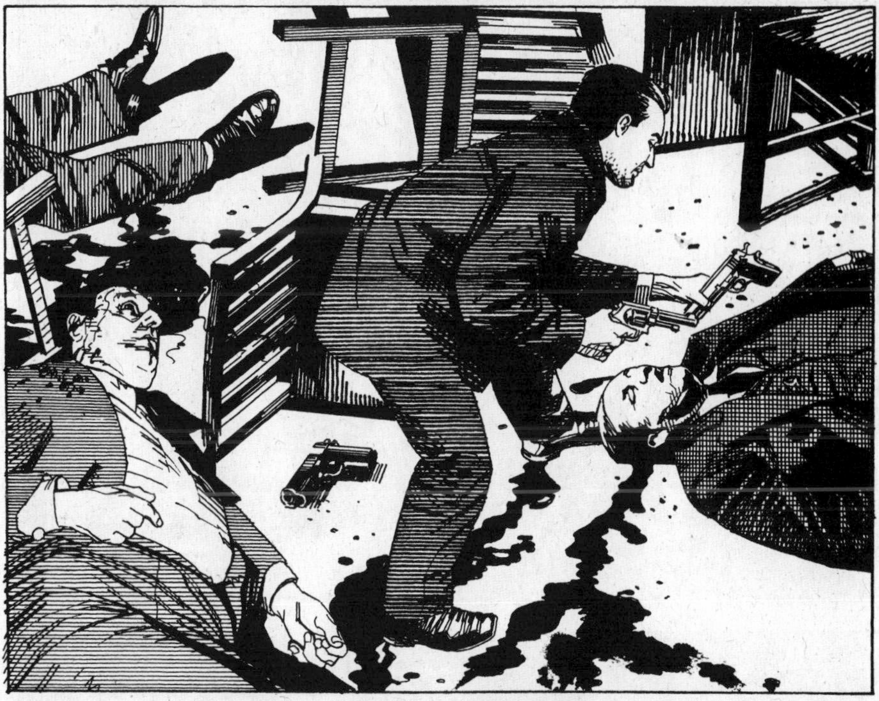

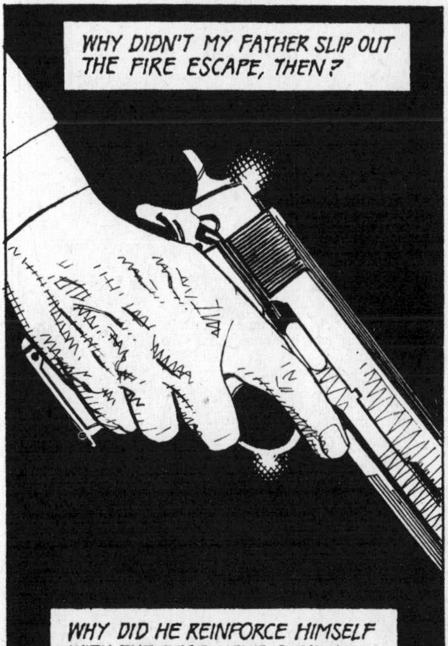
WHY DIDN'T MY FATHER SLIP OUT THE FIRE ESCAPE, THEN?
WHY DID HE REINFORCE HIMSELF WITH THE DEAD MEN'S GUNS AND GO OUT INTO INEVITABLE CARNAGE?

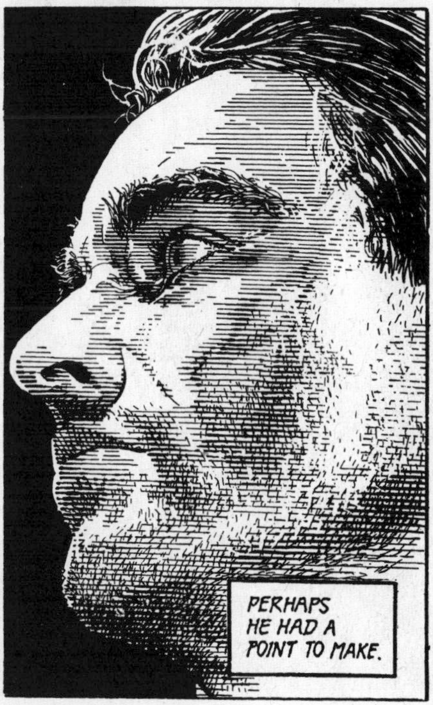
PERHAPS HE HAD A POINT TO MAKE.

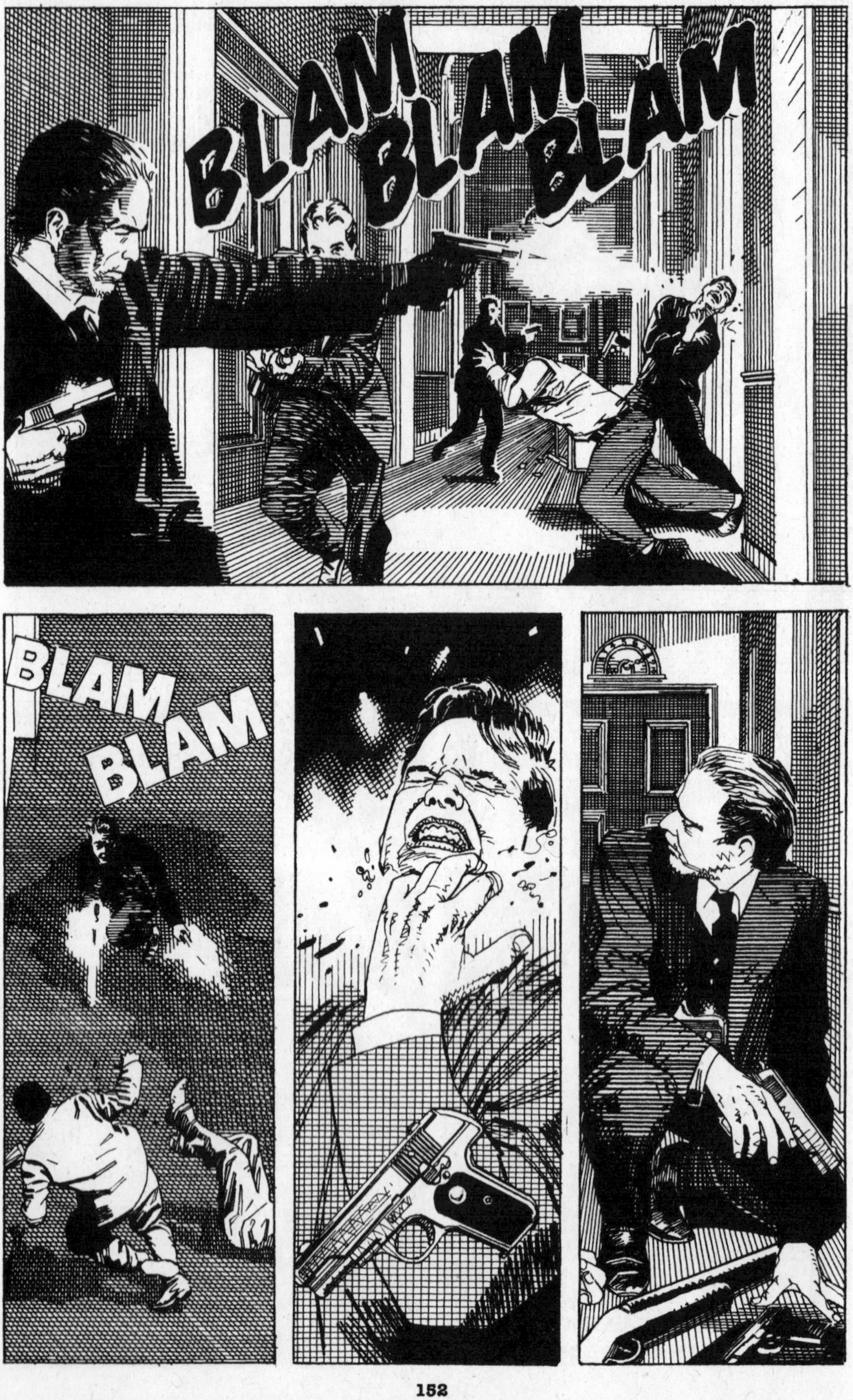
BLAM BLAM BLAM
BLAM BLAM

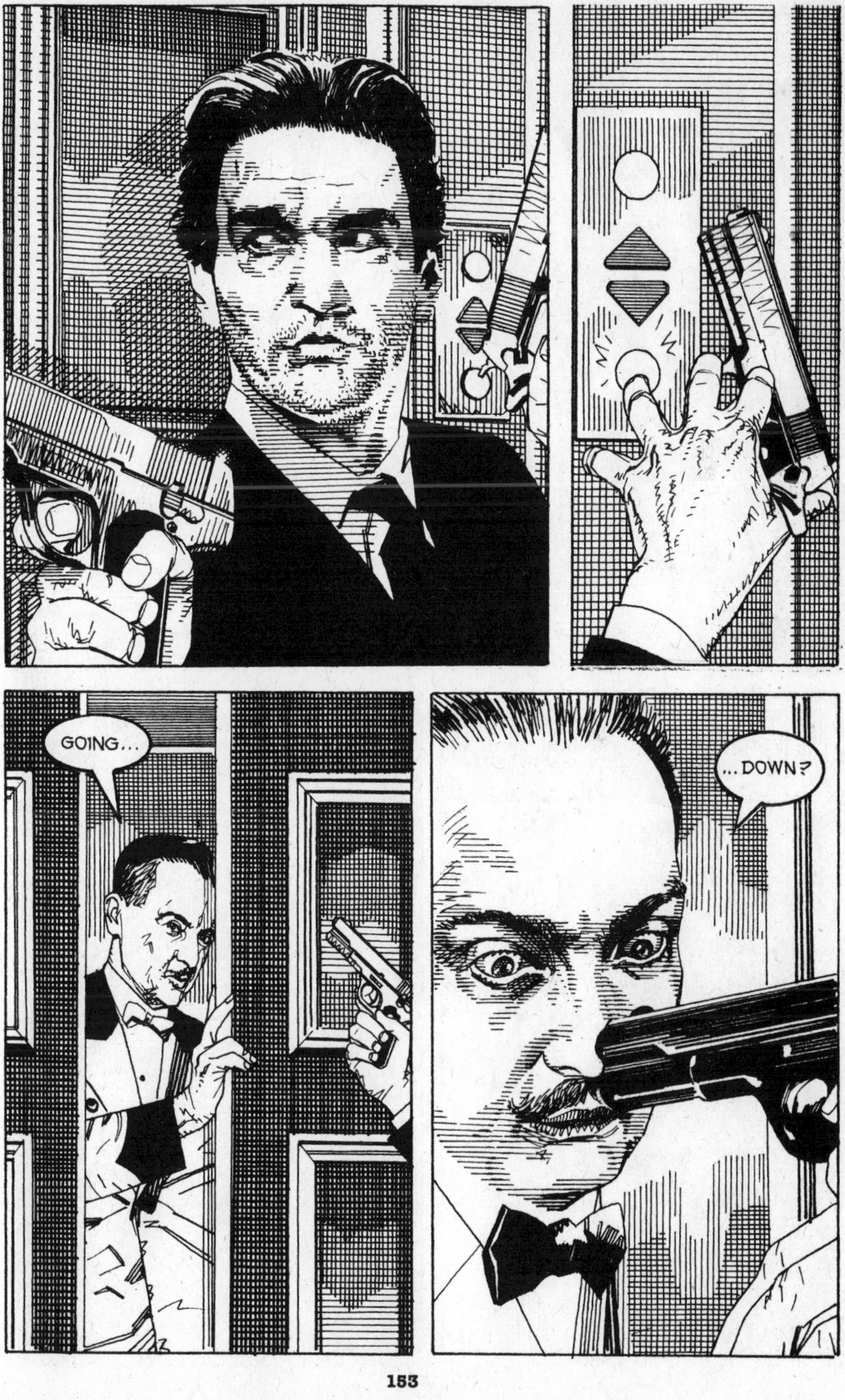
GOING...
...DOWN?

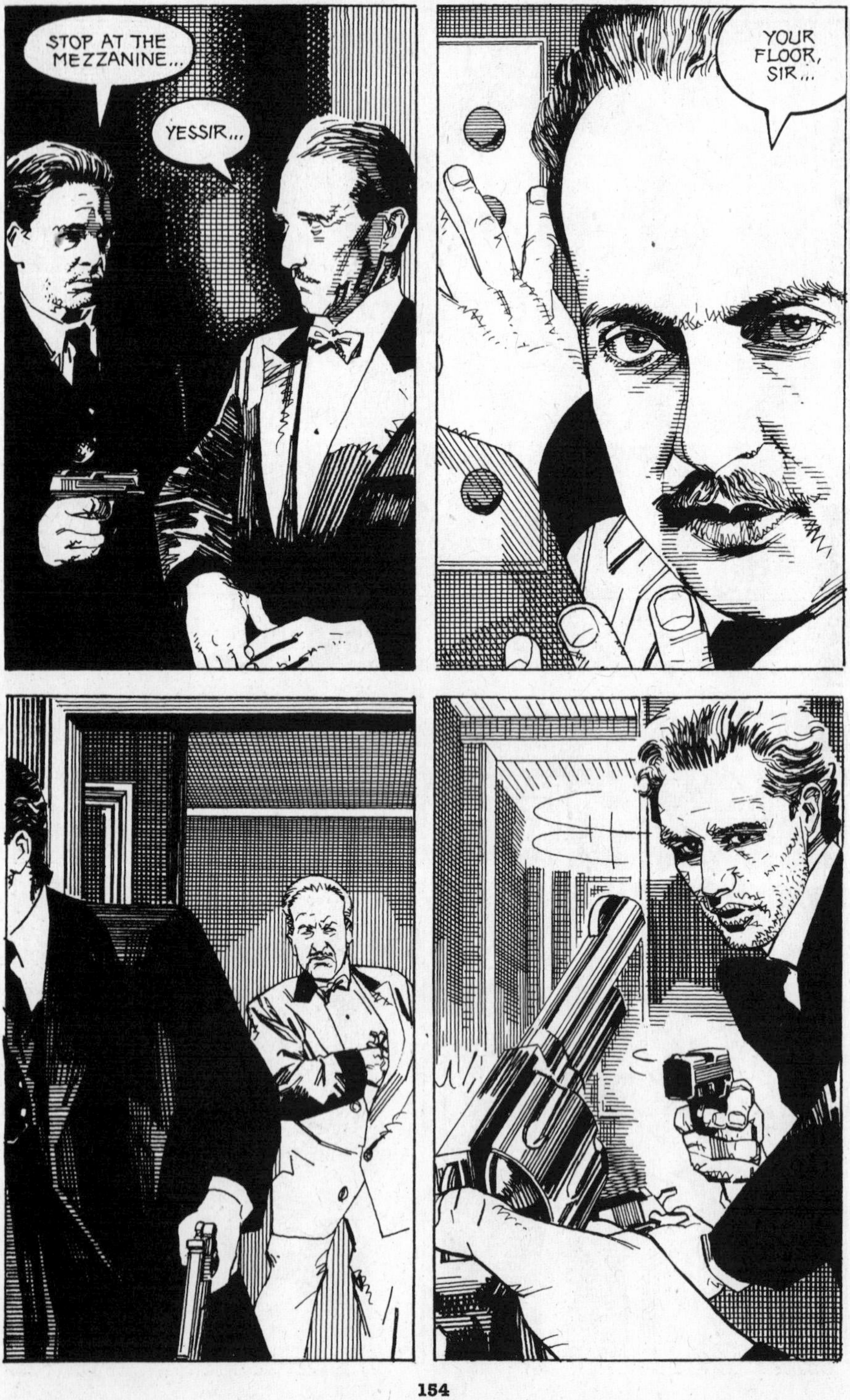
STOP AT THE MEZZANINE...
YESSIR...
YOUR FLOOR, SIR...

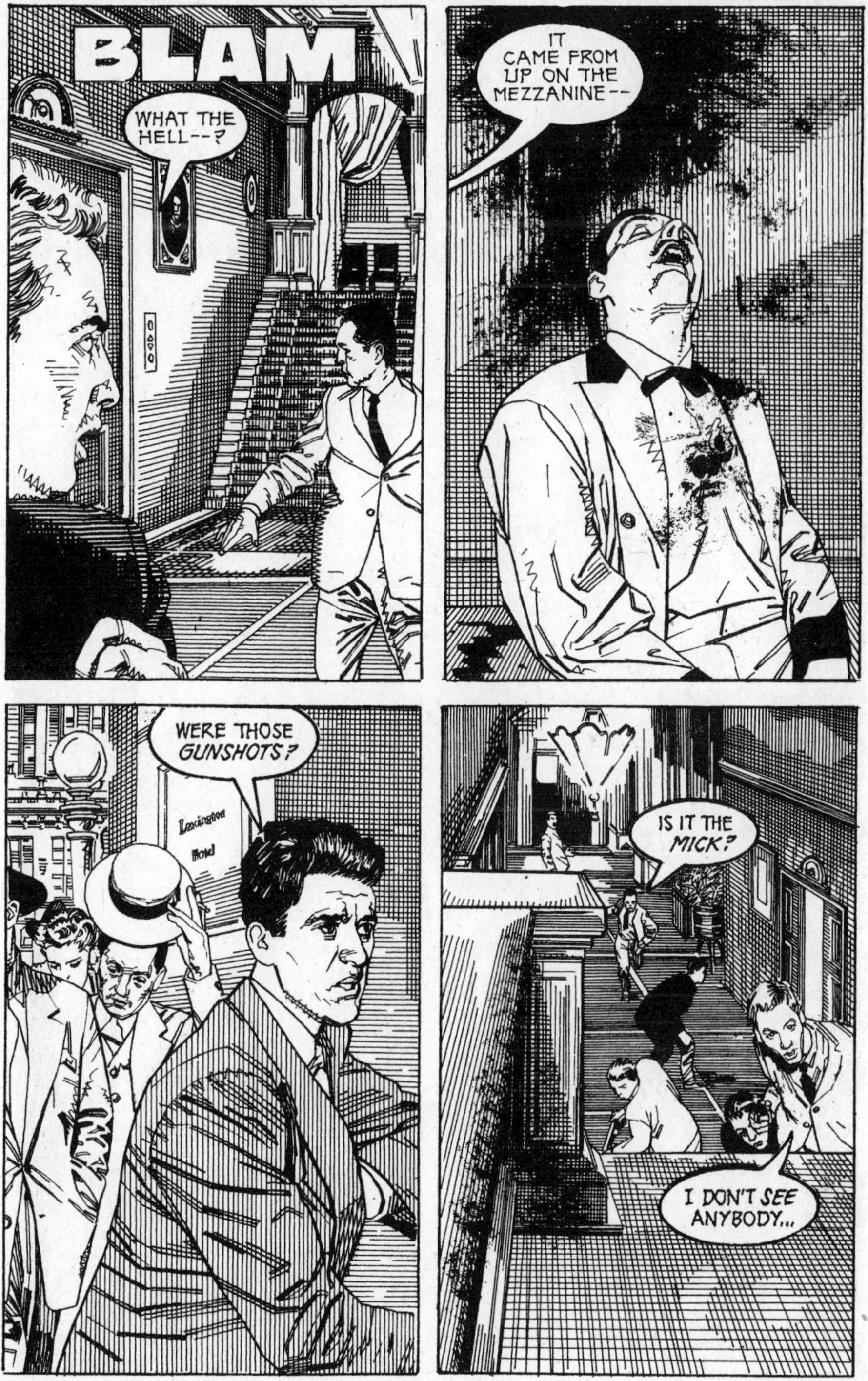
BLAM
WHAT THE HELL--?
IT CAME FROM UP ON THE MEZZANINE--
WERE THOSE GUNSHOTS?
IS IT THE MICK?
I DON'T SEE ANYBODY...

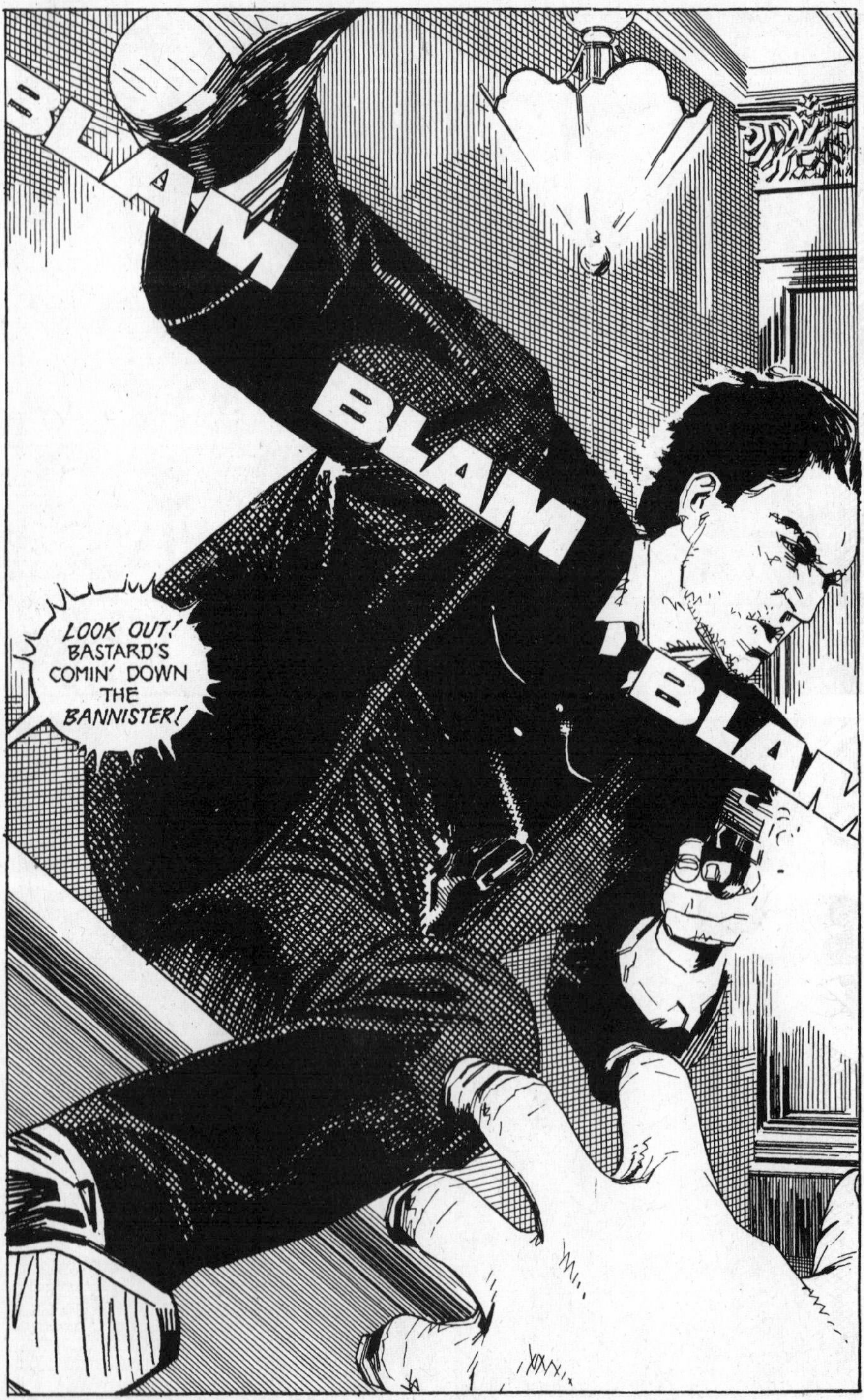
BLAM
BLAM
LOOK OUT! BASTARD'S COMIN' DOWN THE BANNISTER!
BLAM

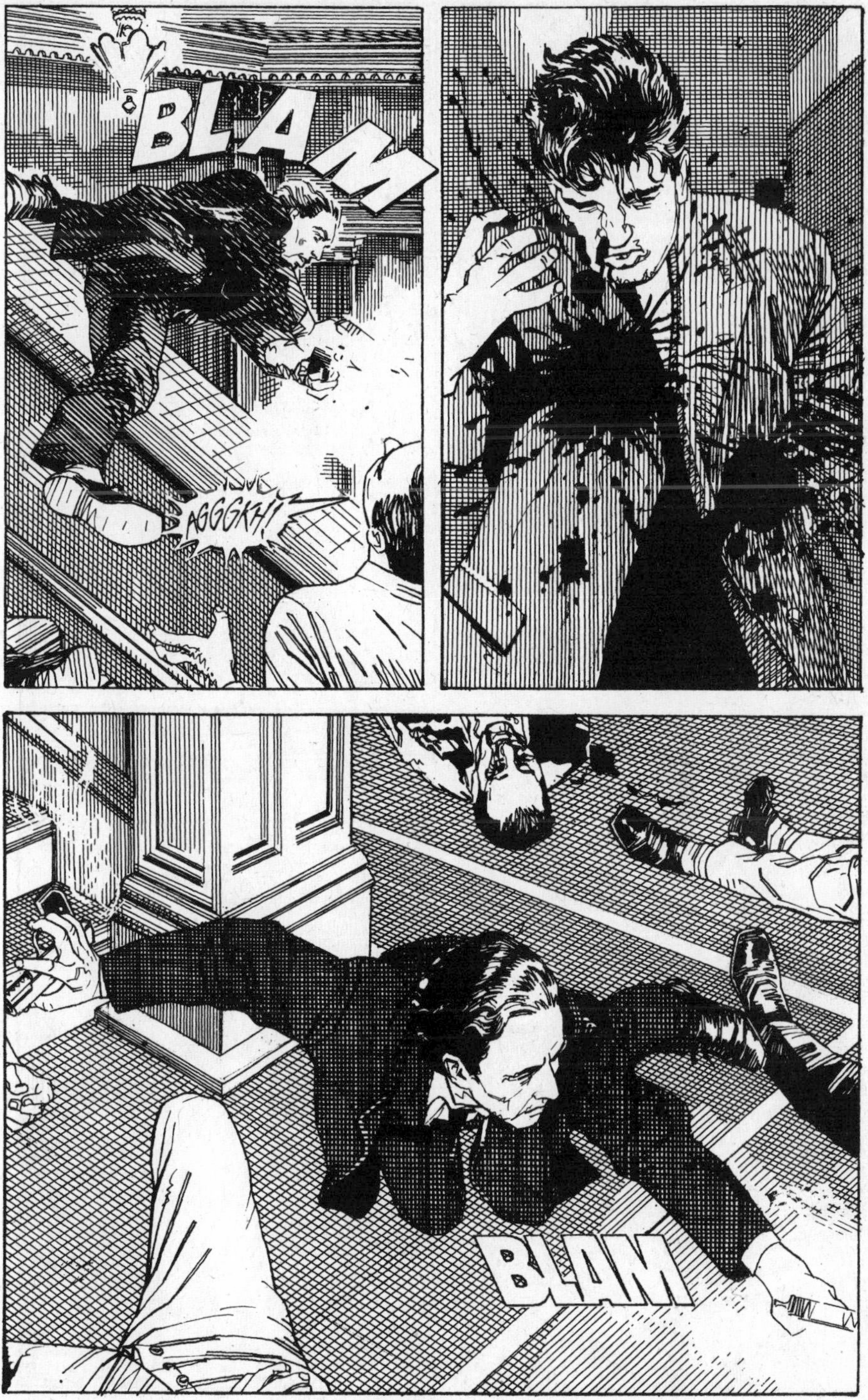
BLAM
AGGGKH!
BLAM

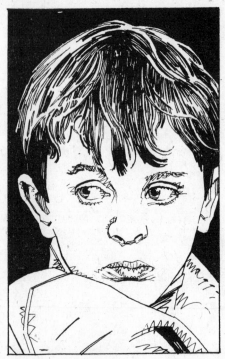

MY FATHER LOOKED CALM EXITING THE FRONT OF THE HOTEL....

SCOOT OVER, SON. NOT TIME FOR YOUR SECOND DRIVING LESSON JUST YET.

I HEARD SHOTS.

WHY DIDN'T YOU LEAVE?

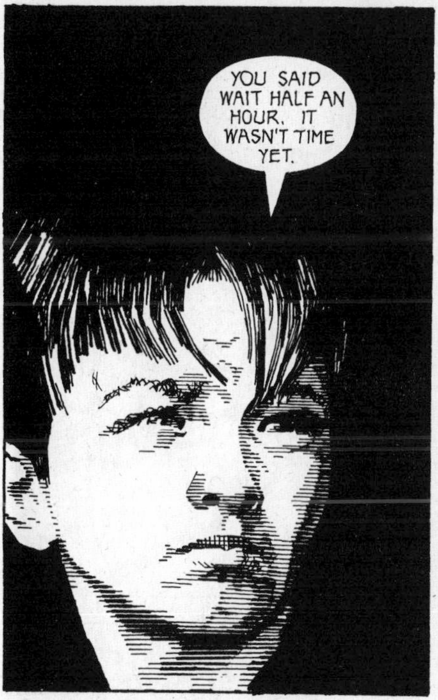
YOU SAID WAIT HALF AN HOUR. IT WASN'T TIME YET.

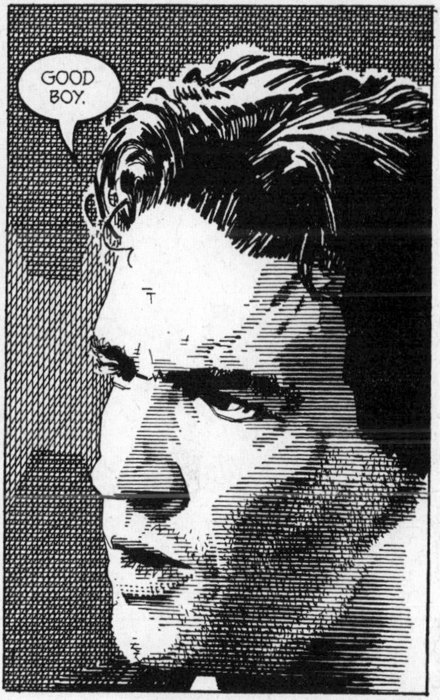
GOOD BOY.

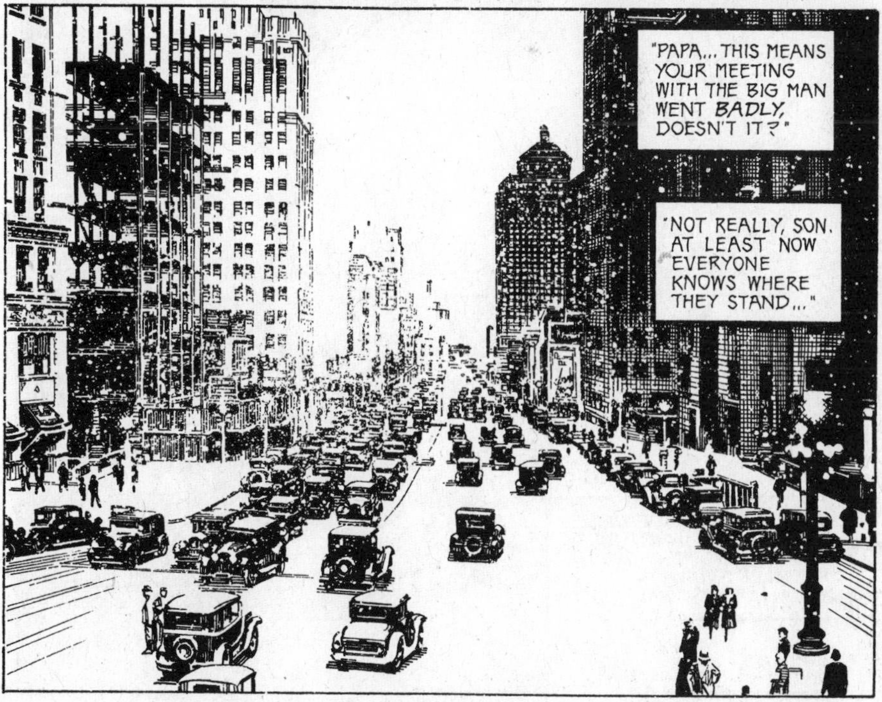
"PAPA... THIS MEANS YOUR MEETING WITH THE BIG MAN WENT *BADLY*, DOESN'T IT?"
"NOT REALLY, SON. AT LEAST NOW EVERYONE KNOWS WHERE THEY STAND..."

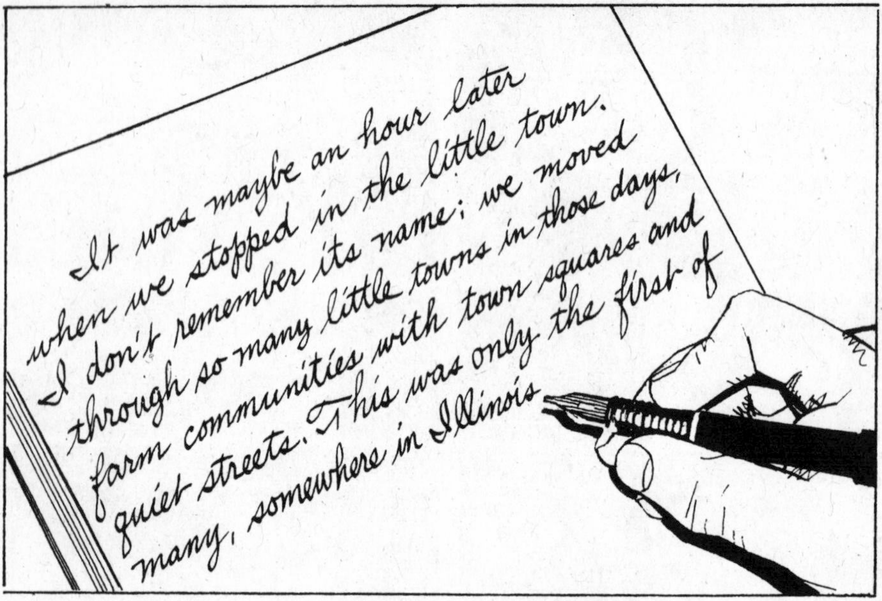
It was maybe an hour later
when we stopped in the little town.
I don't remember its name; we moved
through so many little towns in those days,
farm communities with town squares and
quiet streets. This was only the first of
many, somewhere in Illinois

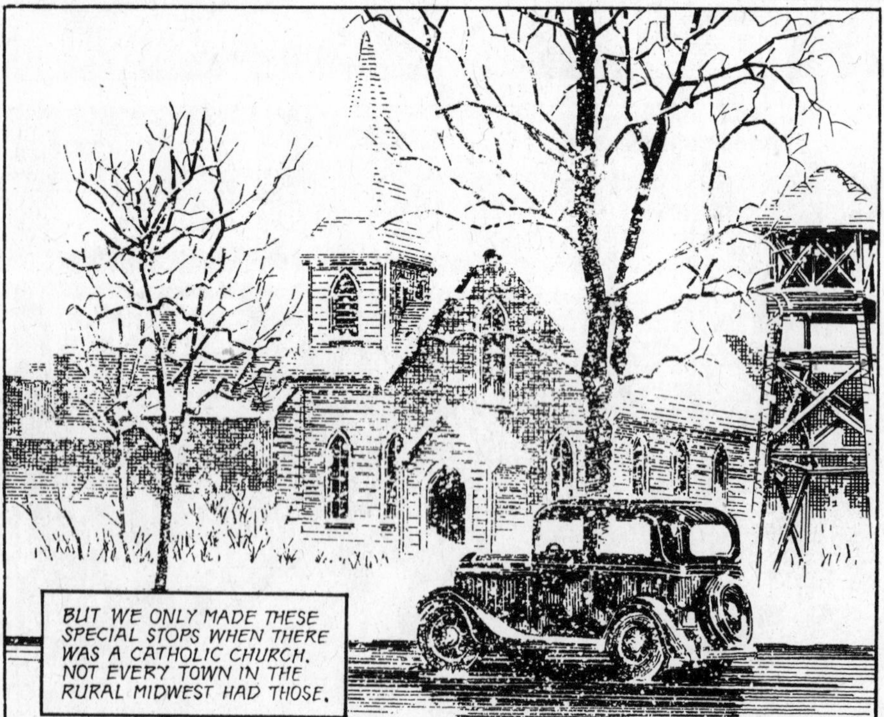
BUT WE ONLY MADE THESE SPECIAL STOPS WHEN THERE WAS A CATHOLIC CHURCH. NOT EVERY TOWN IN THE RURAL MIDWEST HAD THOSE.

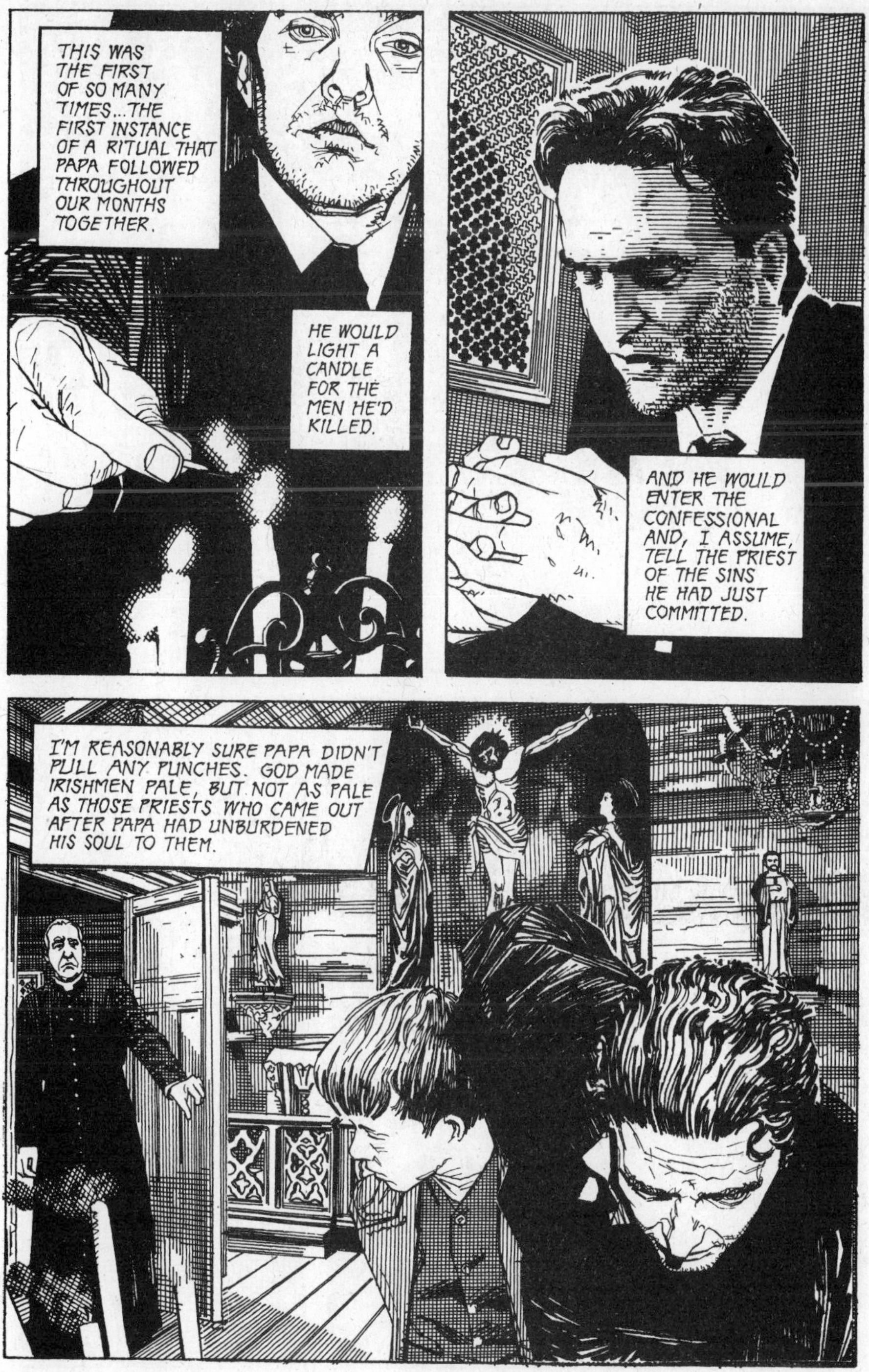
THIS WAS THE FIRST OF SO MANY TIMES... THE FIRST INSTANCE OF A RITUAL THAT PAPA FOLLOWED THROUGHOUT OUR MONTHS TOGETHER.
HE WOULD LIGHT A CANDLE FOR THE MEN HE'D KILLED.
AND HE WOULD ENTER THE CONFESSIONAL AND, I ASSUME, TELL THE PRIEST OF THE SINS HE HAD JUST COMMITTED.
I'M REASONABLY SURE PAPA DIDN'T PULL ANY PUNCHES. GOD MADE IRISHMEN PALE, BUT NOT AS PALE AS THOSE PRIESTS WHO CAME OUT AFTER PAPA HAD UNBURDENED HIS SOUL TO THEM.

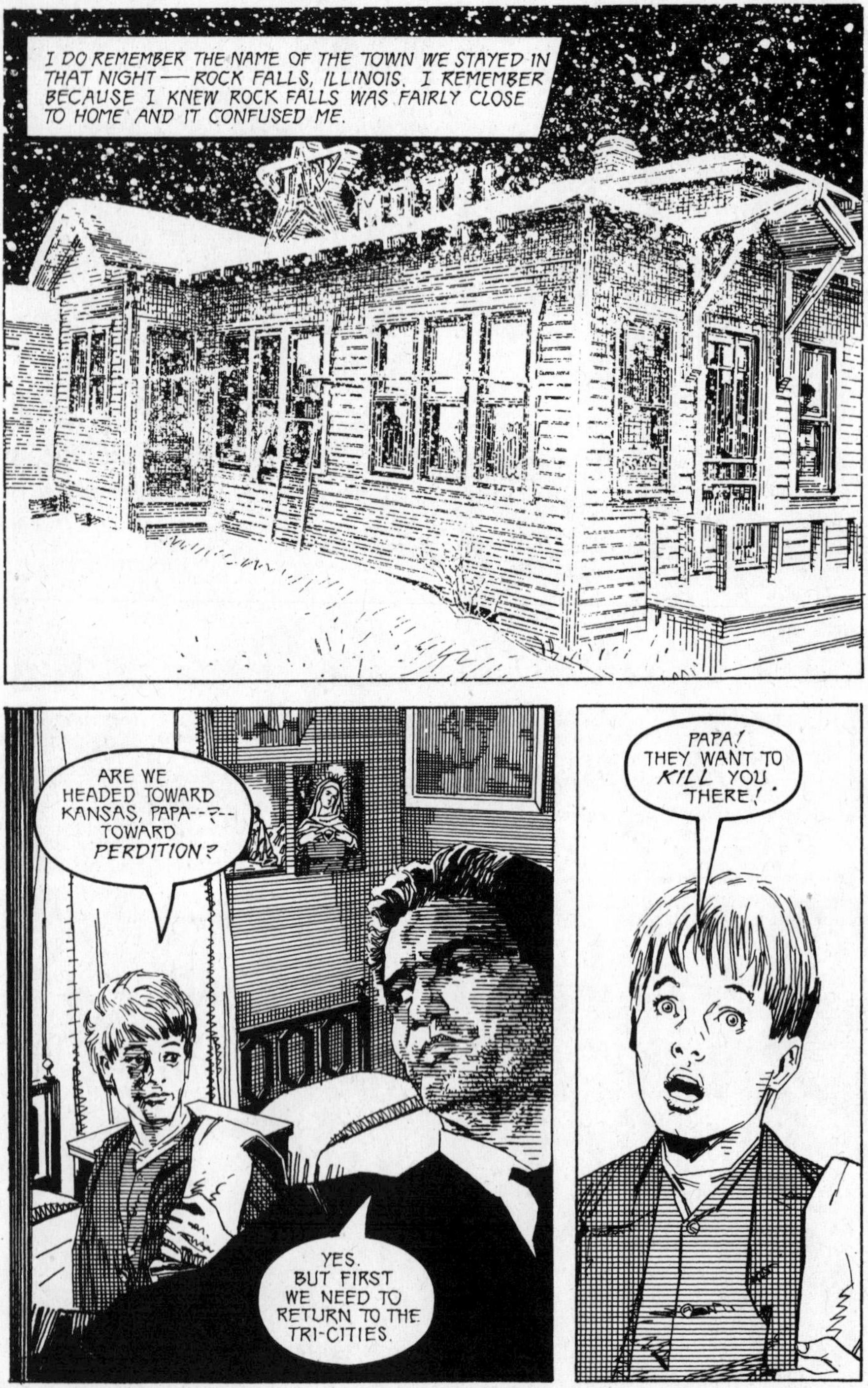
I DO REMEMBER THE NAME OF THE TOWN WE STAYED IN THAT NIGHT — ROCK FALLS, ILLINOIS. I REMEMBER BECAUSE I KNEW ROCK FALLS WAS FAIRLY CLOSE TO HOME AND IT CONFUSED ME.
ARE WE HEADED TOWARD KANSAS, PAPA--?-- TOWARD PERDITION?
YES. BUT FIRST WE NEED TO RETURN TO THE TRI-CITIES.
PAPA! THEY WANT TO KILL YOU THERE!

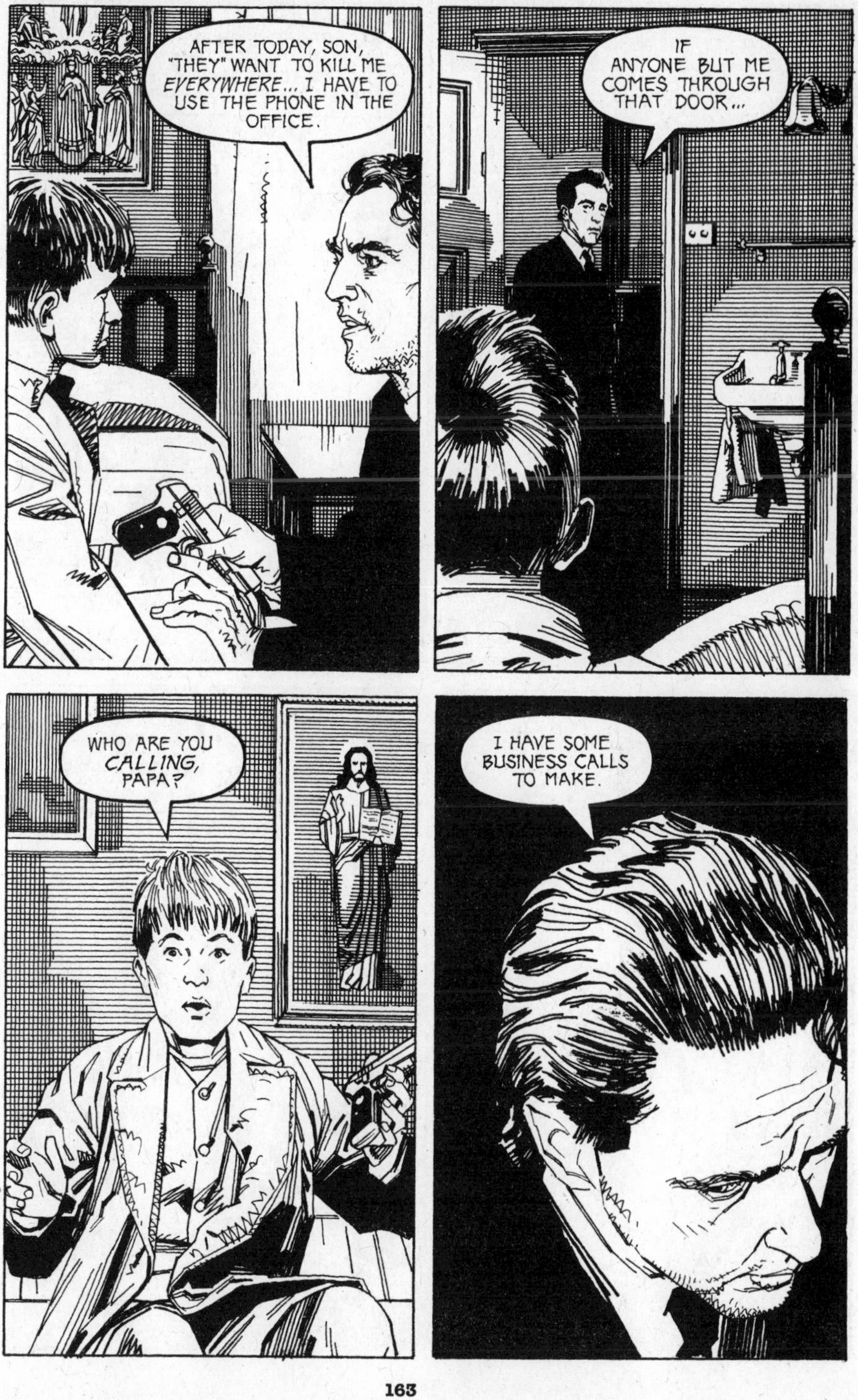
AFTER TODAY, SON, "THEY" WANT TO KILL ME EVERYWHERE... I HAVE TO USE THE PHONE IN THE OFFICE.
IF ANYONE BUT ME COMES THROUGH THAT DOOR...
WHO ARE YOU CALLING, PAPA?
I HAVE SOME BUSINESS CALLS TO MAKE.

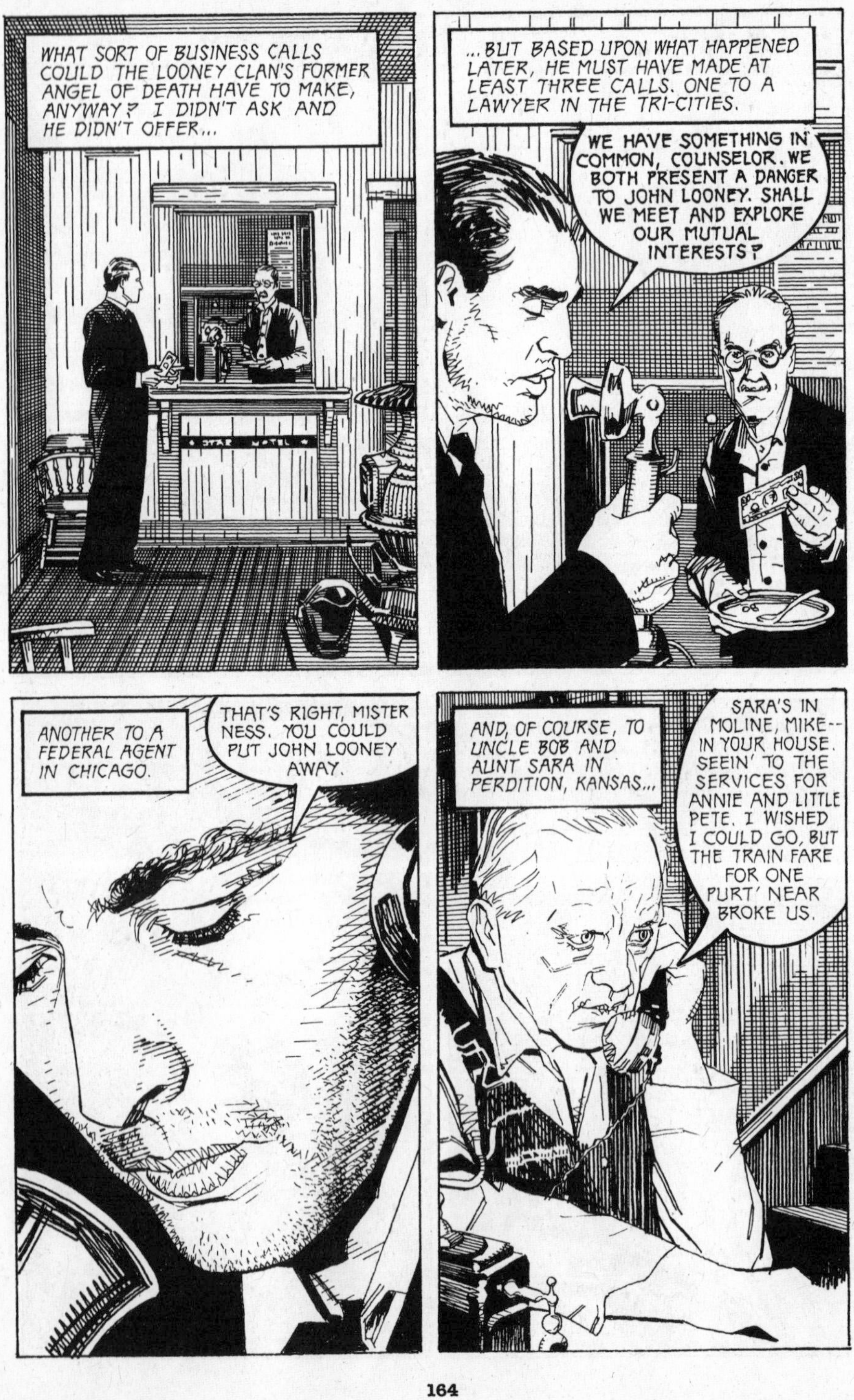

WHAT SORT OF BUSINESS CALLS COULD THE LOONEY CLAN'S FORMER ANGEL OF DEATH HAVE TO MAKE, ANYWAY? I DIDN'T ASK AND HE DIDN'T OFFER...
STAR MOTEL
...BUT BASED UPON WHAT HAPPENED LATER, HE MUST HAVE MADE AT LEAST THREE CALLS. ONE TO A LAWYER IN THE TRI-CITIES.
WE HAVE SOMETHING IN COMMON, COUNSELOR. WE BOTH PRESENT A DANGER TO JOHN LOONEY. SHALL WE MEET AND EXPLORE OUR MUTUAL INTERESTS?
ANOTHER TO A FEDERAL AGENT IN CHICAGO.
THAT'S RIGHT, MISTER NESS. YOU COULD PUT JOHN LOONEY AWAY.
AND, OF COURSE, TO UNCLE BOB AND AUNT SARA IN PERDITION, KANSAS...
SARA'S IN MOLINE, MIKE-- IN YOUR HOUSE. SEEIN' TO THE SERVICES FOR ANNIE AND LITTLE PETE. I WISHED I COULD GO, BUT THE TRAIN FARE FOR ONE PURT' NEAR BROKE US.

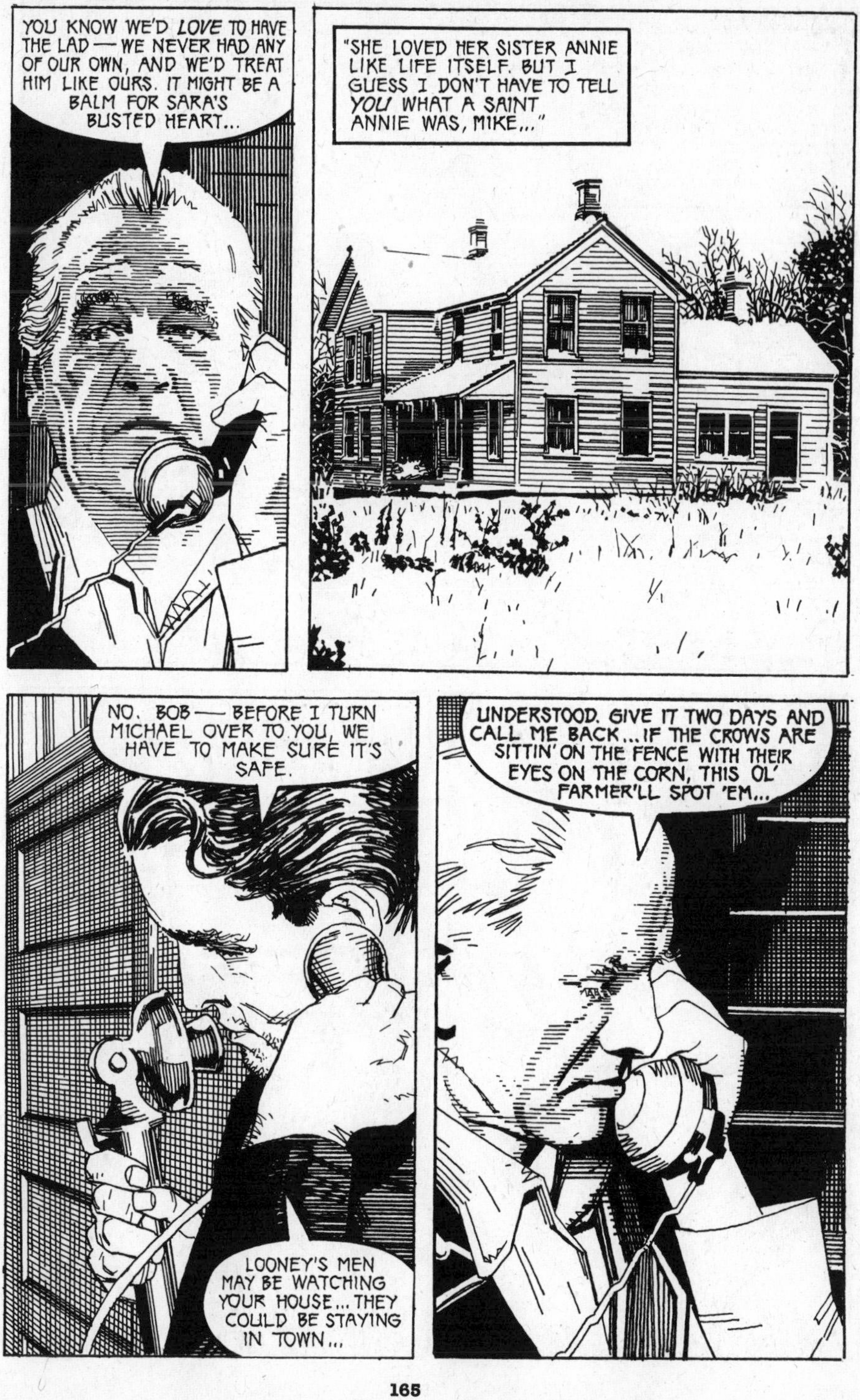
YOU KNOW WE'D *LOVE* TO HAVE THE LAD — WE NEVER HAD ANY OF OUR OWN, AND WE'D TREAT HIM LIKE OURS. IT MIGHT BE A BALM FOR SARA'S BUSTED HEART...
"SHE LOVED HER SISTER ANNIE LIKE LIFE ITSELF. BUT I GUESS I DON'T HAVE TO TELL *YOU* WHAT A SAINT ANNIE WAS, MIKE..."
NO. BOB — BEFORE I TURN MICHAEL OVER TO YOU, WE HAVE TO MAKE SURE IT'S SAFE.
LOONEY'S MEN MAY BE WATCHING YOUR HOUSE... THEY COULD BE STAYING IN TOWN...
UNDERSTOOD. GIVE IT TWO DAYS AND CALL ME BACK... IF THE CROWS ARE SITTIN' ON THE FENCE WITH THEIR EYES ON THE CORN, THIS OL' FARMER'LL SPOT 'EM...

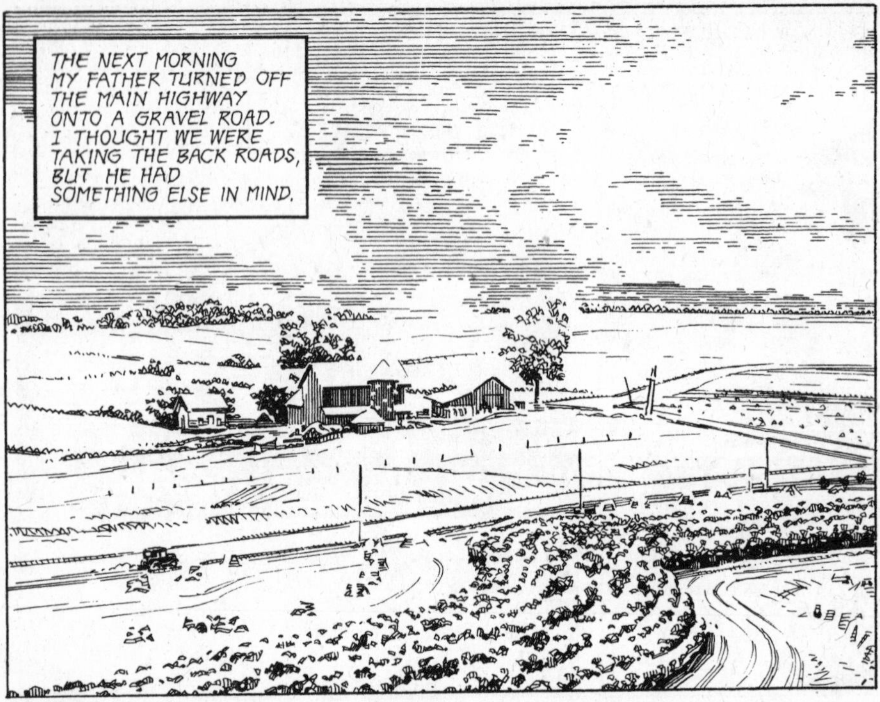
THE NEXT MORNING MY FATHER TURNED OFF THE MAIN HIGHWAY ONTO A GRAVEL ROAD. I THOUGHT WE WERE TAKING THE BACK ROADS, BUT HE HAD SOMETHING ELSE IN MIND.

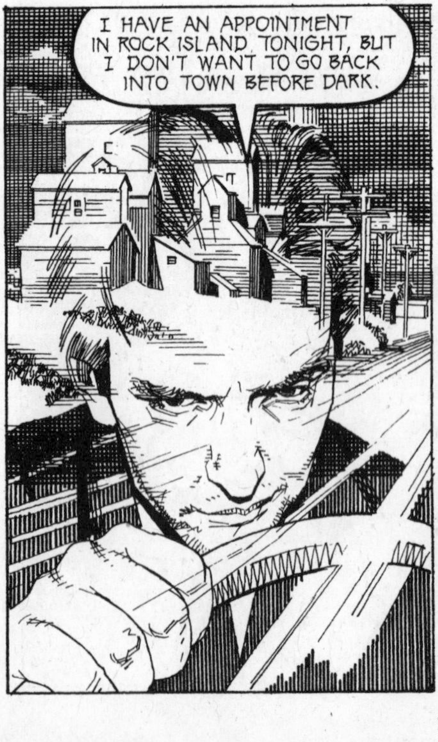
I HAVE AN APPOINTMENT IN ROCK ISLAND TONIGHT, BUT I DON'T WANT TO GO BACK INTO TOWN BEFORE DARK.

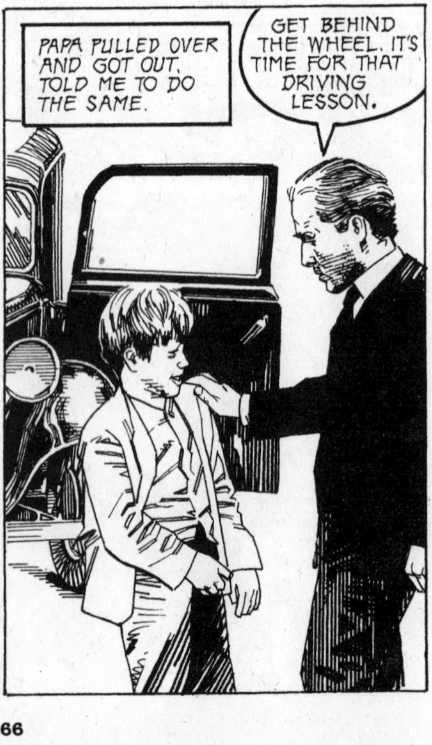
PAPA PULLED OVER AND GOT OUT, TOLD ME TO DO THE SAME.
GET BEHIND THE WHEEL. IT'S TIME FOR THAT DRIVING LESSON.

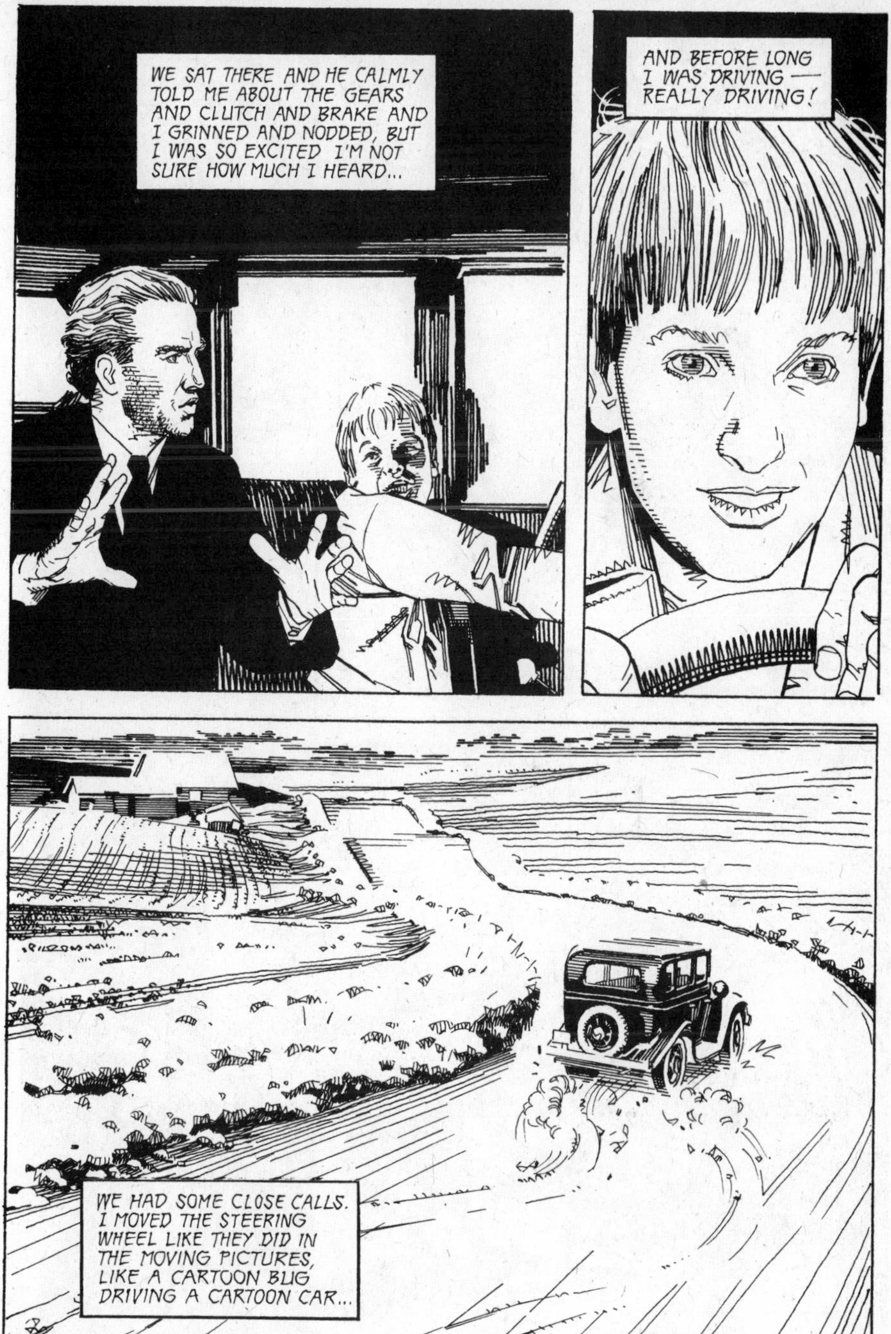
WE SAT THERE AND HE CALMLY TOLD ME ABOUT THE GEARS AND CLUTCH AND BRAKE AND I GRINNED AND NODDED, BUT I WAS SO EXCITED I'M NOT SURE HOW MUCH I HEARD...
AND BEFORE LONG I WAS DRIVING — REALLY DRIVING!
WE HAD SOME CLOSE CALLS. I MOVED THE STEERING WHEEL LIKE THEY DID IN THE MOVING PICTURES, LIKE A CARTOON BUG DRIVING A CARTOON CAR...

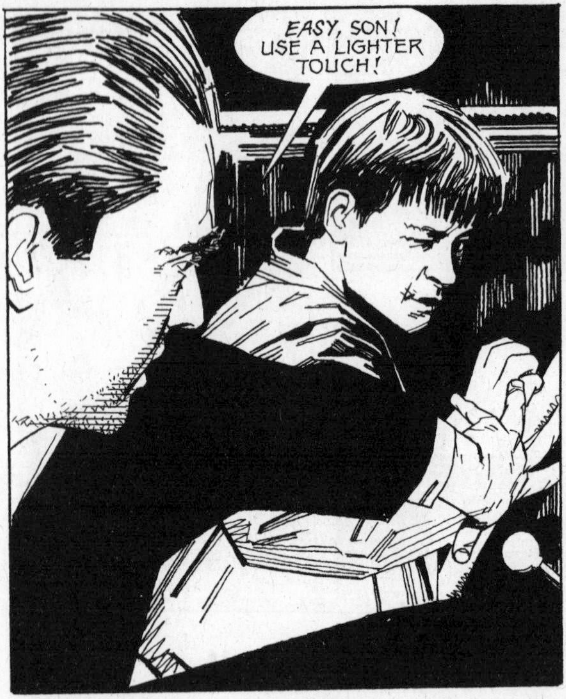
EASY, SON! USE A LIGHTER TOUCH!

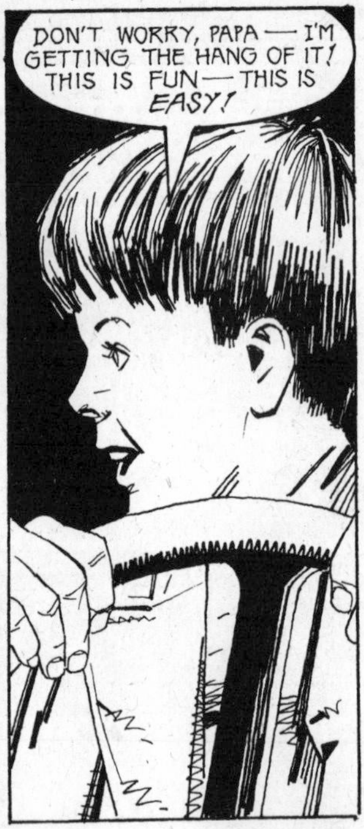
DON'T WORRY, PAPA — I'M GETTING THE HANG OF IT! THIS IS FUN — THIS IS EASY!

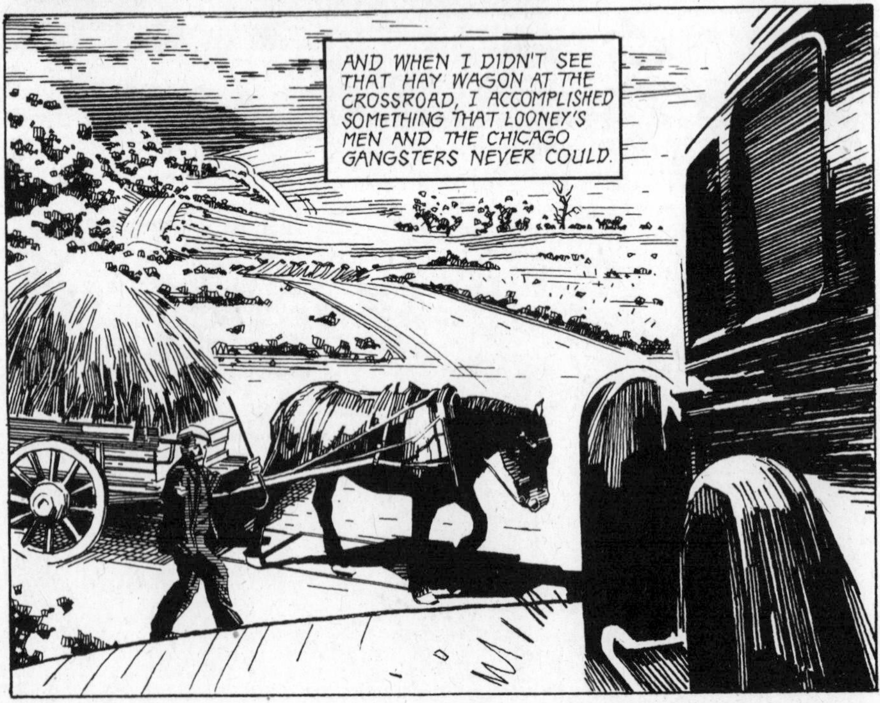
AND WHEN I DIDN'T SEE THAT HAY WAGON AT THE CROSSROAD, I ACCOMPLISHED SOMETHING THAT LOONEY'S MEN AND THE CHICAGO GANGSTERS NEVER COULD.

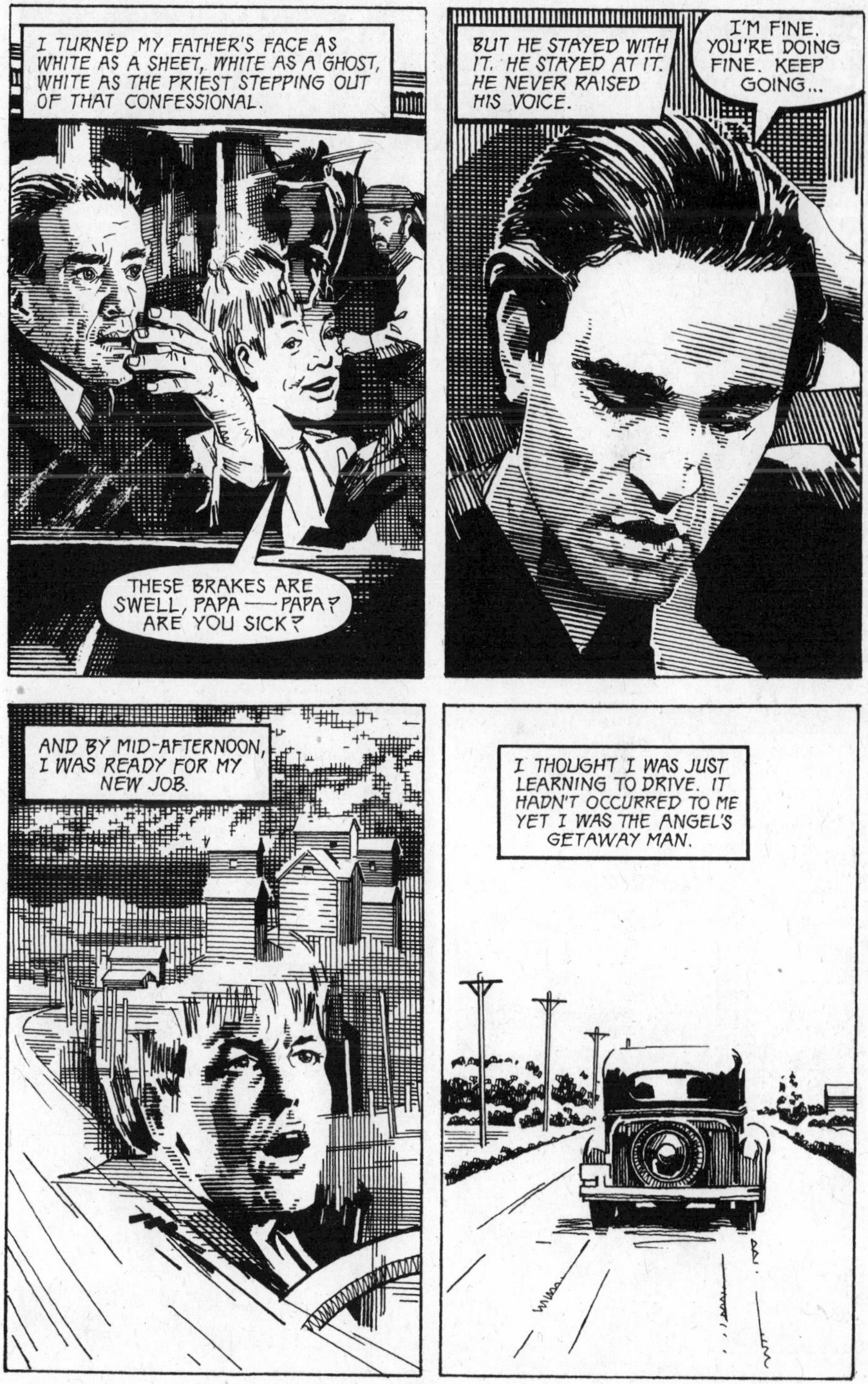
I TURNED MY FATHER'S FACE AS WHITE AS A SHEET, WHITE AS A GHOST, WHITE AS THE PRIEST STEPPING OUT OF THAT CONFESSIONAL.
THESE BRAKES ARE SWELL, PAPA — PAPA? ARE YOU SICK?
BUT HE STAYED WITH IT. HE STAYED AT IT. HE NEVER RAISED HIS VOICE.
I'M FINE. YOU'RE DOING FINE. KEEP GOING...
AND BY MID-AFTERNOON, I WAS READY FOR MY NEW JOB.
I THOUGHT I WAS JUST LEARNING TO DRIVE. IT HADN'T OCCURRED TO ME YET I WAS THE ANGEL'S GETAWAY MAN.

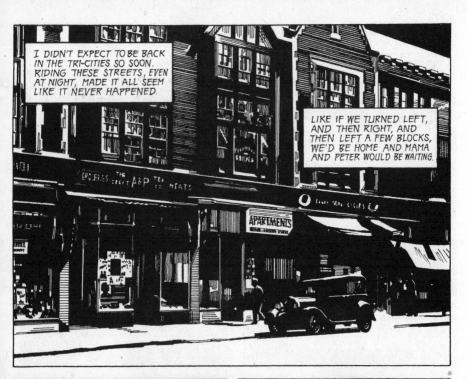

I DIDN'T EXPECT TO BE BACK IN THE TRI-CITIES SO SOON. RIDING THESE STREETS, EVEN AT NIGHT, MADE IT ALL SEEM LIKE IT NEVER HAPPENED.

LIKE IF WE TURNED LEFT, AND THEN RIGHT, AND THEN LEFT A FEW BLOCKS, WE'D BE HOME AND MAMA AND PETER WOULD BE WAITING.

MY FATHER DIDN'T GIVE ME ANY INSTRUCTIONS THIS TIME. HE DIDN'T TELL ME THINGS TWICE.

I SAW HIM GLANCING UP, I THINK AT A WINDOW ON THE SECOND FLOOR OF THE BUILDING. IT WAS THE ONLY LIGHT THAT WAS ON.

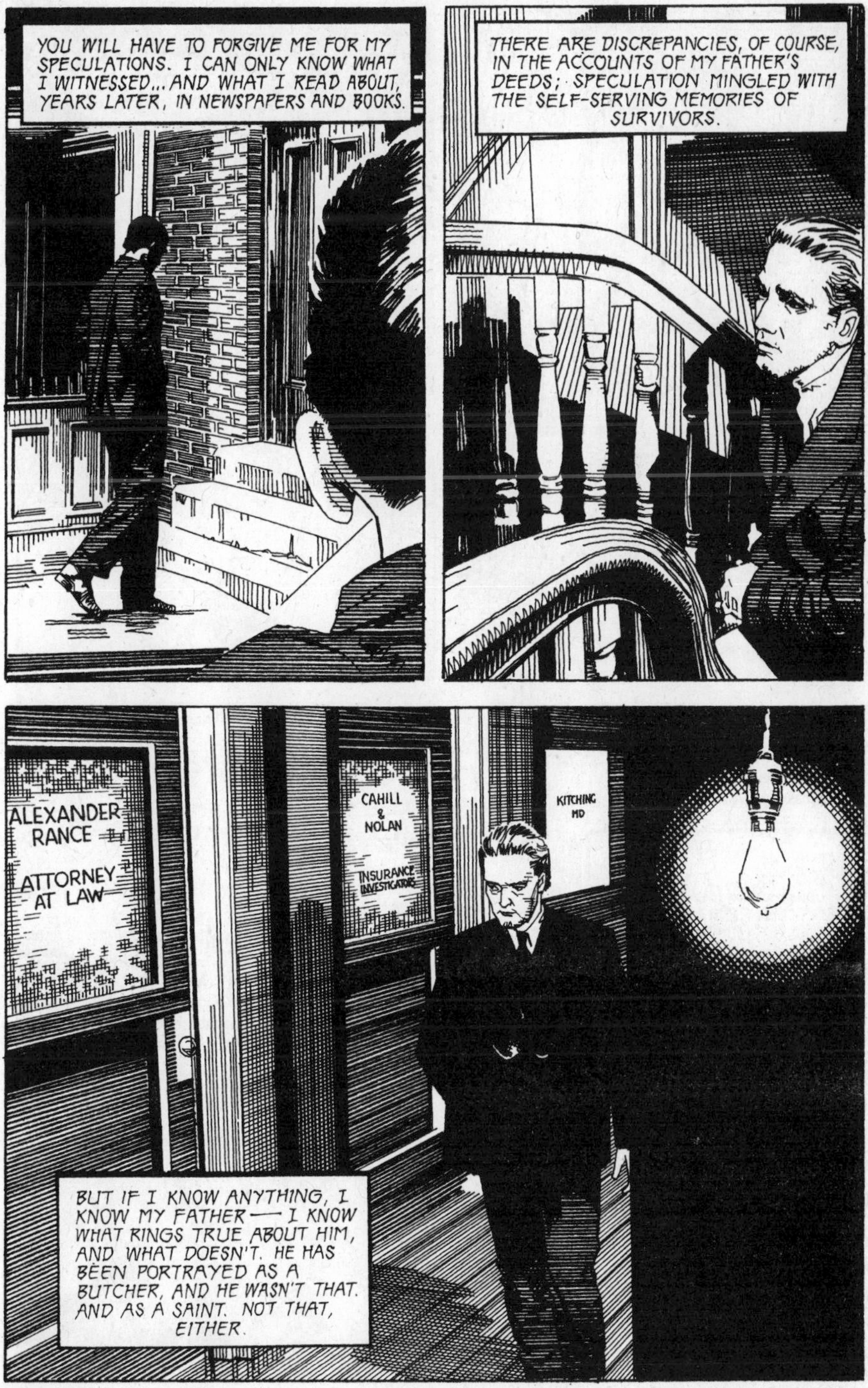
YOU WILL HAVE TO FORGIVE ME FOR MY SPECULATIONS. I CAN ONLY KNOW WHAT I WITNESSED... AND WHAT I READ ABOUT, YEARS LATER, IN NEWSPAPERS AND BOOKS.
THERE ARE DISCREPANCIES, OF COURSE, IN THE ACCOUNTS OF MY FATHER'S DEEDS; SPECULATION MINGLED WITH THE SELF-SERVING MEMORIES OF SURVIVORS.
ALEXANDER RANCE ATTORNEY AT LAW
CAHILL & NOLAN INSURANCE INVESTIGATORS
KITCHING MD
BUT IF I KNOW ANYTHING, I KNOW MY FATHER — I KNOW WHAT RINGS TRUE ABOUT HIM, AND WHAT DOESN'T. HE HAS BEEN PORTRAYED AS A BUTCHER, AND HE WASN'T THAT. AND AS A SAINT. NOT THAT, EITHER.

ALEXAN
RANC

ATTOR

HELLO, RANCE. HOPE YOU DON'T MIND ME STOPPING BY A LITTLE EARLY.

NO! NO. NOT AT ALL.

YOU SEE, IF I CAN FIGURE OUT THAT YOU'VE GOT GABEL'S CANCELED CHECKS, OLD MAN LOONEY CAN DO THE SAME.

ALEXANDER RANCE

ATTORNEY AT LAW

BILL GABEL WAS MY BROTHER-IN-LAW. LOONEY'S SON CONNOR SLAUGHTERED HIM. CAN YOU IMAGINE I'D EVER DO BUSINESS WITH BILL'S MURDERERS?

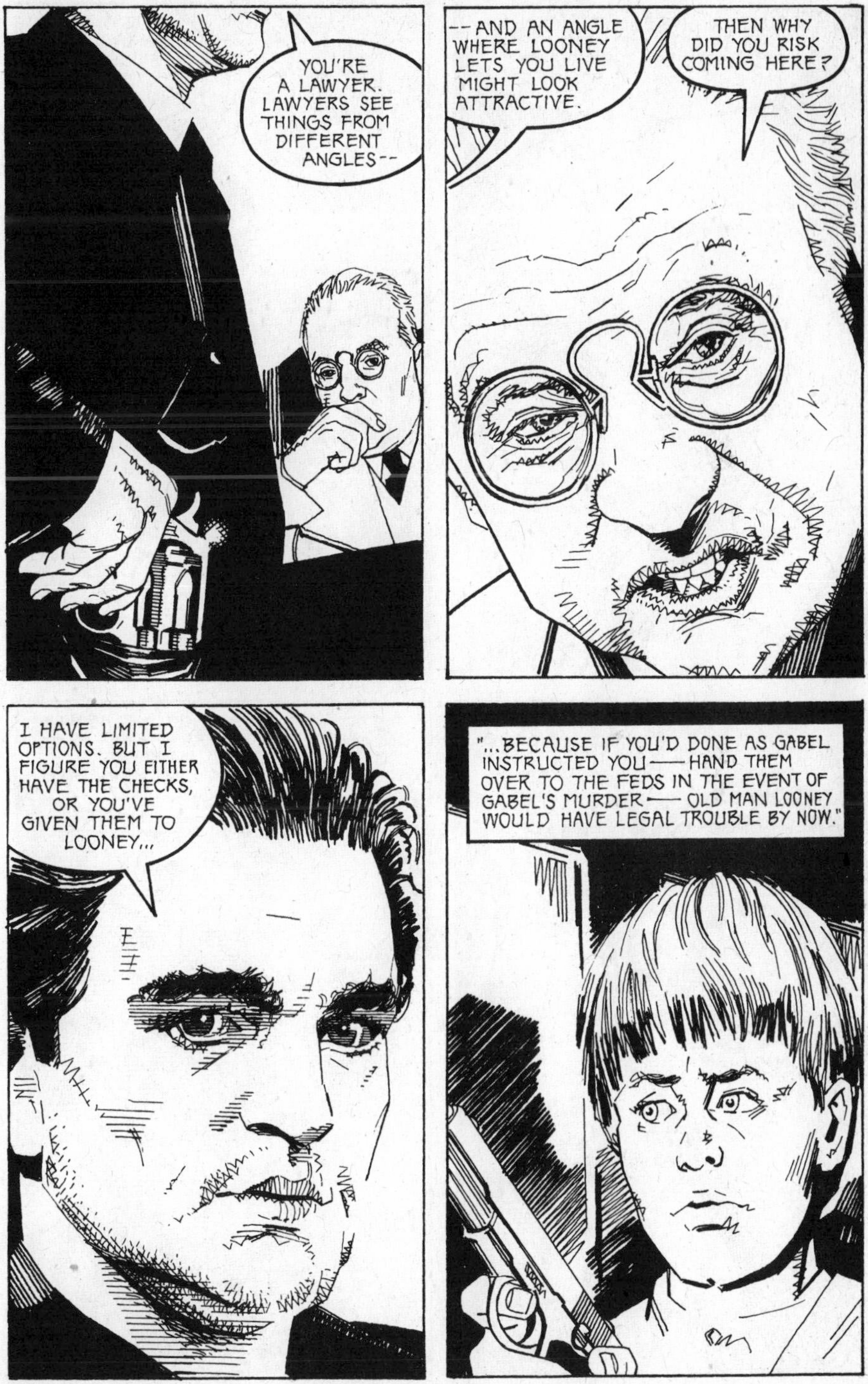
YOU'RE A LAWYER. LAWYERS SEE THINGS FROM DIFFERENT ANGLES--
--AND AN ANGLE WHERE LOONEY LETS YOU LIVE MIGHT LOOK ATTRACTIVE.
THEN WHY DID YOU RISK COMING HERE?
I HAVE LIMITED OPTIONS. BUT I FIGURE YOU EITHER HAVE THE CHECKS, OR YOU'VE GIVEN THEM TO LOONEY...
"...BECAUSE IF YOU'D DONE AS GABEL INSTRUCTED YOU — HAND THEM OVER TO THE FEDS IN THE EVENT OF GABEL'S MURDER — OLD MAN LOONEY WOULD HAVE LEGAL TROUBLE BY NOW."

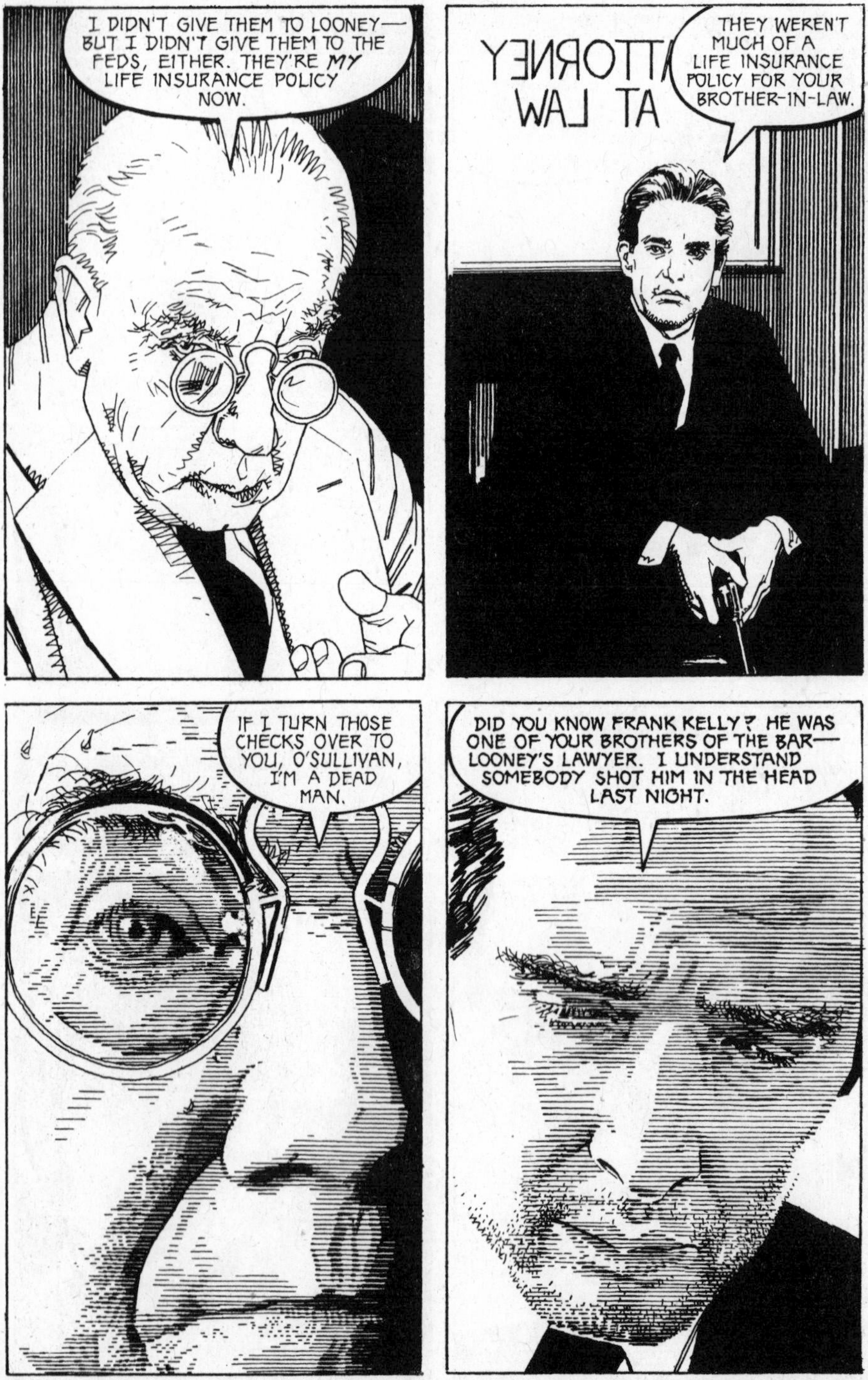
I DIDN'T GIVE THEM TO LOONEY— BUT I DIDN'T GIVE THEM TO THE FEDS, EITHER. THEY'RE *MY* LIFE INSURANCE POLICY NOW.
ATTORNEY AT LAW
THEY WEREN'T MUCH OF A LIFE INSURANCE POLICY FOR YOUR BROTHER-IN-LAW.
IF I TURN THOSE CHECKS OVER TO YOU, O'SULLIVAN, I'M A DEAD MAN.
DID YOU KNOW FRANK KELLY? HE WAS ONE OF YOUR BROTHERS OF THE BAR— LOONEY'S LAWYER. I UNDERSTAND SOMEBODY SHOT HIM IN THE HEAD LAST NIGHT.

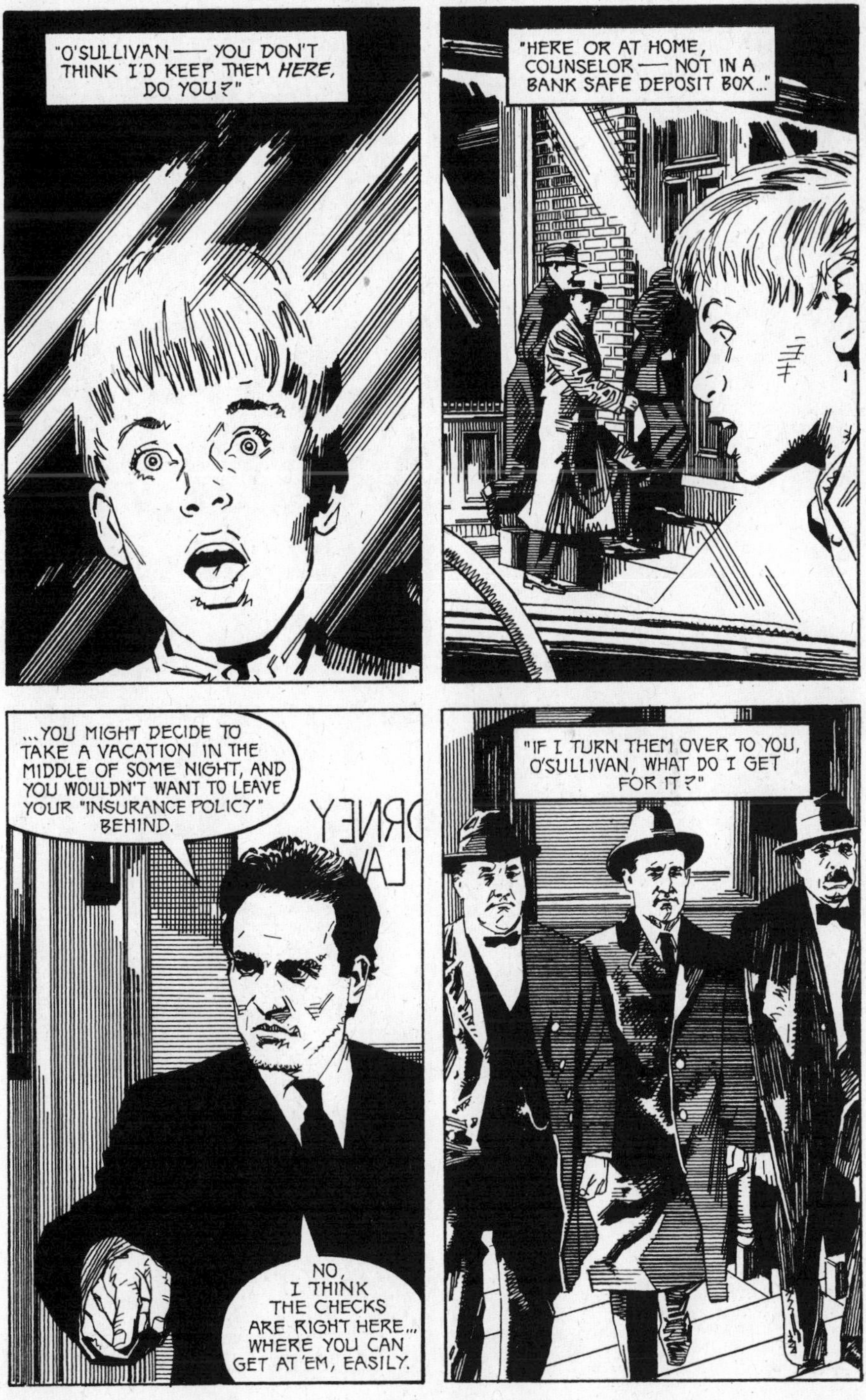
"O'SULLIVAN — YOU DON'T THINK I'D KEEP THEM *HERE*, DO YOU?"
"HERE OR AT HOME, COUNSELOR — NOT IN A BANK SAFE DEPOSIT BOX..."
...YOU MIGHT DECIDE TO TAKE A VACATION IN THE MIDDLE OF SOME NIGHT, AND YOU WOULDN'T WANT TO LEAVE YOUR "INSURANCE POLICY" BEHIND.
NO, I THINK THE CHECKS ARE RIGHT HERE... WHERE YOU CAN GET AT 'EM, EASILY.
"IF I TURN THEM OVER TO YOU, O'SULLIVAN, WHAT DO I GET FOR IT?"

I MEAN, SUPPOSING OLD MAN LOONEY HAD OFFERED TO LET ME TAKE FRANK KELLY'S POSITION...DO YOU KNOW HOW LUCRATIVE THAT COULD BE, BEING LOONEY'S ATTORNEY?

"OF COURSE, THERE ARE THOSE WHO SAY ALL THE VIOLENCE OF THE PAST SEVERAL DAYS IS GOING TO BRING DOWN THE LAW ON LOONEY. THE PUBLIC IS OUTRAGED, FEARFUL..."

CAHILL & NOLAN

INSURAN

SO THIS MAY NOT BE THE POINT IN TIME A PERSON LIKE MYSELF MIGHT WANT TO ALIGN HIMSELF WITH THE LOONEYS.

ALEXANDER RANCE

ATTORNEY AT LAW

I COULD REPRESENT YOU, MR. O'SULLIVAN— IF YOU COULD PRESENT ME WITH A RETAINER OF, SAY, TEN THOUSAND DOLLARS, I MIGHT BE ABLE TO..."VACATION" SOMEWHERE UNTIL THE LAW HAD TAKEN CARE OF MR. LOONEY...

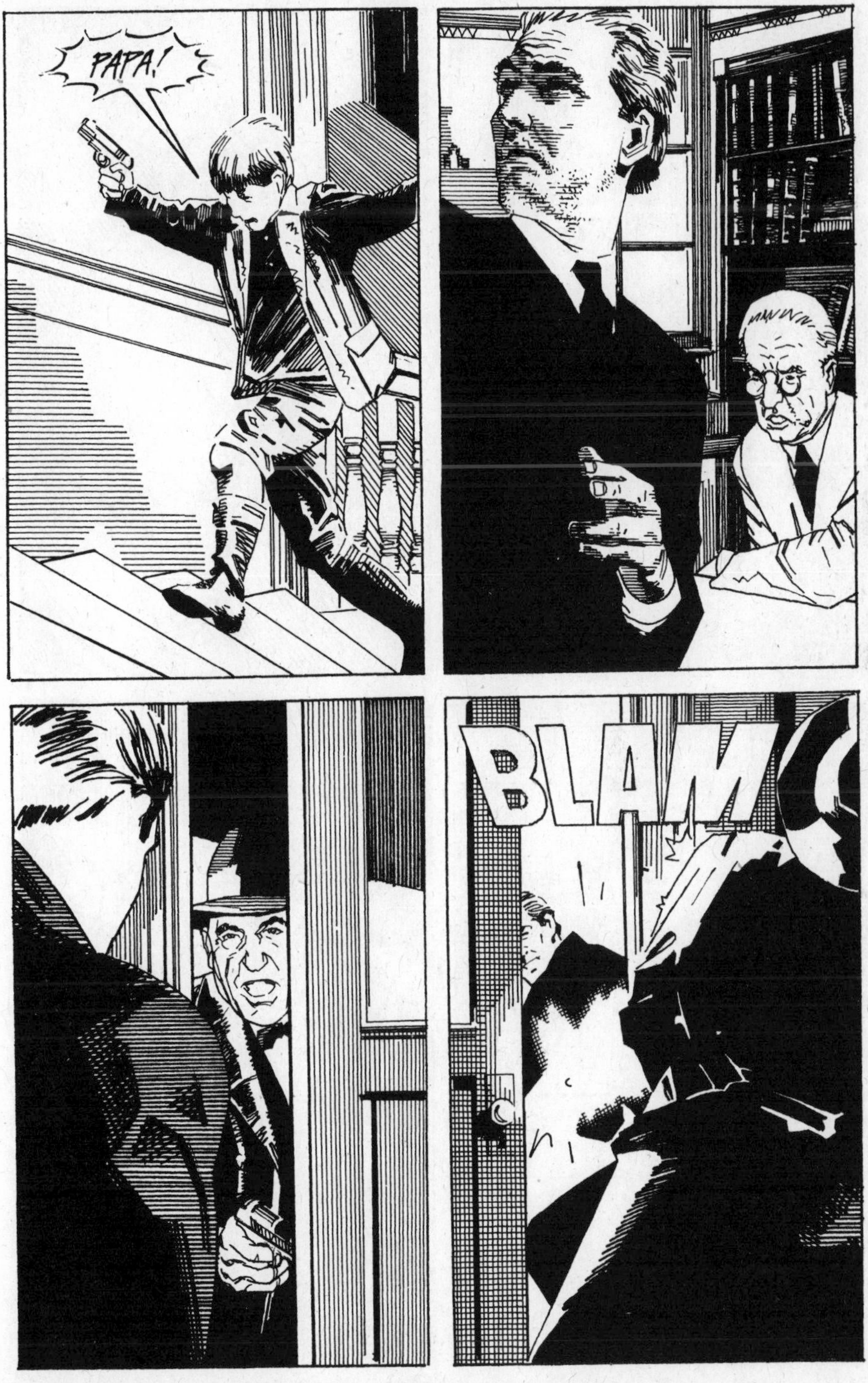
PAPA!
BLAM

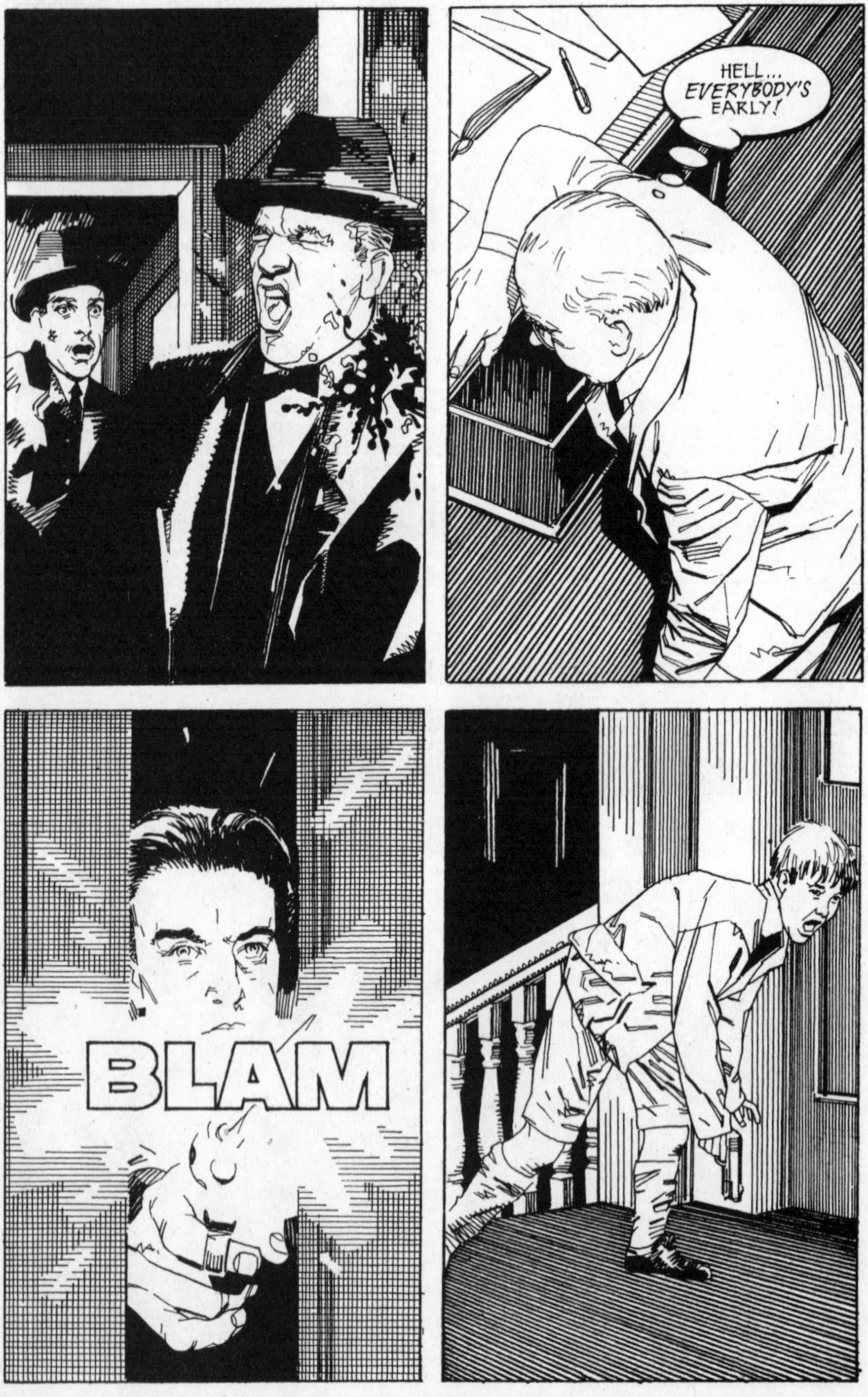
HELL... EVERYBODY'S EARLY!
BLAM

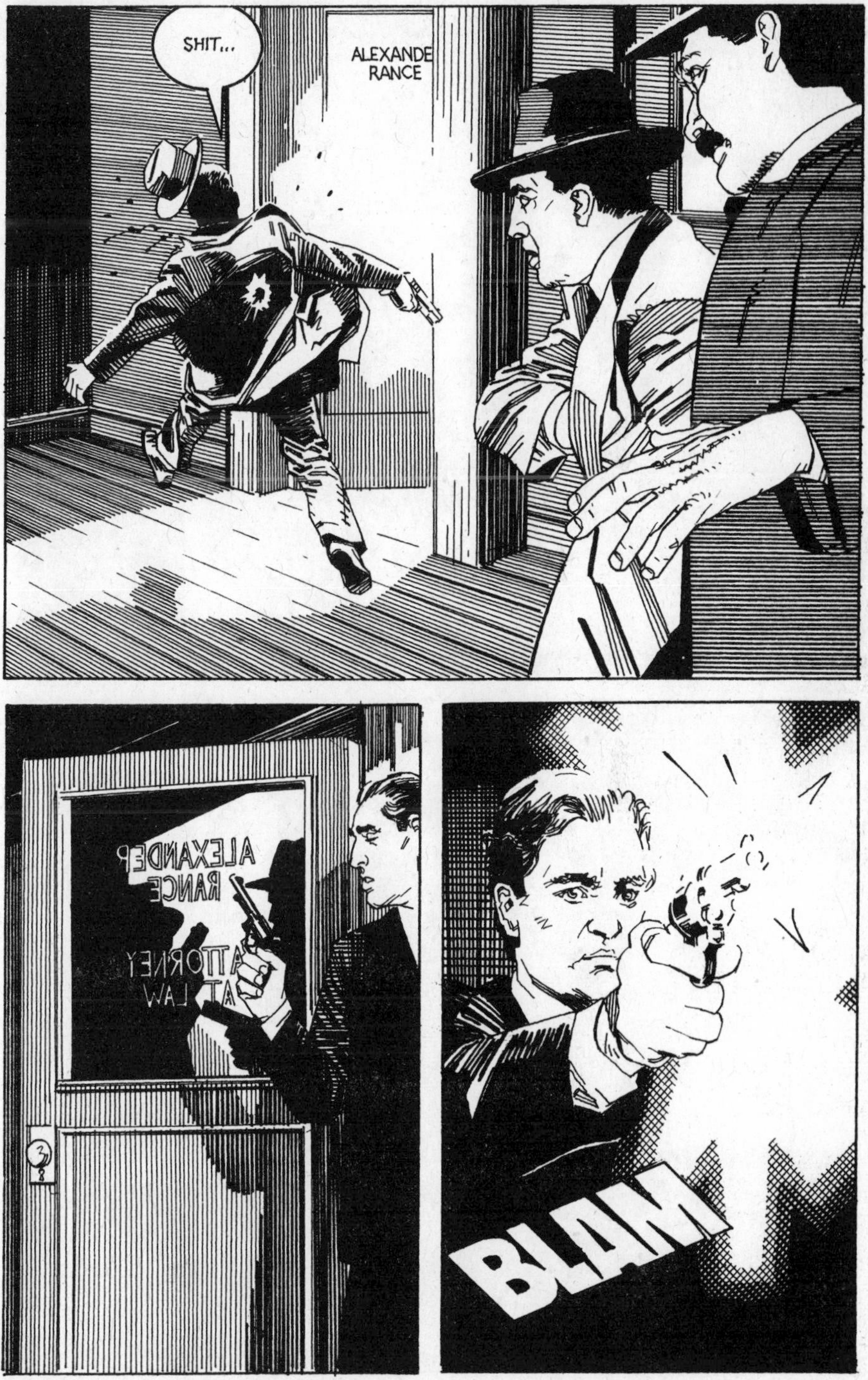
SHIT...
ALEXANDE
RANCE
ALEXANDER
RANCE
ATTORNEY
AT LAW
BLAM

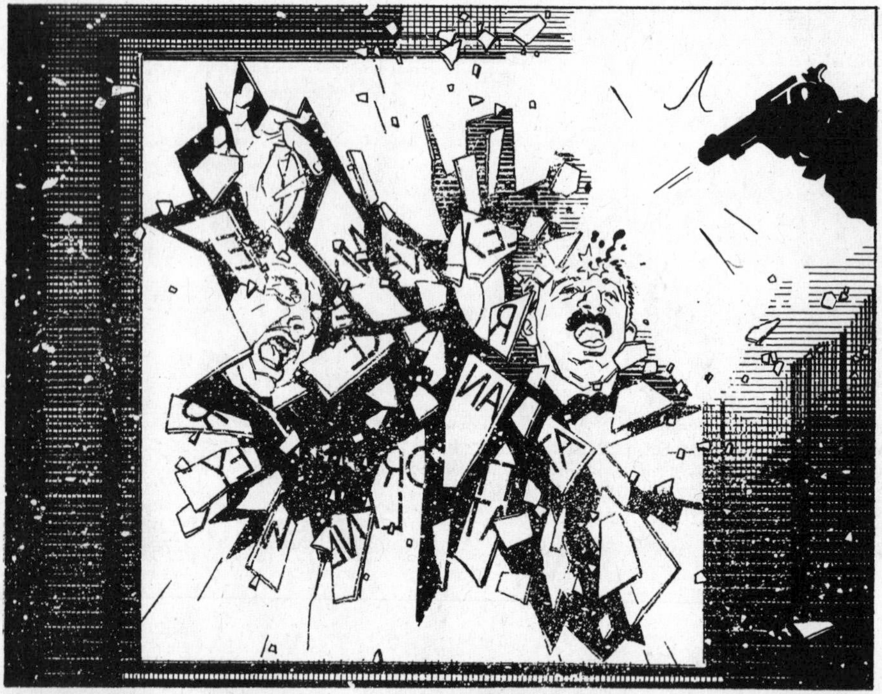

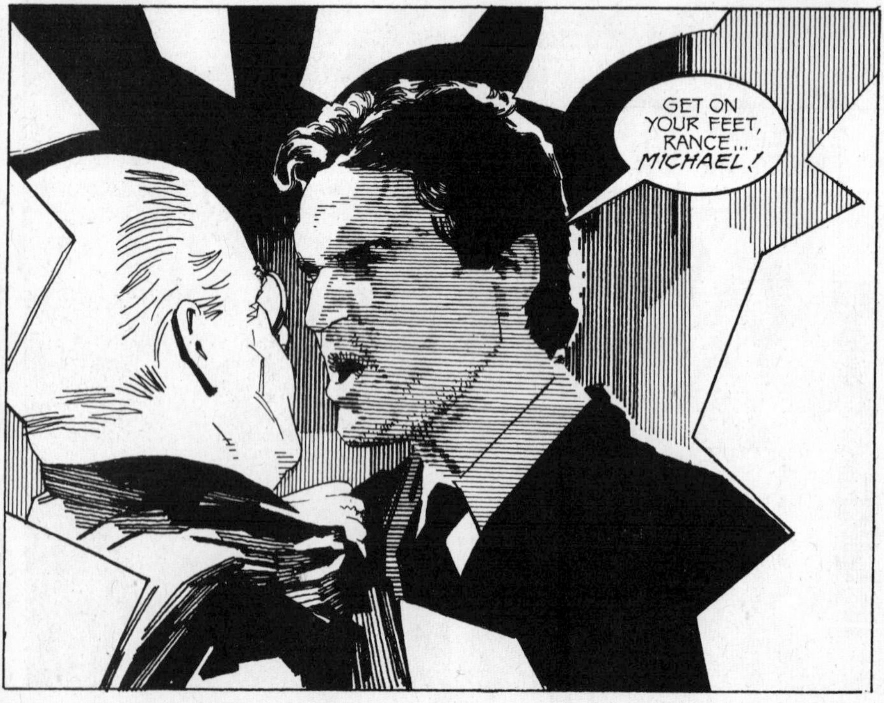
GET ON YOUR FEET, RANCE... MICHAEL!

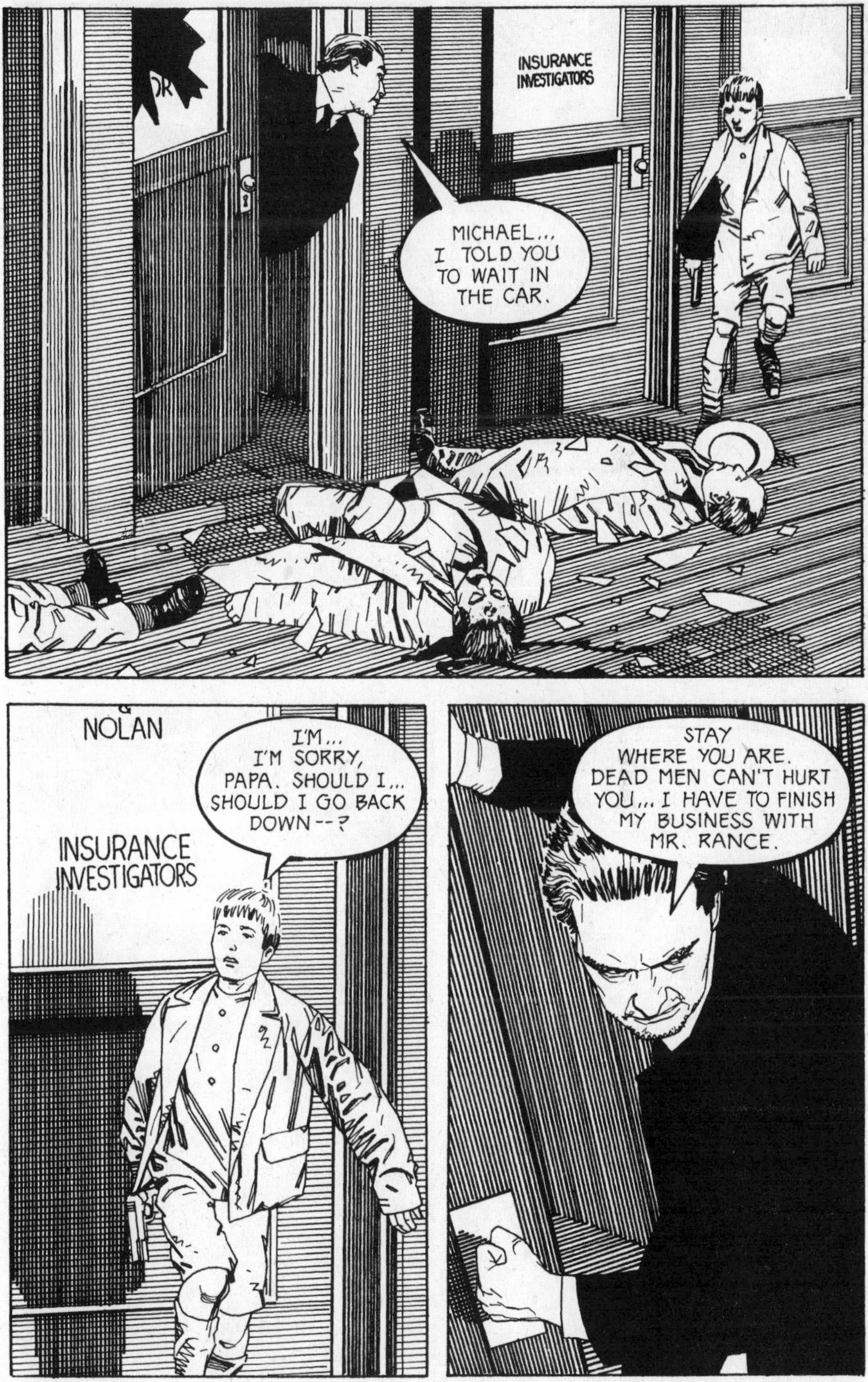
INSURANCE INVESTIGATORS
MICHAEL... I TOLD YOU TO WAIT IN THE CAR.
NOLAN
INSURANCE INVESTIGATORS
I'M... I'M SORRY, PAPA. SHOULD I... SHOULD I GO BACK DOWN--?
STAY WHERE YOU ARE. DEAD MEN CAN'T HURT YOU... I HAVE TO FINISH MY BUSINESS WITH MR. RANCE.

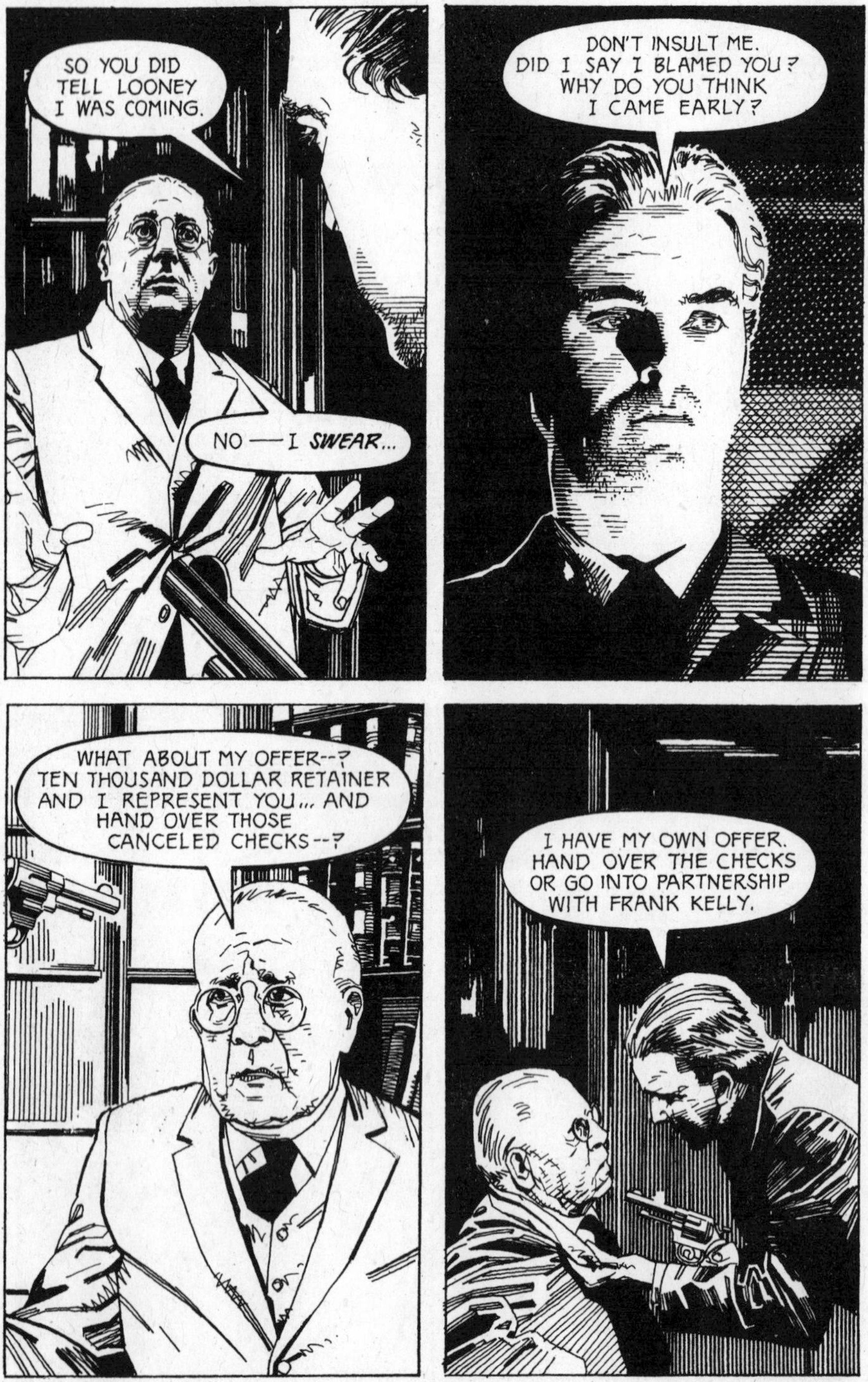
SO YOU DID TELL LOONEY I WAS COMING.
NO — I *SWEAR*...
DON'T INSULT ME. DID I SAY I BLAMED YOU? WHY DO YOU THINK I CAME EARLY?
WHAT ABOUT MY OFFER--? TEN THOUSAND DOLLAR RETAINER AND I REPRESENT YOU... AND HAND OVER THOSE CANCELED CHECKS--?
I HAVE MY OWN OFFER. HAND OVER THE CHECKS OR GO INTO PARTNERSHIP WITH FRANK KELLY.

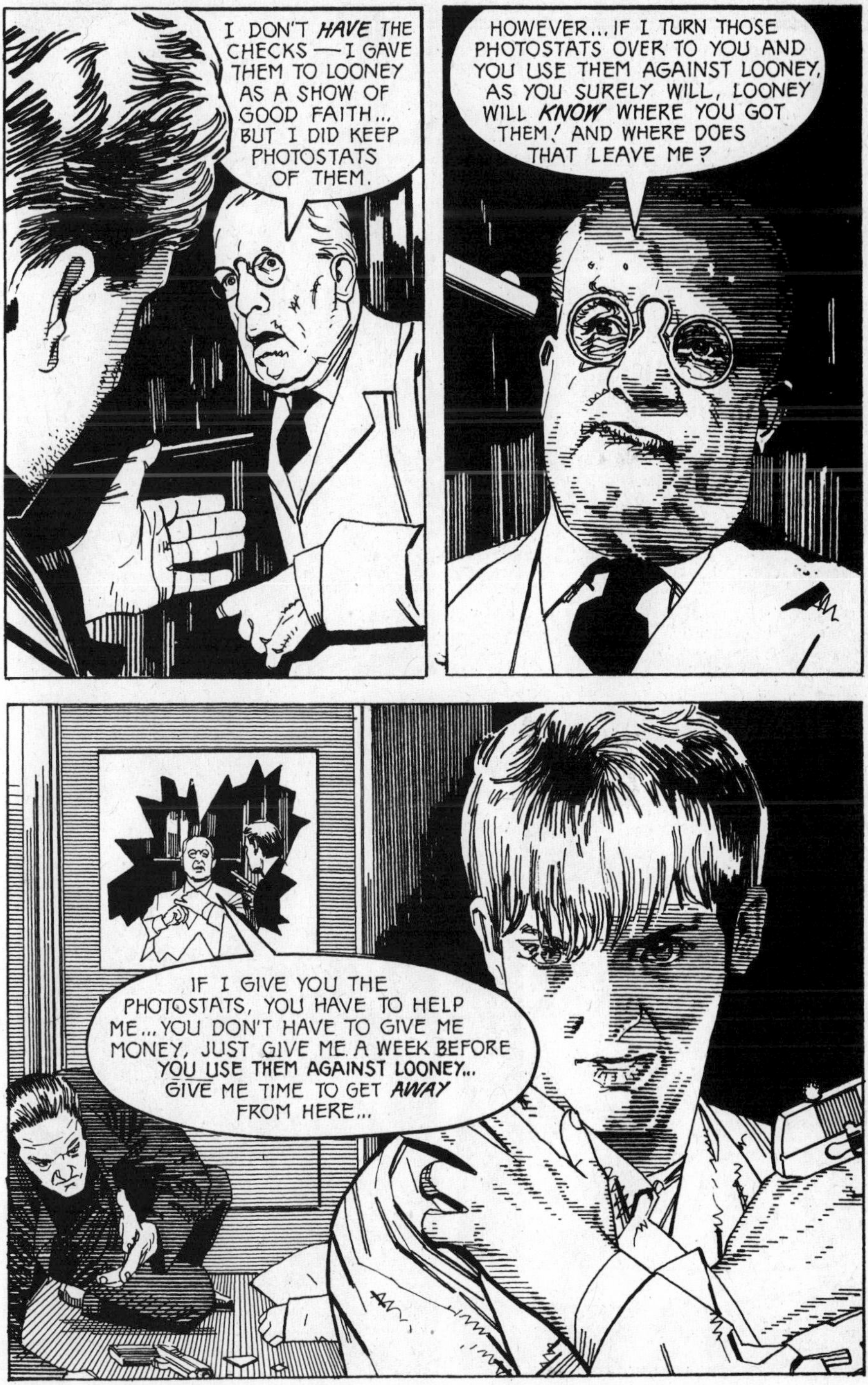
I DON'T HAVE THE CHECKS — I GAVE THEM TO LOONEY AS A SHOW OF GOOD FAITH... BUT I DID KEEP PHOTOSTATS OF THEM.
HOWEVER... IF I TURN THOSE PHOTOSTATS OVER TO YOU AND YOU USE THEM AGAINST LOONEY, AS YOU SURELY WILL, LOONEY WILL KNOW WHERE YOU GOT THEM! AND WHERE DOES THAT LEAVE ME?
IF I GIVE YOU THE PHOTOSTATS, YOU HAVE TO HELP ME... YOU DON'T HAVE TO GIVE ME MONEY, JUST GIVE ME A WEEK BEFORE YOU USE THEM AGAINST LOONEY... GIVE ME TIME TO GET AWAY FROM HERE...

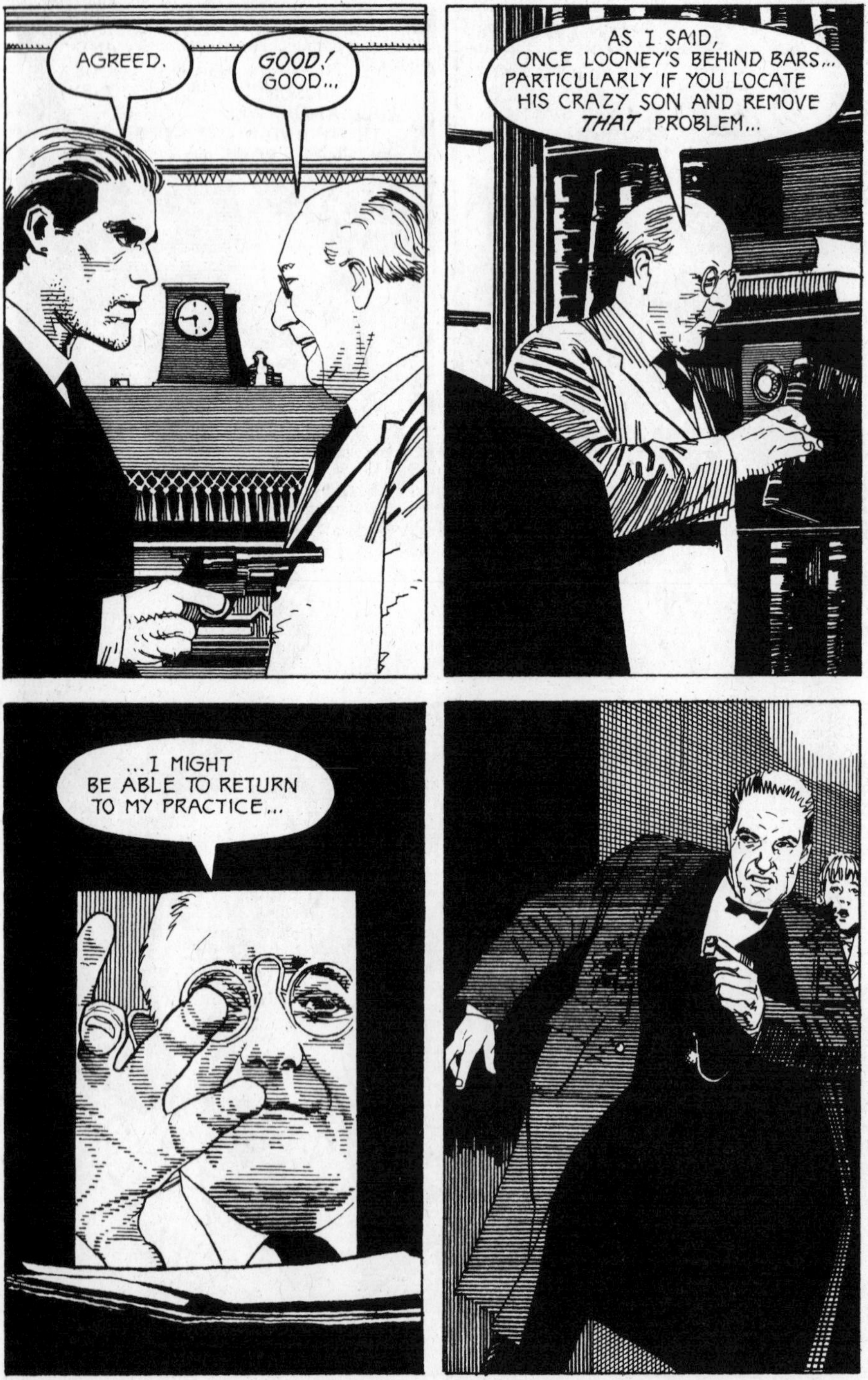
AGREED.
GOOD! GOOD...
AS I SAID, ONCE LOONEY'S BEHIND BARS... PARTICULARLY IF YOU LOCATE HIS CRAZY SON AND REMOVE THAT PROBLEM...
...I MIGHT BE ABLE TO RETURN TO MY PRACTICE...

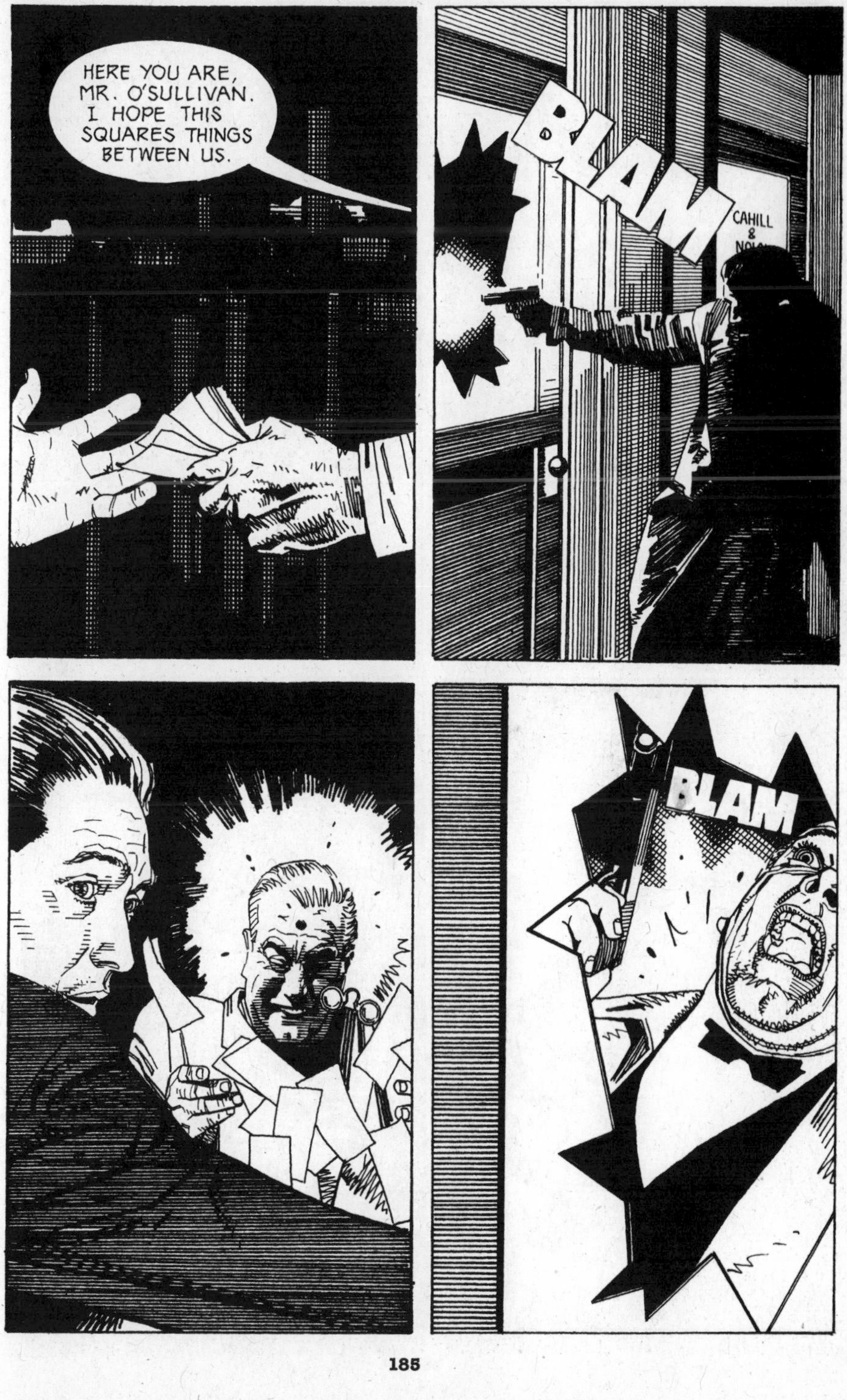
HERE YOU ARE, MR. O'SULLIVAN. I HOPE THIS SQUARES THINGS BETWEEN US.
BLAM
CAHILL & NOL
BLAM

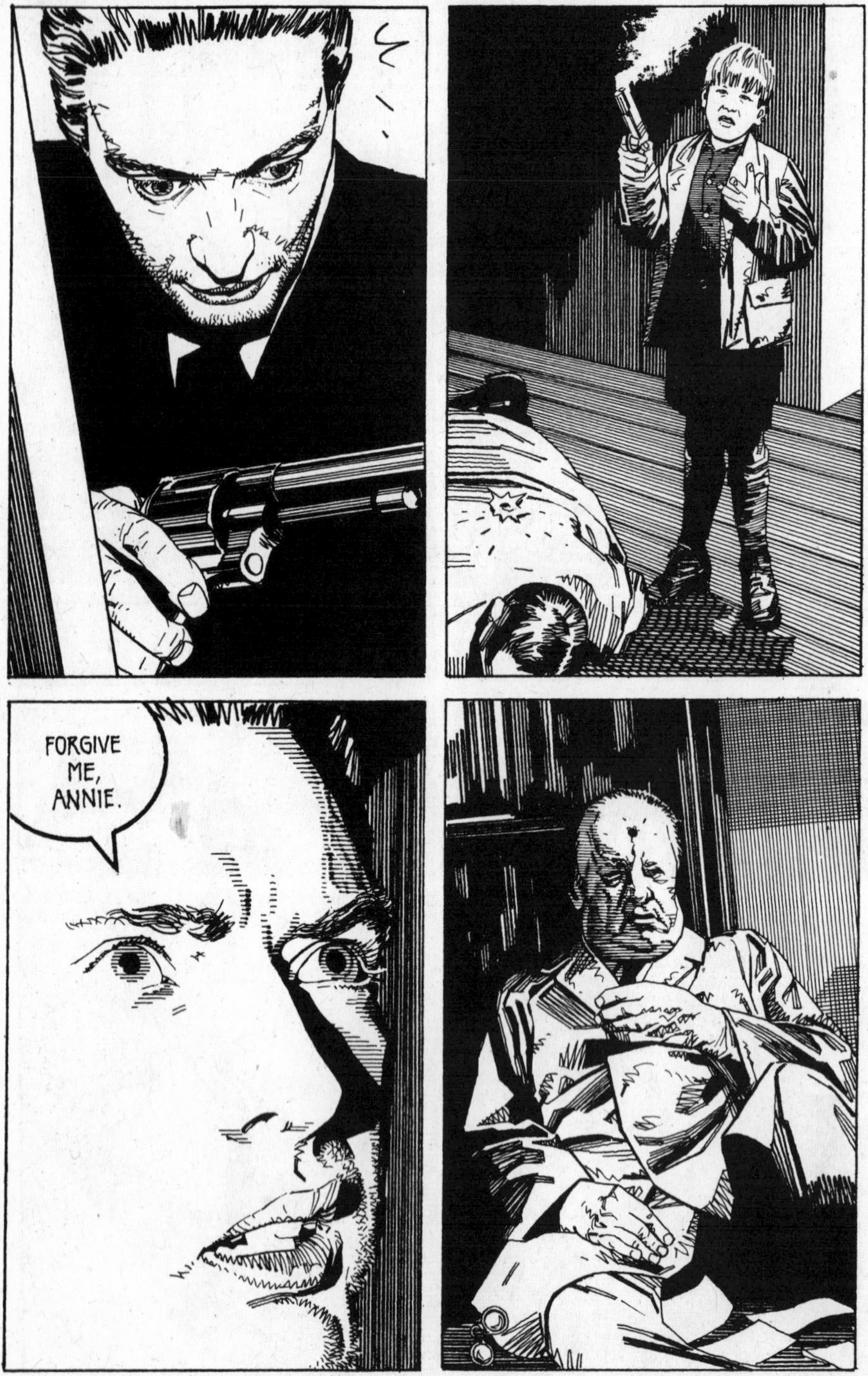
FORGIVE ME, ANNIE.

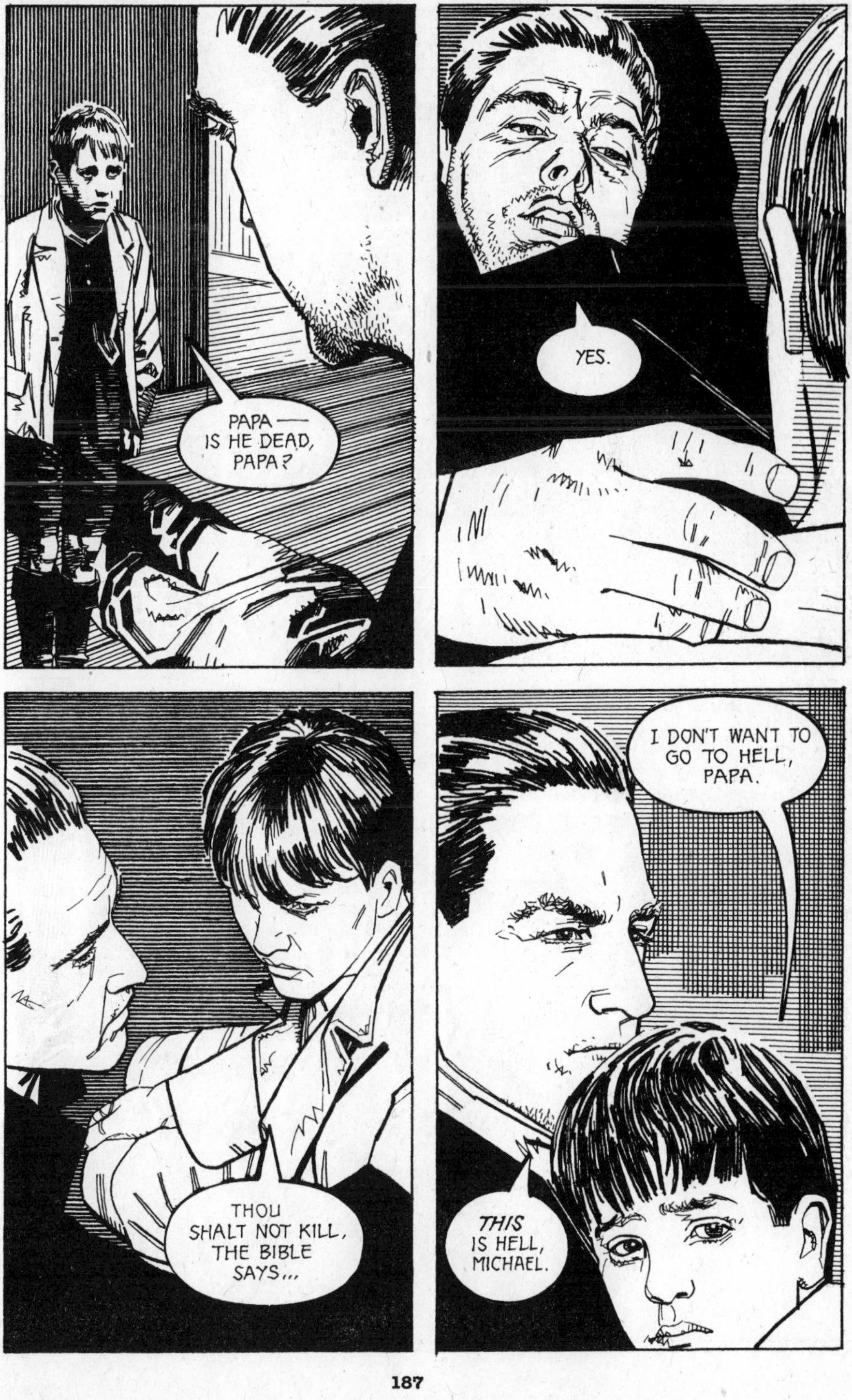
PAPA— IS HE DEAD, PAPA?
YES.
THOU SHALT NOT KILL, THE BIBLE SAYS...
I DON'T WANT TO GO TO HELL, PAPA.
THIS IS HELL, MICHAEL.

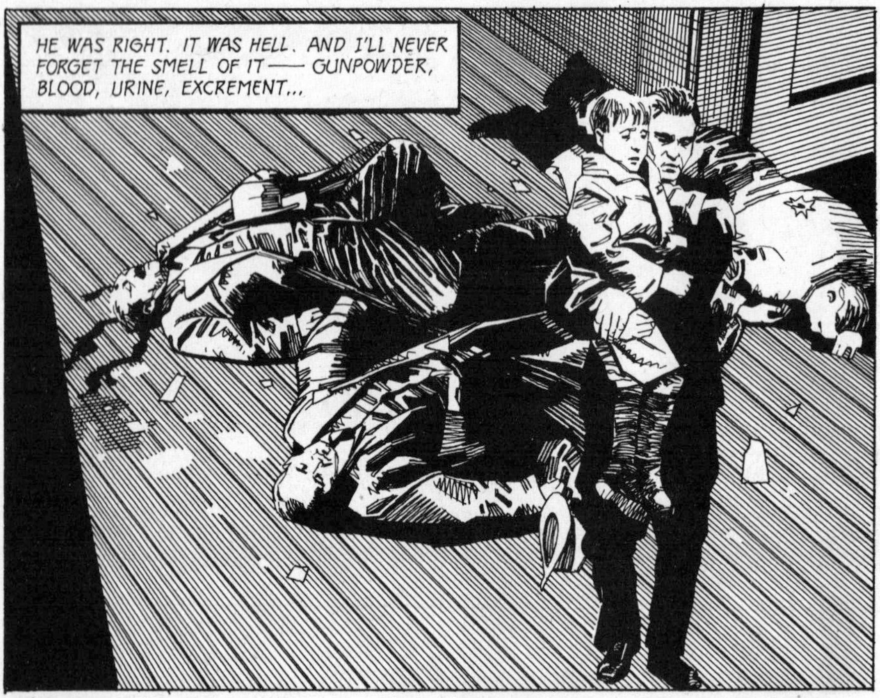
HE WAS RIGHT. IT WAS HELL. AND I'LL NEVER FORGET THE SMELL OF IT — GUNPOWDER, BLOOD, URINE, EXCREMENT...

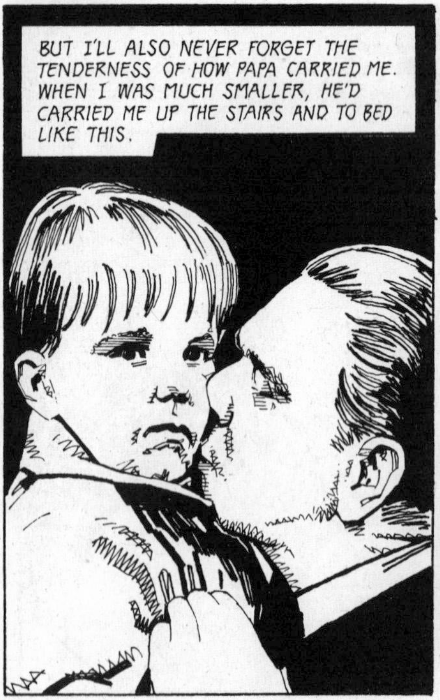
BUT I'LL ALSO NEVER FORGET THE TENDERNESS OF HOW PAPA CARRIED ME. WHEN I WAS MUCH SMALLER, HE'D CARRIED ME UP THE STAIRS AND TO BED LIKE THIS.

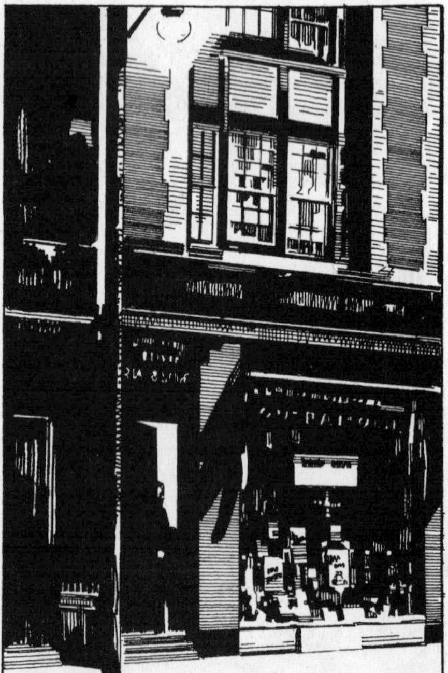

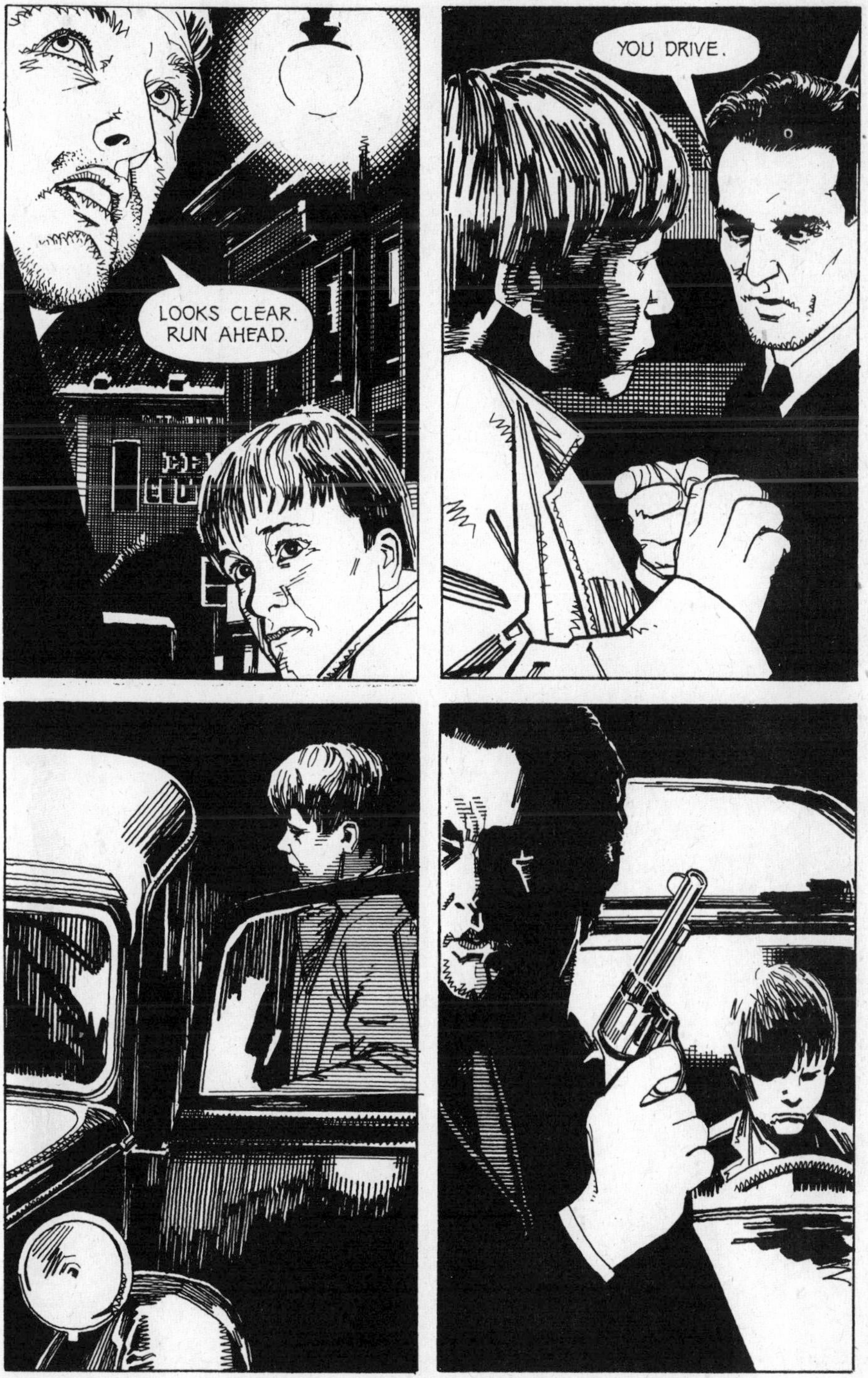
LOOKS CLEAR. RUN AHEAD.
YOU DRIVE.

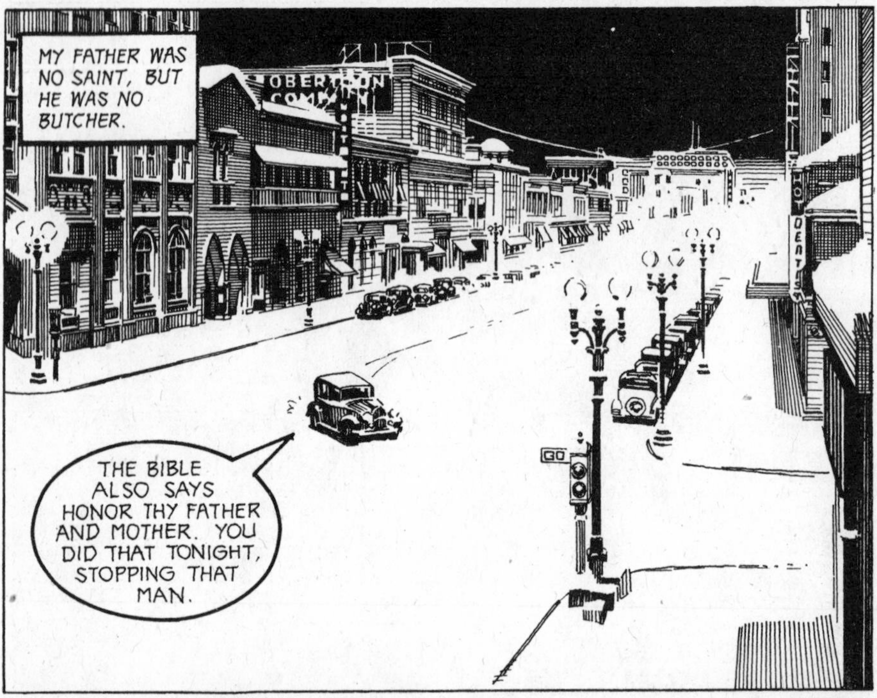
MY FATHER WAS NO SAINT, BUT HE WAS NO BUTCHER.
THE BIBLE ALSO SAYS HONOR THY FATHER AND MOTHER. YOU DID THAT TONIGHT, STOPPING THAT MAN.

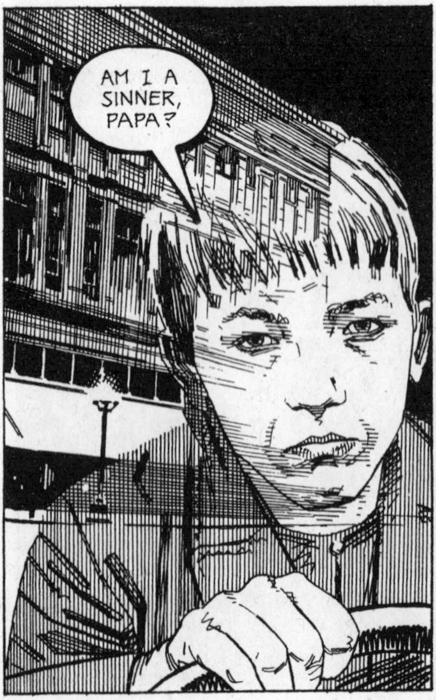
AM I A SINNER, PAPA?

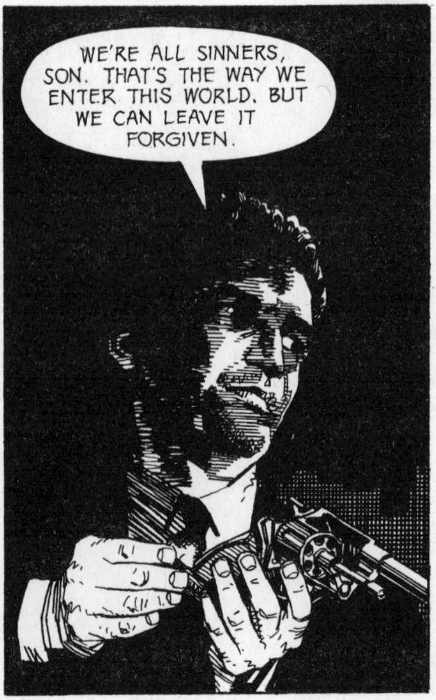
WE'RE ALL SINNERS, SON. THAT'S THE WAY WE ENTER THIS WORLD. BUT WE CAN LEAVE IT FORGIVEN.

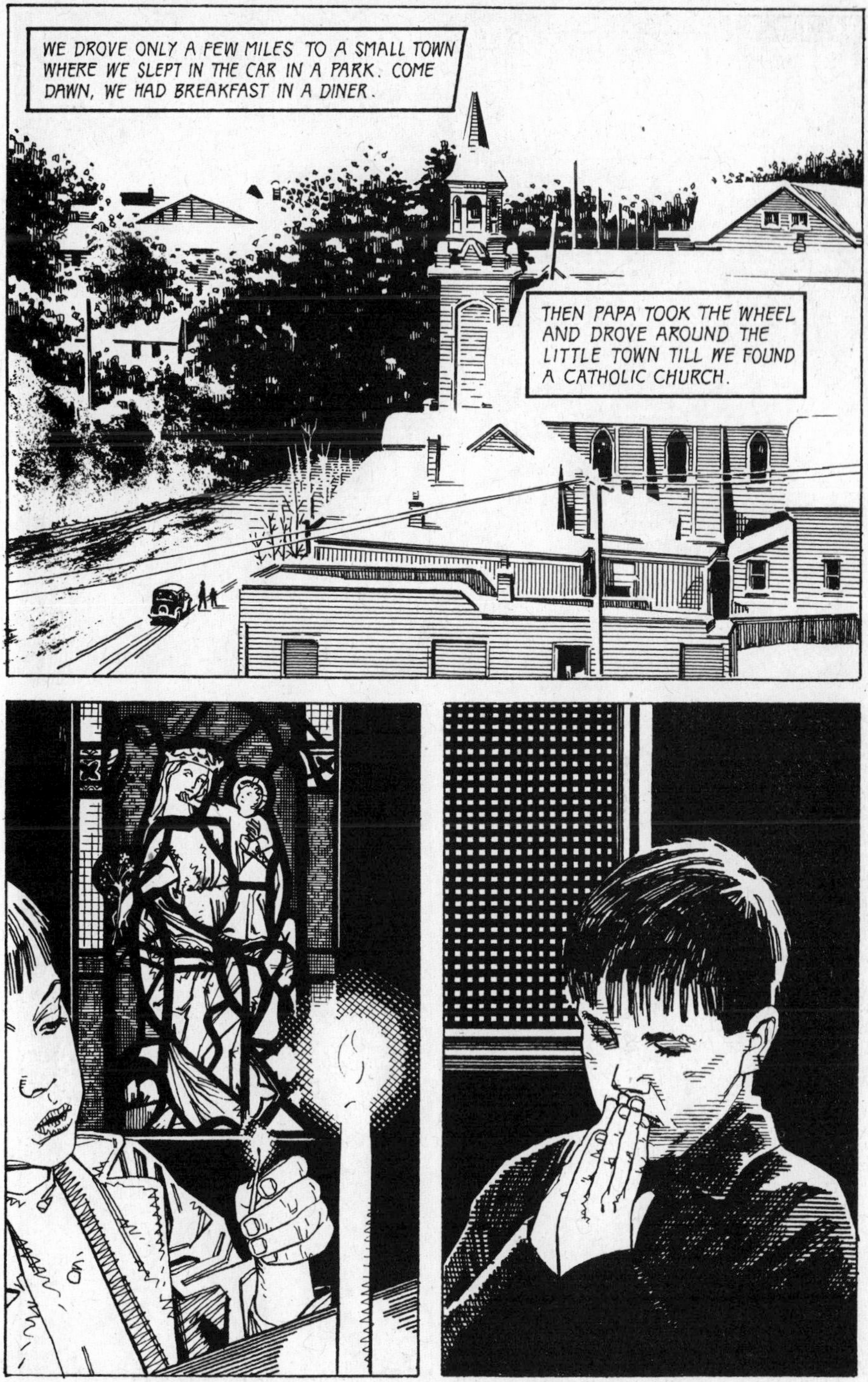
WE DROVE ONLY A FEW MILES TO A SMALL TOWN WHERE WE SLEPT IN THE CAR IN A PARK. COME DAWN, WE HAD BREAKFAST IN A DINER.
THEN PAPA TOOK THE WHEEL AND DROVE AROUND THE LITTLE TOWN TILL WE FOUND A CATHOLIC CHURCH.

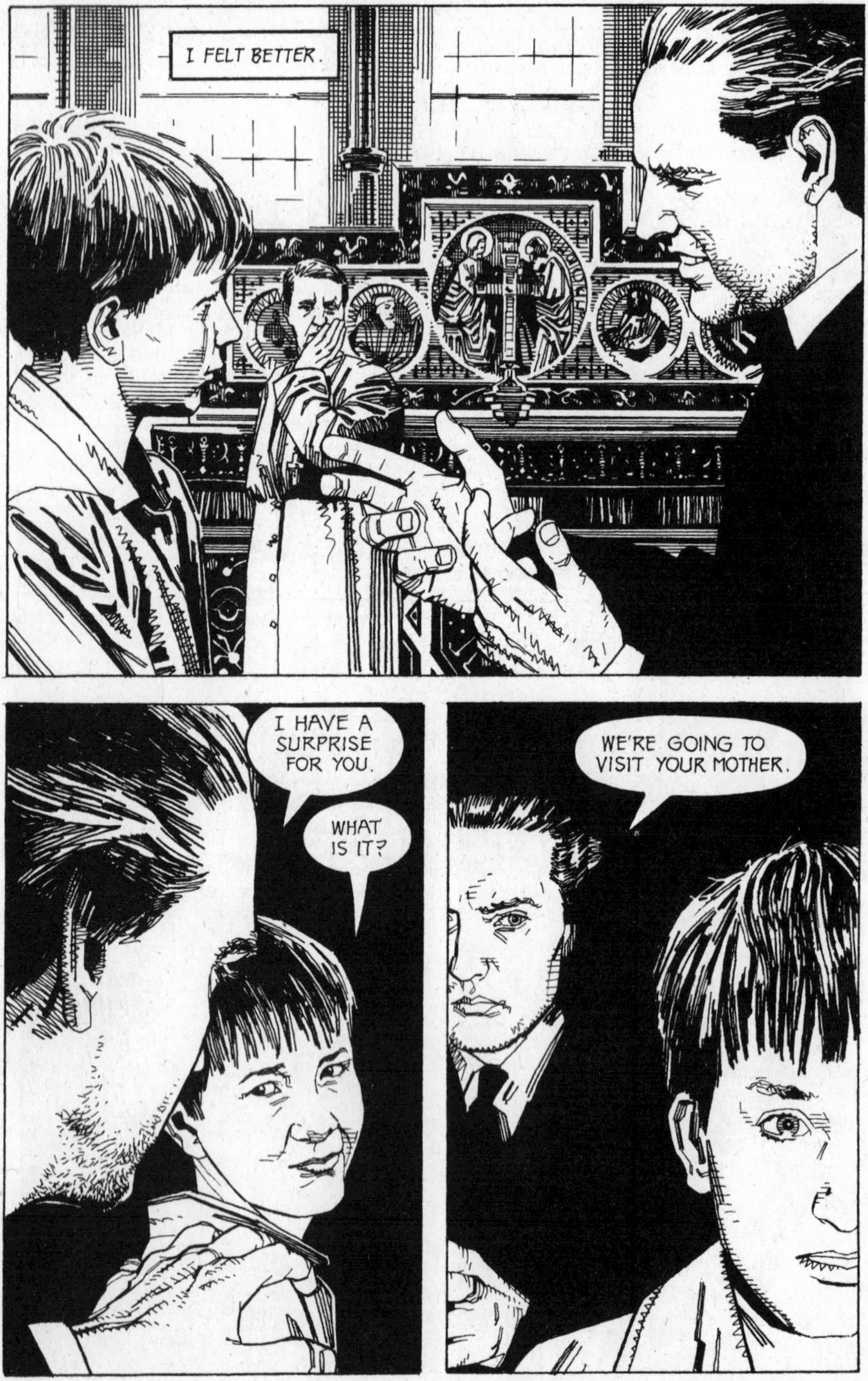
I FELT BETTER.
I HAVE A SURPRISE FOR YOU.
WHAT IS IT?
WE'RE GOING TO VISIT YOUR MOTHER.

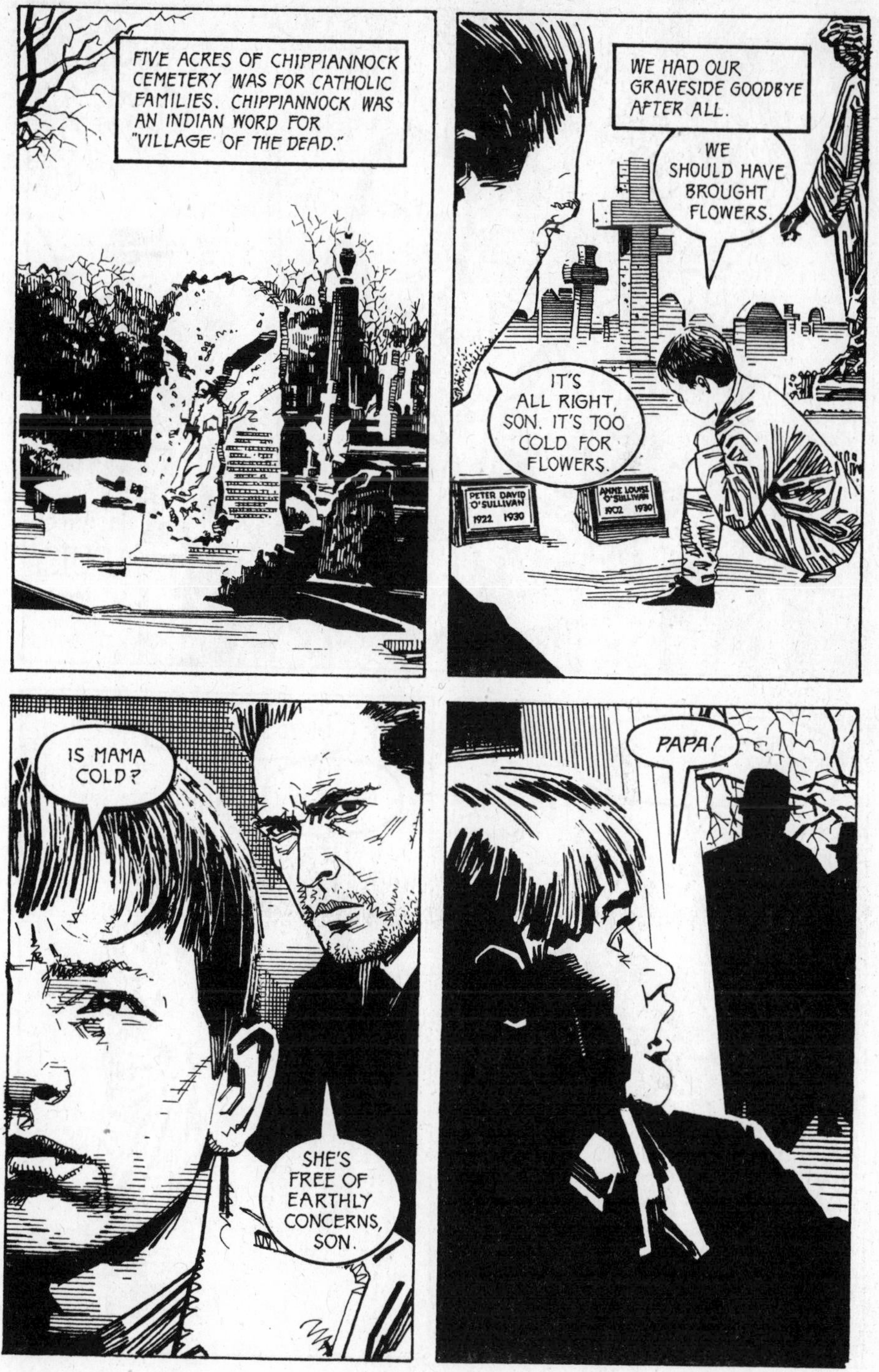
FIVE ACRES OF CHIPPIANNOCK CEMETERY WAS FOR CATHOLIC FAMILIES. CHIPPIANNOCK WAS AN INDIAN WORD FOR "VILLAGE OF THE DEAD."
WE HAD OUR GRAVESIDE GOODBYE AFTER ALL.
WE SHOULD HAVE BROUGHT FLOWERS.
IT'S ALL RIGHT, SON. IT'S TOO COLD FOR FLOWERS.
PETER DAVID O'SULLIVAN 1922 1930
ANNE LOUISE O'SULLIVAN 1902 1930
IS MAMA COLD?
SHE'S FREE OF EARTHLY CONCERNS, SON.
PAPA!

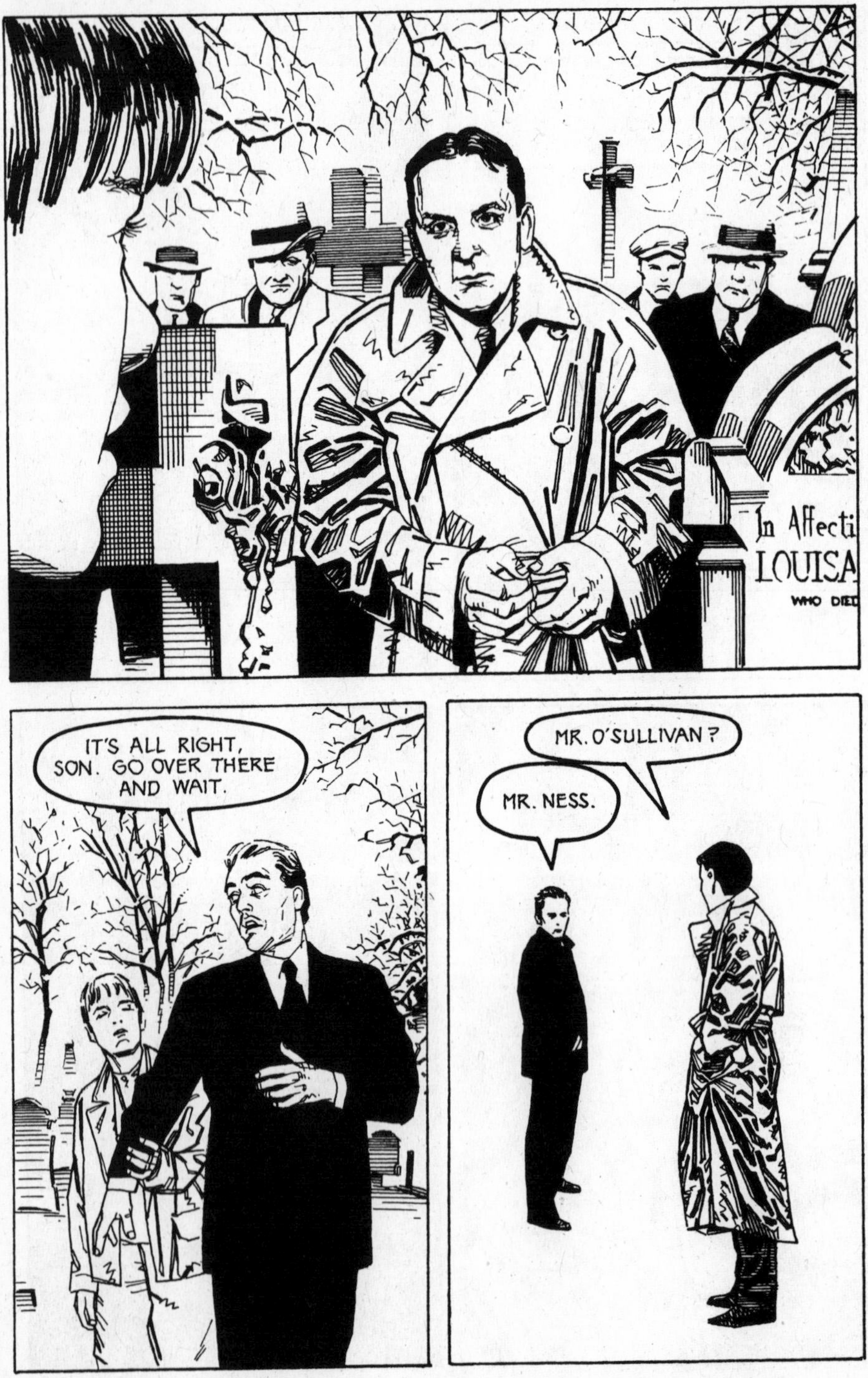
In Affecti
LOUISA
WHO DIED
IT'S ALL RIGHT, SON. GO OVER THERE AND WAIT.
MR. O'SULLIVAN?
MR. NESS.

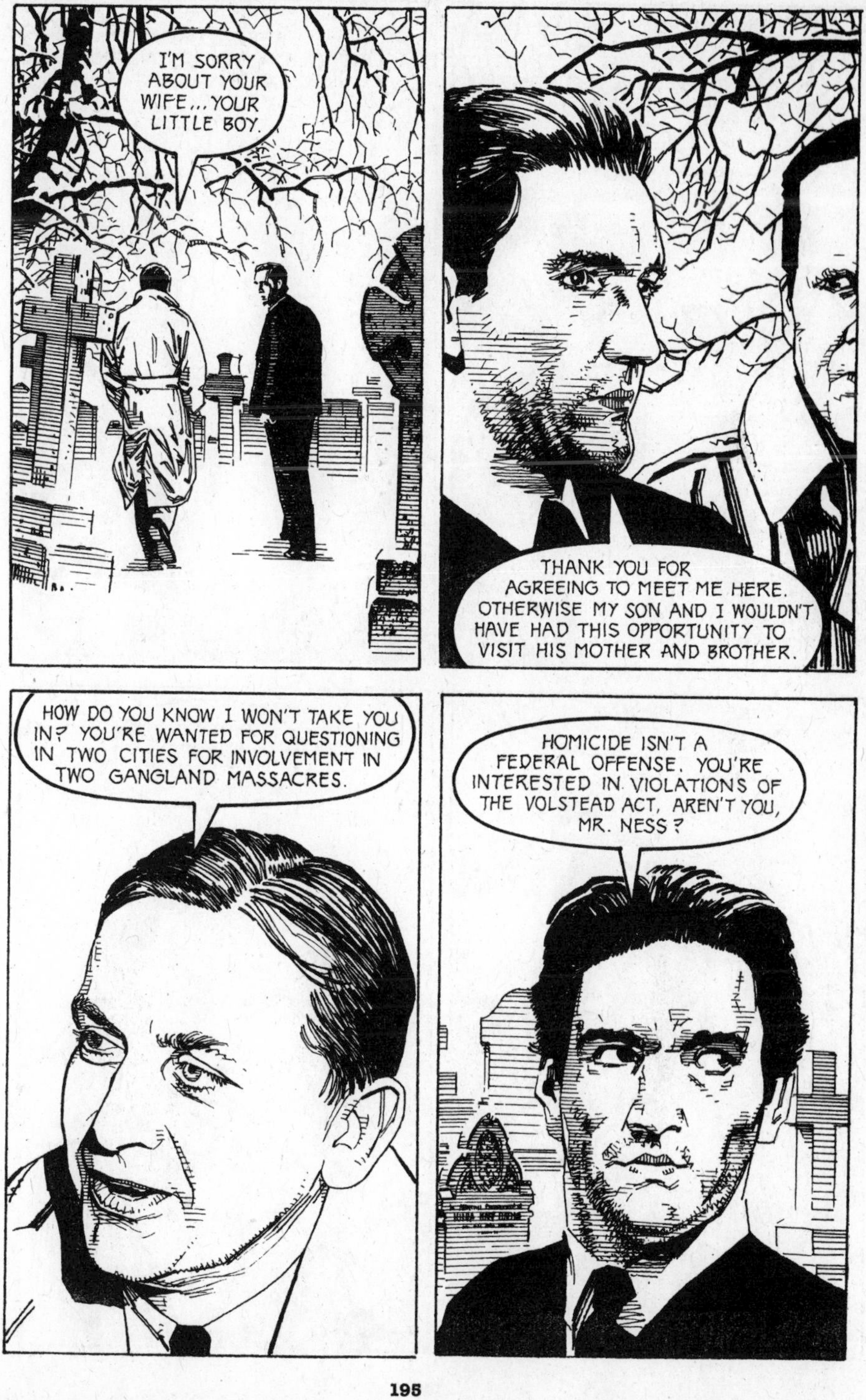
I'M SORRY ABOUT YOUR WIFE... YOUR LITTLE BOY.
THANK YOU FOR AGREEING TO MEET ME HERE. OTHERWISE MY SON AND I WOULDN'T HAVE HAD THIS OPPORTUNITY TO VISIT HIS MOTHER AND BROTHER.
HOW DO YOU KNOW I WON'T TAKE YOU IN? YOU'RE WANTED FOR QUESTIONING IN TWO CITIES FOR INVOLVEMENT IN TWO GANGLAND MASSACRES.
HOMICIDE ISN'T A FEDERAL OFFENSE. YOU'RE INTERESTED IN VIOLATIONS OF THE VOLSTEAD ACT, AREN'T YOU, MR. NESS?

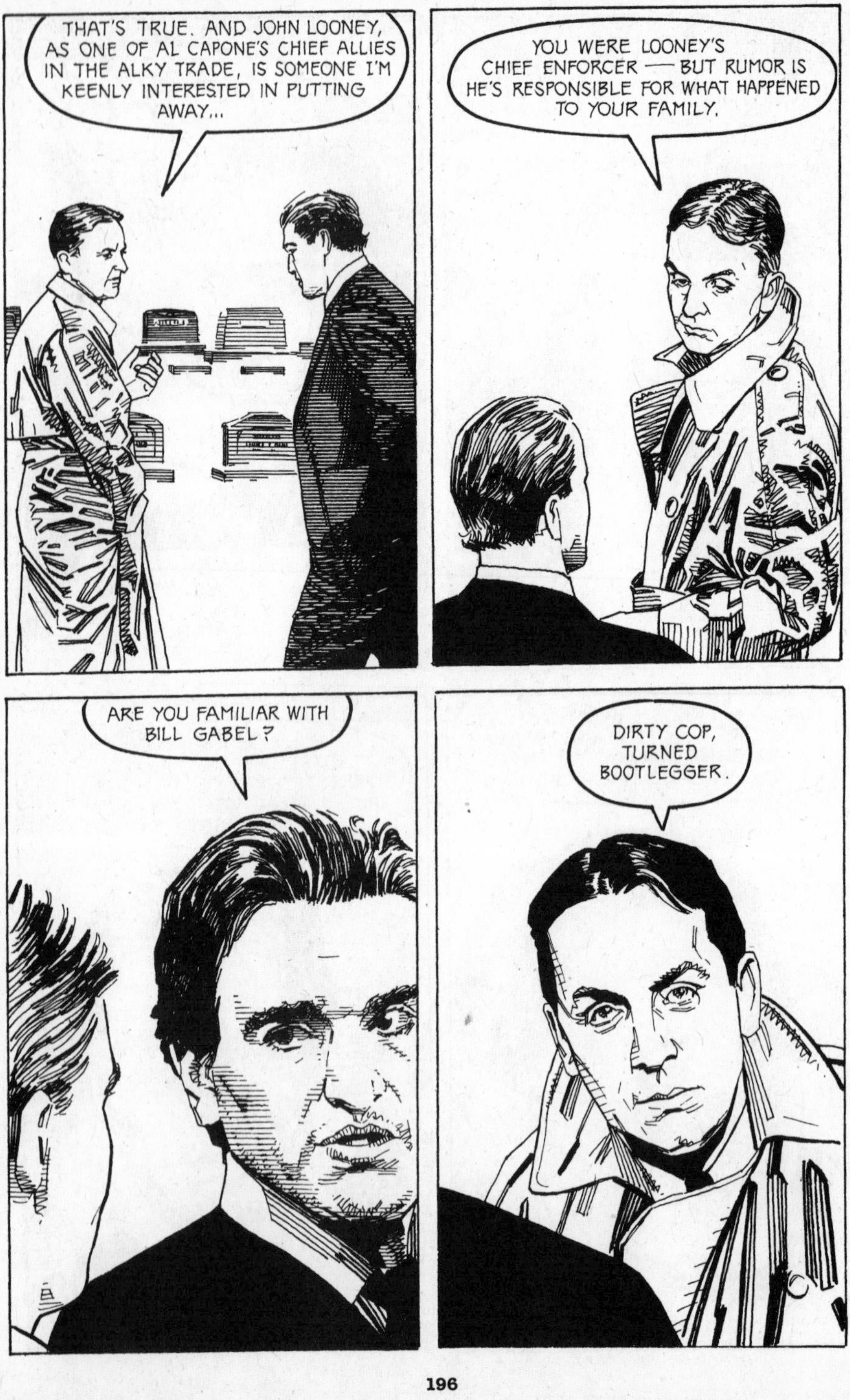
THAT'S TRUE. AND JOHN LOONEY, AS ONE OF AL CAPONE'S CHIEF ALLIES IN THE ALKY TRADE, IS SOMEONE I'M KEENLY INTERESTED IN PUTTING AWAY...
YOU WERE LOONEY'S CHIEF ENFORCER — BUT RUMOR IS HE'S RESPONSIBLE FOR WHAT HAPPENED TO YOUR FAMILY.
ARE YOU FAMILIAR WITH BILL GABEL?
DIRTY COP, TURNED BOOTLEGGER.

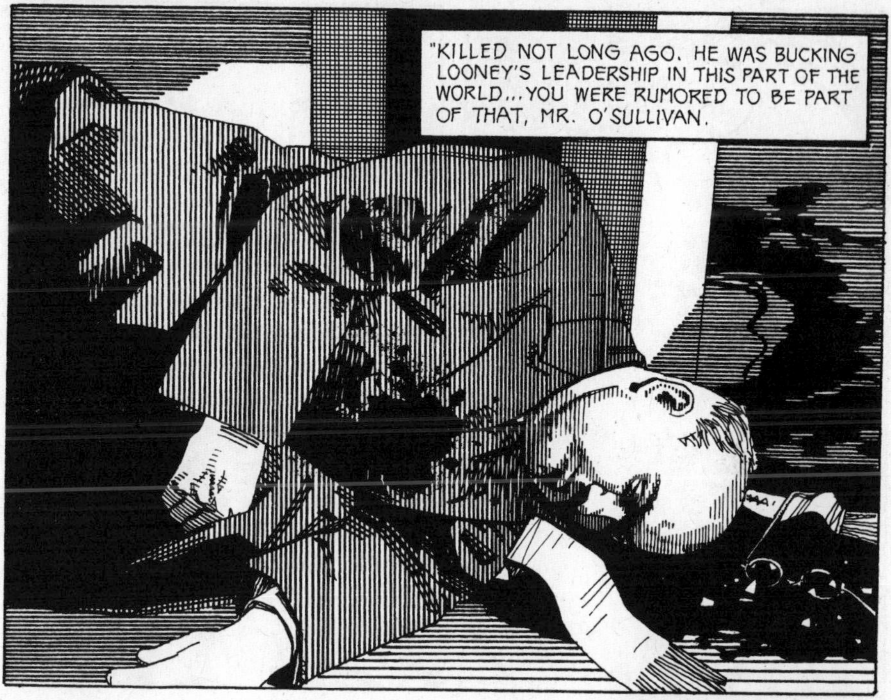
"KILLED NOT LONG AGO. HE WAS BUCKING LOONEY'S LEADERSHIP IN THIS PART OF THE WORLD... YOU WERE RUMORED TO BE PART OF THAT, MR. O'SULLIVAN.
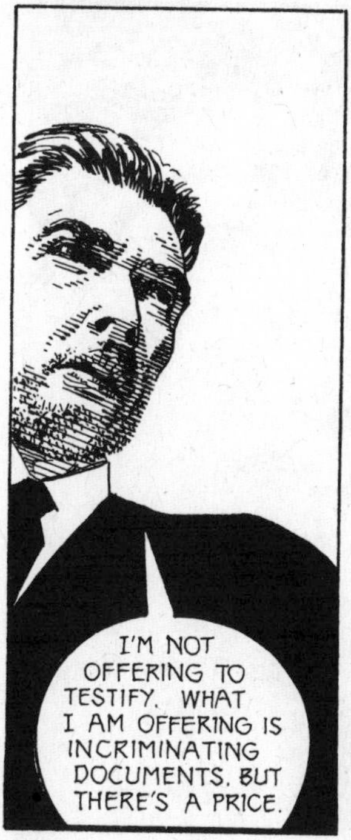
I'M NOT OFFERING TO TESTIFY. WHAT I AM OFFERING IS INCRIMINATING DOCUMENTS. BUT THERE'S A PRICE.
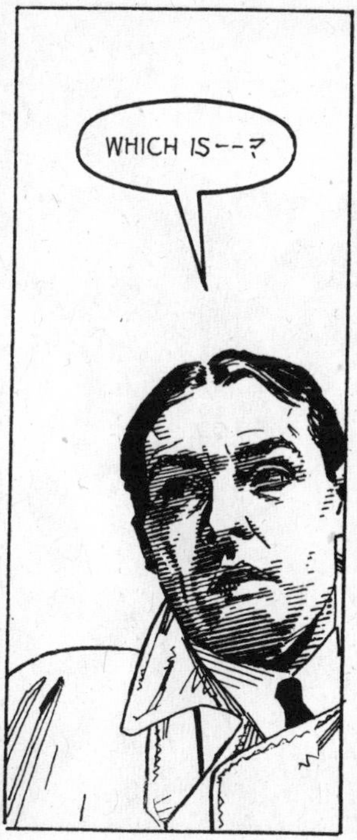
WHICH IS--?
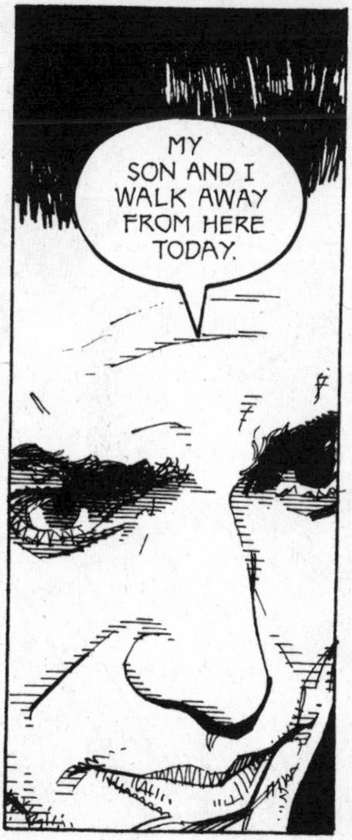
MY SON AND I WALK AWAY FROM HERE TODAY.

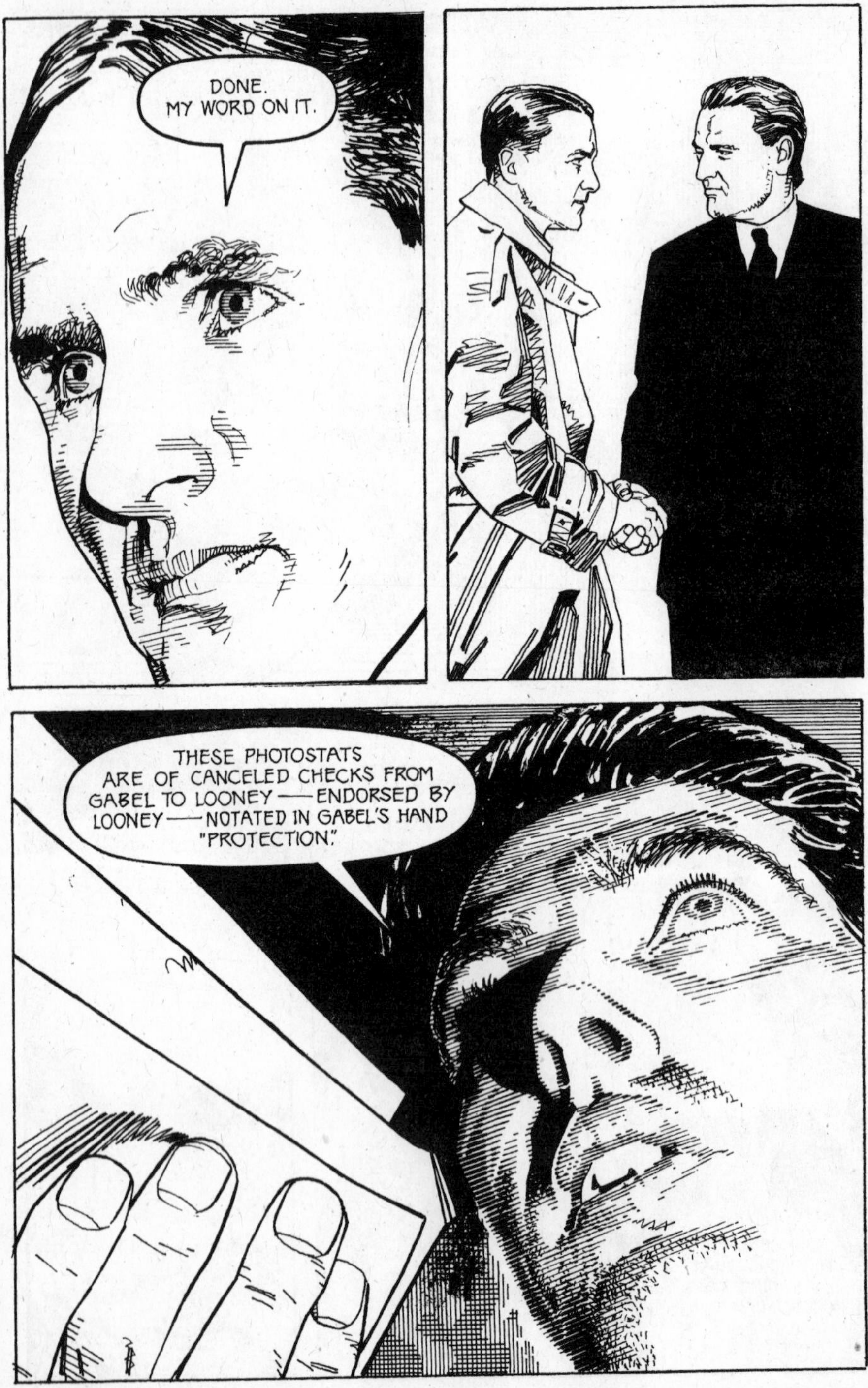
DONE. MY WORD ON IT.
THESE PHOTOSTATS ARE OF CANCELED CHECKS FROM GABEL TO LOONEY—ENDORSED BY LOONEY—NOTATED IN GABEL'S HAND "PROTECTION."

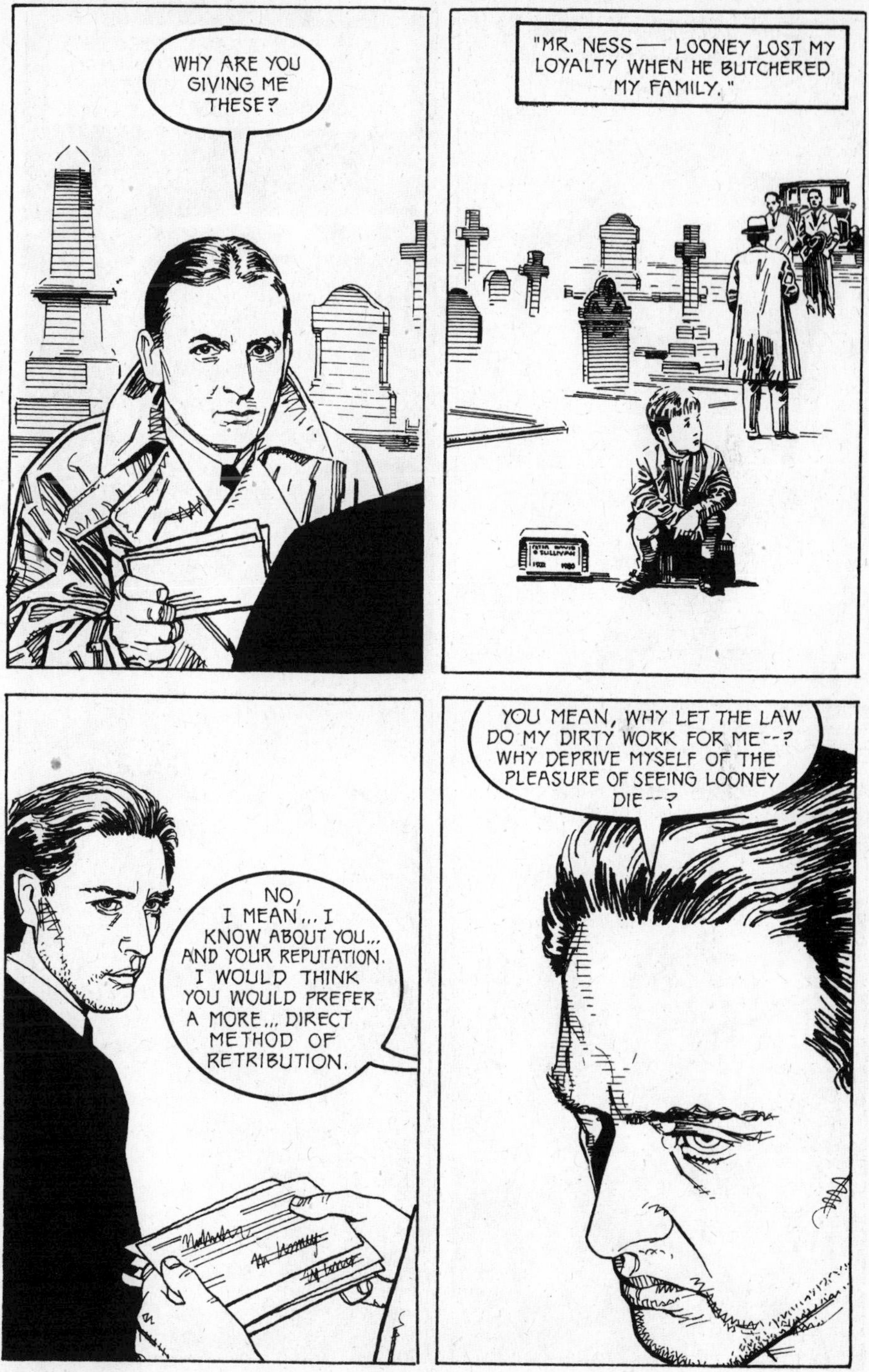
WHY ARE YOU GIVING ME THESE?
"MR. NESS — LOONEY LOST MY LOYALTY WHEN HE BUTCHERED MY FAMILY."
NO, I MEAN... I KNOW ABOUT YOU... AND YOUR REPUTATION. I WOULD THINK YOU WOULD PREFER A MORE... DIRECT METHOD OF RETRIBUTION.
YOU MEAN, WHY LET THE LAW DO MY DIRTY WORK FOR ME--? WHY DEPRIVE MYSELF OF THE PLEASURE OF SEEING LOONEY DIE--?

SOMETHING LIKE THAT.

"LOONEY'S AN OLD MAN. I PREFER TO SEE HIM DIE SLOWLY...IN PRISON... LIVING WITH THE KNOWLEDGE THAT HIS SON DIED VIOLENTLY.

CONNOR LOONEY KILLED--? WHEN DID THIS HAPPEN?

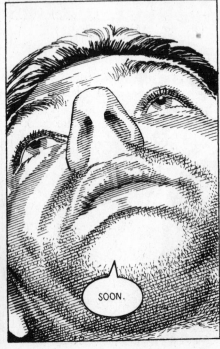

SOON.

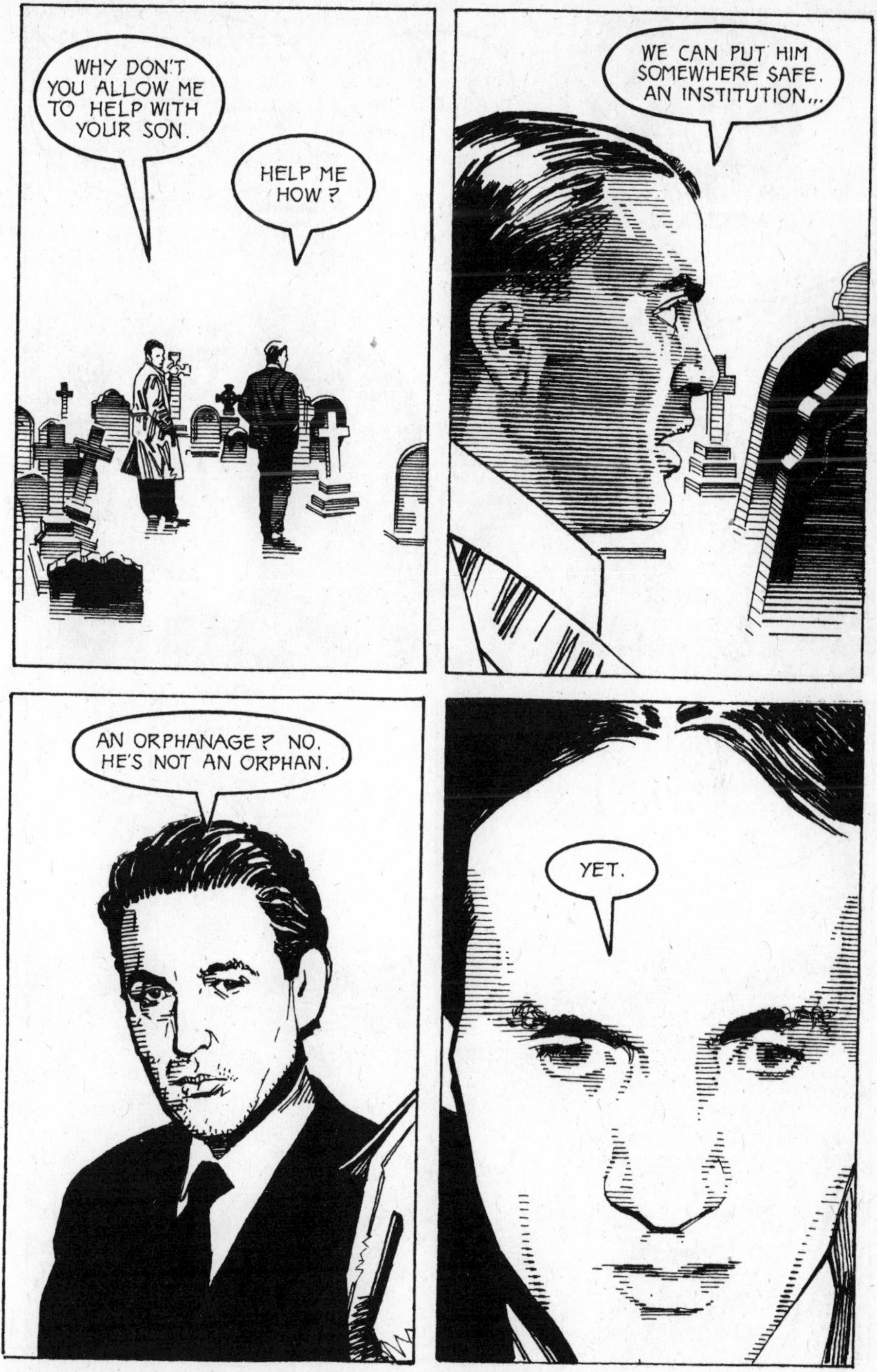
WHY DON'T YOU ALLOW ME TO HELP WITH YOUR SON.
HELP ME HOW?
WE CAN PUT HIM SOMEWHERE SAFE. AN INSTITUTION...
AN ORPHANAGE? NO. HE'S NOT AN ORPHAN.
YET.

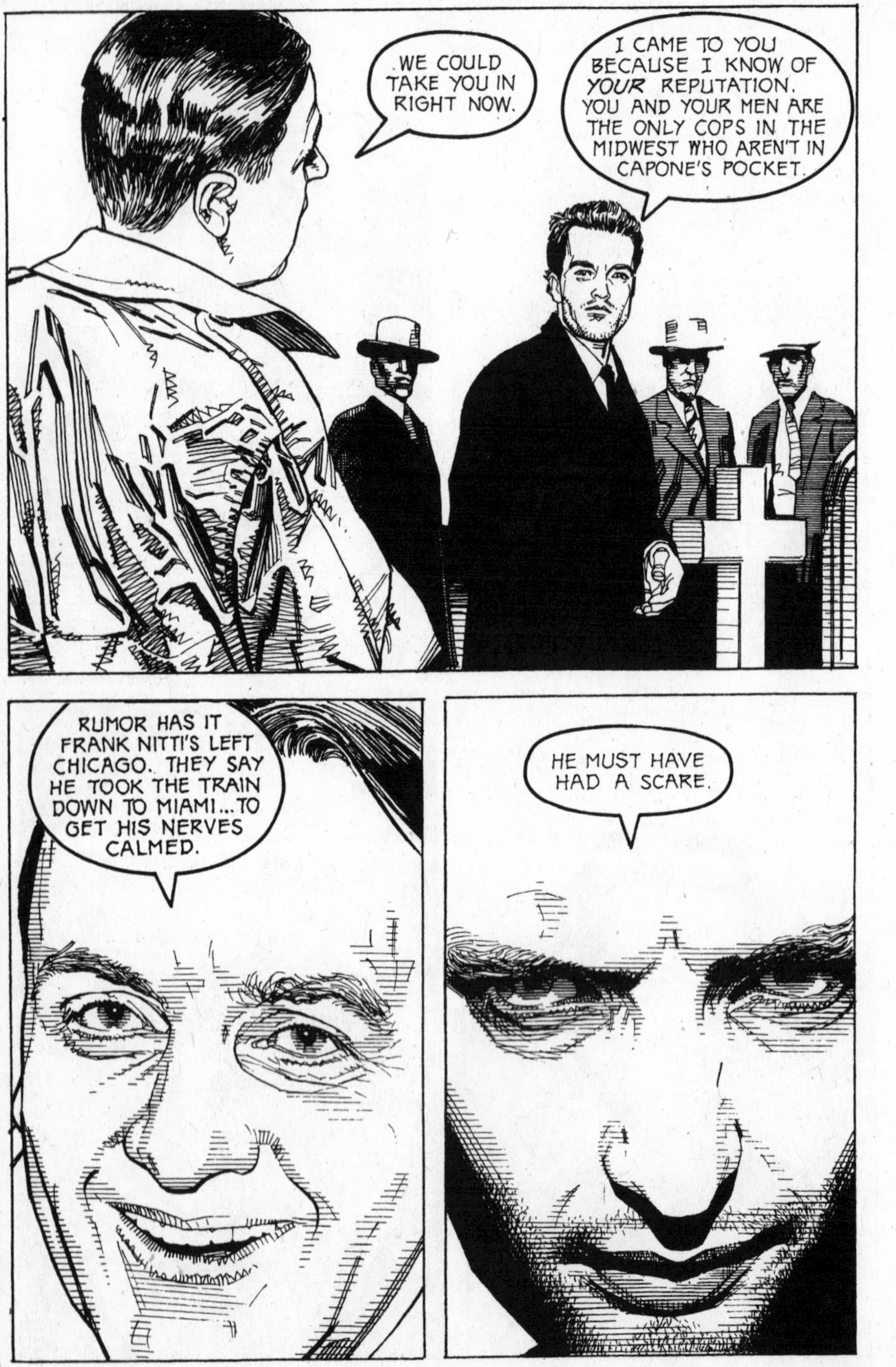
WE COULD TAKE YOU IN RIGHT NOW.
I CAME TO YOU BECAUSE I KNOW OF *YOUR* REPUTATION. YOU AND YOUR MEN ARE THE ONLY COPS IN THE MIDWEST WHO AREN'T IN CAPONE'S POCKET.
RUMOR HAS IT FRANK NITTI'S LEFT CHICAGO. THEY SAY HE TOOK THE TRAIN DOWN TO MIAMI...TO GET HIS NERVES CALMED.
HE MUST HAVE HAD A SCARE.

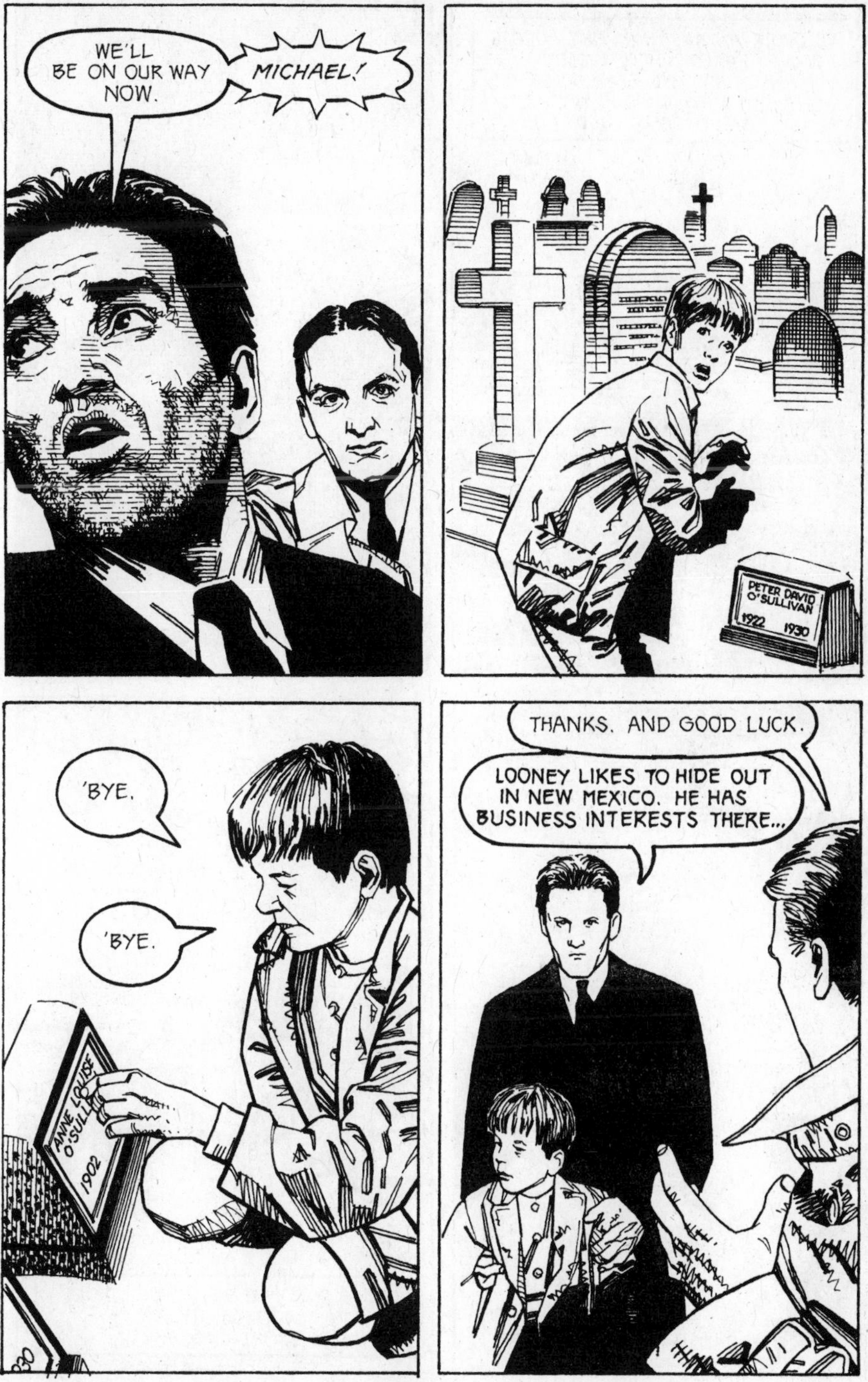
WE'LL BE ON OUR WAY NOW.
MICHAEL!
PETER DAVID O'SULLIVAN
1922 1930
'BYE.
'BYE.
ANNE LOUISE
1902
THANKS. AND GOOD LUCK.
LOONEY LIKES TO HIDE OUT IN NEW MEXICO. HE HAS BUSINESS INTERESTS THERE...

WE DROVE A LONG TIME. CUT ACROSS IOWA AND A CORNER OF MISSOURI, WHICH IS WHERE WE STAYED FOR THE NIGHT. WE WERE ON OUR WAY TO KANSAS, PAPA SAID.

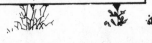

BOB — ANY CROWS ON THE FENCE--?

'FRAID SO.

"MIKE, THEY'RE SITTIN' RIGHT OUT IN FRONT OF THE PLACE IN BROAD DAYLIGHT."

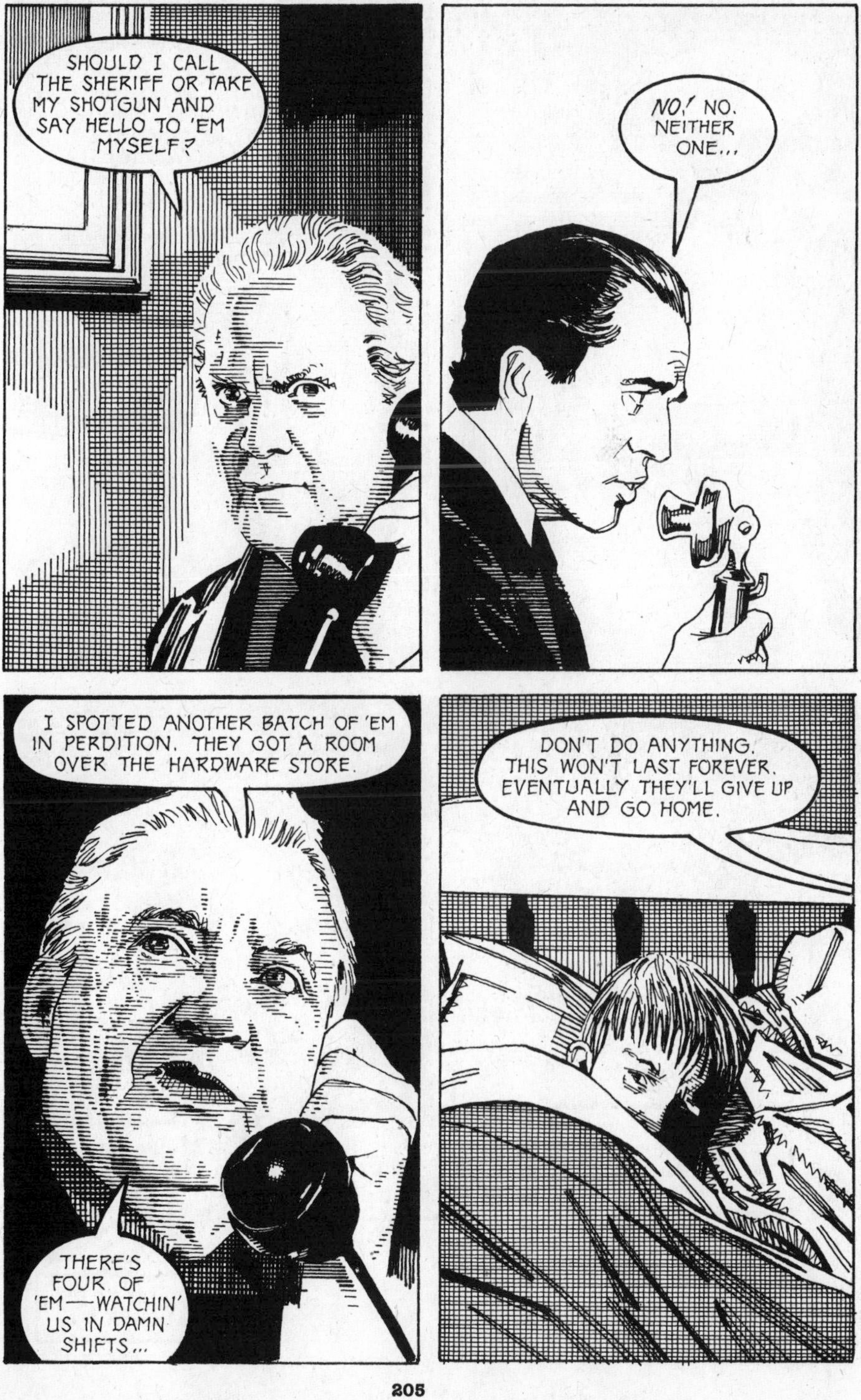
SHOULD I CALL THE SHERIFF OR TAKE MY SHOTGUN AND SAY HELLO TO 'EM MYSELF?
NO! NO. NEITHER ONE...
I SPOTTED ANOTHER BATCH OF 'EM IN PERDITION. THEY GOT A ROOM OVER THE HARDWARE STORE.
THERE'S FOUR OF 'EM—WATCHIN' US IN DAMN SHIFTS...
DON'T DO ANYTHING. THIS WON'T LAST FOREVER. EVENTUALLY THEY'LL GIVE UP AND GO HOME.

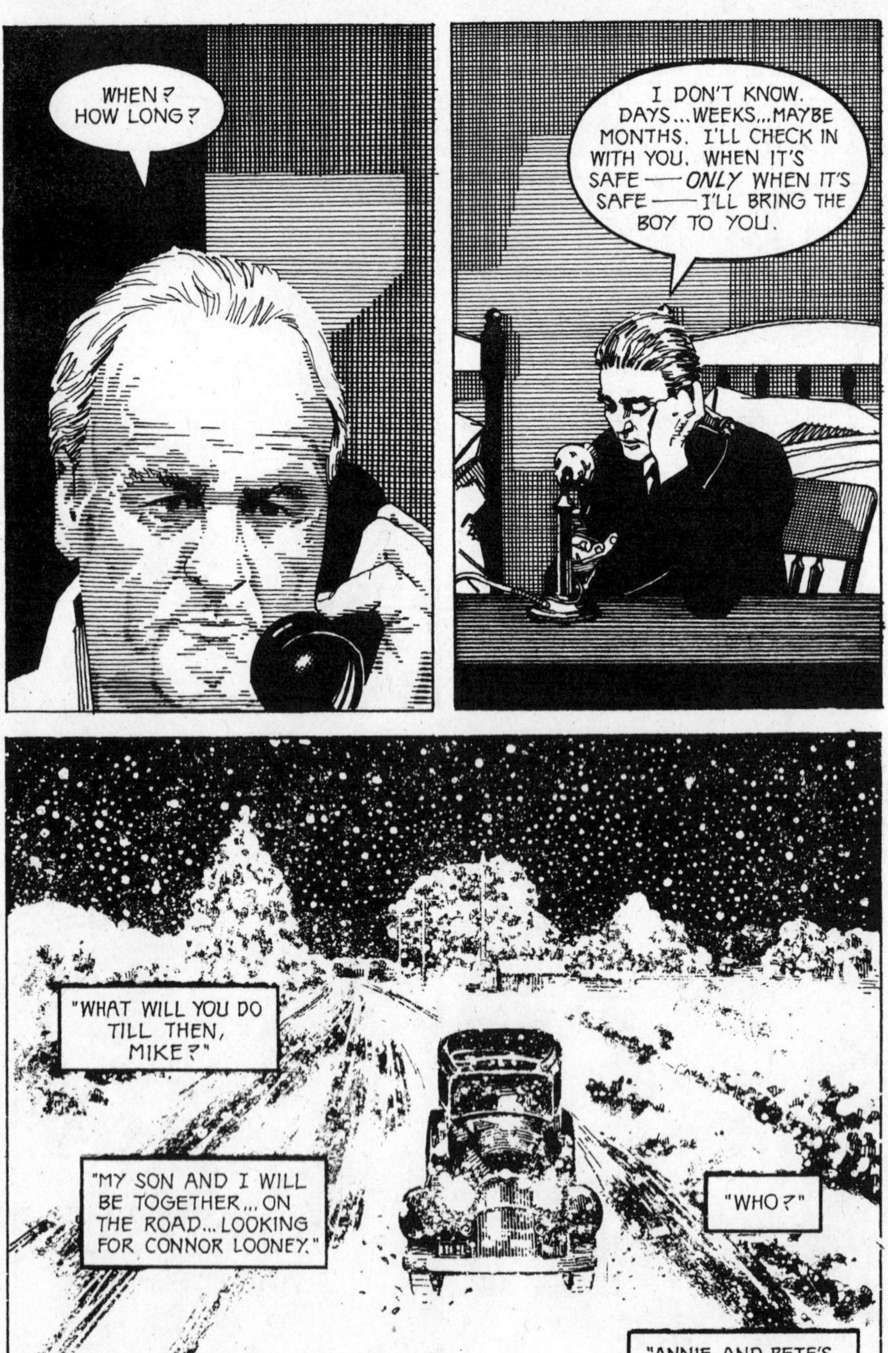
WHEN? HOW LONG?
I DON'T KNOW. DAYS...WEEKS...MAYBE MONTHS. I'LL CHECK IN WITH YOU. WHEN IT'S SAFE — ONLY WHEN IT'S SAFE — I'LL BRING THE BOY TO YOU.
"WHAT WILL YOU DO TILL THEN, MIKE?"
"MY SON AND I WILL BE TOGETHER... ON THE ROAD... LOOKING FOR CONNOR LOONEY."
"WHO?"
"ANNIE AND PETE'S MURDERER."

CHAPTER THREE:

ROAD

WITHOUT END

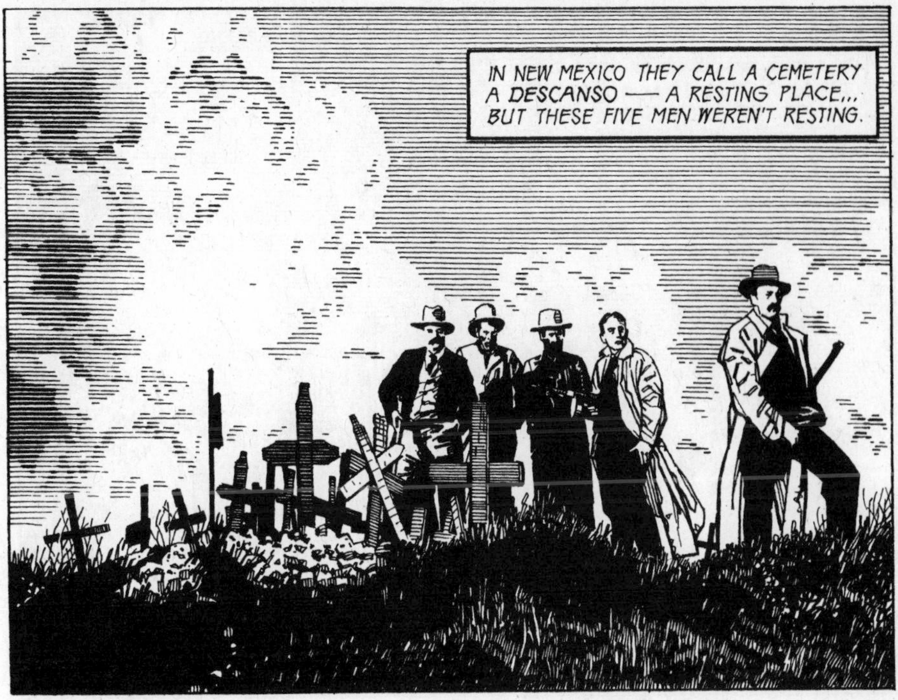
IN NEW MEXICO THEY CALL A CEMETERY A DESCANSO — A RESTING PLACE... BUT THESE FIVE MEN WEREN'T RESTING.

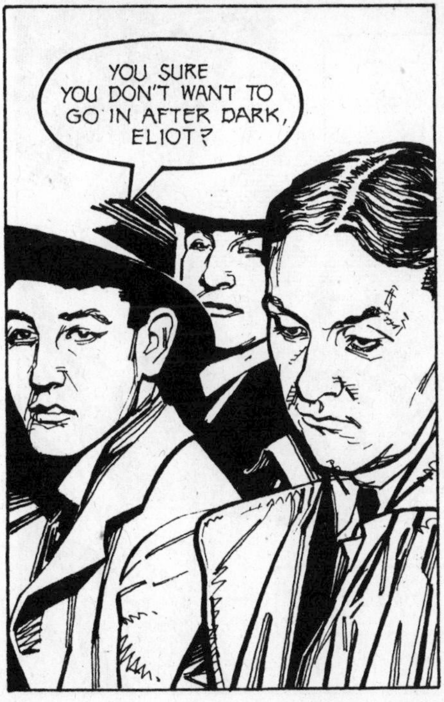
YOU SURE YOU DON'T WANT TO GO IN AFTER DARK, ELIOT?

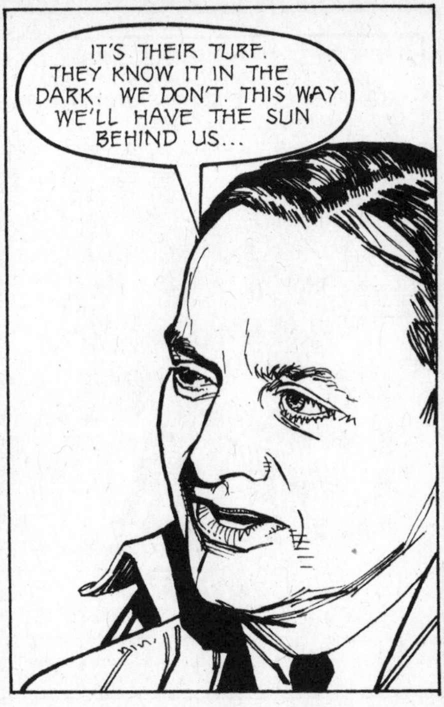
IT'S THEIR TURF. THEY KNOW IT IN THE DARK. WE DON'T. THIS WAY WE'LL HAVE THE SUN BEHIND US...

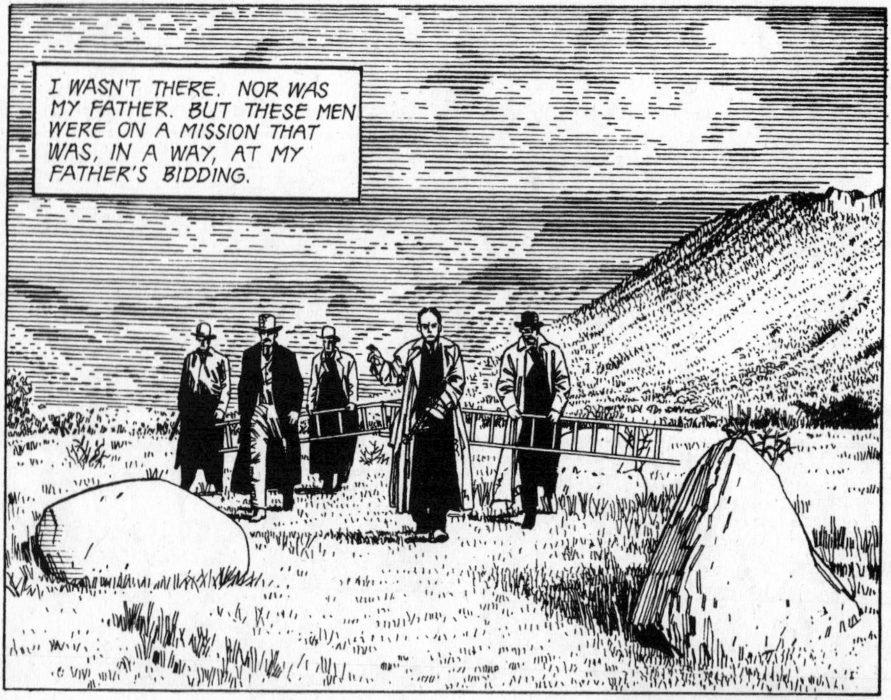
I WASN'T THERE. NOR WAS MY FATHER. BUT THESE MEN WERE ON A MISSION THAT WAS, IN A WAY, AT MY FATHER'S BIDDING.

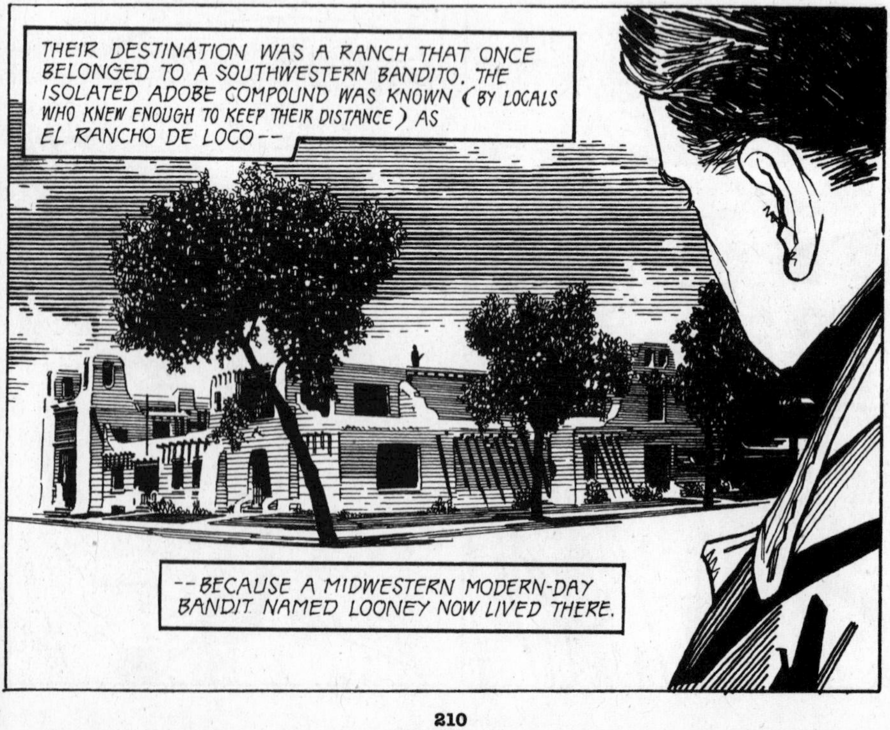
THEIR DESTINATION WAS A RANCH THAT ONCE BELONGED TO A SOUTHWESTERN BANDITO. THE ISOLATED ADOBE COMPOUND WAS KNOWN (BY LOCALS WHO KNEW ENOUGH TO KEEP THEIR DISTANCE) AS EL RANCHO DE LOCO--
--BECAUSE A MIDWESTERN MODERN-DAY BANDIT NAMED LOONEY NOW LIVED THERE.

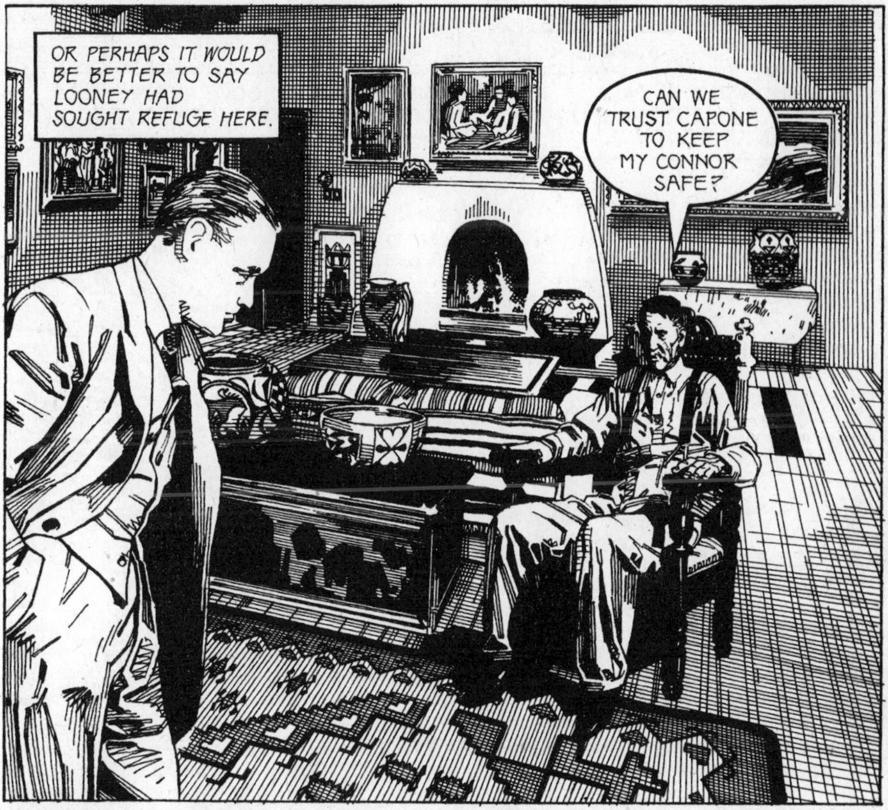
OR PERHAPS IT WOULD BE BETTER TO SAY LOONEY HAD SOUGHT REFUGE HERE.
CAN WE TRUST CAPONE TO KEEP MY CONNOR SAFE?

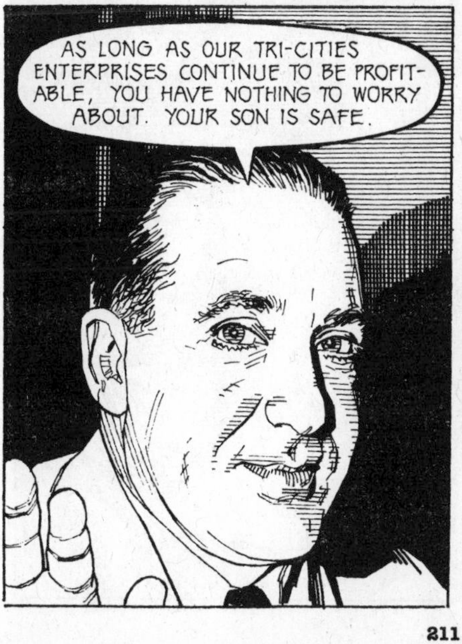
AS LONG AS OUR TRI-CITIES ENTERPRISES CONTINUE TO BE PROFIT-ABLE, YOU HAVE NOTHING TO WORRY ABOUT. YOUR SON IS SAFE.

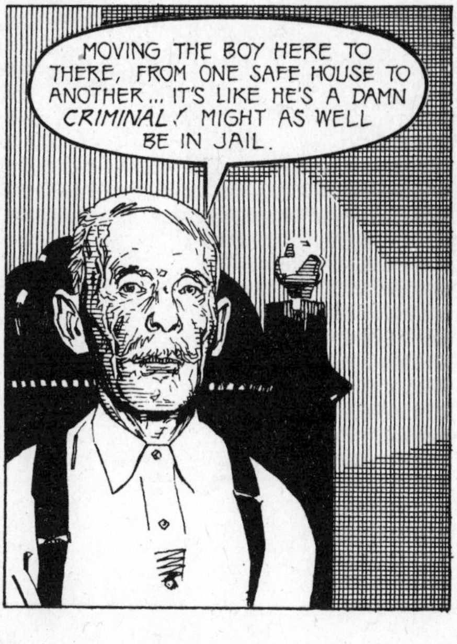
MOVING THE BOY HERE TO THERE, FROM ONE SAFE HOUSE TO ANOTHER... IT'S LIKE HE'S A DAMN *CRIMINAL!* MIGHT AS WELL BE IN JAIL.

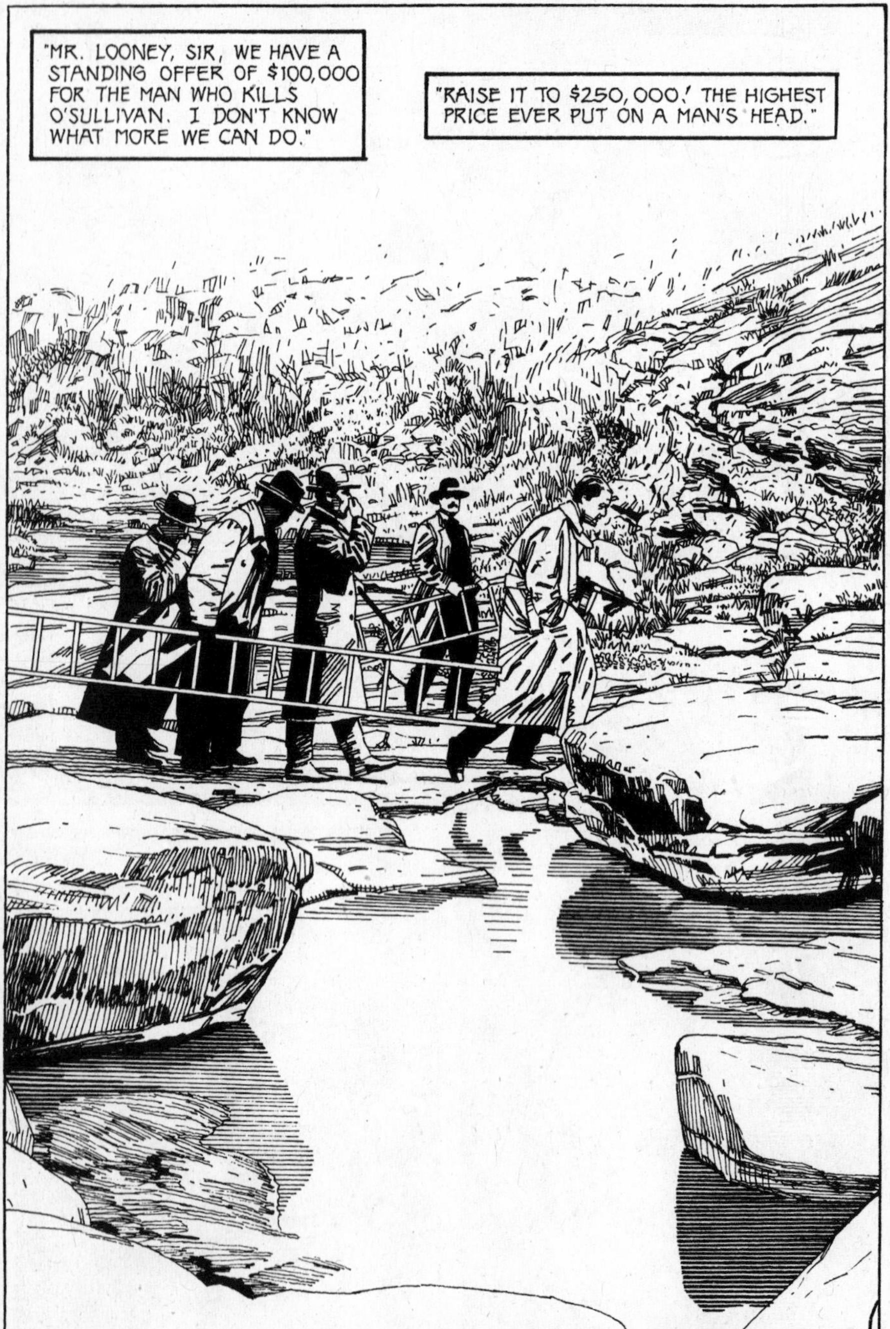
"MR. LOONEY, SIR, WE HAVE A STANDING OFFER OF $100,000 FOR THE MAN WHO KILLS O'SULLIVAN. I DON'T KNOW WHAT MORE WE CAN DO."
"RAISE IT TO $250,000! THE HIGHEST PRICE EVER PUT ON A MAN'S HEAD."

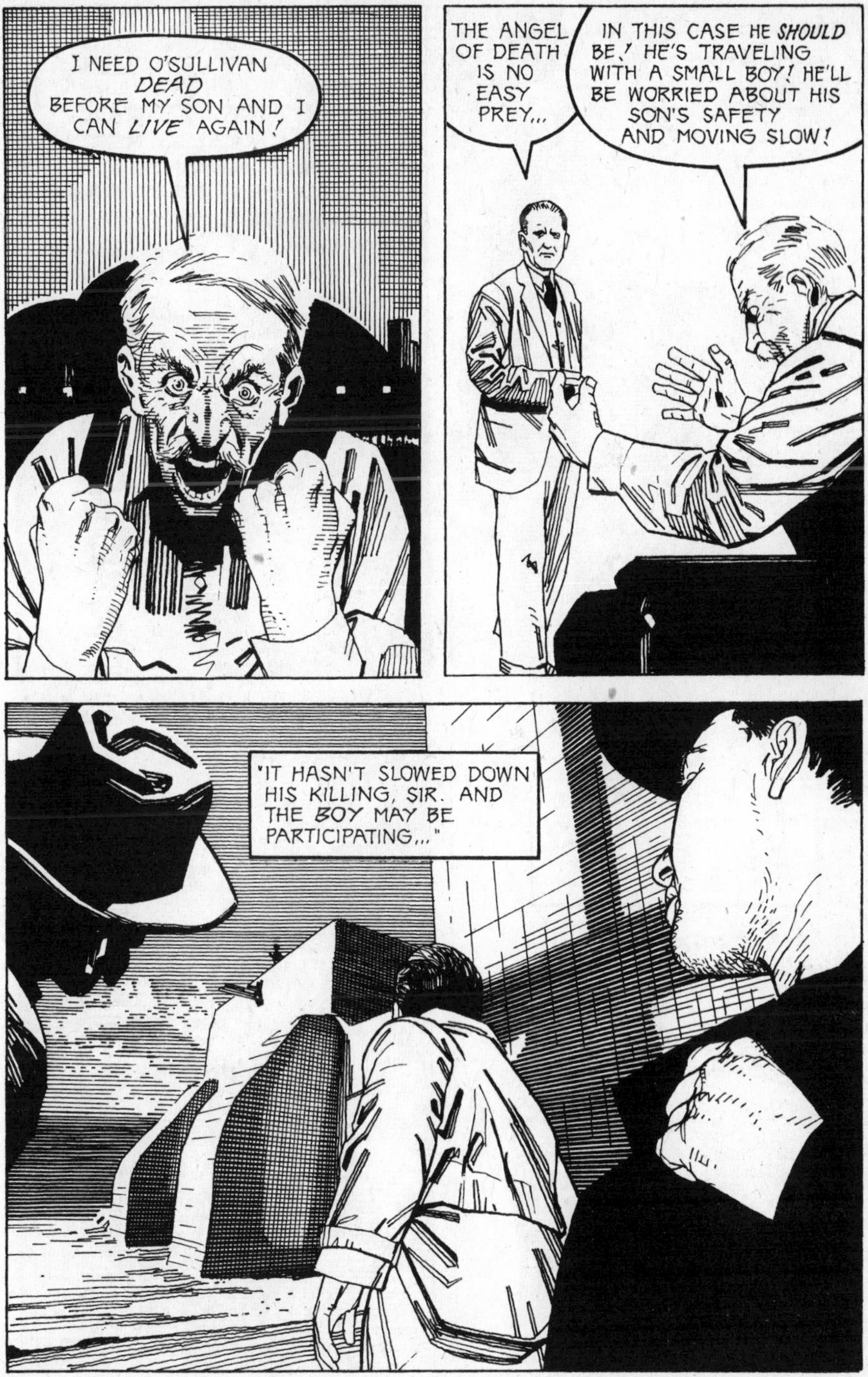
I NEED O'SULLIVAN DEAD BEFORE MY SON AND I CAN LIVE AGAIN!
THE ANGEL OF DEATH IS NO EASY PREY...
IN THIS CASE HE SHOULD BE! HE'S TRAVELING WITH A SMALL BOY! HE'LL BE WORRIED ABOUT HIS SON'S SAFETY AND MOVING SLOW!
"IT HASN'T SLOWED DOWN HIS KILLING, SIR. AND THE BOY MAY BE PARTICIPATING..."

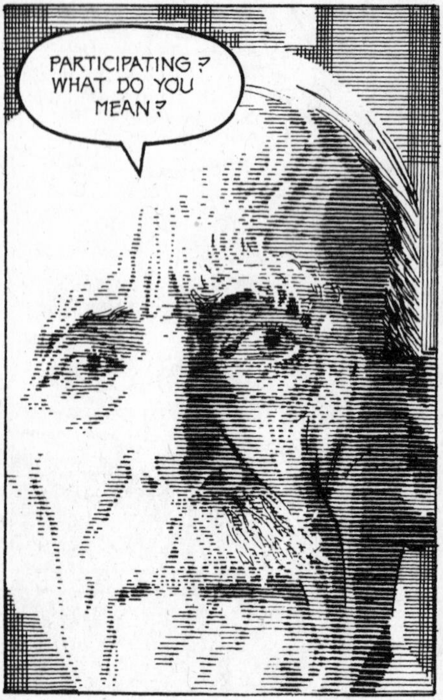
PARTICIPATING? WHAT DO YOU MEAN?

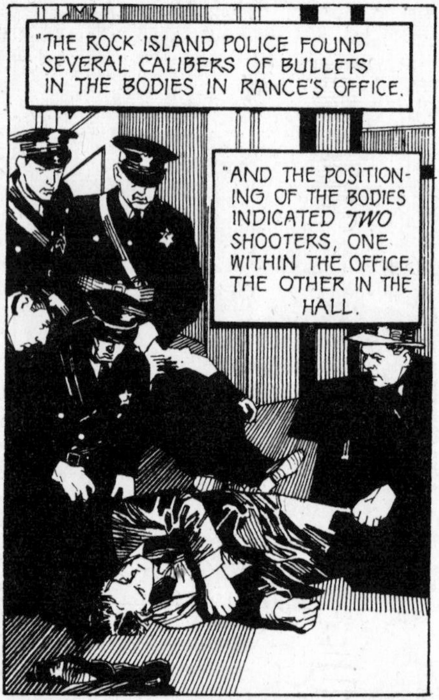
"THE ROCK ISLAND POLICE FOUND SEVERAL CALIBERS OF BULLETS IN THE BODIES IN RANCE'S OFFICE.
"AND THE POSITIONING OF THE BODIES INDICATED *TWO* SHOOTERS, ONE WITHIN THE OFFICE, THE OTHER IN THE HALL.

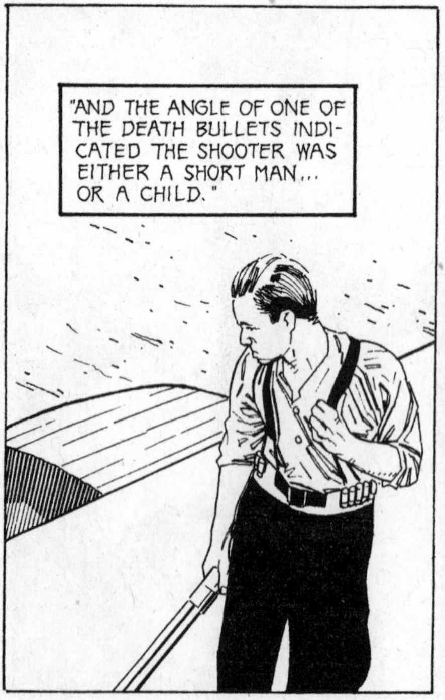
"AND THE ANGLE OF ONE OF THE DEATH BULLETS INDICATED THE SHOOTER WAS EITHER A SHORT MAN... OR A CHILD."

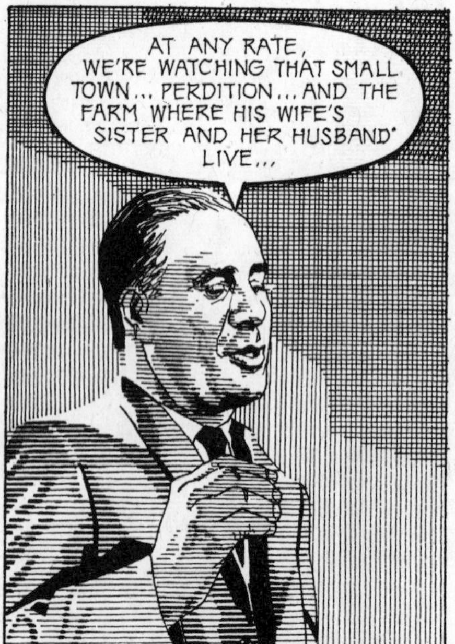
AT ANY RATE, WE'RE WATCHING THAT SMALL TOWN... PERDITION... AND THE FARM WHERE HIS WIFE'S SISTER AND HER HUSBAND LIVE...

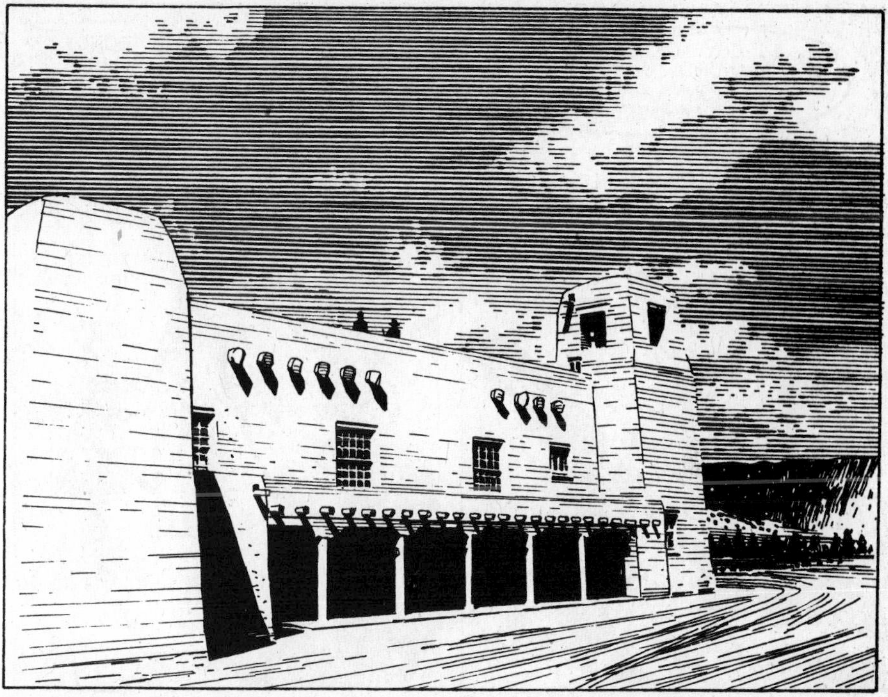

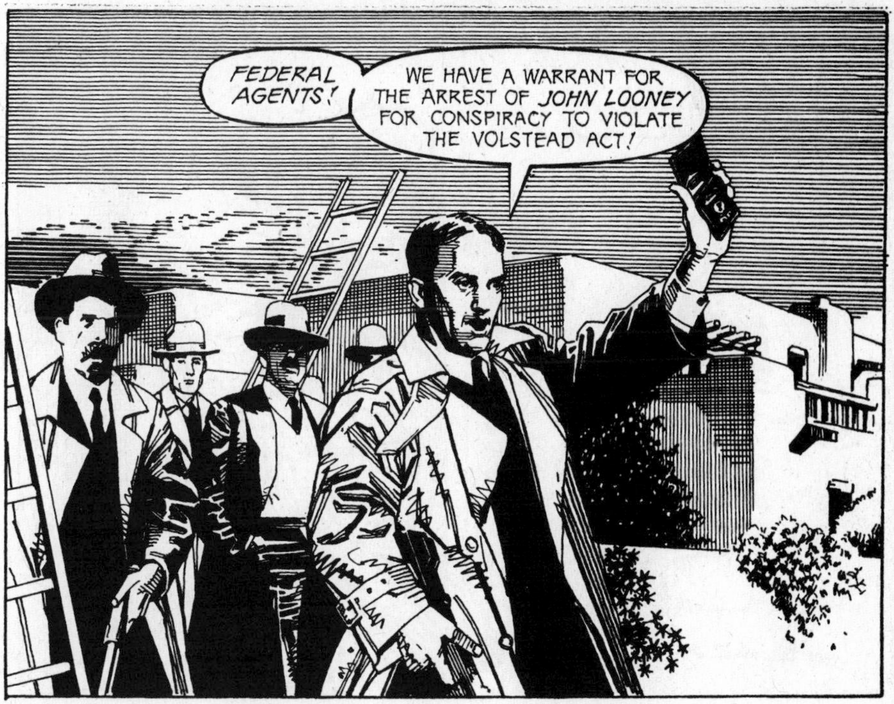
FEDERAL AGENTS!
WE HAVE A WARRANT FOR THE ARREST OF JOHN LOONEY FOR CONSPIRACY TO VIOLATE THE VOLSTEAD ACT!

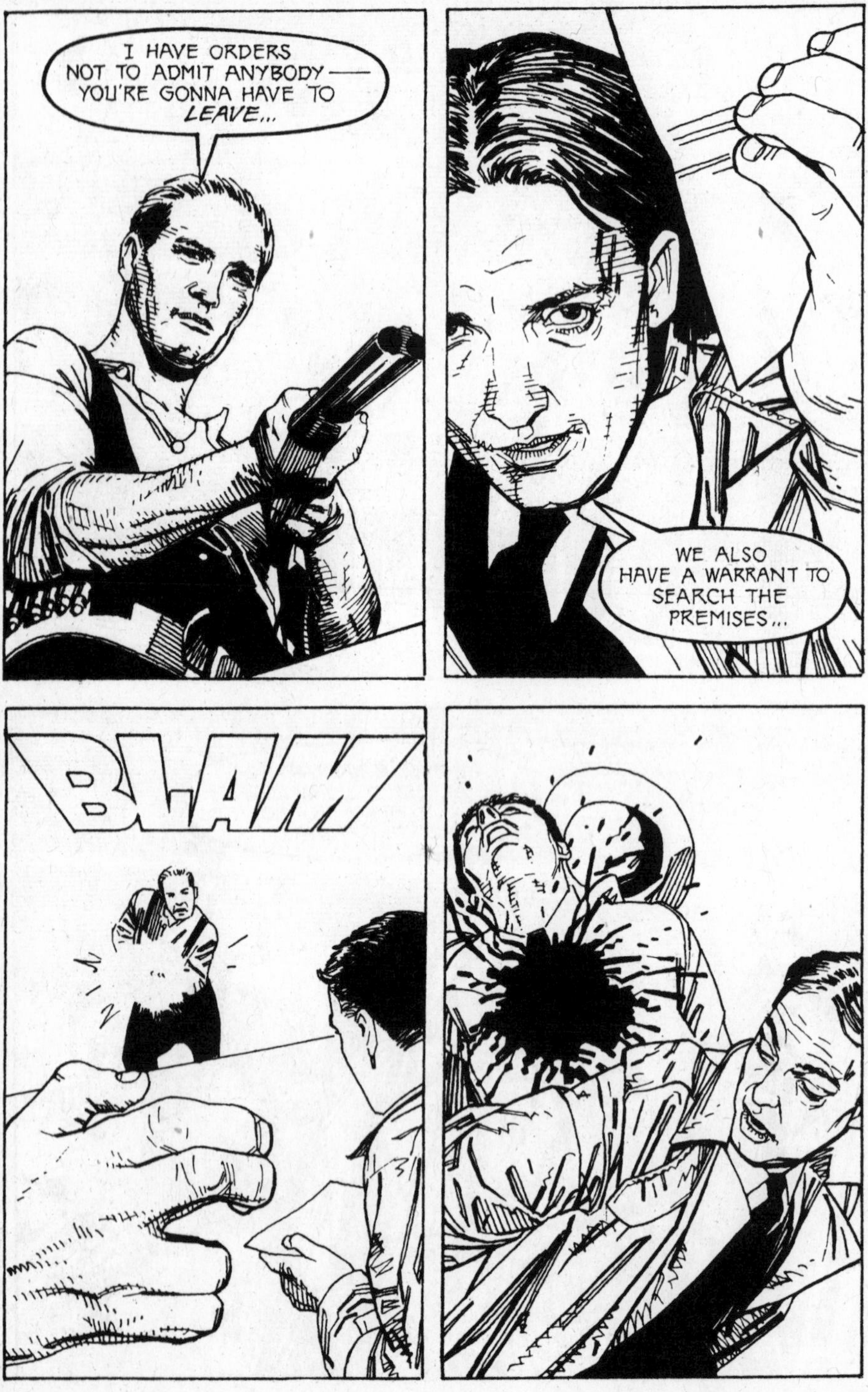
I HAVE ORDERS NOT TO ADMIT ANYBODY—— YOU'RE GONNA HAVE TO *LEAVE*...
WE ALSO HAVE A WARRANT TO SEARCH THE PREMISES...
BLAM

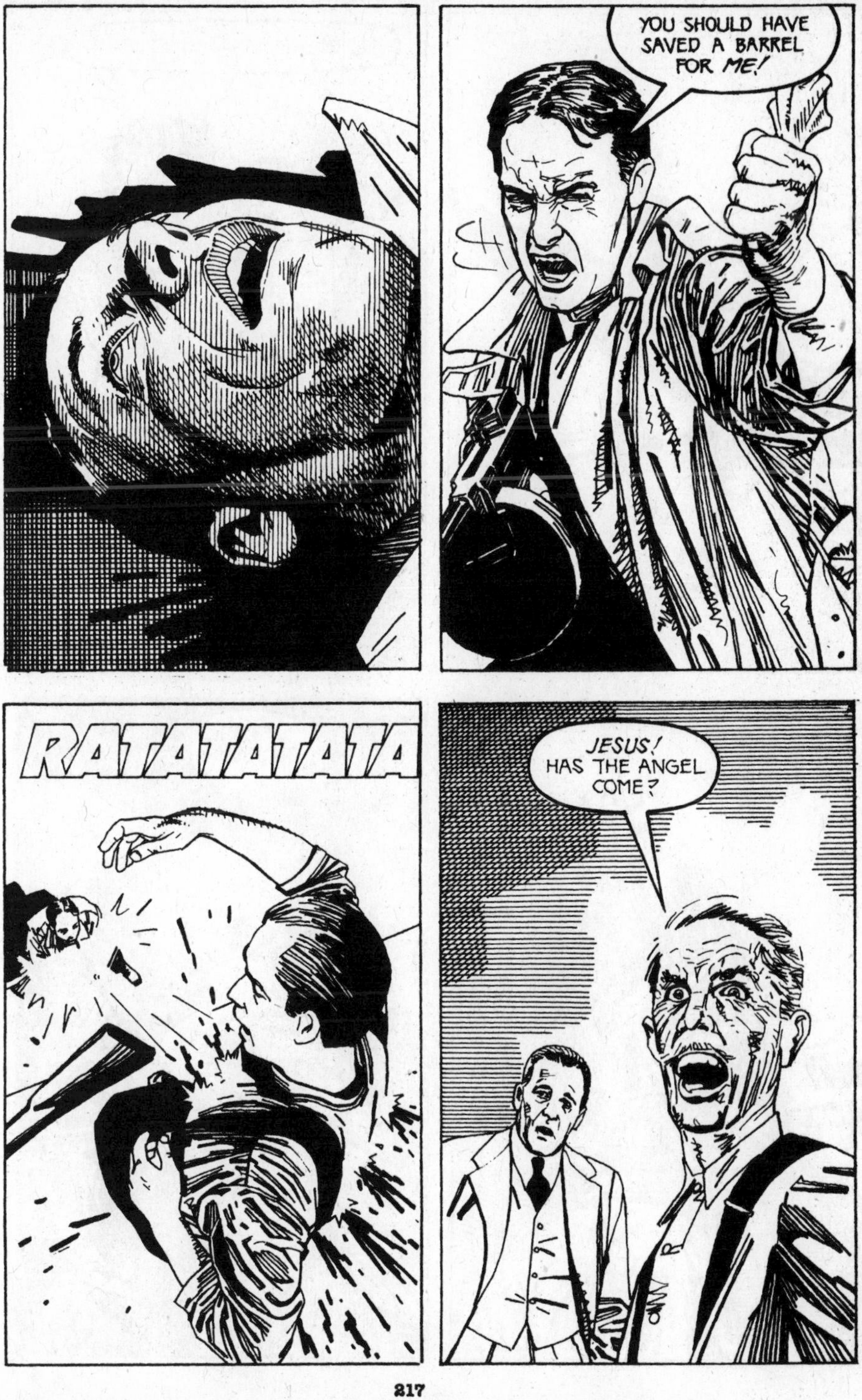
YOU SHOULD HAVE SAVED A BARREL FOR *ME!*
RATATATATA
JESUS! HAS THE ANGEL COME?

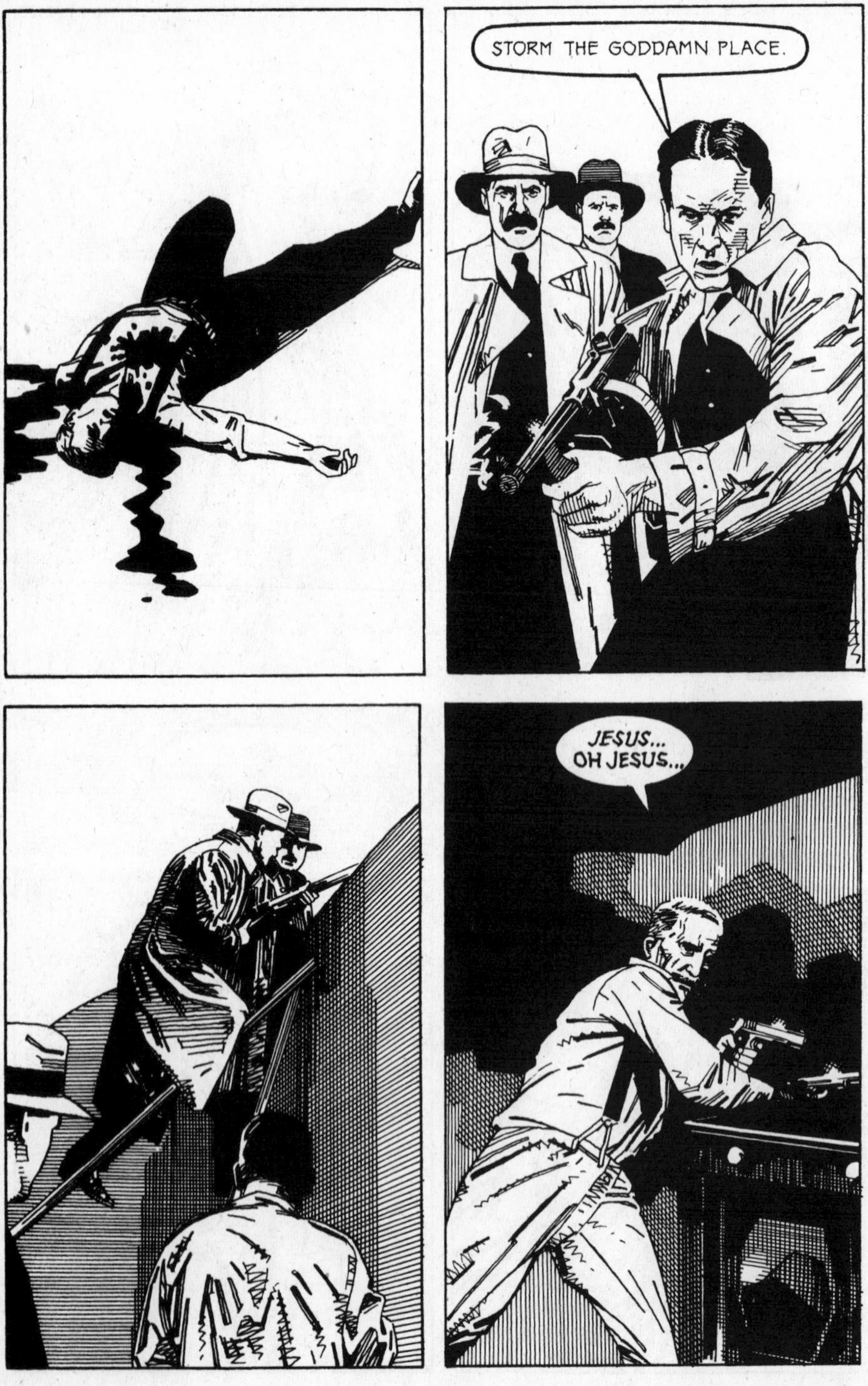
STORM THE GODDAMN PLACE.
JESUS... OH JESUS...

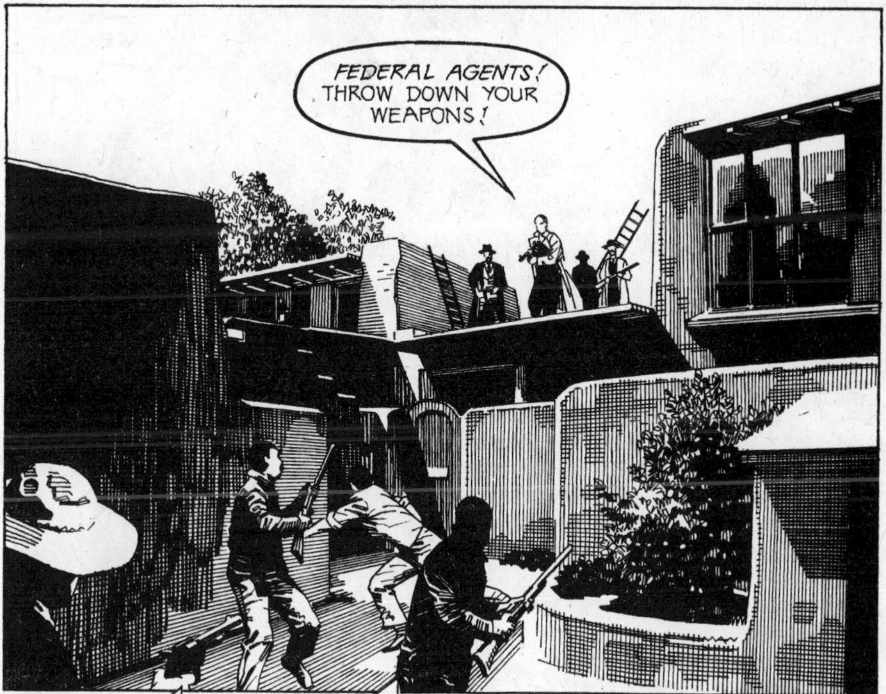
FEDERAL AGENTS! THROW DOWN YOUR WEAPONS!

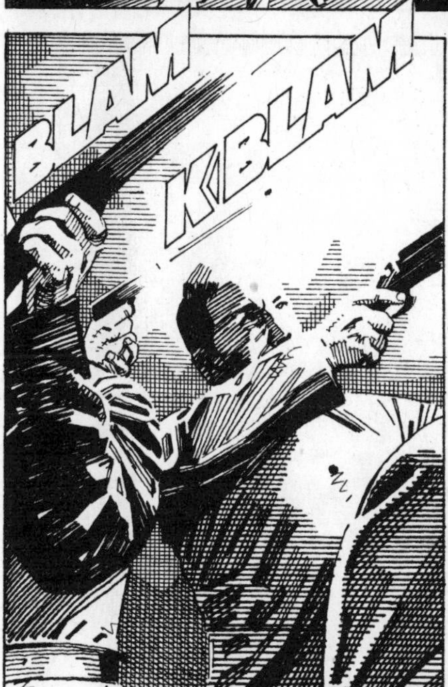
BLAM
KBLAM

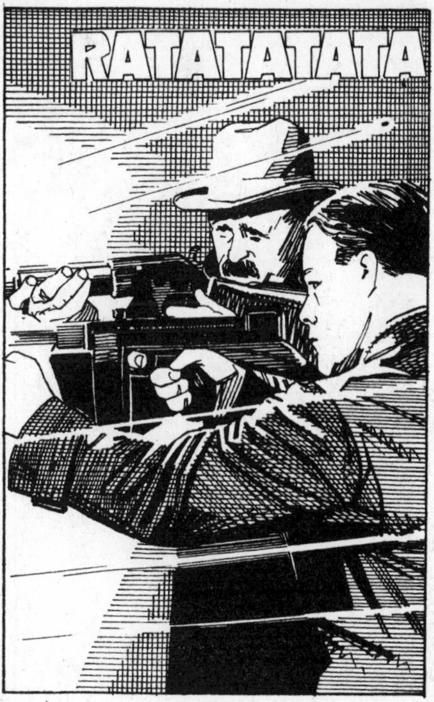
RATATATATA

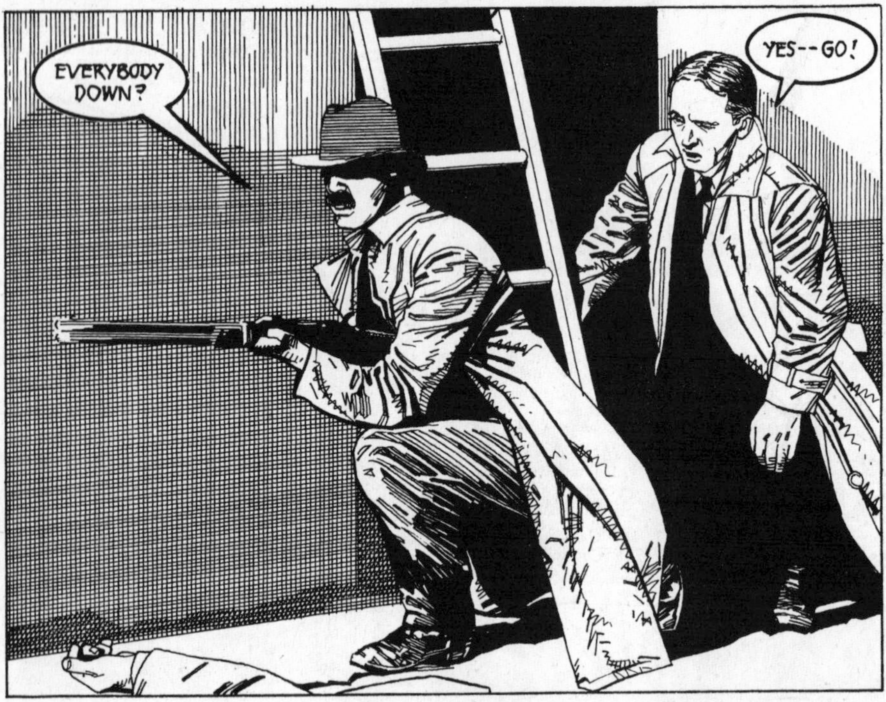
EVERYBODY DOWN?
YES--GO!

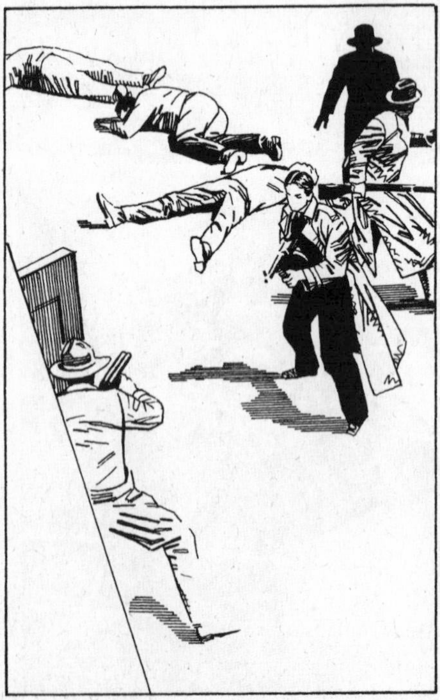

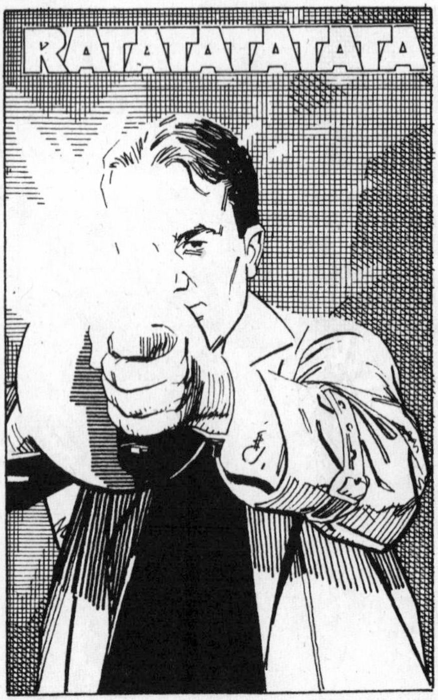
RATATATATATA

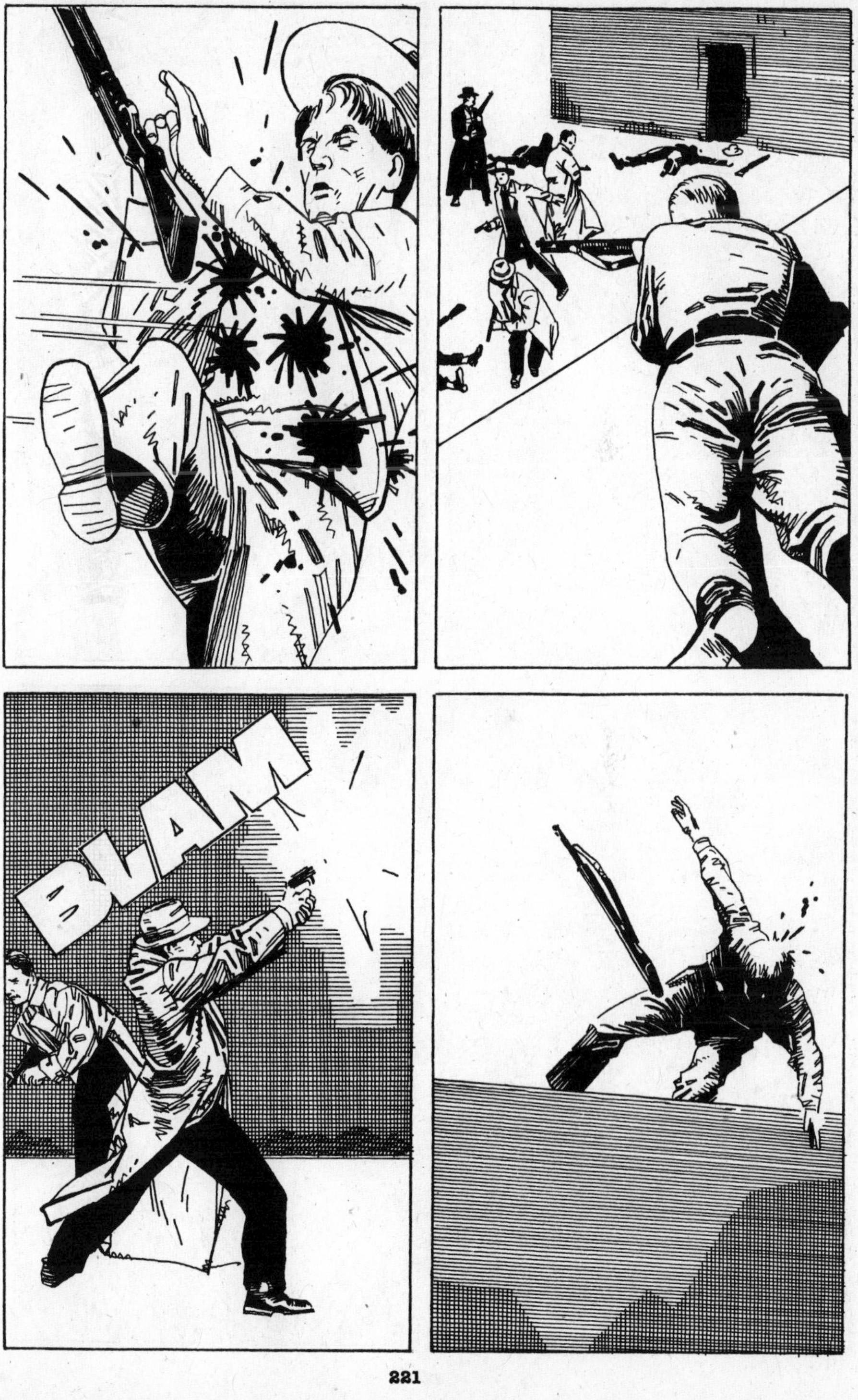
BLAM

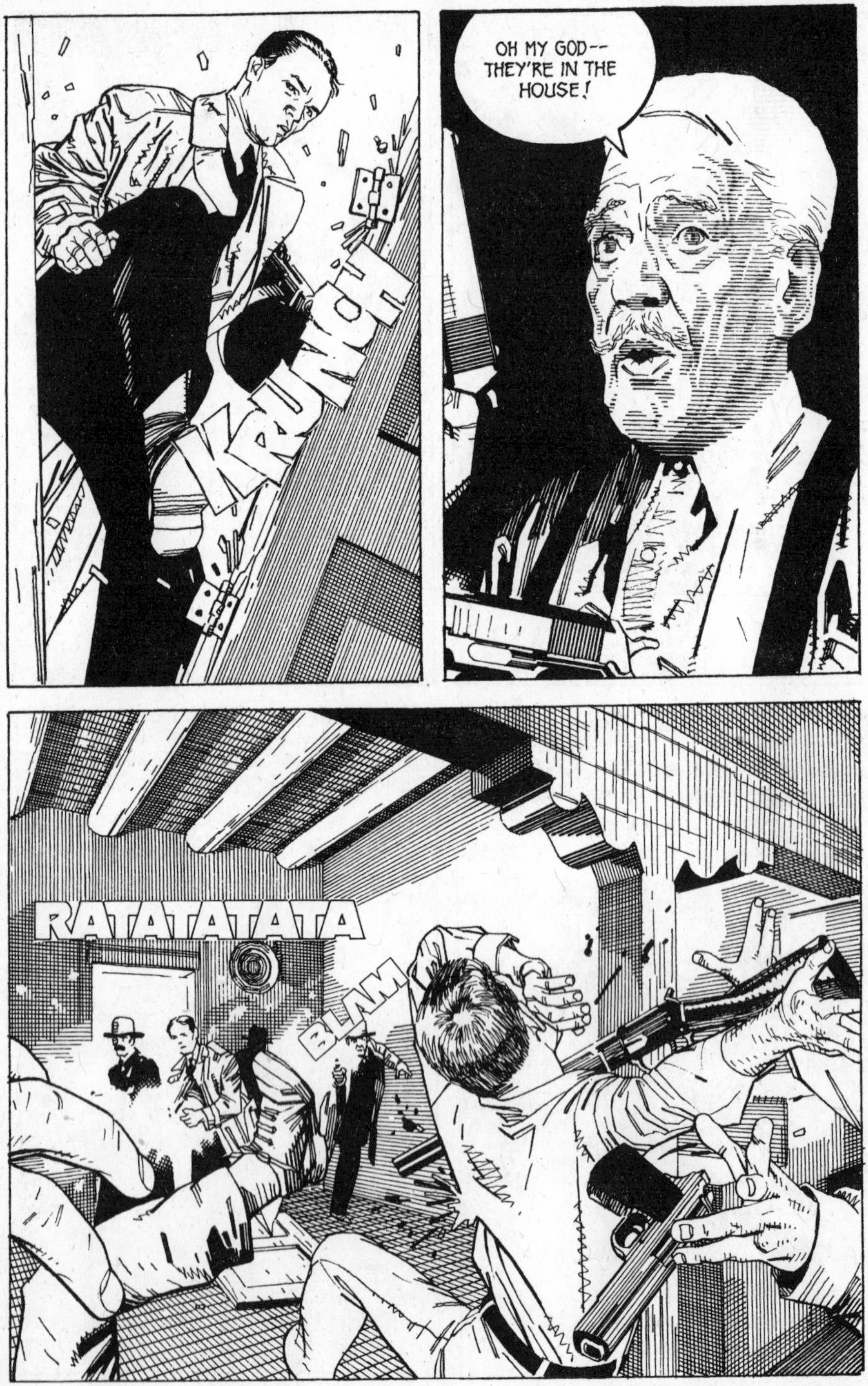
KRUNCH
OH MY GOD-- THEY'RE IN THE HOUSE!
RATATATATA
BLAM

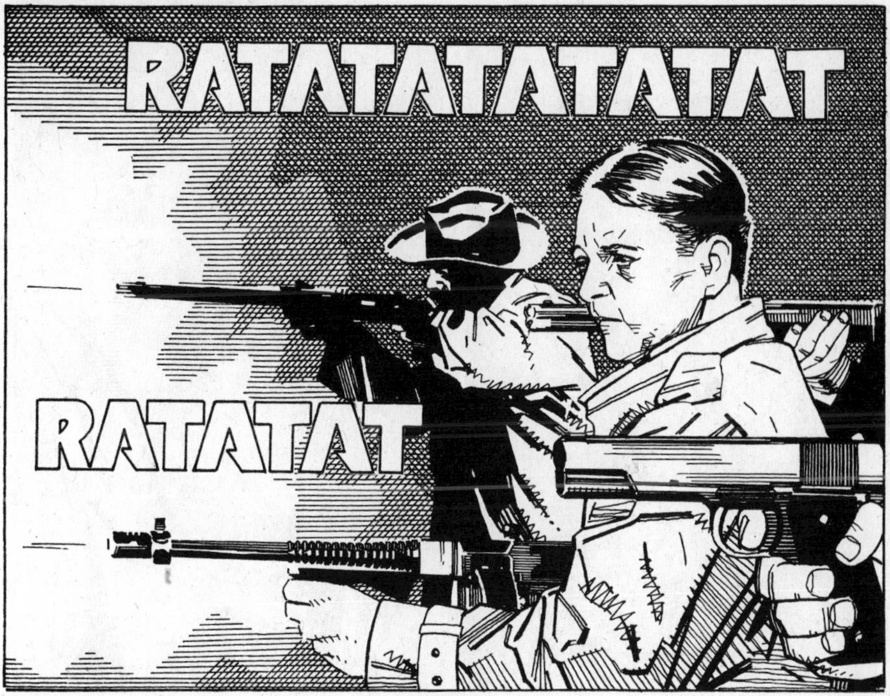
RATATATATATATAT
RATATAT

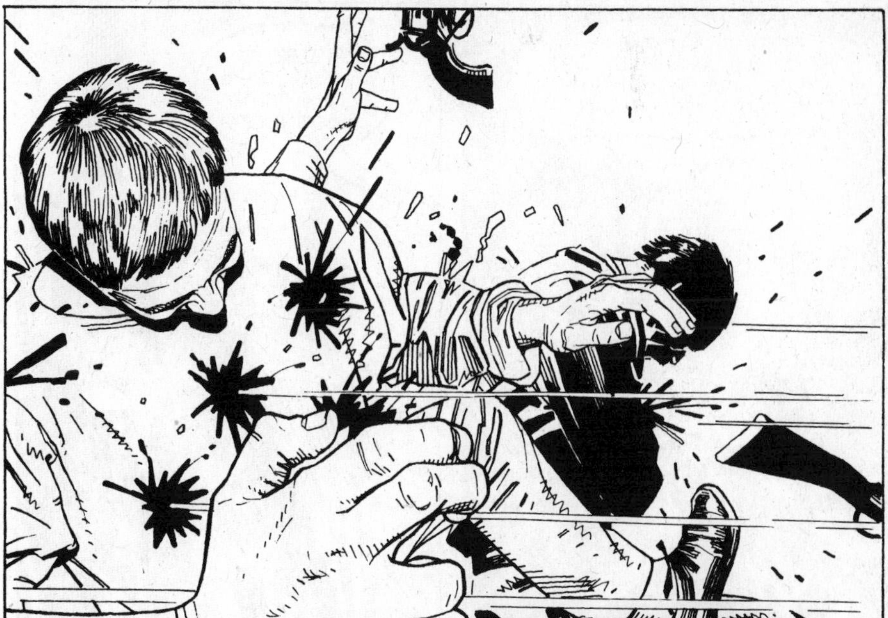

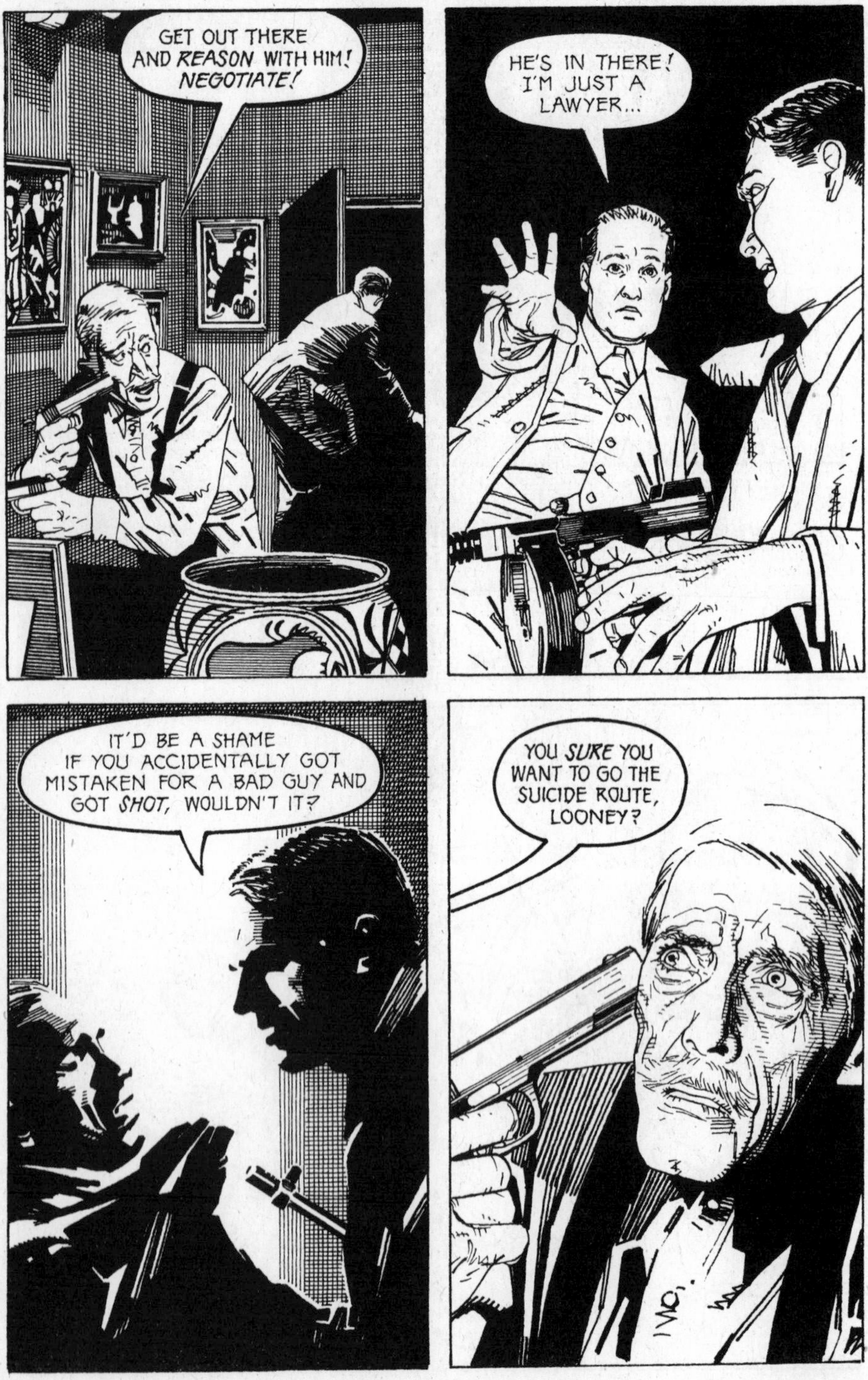
GET OUT THERE AND REASON WITH HIM! NEGOTIATE!
HE'S IN THERE! I'M JUST A LAWYER...
IT'D BE A SHAME IF YOU ACCIDENTALLY GOT MISTAKEN FOR A BAD GUY AND GOT SHOT, WOULDN'T IT?
YOU SURE YOU WANT TO GO THE SUICIDE ROUTE, LOONEY?

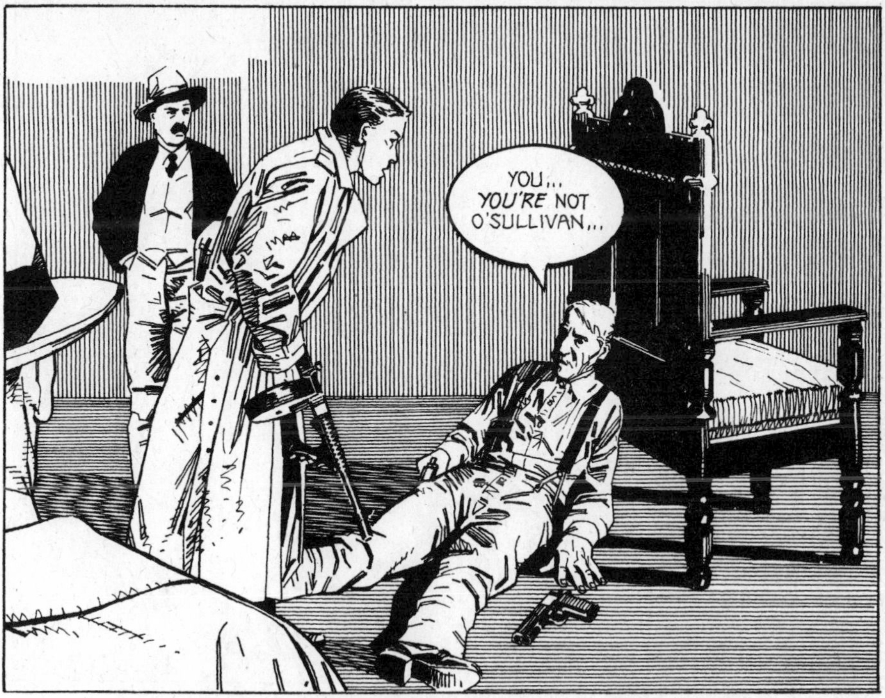
YOU... *YOU'RE* NOT O'SULLIVAN...

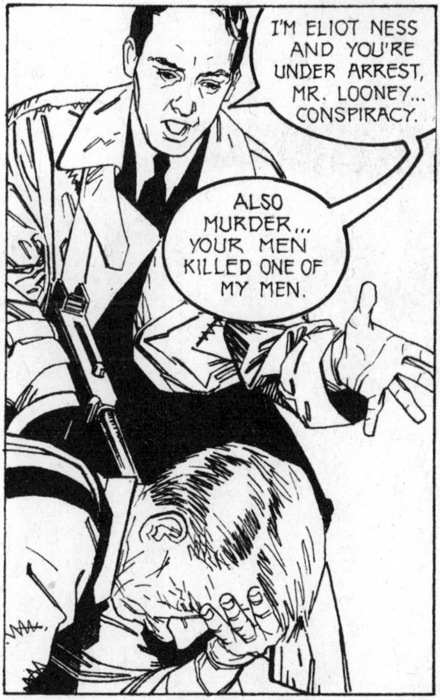
I'M ELIOT NESS AND YOU'RE UNDER ARREST, MR. LOONEY... CONSPIRACY.
ALSO MURDER... YOUR MEN KILLED ONE OF MY MEN.

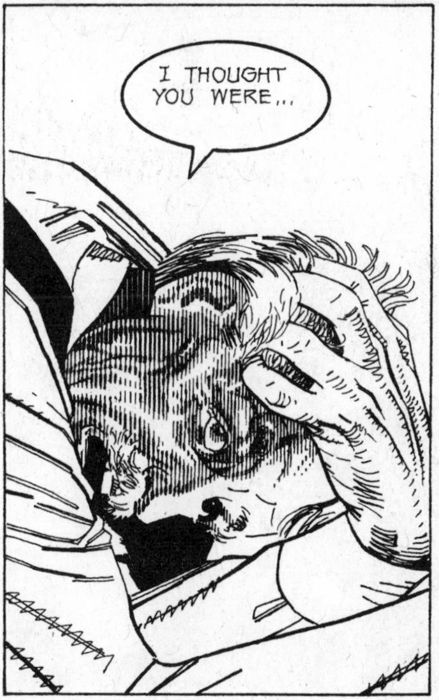
I THOUGHT YOU WERE...

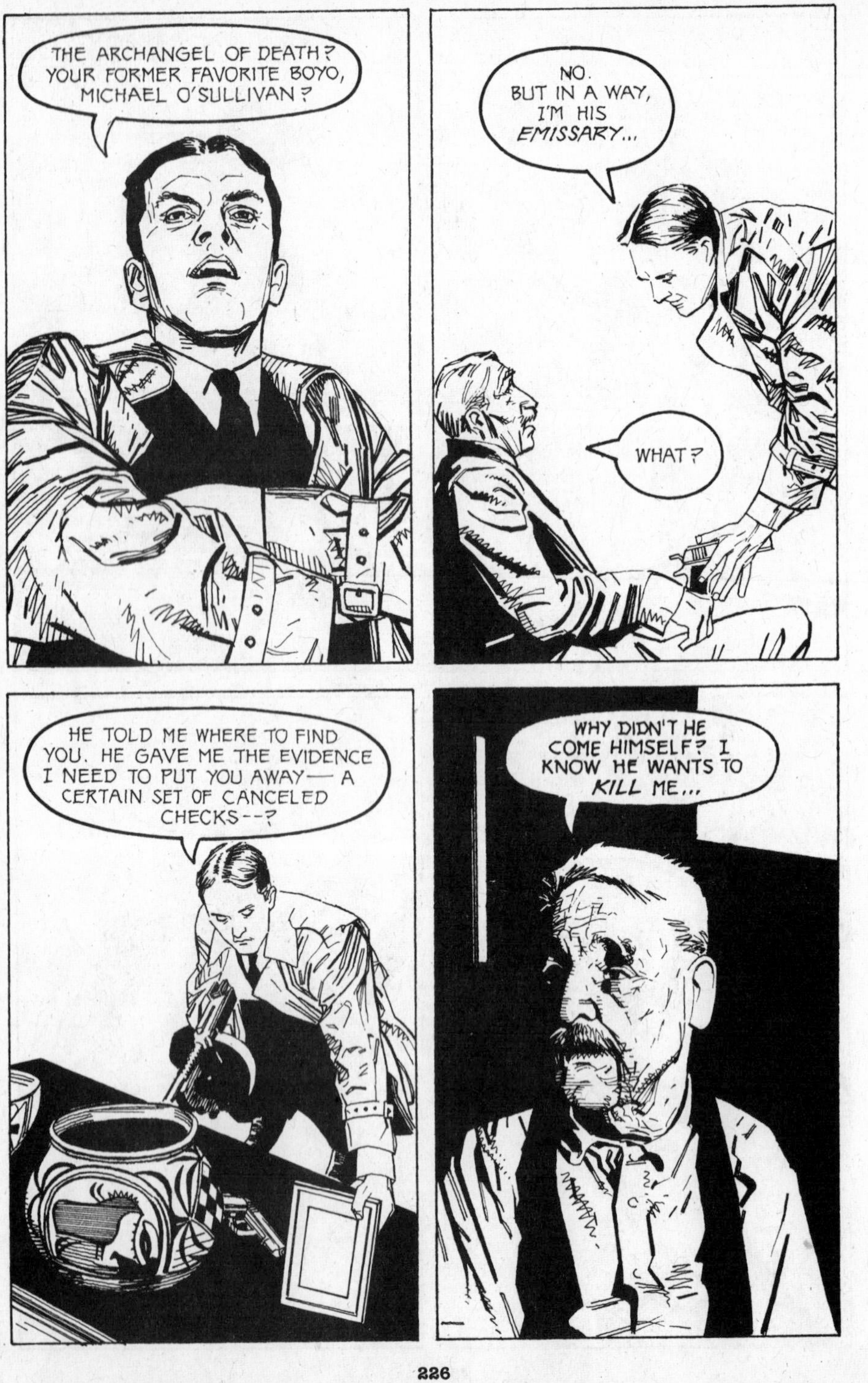
THE ARCHANGEL OF DEATH? YOUR FORMER FAVORITE BOYO, MICHAEL O'SULLIVAN?
NO. BUT IN A WAY, I'M HIS *EMISSARY*...
WHAT?
HE TOLD ME WHERE TO FIND YOU. HE GAVE ME THE EVIDENCE I NEED TO PUT YOU AWAY— A CERTAIN SET OF CANCELED CHECKS--?
WHY DIDN'T HE COME HIMSELF? I KNOW HE WANTS TO *KILL* ME...

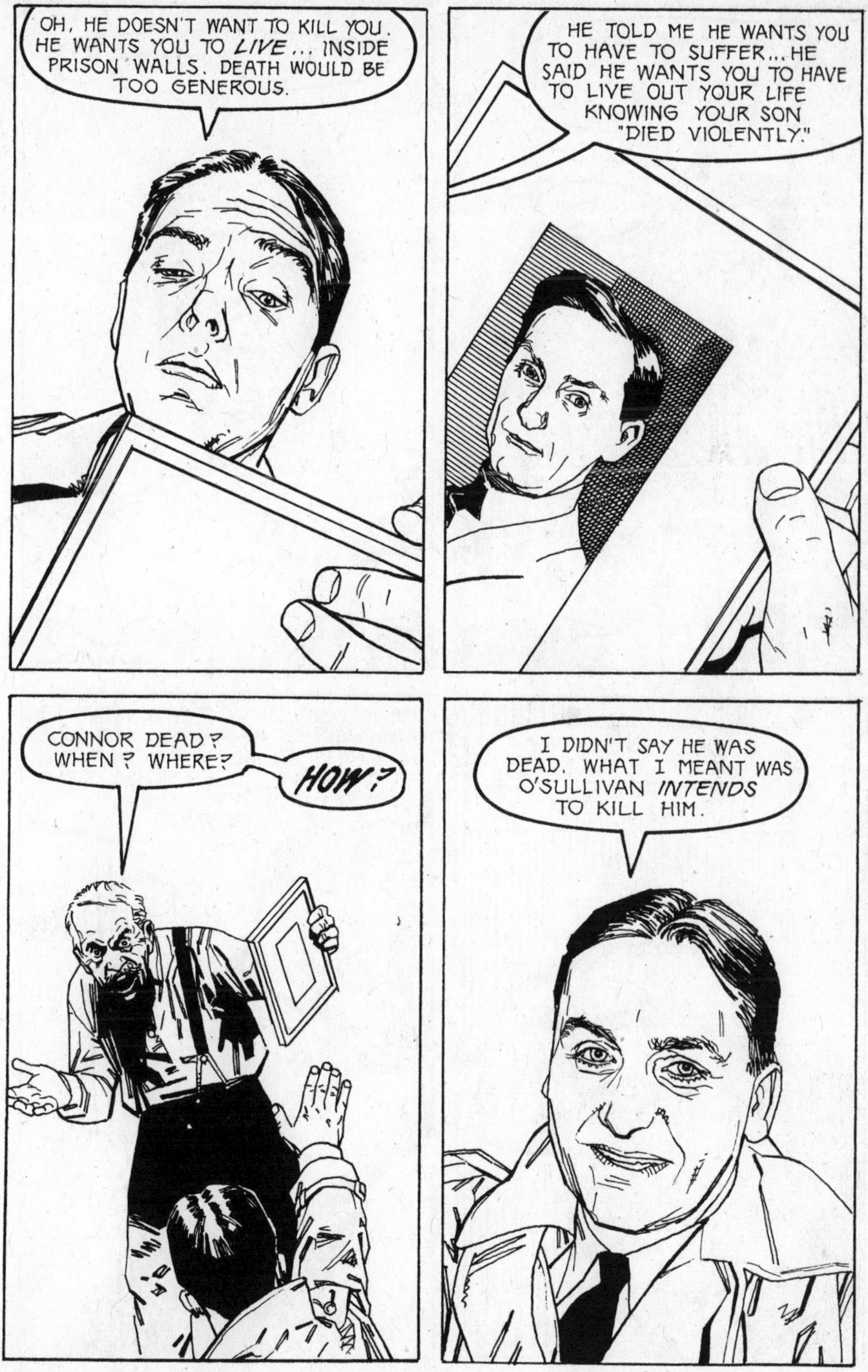
OH, HE DOESN'T WANT TO KILL YOU. HE WANTS YOU TO *LIVE*... INSIDE PRISON WALLS. DEATH WOULD BE TOO GENEROUS.
HE TOLD ME HE WANTS YOU TO HAVE TO SUFFER... HE SAID HE WANTS YOU TO HAVE TO LIVE OUT YOUR LIFE KNOWING YOUR SON "DIED VIOLENTLY."
CONNOR DEAD? WHEN? WHERE?
HOW?
I DIDN'T SAY HE WAS DEAD. WHAT I MEANT WAS O'SULLIVAN *INTENDS* TO KILL HIM.

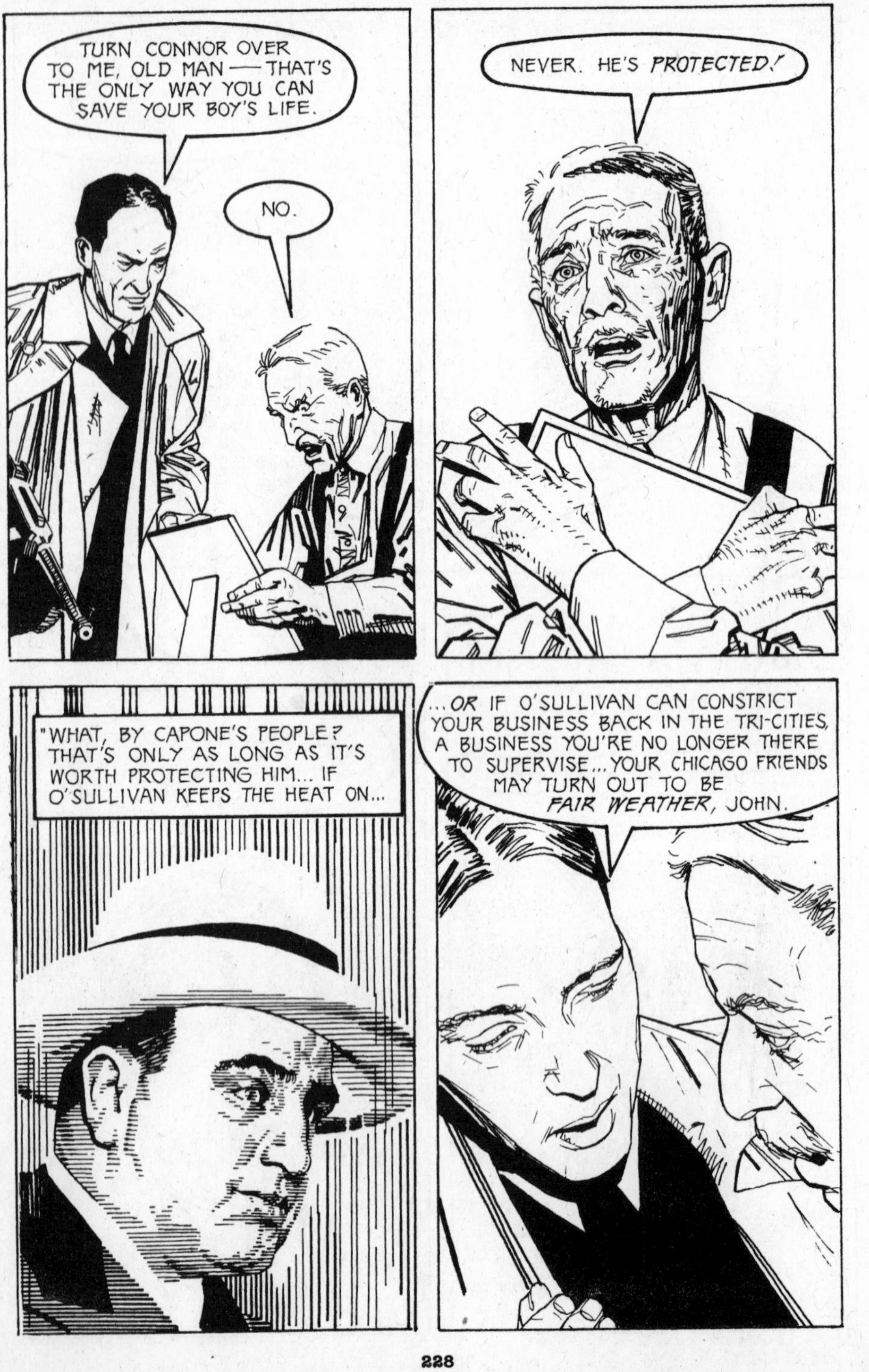
TURN CONNOR OVER TO ME, OLD MAN — THAT'S THE ONLY WAY YOU CAN SAVE YOUR BOY'S LIFE.
NO.
NEVER. HE'S *PROTECTED!*
"WHAT, BY CAPONE'S PEOPLE? THAT'S ONLY AS LONG AS IT'S WORTH PROTECTING HIM... IF O'SULLIVAN KEEPS THE HEAT ON...
...*OR* IF O'SULLIVAN CAN CONSTRICT YOUR BUSINESS BACK IN THE TRI-CITIES, A BUSINESS YOU'RE NO LONGER THERE TO SUPERVISE... YOUR CHICAGO FRIENDS MAY TURN OUT TO BE *FAIR WEATHER*, JOHN.

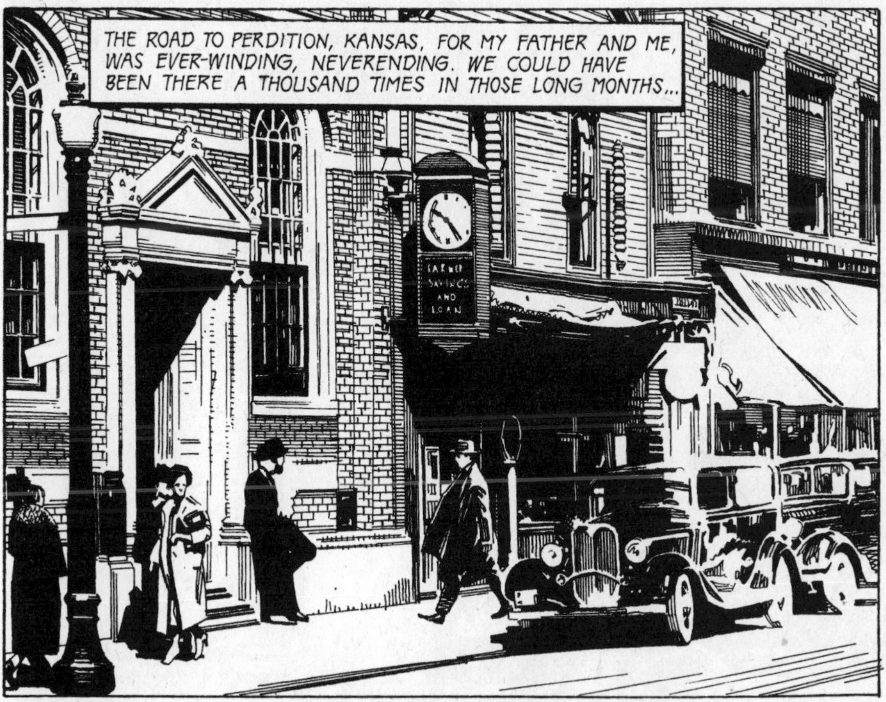
THE ROAD TO PERDITION, KANSAS, FOR MY FATHER AND ME, WAS EVER-WINDING, NEVERENDING. WE COULD HAVE BEEN THERE A THOUSAND TIMES IN THOSE LONG MONTHS...

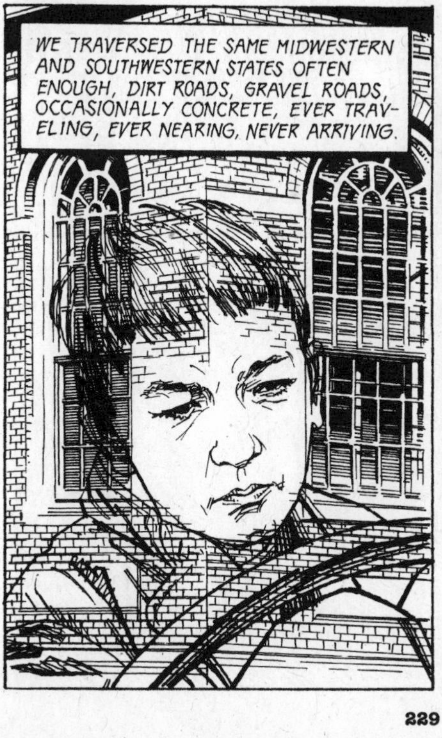
WE TRAVERSED THE SAME MIDWESTERN AND SOUTHWESTERN STATES OFTEN ENOUGH, DIRT ROADS, GRAVEL ROADS, OCCASIONALLY CONCRETE, EVER TRAVELING, EVER NEARING, NEVER ARRIVING.

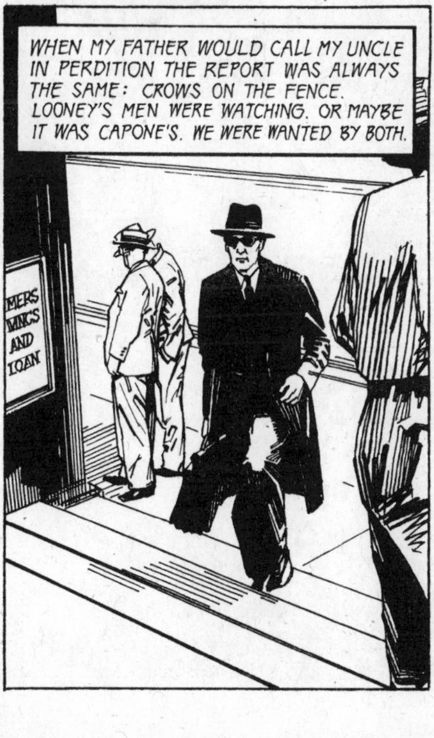
WHEN MY FATHER WOULD CALL MY UNCLE IN PERDITION THE REPORT WAS ALWAYS THE SAME: CROWS ON THE FENCE. LOONEY'S MEN WERE WATCHING. OR MAYBE IT WAS CAPONE'S. WE WERE WANTED BY BOTH.

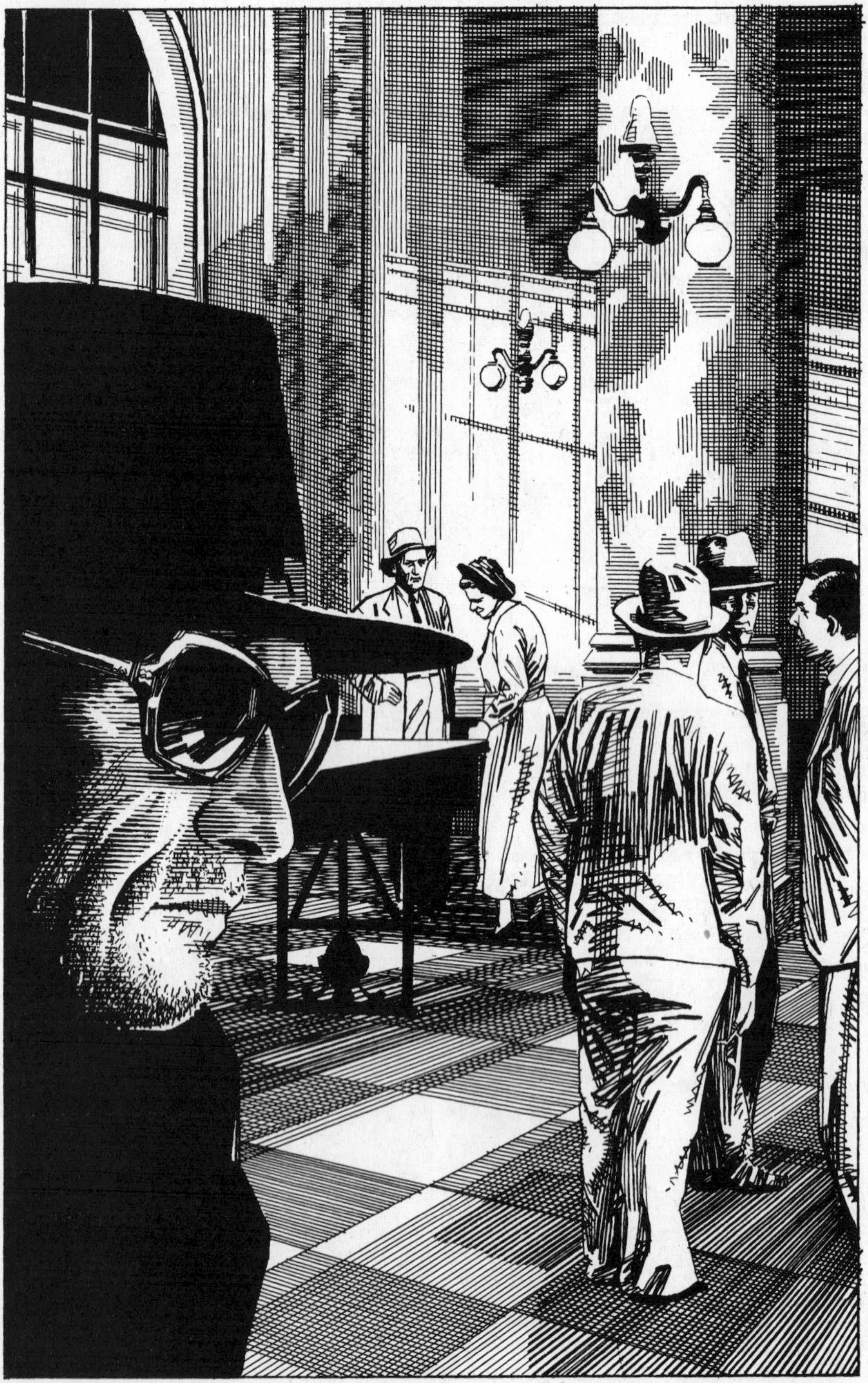

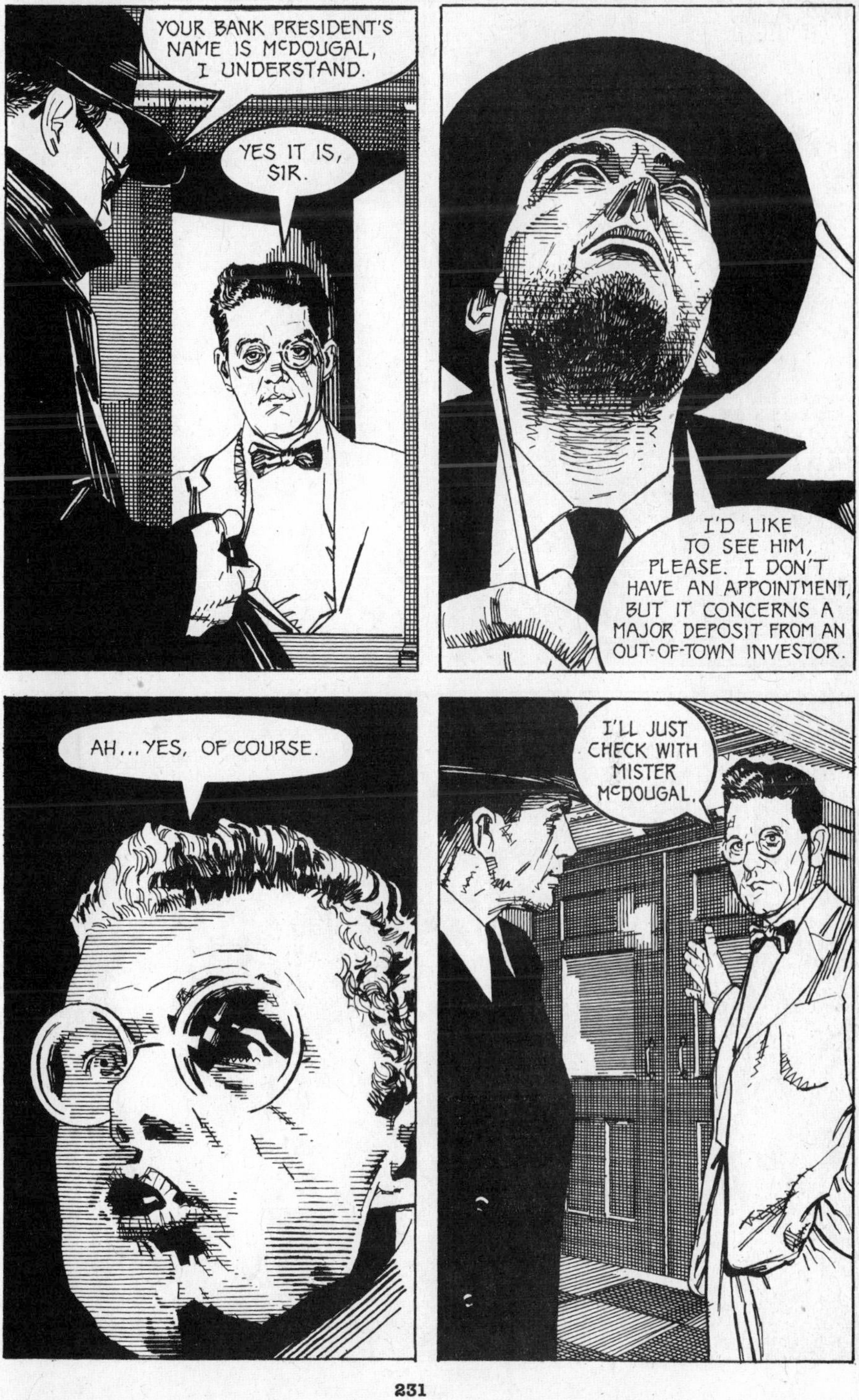
YOUR BANK PRESIDENT'S NAME IS McDOUGAL, I UNDERSTAND.
YES IT IS, SIR.
I'D LIKE TO SEE HIM, PLEASE. I DON'T HAVE AN APPOINTMENT, BUT IT CONCERNS A MAJOR DEPOSIT FROM AN OUT-OF-TOWN INVESTOR.
AH...YES, OF COURSE.
I'LL JUST CHECK WITH MISTER McDOUGAL.

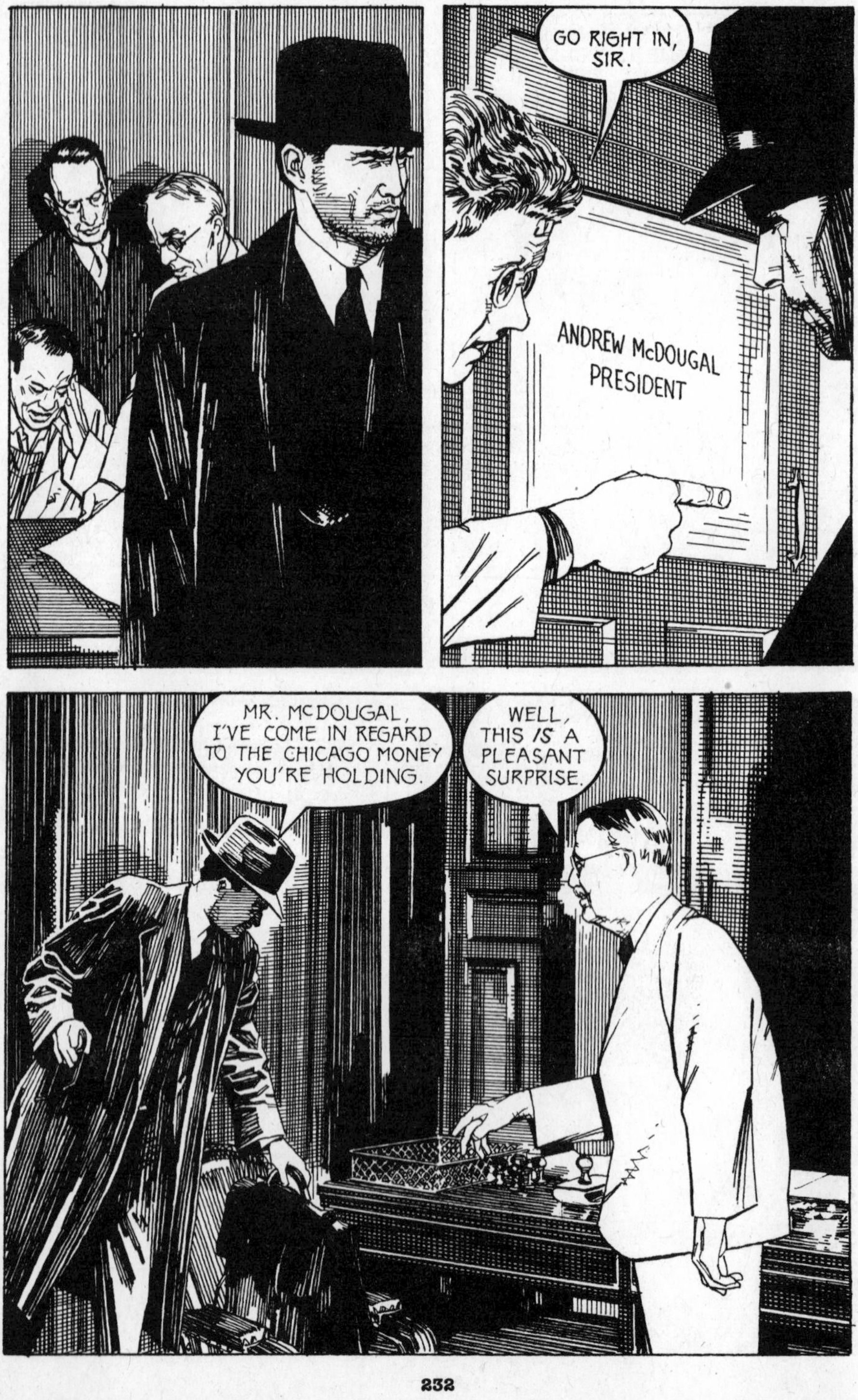
GO RIGHT IN, SIR.
ANDREW McDOUGAL PRESIDENT
MR. McDOUGAL, I'VE COME IN REGARD TO THE CHICAGO MONEY YOU'RE HOLDING.
WELL, THIS *IS* A PLEASANT SURPRISE.

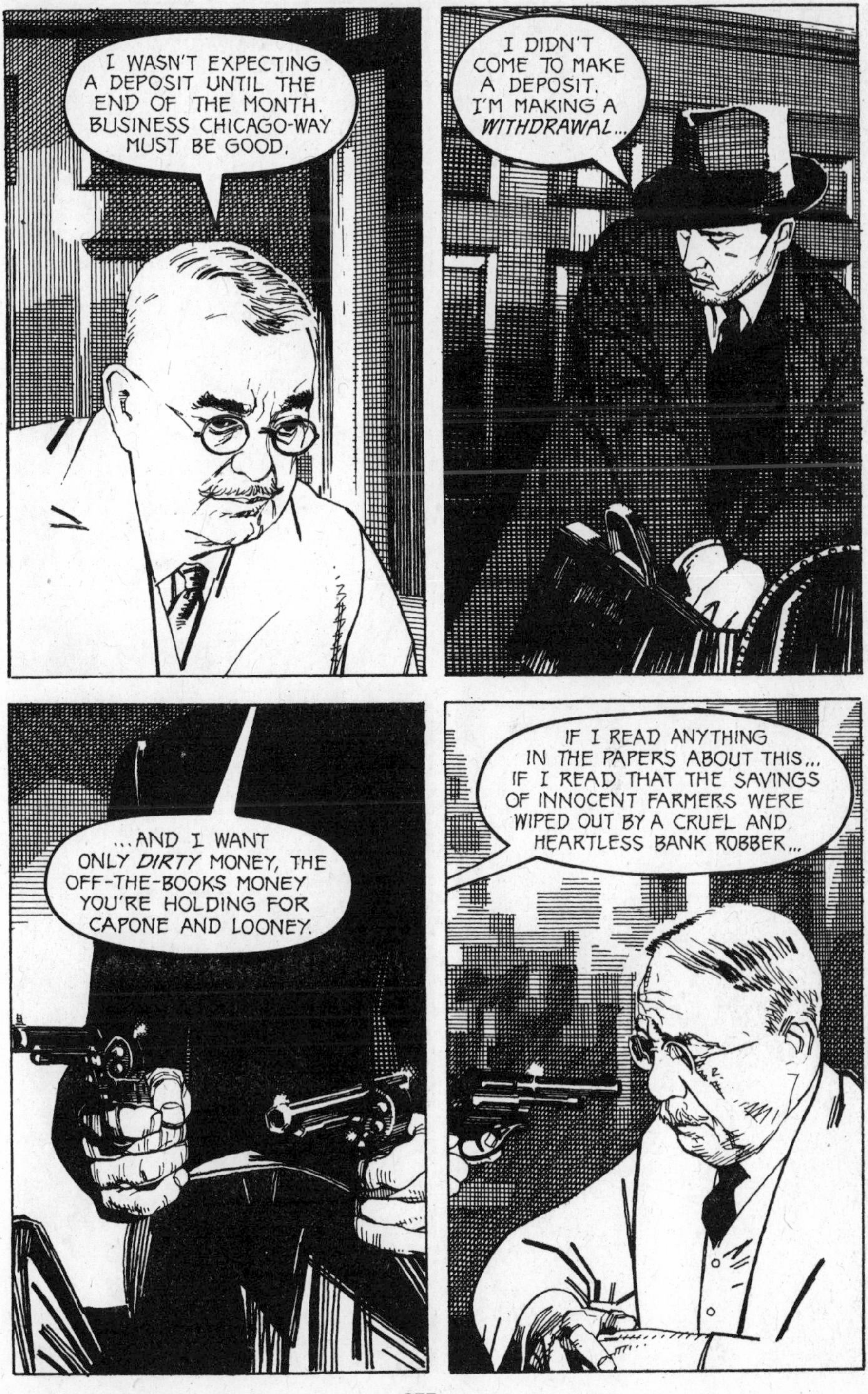
I WASN'T EXPECTING A DEPOSIT UNTIL THE END OF THE MONTH. BUSINESS CHICAGO-WAY MUST BE GOOD.
I DIDN'T COME TO MAKE A DEPOSIT. I'M MAKING A *WITHDRAWAL*...
...AND I WANT ONLY *DIRTY* MONEY, THE OFF-THE-BOOKS MONEY YOU'RE HOLDING FOR CAPONE AND LOONEY.
IF I READ ANYTHING IN THE PAPERS ABOUT THIS... IF I READ THAT THE SAVINGS OF INNOCENT FARMERS WERE WIPED OUT BY A CRUEL AND HEARTLESS BANK ROBBER...

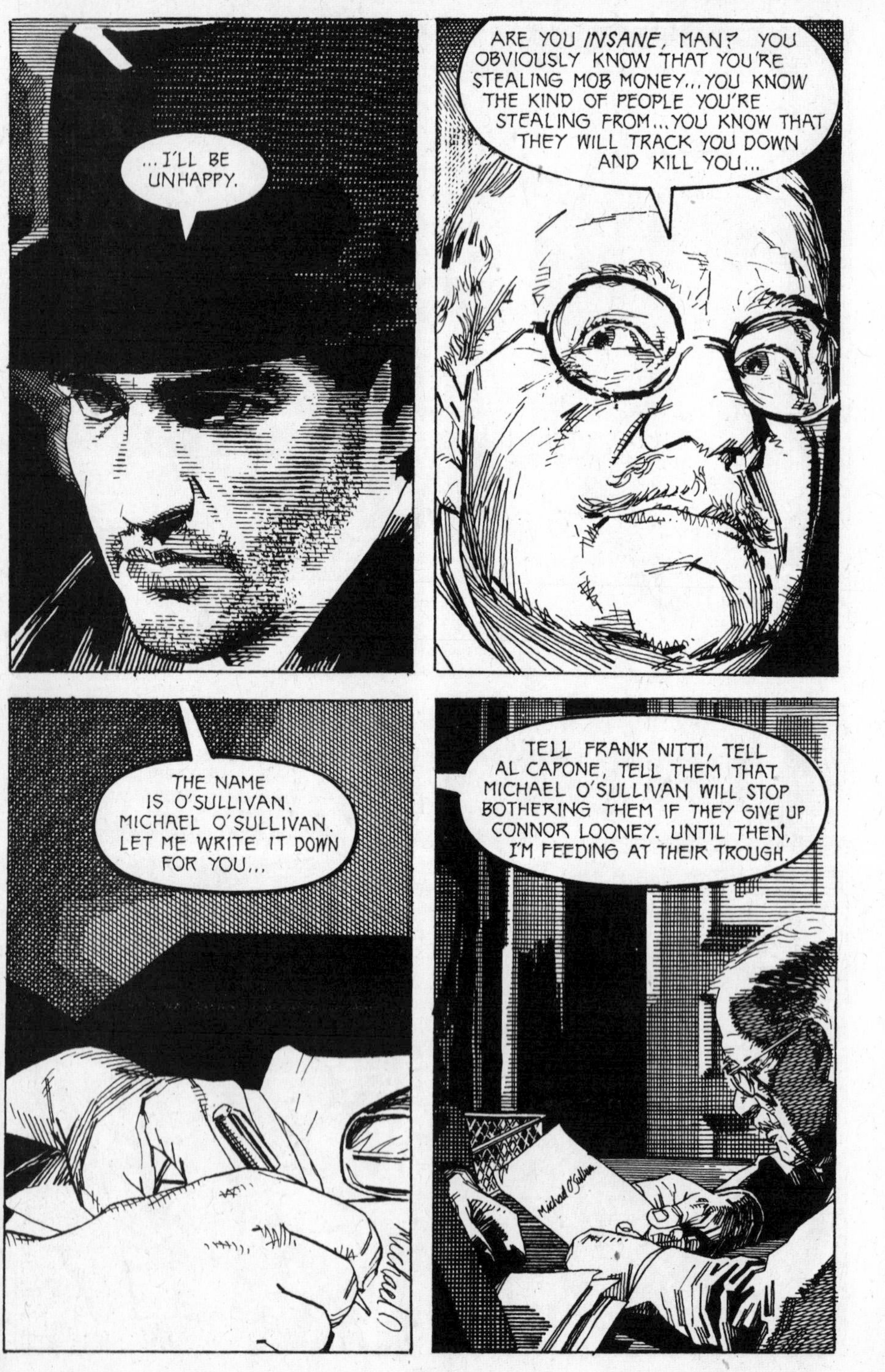
...I'LL BE UNHAPPY.
ARE YOU *INSANE*, MAN? YOU OBVIOUSLY KNOW THAT YOU'RE STEALING MOB MONEY... YOU KNOW THE KIND OF PEOPLE YOU'RE STEALING FROM... YOU KNOW THAT THEY WILL TRACK YOU DOWN AND KILL YOU...
THE NAME IS O'SULLIVAN. MICHAEL O'SULLIVAN. LET ME WRITE IT DOWN FOR YOU...
TELL FRANK NITTI, TELL AL CAPONE, TELL THEM THAT MICHAEL O'SULLIVAN WILL STOP BOTHERING THEM IF THEY GIVE UP CONNOR LOONEY. UNTIL THEN, I'M FEEDING AT THEIR TROUGH.
Michael O'Sullivan

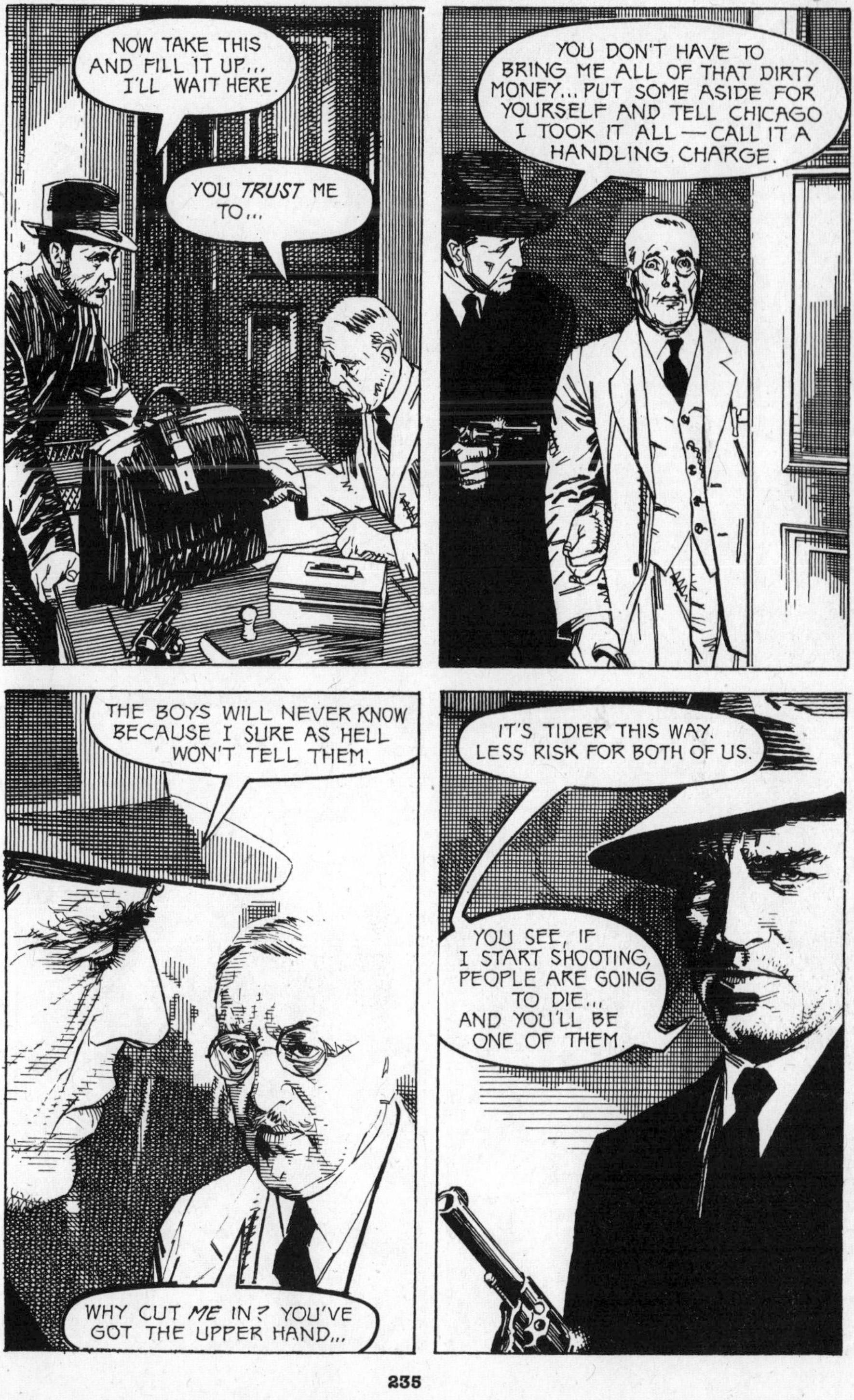
NOW TAKE THIS AND FILL IT UP... I'LL WAIT HERE.
YOU *TRUST* ME TO...
YOU DON'T HAVE TO BRING ME ALL OF THAT DIRTY MONEY... PUT SOME ASIDE FOR YOURSELF AND TELL CHICAGO I TOOK IT ALL — CALL IT A HANDLING CHARGE.
THE BOYS WILL NEVER KNOW BECAUSE I SURE AS HELL WON'T TELL THEM.
WHY CUT *ME* IN? YOU'VE GOT THE UPPER HAND...
IT'S TIDIER THIS WAY. LESS RISK FOR BOTH OF US.
YOU SEE, IF I START SHOOTING, PEOPLE ARE GOING TO DIE... AND YOU'LL BE ONE OF THEM.

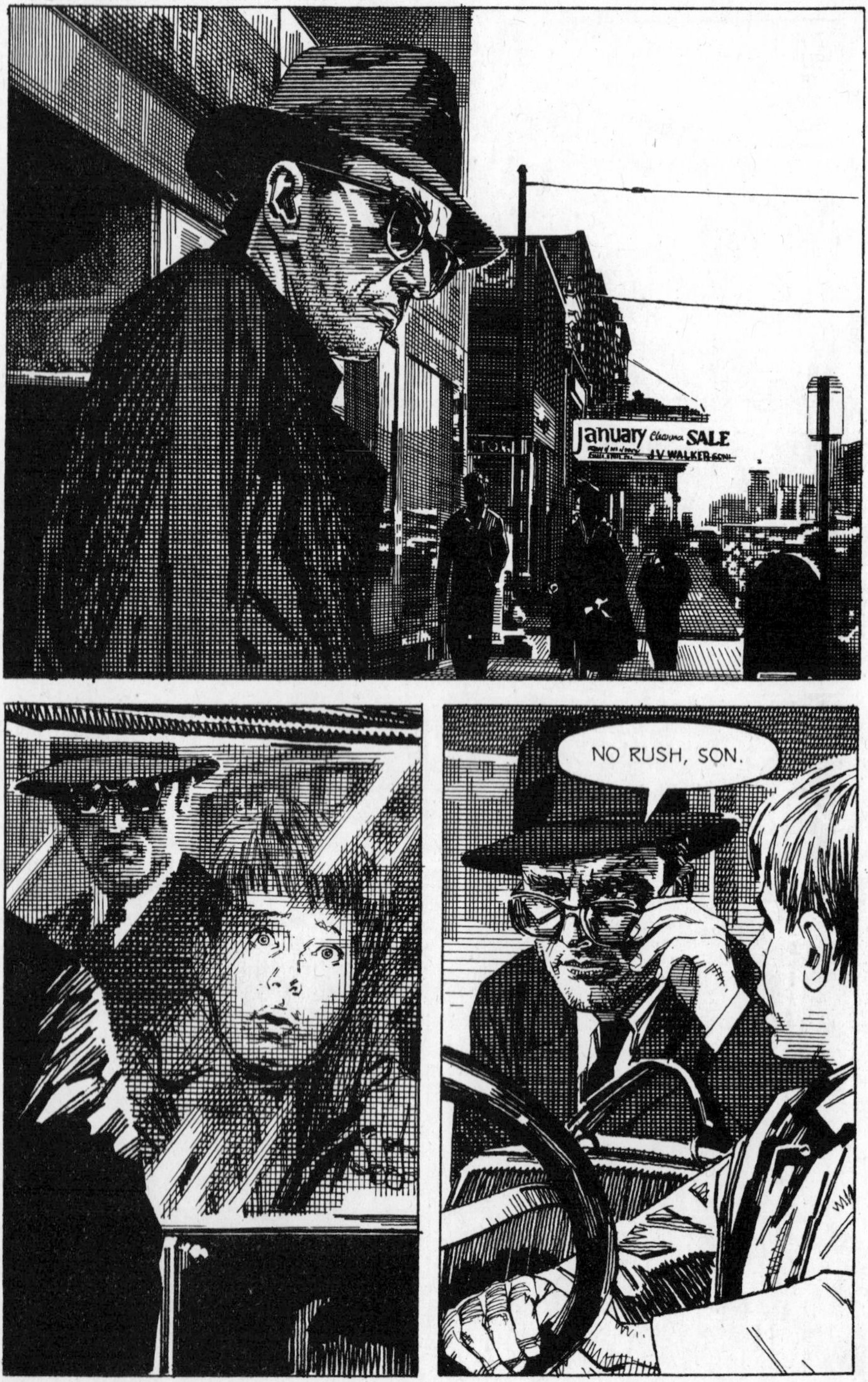
January Clearance SALE
J V WALKER
NO RUSH, SON.

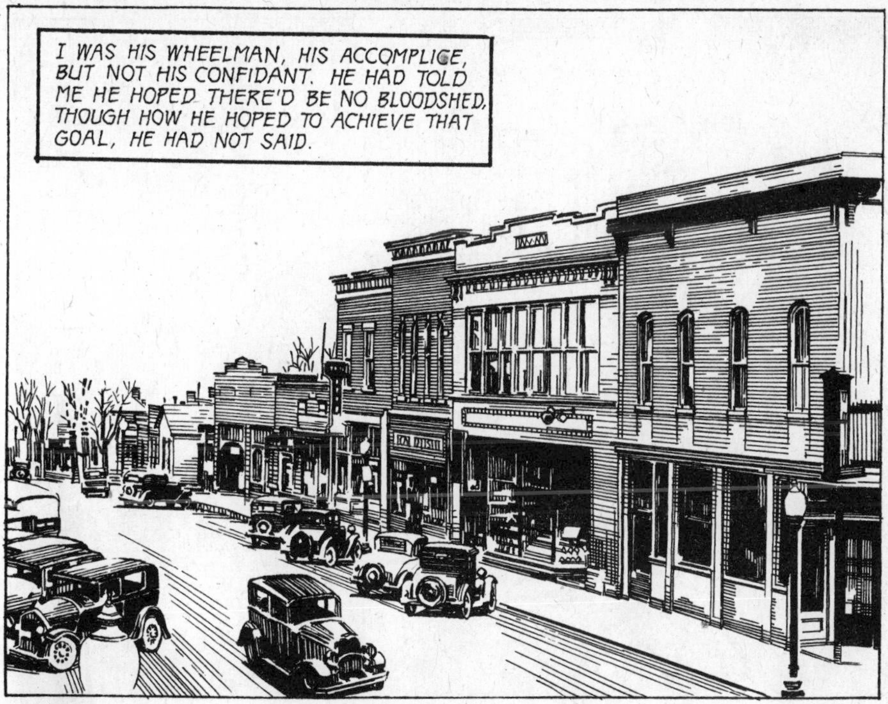
I WAS HIS WHEELMAN, HIS ACCOMPLICE, BUT NOT HIS CONFIDANT. HE HAD TOLD ME HE HOPED THERE'D BE NO BLOODSHED, THOUGH HOW HE HOPED TO ACHIEVE THAT GOAL, HE HAD NOT SAID.
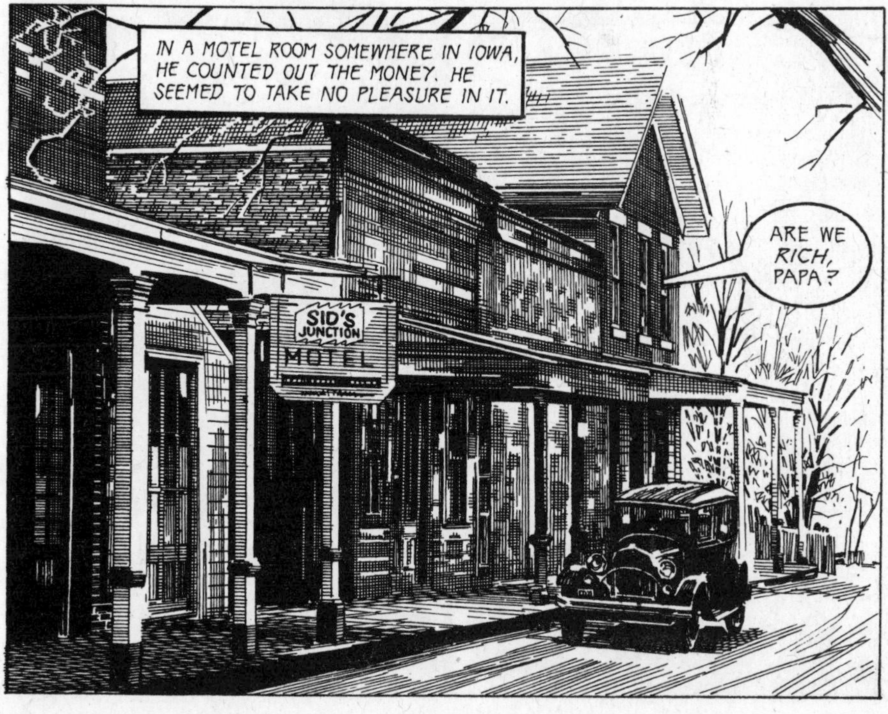
IN A MOTEL ROOM SOMEWHERE IN IOWA, HE COUNTED OUT THE MONEY. HE SEEMED TO TAKE NO PLEASURE IN IT.
SID'S JUNCTION MOTEL
ARE WE *RICH*, PAPA?

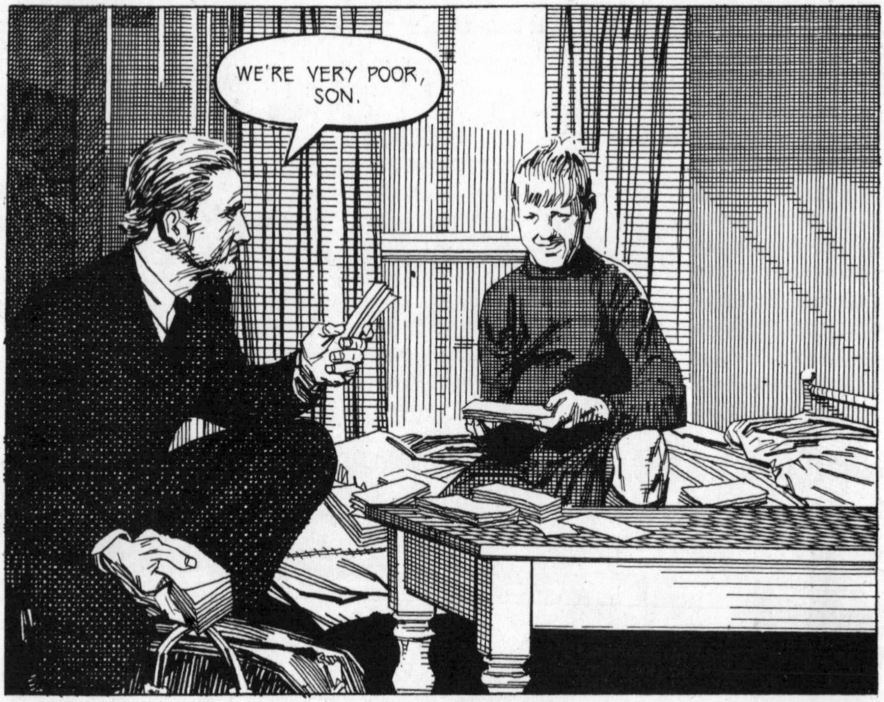
WE'RE VERY POOR, SON.

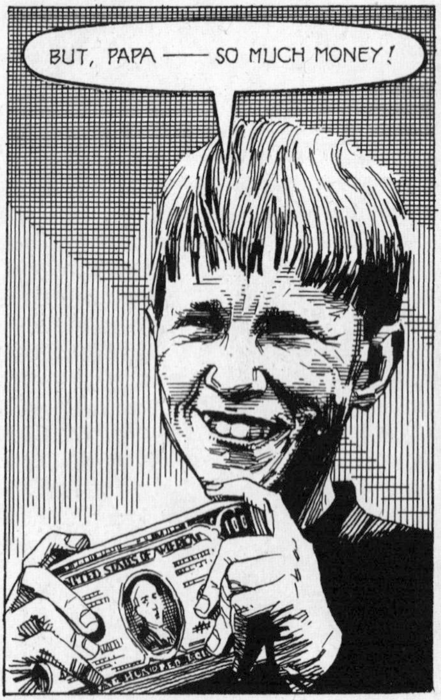
BUT, PAPA —— SO MUCH MONEY!

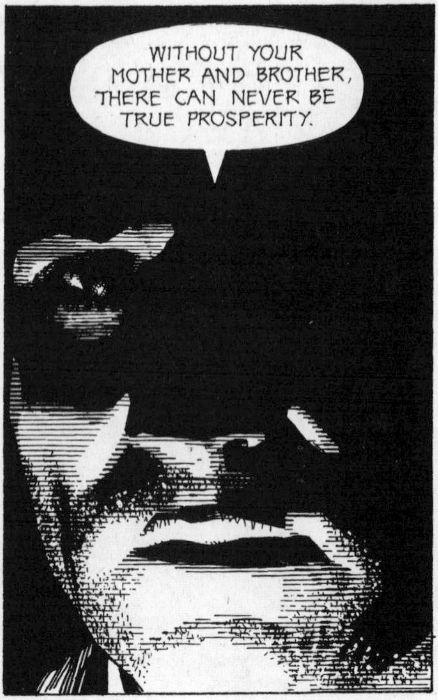
WITHOUT YOUR MOTHER AND BROTHER, THERE CAN NEVER BE TRUE PROSPERITY.

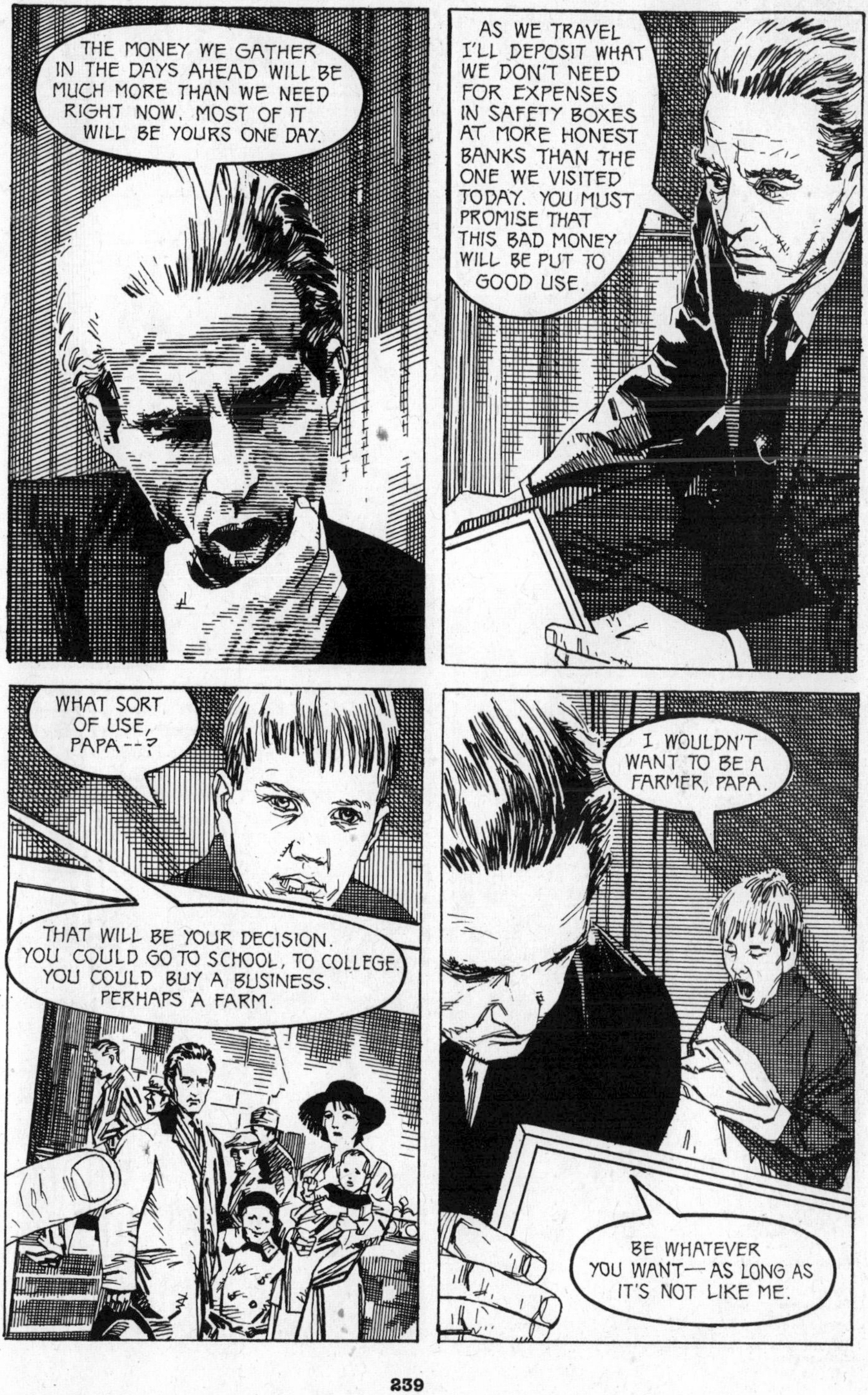
THE MONEY WE GATHER IN THE DAYS AHEAD WILL BE MUCH MORE THAN WE NEED RIGHT NOW. MOST OF IT WILL BE YOURS ONE DAY.
AS WE TRAVEL I'LL DEPOSIT WHAT WE DON'T NEED FOR EXPENSES IN SAFETY BOXES AT MORE HONEST BANKS THAN THE ONE WE VISITED TODAY. YOU MUST PROMISE THAT THIS BAD MONEY WILL BE PUT TO GOOD USE.
WHAT SORT OF USE, PAPA--?
THAT WILL BE YOUR DECISION. YOU COULD GO TO SCHOOL, TO COLLEGE. YOU COULD BUY A BUSINESS. PERHAPS A FARM.
I WOULDN'T WANT TO BE A FARMER, PAPA.
BE WHATEVER YOU WANT— AS LONG AS IT'S NOT LIKE ME.

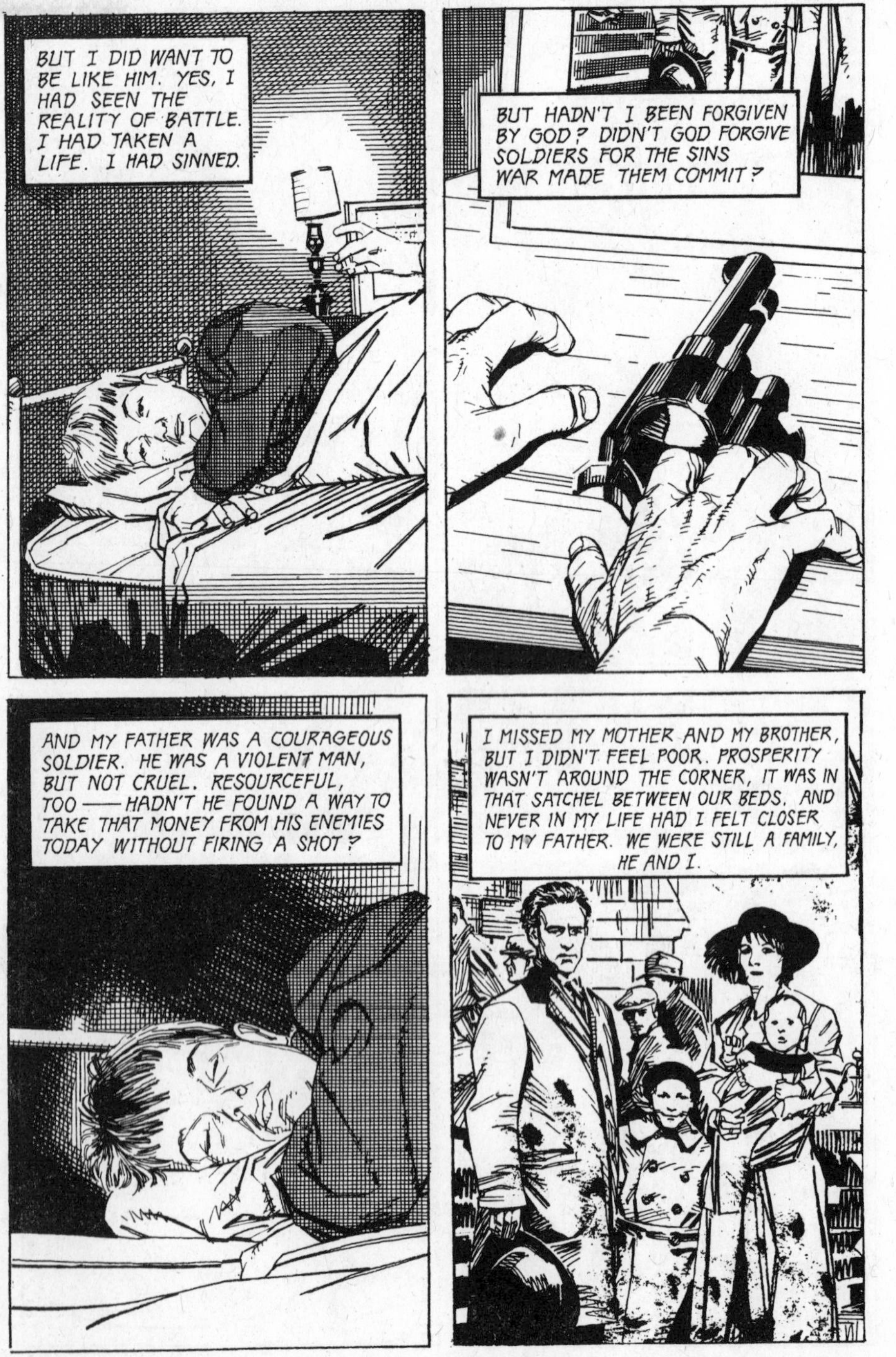
BUT I DID WANT TO BE LIKE HIM. YES, I HAD SEEN THE REALITY OF BATTLE. I HAD TAKEN A LIFE. I HAD SINNED.
BUT HADN'T I BEEN FORGIVEN BY GOD? DIDN'T GOD FORGIVE SOLDIERS FOR THE SINS WAR MADE THEM COMMIT?
AND MY FATHER WAS A COURAGEOUS SOLDIER. HE WAS A VIOLENT MAN, BUT NOT CRUEL. RESOURCEFUL, TOO —— HADN'T HE FOUND A WAY TO TAKE THAT MONEY FROM HIS ENEMIES TODAY WITHOUT FIRING A SHOT?
I MISSED MY MOTHER AND MY BROTHER, BUT I DIDN'T FEEL POOR. PROSPERITY WASN'T AROUND THE CORNER, IT WAS IN THAT SATCHEL BETWEEN OUR BEDS. AND NEVER IN MY LIFE HAD I FELT CLOSER TO MY FATHER. WE WERE STILL A FAMILY, HE AND I.

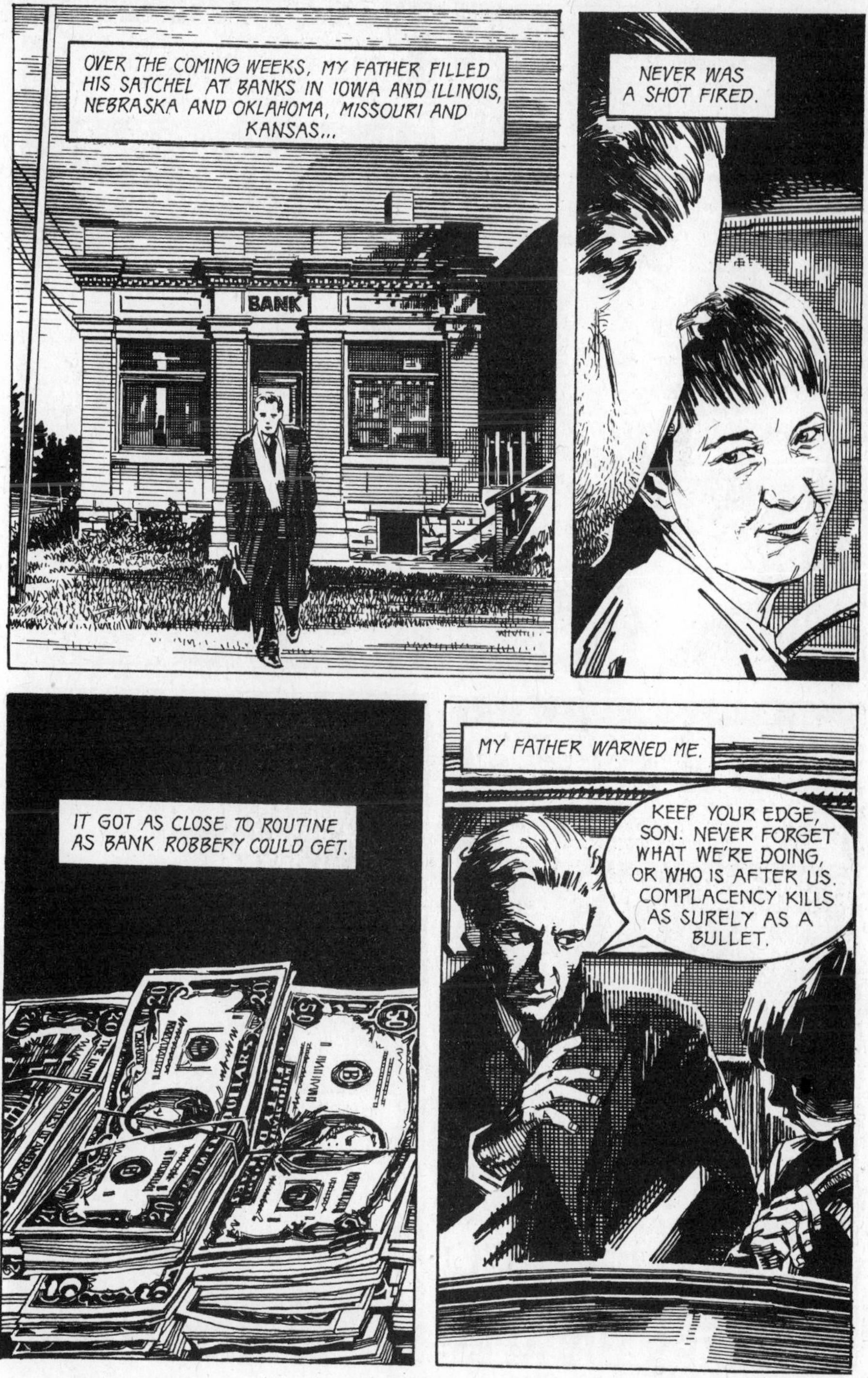
OVER THE COMING WEEKS, MY FATHER FILLED HIS SATCHEL AT BANKS IN IOWA AND ILLINOIS, NEBRASKA AND OKLAHOMA, MISSOURI AND KANSAS...
BANK
NEVER WAS A SHOT FIRED.
IT GOT AS CLOSE TO ROUTINE AS BANK ROBBERY COULD GET.
MY FATHER WARNED ME.
KEEP YOUR EDGE, SON. NEVER FORGET WHAT WE'RE DOING, OR WHO IS AFTER US. COMPLACENCY KILLS AS SURELY AS A BULLET.

WE DID STOP AT OTHER BANKS, NOT TO ROB THEM, BUT FOR MY FATHER TO DEPOSIT OUR EXCESS CASH.

HE READ THE PAPERS RELIGIOUSLY LOOKING FOR MENTION OF OUR ROBBERIES, NEVER FINDING ANYTHING. THAT, HE LIKED.

EXTRA
St Louis Gazette
MASSACRE OF DORAN GANG
VICTIMS ARE LINED AGAINST WAL... VOLLEY KILLS AL...

HE WAS LESS HAPPY ABOUT THE LACK OF OTHER NEWS. HE NEVER SAID, BUT LOOKING BACK, I REALIZE HE WAS LOOKING FOR MENTION OF CONNOR LOONEY'S BODY TURNING UP IN A DITCH SOMEWHERE.

REE CENTS
THE CHICAGO
54TH YEAR '91 IN THE CHICAGO DAILY NEWS
IS TAKES HAND IN

AND HE WOULD STOP TO MAKE PHONE CALLS. SOME WERE TO MY UNCLE, WHO CONTINUED TO REPORT THAT CROWS WERE ON THE FENCE. OTHERS, I CAN ONLY SPECULATE ABOUT.

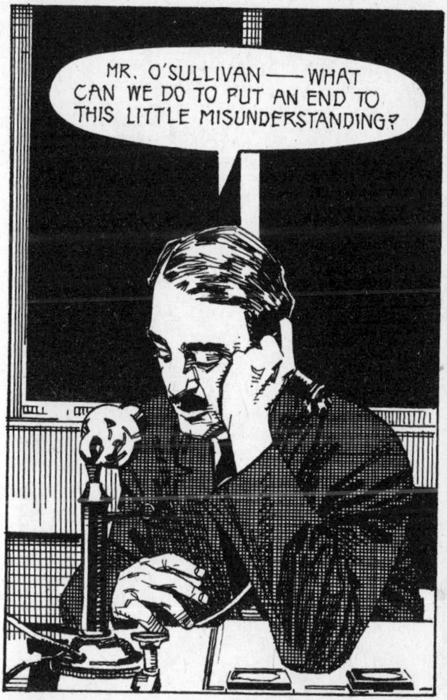
MR. O'SULLIVAN — WHAT CAN WE DO TO PUT AN END TO THIS LITTLE MISUNDERSTANDING?
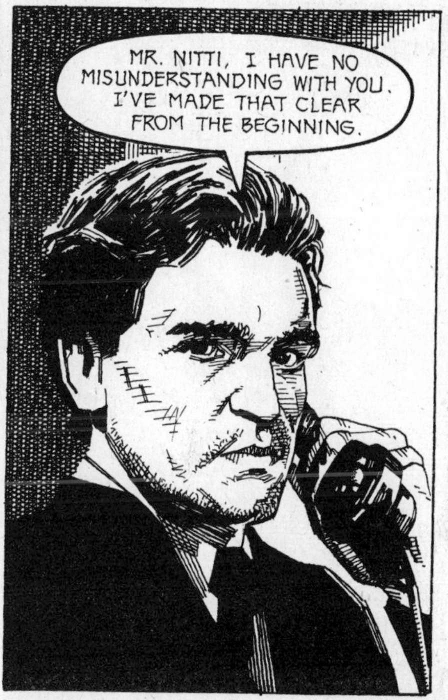
MR. NITTI, I HAVE NO MISUNDERSTANDING WITH YOU. I'VE MADE THAT CLEAR FROM THE BEGINNING.
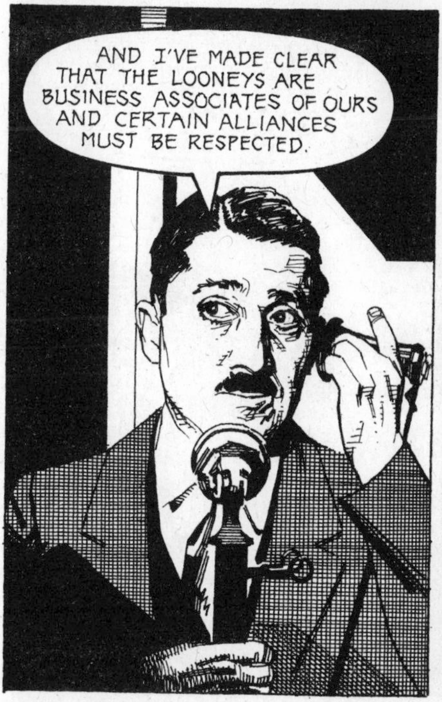
AND I'VE MADE CLEAR THAT THE LOONEYS ARE BUSINESS ASSOCIATES OF OURS AND CERTAIN ALLIANCES MUST BE RESPECTED.
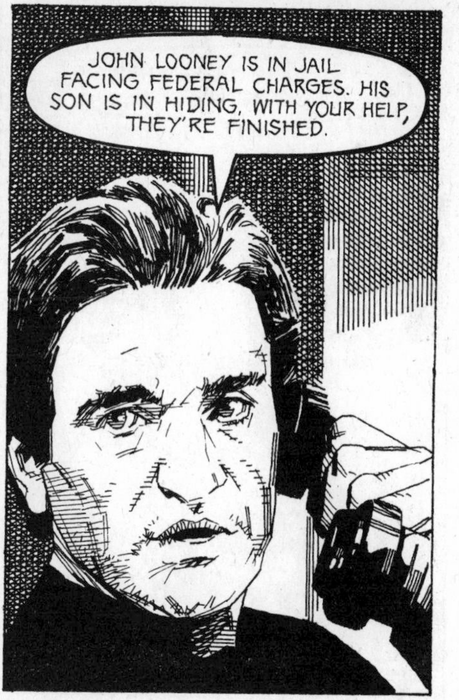
JOHN LOONEY IS IN JAIL FACING FEDERAL CHARGES. HIS SON IS IN HIDING, WITH YOUR HELP, THEY'RE FINISHED.

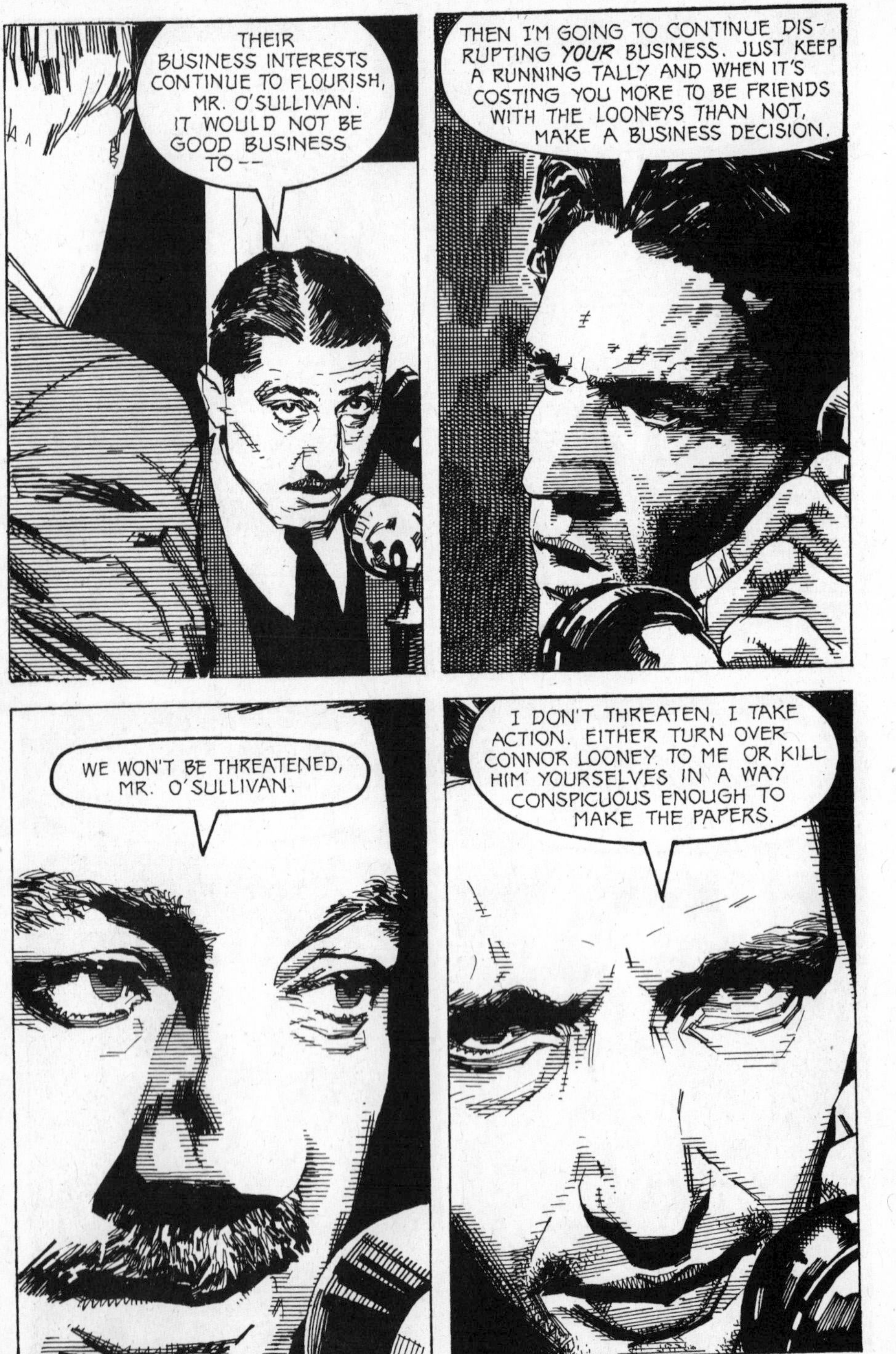
THEIR BUSINESS INTERESTS CONTINUE TO FLOURISH, MR. O'SULLIVAN. IT WOULD NOT BE GOOD BUSINESS TO --
THEN I'M GOING TO CONTINUE DISRUPTING *YOUR* BUSINESS. JUST KEEP A RUNNING TALLY AND WHEN IT'S COSTING YOU MORE TO BE FRIENDS WITH THE LOONEYS THAN NOT, MAKE A BUSINESS DECISION.
WE WON'T BE THREATENED, MR. O'SULLIVAN.
I DON'T THREATEN, I TAKE ACTION. EITHER TURN OVER CONNOR LOONEY TO ME OR KILL HIM YOURSELVES IN A WAY CONSPICUOUS ENOUGH TO MAKE THE PAPERS.

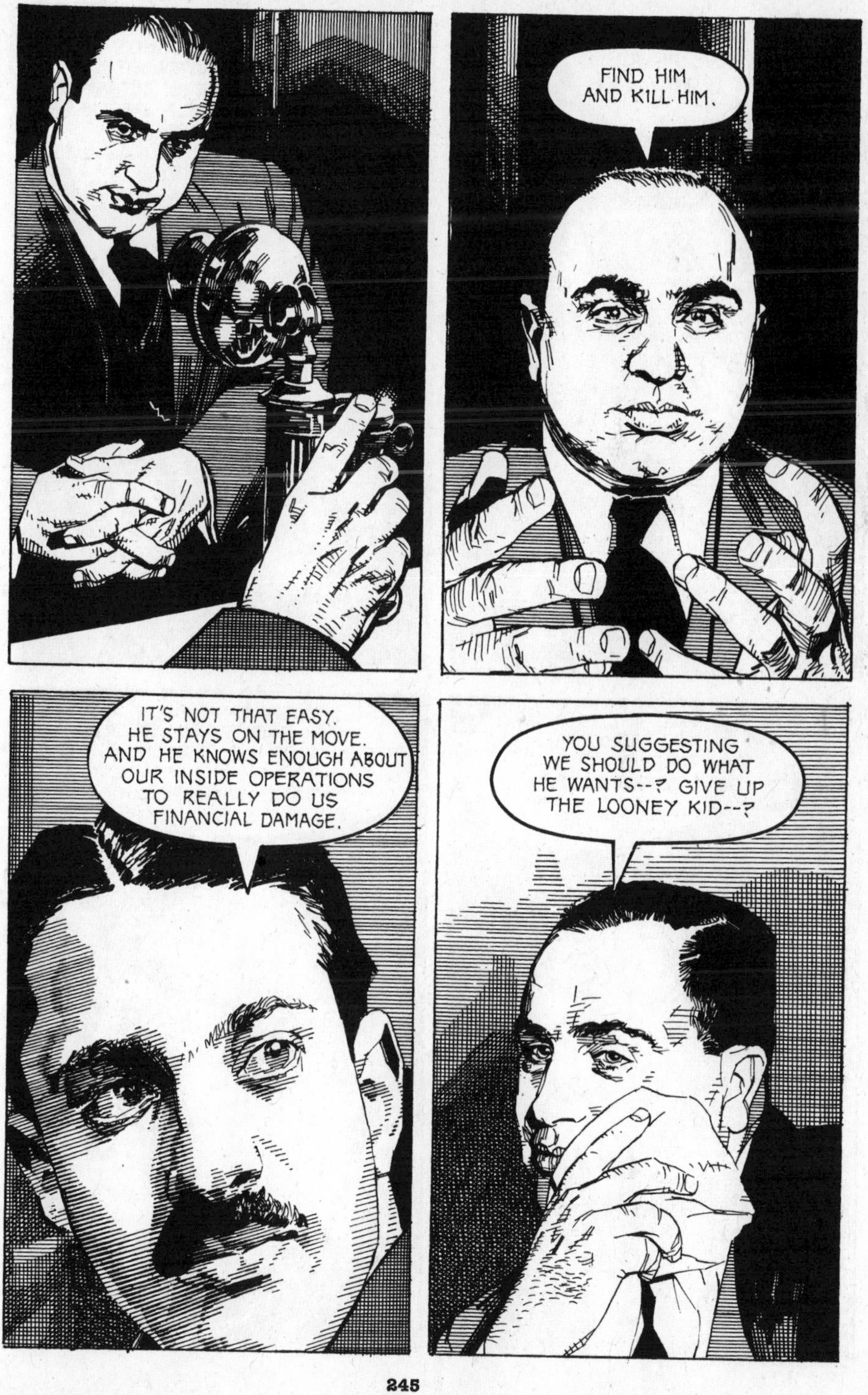
FIND HIM AND KILL HIM.
IT'S NOT THAT EASY. HE STAYS ON THE MOVE. AND HE KNOWS ENOUGH ABOUT OUR INSIDE OPERATIONS TO REALLY DO US FINANCIAL DAMAGE.
YOU SUGGESTING WE SHOULD DO WHAT HE WANTS--? GIVE UP THE LOONEY KID--?

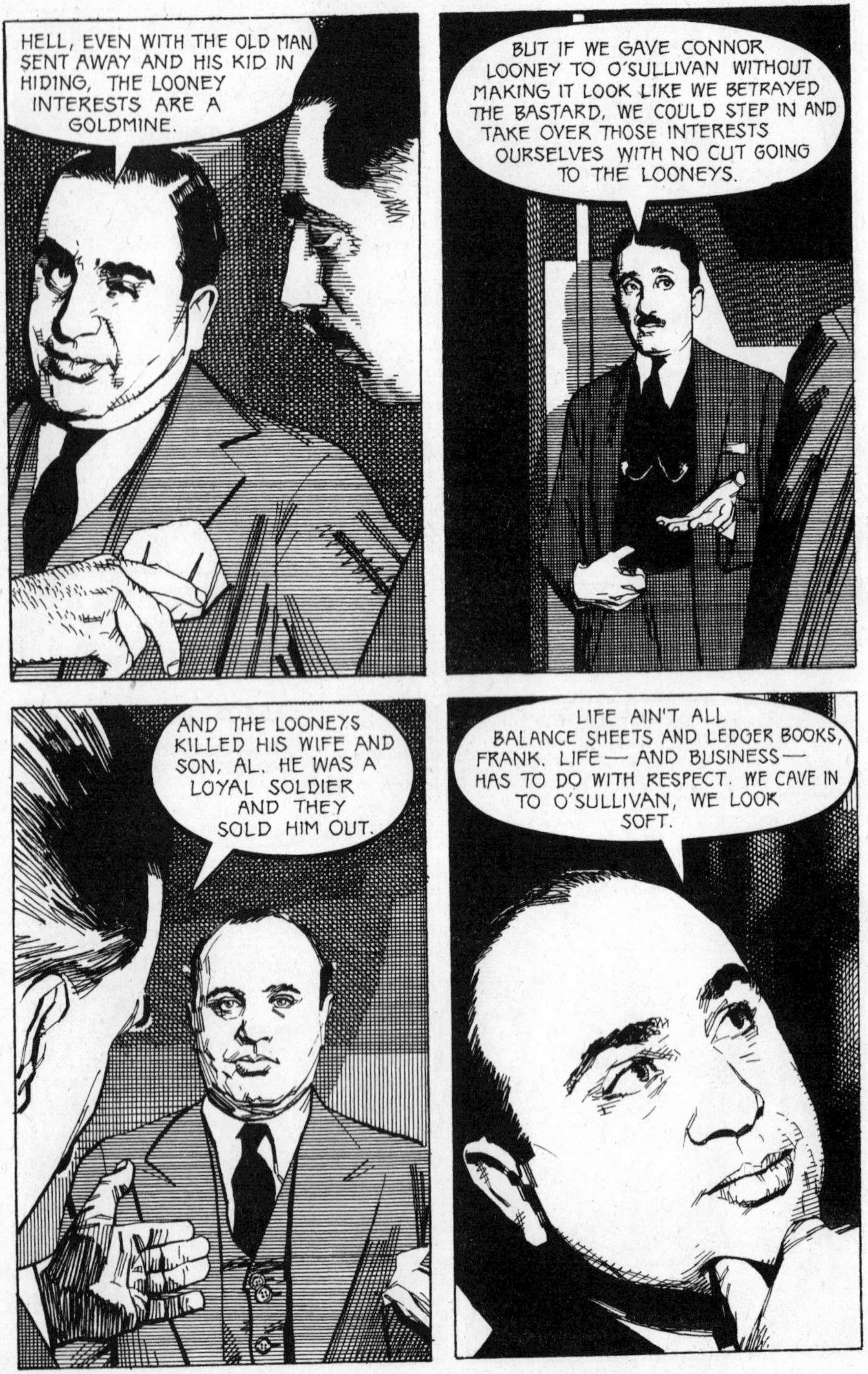
HELL, EVEN WITH THE OLD MAN SENT AWAY AND HIS KID IN HIDING, THE LOONEY INTERESTS ARE A GOLDMINE.
BUT IF WE GAVE CONNOR LOONEY TO O'SULLIVAN WITHOUT MAKING IT LOOK LIKE WE BETRAYED THE BASTARD, WE COULD STEP IN AND TAKE OVER THOSE INTERESTS OURSELVES WITH NO CUT GOING TO THE LOONEYS.
AND THE LOONEYS KILLED HIS WIFE AND SON, AL. HE WAS A LOYAL SOLDIER AND THEY SOLD HIM OUT.
LIFE AIN'T ALL BALANCE SHEETS AND LEDGER BOOKS, FRANK. LIFE — AND BUSINESS — HAS TO DO WITH RESPECT. WE CAVE IN TO O'SULLIVAN, WE LOOK SOFT.

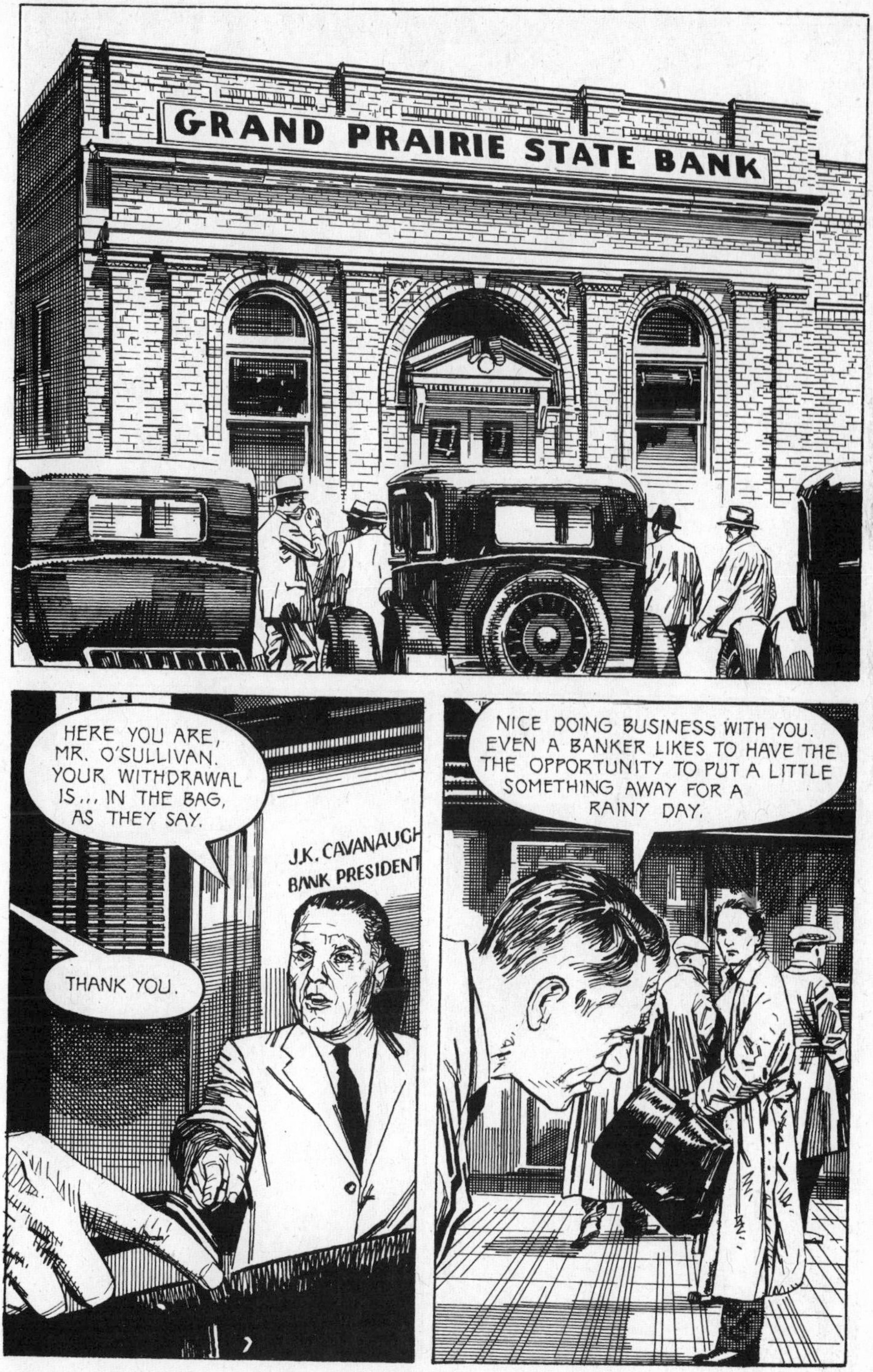
GRAND PRAIRIE STATE BANK
HERE YOU ARE, MR. O'SULLIVAN. YOUR WITHDRAWAL IS... IN THE BAG, AS THEY SAY.
J.K. CAVANAUGH BANK PRESIDENT
THANK YOU.
NICE DOING BUSINESS WITH YOU. EVEN A BANKER LIKES TO HAVE THE THE OPPORTUNITY TO PUT A LITTLE SOMETHING AWAY FOR A RAINY DAY.

GOOD AFTERNOON, SIR. LET ME GET THE DOOR FOR YOU...

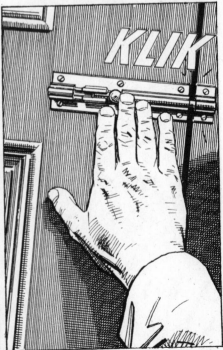

KLIK

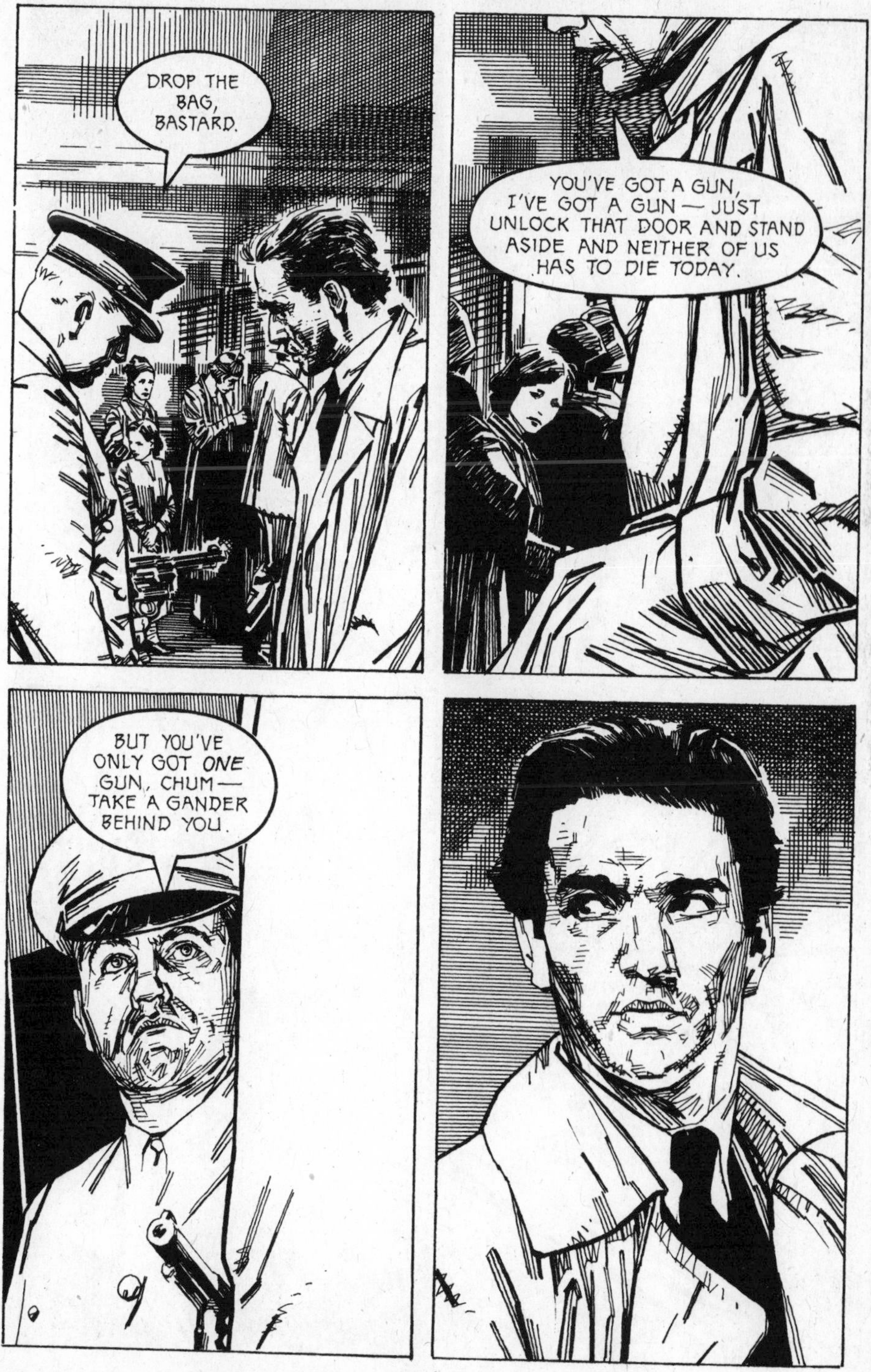
DROP THE BAG, BASTARD.
YOU'VE GOT A GUN, I'VE GOT A GUN — JUST UNLOCK THAT DOOR AND STAND ASIDE AND NEITHER OF US HAS TO DIE TODAY.
BUT YOU'VE ONLY GOT *ONE* GUN, CHUM — TAKE A GANDER BEHIND YOU.

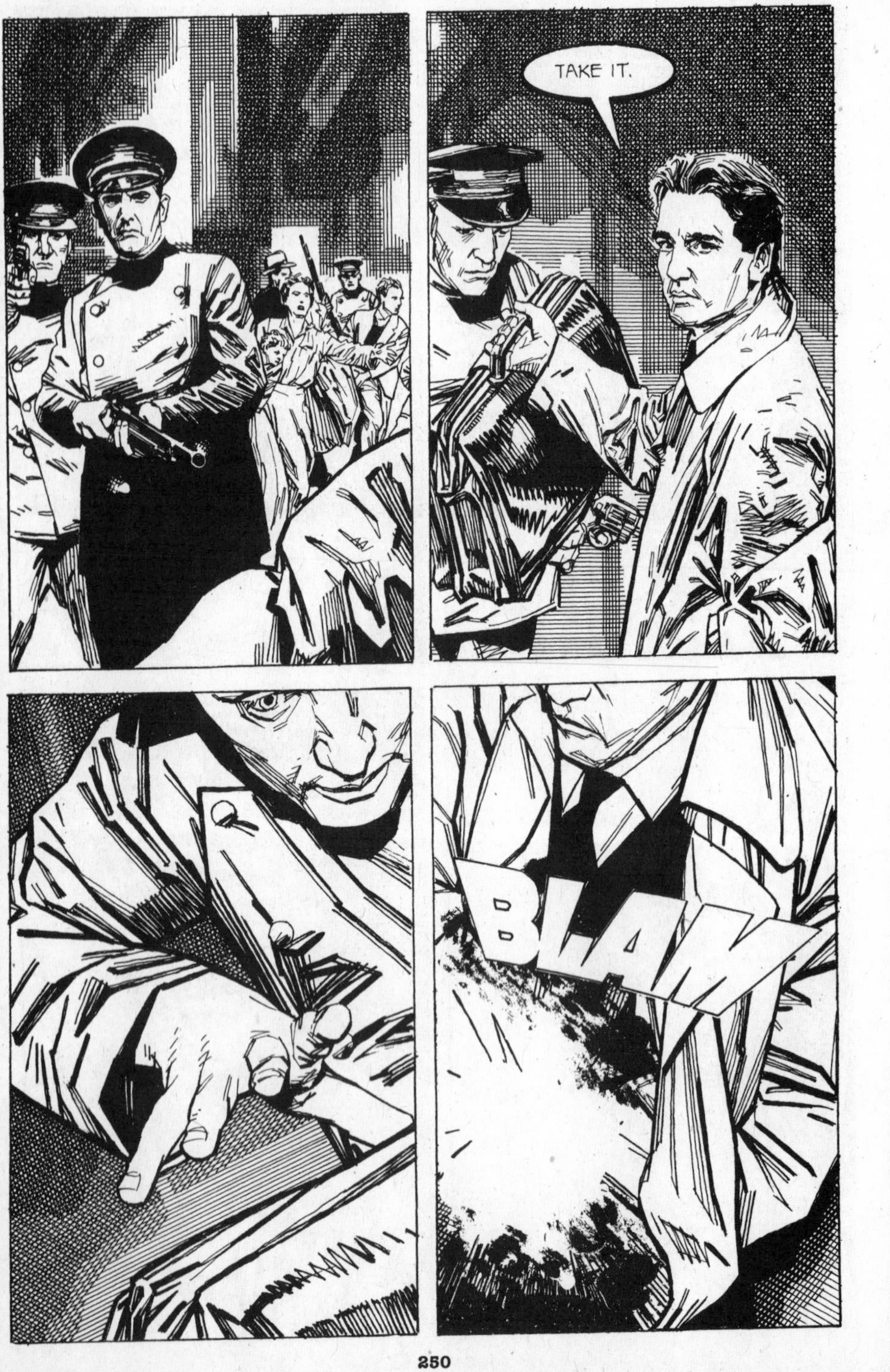
TAKE IT.
BLAM

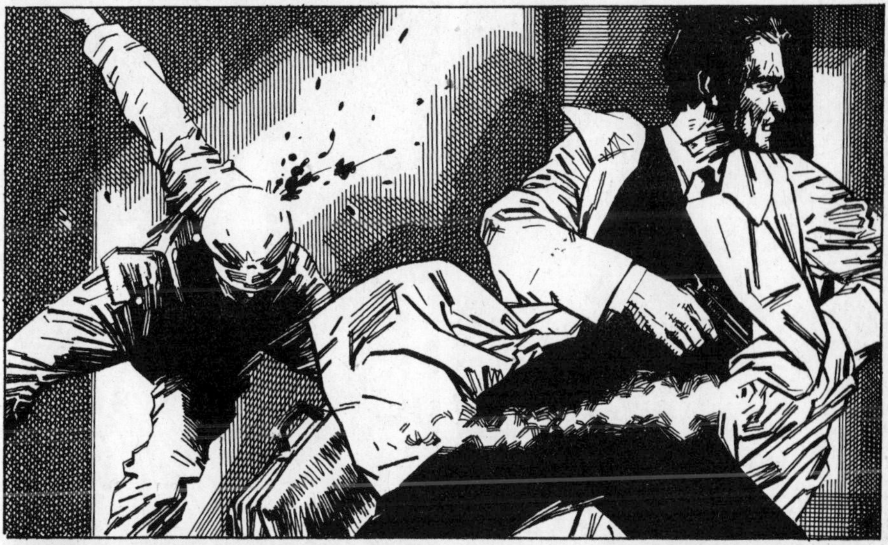

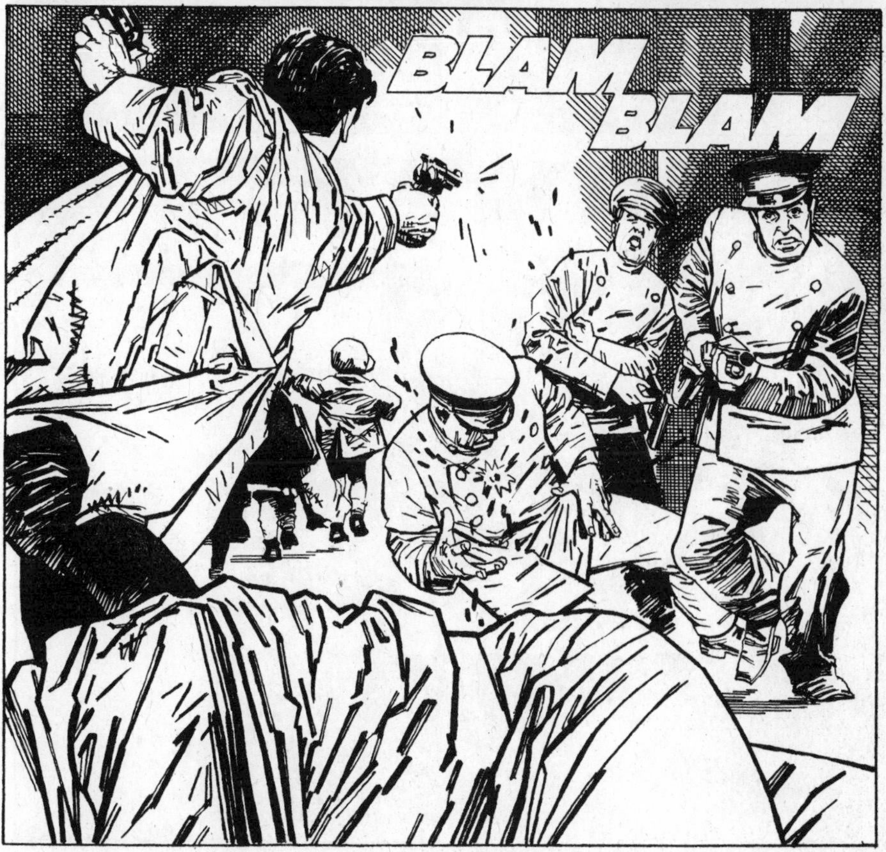
BLAM
BLAM

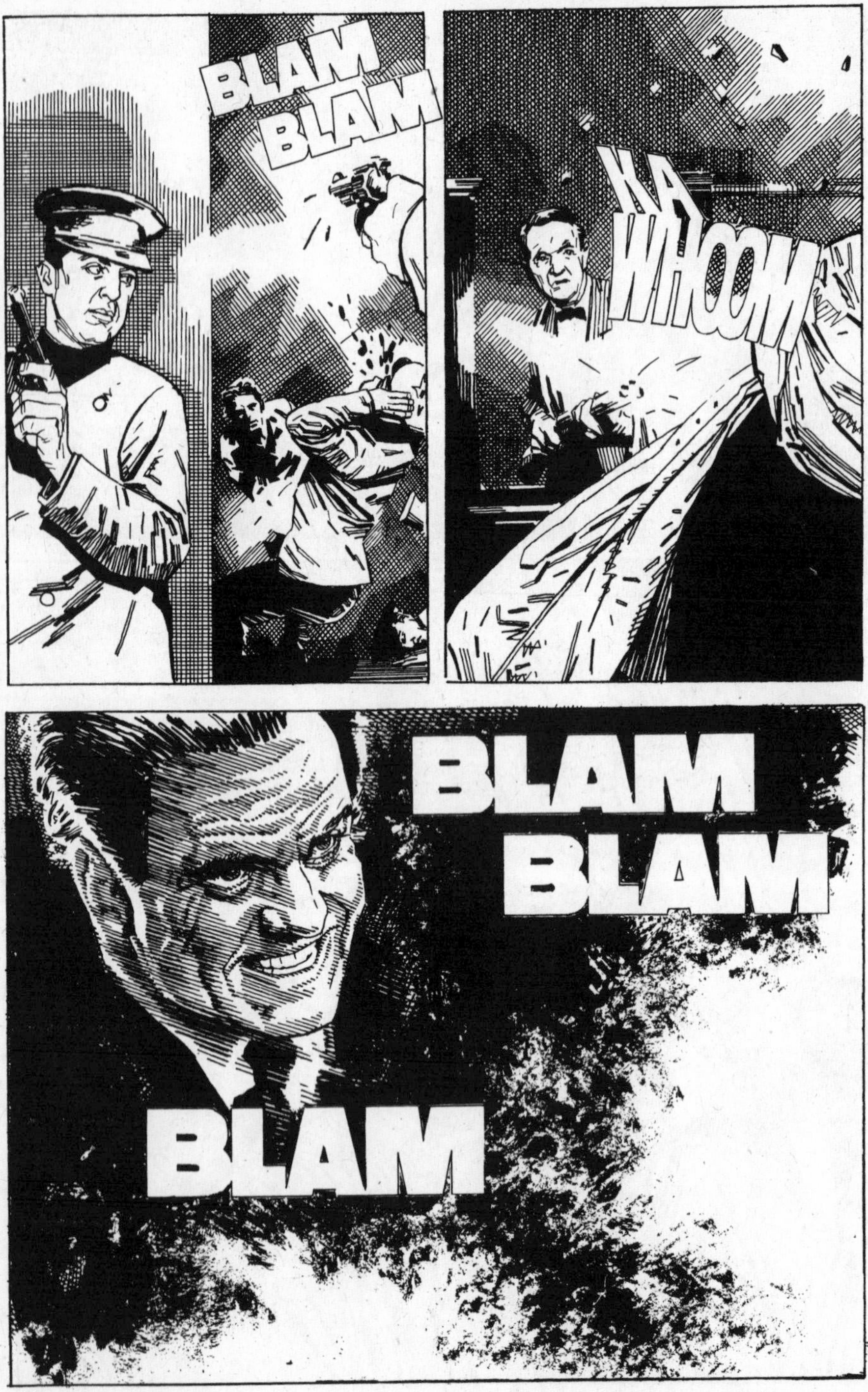
BLAM
BLAM
KA
WHOOM
BLAM
BLAM
BLAM

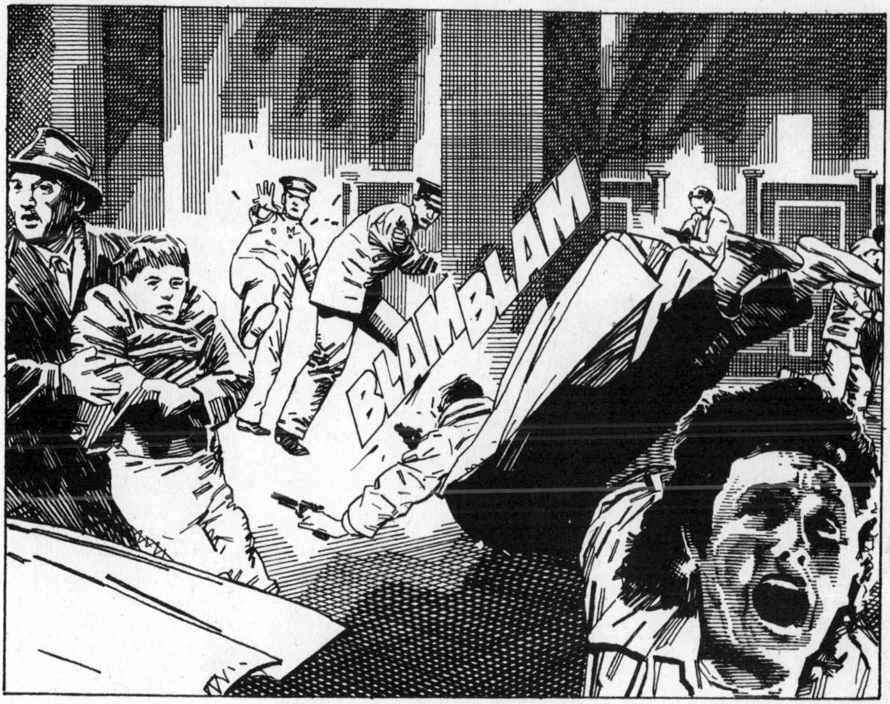
BLAMBLAM
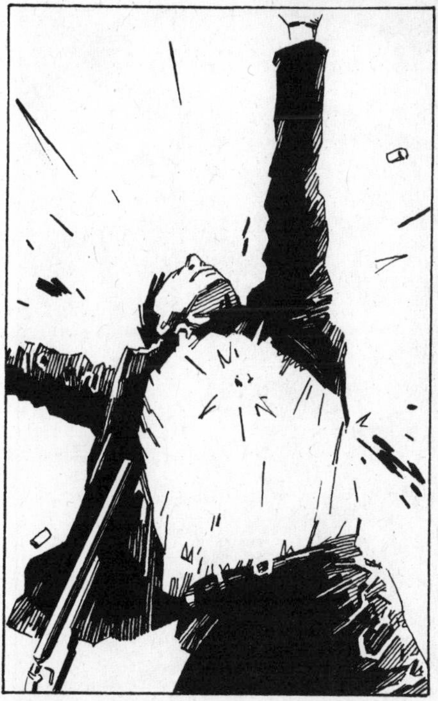
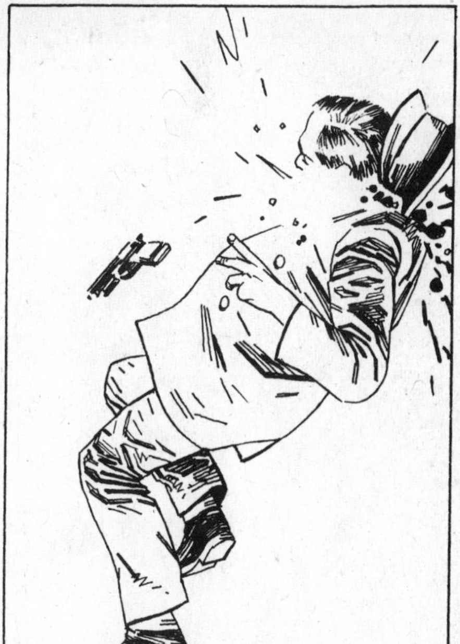

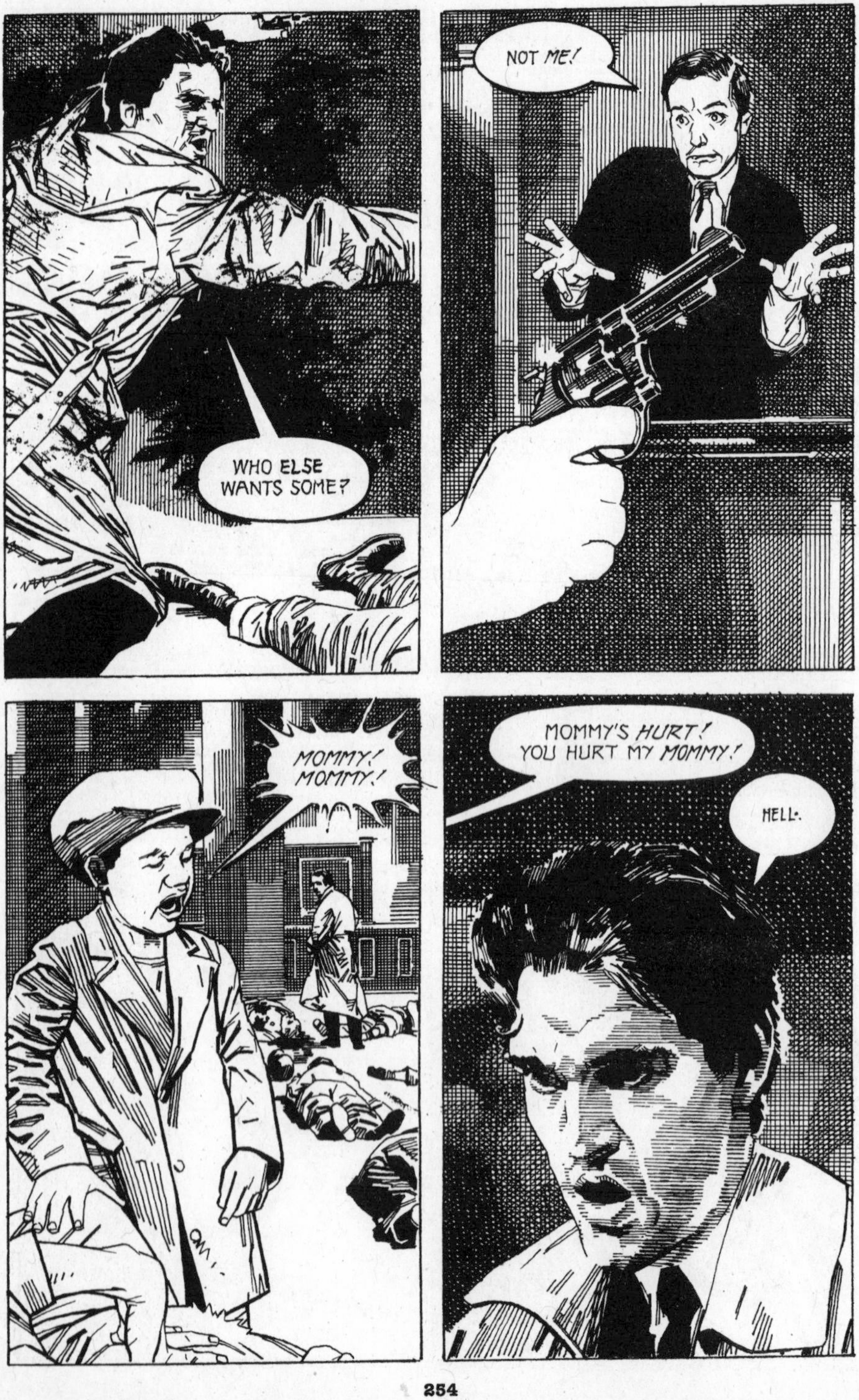
WHO ELSE WANTS SOME?
NOT ME!
MOMMY! MOMMY!
MOMMY'S HURT! YOU HURT MY MOMMY!
HELL.

SOMEBODY TAKE CHARGE OF THIS CHILD.
J K CAVANAU
BANK PRESID
COME WITH ME.
GRAND
PRAIRIE
STATE
BANK
I HAD HEARD SHOTS, BUT PAPA HAD GIVEN ME STRICT ORDERS TO STAY BEHIND THE WHEEL IN SUCH A CASE... AND I WASN'T TO LEAVE WITHOUT HIM UNTIL I HEARD POLICE SIRENS.

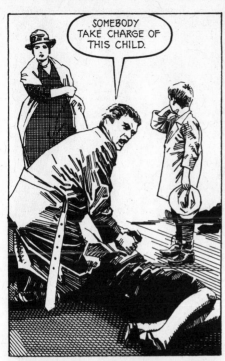

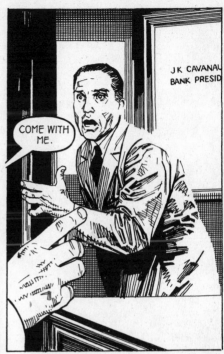

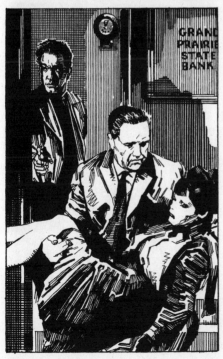

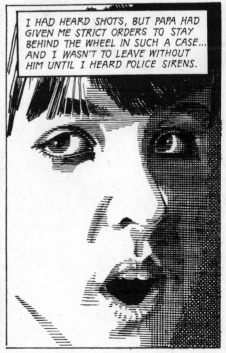

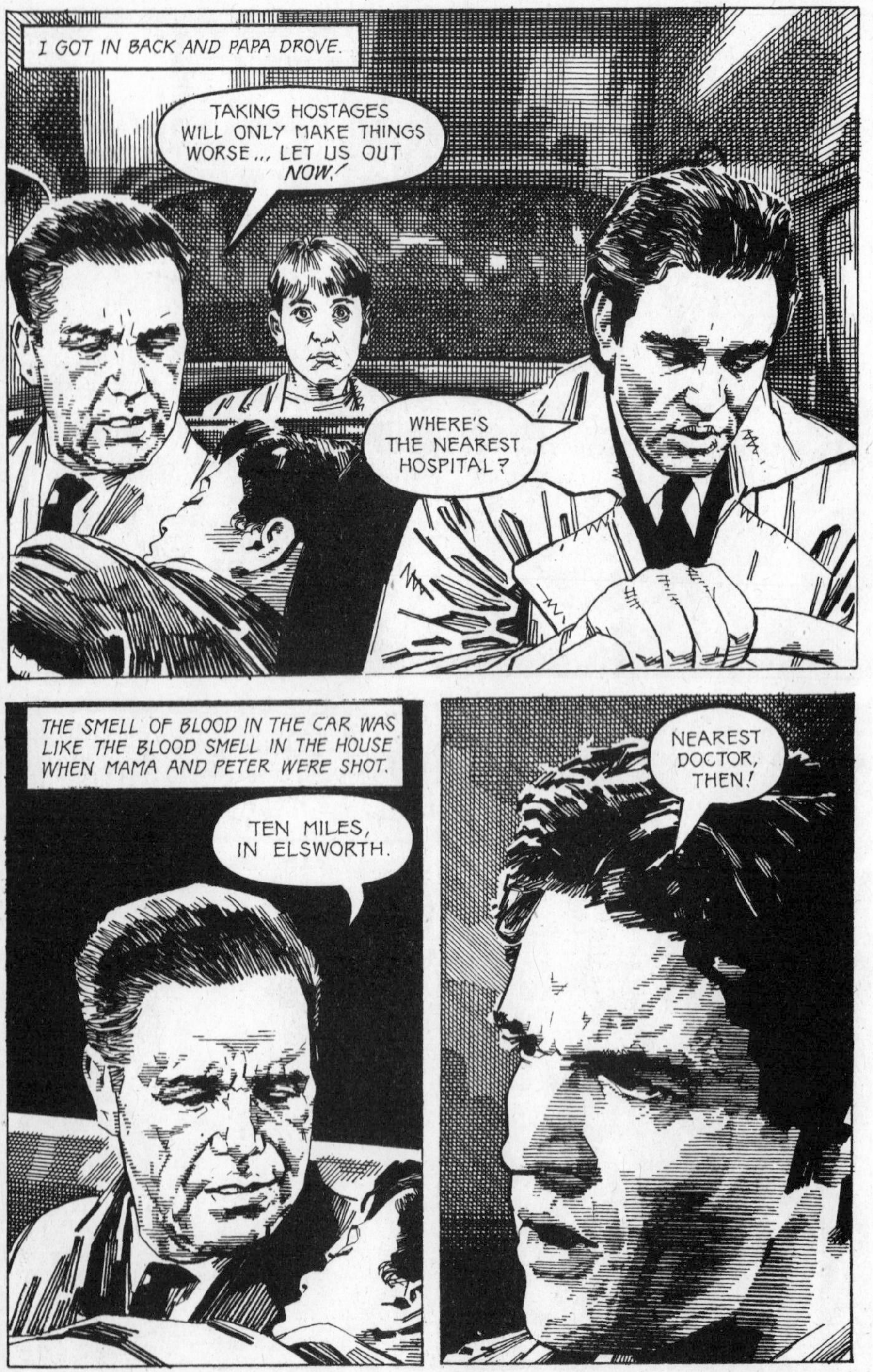
I GOT IN BACK AND PAPA DROVE.
TAKING HOSTAGES WILL ONLY MAKE THINGS WORSE..., LET US OUT *NOW!*
WHERE'S THE NEAREST HOSPITAL?
THE SMELL OF BLOOD IN THE CAR WAS LIKE THE BLOOD SMELL IN THE HOUSE WHEN MAMA AND PETER WERE SHOT.
TEN MILES, IN ELSWORTH.
NEAREST DOCTOR, THEN!

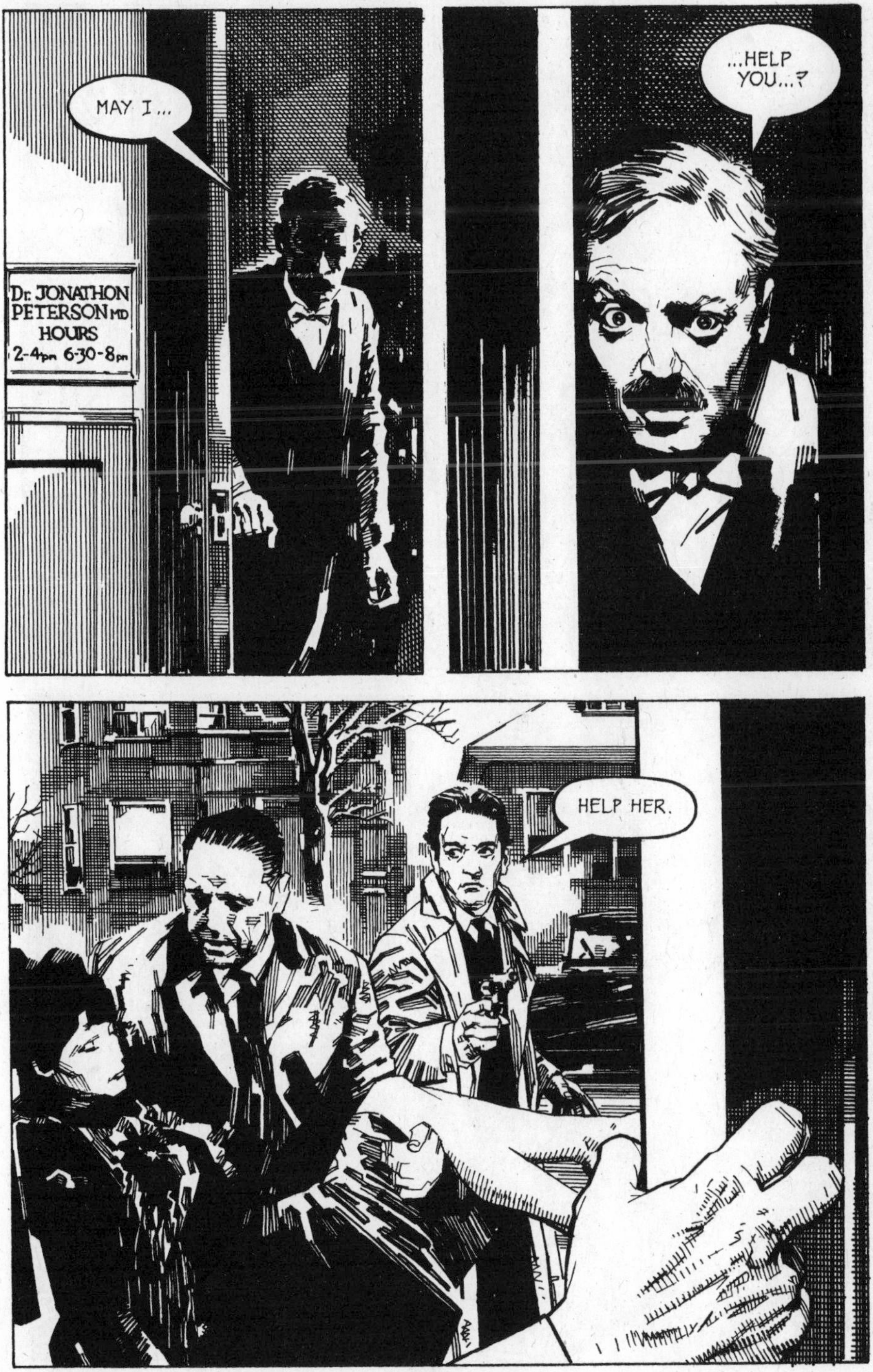
MAY I...
Dr. JONATHON PETERSON MD HOURS 2-4pm 6-30-8pm
...HELP YOU...?
HELP HER.

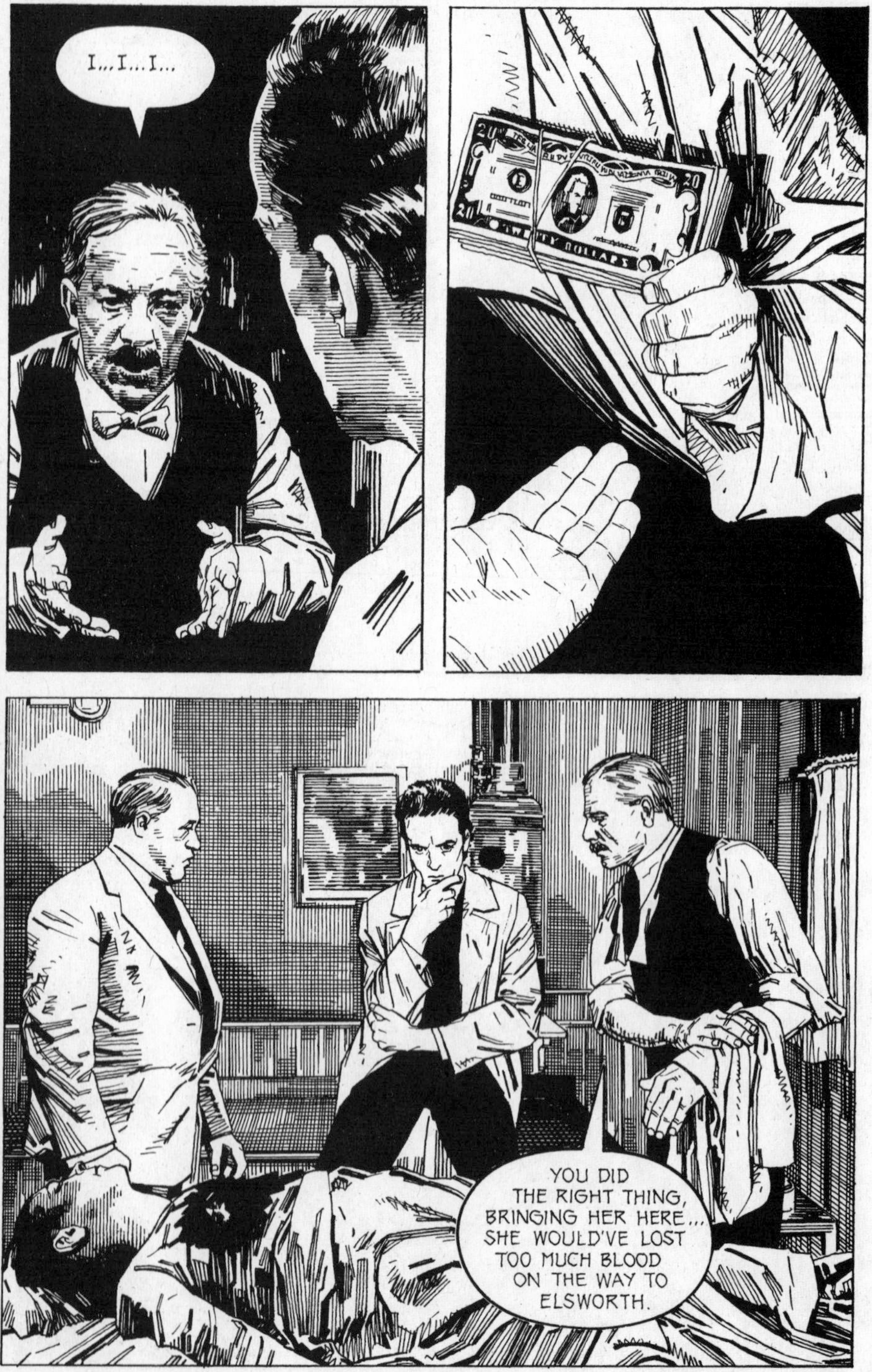
I... I... I...
YOU DID THE RIGHT THING, BRINGING HER HERE... SHE WOULD'VE LOST TOO MUCH BLOOD ON THE WAY TO ELSWORTH.

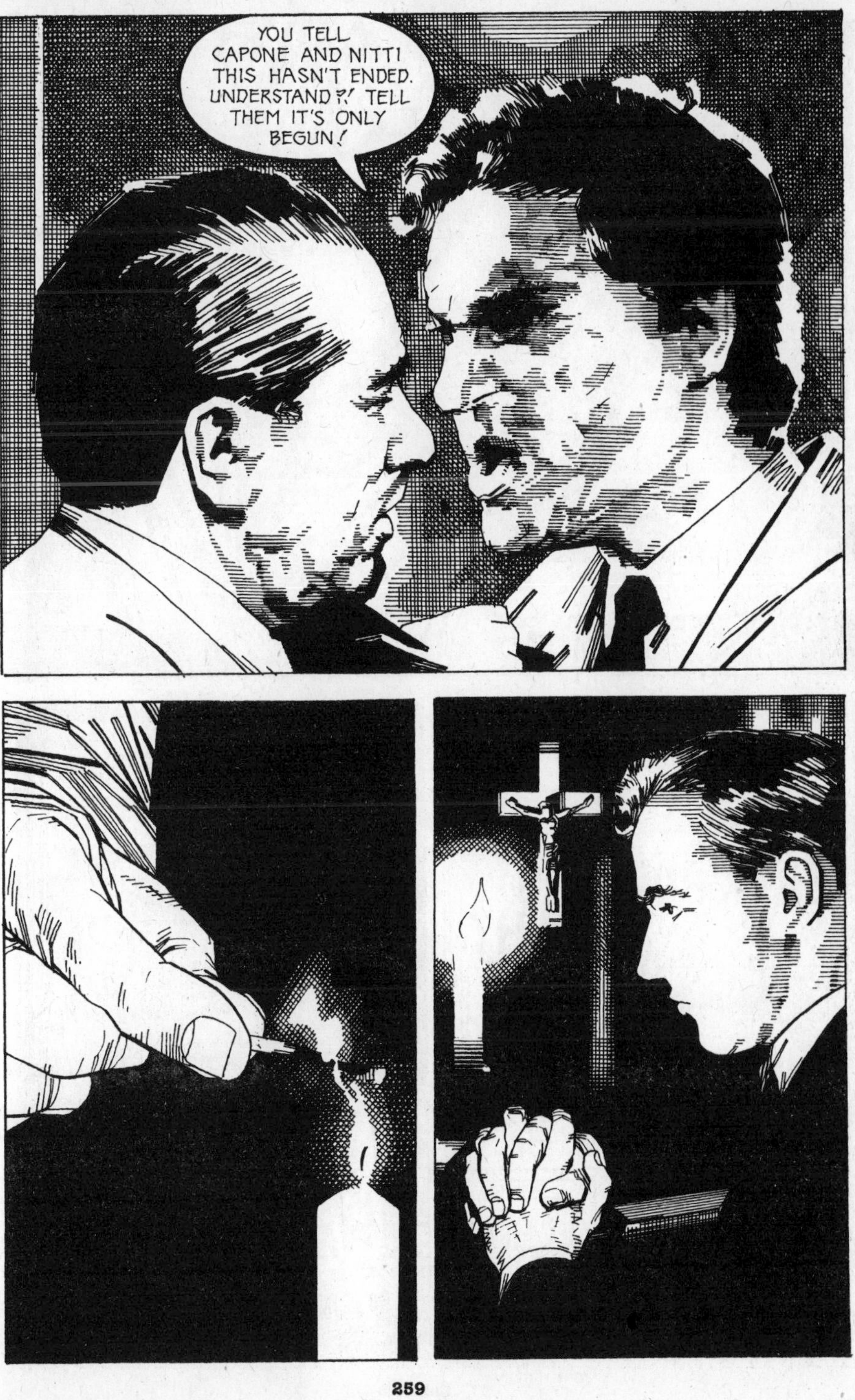
YOU TELL CAPONE AND NITTI THIS HASN'T ENDED. UNDERSTAND?! TELL THEM IT'S ONLY BEGUN!

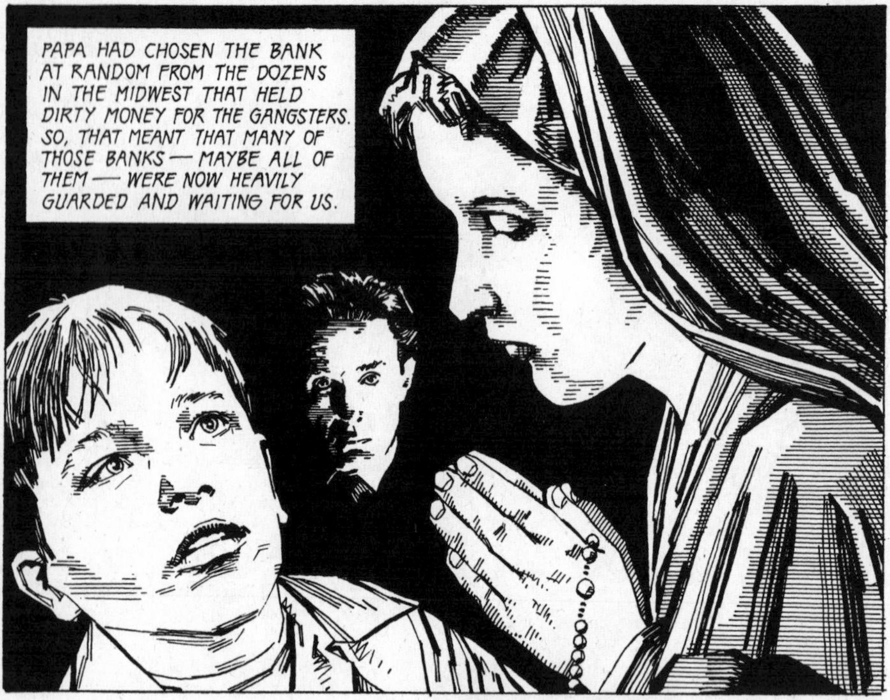
PAPA HAD CHOSEN THE BANK AT RANDOM FROM THE DOZENS IN THE MIDWEST THAT HELD DIRTY MONEY FOR THE GANGSTERS. SO, THAT MEANT THAT MANY OF THOSE BANKS — MAYBE ALL OF THEM — WERE NOW HEAVILY GUARDED AND WAITING FOR US.

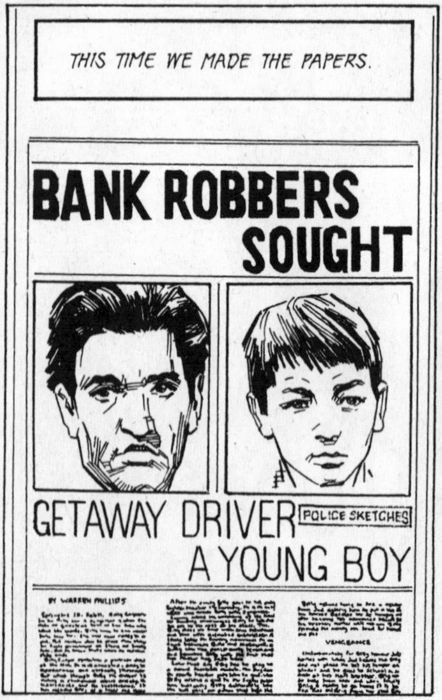
THIS TIME WE MADE THE PAPERS.
BANK ROBBERS SOUGHT
GETAWAY DRIVER
POLICE SKETCHES
A YOUNG BOY

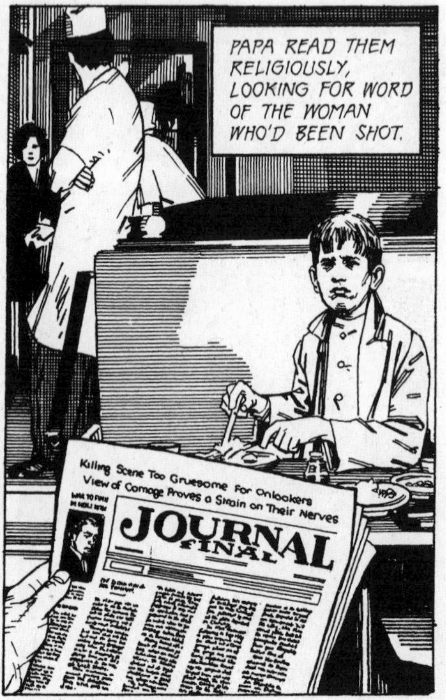
PAPA READ THEM RELIGIOUSLY, LOOKING FOR WORD OF THE WOMAN WHO'D BEEN SHOT.
Killing Scene Too Gruesome For Onlookers
View of Carnage Proves a Strain on Their Nerves
JOURNAL
FINAL

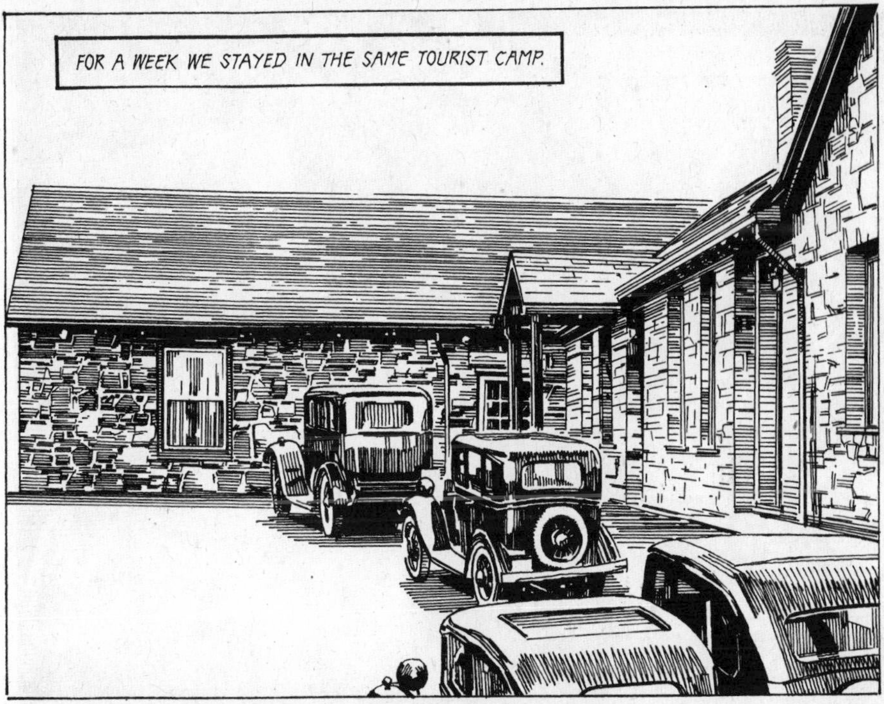
FOR A WEEK WE STAYED IN THE SAME TOURIST CAMP.

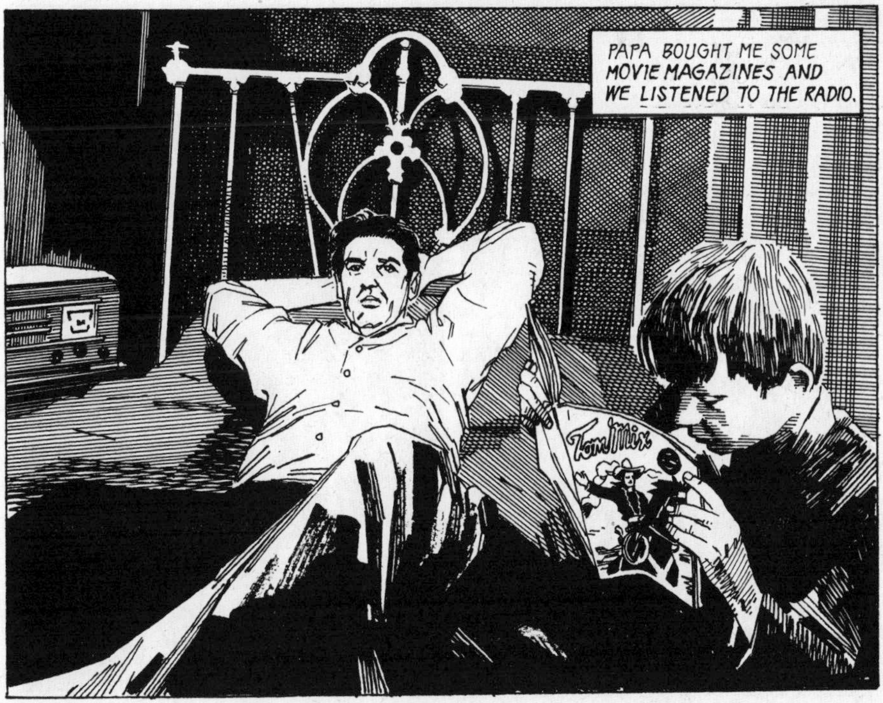
PAPA BOUGHT ME SOME MOVIE MAGAZINES AND WE LISTENED TO THE RADIO.
Tom Mix

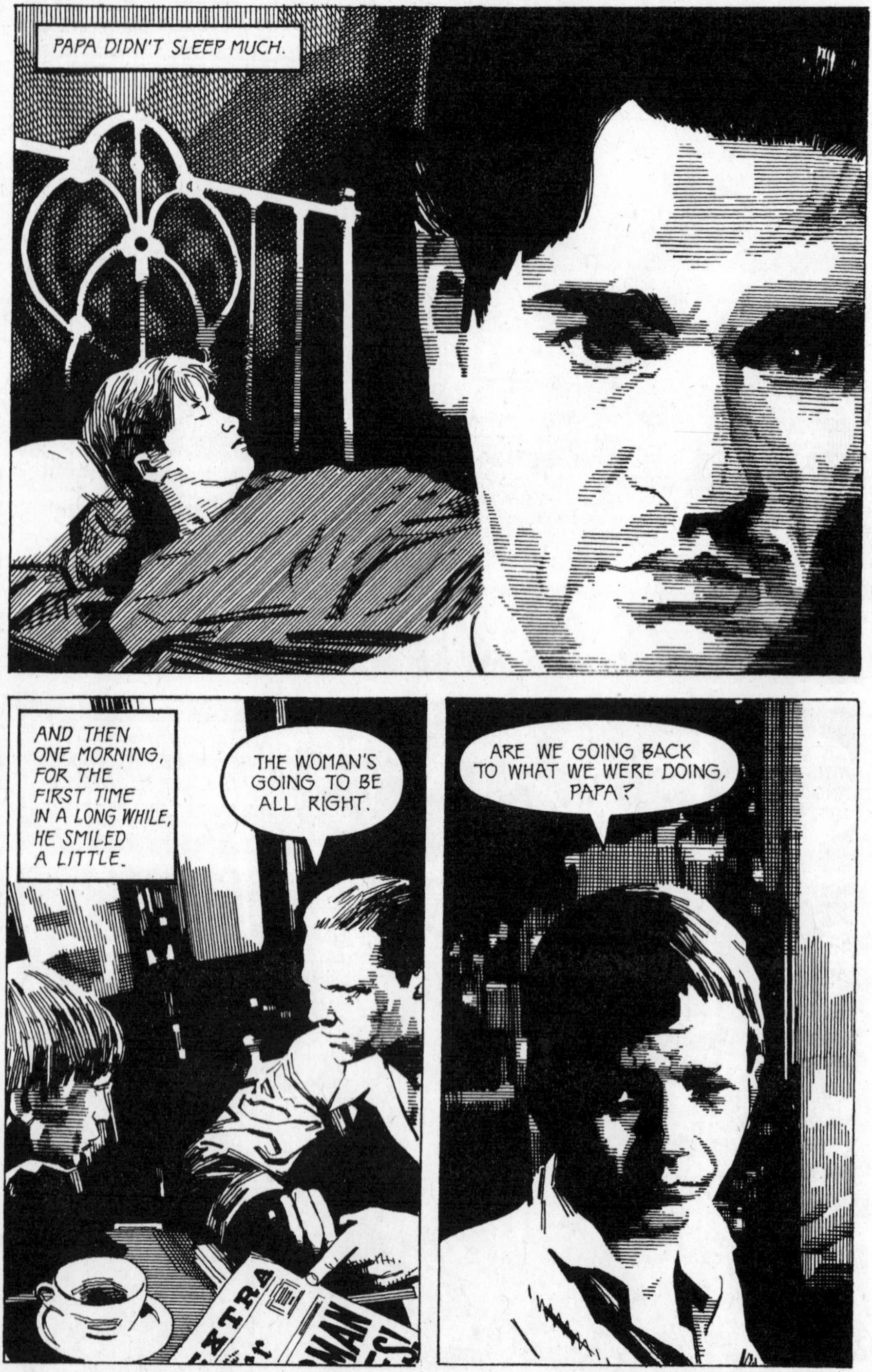
PAPA DIDN'T SLEEP MUCH.
AND THEN ONE MORNING, FOR THE FIRST TIME IN A LONG WHILE, HE SMILED A LITTLE.
THE WOMAN'S GOING TO BE ALL RIGHT.
EXTRA
ARE WE GOING BACK TO WHAT WE WERE DOING, PAPA?

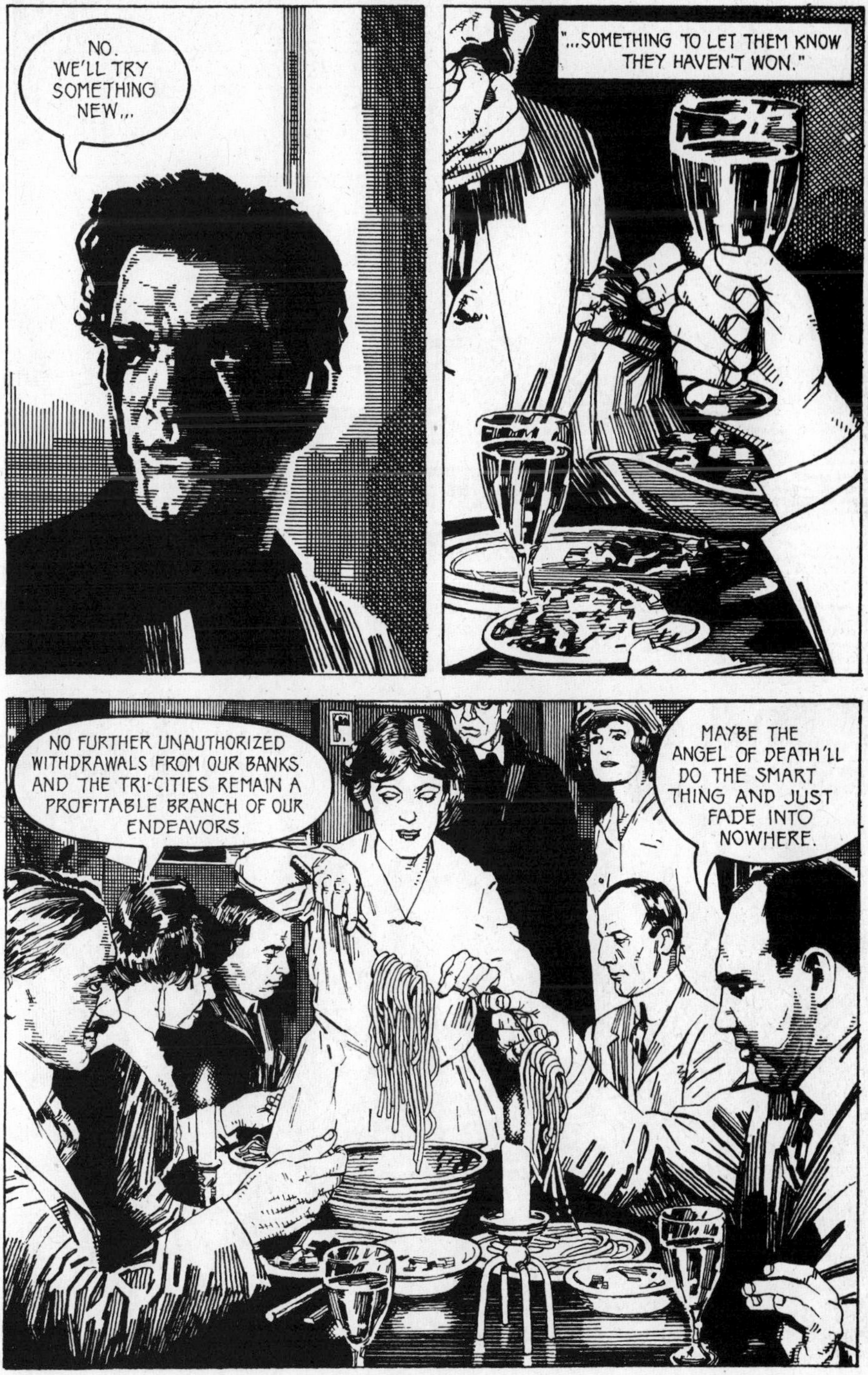
NO. WE'LL TRY SOMETHING NEW...
"...SOMETHING TO LET THEM KNOW THEY HAVEN'T WON."
NO FURTHER UNAUTHORIZED WITHDRAWALS FROM OUR BANKS. AND THE TRI-CITIES REMAIN A PROFITABLE BRANCH OF OUR ENDEAVORS.
MAYBE THE ANGEL OF DEATH'LL DO THE SMART THING AND JUST FADE INTO NOWHERE.

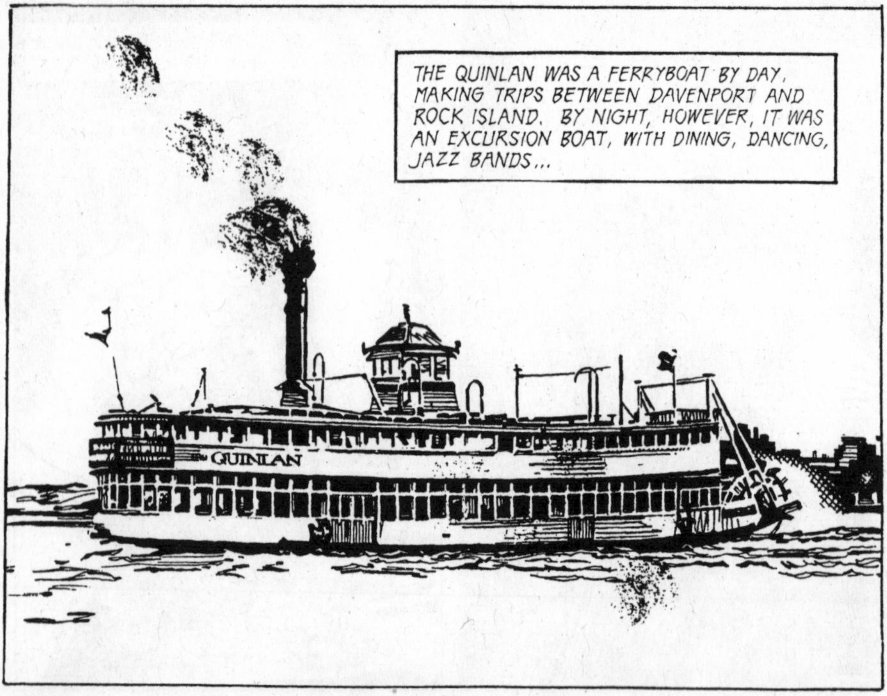
THE QUINLAN WAS A FERRYBOAT BY DAY, MAKING TRIPS BETWEEN DAVENPORT AND ROCK ISLAND. BY NIGHT, HOWEVER, IT WAS AN EXCURSION BOAT, WITH DINING, DANCING, JAZZ BANDS...
QUINLAN

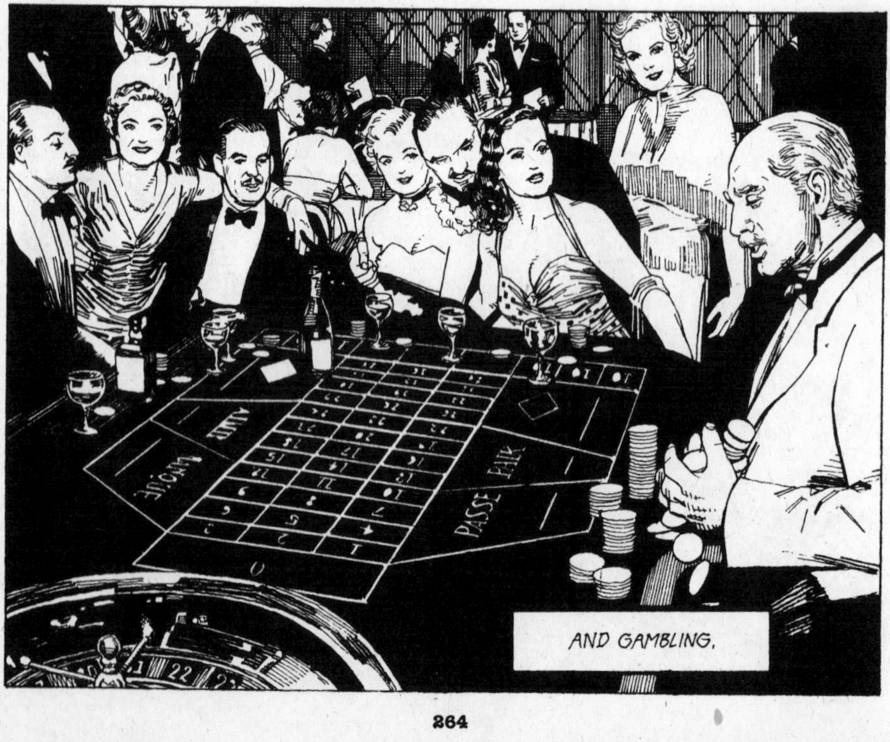
PASSE
PAIR
AND GAMBLING.

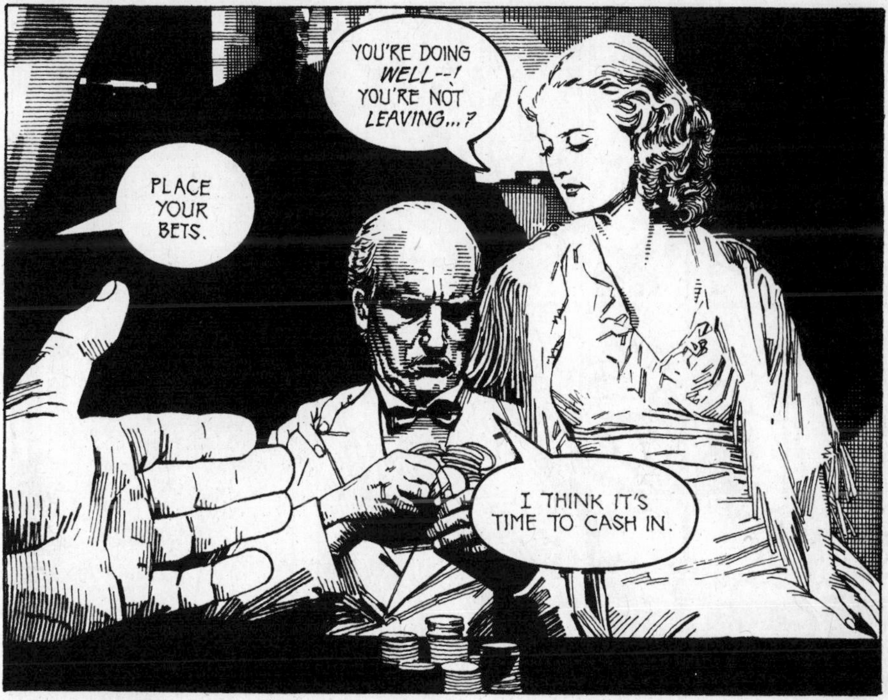
YOU'RE DOING WELL--! YOU'RE NOT LEAVING...?
PLACE YOUR BETS.
I THINK IT'S TIME TO CASH IN.

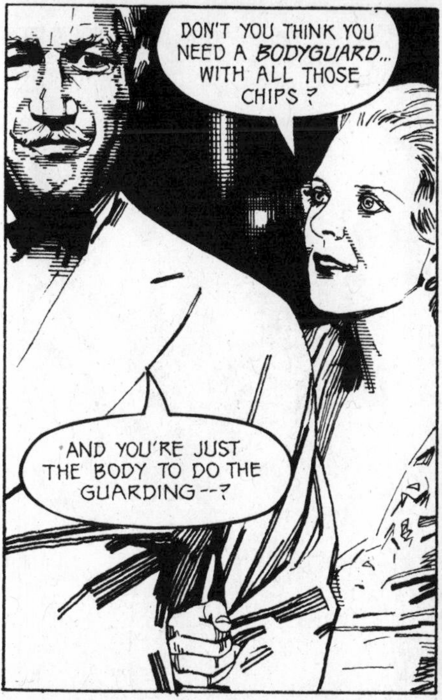
DON'T YOU THINK YOU NEED A BODYGUARD... WITH ALL THOSE CHIPS?
AND YOU'RE JUST THE BODY TO DO THE GUARDING--?

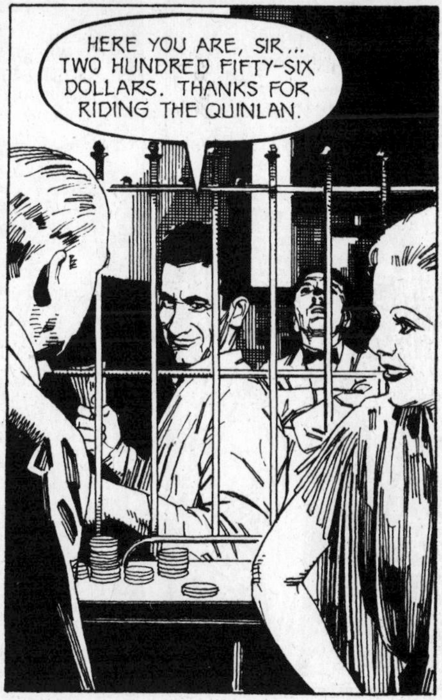
HERE YOU ARE, SIR... TWO HUNDRED FIFTY-SIX DOLLARS. THANKS FOR RIDING THE QUINLAN.

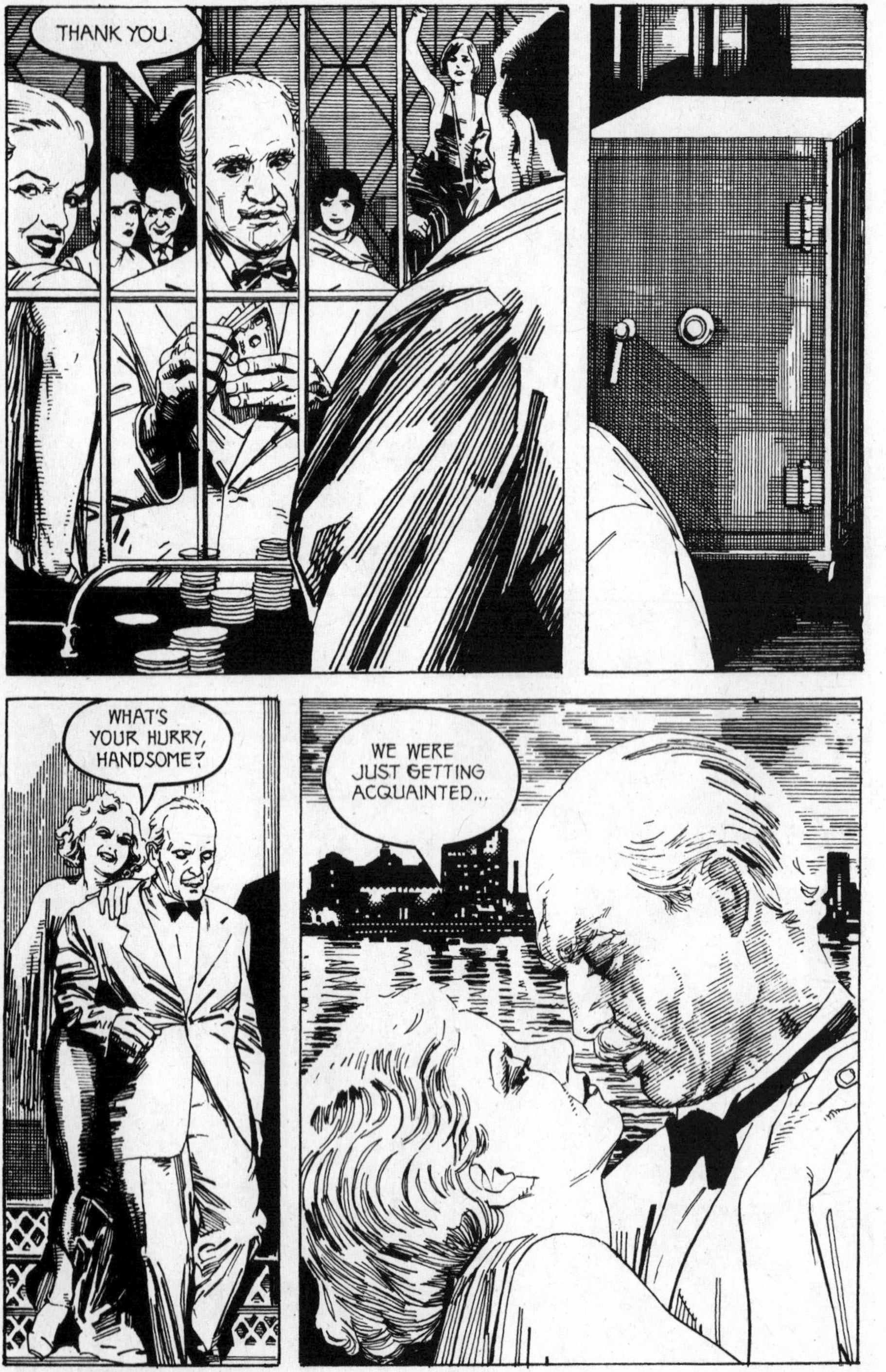
THANK YOU.
WHAT'S YOUR HURRY, HANDSOME?
WE WERE JUST GETTING ACQUAINTED...

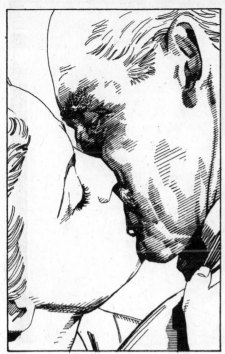

WHY'S A PRETTY KID LIKE YOU INTERESTED IN A FAT OLD CODGER LIKE ME?

YOU GOT A NICE FACE... AND I DON'T THINK YOU'RE SO FAT... BESIDES, MAYBE THIS IS A MONEY BELT...

IS -- IS THAT A *GUN?*

MAYBE I'M JUST GLAD TO SEE YOU.

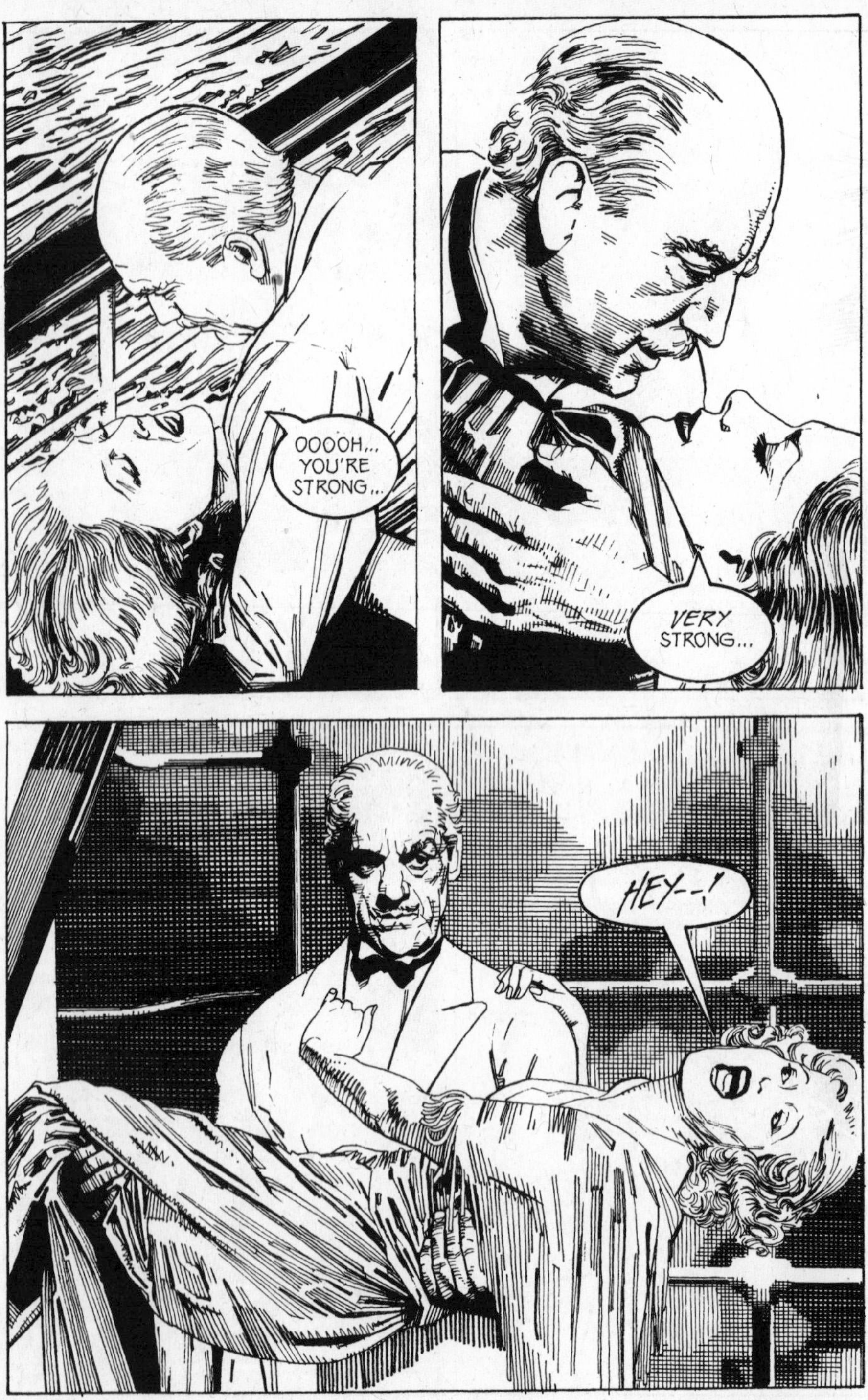
OOOOH... YOU'RE STRONG...
VERY STRONG...
HEY--!

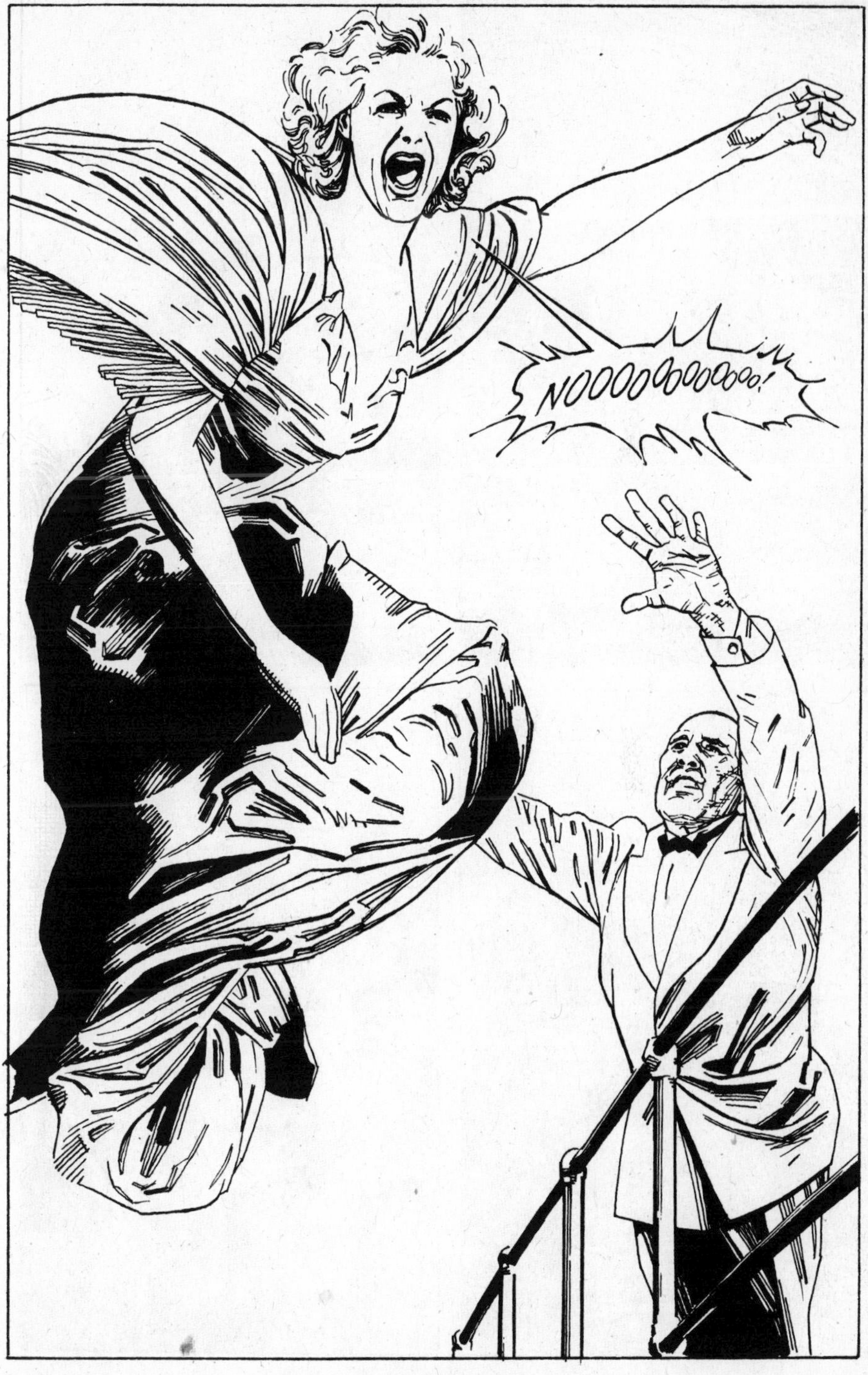
NOOOOOOOOOOOO!

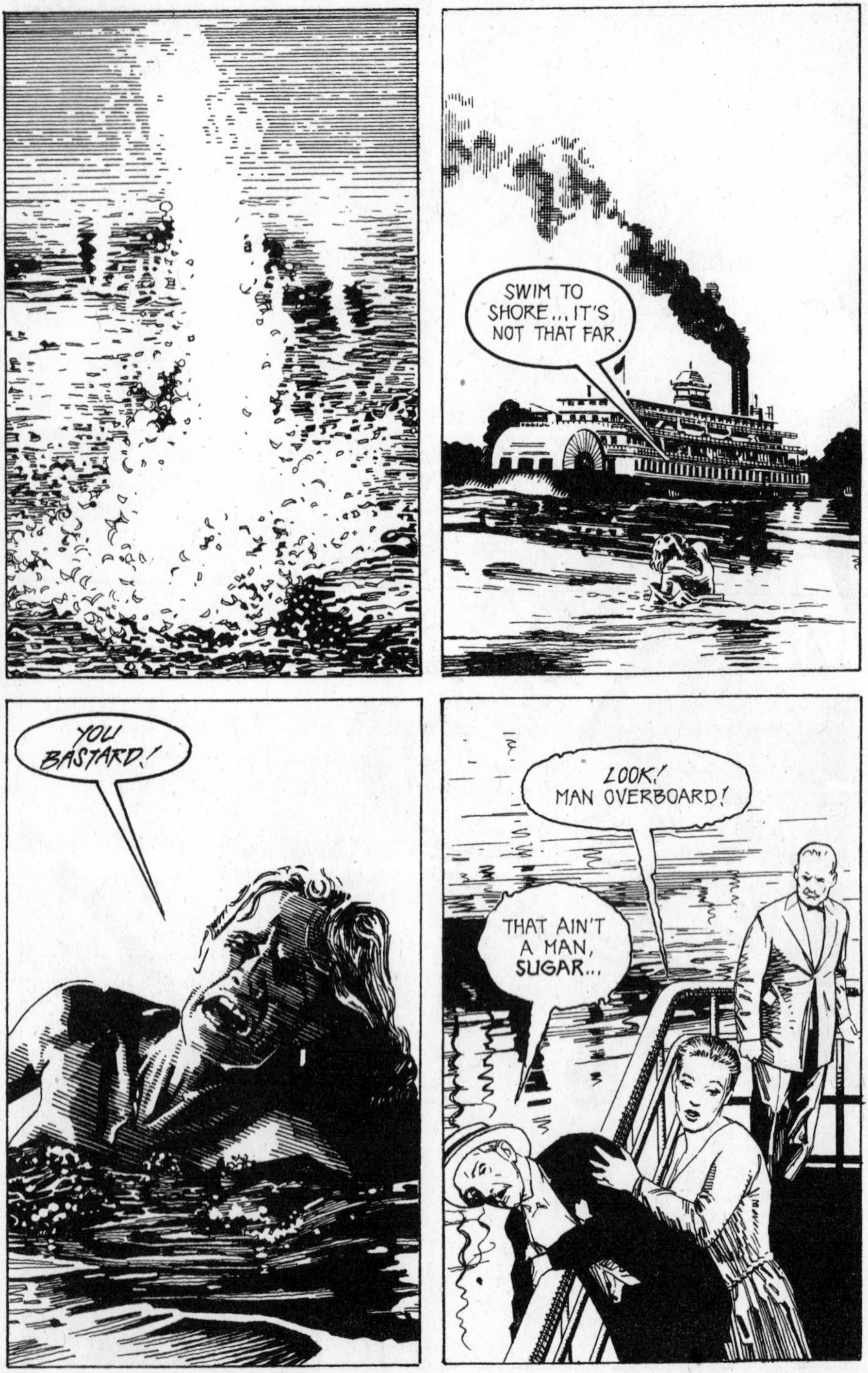
SWIM TO SHORE... IT'S NOT THAT FAR.
YOU BASTARD!
LOOK! MAN OVERBOARD!
THAT AIN'T A MAN, SUGAR...

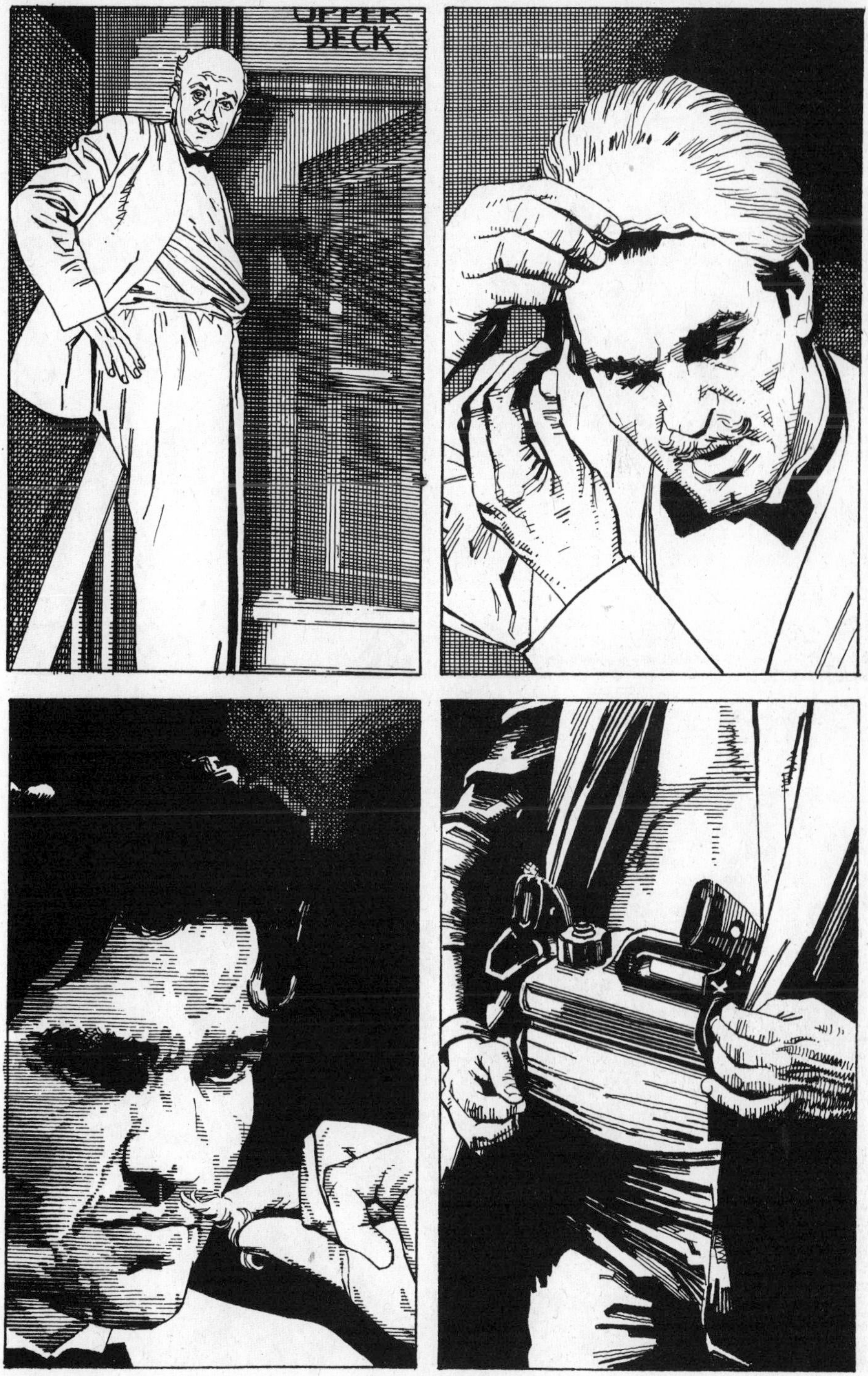
UPPER DECK

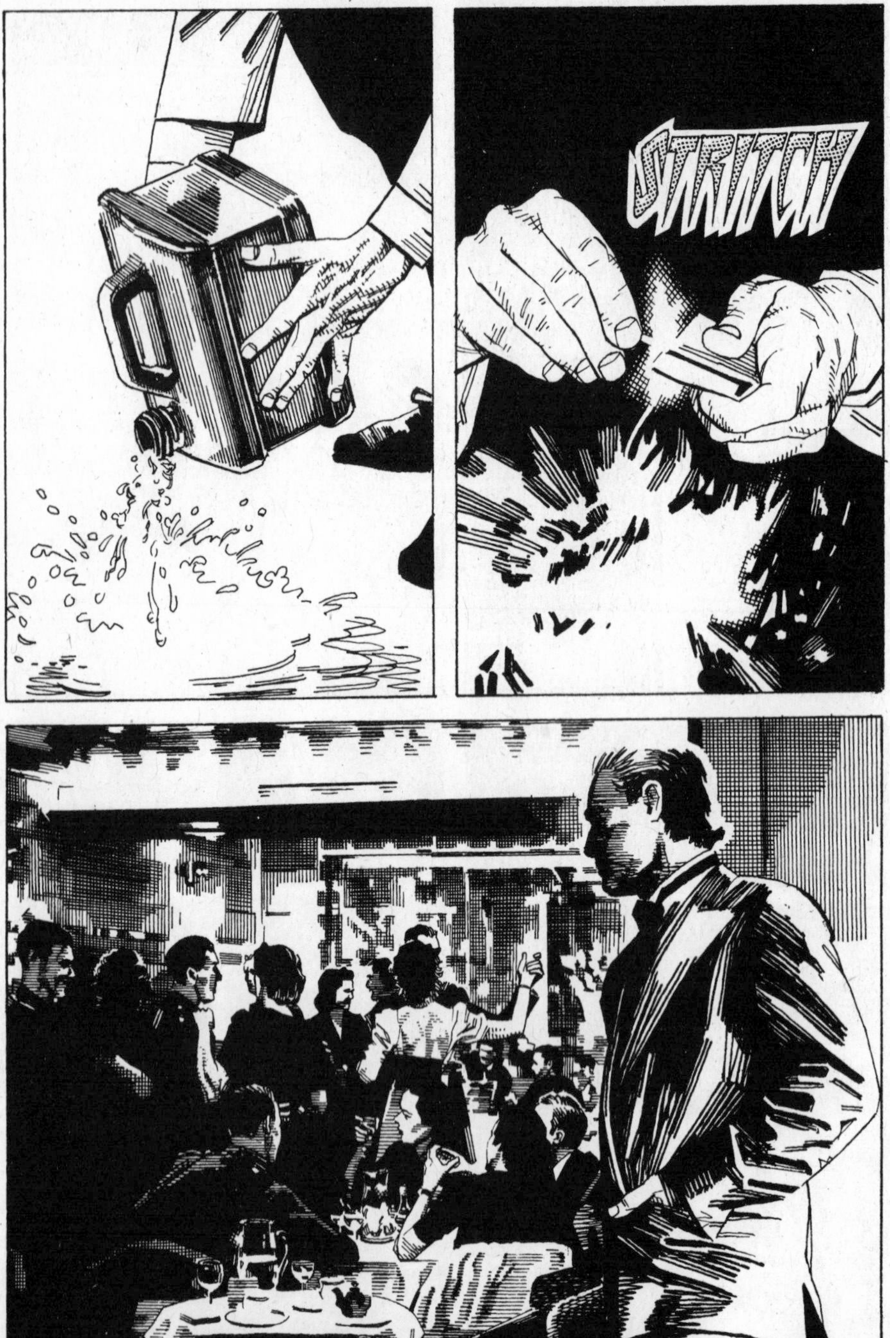
STRITCH

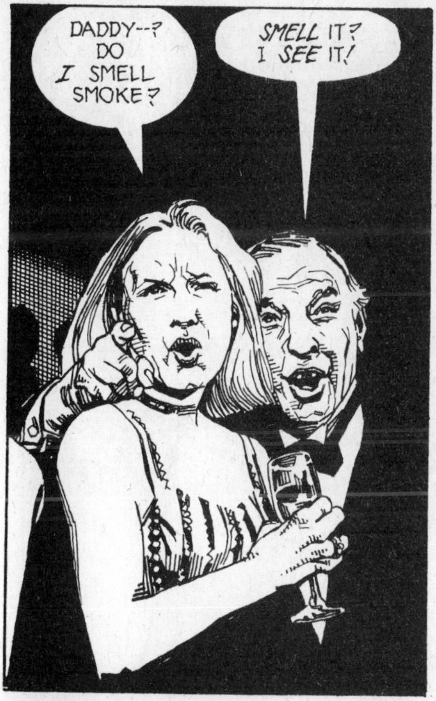
DADDY--? DO *I* SMELL SMOKE?
SMELL IT? I *SEE* IT!
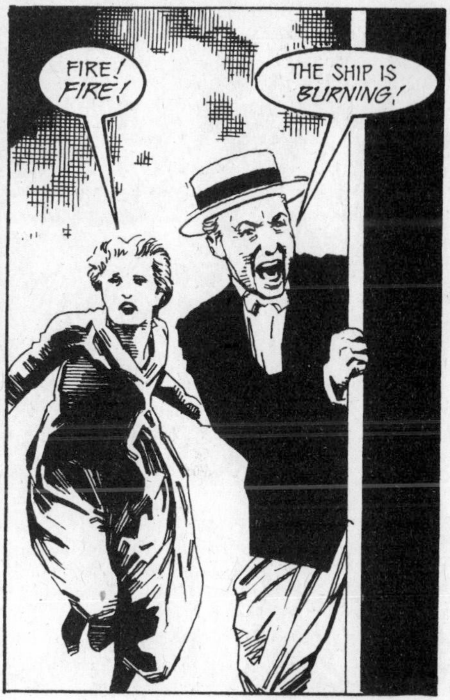
FIRE! *FIRE!*
THE SHIP IS *BURNING!*
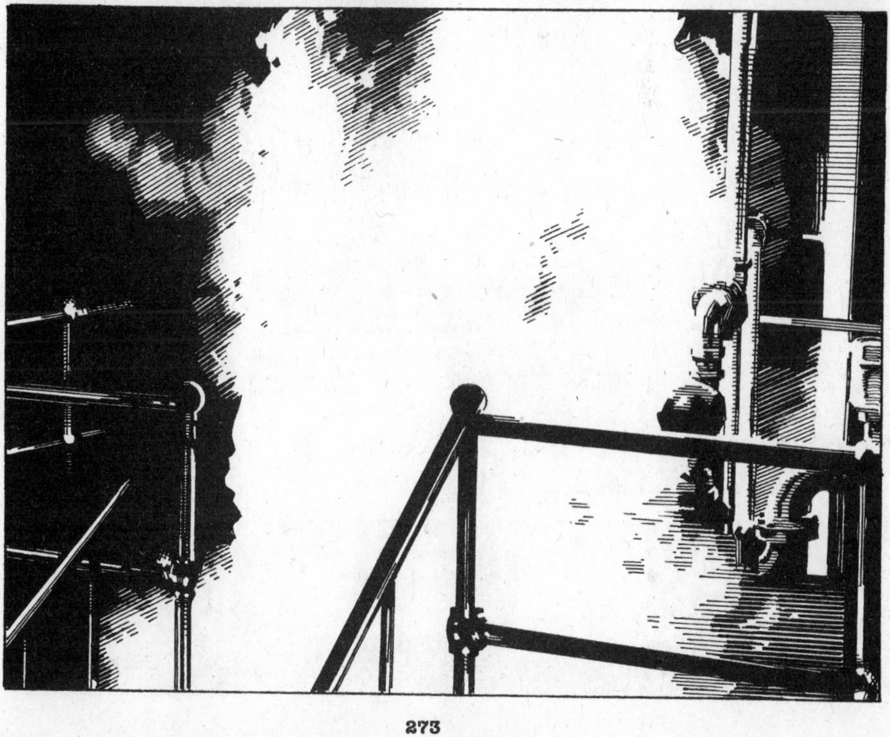

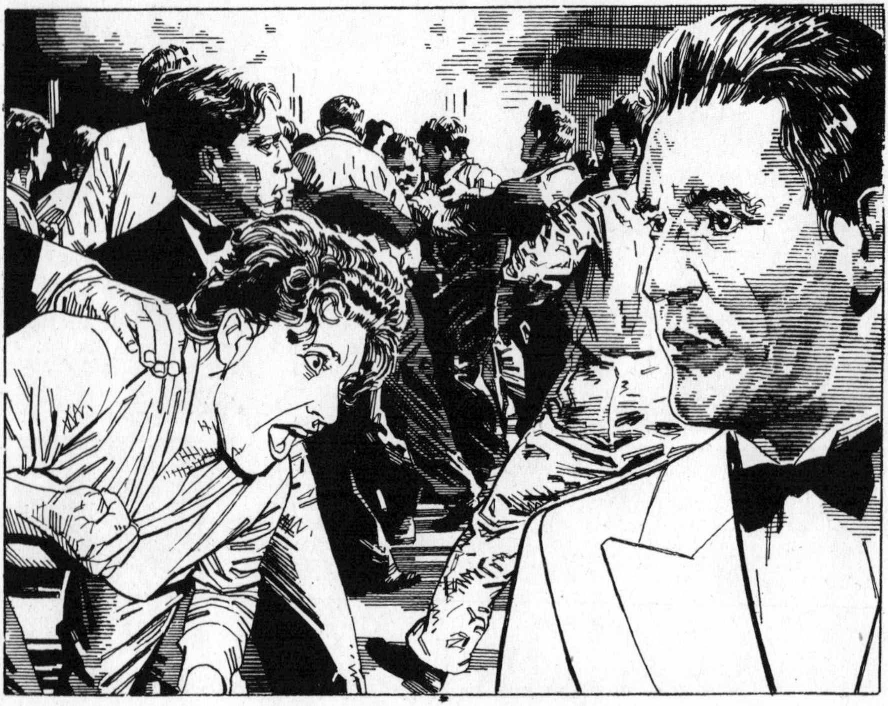

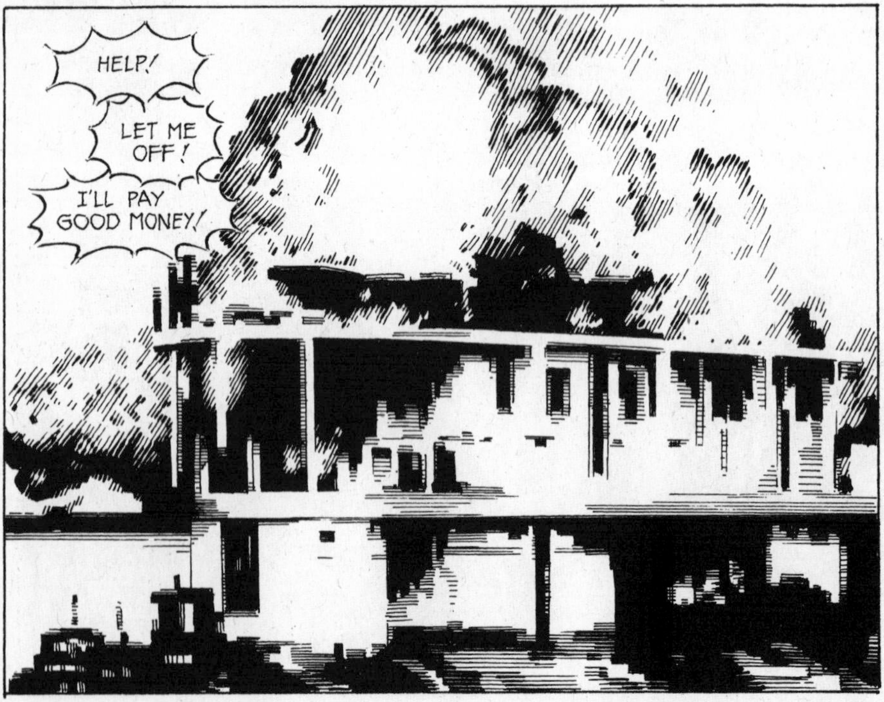
HELP!
LET ME OFF!
I'LL PAY GOOD MONEY!

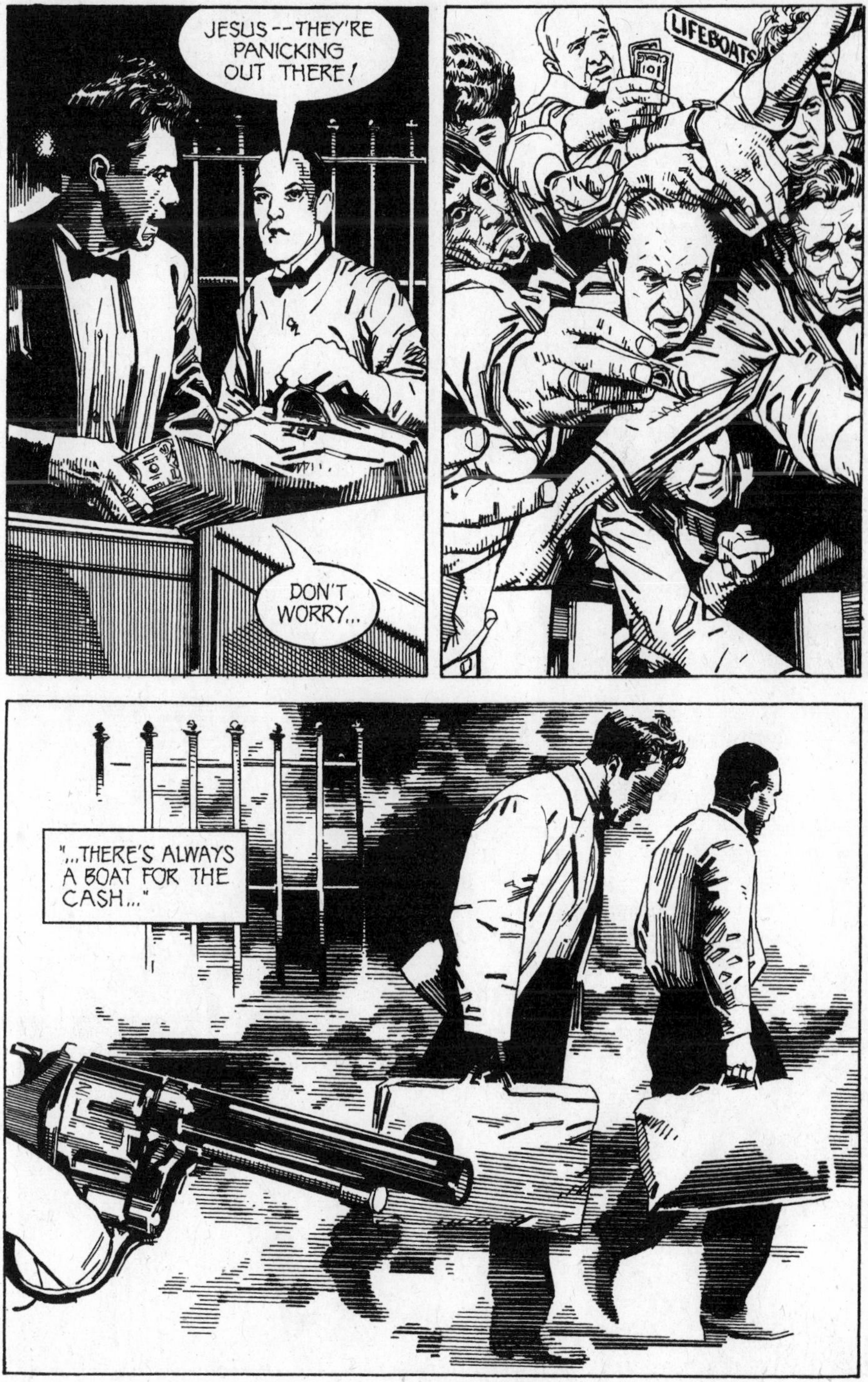
JESUS--THEY'RE PANICKING OUT THERE!
DON'T WORRY...
LIFEBOATS
"...THERE'S ALWAYS A BOAT FOR THE CASH..."

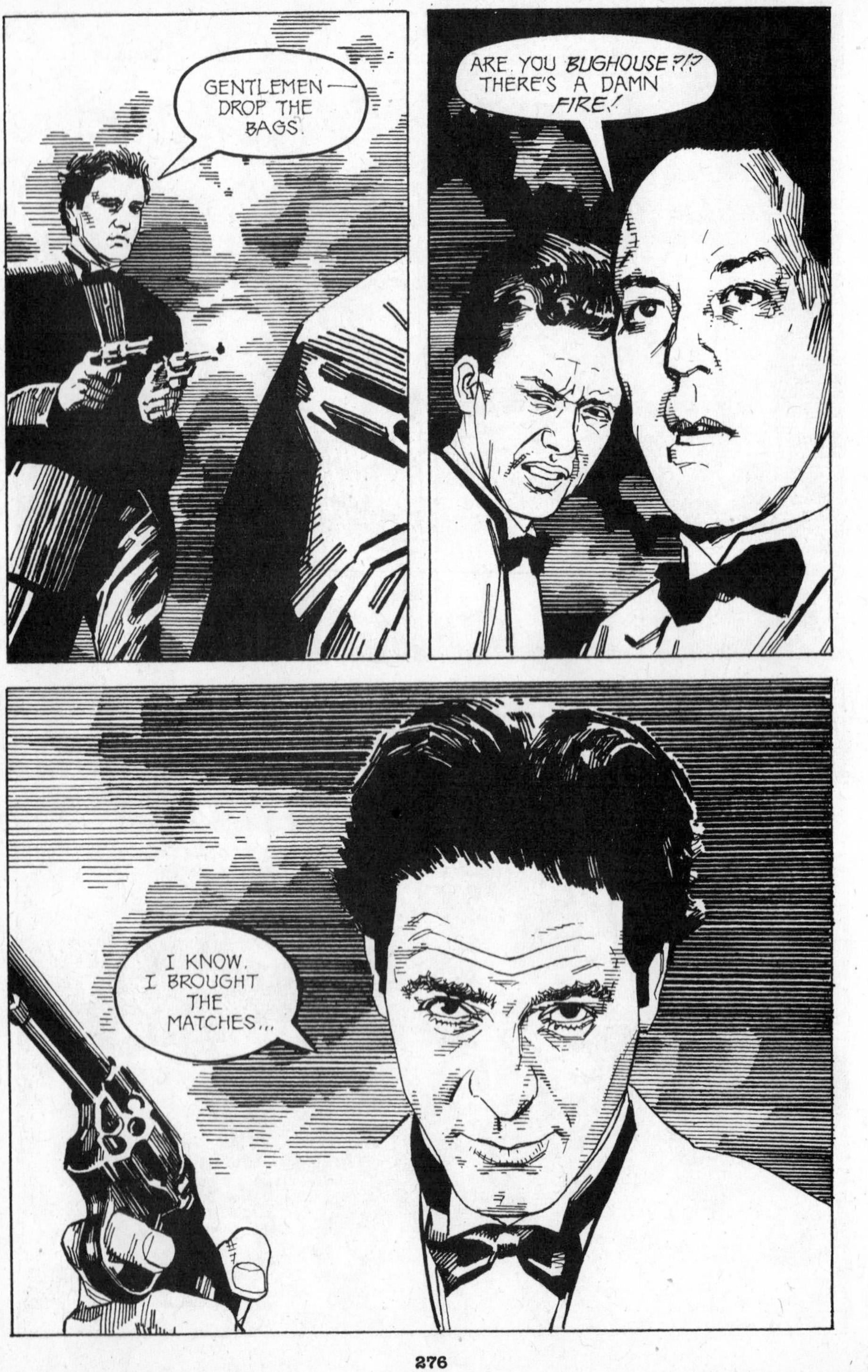
GENTLEMEN— DROP THE BAGS.
ARE YOU BUGHOUSE?!? THERE'S A DAMN FIRE!
I KNOW. I BROUGHT THE MATCHES...

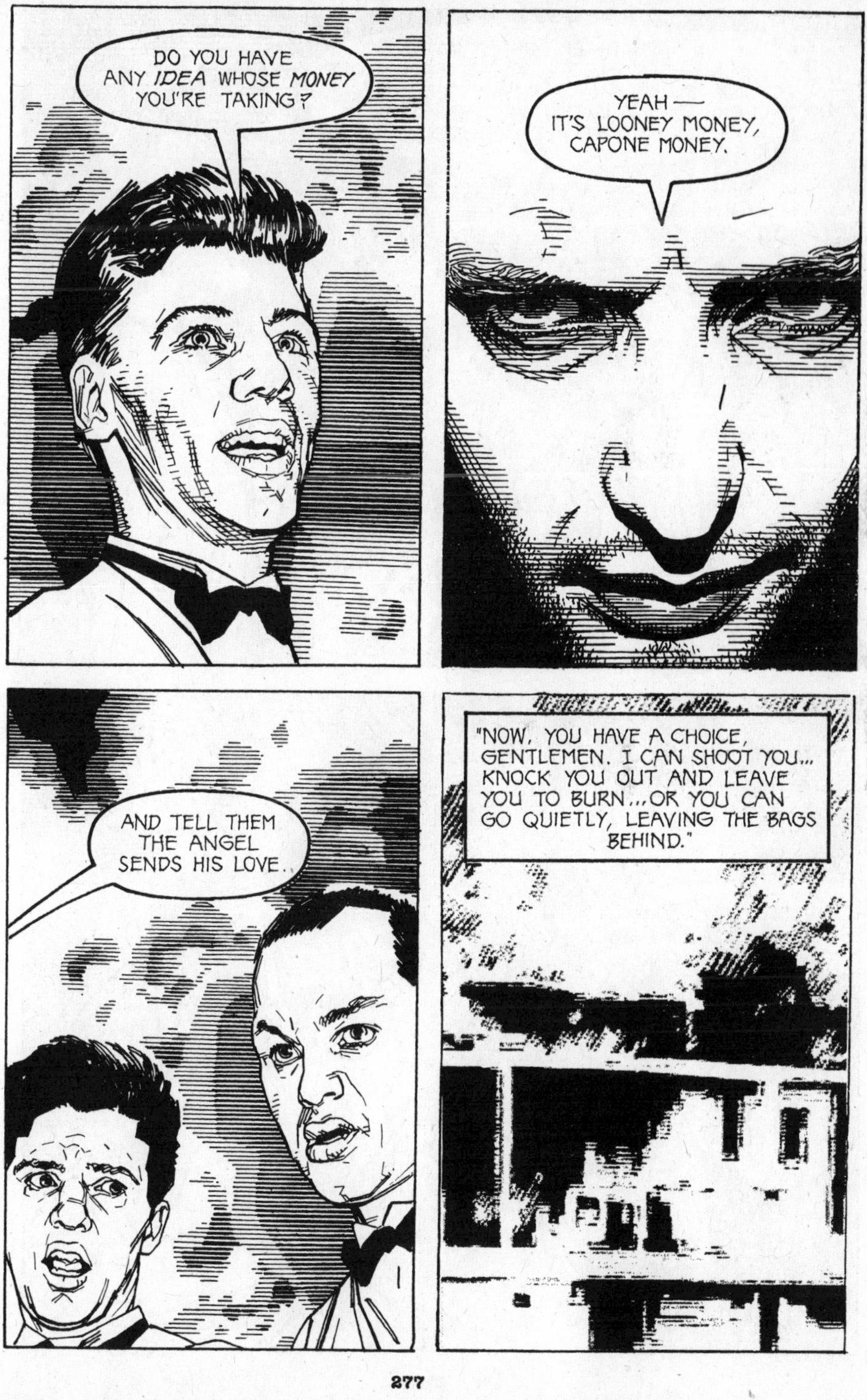

DO YOU HAVE ANY *IDEA* WHOSE *MONEY* YOU'RE TAKING?
YEAH— IT'S LOONEY MONEY, CAPONE MONEY.
AND TELL THEM THE ANGEL SENDS HIS LOVE.
"NOW, YOU HAVE A CHOICE, GENTLEMEN. I CAN SHOOT YOU... KNOCK YOU OUT AND LEAVE YOU TO BURN...OR YOU CAN GO QUIETLY, LEAVING THE BAGS BEHIND."

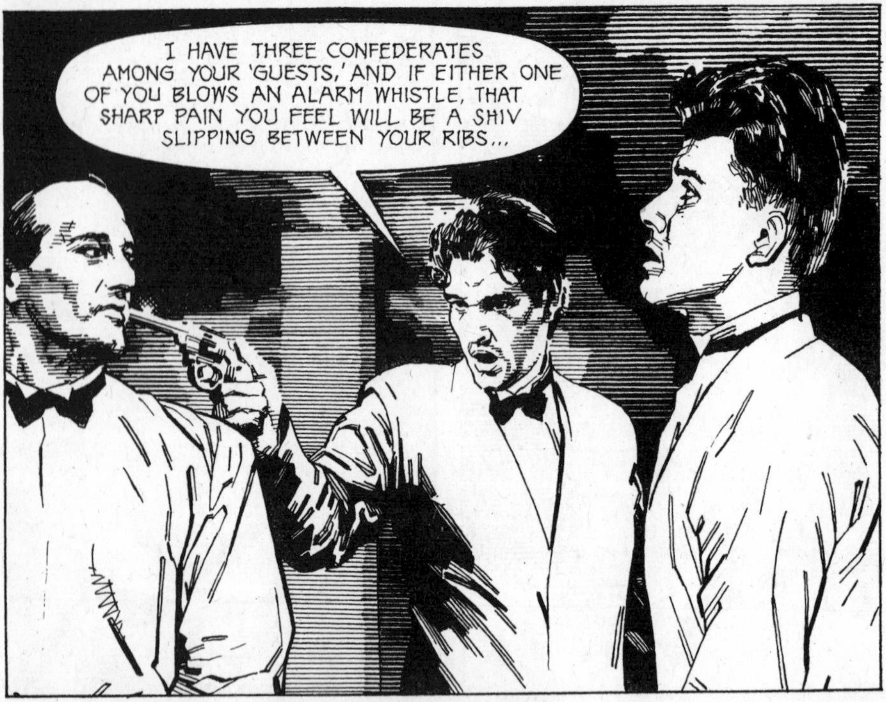
I HAVE THREE CONFEDERATES AMONG YOUR 'GUESTS,' AND IF EITHER ONE OF YOU BLOWS AN ALARM WHISTLE, THAT SHARP PAIN YOU FEEL WILL BE A SHIV SLIPPING BETWEEN YOUR RIBS...

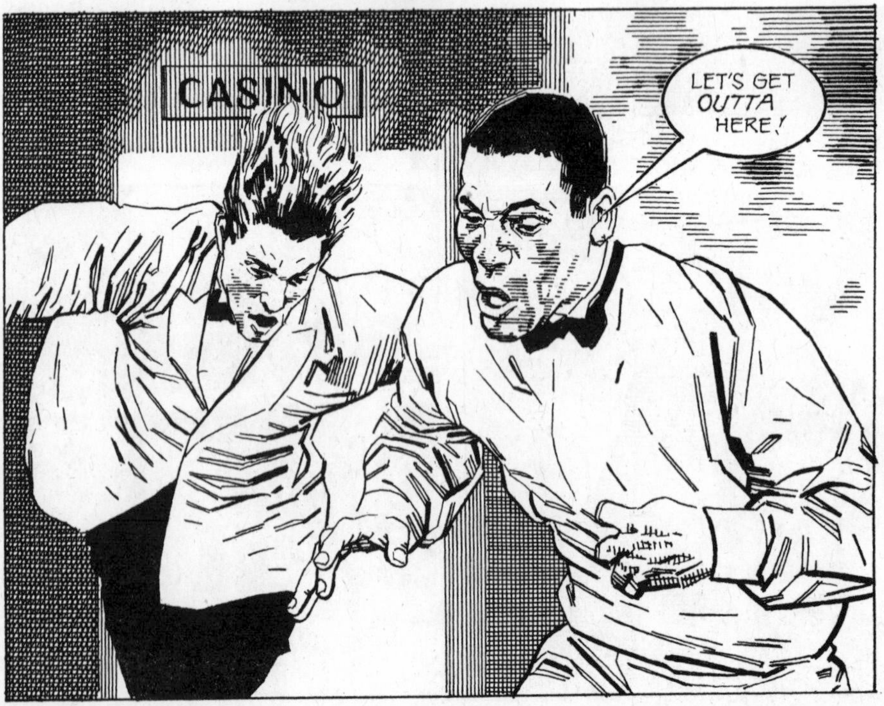
CASINO
LET'S GET *OUTTA* HERE!

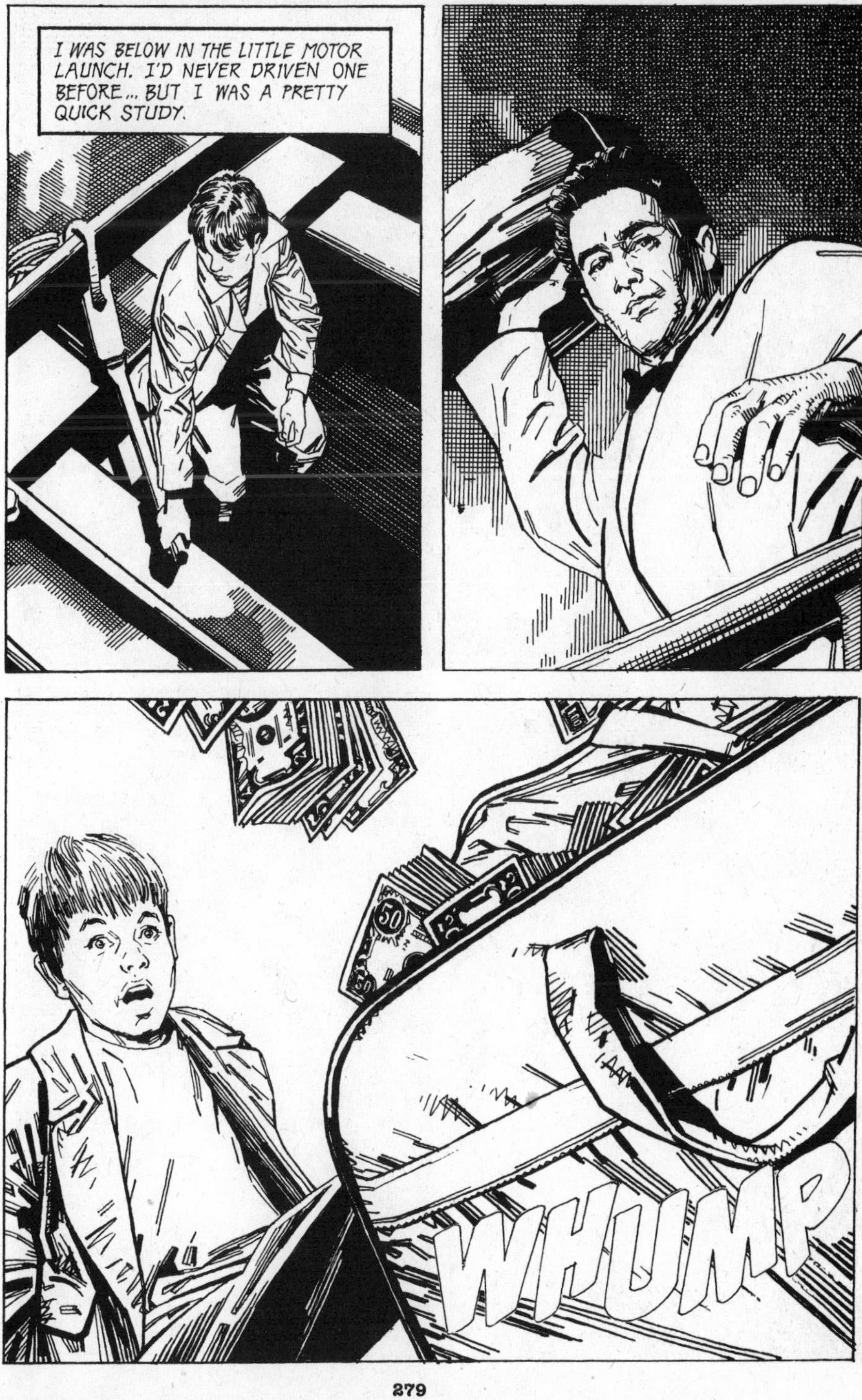
I WAS BELOW IN THE LITTLE MOTOR LAUNCH. I'D NEVER DRIVEN ONE BEFORE... BUT I WAS A PRETTY QUICK STUDY.
WHUMP

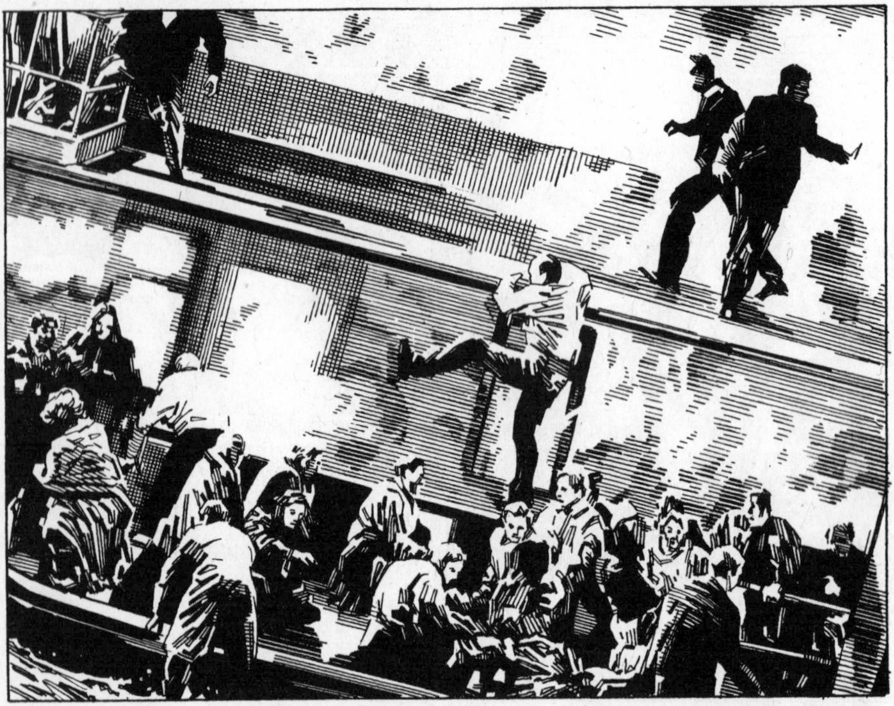

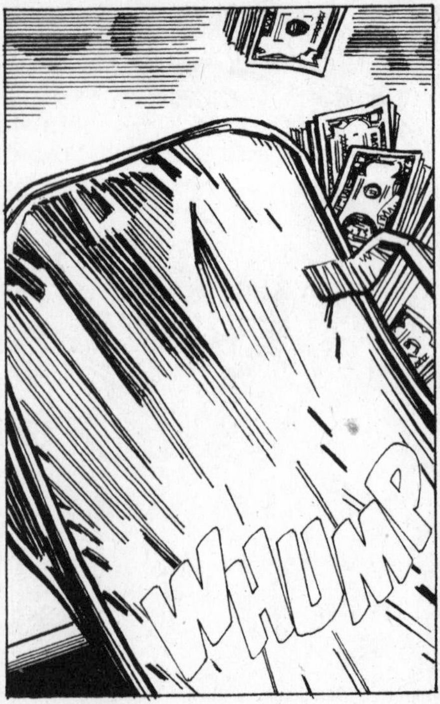
WHUMP

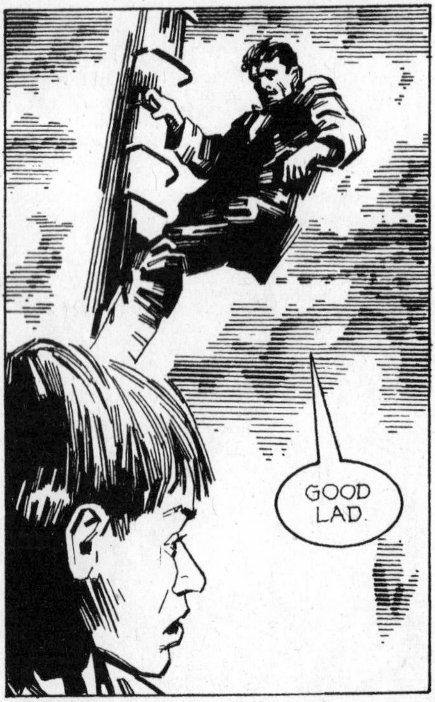
GOOD LAD.

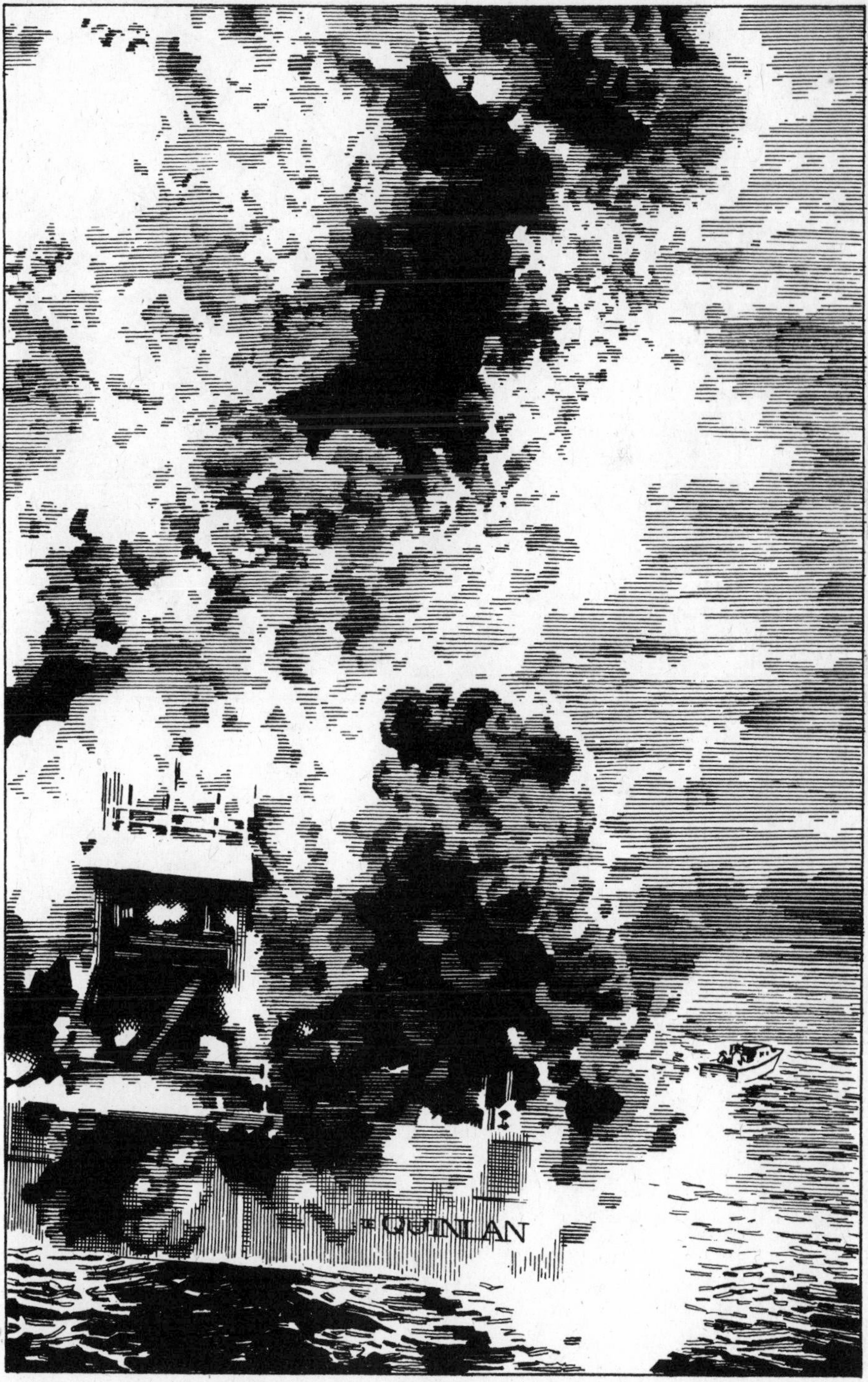
QUINLAN

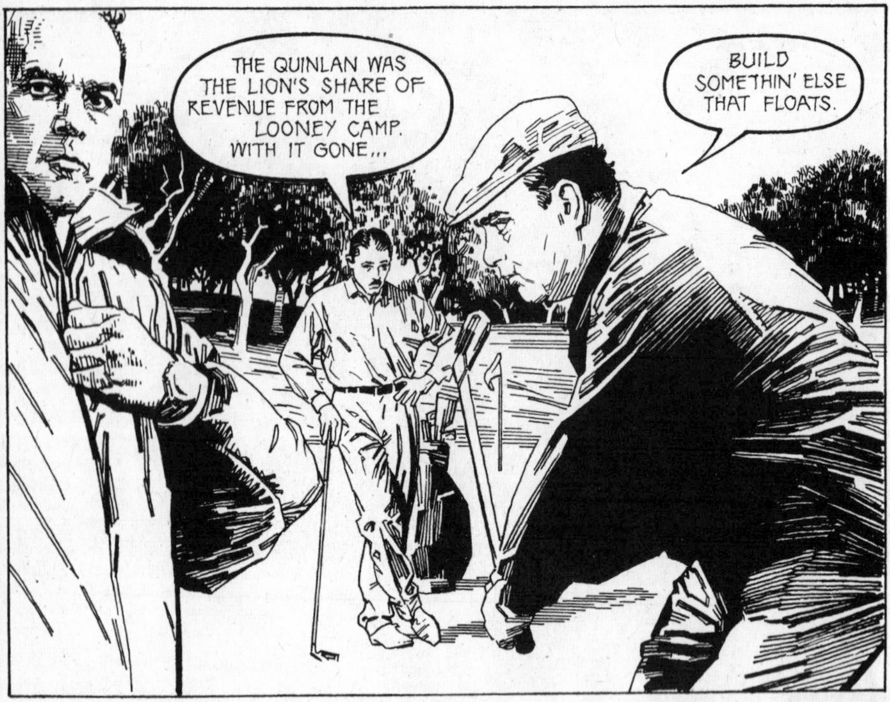
THE QUINLAN WAS THE LION'S SHARE OF REVENUE FROM THE LOONEY CAMP. WITH IT GONE...
BUILD SOMETHIN' ELSE THAT FLOATS.

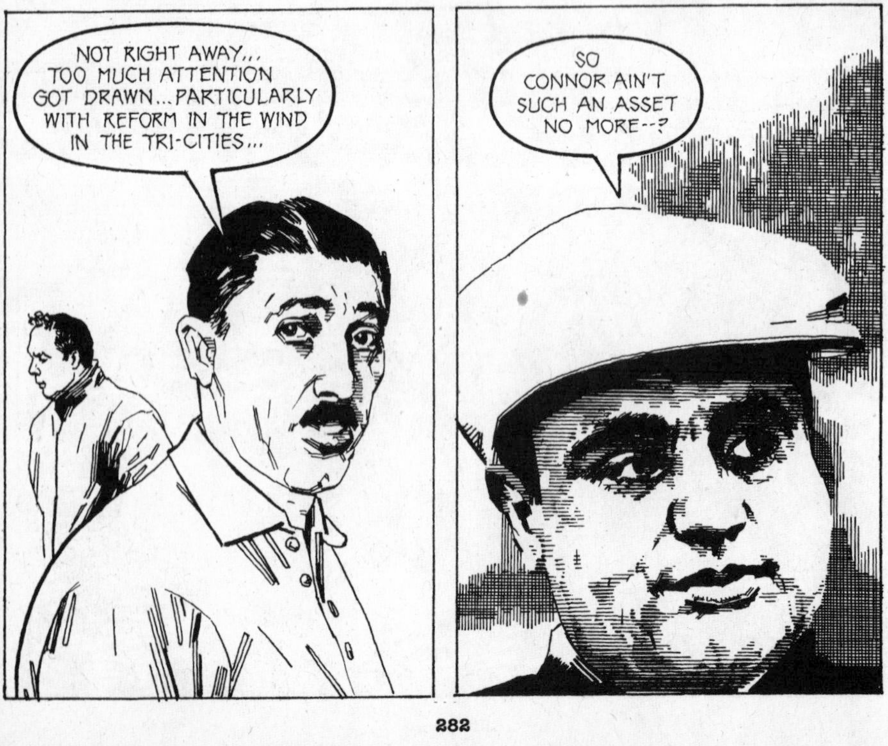
NOT RIGHT AWAY... TOO MUCH ATTENTION GOT DRAWN...PARTICULARLY WITH REFORM IN THE WIND IN THE TRI-CITIES...
SO CONNOR AIN'T SUCH AN ASSET NO MORE--?

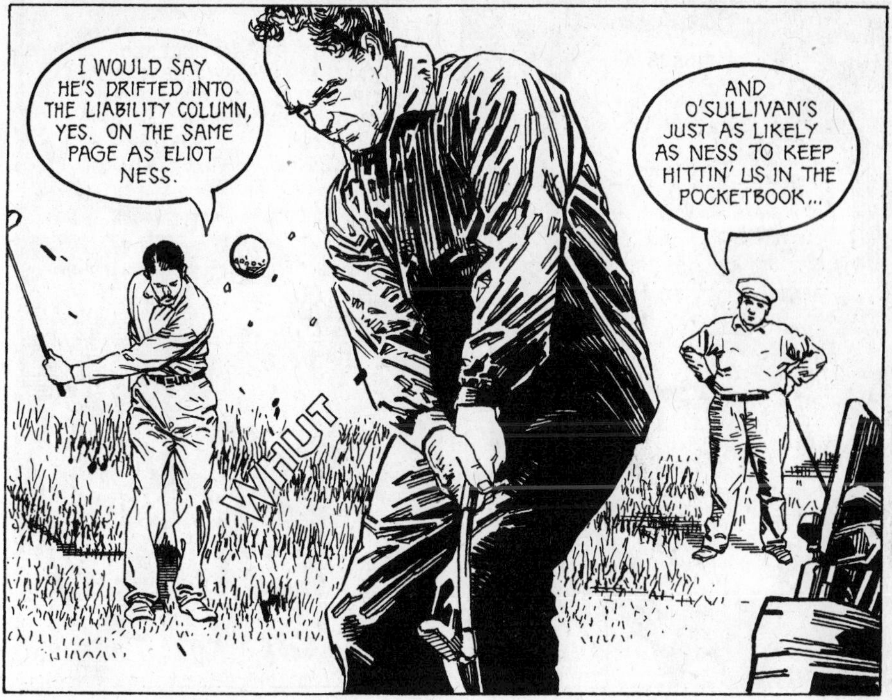
I WOULD SAY HE'S DRIFTED INTO THE LIABILITY COLUMN, YES. ON THE SAME PAGE AS ELIOT NESS.
AND O'SULLIVAN'S JUST AS LIKELY AS NESS TO KEEP HITTIN' US IN THE POCKETBOOK...
WHUT

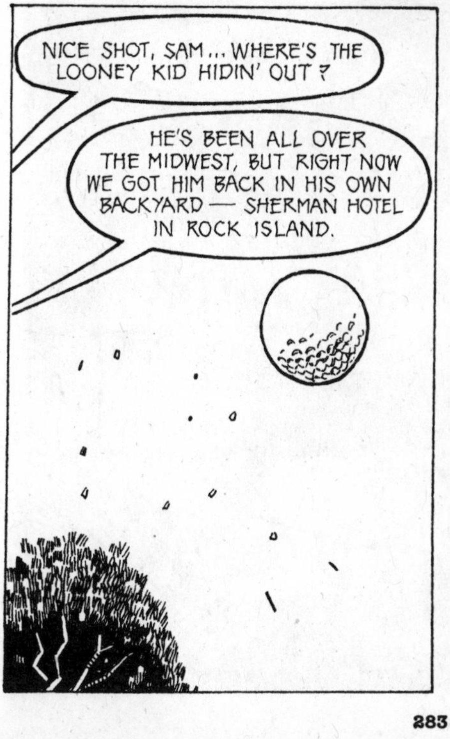
NICE SHOT, SAM... WHERE'S THE LOONEY KID HIDIN' OUT?
HE'S BEEN ALL OVER THE MIDWEST, BUT RIGHT NOW WE GOT HIM BACK IN HIS OWN BACKYARD — SHERMAN HOTEL IN ROCK ISLAND.

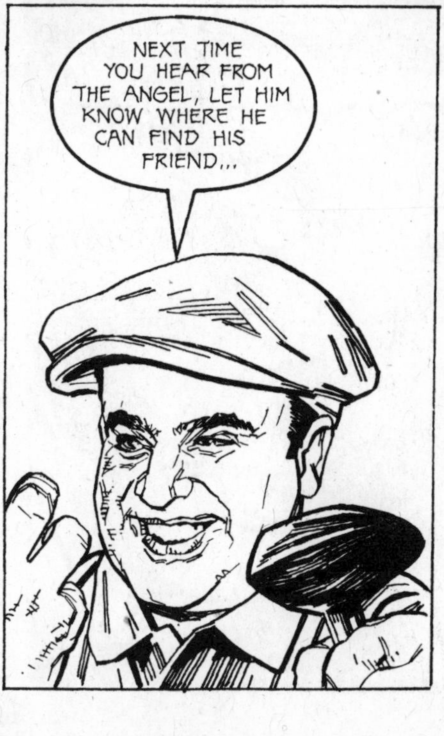
NEXT TIME YOU HEAR FROM THE ANGEL, LET HIM KNOW WHERE HE CAN FIND HIS FRIEND...

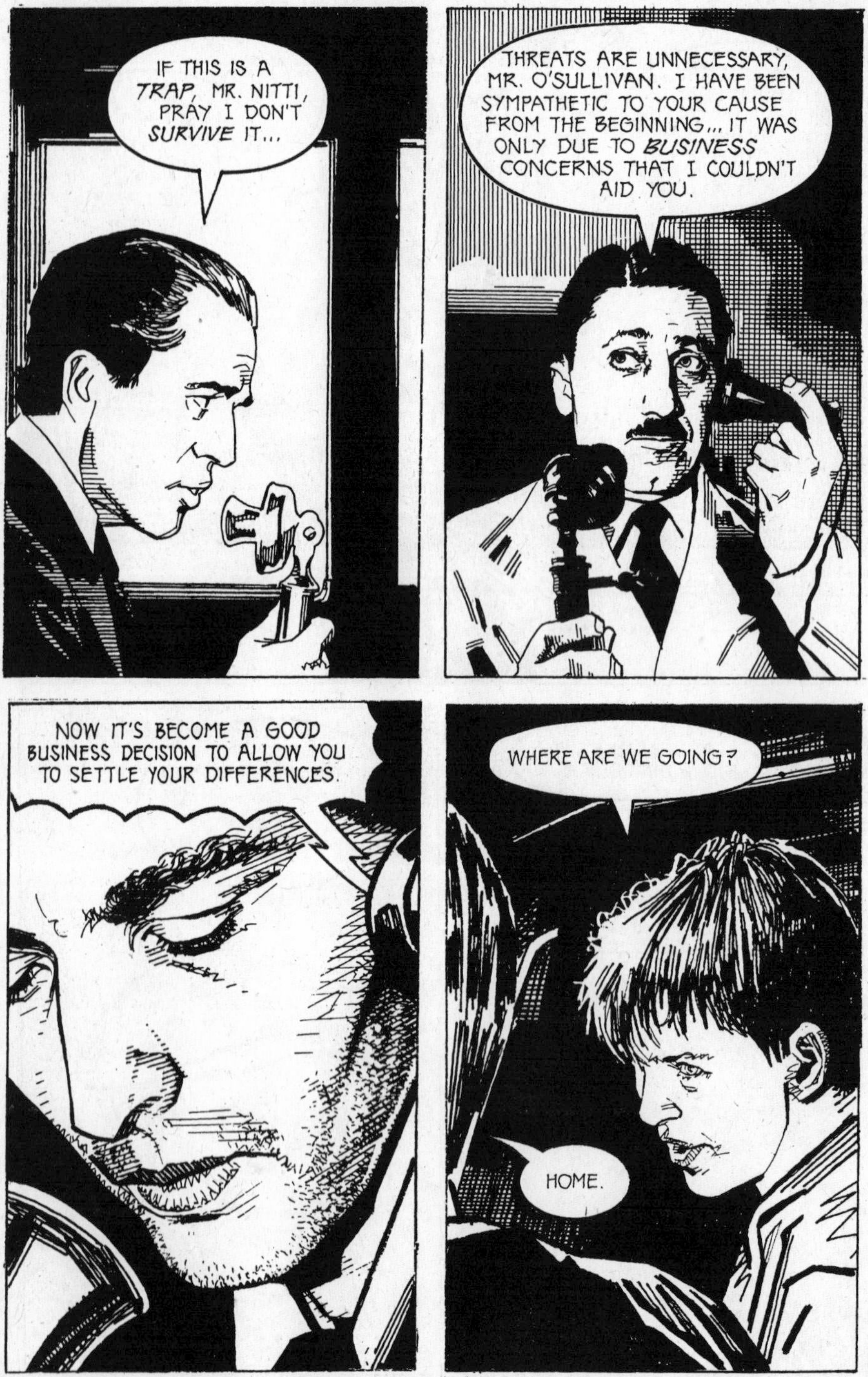
IF THIS IS A TRAP, MR. NITTI, PRAY I DON'T SURVIVE IT...
THREATS ARE UNNECESSARY, MR. O'SULLIVAN. I HAVE BEEN SYMPATHETIC TO YOUR CAUSE FROM THE BEGINNING... IT WAS ONLY DUE TO BUSINESS CONCERNS THAT I COULDN'T AID YOU.
NOW IT'S BECOME A GOOD BUSINESS DECISION TO ALLOW YOU TO SETTLE YOUR DIFFERENCES.
WHERE ARE WE GOING?
HOME.

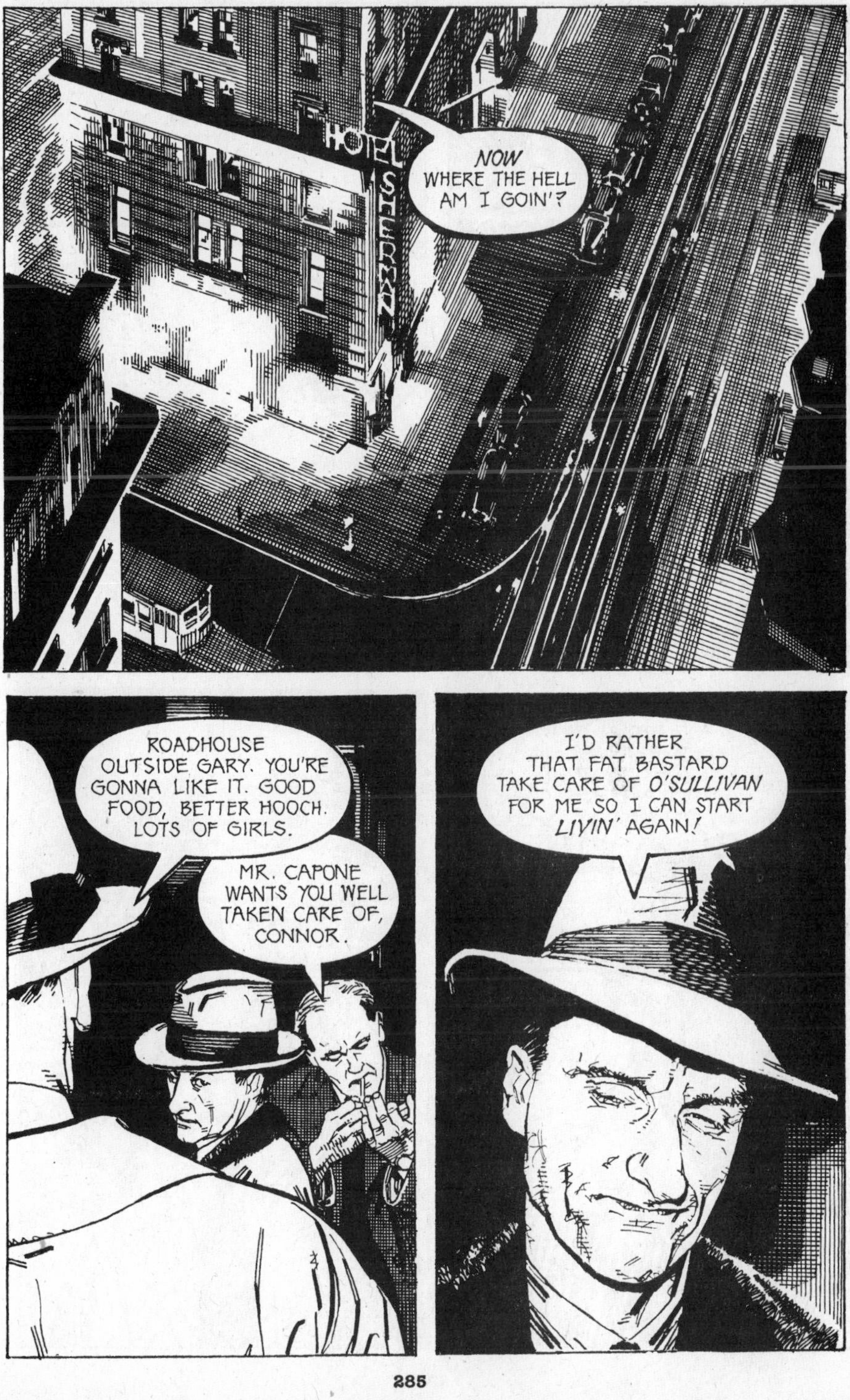
HOTEL SHERMAN
NOW WHERE THE HELL AM I GOIN'?
ROADHOUSE OUTSIDE GARY. YOU'RE GONNA LIKE IT. GOOD FOOD, BETTER HOOCH. LOTS OF GIRLS.
MR. CAPONE WANTS YOU WELL TAKEN CARE OF, CONNOR.
I'D RATHER THAT FAT BASTARD TAKE CARE OF O'SULLIVAN FOR ME SO I CAN START LIVIN' AGAIN!

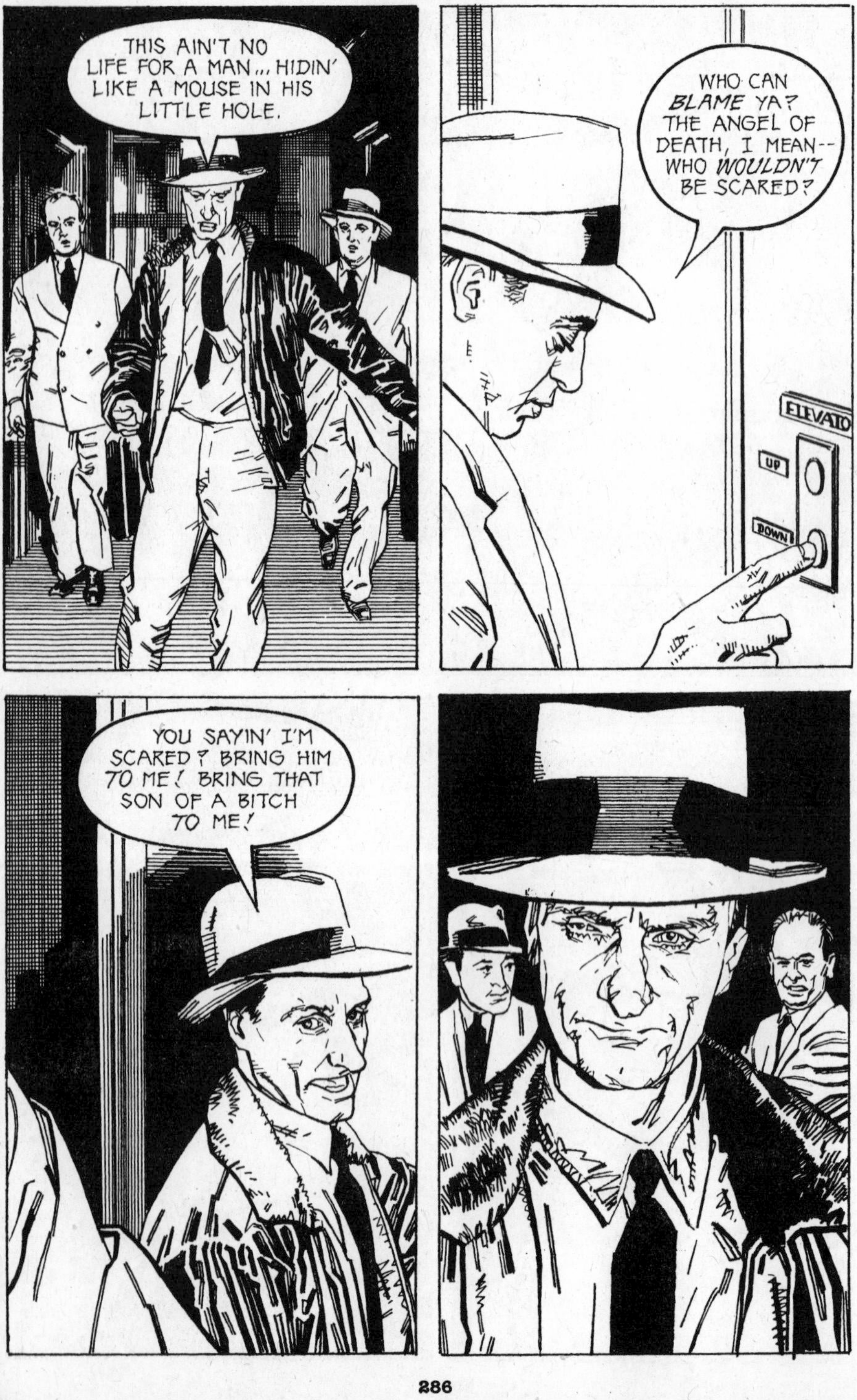
THIS AIN'T NO LIFE FOR A MAN... HIDIN' LIKE A MOUSE IN HIS LITTLE HOLE.
WHO CAN *BLAME* YA? THE ANGEL OF DEATH, I MEAN-- WHO *WOULDN'T* BE SCARED?
ELEVATO
UP
DOWN
YOU SAYIN' I'M SCARED? BRING HIM *TO ME!* BRING THAT SON OF A BITCH *TO ME!*

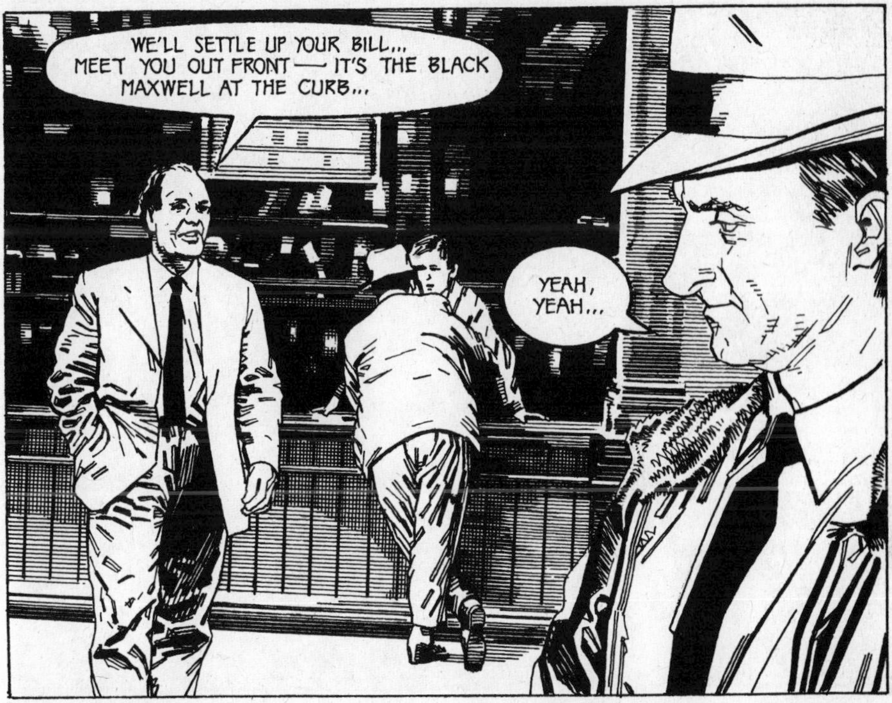
WE'LL SETTLE UP YOUR BILL... MEET YOU OUT FRONT — IT'S THE BLACK MAXWELL AT THE CURB...
YEAH, YEAH...
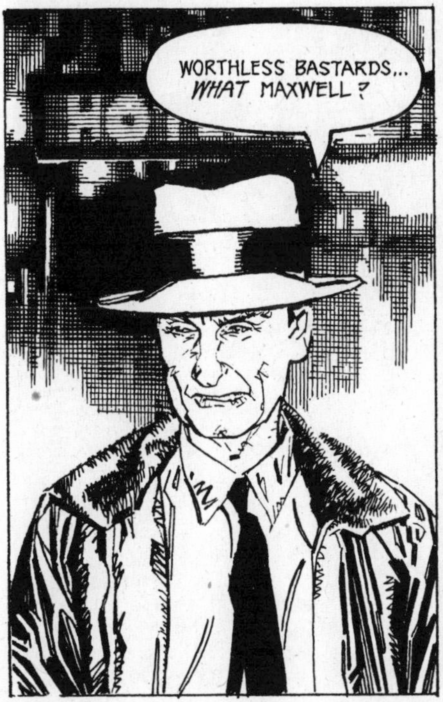
WORTHLESS BASTARDS... *WHAT* MAXWELL ?
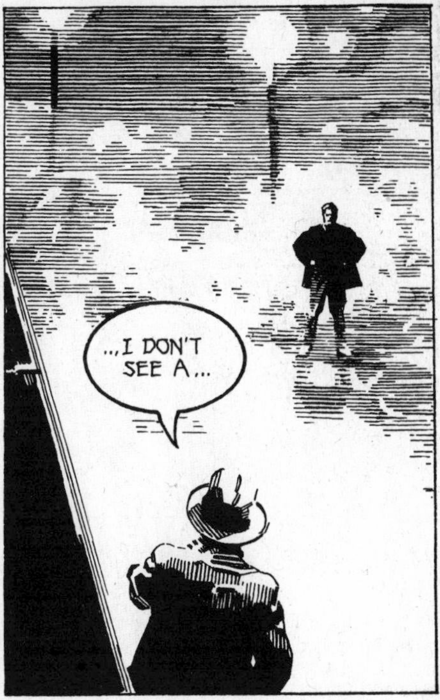
...I DON'T SEE A...

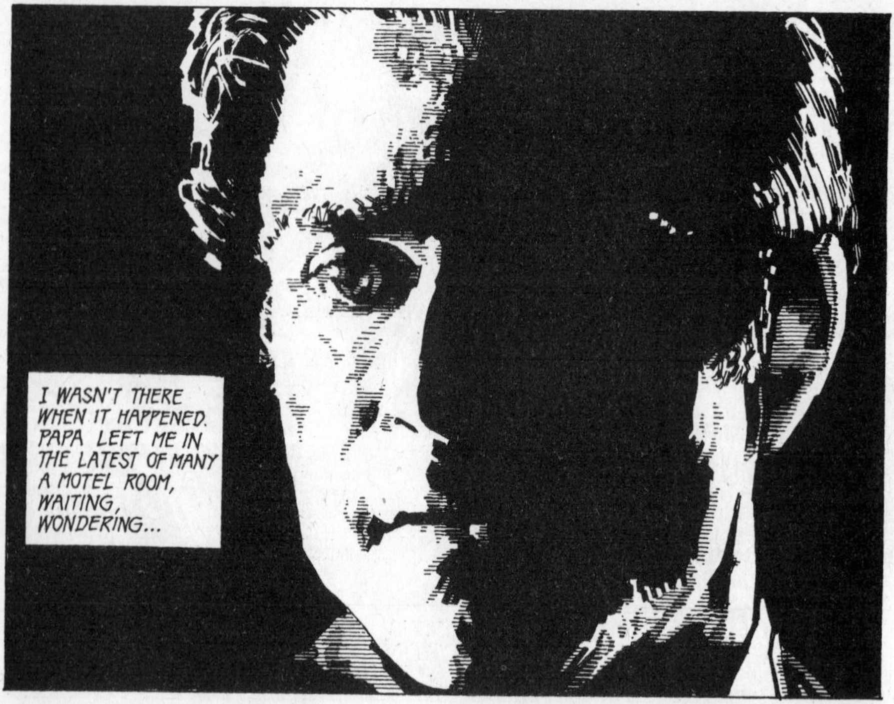
I WASN'T THERE WHEN IT HAPPENED. PAPA LEFT ME IN THE LATEST OF MANY A MOTEL ROOM, WAITING, WONDERING...
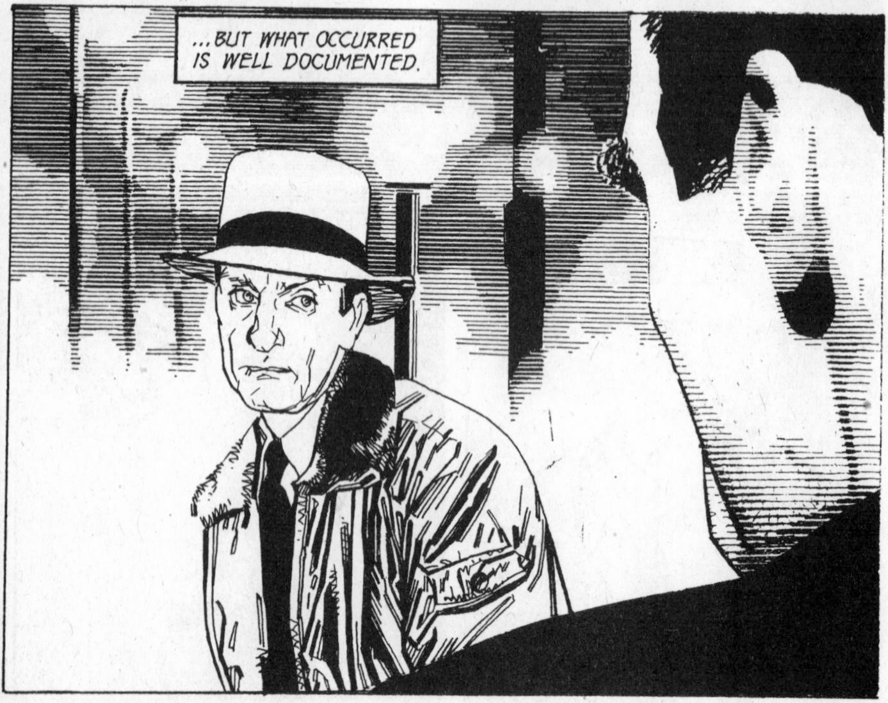
...BUT WHAT OCCURRED IS WELL DOCUMENTED.

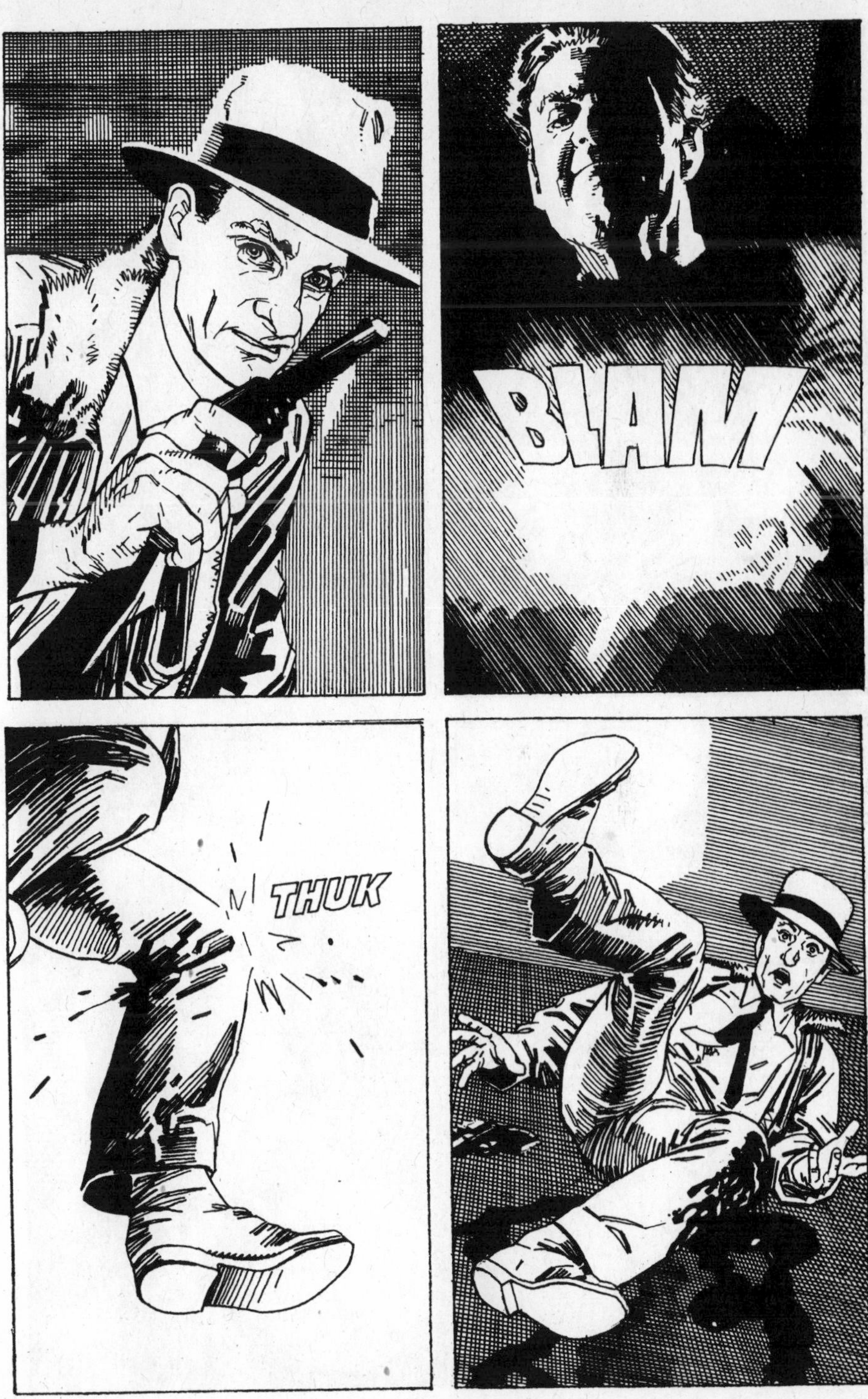
BLAM
THUK

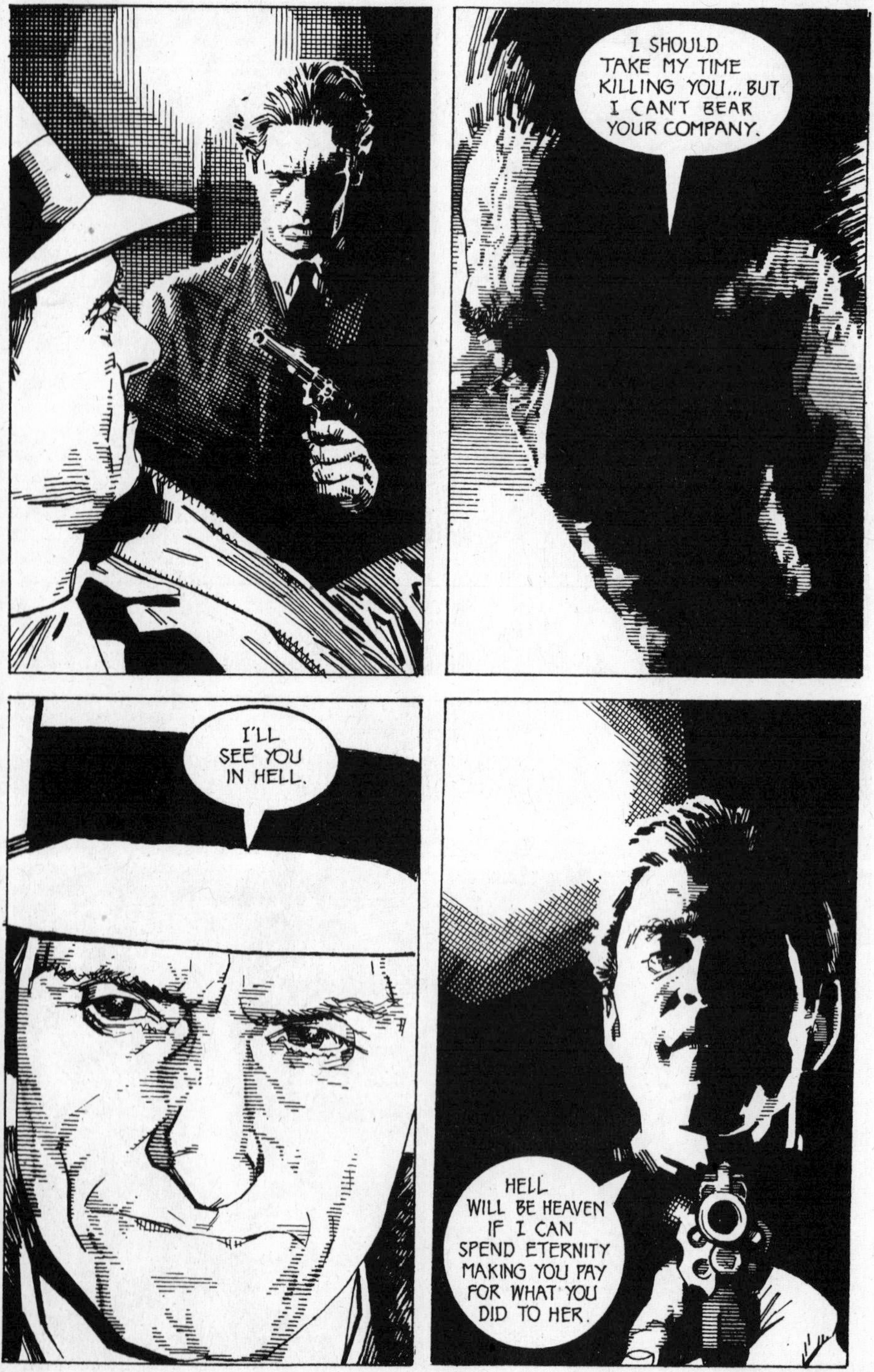
I SHOULD TAKE MY TIME KILLING YOU... BUT I CAN'T BEAR YOUR COMPANY.
I'LL SEE YOU IN HELL.
HELL WILL BE HEAVEN IF I CAN SPEND ETERNITY MAKING YOU PAY FOR WHAT YOU DID TO HER.

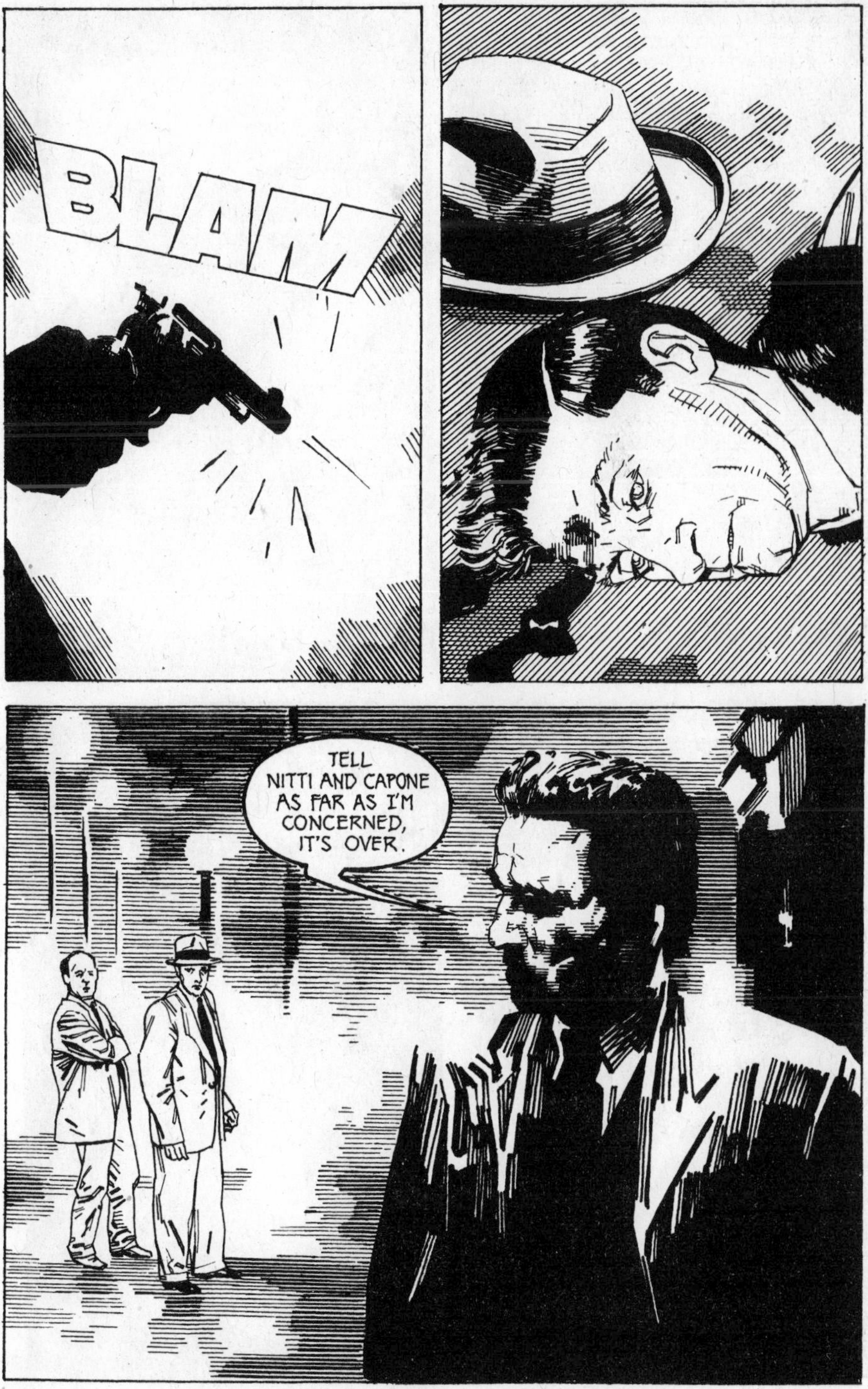
BLAM
TELL NITTI AND CAPONE AS FAR AS I'M CONCERNED, IT'S OVER.

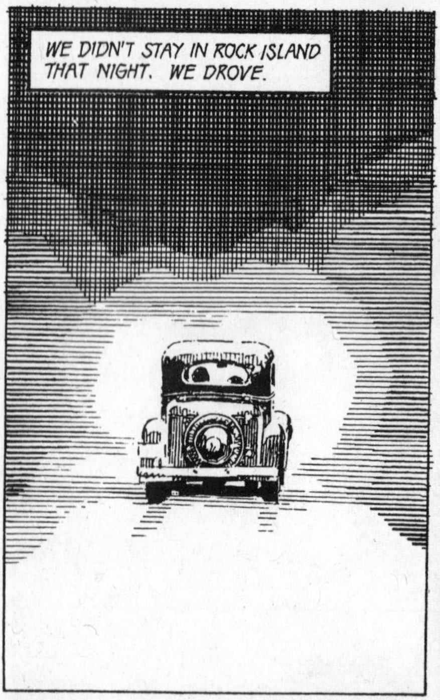
WE DIDN'T STAY IN ROCK ISLAND THAT NIGHT. WE DROVE.

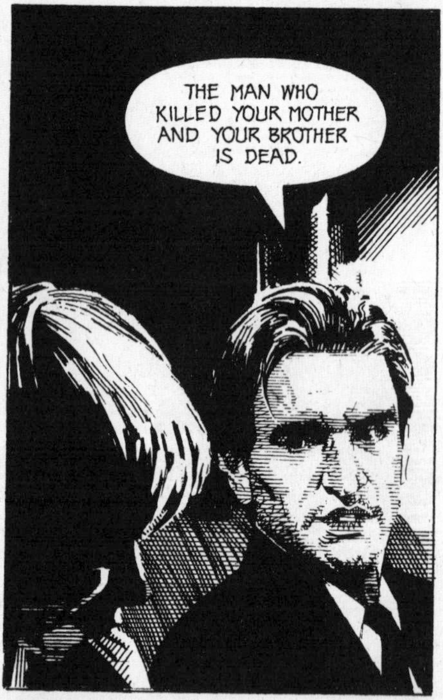
THE MAN WHO KILLED YOUR MOTHER AND YOUR BROTHER IS DEAD.

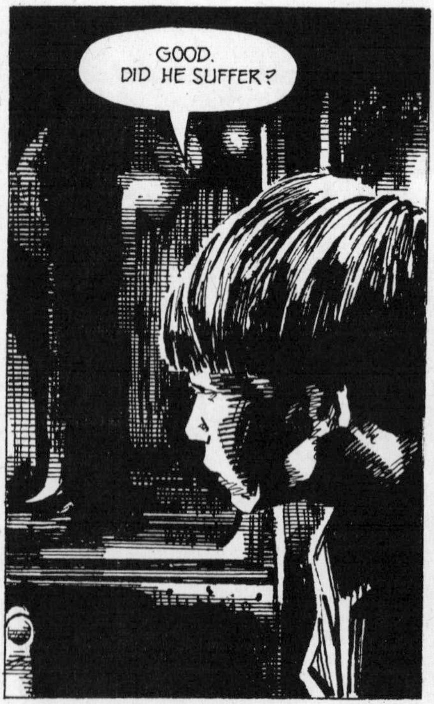
GOOD. DID HE SUFFER?

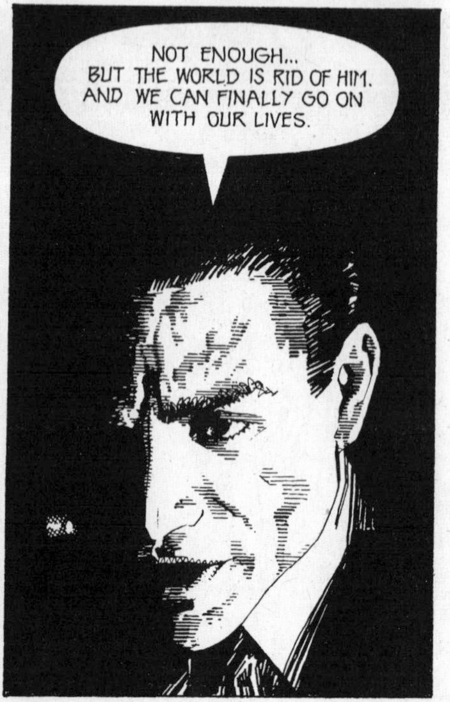
NOT ENOUGH... BUT THE WORLD IS RID OF HIM. AND WE CAN FINALLY GO ON WITH OUR LIVES.

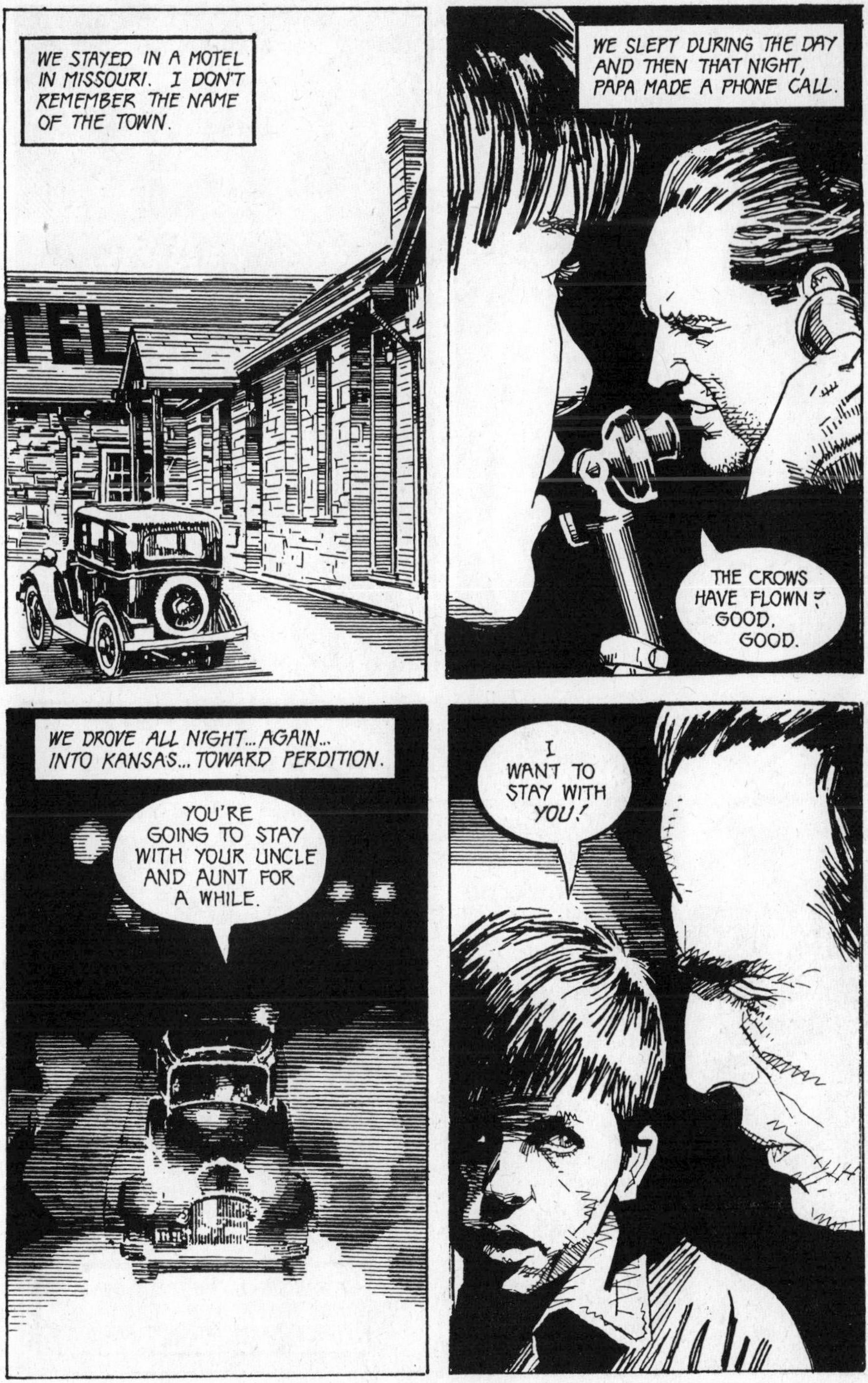
WE STAYED IN A MOTEL IN MISSOURI. I DON'T REMEMBER THE NAME OF THE TOWN.
TEL
WE SLEPT DURING THE DAY AND THEN THAT NIGHT, PAPA MADE A PHONE CALL.
THE CROWS HAVE FLOWN? GOOD. GOOD.
WE DROVE ALL NIGHT... AGAIN... INTO KANSAS... TOWARD PERDITION.
YOU'RE GOING TO STAY WITH YOUR UNCLE AND AUNT FOR A WHILE.
I WANT TO STAY WITH *YOU!*

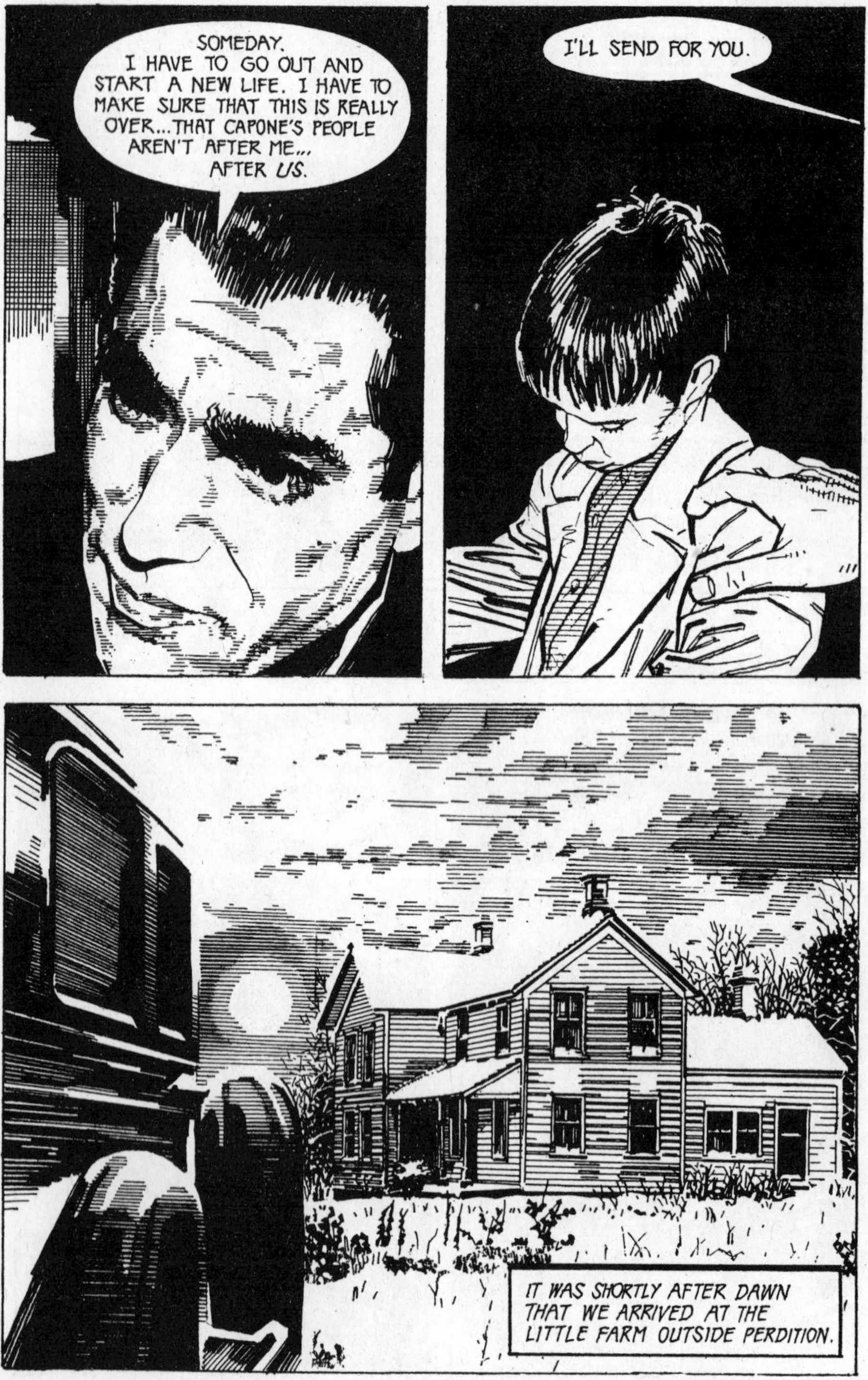
SOMEDAY. I HAVE TO GO OUT AND START A NEW LIFE. I HAVE TO MAKE SURE THAT THIS IS REALLY OVER...THAT CAPONE'S PEOPLE AREN'T AFTER ME... AFTER *US*.
I'LL SEND FOR YOU.
IT WAS SHORTLY AFTER DAWN THAT WE ARRIVED AT THE LITTLE FARM OUTSIDE PERDITION.

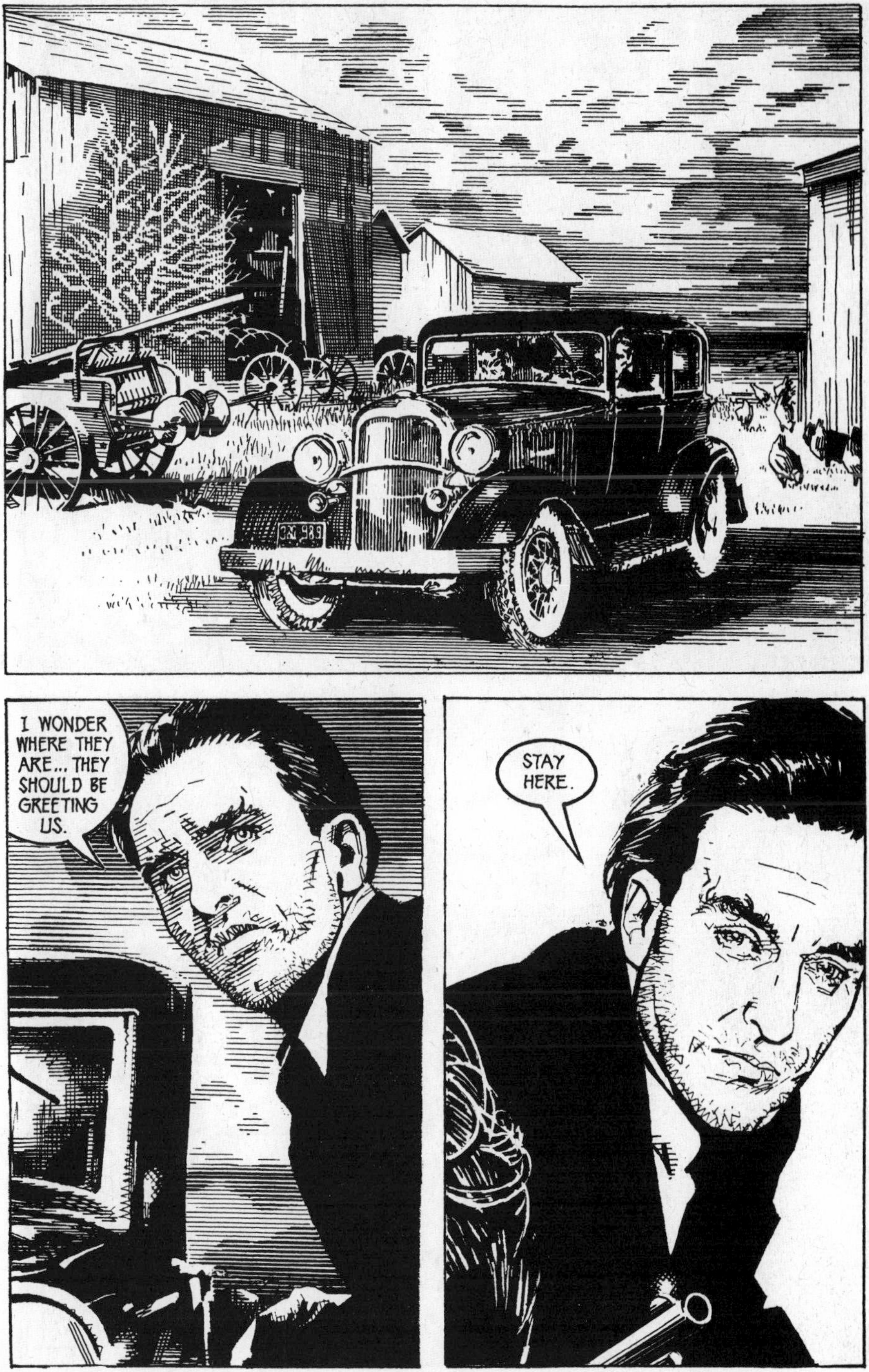
I WONDER WHERE THEY ARE... THEY SHOULD BE GREETING US.
STAY HERE.

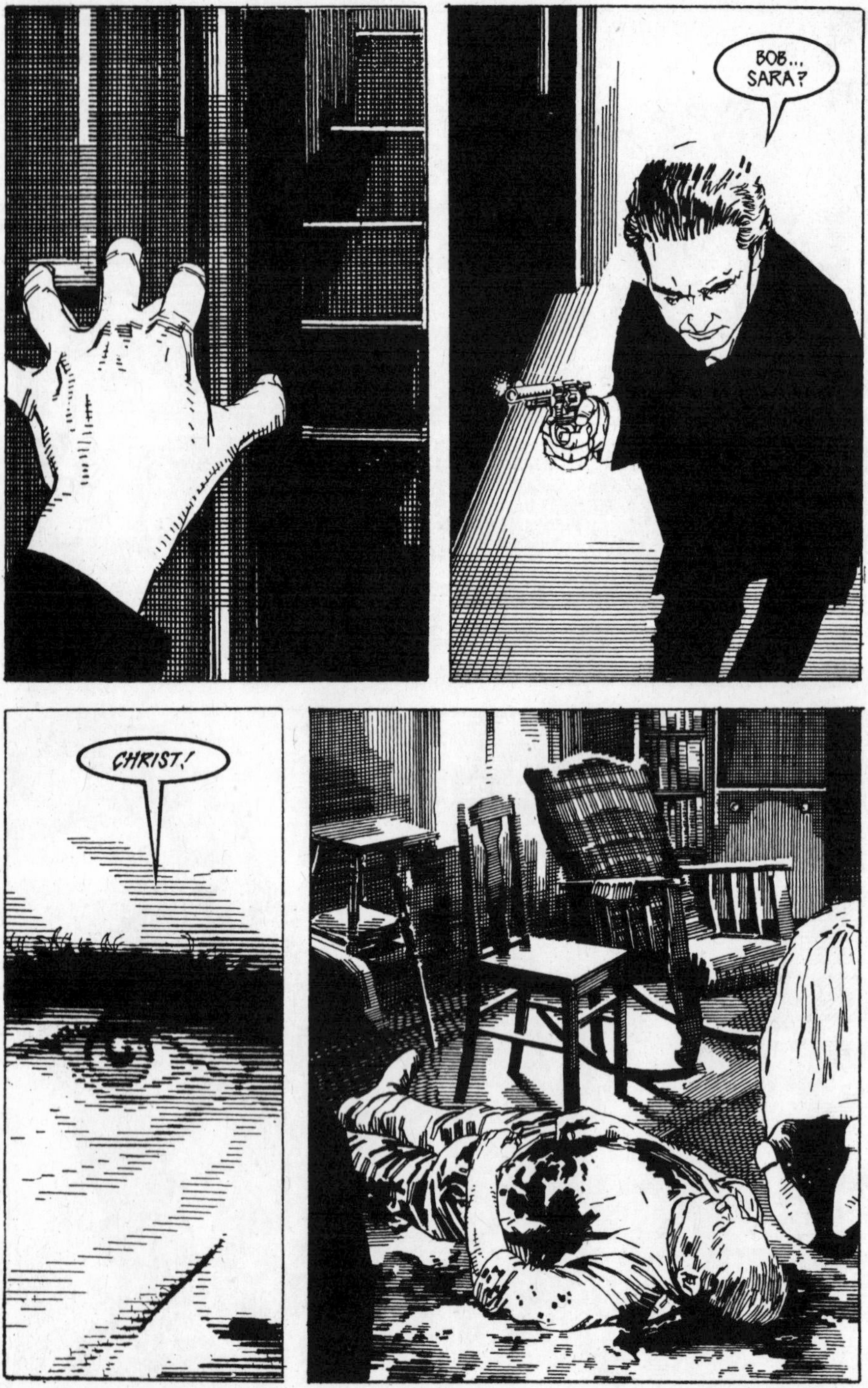
BOB... SARA?
CHRIST!

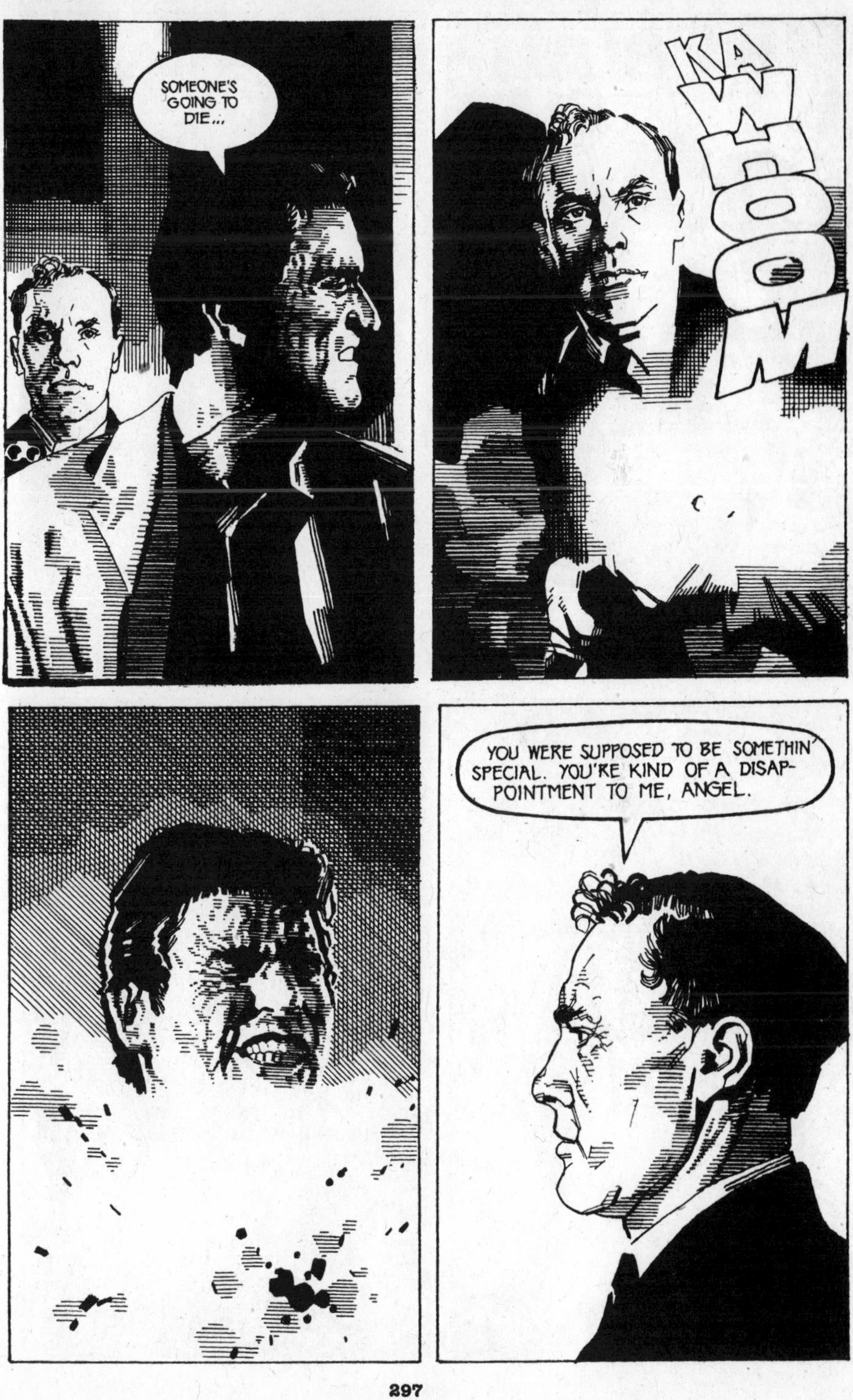
SOMEONE'S GOING TO DIE...
KAWHOOM
YOU WERE SUPPOSED TO BE SOMETHIN' SPECIAL. YOU'RE KIND OF A DISAP-POINTMENT TO ME, ANGEL.

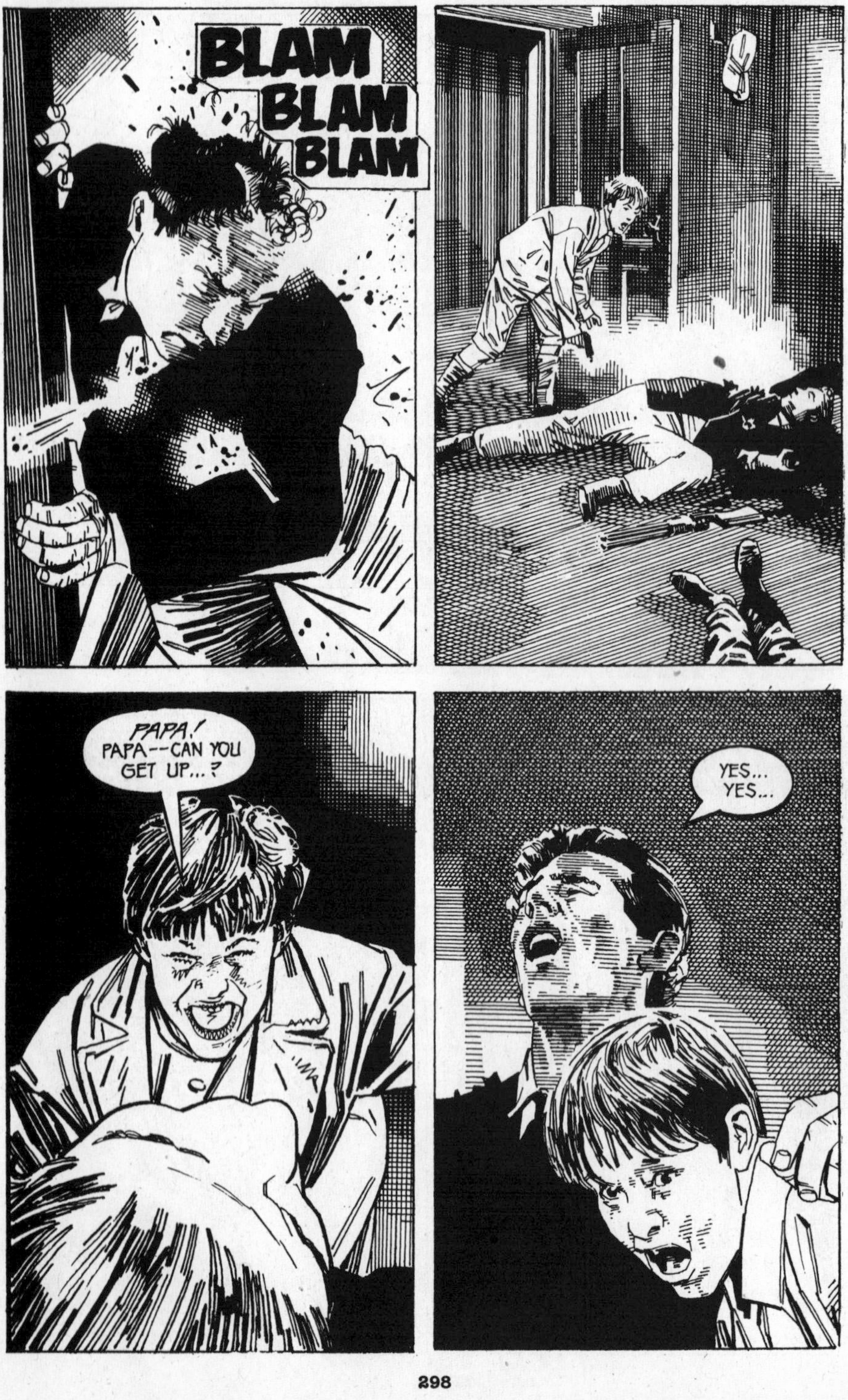
BLAM
BLAM
BLAM
PAPA!
PAPA--CAN YOU GET UP...?
YES... YES...

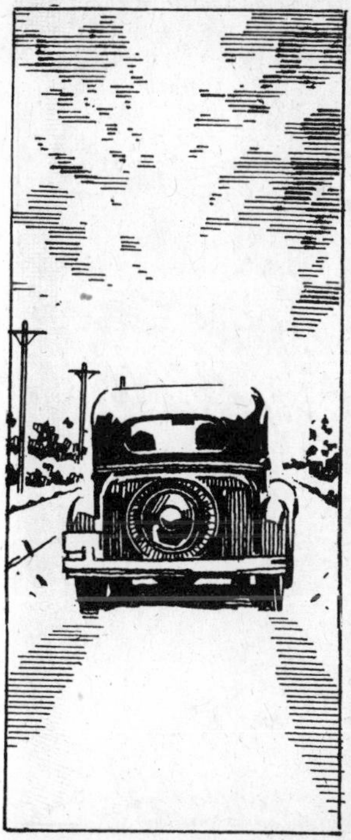

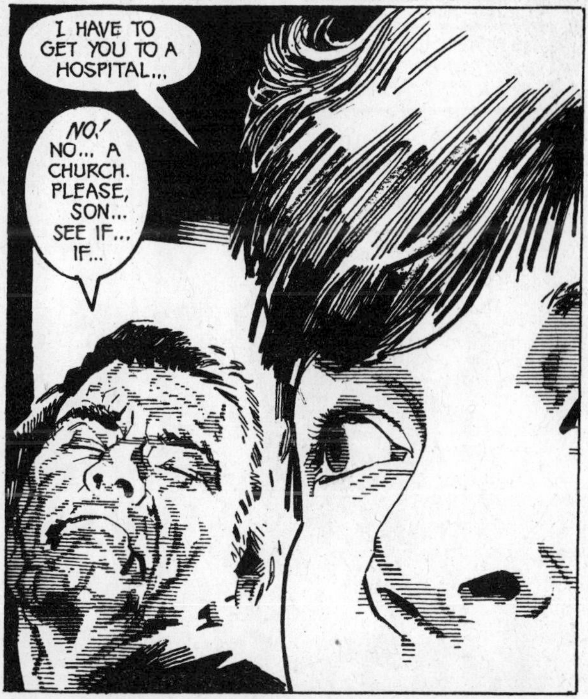
I HAVE TO GET YOU TO A HOSPITAL...
NO! NO... A CHURCH. PLEASE, SON... SEE IF... IF...

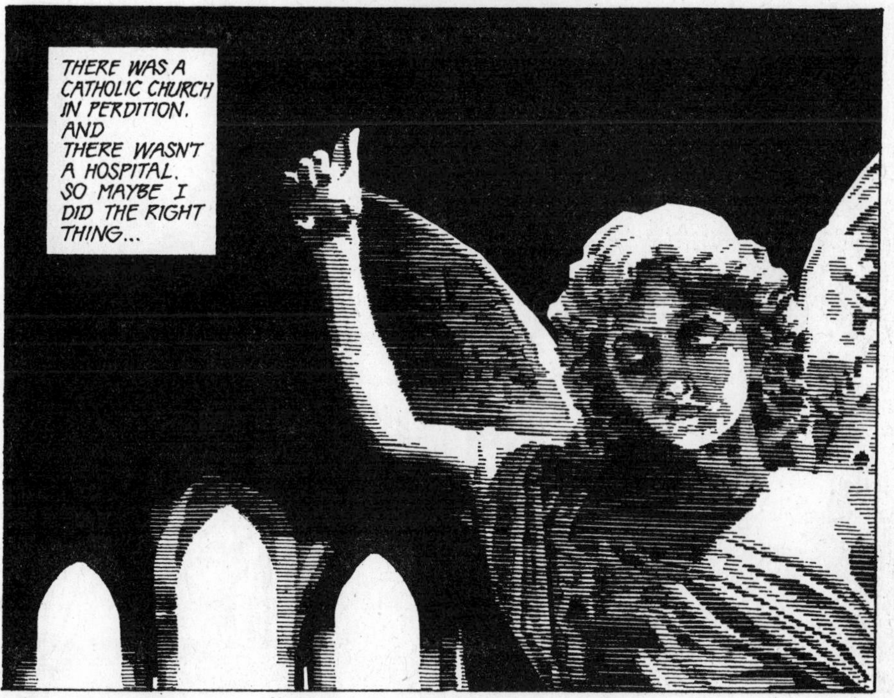
THERE WAS A CATHOLIC CHURCH IN PERDITION. AND THERE WASN'T A HOSPITAL. SO MAYBE I DID THE RIGHT THING...

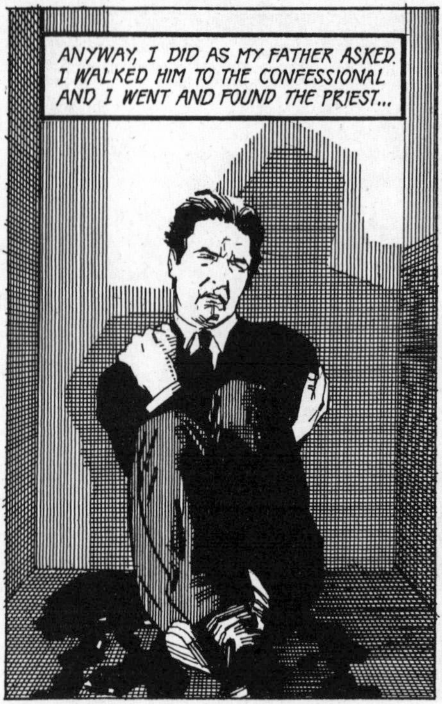
ANYWAY, I DID AS MY FATHER ASKED. I WALKED HIM TO THE CONFESSIONAL AND I WENT AND FOUND THE PRIEST...

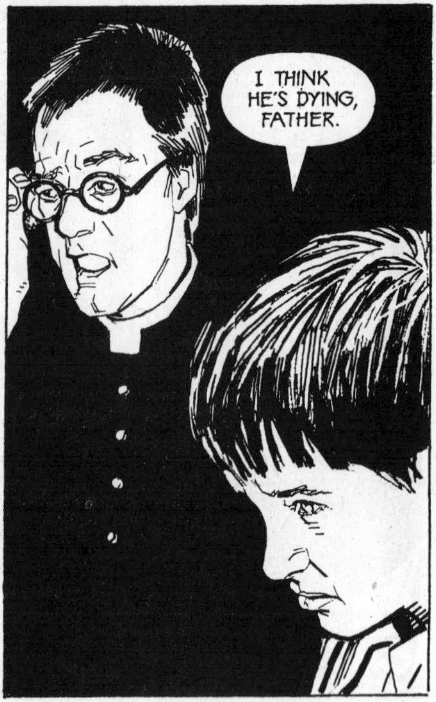
I THINK HE'S DYING, FATHER.

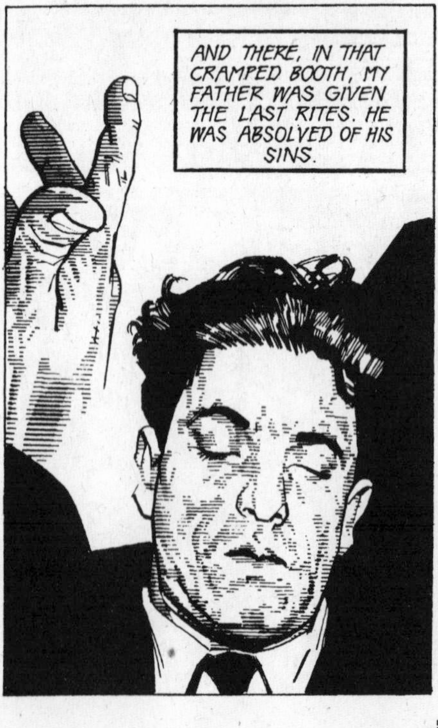
AND THERE, IN THAT CRAMPED BOOTH, MY FATHER WAS GIVEN THE LAST RITES. HE WAS ABSOLVED OF HIS SINS.

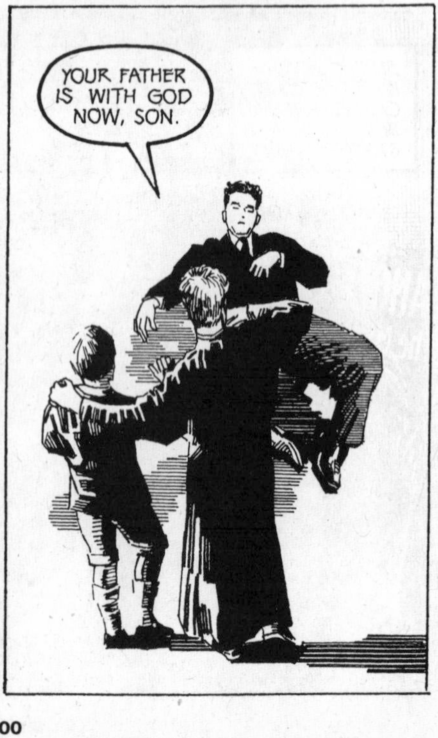
YOUR FATHER IS WITH GOD NOW, SON.

I WAS GLAD HE WAS WITH GOD. BUT WHAT I REALLY HOPED WAS THAT HE WAS WITH MOTHER. AND PETER.

AND SO WE FINALLY REACHED PERDITION, THOUGH I NEVER LIVED THERE. THE CATHOLIC BOY'S ORPHANAGE WAS IN ANOTHER, SLIGHTLY LARGER TOWN.

ST PETER'S HOME FOR BOYS

AND I GREW UP AND THROUGH THE YEARS I READ WHAT WAS WRITTEN ABOUT MY FATHER. SOME CALLED HIM A FIEND. OTHERS AN AVENGING ANGEL. BUT I KNEW ONE DAY I'D HAVE TO WRITE THE STORY OF THE MAN I HAD KNOWN...

ANGEL OF DEATH
The Michael O'Sullivan Story
By BRANDAN CLEMENTS

LOONEY DAYS
by B J EISNER

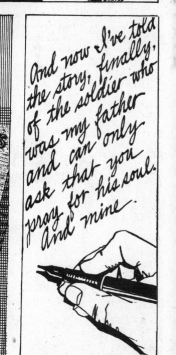

And now I've told the story, finally, of the soldier who was my father and can only ask that you pray for his soul. And mine.

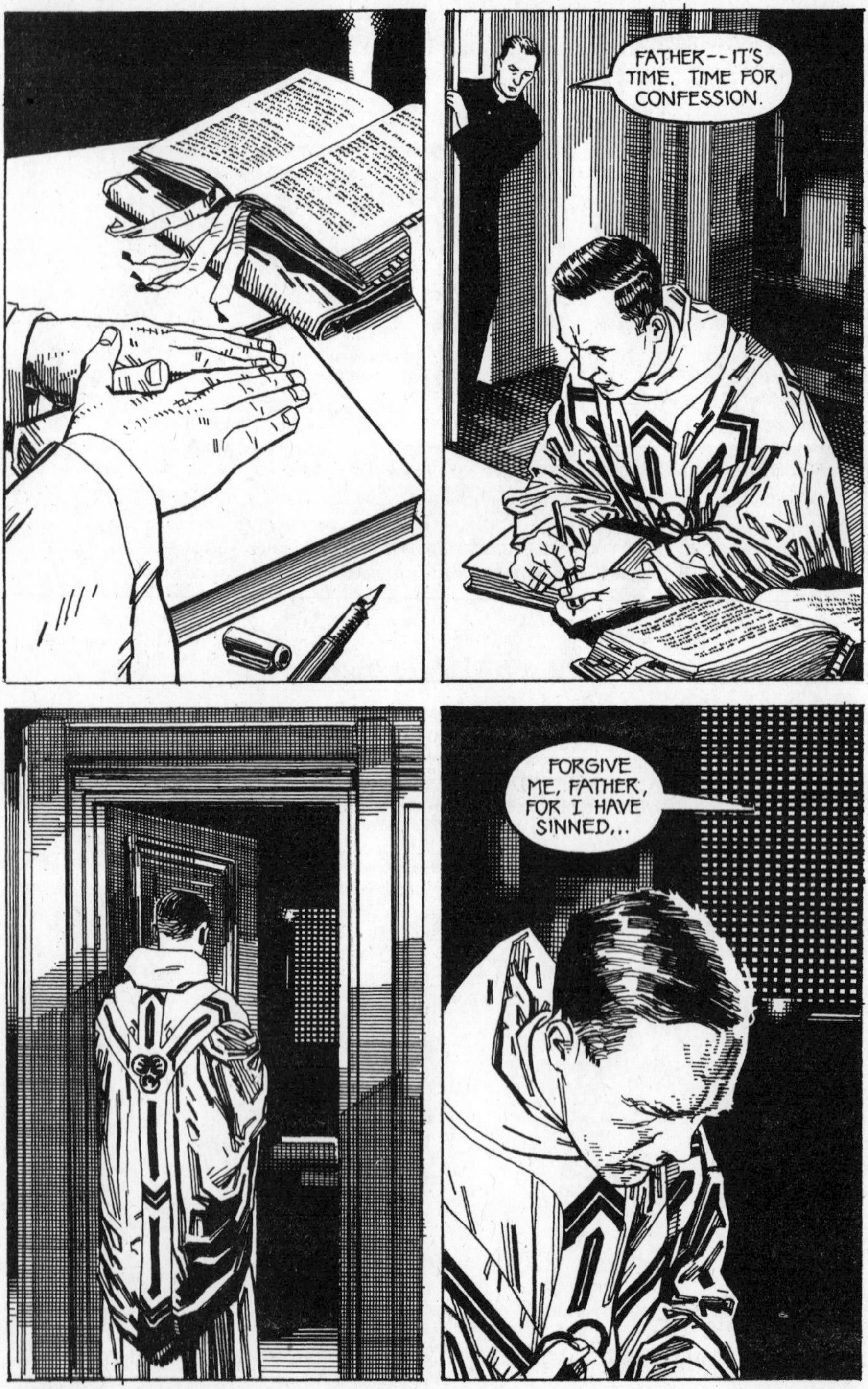
FATHER--IT'S TIME. TIME FOR CONFESSION.
FORGIVE ME, FATHER, FOR I HAVE SINNED...

A TIP OF THE FEDORA

This story is true — or at least, true enough. Capone, Nitti, and Ness are historical figures, of course; but Bill Gabel also existed, as did a betrayed lieutenant of John Looney, and the riverboat *Quinlan* did burn. From the storming of Looney's New Mexico stronghold to the Sherman Hotel shoot-out in Rock Island, this happened. More or less.

My thanks to Andy Helfer for giving me this opportunity, and for his many insightful suggestions and comments, as well as digging in for inventive post-production revisions; his instincts from the beginning of this long-in-the-making project have been frustratingly unerring. I would also like to acknowledge my research associate George Hagenauer as well as B.J. Elsner, whose book *Rock Island: Yesterday, Today, and Tomorrow* (1988) was a key reference work for ROAD TO PERDITION, and *Quad City Times* columnist Bill Wundram, who sparked my interest in Rock Island's notorious Looney clan. As of this writing, I have not had the pleasure of meeting my gifted collaborator, Richard Piers Rayner, but I am grateful to him for bringing this story to life and accompanying me on a ride that has been the most rewarding of my comics-scripting career.

M.A.C.

MAX ALLAN COLLINS

Max Allan Collins is a two-time winner of the Private Eye Writers of America's Shamus award for his Nathaniel Heller historical thrillers *True Detective* (1983) and *Stolen Away* (1991). Author of such movie tie-in bestsellers as *In the Line of Fire* and *Air Force One*, he is the screenwriter/director of the cult favorite suspense films *Mommy* (1995) and *Mommy's Day* (1997). His comics credits include *Dick Tracy, Batman, Ms. Tree* and *Mike Danger.*

RICHARD PIERS RAYNER

Richard Piers Rayner was born and raised in Middlesbrough, England, and began reading American comics at the tender age of four years old. Since breaking into the world of professional comics in 1988, he has illustrated a variety of series for both DC and Marvel Comics including *Hellblazer, Swamp Thing, L.E.G.I.O.N., Dr. Fate* and *Dr. Who.* Additionally, he is a frequent contributor to Paradox Press's Big Book series. All his work is characterized by a meticulous attention to detail — nowhere more evident than in ROAD TO PERDITION, a labor of love that has taken Rayner four years to complete.